The Last Days of the Kingdom of Israel

Beihefte zur Zeitschrift für die alttestamentliche Wissenschaft

Herausgegeben von
John Barton, Reinhard G. Kratz, Nathan MacDonald,
Carol A. Newsom and Markus Witte

Band 511

The Last Days of the Kingdom of Israel

Edited by
Shuichi Hasegawa, Christoph Levin and Karen Radner

DE GRUYTER

ISBN 978-3-11-071051-9
e-ISBN (PDF) 978-3-11-056660-4
e-ISBN (EPUB) 978-3-11-056418-1
ISSN 0934-2575

Library of Congress Cataloging-in-Publication Data
Names: Hasegawa, Shuichi, 1971- editor. | Levin, Christoph, 1950- editor. | Radner, Karen, editor.
Title: The last days of the Kingdom of Israel / edited by Shuichi Hasegawa, Christoph Levin, Karen Radner.
Description: First edition. | Berlin; Boston : Walter de Gruyter, [2018] | Series: Beihefte zur Zeitschrift fur die alttestamentliche Wissenschaft, ISSN 0934-2575 ; Band 511
Identifiers: LCCN 2018023384 | ISBN 9783110564167
Subjects: LCSH: Jews--History--953-586 B.C. | Assyria--History. | Bible. Old Testament--Criticism, interpretation, etc. | Assyro-Babylonian literature--History and criticism.
Classification: LCC DS121.6 .L37 2018 | DDC 933/.03--dc23 LC record available at https://lccn.loc.gov/2018023384

Bibliografische Information der Deutschen Nationalbibliothek
The Deutsche Nationalbibliothek lists this publication in the Deutsche Nationalbibliografie; detailed bibliografic data are available on the Internet at http://dnb.dnb.de.

© 2020 Walter de Gruyter GmbH, Berlin/Boston
This volume is text- and page-identical with the hardback published in 2019.
Druck und Bindung: CPI books GmbH, Leck

www.degruyter.com

Table of Contents

Shuichi Hasegawa
The Last Days of the Northern Kingdom of Israel
　　Introducing the Proceedings of a Multi-Disciplinary Conference —— 1

Part I: Setting the Scene

Bob Becking
How to Encounter an Historical Problem?
　　"722–720 BCE" as a Case Study —— 17

Part II: Approaching the Fall of Samaria from Contemporary Assyrian and Egyptian Sources

Jamie Novotny
Contextualizing the Last Days of the Kingdom of Israel: What Can Assyrian Official Inscriptions Tell Us? —— 35

Eckart Frahm
Samaria, Hamath, and Assyria's Conquests in the Levant in the Late 720s BCE
　　The Testimony of Sargon II's Inscriptions —— 55

Frederick Mario Fales
Why Israel?
　　Reflections on Shalmaneser V's and Sargon II's Grand Strategy for the Levant —— 87

Karen Radner
The "Lost Tribes of Israel" in the Context of the Resettlement Programme of the Assyrian Empire —— 101

Robert G. Morkot
The End of the Kingdom of Israel: A View from the Nile Valley —— 125

Part III: Views from Archaeology

Ron E. Tappy
The Annals of Sargon II and the Archaeology of Samaria: Rhetorical Claims, Empirical Evidence —— 147

Norma Franklin
Megiddo and Jezreel Reflected in the Dying Embers of the Northern Kingdom of Israel —— 189

Part IV: Working with the Book of Kings: the Text

Timo Tekoniemi
Between Two Differing Editions: Some Notable Text-Critical Variants in 2 Kings 17 —— 211

Dan'el Kahn
The Fall of Samaria: an Analysis of the Biblical Sources —— 229

Christoph Levin
In Search of the Original Biblical Record of the Assyrian Conquest of Samaria —— 251

Part V: Working with the Book of Kings: the Chronological Framework

Kristin Weingart
2 Kings 15–18: a Chronological Conundrum? —— 267

Steven L. McKenzie
The Last Days of Israel: Chronological Considerations —— 289

Part VI: Working with the Book of Kings: the Narrative

Christian Frevel
Wicked Usurpers and the Doom of Samaria
  Further Views on the Angle of 2 Kings 15–17 —— 303

Michael Pietsch
Hoshea ben Elah, the Last King of Israel: Narrative and History in 2 Kings 17:1–6 —— 335

Georg Hentschel
Did Hoshea of Israel Continue the Foreign Policy of His Predecessors? —— 355

Part VII: Reflections in the Prophets

Martti Nissinen
The Book of Hosea and the Last Days of the Northern Kingdom
  The Methodological Problem —— 369

H. G. M. Williamson
Isaiah and the Fall of the Kingdom of Israel —— 383

Indices

1 **General index —— 401**

2 **Words —— 411**

3 **Texts —— 413**

Shuichi Hasegawa
The Last Days of the Northern Kingdom of Israel

Introducing the Proceedings of a Multi-Disciplinary Conference

1 The Conference

The Northern Kingdom of Israel ruled the northern part of the Southern Levant for about 200 years from the mid-tenth century to the late eighth century BCE. The kingdom was conquered by the Assyrian Empire after the latter had persistently conducted military campaigns into the Levant from the mid-ninth century BCE onwards.

Despite considerable scholarly efforts over many years, the events of the last three decades of the Northern Kingdom of Israel are still hidden beneath the veil of history. A number of questions remain unresolved: the status of the kingdom after Tiglath-pileser III, king of Assyria, annexed its larger part in 732 BCE; the date of the conquest and the identity of the conqueror of Samaria, the capital of the kingdom; the fate of Hoshea, the Northern Kingdom's last king; or the circumstances under which Samaria joined the anti-Assyrian coalition after its fall. One of the primary reasons for this situation lies in the discrepancies to be found in the available textual sources, namely the Hebrew Bible (chiefly, Book of Kings, Isaiah and Hosea) and the Assyrian material, most importantly royal inscriptions and letters from the state correspondence. The gaps in the sources are not easy to bridge, also because Bible Studies and Assyriology are separate disciplines with distinct agendas and methodologies.

In the period in question, the Northern Kingdom played a significant role within and beyond the Levant. Elucidating its fall is not only critical for reconstructing the history of the kingdom itself, but can also contribute greatly to our understanding of biblical and ancient Near Eastern historiography, for it is extremely rare that the textual sources both of the conqueror and of the conquered are at our disposal. In addition, the modern state of Israel is the most exhaustively and most intensively excavated region in the Middle East, and this provides us with much relevant archaeological information. To investigate the period in question is also meaningful in order to reconstruct Assyria's diplomatic and military strategies toward its client kingdoms and its policies in its administrative provinces. Our topic serves to elucidate the structure of imperial domination of this first empire of the ancient Near East, and to determine the difference in its treatment between the Northern Kingdom of Israel and the Southern Kingdom of Judah, which persisted as an Assyrian client state and was never integrated into the Assyrian provincial system.

To be in any position to attempt to reconstruct "what really happened" in the last days of the Northern Kingdom, one must first analyse all these sources critically and independently, and only then move on to synthesizing the results. Only in this way, do we stand a chance to elucidate the background, the course, and the results of the Syro-Ephraimite War, and to determine the date of the fall of Samaria, the identity of its conqueror and the aftermath of the conquest. The critical analysis of the available sources was therefore the remit of the conference "The Last Days of the Northern Kingdom of Israel," whose proceedings constitute the present volume.

The multi-disciplinary conference was organized by Shuichi Hasegawa (Rikkyo University Tokyo), Christoph Levin and Karen Radner (both LMU Munich) in order to elucidate "The Last Days of the Northern Kingdom of Israel" and to explore with fresh eyes key issues connected with the Fall of Samaria and its narrative that have fuelled scholarly debates since the 19th century. It was held at the building of the Carl Friedrich von Siemens Stiftung in Munich from 15–17 March 2017 and brought together speakers from Finland, Germany, Israel, Italy, Japan, the Netherlands, the United Kingdom and the United States. It received generous funding from a Fostering Joint International Research grant of the Japan Society for the Promotion of Science (KAKENHI; Subject No. 15KK0061) awarded to Hasegawa, with additional financial support provided by the Carl Friedrich von Siemens Stiftung and the Alexander von Humboldt Foundation, the latter through the Alexander von Humboldt chair in the Ancient History of the Near and Middle East held by Radner (who hosted Hasegawa at LMU Munich during the academic year 2016/17). We wish to thank Denise Bolton for carefully proof-reading and, where necessary, language-editing the contributions to this volume, Alexa Bartelmus and Nikola Wenner for compiling the index and De Gruyter's Sabina Dabrowski, Katrin Mittmann and Sophie Wagenhofer for their support, care and speed in preparing this publication.

2 Introducing the Sources

It will be helpful to offer a short summary of the types and nature of the available sources and to briefly highlight the problems relating to them. I will use the following categories: (1) extra-biblical sources; (2) biblical sources; and (3) archaeological data.

2.1 Extra-Biblical Sources

Part II of this volume is devoted to this material which includes (1) Assyrian royal inscriptions, (2) the Assyrian Eponym Chronicle, (3) the Babylonian Chronicles, and (4) various Assyrian archival texts.

2.1.1 Assyrian Royal Inscriptions

In the second half of the eighth century BCE, the rulers of the Assyrian Empire conducted a number of military campaigns into the Levant and recorded accounts of these campaigns in their royal annals and other official inscriptions. These mention information such as the names of the kings of the Northern Kingdom, their tribute, and details of the Assyrian campaigns against the kingdom. The significance of these inscriptions lies in the fact that they were composed shortly after the time of the described events.

Three monarchs ruled the Assyrian Empire during the last years of the Northern Kingdom of Israel: Tiglath-pileser III reigned between 745–727 BCE, his son and crown prince Shalmaneser V succeeded him and ruled from 727 to 722 BCE, when his brother Sargon II took the throne by force and reigned from 722 to 705 BCE.[1]

After a period of decline, the ascent of Tiglath-pileser to the throne of Assyria marked a new stage in the empire's history. Dozens of his royal inscriptions survive although most of them in a very fragmentary state of preservation. This king's extensive military campaigns are recorded in annals that present his deeds in chronological order and in summary inscriptions that summarize his activities according to geographical considerations.[2]

The Hebrew Bible refers to Tiglath-pileser quite often, explicitly as well as indirectly (2Kgs 15–16; Isa 7; 8:1–10, 23; 10:9; 17:1–3; Amos 6:2; 1Chr 5:6, 26; 2Chr 28:16–21), and this mirrors his profound influence on the history of the Northern Kingdom. These passages seemingly reflect the collective memory and the developed tradition of this Assyrian ruler and his activities.

---

[1] E.g., Albert Kirk Grayson, "Assyria: Tiglath-pileser III to Sargon II (744–705 B.C.)," in *The Cambridge Ancient History*, Vol. III/2, second edition, eds. John Boardman, I. E. S. Edwards, E. Sollberger, and N. G. L. Hammond (Cambridge: Cambridge University Press, 1992), 71–102.
[2] Rykle Borger and Hayim Tadmor, "Zwei Beiträge zur alttestamentlichen Wissenschaft aufgrund der Inschriften Tiglathpilesers III.," *ZAW* 94 (1984): 244–51; Hayim Tadmor and Shigeo Yamada, *The Royal Inscriptions of Tiglath-pileser III (747–727 BC), and Shalmaneser V (726–722 BC), Kings of Assyria* (Winona Lake IN: Eisenbrauns, 2011), 106: 17–19; 132: 10–11.

Very few royal inscriptions of Shalmaneser V, the successor of Tiglath-pileser III, and especially no annals have survived. The key information on his reign is known from the Assyrian Eponym Chronicle and the Babylonian Chronicles, which we will discuss below.

Sargon II, the successor of Shalmaneser V, further expanded Assyria's territory by extensive military campaigning. He states in his inscriptions that he conquered Samaria and the Land of Humri, as the Northern Kingdom of Israel is conventionally designated in the Assyrian royal inscriptions. It seems that several passages in the Hebrew Bible also refer to this Assyrian king (2Kgs 17:1–24; 18:1–12; Isa 10:27–32; 14:4b–21; 20:1).

Considering the contemporariness of their composition to the events described, the information found in the Assyrian royal inscriptions and especially their chronological sequence is usually deemed reliable. But the available inscriptions refer to the Northern Kingdom of Israel only in passing and thus do not provide adequate information for reconstructing this specific sequence of events. In addition, the accounts are in no way unbiased as the royal inscriptions were primarily designed to convey Assyrian royal ideology.[3]

2.1.2 The Assyrian Eponym Chronicle

The elaborate version of the Assyrian Eponym List, dubbed the Assyrian Eponym Chronicle, is another important historical source.[4] Since the late second millennium BCE, *limmu* (or *līmu*) is the Assyrian designation for an official one-year position, whose holder lends his name to the year in which he holds this office. We therefore translate the term as "eponym." The Eponym List enumerates the holders of the *limmu* office in chronological order, and the Eponym Chronicle supplements this with information about key events affecting all of Assyria, usually just one per year. Although the source is less biased than the inscriptions, it offers only limited information pertaining to the Northern Kingdom of Israel.

---

[3] Cf. Shuichi Hasegawa, "Adad-nērārī III's Fifth Year in the Saba'a Stela: Historiographical Background," *RA* 102 (2008): 89–98; id., "Historical and Historiographical Notes on the Pazarcık Stela," *Akkadica* 131 (2010): 1–9.
[4] Alan R. Millard, *The Eponyms of the Assyrian Empire 910–612 BC* (Helsinki: The Neo-Assyrian Text Corpus Project, 1994).

2.1.3 The Babylonian Chronicles

The Babylonian Chronicles laconically record the key events in the history of Babylon. As several Assyrian kings, including Tiglath-pileser III, Shalmaneser V and, intermittently, Sargon II held the crown of Babylon, the Chronicles sometimes incorporate events pertaining to the Assyrian Empire, including the mention of the conquest of Samaria under Shalmaneser V.[5]

2.1.4 Assyrian Archival Texts

Samaria and its population are occasionally mentioned in Assyrian archival texts, such as letters from the state correspondence, administrative texts or private legal documents. These sources usually date to the period after the conquest of the Northern Kingdom.

2.2 Biblical Sources

Relevant source materials are included in (1) the Book of Kings and (2) the Books of the Prophets.

2.2.1 The Book of Kings: 2Kgs 15–18

The most detailed information on the final years of the Northern Kingdom derives from 2Kgs 15–18 in the Hebrew Bible. This source provides details such as the names of the kings, the year of their enthronement and the length of their reign, major events, circumstances of coups d'état, and this is useful in creating a basic chronological framework to reconstruct the history of the kingdom. Yet, there are some problems in the biblical chronology that remain unsolved. Part V of this volume addresses the chronological framework of the Book of Kings.

The text is mostly formulaic in style, describing in brief the reigns of the kings of the Northern Kingdom. It is generally assumed that parts of the accounts

---

[5] Albert Kirk Grayson, *Assyrian and Babylonian Chronicles* (New York: J. J. Augustin, 1975), 69–87; Jean-Jacques Glassner, *Chroniques mésopotamiennes* (Paris: Les belles lettres, 1993), 179–87.

of a given king's reign go back to original archival records. On the other hand, later redactors are assumed to have added to this material, and the resultant text cannot be regarded as historically accurate. To understand the nature of the text, literary analysis is therefore indispensable. The narrative art of the Book of Kings is investigated in Part VI of this volume.

Most previous studies are based mainly on the Masoretic Text of the Book of Kings and failed to scrutinize the textual history of the Book of Kings. But recent studies demonstrate that the ancient Greek translations of the old Hebrew text of the Book of Kings, such as the Antiochian text widely known as the Lucianic recension of the Septuagint, sometimes preserve older readings.[6]

The Septuagint is a Greek translation of the Hebrew Bible whose origins may go back to the third century BCE. The Antiochian text, a revised version of an Old Greek translation of the Hebrew Bible, survives in the form of manuscripts from the fourth century CE. Yet, the revision was unequivocally based on a text older than the oldest extant manuscripts of the Septuagint. Thus, the Antiochian text should play an important role in reconstructing an older text of the Book of Kings. Moreover, it has recently been argued that the text of the Book of Kings as preserved in the Vetus Latina, a Latin translation of the Old Greek text of the Hebrew Bible, is highly important as well, although the extant manuscript tradition only partially provides the text of the Book of Kings.[7]

The older text does not always corroborate the historical authenticity of the information that it contains. If the text itself is a fiction, regardless of its age, historically accurate information cannot be expected in it. On the other hand, even though the text depends on an older source, information included in the text could have been altered by later editing. For this reason, it is imperative to reconstruct as old a text of the Book of Kings as possible, before using it as historical source for reconstructing the last days of the Northern Kingdom. Part IV of this volume concentrates on the various textual witnesses of the Book of Kings and the reliability of the information they provide.

---

[6] For example, see Shuichi Hasegawa, "The Conquests of Hazael in 2 Kgs 13:22 in the Antiochian Text," *JBL* 133 (2014): 61–76

[7] Natalio Fernández Marcos "Der antiochenische Text der griechischen Bibel in den Samuel- und Königsbüchern (1–4 Kön LXX)," in *Im Brennpunkt: Die Septuaginta, Studien zur Entstehung und Bedeutung der Griechischen Bibel*, Band 2, ed. Siegfried Kreuzer and Jürgen Peter Lesch (Stuttgart: Kohlhammer, 2004): 177–213; Alexander Fischer, *Der Text des Alten Testaments, Neubearbeitung der Einführung in die Biblia Hebraica von Ernst Würthwein* (Tübingen: Deutsche Bibelgesellschaft, 2009), 138–42; Emmanuel Tov, *Textual Criticism of the Hebrew Bible*, Third Edition, Revised and Expanded (Minneapolis MN: Fortress Press, 2012), 146–47.

2.2.2 The Books of the Prophets

There are other books in the Hebrew Bible that may contain important information on the last days of the Northern Kingdom. Isa 7–8 refers to the Syro-Ephraimite War, a conflict between the Southern Kingdom of Judah and the anti-Judaean league of the Northern Kingdom and Aram-Damascus, which is also recorded in 2Kgs 16. In addition, part of the Book of Hosea is sometimes assumed to allude to the situation on the eve of the fall of the Northern Kingdom.

It is generally assumed that collections of the prophets' words or oral traditions concerning their activities lie at the core of the books of the Prophets such as Isaiah and Hosea. Therefore, in order to extract historical information from these books, an approach is required that is different from that employed for the analysis of the Book of Kings, part of which is assumed to be derived from archival sources.

Recently, the difficulty in locating the original words of the prophets, which had been assumed to be the nuclei in the prophetical books, has been recognized, since the prophetical books too have been subject to extensive editing. As a result, the prophetical books are used less when discussing the prophetic figures in the time of the kingdoms and also as a historical source for reconstructing the history of the kingdoms.[8]

On the other hand, some scholars recently argued that, with adequate caution, one can still extract historical information on the last days of the Northern Kingdom from the early prophecies in the Book of Hosea.[9] Regardless of the validity of this argument, it reflects the view that the state of affairs as described in the Book of Hosea corresponds to the historical situation "at that time." If so, one must first aim to reconstruct the historical situation "at that time" on the basis of other historical sources before judging the value of the Book of Hosea as a historical source. For this purpose, one must build a rough historical framework based on these other sources and then examine whether or not the description in the Book of Hosea fits in there.

At any rate, because of the process required to examine their historical reliability, and due to the fact that they do not derive from archival sources, the prophetical books can serve only as subsidiary sources for reconstructing the last

---

[8] Ehud Ben-Zvi, "The Concept of Prophetic Books and Its Historical Setting," in *The Production of Prophecy: Constructing Prophecy and Prophets in Yehud*, eds. Diana V. Edelman and Ehud Ben Zvi (London: Routledge, 2009): 73–95.

[9] E.g., Nadav Na'aman, "The Book of Hosea as a Source for the Last Days of the Kingdom of Israel," *BZ* 59 (2015): 232–56.

days of the Northern Kingdom of Israel. The prophetical books and their historical value for our topic are discussed in Part VIII of this volume.

2.3 Archaeological Data

Excavations in the Southern Levant have been under way for more than 150 years. Recently, archaeological information has been increasingly consulted for reconstructing the history of ancient Israel.[10] At many of the ruins of the cities in the Northern Kingdom, large-scale destruction layers have been detected that allegedly date to the period of its conquest, as they have been conventionally understood as the results of Tiglath-pileser III's military campaigns.

Samaria, the last capital of the Northern Kingdom, was excavated twice, first in the beginning and then in the middle of the twentieth century.[11] In the 1990s, the results of the excavations were re-evaluated by Ron Tappy through extensive analysis of the original field notes and by adopting an updated methodology, which offered a new archaeological basis for considering the conquest of Samaria.[12]

Recent excavations, for example those at Megiddo and Jezreel, have also shed new light on the Assyrian administrative and economic strategy after these sites had been incorporated into the Empire. Archaeological issues concerning the last days of the Northern Kingdom of Israel are discussed in Part III of this volume.

---

10 This problem is recently discussed in detail in Shuichi Hasegawa, "David and Goliath: Towards a Dialogue between Archaeology and Biblical Studies," in *"Now It Happened in Those Days": Studies in Biblical, Assyrian and Other Ancient Near Eastern Historiography Presented to Mordechai Cogan on His 75th Birthday*, eds. Shmuel Aḥituv, Amitai Baruch-Unna, Israel Ephʻal, Tova Forti, and Jeffrey H. Tiggay (Winona Lake IN: Eisenbrauns, 2017), 607–22.
11 George Andrew Reisner, Clarence Stanley Fisher and D. G. Lyon, *Harvard Excavations at Samaria, 1908–1910*, 2 vols. (Cambridge MA: Harvard University Press, 1924); John Winter Crowfoot and Grace M. Crowfoot, *Samaria-Sebaste 2: Early Ivories from Samaria* (London: Palestine Exploration Fund, 1938); John Winter Crowfoot, Kathleen Mary Kenyon and Eleazar Lipa Sukenik, *The Buildings at Samaria* (London: Palestine Exploration Fund, 1942); John Winter Crowfoot, Grace M. Crowfoot and Kathleen Mary Kenyon, *Samaria-Sebaste III: The Objects* (London: Palestine Exploration Fund, 1957).
12 Ron E. Tappy, *The Archaeology of Israelite Samaria, Volume I: Early Iron Age through the Ninth Century B.C.E.* (Winona Lake IN: Eisenbrauns, 1992); id., *The Archaeology of Israelite Samaria, Volume II: The Eighth Century B.C.E.* (Winona Lake IN: Eisenbrauns, 2001).

3 A Brief Synopsis of Previous Research

Although many books are devoted to the history of ancient Israel, no single volume comprehensively deals with the final years of the Northern Kingdom. In this short overview of the history of research, we shall concentrate on the two topics that have been the main focus of historical research on this period: one is the Syro-Ephraimite War, the other the exact date of the conquest of Samaria.

Regarding the Syro-Ephraimite War, Stuart A. Irvine discussed the historical situation of the Southern Kingdom of Judah during this conflict in its international setting in a 1990 monograph, based on the analysis of the Hebrew Bible and the Assyrian royal inscriptions.[13] According to Irvine, Ahaz's request for help from Assyria, as described in 2Kgs 16, is a dramatization by the Deuteronomist and therefore cannot be regarded as historically factual. Whether one accepts Irvine's view or not, his observation that the description in the Book of Kings does not reflect the historical event is reasonable.

Irvine's primary interest lies in the historical circumstances of the prophecies in Isa 6–9, and how a prophet in the Hebrew Bible can be understood in relation to kingship. Hence, although Irvine paid attention also to the Northern Kingdom, his main focus rests on the situation in the Southern Kingdom. The traditional view of historical biblical scholarship that uncritically relies on the text in Isa 7 is to assume an anti-Assyrian alliance between Aram-Damascus and the Northern Kingdom of Israel.[14] According to this line of research, the Northern Kingdom and Aram-Damascus allied in order to attack the Southern Kingdom of Judah, which had refused to join the anti-Assyrian alliance, with a view to replace the Judahite king with a puppet ruler of their choosing who would join the alliance. However, no source other than Isa 7 attests to that purpose of the anti-

---

[13] Stuart A. Irvine, *Isaiah, Ahaz, and the Syro-Ephraimitic Crisis* (Atlanta GA: Scholars Press, 1990).

[14] Joachim Begrich, "Der syrisch-ephraimitische Krieg und seine weltpolitischen Zusammenhänge," *ZDMG* 83 (1929): 213–37; Bustenay Oded, "The Historical Background of the Syro-Ephraimite War Re-Considered," *CBQ* 34 (1972): 153–65; Herbert Donner, *Geschichte des Volkes Israel und seiner Nachbarn in Grundzügen, Teil 2: Von der Königszeit bis zu Alexander dem Großen mit einem Ausblick auf die Geschichte des Judentums bis Kochba*, 4th edition (Göttingen: Vandenhoeck & Ruprecht, 1986), 337; Martin Noth, *Geschichte Israels*, 10th edition (Göttingen: Vandenhoeck & Ruprecht, 1986), 235; Nadav Na'aman, "Forced Participation in Alliances in the Course of the Assyrian Campaigns to the West," in *Ah Assyria... Studies in Assyrian History and Ancient Near Eastern Historiography Presented to Hayim Tadmor*, ed. Mordechai Cogan and Israel Eph'al (Jerusalem: Magnes 1991): 80–98, esp. 91–94; Christian Frevel, *Geschichte Israels* (Stuttgart: Kohlhammer, 2016), 240.

Assyrian alliance. It is therefore requisite to examine once again the actions of other kingdoms in the region, as mentioned in the Assyrian inscriptions, in order to gauge just how likely this hypothesis is.

Turning to the conquest of Samaria, Bob Becking has published a monograph on this topic in 1992.[15] Using three sources, namely, 2Kgs, the Assyrian royal inscriptions, and the Babylonian Chronicles, Becking supported Hugo Winckler's and Hayim Tadmor's view that Samaria was conquered twice.[16] He dated the first conquest to 723 BCE (Tadmor: 722 BCE) and the second to 720 BCE. Becking also elucidated the deportation of people to the territory that previously belonged to the Northern Kingdom, as well as the deportation of the Israelites to other regions, by using various Assyrian and Babylonian sources. His most recent views on the subject are presented in Part I of this volume.

No single available source relates two consecutive conquests of Samaria. The two-conquest hypothesis was forwarded in order to explain the inconsistency seen in the description of the conqueror of Samaria between 2Kgs 17:3–6// 18:9–10 and the Babylonian Chronicles on the one hand, and the Assyrian royal inscriptions on the other hand. The first two identify the conqueror as Shalmaneser V (727–722 BCE), whereas the inscriptions of Sargon II (722–705 BCE) describe the conquest of Samaria as a major achievement of this ruler's early years. It seems significant that the Book of Kings and the Babylonian Chronicles, although different in viewpoint and language, agree on the identity of the conqueror of Samaria, and this has led to the formulation of the two-conquests hypothesis.

On the other hand, there are scholars who suggest that only one conquest of Samaria took place. Nadav Na'aman suggested that Samaria, even if it was besieged by Shalmaneser V, was conquered only once by Sargon II in 720 BCE.[17] S. J. Park tried to solve the above-mentioned problem by explaining that Sargon II conquered Samaria under Shalmaneser V, before his enthronement (722 BCE).[18]

---

[15] Bob Becking, *The Fall of Samaria: An Historical and Archaeological Study* (Leiden: Brill, 1992).

[16] Hugo Winckler, "Beiträge zur quellenscheidung der Königsbücher," in id., *Alttestamentliche Untersuchungen* (Leipzig: Pfeiffer, 1892): 1–54, esp. 15–20; Hayim Tadmor, "The Campaigns of Sargon II of Assur: A Chronological-Historical Study," *JCS* 12 (1958): 33–40; Kyle Lawson Younger, Jr., "The Fall of Samaria in Light of Recent Research," *CBQ* 61 (1999): 461–82.

[17] Nadav Na'aman, "The Historical Background to the Conquest of Samaria," *Bib* 71 (1990): 206–25; Julian E. Reade, "Sargon's Campaigns of 720, 716, and 715 B.C.: Evidence from the Sculptures," *JNES* 35 (1076): 100–101; M. Christine Tetley, "The Date of Samaria's Fall as a Reason for Rejecting the Hypothesis of Two Conquests," *CBQ* 64 (2002): 59–77.

[18] Sung Jin Park, "A New Historical Reconstruction of the Fall of Samaria," *Bib* 93 (2012): 98–106.

Overall, there is no scholarly consensus as to the date of the conquest and the conqueror of Samaria.[19]

4 The Contributions Offered in the Present Volume

Leading scholars from several disciplines contribute to the debate by presenting the results of their research in this volume.

With methodological reflections on his previous work, Bob Becking attempts to reconsider the fall of Samaria in a way that deliberately gives less priority to highly biased textual sources such as the Hebrew Bible and the Assyrian royal inscriptions. Based primarily on archaeological data, Becking points out that the Assyrian Empire's interest in the conquest of the Southern Levant in the second half of the eighth century BCE was economically oriented rather than political.

Based on the extant Assyrian royal inscriptions, Jamie Novotny suggests that more information on the last days of the Northern Kingdom may once have been given in the "now-lost sources" of the three Assyrian monarchs Tiglath-pileser III, Shalmaneser V, and Sargon II. He concludes that especially inscriptions of the first two kings may well have contained more detailed information on the subject of Samaria.

Eckart Frahm presents new editions of eighteen passages from inscriptions of Sargon II of Assyria that deal with the fall of Samaria. He demonstrates how misleading the information from Assyrian royal inscriptions can be at times and highlights the resultant difficulty in reconstructing the history of the last days of the Northern Kingdom. Taking into account all the available data, Frahm reaches the provisional conclusion that Shalmaneser V was the Assyrian king who was solely responsible for the conquest of Samaria, while the deportation of its inhabitants took place under Sargon II's command.

F. Mario Fales, while following Nadav Na'aman's hypothesis of a single conquest of Samaria, explains the possible economic motivation ("grand strategy") behind Assyria's thrust into the Northern Kingdom, such as better access to olive oil and wine, to the maritime trade of the Phoenicians, to army horses and spe-

---

19 Cf. John H. Hayes and Jeffrey K. Kuan, "The Final Years of Samaria (730–720 B.C.)," *Bib* 72 (1991): 153–81; Gershon Galil, "The Last Years of the Kingdom of Israel and the Fall of Samaria," *CBQ* 57 (1995): 52–64.

cialized military professionals. Fales regards the supposed three-year-siege of Samaria as non-real event.

Karen Radner deals with the fate of its people after the fall of Samaria within the framework of the well-organized management of the populations of the vast lands under Assyrian rule. A variety of contemporary Assyrian sources show that Samarians with specific and specialized skill sets seemingly enjoyed comparatively high status, once resettled.

Robert G. Morkot summarizes the ongoing debates over the complicated Egyptian chronology in the period of the last days of the Northern Kingdom. Morkot suggests that the Northern Kingdom most probably had commercial and possibly also close political relations with the Libyan rulers in the Delta, rather than with the Kushite power in the south.

Exploring the language of conquest in Sargon II's annals and the archaeological record of the old excavations of Samaria, Ron E. Tappy points out the problems in the excavators' dating of Samaria's stratigraphical sequence. He concludes that Samaria escaped wholesale destruction at the hands of the Assyrian forces.

Based on updated archaeological information, Norma Franklin reassesses the function of Megiddo and Jezreel before and after the campaigns of Tiglath-pileser III of Assyria to the region. Well integrated into the Assyrian provincial system, both continued to function as key military and administrative sites in the region.

Timo Tekoniemi's critical analysis of 2Kgs 17 demonstrates the significance of text-critical study of the biblical text before using it as a historical source. There are a few instances in which the Old Greek text and the Masoretic text of the chapter do not agree and, although most commentators have uncritically given priority to the Masoretic text, Tekoniemi argues that there are good reasons to take the Old Greek Text more seriously into account.

A close literary analysis of 2Kgs 17:3–6 and 18:9–11 leads Dan'el Kahn to propose that the former is topically organized, derived from an official Israelite source, while the latter is a late redactional insertion, lacking any historically reliable information.

Christoph Levin likewise regards 2Kgs 18:9–11 as secondary but he finds secondary elements also in 2Kgs 17:3–4 which largely comprises later theological comments. Levin reconstructs the original record using 2Kgs 17:5–6 and 18:9–11 as a succinct account of Shalmaneser V's conquest of Samaria and his deportation of its inhabitants to various places in the Assyrian Empire.

Kristin Weingart challenges an old conundrum of biblical chronology in 2Kgs 15–18. Assuming the change of the New Year in the Northern Kingdom under Assyrian influence during Menahem's reign, and identifying Jotham and

Ahaz as one and the same person, Weingart provides an ingenious solution for the difficulties encountered in the text.

Steven L. McKenzie discusses the same chronological issue. Reconsidering the merits and problems of previous scholarly suggestions, McKenzie cannot find an ultimate solution and regards the chronological data in 2Kgs 15 as "unusable for historical reconstruction."

Analyzing the description of the kings of the Northern Kingdom in 2Kgs 15, Christian Frevel draws attention to their negative portrayal, which he sees as a deliberate strategy by the author. Frevel warns against using the information in the chapter for historical reconstructions.

Basing his view on the analysis of the literary structure and the narrative pragmatic of 2Kgs 17, Michael Pietsch regards the text as a unit, while he rejects the idea that the information given would have originated at the Northern court. For him, the complexity of the source allows us neither to reconstruct the course of events nor to identify the Assyrian conqueror of Samaria.

Georg Hentschel attempts to perceive in the descriptions in 2Kgs 15 and 17 the change of foreign policy toward the Assyrian Empire during the last years of the Northern Kingdom and highlights how Assyria's presence in the region might have exerted influence upon the chain of events that finally led the Northern Kingdom to its fall.

With a focus on methodological considerations, Martti Nissinen discusses the difficulty in gleaning historically reliable information from the Book of Hosea because of its later editing, despite the fact that parts of the Book date to the last days of the Northern Kingdom.

Hugh G. M. Williamson sifts through the Book of Isaiah to identify passages that possibly go back to the prophet who employs the terms "Ephraim," "Samaria," and once "Jacob" for designating the Northern Kingdom. Williamson defends the view that the concept of "Israel" for the two nations must have existed even before the Fall of Samaria as reflected in Isaiah's usage of the term.

With these papers, our volume brings together leading scholars from different fields of research and, for the first time, all available data in order to discuss the problems concerning the last days of the Northern Kingdom from various perspectives. This will help, I would hope, to reach a better and deeper understanding of this crucial period of Levantine history. It is possible to argue that it was these events that triggered the birth of a "New Israel" in the Southern Kingdom of Judah in the following decades, and that eventually led to the formation of the Hebrew Bible and its underlying theology.

Reader of this volume should keep in mind that, although its contributors have tackled the historical issues from different perspectives, many are still inconclusive and thus open for further discussion. At times, the conclusions of individual contributors are at odds with those reached by others. As ever, we can yearn for the discovery of additional sources that might resolve difficulties and achieve consensus. But in the meantime, I sincerely hope that the present volume, with its interdisciplinary approach, will provide rich material for future research on the Northern Kingdom of Israel.

Abbreviations in this volume follow *The SBL Handbook of Style*, 2nd ed. (Atlanta GA: SBL Press, 2014).

Part I: **Setting the Scene**

Bob Becking
How to Encounter an Historical Problem?
"722–720 BCE" as a Case Study

1 De ondergang van Samaria (1985)

In November 1985, I defended my doctoral thesis at Utrecht University. I wrote my dissertation on the Assyrian conquest of the capital city of the Northern Kingdom of Israel from an historical as well as from an exegetical point of view.[1] Although I tried to escape the traditional way of history-writing as a narrative about kings and battles, I now see that I was too event-oriented and influenced by written sources. In other words, I took texts, especially the Hebrew Bible, as a starting point for my investigation then looked for support in other pieces of evidence. Additionally, I was too focused on verifying isolated events. Rethinking my approach leads me to three questions:
a. What is a text?
b. How does one properly encounter the past?
c. What about the *histoire conjoncturelle?*

2 What is a Text?

What is a text? Or more specifically: how does a text relate to an event? The Hebrew Bible is a text, or better, a collection of texts partly of a literary character. This observation opens a whole line of questions. There seems to be a dichotomy in the basic interpretation of texts. Novels, for instance, are generally understood to be fictional. When Biblical texts are labelled as literary texts, are they by im-

---

I would like to thank Shuichi Hasegawa for inviting me to the stimulating meeting in Munich. I have learned much from all the other papers and from the fine and open discussion. Steven McKenzie and Ronald Tappy kindly provided some suggestions to improve my English while Denise Bolton (Munich) language-edited the complete manuscript. All remaining errors are of course mine.

1 Bob Becking, *De ondergang van Samaria: Historische, exegetische en theologische opmerkingen bij II Koningen 17* (Diss. Utrecht; Meppel: Krips Repro, 1985); the historical introduction was reworked into English: Bob Becking, *The Fall of Samaria: An Historical and Archaeological Study* (Leiden: Brill, 1992).

plication fictional? And the other way around: are non-fiction texts by implication not literary? I will try to elucidate this point with an example. Many good books on history are praised for their literary quality. A good style and mastery of the language often leads to books that are both informative and a pleasure to read. The question is: how do such books relate to reality? They certainly refer to events that happened in real-time. They are, however, not equal to the event(s). Such texts do relate to reality since they are descriptions of the events.

In a comparable way, Biblical texts – of whatever literary quality – should be construed as descriptions of (parts of) reality. In fact, they are to be understood as interpretations of what might have happened. Even when a Biblical text refers to an event that with great certainty can be classified in the category 'did really happen' the text does not equal the event. It is – not unlike a restaurant bill – a selection of parts of the event presented from a specific point of view. Texts inform the reader about the view of the author on the past.[2]

As for the period of the last days of the Kingdom of Israel, it should be kept in mind that neither the Biblical accounts[3] nor the Assyrian inscriptions[4] equal the event. Both sets inform the reader about the view of their authors on the assumed events, and give hints about those events.

3 The Source as a Container of Evidence

This brings me to the following remark. Texts are historical sources in the same way that artefacts are. There is, however, a problem. This problem is connected to the fact that texts are complex by nature: They are built up in a way comparable to atoms. In a text we can find particles and forces, i.e. fermions and gluons.[5] In this metaphor, the particles are the singular statements about the past – such as "Sargon II conquered the city of Samaria". The gluons in a text are the ideology and the narrative structure that hold these particles together. In other words, a

---

[2] See Chris Lorenz, *Konstruktion der Vergangenheit: eine Einführung in die Geschichtstheorie* (Wien/Köln/Weimar: Böhlau, 1997).
[3] 2Kgs 17:1–6; 18:9–11.
[4] Cf. the essays by Eckart Frahm and Jamie Novotny in this volume. The material is presented and discussed in e.g. Becking, *The Fall of Samaria*, 21–45 and Kyle Lawson Younger Jr., "The Fall of Samaria in Light of Recent Research," *CBQ* 61 (1999): 461–82 is incomplete due to publication of new Assyrian texts.
[5] See on these particles Toshiyuki Morii, Chong-Sa Lim and Soumyendra N. Mukherjee, *The Physics of the Standard Model and Beyond* (Singapore: World Scientific Publishing Company, 2004).

distinction should be made between individual clauses – and their historical (im)possibility – and the narrative as a whole. The narrative structure as a whole is the matrix that is created by the narrator, or historian, to convince the reader of the truth of his or her view on the events. It is for this reason that a historian has to deconstruct a given source in search of trustworthy particles. Only then can the Hebrew Bible be seen as a "source of information" at the level of its various particles, but not at the level of the text as a whole.

A warning should be taken from the philosophy of history of Robin G. Collingwood.[6] Collingwood was looking for a way out of the dilemma between "realism" and "scepticism". Realism is the position that the sources inform us in a realistic way about the past. A sceptic is of the opinion that the past is inaccessible. By implication, we do not have any real knowledge of the past. Collingwood tried to overcome this dilemma by elaborating a view on the character of so-called historical sources. These traces of the past are available and knowable in the present. All the historian has in hand are the particles of evidence mirroring the past. The evidence makes it possible to know the past, but only in a restricted way. The task of the historian is to collect as much evidence as possible and then construct a personal image of the past. In this re-enactment, models and imagination play a role. The historian cannot do without metaphorical language to describe in an approximate and incomplete way the events mirrored in the sources.

In combining both these approaches to the character of written evidence, I have come to the position that the Old Testament text should be treated primarily as a collection of trace evidence. The Old Testament supplies its readers with diverse vestiges of the past that, one way or another, mirror the past. These traces can be (and have been) treated differently. This difference is partly related to the ideology of the historian – be it minimalistic, or maximalistic, or something in between. Of greater importance, however, is the awareness of other traces of evidence and the matrix in which the historian "reads" this variety of evidence.[7]

---

[6] Robin G. Collingwood, The Idea of History: Revised Edition with Lectures 1926–1928 (Oxford: Clarendon Press, 1994). On Collingwood's historiography see now Dale Jacquette, "Collingwood on Historical Authority and Historical Imagination," Journal of the Philosophy of History 3 (2009): 55–78, and Jan van der Dussen, History as a Science: The Philosophy of R. G. Collingwood (Dordrecht: Springer, 2012).

[7] Interesting remarks on this can be found in David Henige, Historical Evidence and Argument (Madison WI: University of Wisconsin Press, 2005); Kimberly Anderson, "The Footprint and the Stepping Foot: Archival Records, Evidence, and Time," Archival Science 12 (2012): 1–23; and Tim Kenyon, "Oral History and the Epistemology of Testimony," Social Epistemology 30 (2016): 45–66.

I will come back to this below. In other words, texts – as I see it now – are minor pieces of evidence: disconnected footprints in the disturbed snow of the past. They also contain "clues": references to the past that go beyond the direct context of the given piece of evidence and which inform in an indirect way about the past.[8] These traces and clues, however, are wrapped in an often biased narrative.

4 The Point of View as a Power Position

Texts are not neutral containers. The focalization-theory of Gérard Genette argues that the information in a text is always steered by the narrator.[9] The narrator makes the selection out of the available material and connects this selection into the order of the given text. The reader is thus forced to look at the *fable* – a term for the basic narration that became text in a narrative[10] – the way the narrator wants the reader to look at it. The narrator is like the hole in a shoebox through which a diorama can be seen. Hence the narrator of a text is in a power position and the reader is dependent on this sluice. It is the narrator who forces one to look at the ensemble of the narrative from his or her point of view. With regard to the Hebrew Bible, this implies that historians should at least be aware of the fact that information about the past is sluiced through a specific point of view. It is not neutral reports that are presented.

In view of the written evidence concerning the Assyrian conquest of Samaria, it should be noted that we are forced to look at the short narratives in the Book of Kings, as well as the seemingly objective reports in the Assyrian royal inscriptions, through a specific lens. 2Kgs 17:1–6 and 18:9–11 represent the

---

[8] Carlo Ginzburg, *Clues, Myths and the Historical Method* (Baltimore MD: Johns Hopkins University Press, 1989; translated from the 1986 Italian publication).
[9] Gérard Genette, "Discours du récit: essaie de méthode," in id., Figures III (Paris: Édition du Seuil, 1972); id., Nouveau discours du récit (Paris: Édition du Seuil, 1983) = id., Narrative Discourse Revisited (New York: Cornell University Press, 1989); see also Willem Bronzwaer, "Implied Author, Extradiegetic Narrator and Public Reader: Gérard Genette's Narratological Model and the Reading Version of Great Expectations," Neophilologus 621 (1978): 1–18; Mieke Bal, "The Narrating and the Focalizing: a Theory of the Agents in Narrative," Style 17 (1983): 234–69; François Tolmie, Narratology and Biblical Narratives: a Practical Guide (Eugene OR: Wipf and Stock Publishers, 1999), esp. 29–38; Michael Hoey, Textual Interaction: an Introduction to Written Discourse Analysis (London/New York: Routledge, 2001).
[10] This concept should not be confused with the fable as a form in folk literature, such as the fables of Aesop or de la Fontaine.

view of the Deuteronomistic historian(s) on the past.¹¹ The pertinent inscriptions of Sargon II reveal the view of the Assyrian court-writers and their royal ideology.¹² They are written to impress the populace, especially those who visited the royal palace, as well as to account for the responsibilities of the Assyrian ruler given to him by the Assyrian gods.

Although deportations are referred to, the effect that those events would have had on the lives of "ordinary people" is silenced, both in the Hebrew Bible and the Assyrian inscriptions. The reports on exile and deportation are narrated from the focus of temple and court.

In sum, it is possible to take written texts as the starting point for an historical inquest. In view of the remarks made, it is better not to take these written texts as a starting point for finding the answer(s) of the historical problem(s). How then to proceed?

5 A Five Dimensional Matrix

More than twenty years ago, Manfred Weippert wrote a very interesting contribution to ancient Israelite historiography.¹³ I agree with him that the historiography of ancient Israel had arrived at a crossroads around 1990 and that it was important to take the right turn. Weippert hinted at two methodological weaknesses in ancient Israelite historiography.

Firstly, he argued that much of the traditional historiography is too "event-oriented". Histories of ancient Israel focus on important events in the assumed history. This implies that an important tendency in "general" historiography is

---

11 From the abundance of literature on the Deuteronomistic historian(s), I only refer to the synthesizing work by Thomas C. Römer, *The So-called Deuteronomistic History: a Sociological, Historical and Literary Introduction* (London/New York: Continuum, 2005).
12 Much has been written on Mesopotamian royal ideology, see recently: Douglas J. Green, *"I Undertook Great Works": The Ideology of Domestic Achievements in West Semitic Royal Inscriptions* (Tübingen: Mohr Siebeck, 2010); Linda T. Darling, *A History of Social Justice and Political Power in the Middle East: The Circle of Justice from Mesopotamia to Globalization* (London/New York: Routledge, 2013), 15–31; Vladimir Sazonov, "Some Remarks Concerning the Development of the Theology of War in Ancient Mesopotamia," in *The Religious Aspects of War in the Ancient Near East, Greece, and Rome*, ed. Krzysztof Ulanowski (Leiden: Brill, 2016): 23–50; David T. Rowlands, "Imperial Ideology in the Neo-Assyrian Empire," *Teaching History* 50 (2016): 4–7.
13 Manfred Weippert, "Geschichte Israels am Scheideweg," TRu 58 (1993): 71–103; the article is in fact a lengthy review of Herbert Donner, Geschichte des Volkes Israel und seiner Nachbarn in Grundzügen (Göttingen: Vandenhoeck und Ruprecht, 1984), and its reprint in one volume in 1987.

passed by. The French historiographical revolution known as the "Annales School"[14] is overlooked by almost all historians of ancient Israel. This implies that there is seldom a window into daily life. Weippert observed that the inclination of historians of ancient Israel to focus on events often results in closing the ways that would lead to an understanding of processes in ancient Israel at the level of *longue durée* or even at the level of the *histoire conjuncturelle*.[15] Fortunately, in the 20 years following this remarkable contribution, we have seen some shifts in the field.[16]

Secondly, Weippert argues that scholars – especially biblical scholars – writing a "History of Israel" too easily take the biblical narrative at face value and use it as the backbone of their (re)construction.

In order to overcome these weaknesses, Weippert proposes approaching the past through a set of five windows. In his opinion, the following five dimensions need to be explored: (1) landscape; (2) climate; (3) archaeology; (4) epigraphy; and (5) biblical texts. The past needs to be looked at through these five windows and in the order given.[17] On the basis of the evidence found, a *histoire conjuncturelle*[18] can be designed. In the next sections, I will apply this approach in connection with the "The Last Days of the Kingdom of Israel".

5.1 Landscape

A look at the landscape of ancient Israel/Palestine makes clear that this was a hilly area that contained various and differing zones. The mountainous core of Judah and Samaria was blessed with fertile soil. However, this core area, as

---

[14] A good introduction is to be found in Peter Burke, The French Historical Revolution: the Annales School, 1929–89 (Stanford CA: Stanford University Press, 1990).
[15] On this concept see Fernand Braudel, "Histoire et sciences sociales: La longue durée," *Annales. Histoire, Sciences Sociales* 13 (1958): 725–53.
[16] Important voices being Hans M. Barstad, *History and the Hebrew Bible: Studies in Ancient Israelite and Ancient near Eastern Historiography* (Tübingen: Mohr Siebeck, 2008); Kurt L. Noll, *Canaan and Israel in Antiquity: a Textbook on History and Religion Second Edition* (London/New York: Bloomington, 2013), 23–65; Christian Frevel, *Geschichte Israels* (Stuttgart: Kohlhammer, 2015), 17–41; Lester L. Grabbe, *Ancient Israel: What Do We Know and How Do We Know it?* (London/New York: Bloomington, 2017; rev. ed.), 3–38.
[17] This matrix is more fruitful than that proposed by Heather Gerow, "Methodology in Ancient History: Reconstructing the Fall of Samaria," *Constellations* 2 (2010): no. 1, who operates with the model to start by the Hebrew Bible and look for corroborations in other sources and findings.
[18] On this concept see Braudel, "Histoire et Sciences'; with critical remarks by Gerrit van Roon, "Historians and long waves," *Futures* 13 (1981): 383–88.

well as the surrounding semi-arid zones, constantly required rainwater and a technology to prevent run-off. In other words, the area had great agricultural potential but needed an intelligent cultivator. The territory of the Northern Kingdom was divided into various zones. The presence of hills and mountains created a patchwork of semi-independent agricultural entities. This element certainly slowed the pace of nation-building after the collapse of the Bronze Age culture. The Hebrew Bible describes the Northern Kingdom as a complex of ten different tribes. I will not argue for the historicity of this tradition, but only note that the landscape was ripe for regionalization. These tribal areas might eventually have unified.[19] However, the different identities might have survived for considerable time. Pride in one's tribal identity in addition or opposition to the overarching national identity probably endured until the Babylonian Exile. The presence of various tribal factions – and their different ambitions – might have negatively affected the alertness of the central organs of power, an issue that could have contributed to the internal weakness of the Northern Kingdom at the eve of destruction.[20]

5.2 Climate

Having a semi-arid climate, the territory of the Kingdom of Israel was strongly dependent on rainfall for its agriculture. The way in which the population coped with this problem will be discussed in the next section. The Iron Age I–II period coincided with a period of global cooling. Climate in the Iron Age II–III period remained stable in ancient Israel.[21] We can therefore assume that no specific impulses from a (sudden) change in climate would have influenced the course of events leading to the end of the kingdom.

---

[19] On this process see Alexander H. Joffe, "The Rise of Secondary States in the Iron Age Levant," *JESHO* 45 (2002): 425–67.
[20] This view, for instance in an antagonism between 'Gileadites' and 'Manassites' as argued for by John Gray, *I & II Kings* (London: SCM Press, 1977; third ed.) or William H. Shea, "The Date and Significance of the Samaria Ostraca," *IEJ* 27 (1977): 16–27, is difficult to test.
[21] See, e.g. Arie S. Issar, Water Shall Flow from the Rock: Hydrology and Climate in the Lands of the Bible (Berlin/New York: Springer, 1990); Lester L. Grabbe, "The Kingdom of Israel from Omri to the Fall of Samaria: If We Only Had the Bible …," in Ahab Agonistes: The Rise and Fall of the Omri Dynasty, ed. Lester L. Grabbe (London/New Tork: T&T Clark, 2007): 54–99.

5.3 Archaeology

In my monograph on the Assyrian conquest, I briefly discussed the archaeological evidence.[22] As I now see it, I was then much too focused on the military and administrative aspects of events. I scrutinized the archaeological evidence for traces of destruction at a variety of sites, as well as for traces of the administrative take-over by the Assyrians, by looking at the construction of buildings that could be interpreted as Assyrian bureaucratic centers. I now have quite a different set of questions with which to "read" the archaeological evidence. Firstly, does the evidence support or challenge the assumption that the change in political power had little influence on rural communities in the territory.[23] Secondly, what happened in Samaria? And thirdly, what do we know about the Assyrian military presence in the area?

I will start with a side remark. As a matter of fact, in my earlier thesis, I drew the correct conclusion that the archaeological evidence was insufficient to solve the chronological riddle.[24]

Regarding the first question, the archaeological data from areas outside Samaria provides no evidence for the complete destruction or disruption of the Israelite countryside.[25] The fact that the agricultural terraces remained intact can be seen as a clue to the Assyrian interest in maintaining food production. During the Iron Age II period some technological improvements in the system of terrace agriculture took place. This system is a typical element of the *longue durée*. In the Levant, the construction of terraces on hill slopes has very ancient (even pre-historic) roots.[26] During the Early Bronze Age I period, this terrace technique was

---

[22] Becking, *The Fall of Samaria*, 56–60.
[23] A good starting point for this exercise is to be found in Magen Broshi and Israel Finkelstein, "The Population of Palestine in Iron Age II," *BASOR* 287 (1992): 47–60.
[24] Becking, *The Fall of Samaria*, 56–60.
[25] See also Frevel, *Geschichte Israels*, 242–43.
[26] From the Natufian site Nahal Oren four architectural terraces are known that supported a settlement of about 13 hut-dwellings, see Moshe Stekelis and Tamar Yizraeli, "Excavations at Nahal Oren: A Preliminary Report," *IEJ* 13 (1963): 1–12; see also Ian Kuijt and Nigel Goring-Morris, "Foraging, Farming, and Social Complexity in the Pre-Pottery Neolithic of the Southern Levant: A Review and Synthesis," *Journal of World Prehistory* 16 (2002): 361–440; Guy Bar-Oz, Tamar Dayan, Daniel Kaufman and Mina Weinstein-Evron, "The Natufian Economy at el-Wad Terrace with Special Reference to Gazelle Exploitation Patterns," *Journal of Archaeological Science* 31 (2004): 217–31.

implemented on a larger scale.[27] This technology helped to arrest the run-off water, making it useful for agricultural purposes. Additionally, the terrace system meant that more horizontal surfaces for agricultural use came into existence, which made the work for the cultivator much easier. A system of terraces is also very helpful in avoiding erosion.[28] The presence of a developed system of agricultural terraces contains an important clue. The system hints at an advanced level of agricultural development. Combining the terrace system with the deployment of the iron-tipped plough[29] farmers were able to produce more than their local need. This surplus was important as a reserve in times of drought or crop failure. On the other hand, the surplus was also needed to pay off local elites in exchange for their protection.[30] In the territory of the Northern Kingdom, the technology of food production on terraces continued after the Assyrians took over the capital city of Samaria.

Moving to the city of Samaria itself, a few remarks must be made. Crowfoot and Kenyon's excavations brought to light various indications of demolition and destruction. Kenyon classified these traces as silent witnesses to a massive Assyrian conquest of the city. In her view, the overwhelming power of the Assyrian army overpowered the Israelite defence-lines by destroying great parts of the city and its buildings.[31] Stig Forsberg challenged this interpretation, suggesting it was biased towards biblical traditions. In his opinion the traces do not refer to a single eighth century destruction of the city but are witnesses to a variety of attacks on the city from tribal conflicts within the Kingdom of Israel as well as from without: from the Assyrians, via the Scythians, up to Roman times. In his view Kathleen Kenyon telescoped evidence from a long time period into the short

---

27 See Nelson Glueck, "Further Explorations in Eastern Palestine," *BASOR* 86 (1942), 14–24; Issar, *Water Shall Flow from the Rock*, 123–40; Pierre de Miroscheddji, "Tel Yarmut, 1992," *IEJ* 42 (1992): 265–72.
28 See, e.g., David C. Hopkins, *The Highlands of Canaan: Agricultural Life in the Early Iron Age* (Sheffield: Sheffield Academic Press, 1985), 173–86; Hendrik J. Bruins, M. Evenari and U. Nessler, "Rainwater-Harvesting for Food Production in Arid Zones," *Applied Geography* 6 (1986): 13–32; Karl W. Butzer, "Environmental History in the Mediterranean World: Cross-Disciplinary Investigation of Cause-and-Effect for Degradation and Soil Erosion," *Journal of Archaeological Science* 32 (2005): 1773–800.
29 See Hopkins, *The Highlands of Canaan*, 217–23.
30 On the development of agriculture see Patrick Nolan and Gerhard Lenski, *Human Societies* (Boulder AZ: Paradigm, 2004).
31 See, e.g., John W. Crowfoot, Grace M. Crowfoot and Kathleen M. Kenyon, *The Objects from Samaria* (London: Palestine Exploration Fund, 1957); Kathleen M. Kenyon, *Royal Cities of the Old Testament* (New York: Schocken, 1971).

time slot of the last days of the Kingdom of Israel.[32] Ron Tappy, too, referred to the methodological weaknesses in Kenyon's reconstruction. According to him, Kenyon's work suffers from the lack of a clear stratigraphy – an argument that parallels Forsberg's. Kenyon's documentation of the find spots of the evidence is – in Tappy's view – sloppy and loose. If I understand him correctly, some of the traces can be connected to the Assyrian assault. The city, however, was not completely devastated. The presence of Israelite-Assyrian pottery indicates that the tell remained occupied.[33]

There are a few archaeological clues about the Assyrian military presence in the area. Fantalkin and Tal have re-examined the remains of a fortress at Tell Qudadi (Tell esh-Shuna), located on the northern bank of the mouth of the Yarkon River. Their analysis of the ceramic assemblage made clear that the site was only established in the second half of the eighth century BCE. They argue that this stronghold should not be interpreted as an Israelite defensive fortress, but as an Assyrian establishment that secured Assyrian trade along the *via maris*.[34] This would indicate that the Assyrian interest was more focused on trade along the Mediterranean coast than it was on the agricultural potential of the hill country. In addition, Finkelstein convincingly argued that the tower excavated by Albright and Lapp at Tell el-Ful[35] was first constructed in the Iron IIC period as an Assyrian watchtower commanding the northern approach to Jerusalem.[36] This military structure needs to be construed as a defensive measure

---

32 Stig Forsberg, *Near Eastern Destruction Datings as Sources for Greek and Near Eastern Iron Age Chronology: Archaeological and Historical Studies: The cases of Samaria (722 BC) and Tarsus (696 BC)* (Uppsala: Acta Universitatis Upsaliensis, 1995), esp. 25–36.
33 Ron E. Tappy, *The Archaeology of Israelite Samaria, Volume II: The Eighth Century BCE* (Winona Lake IN: Eisenbrauns, 2001), 351–441; id., "The Final Years of Israelite Samaria: Toward a Dialogue between Texts and Archaeology," in *Up to the Gates of Ekron: Essays on the Archaeology and History of the Eastern Mediterranean in Honor of Seymour Gitin*, ed. Sidnie White Crawford and Amnon Ben-Tor (Jerusalem: W. F. Albright Institute of Archaeological Research/Israel Exploration Society, 2007), 258–79. Note that Israel Finkelstein, *The Forgotten Kingdom: The Archaeology and History of Northern Israel* (Atlanta GA: SBL Press, 2013), does not refer to this question or the work of Tappy.
34 Alexander Fantalkin and Oren Tal, "Re-Discovering the Iron Age Fortress at Tell Qudadi in the Context of Neo-Assyrian Imperialistic Policies," *PEQ* 141 (2009): 188–206; see also Yifat Thareani, "The Empire and the "Upper Sea": Assyrian Control Strategies along the Southern Levantine Coast," *BASOR* 375 (2016): 77–102.
35 See Nancy L. Lapp, "Casemate Walls in Palestine and the Late Iron II Casemate at Tell el-Ful (Gibeah)," *BASOR* 223 (1976): 25–42.
36 Israel Finkelstein, "Tell el-Ful Revisited: The Assyrian and Hellenistic Periods (With a New Identification)," *PEQ* 143 (2011): 106–18.

against a possible attack from Judah. In a different way, the Tell el-Ful tower served the Assyrian interests in the area of the former Kingdom of Israel.

An interesting remark has been made by a group of osteo-archaeologists. According to them, human remains dating from the Iron Age IIB period Levant – when the Assyrian Empire was at its height – only rarely manifest trauma to the skull, left forearm, vertebrae, and ribs. The few existing examples could be interpreted as referring to war-time circumstances. The great majority of intact skeletons hint that the Assyrians were not as cruel and unrelenting towards their enemies as is often supposed by tradition.[37]

In sum, the Assyrian take-over was less brutal than often imagined. The evidence hints that the Assyrians wanted to rule over the territory in order to safeguard their economic interests, such as the trade route along the coast and the remittance of the agricultural surplus.

5.4 Epigraphy

There are no paleo-Hebrew inscriptions that can directly be connected to the Assyrian conquest of Samaria. Unfortunately, there is no counterpart to the Lachish ostraca that describe the fear that arose in this Judaean stronghold during the campaign of Nebuchadnezzar against Jerusalem in the early sixth century BCE.[38] Fortunately, we have some material to work with. The Samaria ostraca document the delivery of wine and oil from various districts to the court in Samaria around the middle of the eighth century BCE.[39] The absence of compara-

---

[37] H. Cohen, V. Slon, A. Barash, H. May, B. Medlej and I. Hershkovitz, "Assyrian Attitude Towards Captive Enemies: a 2700-Year-Old Paleo-Forensic Study," *International Journal of Osteoarchaeology* 23 (2013): 265–80; Susan G. Sheridan, "Bioarchaeology in the Ancient Near East: Challenges and Future Directions for the Southern Levant," *American Journal of Physical Anthropology* 162 (2017): 110–52.
[38] Lak (6):1.1–21; editio princeps: Harry Torczyner, *Lachish I: The Lachish Letters* (London/New York: Oxford University Press, 1938).
[39] Sam (8):1.1–102; see Shea, "The Date and Significance of the Samaria Ostraca." On the administration and the commodities see Baruch Rosen, "Wine and Oil Allocations in the Samaria Ostraca," TA 13/14 (1986–87): 39–45; Meindert Dijkstra, "Chronological Problems of the Eighth Century BCE: a New Proposal for Dating the Samaria Ostraca," in *Past, Present, Future: The Deuteronomistic History and the Prophets*, ed. Johannes C. de Moor and Harry F. van Rooy (Leiden: Brill, 2000): 76–87; Avraham Faust, "Household Economies in the Kingdoms of Israel and Judah," in *Household Archaeology in Ancient Israel and Beyond*, ed. Assaf Yasur-Landau, Jennie R. Ebeling and Laura B. Mazow (Leiden: Brill, 2011): 255–74; Matthew J. Suriano, "Wine Shipments to Samaria from Royal Vineyards," *Tel Aviv* 43 (2016): 99–110; on the archaeological con-

ble documents from the period after the Assyrian conquest of the capital city does not indicate a break in the production of oil and wine in the area. We can only assume that the Assyrian administration found other ways of recording these deliveries.

Epigraphic evidence indicates that the exiled Israelites were carried away to till the fields in Assyria, and that some of them were incorporated into the Assyrian army.[40] According to the documents, at least a part of these exiles lived in restricted freedom. Some were accepted as witnesses in various contracts. Information about their religion is absent except for the fact that many of them had names with a Yahwistic-theophoric element.[41] Neo-Assyrian inscriptions found in the territory of the former Northern Kingdom – fragmentary and rare as they are – indicate that the 'newcomers', i.e. those exiled from Neo-Babylonian territories who were conquered by the Assyrians, had mingled with the local population.[42]

Royal inscriptions reporting the Assyrian conquest of Samaria supply restricted and biased information on the past. This does not imply that they are of no value for the historian. They should, however, be taken for what they are: expressions of a royal discourse larded with some details that could be correct.[43]

5.5 Hebrew Bible

I will not discuss or summarize the debate on the value of the Hebrew Bible for the reconstruction of the past. The interested reader is referred to the very infor-

---

text of the find of the ostraca see Ron E. Tappy, *The Archaeology of the Ostraca House at Israelite Samaria: Epigraphic Discoveries in Complicated Contexts* (Boston MA: American Schools of Oriental Research, 2016).

40 See Ran Zadok, "Israelites and Judaeans in the Neo-Assyrian Documentation (732–602 BCE): An Overview of the Sources and a Socio-Historical Assessment," *BASOR* 374 (2015), 159–89 and Radner's chapter in this volume.

41 For a survey see Becking, *The Fall of Samaria*, 61–93; with Zadok, "Israelites and Judaeans" and Josette Elayi, *Sargon II, King of Assyria* (Atlanta GA: SBL Press, 2017), 50–51.

42 See Becking, *The Fall of Samaria*, 94–118; see also Karel van der Toorn, "Cuneiform Documents from Syria-Palestine. Texts, Scribes, and Schools," *ZDPV* 116 (2000): 97–113; Wayne Horowitz, Takayoshi Oshima and Seth Sanders, "A Bibliographical List of Cuneiform Inscriptions from Canaan, Palestine/Philistia, and the Land of Israel," *JAOS* 122 (2002): 753–66.

43 The inscriptions are discussed in Becking, *The Fall of Samaria*, 21–45. On Sargon II see now also Sarah C. Melville, *The Campaigns of Sargon II, King of Assyria, 721–705 BC* (Norman OK: University of Oklahoma Press, 2016), 21–55 and Elayi, *Sargon II*.

mative book by Brad Kelle and Megan Bishop Moore.⁴⁴ As for the reports in the Hebrew Bible on the last days of the Kingdom of Israel, scholars hold different positions on the provenance of these textual units and their date of composition. I will not try to summarize that discussion or argue for a specific position.⁴⁵ These textual units can be read in two ways.

Firstly, reading the texts from a factual perspective, it is clear that 2Kgs 17:1–6 and 18:9–11 offer a set of propositions about the event:
1. Hoshea, the last king of the Northern Kingdom, rebelled against his Assyrian overlord.
2. Hoshea unavailingly looked for support in Egypt.
3. Shalmaneser (V), king of Assyria, conquered the city of Samaria.
4. Inhabitants of the Northern Kingdom were carried away in exile to a set of localities controlled by the Assyrian Empire.

These propositions can be rephrased as hypotheses about the past. It is, however, impossible to verify their implied claims. In case it turns out that they are all correct, it should be noted that they can only be interpreted as supplying a skeleton, without flesh, of the events. They only supply surface information on the course of events. The impact of the event on the life of (ordinary) people is not narrated.

Secondly, the Book of Kings offers a view on the reasons for the Assyrian conquest from a perspective comparable to that of the *longue durée*, but quite different from the *Annales*-perspective. The religious ideology of authors presents the fall of Samaria as the result of divine wrath triggered by the illicit conduct of the kings and inhabitants of Israel.⁴⁶ This explanation will not convince the modern, post-modern, or post-post-modern historian. It indicates, however, that the Biblical writers did look at the event from a broader perspective.

---

44 Megan Bishop Moore and Brad E. Kelle, *Biblical History and Israel's Past: The Changing Study of the Bible and History* (Grand Rapids MI/Cambridge: Eerdmans, 2011).
45 See Younger, "The Fall of Samaria," 477–79, the various commentaries on the Book of Kings, and the chapters by Levin, McKenzie and Tekoniemi in this volume.
46 See my analysis of 2Kgs 17:7–20 and 21–23 in Bob Becking, *From David to Gedaliah: the Book of Kings as Story and History* (Fribourg: Universitätsverlag & Göttingen: Vandenhoeck und Ruprecht, 2007), 88–122.

6 The Two-Conquests Theory

Previously, I have defended the "two-conquests theory".[47] This idea was first formulated by Hugo Winckler[48] and later elaborated by Hayim Tadmor.[49] This theory reconciles the claims by two Assyrian kings to have conquered Samaria. Both Shalmaneser V and Sargon II are described as conqueror of the capital of the Kingdom of Israel. In the Babylonian Chronicle it is said that Shalmaneser "destroyed Samaria" (^{uru}šá-ma-ra-'-in iḫ-te-pi).[50] In the royal inscriptions narrating the deeds of Sargon II, this king is presented as the one who "besieged and conquered Samerina" (^{uru}sa-me-ri-na al-me ak-šud) over half a dozen times.[51] In my opinion, the chronological riddle can best be solved by assuming a twofold Assyrian take-over: firstly by Shalmaneser V, and after the premature death of this king, by his successor Sargon II.[52]

The re-reading of the archaeological evidence, however, prompts me to rephrase the theory. The relatively scarce evidence for demolition both in Samaria and in the countryside urges one to rethink the character of the language in the Assyrian inscriptions. With Ron Tappy, I am now convinced that the tough language in these inscriptions is primarily hyperbolic.[53] The martial expression of conquest and demolition functioned to impress the audience at home in Assyria.

---

[47] Becking, *Fall of Samaria*, 21–45.
[48] Hugo Winckler, *Alttestamentliche Untersuchungen* (Leipzig: Pfeiffer, 1892), 15–20.
[49] Hayim Tadmor, "The Campaigns of Sargon II of Assur: a Chronological-Historical Study," *JCS* 12 (1958): 22–40, 77–100. Tadmor does not refer to Winckler, however.
[50] Babylonian Chronicle I i 28; see A. Kirk Grayson, *Assyrian and Babylonian Chronicles* (Locust Valley NY: Augustin, 1975), 69–87; Tadmor, "Campaigns of Sargon II," 39; Becking, *Fall of Samaria*, 22–25; Younger, "The Fall of Samaria," 464–8; Peter Dubovský, "Did Shalmaneser V Conquer the City of Samaria? An Investigation into the *ma/ba*-sign in Chronicle 1," *Or* 80 (2011): 423–38; Ariel M. Bagg, *Die Assyrer und das Westland: Studien zur historischen Geographie und Herrschaftspraxis in der Levante im 1. Jt. v.u.Z.* (Leuven: Peeters, 2011), 227–28; Grabbe, *Ancient Israel*, 171; Elayi, *Sargon II*, 46–47.
[51] Thus the Khorsabad Display Inscription, i 23. In other texts, the wording differs but always has a military flavour.
[52] This view is accepted by a majority of scholars; see, e.g., Nadav Na'aman, "The Historical Background to the Conquest of Samaria (720 BC)," *Bib* (1990): 206–25; Tappy, *Archaeology of Israelite Samaria, Volume II*, 558–75; Younger, "The Fall of Samaria"; Grabbe, *Ancient Israel*, 192; Elayi, *Sargon II*, 48–50. M. Christine Tetley, "The Date of Samaria's Fall as a Reason for Rejecting the Hypothesis of Two Conquests," *CBQ* 64 (2002): 59–77; Sung Jin Park, "A New Historical Reconstruction of the Fall of Samaria," *Bib* 93 (2012): 98–106, unconvincingly argued against this view taking their starting point in the Biblical narrative; see Frevel, *Geschichte Israels*, 242.
[53] Tappy, "The Final Years of Israelite Samaria."

These sources are not reliable descriptions of the event(s). Although I do not think that the Assyrian takeover of Samaria was a completely peaceful action, I am of the opinion that the aim of the Assyrians was to gain control over the area with as little damage to it as possible in order to be able to gather as much in taxes as possible – in the form of food products – and to secure their trade interests along the *via maris*.[54] The character of this control can best be labelled with a term from colonial studies: "dominance without hegemony".[55] The Assyrians dominated the trade and were the receivers of the agricultural surplus, but their power structure did not influence the area in its remoter parts.

7 Event and Waves of History: *histoire conjuncturelle*

Archaeology and climate studies are of great importance for the construction of processes of *longue durée* in an area. The picture that emerges from this type of analysis is that of Ancient[56] Israel as an agricultural society that slowly developed from a loosely connected network of self-supplying communities into a more closely knit network in which trade and surplus production became increasingly important to supply the needs of court, temple, and later, the foreign suzerain.[57]

At the level of the *histoire conjuncturelle* it must be noted that Samaria fell prey to the Neo-Assyrian expansion. This expansion had its own internal mechanism and almost inevitable necessity. The will to govern over regions beyond the border of the Assyrian homeland necessitated building a strong army. The Assyrian armed forces and their campaigns needed to be financed. This financial pressure, in combination with the growing need for luxury in and around the court (including food to feed the otherwise unproductive court officials), was basic to the Neo-Assyrian system of raising tribute from conquered areas.[58] Avra-

---

54 See Younger, "The Fall of Samaria," 481.
55 See Ranajit Guha, *Dominance without Hegemony: History and Power in Colonial India* (Cambridge MA: Harvard University Press, 1997); Bagg, *Die Assyrer und das Westland*, 301–308.
56 Or 'Ancient' Israel; Iron Age Israel; Palestine; Southern Levant.
57 See, e. g., Paula McNutt, *Reconstructing the Society of Ancient Israel* (Louisville KY: Westminster John Knox Press, 1999).
58 See, e. g., Jürgen Bär, *Der assyrische Tribut und seine Darstellung: eine Untersuchung zur imperialen Ideologie im neuassyrischen Reich* (Neukirchen-Vluyn: Neukirchener Verlag, 1996); Karen Radner, "Abgaben an den König von Assyrien aus dem In- und Ausland," in *Geschenke und Steuern, Zölle und Tribute: Antike Abgabenformen in Anspruch und Wirklichkeit*, ed. Hilmar

ham Faust has elaborated this view by analysing the Assyrian demand for olive oil to be supplied from the Ekron area.[59] Supported by an incomparably strong military technology[60] this fly-wheel raged through the world of the Iron Age II period. When this almost unstoppable military machine reached the territory of the Northern Kingdom of Israel, it was only a matter of time till conquest of Samaria took place. I will not argue that the Assyrian take-over of Samaria was an inevitable fact that had to take place. History is too much an open process for such a claim.[61] In hindsight, however, the end of the Kingdom of Israel seems an appropriate outcome of the political-military game of those days. It is only against the background of this *histoire conjuncturelle* that the Biblical report on this event makes sense.

In sum and by way of re-enactment:

1. Event: The inhabitants of the city of Samaria had to bow to the military superiority of the Assyrians. The death of Shalmaneser V and subsequent diplomatic intrigue only led to the delay of the seemingly inevitable. After the struggle, parts of the population were deported and new settlers came in.
2. Wave: The military conquest might not have been inevitable, but in view of the machinery of Assyrian expansion politics, this was an understandable outcome.
3. *Longue durée:* The area maintained its agricultural function. Food production was the basis of its economy. The agricultural surplus now had to be given to foreigners who ruled the area, although they were far away.

Klinkott, Sabine Kubisch and Renate Müller-Wollermann (Leiden: Brill, 2007): 213–30; Peter R. Bedford, "The Assyrian Empire," in *The Dynamics of Ancient Empires: State Power from Assyria to Byzantium*, ed. Ian Morris and Walter Scheidel (Oxford: Oxford University Press, 2009): 30–65.
59 Avraham Faust, "The Interests of the Assyrian Empire in the West: Olive Oil Production as a Test-Case," *JESHO* 54 (2011): 62–86.
60 See e.g. Walter Mayer, *Politik und Kriegskunst der Assyrer* (Münster: Ugarit-Verlag, 1995).
61 There are no such things as 'laws of history' which make events inevitable and necessary and by which the outcome of a process can be calculated; *pace* Graeme D. Snooks, *The Laws of History* (London/New York: Routledge, 2002).

Part II: **Approaching the Fall of Samaria from Contemporary Assyrian and Egyptian Sources**

Jamie Novotny
Contextualizing the Last Days of the Kingdom of Israel: What Can Assyrian Official Inscriptions Tell Us?

1 Introduction

Considerable scholarly effort has been made trying to lift the heavy veil shrouding the details of the history of the final two decades of the kingdom of Israel, including the identity of the Assyrian ruler who conquered its capital Samaria and captured its last king Hoshea. Because there are significant discrepancies in extant primary sources, in particular between the Old Testament and Assyrian inscriptions, scholars have yet to satisfactorily answer the most important questions about this crucial period in the history of the Levant. Assyrian sources, especially royal inscriptions, may provide some key pieces to the puzzle, but what can they tell us about the last twenty to thirty years of the kingdom of Israel, the fall of Samaria, and the fate of Hoshea?[1] This paper will examine the available inscriptions of the eighth- and seventh-century Assyrian kings in order to eluci-

---

Support for my research on Assyrian (and Babylonian) inscriptions is provided by the Alexander von Humboldt Foundation (through the establishment of the Alexander von Humboldt Professorship for Ancient History of the Near and Middle East) and Ludwig-Maximilians-Universität München (Historisches Seminar – Abteilung Alte Geschichte). I would like to thank Karen Radner for reading through and commenting on a draft of this manuscript. Her time and care are greatly appreciated. Any errors or omissions are solely my responsibility. Because this conference volume contains numerous topic-specific studies on the last days of Israel and because this chapter is to serve as an introduction to Part I of the proceedings, footnotes and bibliography are kept to a minimum. For the Assyrian material, see the chapters by Eckart Frahm and Karen Radner. All dates are BC(E), except, of course, in bibliographical references.

[1] For (general) studies on royal inscriptions, see in particular Albert Kirk Grayson, "Assyria and Babylonia," *Or* NS 49 (1980): 140–93; Johannes Renger "Königsinschriften. B. Akkadisch," in *RlA*, vol. 6/1–2, ed. Dietz Otto Edzard (Berlin: de Gruyter, 1980), 65–77 (especially 71–77); Hayim Tadmor, "Propaganda, Literature, Historiography: Cracking the Code of the Assyrian Royal Inscriptions," *Assyria 1995: Proceedings of the 10th Anniversary Symposium of the Neo-Assyrian Text Corpus Project*, ed. Simo Parpola and Robert M. Whiting (Helsinki: Neo-Assyrian Text Corpus Project, 1997), 325–38; and Frederick Mario Fales, "Assyrian Royal Inscriptions: Newer Horizons," *SAAB* 13 (1999–2001): 115–44.

https://doi.org/10.1515/9783110566604-003

date what information that genre of Akkadian text can and cannot provide with regard to the history of Israel. Special attention will be given to potential lost sources to determine if new Assyrian texts could really help scholars solve some of the mysteries of the Bible.

This paper will serve as a general introduction to the more topic-specific papers given in Part I of this book. Nevertheless, I do hope to say a few things not covered in the other chapters. As a word of warning, at least one section of this paper will be purely speculative. However, these conjectures will be deeply rooted in the extant source material of Tiglath-pileser III and Sargon II.

2 Background Information: What Do We Know about Shalmaneser V?[2]

Before diving into the heart of matters, let me introduce Shalmaneser V, the chief protagonist of our story according to a Babylonian chronicle, the Bible, and the classical historian Josephus.

From Babylonian King List A, the Ptolemaic Canon, and several Neo-Assyrian letters, we know that the man who would be the fifth Assyrian king with the name Shalmaneser also went by the name Ulūlāyu, his nickname or birth name.[3]

---

[2] For details on Shalmaneser V/Ulūlāyu, see Albert Kirk Grayson, "Assyria: Tiglath-pileser III to Sargon II (744–705 B.C.)," in *The Assyrian and Babylonian Empires and other States of the Near East, from the Eighth to the Sixth Centuries B.C.*, The Cambridge Ancient History 3/2, second edition, ed. John Boardman et al. (Cambridge: Cambridge University Press, 1991): 85–86; Heather D. Baker, "Salmānu-ašarēd," in *The Prosopography of the Neo-Assyrian Empire*, vol. 3/I, ed. Heather D. Baker (Helsinki: Neo-Assyrian Text Corpus Project, 2002), 1077 no. 5; Heather D. Baker, "Salmaneser V.," in *RlA*, vol. 11/7–8, ed. Michael P. Streck (Berlin: de Gruyter, 2008), 585–87; Karen Radner, "Ulūlāiu," in *The Prosopography of the Neo-Assyrian Empire*, vol. 3/II, ed. Heather D. Baker (Helsinki: Neo-Assyrian Text Corpus Project, 2011), 1375 no. 3; Hayim Tadmor and Shigeo Yamada, *The Royal Inscriptions of Tiglath-pileser III (744–727 BC) and Shalmaneser V (726–722 BC), Kings of Assyria* (Winona Lake IN: Eisenbrauns, 2011), 14; Karen Radner, "Shalmaneser V, king of Assyria (726–722 BC)," in *Assyrian Empire Builders* (London: University College London, 2012), http://www.ucl.ac.uk/sargon/essentials/kings/shalmaneserv/ (accessed 10/2017); and Keiko Yamada and Shigeo Yamada, "Shalmaneser V and His Era, Revisited," in *'Now It Happened in Those Days': Studies in Biblical, Assyrian, and Other Ancient Near Eastern Historiography Presented to Mordechai Cogan on His 75th Birthday*, eds. Amitai Baruchi-Unna, Tova Forti, Shmuel Aḥituv, Israel Eph'al and Jeffrey H. Tigay (Winona Lake IN: Eisenbrauns, 2017): 387–442.

[3] For the relevant sections of Babylonian King List A and the Ptolemaic Canon, see Tadmor and Yamada, *Tiglath-pileser III*, 15–16. For details on these texts, see Jamie Novotny, "Babylonian King List A (BM 033332; Rm 3, 005)," in *The Royal Inscriptions of Babylonia online* (Munich:

A handful of royal letters attest to the crown prince Ulūlāyu playing an active role in his father's administration, particularly in the affairs of the western part of the empire. His responsibilities included securing sufficient supplies, coordinating security details for the queen (perhaps his mother), and receiving ambassadorial delegations visiting the capital Calah (Kalḫu; modern Nimrud). His on-the-job training gave him excellent knowledge of Assyria's western vassal kingdoms and prepared him well for his royal duties, once he became king. According to a Babylonian chronicle, Shalmaneser ascended the throne of Assyria without opposition shortly after Tiglath-pileser died; this was in the year 727.[4]

Hard facts about his short reign are rather scarce since textual and archaeological evidence for his stint as king are almost non-existent. This is in part due to that fact that no royal inscription of his has survived, apart from a set of lion-shaped weights.[5] The passage recording events of his reign in the Eponym Chronicle is heavily damaged and the relevant details are completely broken away.[6] Nevertheless, it is fairly certain he stayed at home during his first year as king and that military expeditions were conducted in his second, third, and fourth years on the throne. Unfortunately, the names of his military targets are missing. The kingdom of Bīt-Ḫumria, the Assyrian name for Israel, may have been named in this source since the Bible (2Kgs 17:3–6 and 2Kgs 18:9–12) records that Shalmaneser campaigned in that region.[7] As for what happened in his fifth year as king, nothing is preserved in the Eponym Chronicle. A Babylonian chronicle provides one important piece of information: Shalmaneser is report-

---

Oracc, 2016), http://oracc.museum.upenn.edu/ribo/kinglists/kinglista/ (accessed 10/2017); and Henry Heitmann-Gordon, "First Section of the Ptolemaic Canon," in *The Royal Inscriptions of Babylonia online* (Munich: Oracc, 2016), http://oracc.museum.upenn.edu/ribo/kinglists/ptolemaiccanon/ (accessed 10/2017). For the letters from Calah, see Karen Radner, "Salmanassar V. in den Nimrud Letters," *AfO* 50 (2003–4): 95–104 and Mikko Luukko, *The Correspondence of Tiglath-pileser III and Sargon II from Calah/Nimrud* (Winona Lake IN: Eisenbrauns, 2013), L–LII and 10–13 nos. 8–11.

4 Albert Kirk Grayson, *Assyrian and Babylonian Chronicles* (Locust Valley NY: Augustin, 1975), 73 no. 1 i 24–28; and Tadmor and Yamada, *Tiglath-pileser III*, 18.

5 Tadmor and Yamada, *Tiglath-pileser III*, 171–81 nos. 1–9 and Frederick Mario Fales, "The Assyrian Lion-Weights: A Further Attempt," in *Libiamo ne' lieti calici: Ancient Near Eastern Studies Presented to Lucio Milano*, ed. Paola Corò et al. (Münster: Ugarit-Verlag, 2016): 483–507.

6 Alan Millard, *The Eponyms of the Assyrian Empire 910–612 BC* (Helsinki: Neo-Assyrian Text Corpus Project, 1994), 45–46, 59; and Tadmor and Yamada, *Tiglath-pileser III*, 17–18.

7 For textual references and bibliography, see Ariel M. Bagg, *Die Orts- und Gewässernamen der neuassyrischen Zeit Teil 1: Die Levante* (Wiesbaden: Reichert, 2007), 50. For a recent study of the Assyrian Empire and the west, see Ariel M. Bagg, *Die Assyrer und das Westland: Studien zur historischen Geographie und Herrschaftspraxis in der Levante im 1. Jt. v.u.Z.* (Leuven: Peeters, 2011), especially 213–44.

ed to have ravaged Samaria.⁸ 2Kgs 17 and 18 and Josephus (*Antiquitates Judaicae* IX 15) also credit him with the conquest of Israel's capital; inscriptions of his successor, however, infer that Sargon II captured Samaria.⁹ Exactly when Shalmaneser attacked Israel and when Samaria was captured is uncertain, but it is sometimes thought that Samaria fell towards the end of his reign, possibly in his fifth year. Shalmaneser appears to have added three new provinces to Assyria (Que, Sam'al, and Samaria)¹⁰ and he may have besieged the Phoenician city Tyre, if the account of Josephus (*Antiquitates Judaicae* IX 16) is to be believed.

No building activity by this Shalmaneser is known so far. However, a brick found at Apku, modern Tell Abu Marya, may belong to him, and, assuming the attribution proves correct, then this brick may attest to construction in that city.¹¹

The end of Shalmaneser's reign is known only from a text composed under the auspices of his brother and successor.¹² The "Aššur Charter" portrays Shalmaneser as an oppressive ruler who had robbed the citizens of the city of Aššur of their god-given privileges and imposed hard labor upon them. Because Shalmaneser angered the gods, he was violently removed from the throne and replaced by someone more suitable: his brother, who took the name Šarru-ukīn (Šarru-kēnu/Šarru-kīn).¹³ A Babylonian chronicle states that Shalmaneser died and was succeeded a few days later by Sargon;¹⁴ no reference to the violent

---

8 Grayson, *Chronicles*, 73 no. 1 i 28; and Tadmor and Yamada, *Tiglath-pileser III*, 18.
9 The identity of the Assyrian king who captured Samaria (Shalmaneser V or Sargon II), whether the Assyrians conquered that city once or twice, and when that city fell are still matters of scholarly debate. Those issues fall outside the scope of the present paper, but are addressed elsewhere in this volume. In § 4.3, it is assumed, however, that Samaria may have succumbed to Assyria while Shalmaneser was still on the throne. For summaries and assessments of relevant scholarly discussion see, for example, Kyle Lawson Younger Jr., "The Fall of Samaria in Light of Recent Research," *CBQ* 61 (1999): 461–82 and Kenneth Bergland, "Analysis and Assessment of Chronological Explanations of the Fall of Samaria," *Spes Christiana* 22–23 (2011–12): 63–84; for further bibliographical references, see n. 5 of Frahm's chapter in this volume.
10 Karen Radner, "Provinz. C. Assyrien," in *RlA*, vol. 11/1–2, ed. Michael P. Streck (Berlin: de Gruyter, 2006), 62 nos. 57–59.
11 Tadmor and Yamada, *Tiglath-pileser III*, 183–84.
12 Henry W.F. Saggs, "Historical Texts and Fragments of Sargon II of Assyria: 1. The 'Aššur Charter'," *Iraq* 37 (1975): 11–20; and Galo W. Vera Chamaza, "Sargon II's Ascent to the Throne: The Political Situation," *SAAB* 6/1 (1992): 21–33. See also Text 1 in Frahm's chapter in this volume.
13 For a discussion about the meaning of Sargon's name ("The righteous king" or "He [= the god] made firm the king"), see, e.g., Andreas Fuchs, "Sargon II.," in *RlA*, vol. 12/1–2, ed. Michael P. Streck (Berlin: de Gruyter, 2009): 51–53 § 2; and Andreas Fuchs, "Šarru-kēnu, Šarru-kīn, Šarru-ukīn," in *The Prosopography of the Neo-Assyrian Empire*, vol. 3/II, ed. Heather D. Baker and Robert D. Whiting (Helsinki: Neo-Assyrian Text Corpus Project, 2011): 1239–47 no. 2.
14 Grayson, *Chronicles*, 73 no. 1 i 29–31; and Tadmor and Yamada, *Tiglath-pileser III*, 18.

circumstances of his death is given in that source. We just have Sargon's word on the matter.

No positively identified inscriptions of Shalmaneser V have survived, apart from several bilingual Akkadian-Aramaic lion weights.[15] One expects that more official texts of his must have existed in antiquity; this is suggested by the fact that inscriptions of other Assyrian kings – for example, Sennacherib and Esarhaddon – were written well before their fifth regnal years, as well as in their fifth year as king.[16] Because he is known to have carried out at least three military expeditions (according to the Eponym Chronicle), it would be highly unusual had Shalmaneser not taken the opportunity to record his deeds. Although there is a near complete gap in the textual record for the five years that Shalmaneser was king, we can still speculate about what he may have recorded about himself and what form those royal compositions may have taken.

To put our conjectured now-lost sources into context, we must dive into the extant corpora of Shalmaneser's immediate predecessor and successor. Let us start with those of Tiglath-pileser III.

3 Brief Overview of the Official Inscriptions of Tiglath-pileser III[17]

Thirty-four or thirty-five inscriptions of Tiglath-pileser III, excluding those of his wife Yabâ and several of his subordinates, are known. The complete corpus of texts has been recently published by Hayim Tadmor and Shigeo Yamada for the Royal Inscriptions of the Neo-Assyrian Period Project, directed by Grant

---

15 See n. 5 above.
16 E.g., A. Kirk Grayson and Jamie Novotny, *The Royal Inscriptions of Sennacherib, King of Assyria (704–681 BC), Part 1* (Winona Lake IN: Eisenbrauns, 2012), 29–69 nos. 1–4; and Erle Leichty, *The Royal Inscriptions of Esarhaddon, King of Assyria (680–669 BC)* (Winona Lake IN: Eisenbrauns, 2011), 119–34 nos. 57–59. For the inscriptions of Sargon II written near the beginning of his reign, see Texts 1–3 in Frahm's chapter.
17 For details on Tiglath-pileser III and his reign, see, e.g., Grayson, "Tiglath-pileser III to Sargon II," 71–85; Tadmor and Yamada, *Tiglath-pileser III*, 12–14; Heather D. Baker, "Tukultī-apil-Ešarra," in *The Prosopography of the Neo-Assyrian Empire*, vol. 3/II, ed. Heather D. Baker (Helsinki: Neo-Assyrian Text Corpus Project, 2011), 1329–31 no. 3; Heather D. Baker, "Tiglatpileser III.," in *RlA*, vol. 14/1–2, ed. Michael P. Streck (Berlin: de Gruyter, 2006), 21–4; and Karen Radner, "Tiglath-pileser III, king of Assyria (744–727 BC)," in *Assyrian Empire Builders* (London: University College London, 2012), http://www.ucl.ac.uk/sargon/essentials/kings/tiglatpileseriii/ (accessed 10/2017).

Frame of the University of Pennsylvania.¹⁸ These self-aggrandizing compositions are found on a variety of stone, clay, and metal objects. The most important are written on wall slabs with reliefs, threshold slabs, mud bricks, clay tablets, and a stele. The majority were discovered in the citadel of Calah, in the ruins of the Central and South-West Palaces, while a few others were found at Aššur, Arslan Tash, and western Iran. Following Tadmor, scholars generally divide this king's texts into three categories: (1) chronologically-arranged annals; (2) geographically-organized summary inscriptions; and (3) miscellaneous texts, which include labels and building inscriptions.¹⁹

The most important inscription of Tiglath-pileser is the so-called "Calah Annals."²⁰ This modern conflation of several ancient texts is a long running annalistic account of the events of Tiglath-pileser's reign from his accession year to his fifteenth or seventeenth year as king.²¹ Copies of it were originally inscribed on the walls of rooms and corridors of the Central Palace, usually in a horizontal band separating the sculpted upper and lower registers.²² Due in part to the fact that the seventh-century Assyrian king Esarhaddon dismantled the Central Palace and reused some of the sculpted wall slabs in his own palace, most of Tiglath-pileser's annals have not survived.²³ One third, if not less, of the Calah Annals are known today, and the known pieces may represent parts of four or

---

18 For details on the inscriptions of Tiglath-pileser III (with references to previous scholarly literature), see Tadmor and Yamada, *Tiglath-pileser III* and its online version on *Royal Inscriptions of the Neo-Assyrian Period online* http://oracc.museum.upenn.edu/rinap/rinap1/ (accessed 10/2017). Much of the contents of that volume is based on Hayim Tadmor, *The Inscriptions of Tiglath-pileser III King of Assyria: Critical Edition, with Introductions, Translations, and Commentary* (Jerusalem: The Israel Academy of Sciences and Humanities, 1994).
19 Tadmor, *Tiglath-pileser III King of Assyria*, 22–25. This classification of the corpus is maintained in Tadmor and Yamada, *Tiglath-pileser III*; see pp. 4–10 of that volume.
20 Tadmor, *Tiglath-pileser III King of Assyria*, 27–89, 216–21 and 238–59; and Tadmor and Yamada, *Tiglath-pileser III*, 4–8 and 19–79 nos. 1–34. See also John Malcolm Russell, *The Writing on the Wall: Studies in the Architectural Context of Late Assyrian Palace Inscriptions* (Winona Lake IN: Eisenbrauns, 1999), 88–96.
21 For details, see Tadmor and Yamada, *Tiglath-pileser III*, 4–7. Tadmor's designations for the inscriptions are followed here.
22 For drawings showing the position of the text of the Calah Annals on the extant wall slabs, see Tadmor, *Tiglath-pileser III King of Assyria*, 241–56 (= Figures 11–2).
23 Tadmor, *Tiglath-pileser III King of Assyria*, 10–12 and Richard David Barnett and Margarete Falkner, *The Sculptures of Aššur-naṣir-apli II (883–859 B.C.), Tiglath-pileser III (745–727 B.C.), Esarhaddon (681–669 B.C.) from the Central and South-West Palaces at Nimrud* (London: Trustees of the British Museum, 1962), 1–7 and 20–23 provide good information about the poor condition in which Tiglath-pileser's palace and its inscribed and sculpted wall slabs were discovered. See also § 4.1 (with n. 49) below.

five different texts. The surviving material is divided into three hypothetical series: Series A, the "Hall of the Seven-Line Series"; Series B, the "Hall of the Twelve-Line Series"; and Series C, the "Colossal Slabs (Series)". When all three series are combined, the extant text of the Annals preserves parts of the prologue, reports of Tiglath-pileser's 1st–3rd (745–743), 7th–9th (739–737), 11th (735), 13th (733), and 15th (731) regnal years, and an account of the construction of Tiglath-pileser's palace. This badly damaged set of inscriptions narrated the military achievements of every year of the king's reign, up to his fifteenth or seventeenth regnal year. The Calah Annals are one of the principal Assyrian sources that provide evidence about the last days of Israel. Of note, Menahem of Samaria is said to have paid tribute to Assyria and sixteen districts of Bīt-Ḫumria are reported to have been destroyed.[24]

Annals of the king were written on other media, including provincial steles and rock reliefs.[25] The two best surviving examples are a stele discovered in western Iran and a panel carved into a rock face near Mila Mergi in Kurdistan. Copies of Tiglath-pileser's annals would have been inscribed on clay foundation documents that would have been deposited into the structures of buildings constructed or repaired by him. No such object bearing his annals is known today.[26] Some of these now-lost documents are presumed to have been destroyed in antiquity by Esarhaddon when he built his own royal residence at Calah, or in modern times, by local inhabitants or nineteenth century excavators.[27] There is little doubt in my mind that such texts existed, despite their current lack in the archaeological record.

Several of Tiglath-pileser's so-called "Summary Inscriptions" are also known.[28] These compositions were written on stone pavement slabs and clay tablets near the end of his reign, probably late in 729 or in 728, and they give a summary of his military achievements by geographical region. The résumé of victories usually began with events in the south and then continued with those of the east and north, and concluded with events in the west. The narrative

---

[24] Tadmor and Yamada, *Tiglath-pileser III*, 46 no. 14 line 10, 61–63 nos. 21–22, 70 no. 27 line 3, and 77 no. 32 line 2.
[25] Tadmor, *Tiglath-pileser III King of Assyria*, 90–116; and Tadmor and Yamada, *Tiglath-pileser III*, 8–9 and 79–94 nos. 35–38.
[26] This might not be entirely true as a small clay fragment found at Aššur (VAT 12938) might be inscribed with a version of Tiglath-pileser's annals. Too little of that inscription is preserved to properly classify it.
[27] See n. 23 above and § 4.1 below.
[28] Tadmor, *Tiglath-pileser III King of Assyria*, 117–204; and Tadmor and Yamada, *Tiglath-pileser III*, 9–10 and 94–138 nos. 39–52.

divides the accomplishments of the king as follows: (1) the Babylonia wars; (2) the Zagros campaigns; (3) the wars with Urarṭu and its allies; (4) the conquest of northern Syrian states; and (5) the military operations in southern Syria, Palestine, and Arabia. Two of the summary inscriptions report on Israel: Tiglath-pileser claims to have conquered parts of Bīt-Ḫumria, as well as states that Pekah was killed and Hoshea was installed as king in his stead.[29] Although this type of inscription is less descriptive than annalistic texts, summary inscriptions nevertheless provide important historical information and supplement and compliment details provided by the annals.

With regard to the miscellaneous category of inscriptions,[30] I will briefly mention just one type: epigraphs. Three epigraphs of Tiglath-pileser III survive and these one-word labels help us identify cities shown in reliefs being besieged, destroyed, and looted.[31] This text type is extremely important as such texts often name places not mentioned in other texts.[32] This is the case for all three epigraphs of Tiglath-pileser.

---

29 Tadmor and Yamada, *Tiglath-pileser III*, 106 no. 42 lines 15′b–19′a and 112 no. 44 lines 17′–18′. On the death (murder/assassination) or overthrow of Pekah in these texts, see Tadmor, *Tiglath-pileser III King of Assyria*, 141 (note to line 17′), 277 and 281; and Tadmor and Yamada, *Tiglath-pileser III*, 106 (note to no. 42 line 17′). According to 2Kgs 15:25, Pekah was assassinated by Hoshea, a man whom Tiglath-pileser claims to have installed as king.
30 Tadmor, *Tiglath-pileser III King of Assyria*, 205–15; and Tadmor and Yamada, *Tiglath-pileser III*, 10 and 139–54 nos. 53–64.
31 Tadmor and Yamada, *Tiglath-pileser III*, 143–46 nos. 55–57. The city Gazru in text no. 57 is probably to be identified with biblical Gezer, an Israelite city located in the Vale of Ayalon. This city was probably captured in 733.
32 Although annalistic texts and summary inscriptions name many important opponents, it is certain that those inscriptions did not record the name of every person who was defeated and every place that was captured. Therefore, many epigraphs accompanying reliefs play an important role in reconstructing Assyrian history, since they provide information intentionally omitted in longer descriptions of military expeditions. This is well attested throughout the Neo-Assyrian period. The best-known example is the depiction of Sennacherib's siege of Lachish. This relief, which adorned the walls of Room XXXVI of the Southwest Palace at Nineveh, shows many details of the hard-fought siege of a well-fortified Judean city (not mentioned elsewhere in Sennacherib's annals) and its aftermath. For the Lachish reliefs, see Richard David Barnett, Erika Bleibtreu, and Geoffrey Turner, *Sculptures from the Southwest Palace of Sennacherib at Nineveh*, vol. 2 (London: Trustees of the British Museum, 1998), 322–52.

4 Brief Overview of the Official Inscriptions of Sargon II[33]

To date, approximately 125 inscriptions of Sargon II, excluding those of his wife Atalya and several of his officials, are known. Unfortunately, the complete corpus of texts has yet to be published in a single place; Grant Frame's manuscript of this king's inscriptions are in an advanced state of preparation and should appear in 2019 (or 2020).[34] The major texts from Khorsabad, Nineveh, and Aššur, however, have been carefully edited by Andreas Fuchs.[35] This rich source material is found on a plethora of stone, clay, and metal objects. The most important compositions were written on wall slabs with reliefs, threshold slabs, human-headed bull colossi, prisms, cylinders, and provincial steles. Given this king's efforts to build himself a new royal city, it is little surprise that about half (46%) of the inscriptions were found at Dūr-Šarrukīn, with the highest percentage coming from his own palace. As one expects from a late-eighth-century Assyrian king, many inscriptions of his were discovered in the ruins of Aššur, Calah, and Nineveh. In addition, building inscriptions of his come from Babylon and Uruk, Babylonian cities where he sponsored building, and steles of his commemorating victories on the battlefields have been found in Cyprus, Iran, Israel, Syria, and Turkey. Sargon's scribes wrote out detailed chronologically-arranged annals, geographically-organized summary inscriptions, labels (including epigraphs), dedicatory texts, and building inscriptions. In addition, a few unique compositions have survived; for example, "Sargon's Letter to Aššur," which reports on a campaign conducted against Urarṭu and the city Muṣaṣir, and the "Aššur Char-

---

[33] For details on Sargon II and his reign, see, e.g., Grayson, "Tiglath-pileser III to Sargon II," 86–102; Fuchs, "Sargon II.," 51–61; Fuchs, "Šarru-kēnu, Šarru-kīn, Šarru-ukīn," 1239–47 no. 2; Karen Radner, "Sargon II, king of Assyria (721–705 BC)," in *Assyrian Empire Builders* (London: University College London, 2012), http://www.ucl.ac.uk/sargon/essentials/kings/sargonii/ (accessed 10/2017); and Sarah C. Melville, *The Campaigns of Sargon II, King of Assyria, 721–705 B.C.* (Norman OK: University of Oklahoma Press, 2016). See also Radner's chapter in this volume.

[34] I would like to thank Grant Frame for allowing me use of his unpublished manuscript *The Royal Inscriptions of Sargon II, King of Assyria (721–705 BC)*, prior to its publication as volume 2 in the series *The Royal Inscription of the Neo-Assyrian Period*. Access to his Sargon material facilitated the writing of this section.

[35] Andreas Fuchs, *Die Inschriften Sargons II. aus Khorsabad* (Göttingen: Cuvillier Verlag, 1994); and Andreas Fuchs, *Die Annalen des Jahres 711 v. Chr. nach Prismenfragmenten aus Ninive und Assur* (Helsinki: Neo-Assyrian Text Corpus Project, 1998). This section overlaps to some extent Frahm's chapter in this volume; see that chapter for further details.

ter," which describes his succession to the throne.³⁶ Most of the dateable texts were written during the second half of his reign, between his eighth regnal year, 714, and his sixteenth regnal year, 706; at least one text was written at the very beginning of his reign, probably late in his second regnal year, 720.³⁷

Following in the footsteps of his predecessors, including the powerful ninth-century ruler Ashurnasirpal II, Sargon had his annals inscribed on the walls of his palace; the slabs of Rooms II, V, XIII, XIV, and Court VII bore this text.³⁸ Each of the aforementioned rooms contained a complete version of the inscription. These annalistic texts were always written in a broad horizontal band separating the elaborately sculpted upper and lower registers. The width of the inscribed band, and thereby the number of lines per column, depended on the size of the room; for example, the middle register in Room II accommodated thirteen lines of text, while the central band in Room V was wide enough for seventeen lines of text. Unfortunately, large passages are now missing from each version of Sargon's annals; none are fully preserved. This lengthy text recorded in chronological order the deeds of his first fourteen years and, thus, provides a comprehensive picture of Sargon's seventeen-year reign. Unfortunately, many of the details of his second regnal year, when Samaria and Bīt-Ḫumria participated in a rebellion organized by Hamath, are very fragmentarily preserved in this text; Eckart Frahm, in the following chapter, will provide details about the campaign of 720, as well as editions of the relevant passages. These versions of the annals concluded with a description of the creation of this king's new capital, along with the construction and decoration of Sargon's own palace. This group of texts was composed towards the end of his reign, around 707, his fifteenth regnal

---

36 For "Sargon's Letter to Aššur," see François Thureau-Dangin, *Une relation de la huitième campagne de Sargon* (Paris: Geuthner, 1912); and Walter Mayer, *Assyrien und Urarṭu I: Der Achte Feldzug Sargons II. im Jahr 714 v.Chr.* (Münster: Ugarit-Verlag, 2013). For the "Aššur Charter," see Saggs, "Historical Texts and Fragments of Sargon II of Assyria," 11–20; Vera Chamaza, "Sargon II's Ascent to the Throne," 21–33; and Text 1 in Frahm's chapter.

37 For a helpful chart of the dates of the most important inscriptions of Sargon, see Fuchs, "Sargon II.," 52. The "Tell Asharneh Stele" and "Tell Tayinat Stele" (Texts 2–3 in Frahm's chapter) probably also date to around 720. For details on these two texts, see Grant Frame, "The Tell Acharneh Stela of Sargon II of Assyria," in *Tell Acharneh 1998–2004*, ed. Michel Fortin (Turnhout: Brepols, 2006): 49–68, esp. 49–52; and Jacob Lauinger and Stephen Batiuk, "A Stele of Sargon II at Tell Tayinat," *ZA* 105 (2015): 54–68.

38 Fuchs, *Die Inschriften Sargons II. aus Khorsabad*, 82–188. See also Grant Frame, "The Order of the Wall Slabs with Sargon's Annals in Room V of the Palace at Khorsabad," in *From the Upper Sea to the Lower Sea: Studies on the History of Assyria and Babylonia in Honour of A.K. Grayson*, ed. Grant Frame (Istanbul and Leiden: Netherlands Institute for the Near East, 2004), 89–102; Russell, *The Writing on the Wall*, 111–15; and Texts 7 and 10 in Frahm's chapter.

year; compare the Calah Annals of Tiglath-pileser III, which were composed around his seventeenth year as king. Other annalistic texts of his are attested and these are preserved on prisms, prismatic cylinders, tablets, and steles; many are badly damaged, with much of their original contents missing.[39]

Another important text of Sargon inscribed on the walls of his palace is the so-called "Great Display Inscription."[40] Copies of it were found in Rooms I, IV, VII, VIII, and X and, unlike the annals, this composition described the military expeditions geographically, starting with the east and ending with the southeast. In this inscription, Sargon states that he plundered Samaria and the entire land of Bīt-Ḫumria. A shorter version of this text, the so-called "Small Display Inscription," is also known, and it likewise mentions the defeat of the inhabitants of Bīt-Ḫumria and Samaria in 720.[41] Both compositions were written in or after his fifteenth year (707).

Sargon had his scribes write out at least one inscription that is a perfect blend of a display and building inscription: this is the so-called "Bull Inscription."[42] Numerous human-headed bull colossi flanking the prominent gateways at Khorsabad, including several from Sargon's palace, are inscribed with a text that included a short geographical summary of this ruler's victories and a lengthy account of the creation of Dūr-Šarrukīn. With one known exception, the Bull Inscription was distributed between a pair of bulls. Each colossus had two rectangular panels, one below its belly and one between its hind legs, and was inscribed with approximately half of the text. Thus, the complete text required two bulls and four inscribed surfaces. The Door M, Room VIII colossi, however, were different: each of those bulls bore a complete inscription, written in two inscribed surfaces. The information included in this text, which

---

39 For example, see Cyril J. Gadd, "Inscribed Prisms of Sargon II from Nimrud," *Iraq* 16 (1954): 173–201 (= "Nimrud Prism"); Louis D. Levine, *Two Neo-Assyrian Stelae from Iran* (Toronto: Royal Ontario Museum, 1972) (= "Najafehabad Stele"); Françoise Malbran-Labat, "Section 4: Inscription assyrienne (No. 4001)," in *Kition dans les textes*, Kition-Bamboula 5, ed. Marguerite Yon (Paris: Éditions Recherche sur les Civilisations, 2004): 345–54 (= "Cyprus Stele"); Fuchs, *Die Inschriften Sargons II. aus Khorsabad*, 29–44 and 289–96 (= "Khorsabad Cylinder"); and Fuchs, *Die Annalen des Jahres 711 v. Chr.* (= "Nineveh Prism," "Aššur Prism"). See Texts 4, 6, 8, and 13 in Frahm's chapter.
40 Fuchs, *Die Inschriften Sargons II. aus Khorsabad*, 189–248 and 343–55; and Russell, *The Writing on the Wall*, 111–5. See also Texts 9 and 12 in Frahm's chapter.
41 Fuchs, *Die Inschriften Sargons II. aus Khorsabad*, 75–81 and 307–12. See also Text 16 in Frahm's chapter.
42 Fuchs, *Die Inschriften Sargons II. aus Khorsabad*, 60–74 and 303–307. See also Russell, *The Writing on the Wall*, 103–108, and Text 17 in Frahm's chapter.

was written in or after his fifteenth year (707), compliments what was recorded in the annals and display inscriptions.

Sargon's successes on the battlefield and his building activities at his new capital are also recorded on numerous pavement slabs; five, or possibly six, different inscriptions are known from twenty-one, or twenty-two, threshold slabs.[43] Military matters are mentioned, but only in a very cursory fashion. The longest of the threshold inscriptions refers to the conquest of Bīt-Ḫumria and Samaria.

As mentioned earlier, there are many other sub-genres of official inscriptions composed during the reign of Sargon. As for building inscriptions, texts recording only the construction of a palace or temple, these are attested on a wider variety of objects, in particular clay cylinders and stone and metal foundation tablets. We know from mid-nineteenth century French excavations at Khorsabad that such (stone and metal) tablets were sometimes placed inside alabaster coffers and deposited within the walls of buildings.[44] One unique royal composition from this time is a text often referred to as "Sargon's Eighth Campaign," "Sargon's Letter to God" or "Sargon's Letter to Aššur".[45] The inscription consists of an initial address to the god Aššur, the body of the text, which records in minute detail a campaign directed against Urarṭu and the city Muṣaṣir in the ruler's eighth regnal year (713), and a concluding statement/colophon. This royal report is generally classified as a letter to a god, a rarely attested genre of text, and it is sometimes thought "not to be deposited in silence in the sanctuary, but to be actually read to a public that was to react directly to their contents" and that "they replace in content and most probably in form the customary oral report of the king or his representative on the actual campaign to the city and the priesthood of the capital."[46]

---

43 Fuchs, *Die Inschriften Sargons II. aus Khorsabad*, 249–75 and 356–63. See also Text 18 in Frahm's chapter.

44 Fuchs, *Die Inschriften Sargons II. aus Khorsabad*, 45–52 and 296–300. These tablets made of gold (AO 19933; formerly Nap. III 2897), silver (AO 21371; formerly Nap. III 2898), bronze (AO 21370; formerly Nap. III 2900), and magnesite (Nap. III 2899) were discovered in 1854 inside alabaster coffers embedded in the mud-brick wall between Rooms 17 and 19 of Sargon's palace at Dūr-Šarrukīn.

45 See n. 36 above.

46 A. Leo Oppenheim, "The City of Assur in 714 B. C.," *JNES* 19 (1960): 143. With regard to letters to gods, see, e. g., Rykle Borger, "Gottesbrief," in *RlA*, vol. 3/8, ed. Ernst Weidner and Wolfram von Soden (Berlin: de Gruyter, 1971): 575–76; and Oppenheim, "The City of Assur in 714 B. C.," 133–47.

5 Conjectured now-lost Assyrian inscriptions and their contents

Now that I have given a brief overview of the most important extant Assyrian inscriptions from 744 to 705, let me address what now-lost sources may have told us about the end of the kingdom of Israel.

5.1 Lost inscriptions of Tiglath-pileser III

Compared to kings like Sargon II and Sennacherib, or even Esarhaddon, relatively few inscriptions of Tiglath-pileser III, especially from his own palace, have survived. Now-lost texts of his or passages of known texts that are no longer preserved would have provided some information about Bīt-Ḫumria and its rulers Peqah and Hoshea. Annalistic texts, including now-lost portions of the Calah Annals, would have provided many details about Tiglath-pileser's western campaigns – which took place during his eleventh, twelfth, and thirteenth regnal years – and, thus, would have provided the Assyrian point of view of events recorded in 2Kgs 15 and 16. These texts would have contained more information than what is already known from contemporary summary inscriptions. At present, no annalistic accounts for the years 734 and 732 are extant and what is preserved for the year 733 is too badly damaged for proper assessment.[47] Tiglath-pileser's annals, based on statements in two summary inscriptions, would very likely have described or mentioned Pekah's removal from the throne and/or his death/assassination. It would have been nice to have had contemporary confirmation of the information given in 2Kgs 15:25, which states that Hoshea murdered his successor. On the other hand, it is possible that Assyrian texts would have credited Pekah's death to Tiglath-pileser, as he is the central figure of his

---

[47] The relevant section of one version of the Calah Annals reads: "... [...] *without* ... [... I *utterly demolished* ...] of sixteen dis[tricts of the land *Bīt-Ḫumria* (Israel). I carried off (to Assyria) ...] capti[ves from ...], 226 [captives from ..., ...] captives [from ...], 400 [(and ...) captives from ...], 656 cap[tives from the city Sa..., ...] (altogether) 13,520 [people, ...], with their belongings. [I ... *the cities Arumâ (and) Marum*, (...) *which are*] sit[uated in] rugged mountains" (Tadmor and Yamada, *Tiglath-pileser III*, 61 no. 21 lines 1′–11′). Another version of the annals has: "[...] ... [...] ... [...] I en[veloped] him [like] a (dense) fog [... *I*] ut[terly demolished ... of sixteen] districts of the land *Bīt-Ḫum*[*ria* (Israel). *I carried off (to Assyria)* ... *captives from* the city ...]barâ, 625 captives from the city ...a[..., ... *captives from* the city] Ḫinatuna, 650 captives from the city Ku[..., ... *captives from* the city Ya]ṭbite, 656 captives from the city Sa...[..., ..., *with their belongings*. I ...] the cities Arumâ (and) Marum [...]" (Tadmor and Yamada, *Tiglath-pileser III*, 62 no. 22 lines 1′–8′a).

self-aggrandizing compositions.⁴⁸ Based on what little is preserved in the Calah Annals for the year 733 and what is recorded in extant summary inscriptions, the annals would have provided some details about the Israelite cities and districts conquered, and the number of people deported; we do know that sixteen districts of Bīt-Ḫumria were ravaged by the Assyrian army. Now-lost annalistic texts written closer to the events than the Calah Annals may have given more details. Such inscriptions may have been written on steles and/or on (clay and/or stone) foundation documents. I assume that Tiglath-pileser had texts deposited in the walls of his palace and that many of these foundation documents were lost or destroyed when Esarhaddon had that royal residence dismantled to make use of its building materials.⁴⁹ Exposure to the elements and other lootings of that building, ancient and modern, likely played a part in the near absence of Tiglath-pileser's foundation documents today; the few foundation tablets of his

---

48 Regarding the relevant passage in one of Tiglath-pileser's summary inscriptions (Tadmor and Yamada, *Tiglath-pileser III*, 106 no. 42 line 17′), Tadmor (*Tiglath-pileser III King of Assyria*, 141) correctly points out: "[…]-*du*-⸢x₁⸣-⸢x₂⸣: The possible restoration of the verb describing Peqah's fate is still a riddle. DU is the only completely preserved sign, followed by KU (or UK) and a trace of another sign. One might restore [*i*]-*du*-[*ku-ma*] or even [*a*]-*du*-[*uk-ma*], but in Smith's draft there is space to restore a longer word. Rost's *is-ku-pu-ma* is entirely conjectural. According to 2Kgs 15:25, Peqah was assassinated by Hoshea."

49 For details, see Tadmor, *Tiglath-pileser III King of Assyria*, 10–12 and Barnett and Falkner, *Central and South-West Palaces at Nimrud*, 1–7 and 20–23. The best description of the state of affairs in the Central Palace is provided by Austen Henry Layard for a group of slabs discovered there: "Walls of unbaked bricks could still be traced; but the slabs, with which they had been paneled, were no longer in their places, being scattered about without order, and lying mostly with their faces on the flooring of baked bricks. Upon them were both sculptures and inscriptions. Slab succeeded to slab; and when I had removed nearly twenty tombs, and cleared away the earth from a space of about fifty feet square, the ruins, which had been thus uncovered, presented a very singular appearance. Above one hundred slabs were exposed to view, packed in rows, one against the other, as slabs in a stone-cutter's yard, or as leaves of a gigantic book. Every slab was sculptured; and as they were placed in a regular series, according to the subjects upon them, it was evident that they had been moved, in the order in which they stood, from their original positions against the walls of sundried brick; and had been left as found, preparatory to their removal elsewhere. … These sculptures resembled, in many places, some of the bas-reliefs found in the south-west palace, in which the sculptured faces of the slabs were turned, it will be remembered, towards the walls of unbaked brick. It appeared, therefore, that the centre building had been destroyed, to supply materials for the construction of the more southern edifice." Excerpted from Austen Henry Layard, *Nineveh and Its Remains: A Narrative of an Expedition to Assyria during the years 1845, 1846, & 1847*, vol. 2 (London: John Murray, 1849), 19–20. For images of a trench with a deposit of Tiglath-pileser's reliefs, see Richard Sobolewski, "The Polish Work at Nimrud: Ten Years of Excavation and Study, *ZA* 71 (181): fig. 7; and [anonymous], "Nimrud," in *W Cieniu Wojny* (http://heritage.pcma.uw.edu.pl/en/; accessed 10/2017) s.v. Archaeological Sites, Nimrud.

that we now have are all summary inscriptions, and these were found elsewhere at Calah, in the South-East Palace and in the temple of the god Nabû (Ezida).

As for missing information in summary inscriptions, better preserved texts might have clarified who killed Pekah: Tiglath-pileser, Hoshea, or frightened members of the Israelite court and elite.

5.2 Lost Inscriptions of Sargon II

Jumping ahead to the reign of Sargon II, there is a gap in the textual record, at least up to his eighth year (713). Most extant inscriptions of his referring to Samaria date to Sargon's final years on the throne, when his annals and display inscriptions were engraved on the walls of his palace.[50] Several texts from his second and/or third year as king also record the defeat of the inhabitants of Samaria. All of the known references to Israel's capital in this corpus of texts are to that city's participation in an anti-Assyrian rebellion that took place in 720. Earlier versions of the annals, those written on steles and clay foundation records, might have provided us with only a few more details about what Sargon did in the Levant during his second regnal year (720), thus, giving us only a slightly better picture of the post-fall-of-Samaria landscape and the anti-Assyrian pockets of resistance in the Levant. Because the Great Display Inscription and a version of the king's annals written on clay prisms discovered at Calah, a text written in the year 706, contain rather descriptive accounts of the defeat of the inhabitants of Samaria, I have my doubts that yet-to-be-discovered inscriptions of Sargon would have revealed more than what the known texts already tell us. Perhaps those lost inscriptions would have recorded a different number of deportees and chariots carried off to Assyria. For example, some texts states that the Assyrians took 27,290 inhabitants and 50 chariots, while others appear to increase those numbers to 47,280 (reading not entirely certain) and 200 respectively.[51]

---

50 For editions of the relevant passages concerning Samaria and Bīt-Ḫumria, see Frahm's chapter in this volume.

51 The reading of the number in Nimrud Prism iv 31 is uncertain. Frahm (this volume) reads it as [2]7? LIM 2 ME 80 ("[2]7,280"), while Nadav Na'aman reads it as [4]7? LIM 2 ME 80 ("[4]7,280"). See Nadav Na'aman, "The Number of Deportees from Samaria in the Nimrud Prisms of Sargon II," *NABU* 2000: 1 no. 1. Unfortunately, the original object (IM 67661; ND 2601 + ND 3401 + ND 3403 + ND 3417), which is now in the Iraq Museum (Baghdad), could not be checked to verify the reading of the now-damaged number. The number in Gadd's copy looks more like [2]7 than [4]7; see Gadd, "Inscribed Prisms of Sargon II from Nimrud," pl. XLVI.

5.3 Lost inscriptions of Shalmaneser V

Assuming Shalmaneser V followed in the footsteps of his predecessors, we expect that he recorded his military conquests and building activities on a variety of clay, stone, and metal objects. If we look at what is preserved for other eighth- and seventh-century Assyrian rulers, it is clear that kings started having their scribes writing compositions in their names the first chance they got. For example, Sargon recorded the defeats of Elam and Hamath in inscriptions written in or just after his second year (720);[52] Sennacherib described his successes in Babylonia in texts composed during his third year (702);[53] and Ashurbanipal commemorated the installation of his brother as the king of Babylon and the return of the god Marduk in an inscription written shortly after ascending the throne (early 668).[54] It has sometimes been suggested that because Shalmaneser reigned only five years, that he did not have time to have any inscriptions written in his name.[55] That proposal is not very plausible since texts of other kings are known from their first years on the throne and since Shalmaneser is known to have conducted no less than three campaigns (according to the Eponym Chronicle).[56] However, this would certainly be the case if one was referring to annalistic texts and summary inscriptions carved on wall and pavement slabs. It is clear from the extant texts of his father and brother that such monumental inscriptions were composed after sitting on the throne for more than a decade. Thus, given Shalmaneser's five-year tenure as king, we should only expect more modest texts: in particular annals written on foundation documents and steles; building texts written on foundation documents and bricks; as well as royal dedications and proprietary labels written on a wide variety of objects, including bronze lion weights. Apart from a set of weights,[57] none of these objects have survived. So, what happened to them?

Let me try to answer that question before diving into what the texts might have included. Many of Shalmaneser's foundations documents may have suffered at the hands of his successors (Sargon II and Esarhaddon, in particular)

---

52 See nn. 36–37 above.
53 See n. 16 above.
54 Jamie Novotny, *Selected Royal Inscriptions of Assurbanipal: L³, L⁴, LET, Prism I, Prism T, and Related Texts* (Winona Lake IN: Eisenbrauns, 2014), xvi–xvii, 77–80 and 96–99 no. 18. This text is commonly referred to as the "L[ondon]⁴ Inscription" or "Ashurbanipal's School Days Inscription."
55 Compare Grayson, "Tiglath-pileser III to Sargon II," 85.
56 See n. 6 above.
57 See n. 5 above.

and, thus, did not survive antiquity. At Calah, his inscriptions may have been removed from their original locations when Esarhaddon decided to build a palace for himself. This seventh-century ruler made extensive use of the limestone slabs decorating the walls and floors of Tiglath-pileser's palace.[58] Esarhaddon had the unfinished royal residence of his great grandfather dismantled, numerous wall slabs transported further south, and packed in rows, one against the other. The slabs that were installed in the South-West Palace before Esarhaddon's death had their sculptured surfaces face the mudbrick wall in order to leave their uninscribed surfaces exposed. In a few instances, the slabs were re-cut to make them fit their new spaces.[59] Any foundation document deposited in the Central Palace may not have been treated with respect. If Shalmaneser had continued the work of his father at Calah, then any inscribed object of his in the Central Palace may have been removed during the demolition or left to the elements.[60] Thus, it is possible that many of Shalmaneser's inscriptions disappeared or were placed elsewhere, in a location that has yet to be discovered, during Esarhaddon's reign. Moreover, given the tenor of the Aššur Charter, there is a possibility that Sargon had his brother's texts intentionally destroyed. The near complete absence of official inscriptions from Shalmaneser's reign may be due to Sargon's systematic attempt to erase any trace of his brother's accomplishments as king; this would have included destroying Shalmaneser's foundation records. Of course, there are many other possible scenarios leading to the near complete absence of inscriptions of Shalmaneser.[61]

---

58 See above, §4.1 (especially n. 49). Further details about the reuse of earlier material in the South-West Palace can be found in Barnett and Falkner, *Central and South-West Palaces at Nimrud*, 23–30, which excerpt Layard's descriptions in *Nineveh and Its Remains* 1–2.
59 According to Layard, *Nineveh and Its Remains* 2, 35, some of the edges of the orthostats "had been cut away, several letters of the inscriptions being destroyed, in order to make the stones fit into the wall."
60 In the ninth and eighth centuries, Assyrian kings appear not to have deposited many clay foundation records in their royal residences if those palaces had copies of annals and summary/display inscriptions prominently inscribed on sculpted orthostats. No clay foundation documents of Ashurnasirpal II have so far been found in the North-West Palace at Calah, however, some clay cylinders of Sargon II (the "Khorsabad Cylinder") have been discovered in that king's palace at Dūr-Šarrukīn. None of the summary inscriptions of Tiglath-pileser written on clay tablets (assumed here to be foundation documents rather than archival copies) were discovered in the Central Palace, which could have been the result of their removal by Esarhaddon.
61 One possibility is that Shalmaneser made only relatively minor repairs to buildings and walls worked on by his father and, therefore, did not have foundation records deposited in those structures. Compare, for example, Aššur-etel-ilāni who restored a few rooms of the Nabû temple (Ezida) at Calah and left his mark only in the form of inscribed bricks. It is also likely that some of the temples, palaces, and walls worked on by Shalmaneser were subsequent-

As for the contents and media of these hypothetical texts, I tentatively suggest that Shalmaneser's scribes wrote out annalistic texts, dedicatory inscriptions, building inscriptions, and proprietary labels. Annalistic texts may have been inscribed on stele or on clay foundation tablets. In my opinion, prisms and cylinders were probably not used because tablets were the primary choice of foundation document between 1076 and 721.[62]

We know that Shalmaneser led at least three campaigns, and certainly his scribes would have described one or more of these. Because the targets of the expeditions are not known, apart from Bīt-Ḫumria and Samaria, we cannot speculate too much about the contents of this king's now-lost compositions. Early versions of Shalmaneser's annals, those written in 725 or 724, may have described the destruction of Israel and may have included a statement about its last king's anti-Assyrian behavior; since the siege of Samaria is said to have lasted three years, this campaign likely took place during this king's second or third year. Assuming such accounts existed, contemporary texts would have presumably given us a more comprehensive view of the last days of Israel and may have confirmed or contradicted information provided in 2Kgs 17 and 18, including Hoshea's capture prior to the siege of Samaria. Given the fact that Assyrian kings generally avoided referring to unfinished business, for example, in-prog-

---

ly rebuilt/restored/repaired by Sargon II, who did not return inscriptions of his brother that his workmen had found to their original spots, as many inscriptions request of their successors, but rather had them destroyed. This might explain why no inscriptions of Shalmaneser have been discovered in the ruins of the Aššur temple (Eḫursaggalkurkurra) at Aššur or the Nabû temple (Ezida) at Calah, assuming, of course, that this Assyrian king undertook such projects. Moreover, it is likely that the bricks used for Shalmaneser's repairs were not inscribed (or stamped). Assyrian kings did not always have inscriptions placed on bricks, as is clear from eighth- and seventh-century repairs made to the aforementioned Ezida temple; no inscribed bricks of Sargon II, Sennacherib, Esarhaddon, Ashurbanipal, or Sîn-šarru-iškun have been found in that temple. For the building history of Ezida, see Jamie Novotny and Greta Van Buylaere, "Sîn-šarru-iškun and Ezida in Calah," in *Homeland and Exile: Biblical and Ancient Near Eastern Studies in Honour of Bustenay Oded*, ed. Gershon Galil, Mark Geller and Alan Millard (Leiden: Brill, 2009): 233–35.

62 No prisms or cylinders bearing Assyrian inscriptions are known between the reigns of Tiglath-pileser I and Sargon II. The latter's scribes appear to have reintroduced prisms as a medium for writing out long, descriptive annals and adopted the cylinder format for shorter texts from its southern neighbor Babylonia; a cylinder of Marduk-apla-iddina II (Merodach-baladan of the Bible) from Uruk was brought back to Calah, where it likely served as a model for Sargon's own inscriptions. K. 3751, a clay tablet discovered in the South-East Palace at Calah, is a good example of a clay foundation tablet used during the reign of Shalmaneser V's father; for photographs, see Tadmor and Yamada, *Tiglath-pileser III*, 117 figures 6–7. On prisms see Benjamin Studevent-Hickman, "Prisma," in *RlA*, vol. 11/1–2, ed. Michael P. Streck (Berlin: de Gruyter, 2006), 4–6.

ress sieges, Shalmaneser's scribes may have done their best to not mention Samaria in these first reports. If they did, they presumably found a way to spin the narrative in favor of their royal patron. A good example of this is Sennacherib's siege of Jerusalem, a city whose capture is absent in reports of this king's annals.[63]

Later annalistic texts, those written in the king's fourth and fifth regnal year, assuming such inscriptions existed, may have recorded the capture of Samaria and the deportation of its inhabitants, assuming, of course, that the city was taken while Shalmaneser was still king. Such compositions may have confirmed (or even contradicted) some of the information provided in 2Kgs 17 and 18. It is highly unlikely, however, that Assyrian inscriptions would have admitted that it took three years to capture the city. Statements about the conquest of Samaria and the removal of its population, livestock, and property, would likely have been incorporated into the earlier reports of the destruction of Bīt-Ḫumria. Whether Shalmaneser had time to commemorate the capture of Samaria would have depended on how long before his death the city was taken and how long and tumultuous the revolt that brought his reign and life to an end lasted. If it was captured too close to the tenth month of 722, then it is unlikely that Shalmaneser would have had time to record this event in texts written in his name. However, if Samaria was taken in 723 or early in 722, then it is possible that Shalmaneser proudly boasted about capturing Bīt-Ḫumria's capital.

6 Conclusions

So then, what can now-lost Assyrian inscriptions tell us about the last days of Israel? Potentially a great deal. This is certainly the case for Tiglath-pileser III and possibly the case for Shalmaneser V. Texts of these two kings may have provided important information about the years 734–732 and 725–722 and may have supplemented or contradicted the information provided in 2Kgs 15–18. However, missing inscriptions of Sargon II would probably not improve our knowledge about the anti-Assyrian activities of the inhabitants of Samaria in the year 720, as that information is already known from a number of important texts. Until new sources become available, we can only guess at what the eighth-century Assyrian kings might have said about Bīt-Ḫumria, its last two kings, and its capital.

---

63 E.g., Grayson and Novotny, *Inscriptions of Sennacherib* 1, 65–66 no. 4 lines 52–58, and 176–77 no. 22 iii 27b–49.

Eckart Frahm
Samaria, Hamath, and Assyria's Conquests in the Levant in the Late 720s BCE

The Testimony of Sargon II's Inscriptions

1 Introduction

The fall of Samaria in the late 720s BCE, and the political and military actions leading to and immediately following this fateful event, with its major historical and religious consequences, are documented by several types of historical sources. The available evidence comprises:

> a) Texts from various backgrounds, including the Hebrew Bible, Assyrian royal inscriptions, Assyrian and Babylonian chronographic works, as well as Assyrian administrative and legal documents with references to Israelites,[1]
> b) Images on Assyrian sculptures in Rooms V and VIII of Sargon II's palace in Khorsabad,[2]
> c) Other artifacts, most importantly a substantial number of ivories found in the Assyrian city of Calah and in Samaria itself,[3]
> d) Archaeological traces (albeit all in all modest) of the destruction and later rebuilding

---

[1] The Assyrian royal inscriptions are discussed in this and in Jamie Novotny's contribution to the volume at hand. Notes on the chronographic texts are found in the last section of this chapter. For the Assyrian administrative and legal documents, see the articles by Radner and Fales. Several other contributions to this book provide detailed analyses of the various Biblical texts pertaining to the fall of Samaria.
[2] See Andreas Fuchs, *Die Inschriften Sargons II. aus Khorsabad* (Göttingen: Cuvillier Verlag, 1994), 276–78, 364; Christoph Uehlinger, "'...und wo sind die Götter von Samarien?' Die Wegführung syrisch-palästinischer Kultstatuen auf einem Relief Sargons II. in Ḫorsabad/Dūr-Šarrukīn," in *Und Mose schrieb dieses Lied auf...: Festschrift für Oswald Loretz*, ed. Manfried Dietrich and Ingo Kottsieper (Münster: Ugarit-Verlag, 1998), 739–76; Nadav Na'aman, "No Anthropomorphic Graven Image: Notes on the Assumed Anthropomorphic Cult Statues in the Temples of YHWH in the Pre-Exilic Period," *UF* 31 (1999): 391–415.
[3] It is possible that the ivories found in Room SW 37 of Fort Shalmaneser at Calah (Nimrud) may have come from Assyria's western campaigns in the 720s, when Samaria was conquered. Numerous ivories, perhaps representing the same set, were, in fact, found at Samaria, in layers dating to the Late Hellenistic period, when they were apparently dumped. For discussion and further literature, see Claudia Suter, "Images, Tradition, and Meaning: The Samaria and Other Levantine Ivories," in *A Common Cultural Heritage: Studies on Mesopotamia and the Biblical World in Honor of Barry L. Eichler*, ed. Grant Frame et al. (Bethesda MD: CDL Press, 2011), 219–41, esp. 220–21.

that occurred as a consequence of the Assyrian conquests in the urban setting of Samaria, and the (former) kingdom of Israel in general.⁴

Reviewing this list, it seems no exaggeration to claim that few other major events in ancient Near Eastern history are documented by larger numbers of written documents and other evidence than the end of the kingdom of Israel is. And yet, despite this *embarrassment of riches* – or perhaps rather because of it – Assyriologists and Hebrew Bible scholars such as Hayim Tadmor, Bob Becking, Nadav Na'aman, Andreas Fuchs, Gershon Galil, Christine Tetley, Ariel Bagg, and Sarah Melville, to list only some of the many scholars who have contributed to the discussion, have suggested very different scenarios and chronologies for the events at issue.⁵ Key questions that remain unanswered include whether the Assyrians conquered Samaria once or twice, and when exactly; which roles were played by the Assyrian kings Shalmaneser V (726–722 BCE) and Sar-

---

4 For Samaria, see Ron E. Tappy, *The Archaeology of Israelite Samaria, Volume I, Early Iron Age Through the Ninth Century B.C.E.* (Atlanta GA: Scholars Press, 1992), id., *The Archaeology of Israelite Samaria, Volume II: The Eighth Century B.C.E.* (Winona Lake IN: Eisenbrauns, 2002), id., "The Final Years of Israelite Samaria: Toward a Dialogue between Texts and Archaeology," in *Up to the Gates of Ekron: Essays on the Archaeology and History of the Eastern Mediterranean in Honor of Seymour Gitin*, ed. Sidnie White Crawford and Amnon Ben-Tor (Jerusalem: W. F. Albright Institute of Archaeological Research / Israel Exploration Society, 2007), 258–79; see also the short recent overview by Rupert Chapman, "Samaria – Capital of Israel," *BAR* 43/5 (2017): 24–30, 63. Evidence for destruction by the Assyrian army is virtually non-existent at the site of Samaria, despite claims to the contrary in the very incomplete reports by Kathleen Kenyon on her 1930s excavations, which were heavily based on the Biblical account. For additional information, see the chapters on the archaeology of Samaria and other Israelite sites found elsewhere in this volume.

5 Hayim Tadmor, "The Campaigns of Sargon II of Assur: A Chronological-Historical Study," *JCS* 12 (1958): 22–40, 77–100; Bob Becking, *The Fall of Samaria: An Historical and Archaeological Study* (Leiden: Brill, 1992); Nadav Na'aman, "The Historical Background of the Conquest of Samaria (720 BC)," *Bib* 71 (1990): 206–25; Fuchs, *Die Inschriften Sargons II. aus Khorsabad*, 457–58; Gershon Galil, "The Last Years of the Kingdom of Israel and the Fall of Samaria," *CBQ* 57 (1995): 52–65; M. Christine Tetley, "The Date of Samaria's Fall as a Reason for Rejecting the Hypothesis of Two Conquests," *CBQ* 64 (2002): 59–77; Ariel Bagg, *Die Assyrer und das Westland: Studien zur historischen Geographie und Herrschaftspraxis in der Levante im 1. Jt. v.u.Z.* (Leuven: Peeters, 2011), 227–44; Sarah C. Melville, *The Campaigns of Sargon II, King of Assyria, 721–705 B.C.* (Norman: University of Oklahoma Press, 2016), 65–76. Helpful summaries and critical assessments of the scholarly discussion are provided by Kyle Lawson Younger Jr., "The Fall of Samaria in Light of Recent Research," *CBQ* 61 (1999): 461–82 and Kenneth Bergland, "Analysis and Assessment of Chronological Explanations of the Fall of Samaria," *Spes Christiana* 22–23 (2011–12): 63–84. See now also Mordechai Cogan, "Restoring the Empire: Sargon's Campaign to the West in 720/19 BCE," *IEJ* 67 (1967): 151–67.

gon II (721–705 BCE), respectively, both of whom seem to have been involved in the events; what eventually happened to the last king of Israel, Hoshea; who was in charge in Samaria in the aftermath of his deposition; and finally, whether the three year siege of Samaria mentioned in the Bible (2Kgs 17:5–6) began in 725, 724, or perhaps even as late as 721 BCE, if it ever took place.

Several factors explain why modern scholars have so far failed to reach a consensus on the issues in question. One is that no inscriptions of any importance from the reign of Shalmaneser V have yet been found.[6] Consequently, the statement in the Babylonian Chronicle (I 27–28) that Shalmaneser "ravaged Samaria" at some point during his five year long reign,[7] and similar claims made in the Bible, cannot be paired with more elaborate accounts of this event, written in the name of the king who supposedly brought it about. Equally problematic is that several of the texts from Assyria that are available, most notably the Assyrian Eponym Chronicle and a number of important inscriptions of Sargon II, offer poorly preserved accounts of the events surrounding the fall of Samaria – and that Sargon's inscriptions differ markedly in what they have to say about them. And finally, there is the problem that the most important Biblical accounts, in 2Kgs 17 and 18, provide a number of chronological and historical conundrums, probably due to the fact that they misrepresent, at least to some degree, the chronographic records and other traditions on which they were originally based.

This article does not aim at offering a reconstruction of the events that will settle the discussion once and for all, something that can probably only be achieved if we are lucky enough one day to discover additional sources. What it primarily seeks to provide instead is a presentation and a new assessment of the

---

[6] For the most recent analysis of the inscribed weights from Shalmaneser's reign, the only extant objects with texts written in the name of this king, see Frederick Mario Fales, "The Assyrian Lion-Weights: A Further Attempt," in: *Libiamo ne' lieti calici: Ancient Near Eastern Studies Presented to Lucio Milano*, ed. Paola Corò et al. (Münster: Ugarit-Verlag, 2016), 483–507. Fales suggests, very tentatively, "that the weight-standard 'of the land' which came to be added, only in Aramaic, on the lion-weights from his [scil. Shalmaneser V's] reign enhanced by bronze handles, could have represented a ponderal measure then current in the territories of the Levant or Transeuphratene, such as had been annexed to Assyrian suzerainty by this ruler" (p. 497). For a thorough reevaluation of the reign of Shalmaneser V, see now Keiko Yamada and Shigeo Yamada, "Shalmaneser V and His Era, Revisited," in: *"Now It Happened in Those Days": Studies in Biblical, Assyrian and Other Ancient Near Eastern Historiography Presented to Mordechai Cogan on His 75th Birthday*, ed. Amitai Baruchi-Unna et al. (Winona Lake IN: Eisenbrauns, 2017), 387–442 (an article that appeared too late to be fully taken into consideration here, but which comes to similar historical conclusions).

[7] A. Kirk Grayson, *Assyrian and Babylonian Chronicles* (Locust Valley NY: Augustin, 1975), 73.

various accounts of the victory over Samaria that are found in Sargon II's royal inscriptions – some of which have only recently become known. It is hoped that such an overview will, at the very least, help eliminate some of the less likely historical solutions that have been proposed in the past. Since the fall of Samaria cannot be detached from the events surrounding the wide-ranging rebellion of Yau-bi'di – or Ilu-bi'di – of Hamath,[8] this latter event will feature quite prominently as well.[9]

In the following, I will present the relevant Sargon texts, to the extent possible, in the sequence in which they were written,[10] trusting that such an arrangement will contribute to a better understanding of some chronological issues crucial for a historical analysis of the events under discussion. Even though several students of Assyrian royal inscriptions, most notably Liverani,[11] have shown that later campaign accounts that modify earlier ones should by no means be dismissed as historically worthless (despite their tendency to con-

---

8 It has long been supposed (even though some doubts remain) that the name Yau-bi'di contains the theophoric element YHWH, which could be seen as adding a religious dimension to the alliance between the Hamathean insurgent and the Samarians; see, among others, Stephanie Dalley, "Yahweh in Hamath in the 8th Century BC: Cuneiform Material and Historical Deductions," *VT* 50 (1990): 21–32. One should keep in mind, however, that other members of the anti-Assyrian coalition of 720 BCE, not the least Damascus, were clearly not particularly committed to the worship of YHWH, and that the rebellion, therefore, can hardly be seen as a "holy war" waged in the name of the Israelite god. Ran Zadok, "Israelites and Judaeans in the Neo-Assyrian Documentation (732–602 B.C.E.): An Overview of the Sources and a Socio-Historical Assessment," *BASOR* 374 (2015): 159–89, esp. 160, discusses the possibility that both Yau-bi'di and an earlier Hamathean insurgent with an apparently Yahwistic name, Azri-Yau, "descended from dynastic marriages between Hamathean rulers and North Israelite princesses."
9 On rebellions against the Assyrian crown in general, see Karen Radner, "Revolts in the Assyrian Empire: Succession Wars, Rebellions Against a False King and Independence Movements," in *Revolt and Resistance in the Ancient Classical World and the Near East: In the Crucible of Empire*, ed. John J. Collins and J.G. Manning (Leiden: Brill, 2016), 41–54, and Eckart Frahm, "Revolts in the Neo-Assyrian Empire: A Preliminary Discourse Analysis," in *Revolt and Resistance*, 76–89.
10 For a discussion and convenient overview of the composition dates of Sargon's royal inscriptions, see Andreas Fuchs, *Die Annalen des Jahres 711 v. Chr.* (Helsinki: The Neo-Assyrian Text Corpus Project, 1998), 81–96, and id., "Sargon II.," *RlA* 12, ed. Michael P. Streck (Berlin: de Gruyter, 2009), 51–61, esp. 52. It is important to note that the dates provided by Fuchs are mostly based on the number of campaigns covered in the inscriptions and not on actual date formulas concluding them. Given that there are substantial inconsistencies in the way Sargon's scribes provided chronological markers for the king's military activities, some uncertainty remains.
11 Mario Liverani, "Critique of Variants and the Titulary of Sennacherib," in *Assyrian Royal Inscriptions: New Horizons in Literary, Ideological, and Historical Analysis*, ed. Frederick Mario Fales (Rome: Istituto per l'Oriente, 1981), 225–57.

flate earlier and later historical events), the old rule established by Olmstead,[12] that the very first reports an Assyrian king provides about a given military campaign tend to be the most reliable, remains to some extent valid.

2 The Samaria and Hamath Episodes in Sargon II's Inscriptions

One of the earliest Sargon texts mentioning Samaria is the so-called "Ashur Charter," which is actually a votive inscription for Assur copied from a silver vessel dedicated to the god (see ll. 40–43) onto a clay tablet. The "historical" part of the text, which follows a panegyric introduction praising first the god Assur and then King Sargon, is devoted exclusively to events of Sargon's second regnal year, that is, 720 BCE:

Text 1: Ashur Charter (covers events up to 720 BCE)[13]

16) *i-na* 2-*e* BALA-*ia šá ina* ᵍᶦˢGU.ZA LUGAL-*ti ú-ši-bu-ma a-ge-e be-lu-ti an-na-*[*ap-ru-ma*]
17) ILLAT ᵐᵈ*ḫum-ba-i-ga-áš* MAN KUR *e-lam-ti ú-par-ri-ra áš-ku-na* BAD₅.BAD₅-*šú* ⸢ᵐᵈ⸣[*ia-ú-bi-i'-di*]
18) ⸢ˡᶸ⸣*ḫa-ma-ta-a-a la* EN ᵍᶦˢGU.ZA *la ši-nin-ti* É.GAL *šá ina* SIPA-*ut* UN.MEŠ *ši-mat-s*[*u lā šīmat* (0?)]
19) *a-na* AN.ŠÁR KUR-*šú* UN.MEŠ-*šú* ḪUL-*tu la* DÙG.GA-*tú ú-ba-'u-ú-ma il-qa-a ši-ṭ*[*u-*(*ú-*)*tu* (*ṣimirra dimašqu* (?))]
20) ⸢ᵘʳᵘ⸣*ar-pa-da* ᵘʳᵘ**sa-me-ri-na** *ú-paḫ-ḫir-ma a-na i-di-šú ú-ter-r*[*a mārē aššur ša ina māt ḫamati* (?) (...)]
21) [*ba*?]-⸢*šu*?-*ú*?⸣ GIM DIŠ-*en id-duk-ma*⸣ *na-piš-tú ul e-z*[*ib* x x x x x x x x]
22) [x x] x x x ⸢*qa*?-*ti*?⸣ *áš*⸣-*ši-ma áš-šú ka-šad* KUR *ḫa-ma-t*[*i sakāp Yau-bi'di* (?) x x x]
23) [*ša māt a*]-⸢*mur-re*⸣-*e* DAGAL-*ti am-ḫur-ma* AN.ŠÁR DINGI[R x x x x x x x x x]
24) [*ikrībīya* (?) *i*]*š-me-ma il-qa-a su-pe-ia u*[*m-ma-na-at*(?) *aššur gapšāti*(?) *adkema*(?)]
25) [*ḫarrān māt a-m*]*ur-re-e ú-šá-aṣ-bit* KUR *ḫa-*[*ma-ta* x x x x x x x x x]
26) [x x] x *mu-ṣa-at šá-lam-du ta-nit-t*[*i* x x x x x x x x x x]
27) [*nišē/gimir*(?) *māt a-m*]*ur-re-e a-na* GÌR.2-*ia ú-šak-ni-*[*iš*? *Yau-bi'di / šâšu adi kimtišu* (*mundaḫṣēšu*) (?)]
28) ⸢*a-na*⸣ URU-*ia* ᵘʳᵘ*a-šur ub-la-ma* ......

---

12 Albert Ten Eyck Olmstead, *Assyrian Historiography: A Source Study* (Columbia MO: University of Missouri, 1916).
13 Edition: Henry W. F. Saggs, "Historical Texts and Fragments of Sargon II of Assyria: 1. The 'Aššur Charter'," *Iraq* 37 (1975): 11–20. Collated by the author from a photo posted on the website of the Cuneiform Digital Library Initiative (CDLI); see https://cdli.ucla.edu (accessed 10/2017).

Notes to the text: Line 18 restored after Text 11 ("Mosul Annals"), l. 5; lines 20–22 after Text 11, ll. 14–15, 18 and Text 3 (Tell Tayinat Stele), ll. 5'–7'; line 24 after Text 12 (Khorsabad Display Inscription), l. 34; line 27 after Text 2 (Asharneh Stele), B 11 and other texts. Note the new interpretation of line 26: *mu-ṣa-at* is apparently a feminine singular stative derived from *wuṣṣû/muṣṣû* "to spread out," even though one would rather have expected plural forms here.

"In my second regnal year (*palû*), when I had settled on my royal throne and had been crowned with the lordly crown, I dispersed the forces of Ḫumba(n)igaš, King of Elam, and defeated him.

Yau-bi'di of Hamath, (who was) not the (rightful) throne-holder, (who was) unfit for (living in) a palace, and as whose fate [it had never been decreed] that he would (ever) shepherd the people [(...)], (who) intended (to do) evil, things that were not good, against the god Assur, his land, and his people, and treated (them) with insolence, he gathered [*Ṣimirra, Damascus*], Arpad, and **Samaria**, and brought them to his side. He killed [the citizens of Assyria who] were [in Hamath (...)], all together, and left no one alive.

[...] ... I lifted my hand and prayed for the conquest of the land of Hamath, [the overthrow of Yau-bi'di and the ...] of the vast land of Amurru. Assur, the god [...], listened [to my prayers] and received my supplication.

[*I mobilized the vast*] troops [*of Assur*] and had (them) take [the way to] the land of Amurru. The land of Hamath [...] ... spread out was the corpse, the praise [...]. I made [*the people / all of*] the land of Amurru bow to my feet. [Yau-bi'di (or: Him), together with his *family (and his fighters)*], I brought to my city Ashur (followed by an account of Sargon's favorable treatment of the city of Ashur)."

The Ashur Charter reveals a number of important details:

1) Sargon seems not to have campaigned at all during the last months of 722 BCE, after he had become Assyrian king,[14] and during his entire first regnal year, 721 BCE. Otherwise, he would certainly have mentioned in the Ashur Charter military accomplishments associated with these two years. This makes it very unlikely that the Assyrian army began a siege of Samaria in 721 BCE, as claimed by Tetley.[15] The Ashur Charter also helps establish why Sargon stayed at home during the period in question. The text portrays Sargon's predecessor, Shalmaneser V, as a corrupt ruler who interfered with and harmed the cult of Assur. This negative appreciation strongly suggests that Sargon had come to the throne in

---

[14] According to the Babylonian Chronicle, Sargon ascended the Assyrian throne on the tenth day of Ṭebet (X), 722 BCE, a few days after the death of his predecessor earlier that month: Grayson, *Assyrian and Babylonian Chronicles*, 73: 29–31.

[15] Tetley, "The Date of Samaria's Fall," 59–77. Tetley's arguments suffer from the fact that she ignores much of the relevant Assyriological scholarship, especially the important work on Sargon by Fuchs, thus illustrating the perils of a "Germanica non leguntur" approach. The latter also applies to the study by Sung Jin Park, "A New Historical Reconstruction of the Fall of Samaria," *Bib* 93 (2012): 98–106.

somewhat irregular fashion and had to deal with domestic opposition during the first months of his reign. Other Sargon texts, to be discussed later (see Texts 13–15, below), corroborate this assumption.[16]

2) During the time of domestic unrest in Assyria, Yau-bi'di of Hamath had started a revolt against the Assyrians that was soon joined by numerous important polities of the Westland, including Arpad in northern Syria – and Samaria. Other texts also mention Damascus and Ṣimirra, plus, it seems (in Text 11), some cities whose names are lost.

3) While the Ashur Charter is short on detail, it clearly states that the military actions initiated by Sargon in 720 BCE led to the defeat of the Western coalition (see line 27). Even though it is not explicitly pointed out, it would seem that Samaria gave up its opposition as well; but there is no unequivocal statement in the text that this required a military attack on the city. Moreover, no ruler of Samaria is mentioned, something that applies, however, also to the other states of the enemy coalition.[17]

4) Yau-bi'di, together with his family (and some of his fighters), was brought to Ashur, where he was apparently flayed. This last detail is known, not from the Ashur Charter, but from later Sargon inscriptions (see below Texts 6 and 12) and an epigraph accompanying an image of a tortured enemy in Room VIII of Sargon's palace in Khorsabad.[18]

Did Sargon participate in person in the Western campaign of 720 BCE, or was the campaign conducted by his generals? The Ashur Charter is not quite clear in this regard,[19] but another inscription, on an Assyrian stele erected at Tell Asharneh on the Orontes River shortly after the events, provides an answer to this question:

---

16 The counter-arguments raised by Galo W. Vera Chamaza, "Sargon II's Ascent to the Throne: The Political Situation," *SAAB* 6 (1992): 21–33, do not strike me as particularly convincing.
17 The one exception is Hamath, but it is noteworthy that Yau-bi'di is not presented as the "king" of this polity. Instead, he appears – as in most other Sargon texts (for exceptions, see below note 53) – as "a man from Hamath" (^{lu}ha-ma-ta-a-a). It may well be that Yau-bi'di built his career in opposition to a Hamathean ruler with pro-Assyrian tendencies.
18 For the text, see Fuchs, *Die Inschriften Sargons II. aus Khorsabad*, 278, 364; for a reproduction of an early drawing of the image, see Pauline Albenda, *The Palace of Sargon, King of Assyria* (Paris: Éditions Recherche sur les civilisations, 1986), pl. 78.
19 The Š-stem in l. 25 points towards the latter scenario, but the 1st person singular form in line 28 suggests the former.

Text 2: Tell Asharneh Stele (covers events up to 720 BCE)[20]

Side B
1') [...] x x x [...]
2') [...] *a-na* A.ME[Š x (x)]
3') [...]-*šú ú-qí-ru-m*[*a*]
4') [...] ⸢*i*⸣-*te-e* URU-*šu*
5') [... *a-n*]*a šit-mur* ANŠE.KUR.RA.M[EŠ]
6') [...]-*ti* LÚ x(*e*??) qa? ma?
7') [... *di-ik-ta*(?)-*š*]*ú-nu ma-at-t*[*u*]
8') [... *is*]-⸢*ki*⸣-*ru* ÍD
9') [... *di?-tal?-l*]*i-iš iq-mu-ú-m*[*a*]
10') [x x (x) *ina māt*] *a-ma-at-te iš-ku-nu-m*[*a?*]
11') [...] x *šá-a-šú ga-du kim-ti-*[*šú*]
12') [*a-na qé-re*]*b* URU-*ia aš-šur*ki ⸢*ub-lu*⸣-[*ni*]

Side C
1') [...] x [...]
2') [...]-*ni-ia* [...]
3') [*šá ina tukul*]-*ti* ᵈ*aš-šur* E[N-*ia* ...]
4') [*at?-ta*]-*la-ku ù mim-mu-ú* [(*ša*) *ina māt* (*ḫ*)*am*(*m*)*at*(*t*)*e* / *amurrê* (?)]
5') [*e?-tep*]-*pu-šú áš-ṭu-ra ṣ*[*e-ru-uš-šú-*(*un*)]
6') [*ištēn i*]*na* KUR *ḫa-am-ma-te* 1-*en ina* [...]
7') [*ištēn*] ⸢*i*⸣-*na* ᵘʳᵘ*ḫa-ta-r*[*i-ka* (...)]
8') [*ištēn i*]*na* ᵘʳᵘKUR-⸢*a-a* 1-*en ina* [...]
9') [*ušziz*(?)] *a-lik ar-ki ru ri* x [...]

Side B: "[...] ... for water [...] its/his [...] they made scarce and [...] alongside his city [...] for horses to show their mettle [...] ... [...] a major [*military defeat*] of them [(...) and] blocked up the river [*with their corpses* ...] they burned [...] turning them into [ashes]. They established [*devastation*] in the land of Hamath and [...] .... They brought him (Yau-bi'di) together with [his] family [to] my city Ashur (lines 13'ff. mention offerings for the god Assur)."

Side C: "[...] ... [...] my... [.... What *I* had] *carried out* with faith in Assur, my lord [...] and everything [*I*] had done [in the land of *Hamath / Amurru*], I inscribed upon [it/them]. One (stele) *I had erected*] in the land of Hamath, one in [..., one] in the city of Ḫatarikka [..., one] in the city of KUR'a, (and) one in [...] ... *the one who goes* after ... [...] (lines 10'ff. include blessings and curses)."

While it is regrettable that this interesting text is so poorly preserved, enough is extant to determine, as others have before,[21] that Sargon did apparently not lead the campaign in 720 BCE against the Westland himself. In all likelihood, he participated instead, in the summer of that year, in the fruitless fight in the east

---

20 Edition: Grant Frame, "The Tell Acharneh Stela of Sargon II of Assyria," in *Tell Acharneh 1998–2004*, ed. Michel Fortin (Turnhout: Brepols, 2006), 49–68, esp. 49–52.
21 See, e.g., Fuchs, *Die Inschriften Sargons II. aus Khorsabad*, 421.

against the Elamites at Der, briefly described in the Ashur Charter and several later inscriptions, and also mentioned, and ascribed to Sargon's second year, in the Babylonian Chronicle. The 3rd person plural forms on Side B of the Tell Asharneh stele make it quite clear that the Western campaign was conducted by Assyrian generals.[22]

We learn, moreover, that the battle fought between the Assyrian troops and those of Yau-bi'di involved fighting in and around a city with a nearby river, clearly Qarqar on the Orontes,[23] and major bloodshed and destruction. Samaria is not mentioned in the preserved part of the text, but it is feasible that the city was among the places where Sargon, according to the text on Side C, erected various victory stelae.

Another city where this apparently happened was Kullania, modern Tell Tayinat, on the northern bend of the Orontes River. Fragments of a Sargon stele found there were recently published by Lauinger and Batiuk. Whether the text was written in the immediate aftermath of the quelling of the Yau-bi'di revolt is not certain, but likely. The portion on Samaria reads as follows:

Text 3: Tell Tayinat Stele (covers events up to 720 BCE(?))[24]

1') [...] x [...]
2') [... i-n]a ^{uru}qar-qa-ri ʿú¹-[paḫ-ḫir-ma (...)]
3') [(...) ušbalkit(?) it]-ti-ia ^{uru}a[r-pad-da ṣimirra (...)]
4') [(...) dimašqu (...) ^{uru}s]a-mi¹-ri-i-n[a ...]
5') [mārē aššur ša (?) ina qé-r]eb KUR a-ma-te É/kit x [... bašû kī ištēn (?)]
6') [iddūk qātī (?) aš²-ši²-m]a² ^{d}aš-šur MAN DINGIR.ME[Š (...) aššu (...)]
7') [(...) kašād māt a-ma]-te sa(text: IR)-kap ^{Id}i[a²-ú-bi-i'-di ...]
8') [(...) māt amurrê amḫur (?) ú]-ma-'e-er-ma [...]

---

22 Melville, *The Campaigns of Sargon II*, 61, 237, n. 23, has suggested a slightly different scenario. In her view, Sargon first participated in the battle of Der and then travelled to the West, where he took part in the later stages of the campaign of 720 BCE. One of Melville's arguments is that a relief in Room V of Sargon's palace in Khorsabad depicts the king in his chariot at Ekron. Melville cannot be proven wrong, but some doubts remain, not least because the dating of the Assyrian intervention at Ekron to 720 BCE is not completely certain. One can also ask if the relief really provides an accurate representation of what had actually happened.
23 Qarqar is usually identified with modern Qarqūr, which may well be correct; but one cannot entirely exclude the possibility that the city was actually located at Tell Asharneh, as argued by Nadav Na'aman, "Qarqar = Tell ᶜAsharneh," *NABU* 1999 no. 89. For a discussion see Ariel Bagg, *Die Orts- und Gewässernamen der neuassyrischen Zeit, Teil 1: Die Levante* (Wiesbaden: Reichert, 2007), 194–95.
24 Edition: Jacob Lauinger and Stephen Batiuk, "A Stele of Sargon II at Tell Tayinat," *ZA* 105 (2015): 54–68. The fragment of interest to us is A 27863.

9') [...] ⌈a?-duk??⌉ x [...]
10') [...] x [...]

Notes to the text: For the tentative new restorations in lines 2'–3', and the passage in general, see Text 11 ("Mosul Annals"), ll. 6–11. For lines 6'–8', see Text 1 (Ashur Charter), ll. 22–24, for line 9' see perhaps Text 12 (Khorsabad Display Inscription), l. 35: EN ḫi-iṭ-ṭi a-duk-ma. The size of the gaps at the beginnings and ends of the lines is uncertain.

"He (Yau-bi'di) gathered [... *troops* ...] in the city of Qarqar [and prompted ... (perhaps: the vast land of Amurru) to rebel] against me. Arpad, [Ṣimirra (...), Damascus (...)], and **Samaria** [... (perhaps: he brought to his side). ... *He killed the citizens of Assyria, all together, who were in*] the midst of the land of Hamath ... [...].
[*I lifted my hand(s) and implored*] the god Assur [(to help me) conquer the land of] Hamath, overthrow Yau-bi'di, [*and ... the land of Amurru*]. I ordered [... (perhaps: my ... troops ...)] *I killed* [*those who had committed crimes*])."[25]

The three texts discussed so far were in all likelihood written towards the end or shortly after the Western campaign of 720 BCE. Some four years later, Sargon commissioned two additional texts that mention Yau-bi'di's revolt and its consequences. One is the Najafehabad Stele, erected in 716 BCE by Assyrian troops in the eastern Zagros region. Mostly devoted to the 716 Assyrian campaign to the East, this text also provides some limited information on earlier military ventures, including the Western campaign of 720. The account is very damaged, but seems similar to the versions in three Sargon texts to be discussed later (Texts 10–12). I am grateful to Andreas Fuchs and Grant Frame for providing me with their joint new – but still unpublished – transliteration of the passage, based on a study of a squeeze of the inscription, and to Fuchs for sending me his translation.[26] Much remains, unfortunately, unclear.

Text 4: Najafehabad Stele (covers events up to 716 BCE)[27]

Reverse
4) (x x) x x [ᵐ]⌈ia⌉-ú-bi-i'-di ⌈lúkur⌉⌈ḫa⌉-am-ma-ta-a-⌈a⌉ x x x x (x) [...][28]
5) [(x)] (x x) x x x x x x x x x x x x ma x ú kid? x x x x (x) [...]

---

25 The traces in line 9' are difficult to read.
26 A few of the new readings offered in the following have been established by myself, based on the photos of the text published by Louis D. Levine, *Two Neo-Assyrian Stelae from Iran* (Toronto: Royal Ontario Museum, 1972), pl. VIII and IX. Most of them are, however, owed to Fuchs and Frame, who will publish their collaborative work on the Najafehabad Stele in the near future in volume 2 of the series *The Royal Inscription of the Neo-Assyrian Period*.
27 Edition: Levine, *Two Neo-Assyrian Stelae from Iran*, 25–50.

6) (x) x a x (x) x x ti⁾ x (x) nu ˡᵘ⁺ʼÉRINʼ.MEŠ ʼúʼ-pa-ʼḫirʼ-ma ma-mit ʼDINGIR.MEŠ GAL.MEŠʼ (x) [...]
7) (x) x di x ʼú-terʼ¹-ma ʼa-naʼ e-mu-qi-šú it-ta-ʼkilʼ um-ma-na-at AN.ʼŠÁRʼ gap-š[á-a-ti ad-kema ...]
8) x (x) ʼiʼ diʼ¹ gi-ip-ʼšúʼ¹ x (x) it-ba-a ᵍⁱˢʼGIGIRʼ pit-ḫal-lu ANŠE.ʼKUR.MEŠʼ ina ᵘʳᵘab x [...]
9) [(x)] ʼmaʼ¹ buʼ x (x) riʼ áš ʼdiʼ¹ x x (x) x-šú-nu ÍD na-ba-lu ʼnaʼ-ba-si-iš ʼaṣ-ruʼ-up a x x [...]
10) (x) ʼidʼ é/danʼ uruʼ du/šúʼ¹ x (x) [u]n/aʼ ʼtu/liʼ¹ (x) x x ʼkanʼ¹ ina ᵍⁱˢa-ši-bi ʼdanʼ-ni ʼBÀD-šú karʼ¹-pa-ti-ʼiš úʼ-pa-ʼriʼ-[ir-maʼ ... ᵘʳᵘqarqaru(?)]
11) [(ina)] ʼᵈNEʼ.GI aq-mu šá-a-ʼšú aʼ-di ʼkim-tiʼ-šú ˡᵘmun-daḫ-ṣi-šú a-ʼnaʼ UR[U]-ʼiaʼ ašʼ-šurᵏⁱ ub-la ina IGI ʼKÁʼ.GAL [... mašakšu akūṣ (?) (...)]
12) (x) x x x ʼšuʼ-ut−ˡᵘ⁺ʼSAGʼ.MEŠʼ-ia a-na ˡᵘEN−NAM-ʼúʼ-ti UGU-šú-nu áš-kun KUR ḫa-am-ma-ʼtaʼ (-)[a-aʼ ...]
13) (x x) x ʼidʼ ku/kiʼ¹ x (x) ......

Notes to the text: At the end of line 8, it would have been tempting to read ᵘʳᵘqar-qa-[ri ...],[29] but the sign after URU really seems to be AB and not QAR. Perhaps one should read ᵘʳᵘab-tam-[ma-ku ...] and assume that the city in question is to be identified with Aštammaku, a "royal city" of Hamath during the reign of Shalmaneser III, whose name is once written ᵘʳᵘab-ta-ma-ku.[30] There remains much uncertainty, however. Line 11 is restored after Text 12 (Khorsabad Display Inscription), l. 35 (it cannot be excluded that a-ku-uṣ belongs at the beginning of line 12).

"(In my second regnal year (palû)) ...... Yau-bi'di of Hamath ... [...] ...... [...] ... he gathered his troops and [transgressed] the oath (sworn) by the great gods [...] he brought to his side and trusted in his own force.
[I mobilized] the vast troops of Assur [...] ... massed body ... he rose; chariots, cavalry, and horses in the city of Ab... [...] ...... their ... (with their blood), I dyed the river and the dry land red like red wool ... [...] ...... with a mighty battering ram, I smashed its wall like clay pots [...] I destroyed [the city of Qarqar] by fire. I brought him (Yau-bi'di) together with his family and his fighters to my city Ashur, and in front of the [...] Gate, [I flayed him ...]
... I appointed (one of (?)) my eunuchs over them to serve as provincial governor. The land of Hamath (or: the citizens of Hamath) [...] ... (followed by an account of Sargon's "third palû")."

Unlike the Tell Asharneh Stele, the Najafehabad Stele ascribes all agency for the Western campaign of 720 BCE to Sargon alone. It claims, moreover, that in the wake of the campaign, an Assyrian eunuch was appointed as provincial gover-

---

28 The poorly preserved lines preceding line 4 could have accommodated an account of the battle of Der, but certainly not one of the conquest of Samaria; see Fuchs, Die Annalen des Jahres 711 v. Chr., 85.
29 See the references to Qarqar in Texts 3, 10, 11 and 12.
30 A. Kirk Grayson, Assyrian Rulers of the Early First Millennium BC II (858–754 BC) (Toronto: Toronto University Press, 1996), A.0.102.16: 75'. For further references and possible locations, see Bagg, Die Orts- und Gewässernamen der neuassyrischen Zeit, Teil 1, 33–34.

nor over Hamath. Since this measure is not yet mentioned in the Ashur Charter and the Asharneh Stele (Texts 1 and 2),[31] it seems likely that it was not implemented in 720 BCE but shortly thereafter – when exactly remains unclear.

While later inscriptions (see below Texts 7(?), 8, and 9) claim that Sargon also appointed one of his eunuchs as governor of Samaria, it is noteworthy that the Najafehabad Stele does apparently not yet include such a statement.[32] Considering the emphasis the account in the Stele puts on the events in Hamath, this omission does, however, not necessarily mean that such an appointment had not been made in the meantime.

A rather startling new claim is made in a second Sargon inscription composed around 716 BCE, the so-called Juniper Palace Inscription from Kalḫu in central Assyria. After an introductory passage with royal titles and epithets, the text characterizes the king as follows:

Text 5: Juniper Palace Text (covers events up to 716 BCE)[33]

> 7) NUN *na-a'-du šá ina re-bit* BÀD.AN^{ki} *it-ti* ^{md}*ḫum-ba-ni-ga-áš* LUGAL KUR *e-lam-ti in-nam-ru-ma iš-ku-nu taḫ-ta-šú*
> 8) *mu-šak-niš* **KUR *ia-ú-du*** *šá a-šar-šú ru-ú-qu na-si-iḫ* KUR *ḫa-am-ma-te šá* ^{md}*ia-ú-bi-i'-di ma-lik-šú-nu ik-šu-du* ŠU^{II}-*šú*
>
> "Exalted prince, who met (in battle) with Humbanigaš, king of Elam, in the district of Der and defeated him; subduer of the land of **Judah**, which lies far away; who deported (the people of) Hamath; who captured Yau-bi'di, their king, with his hands."

The Juniper Palace Inscription has some chronological inconsistencies, but the better known episodes to which it alludes in the aforementioned passage all occurred in 720 BCE. Therefore, and because the text covers only events up to 716

---

31 The Tell Tayinat Stele (Text 3) is so damaged that one cannot establish whether it dealt with the Assyrian efforts to reorganize the political landscape of the Westland.
32 At first glance, the strange plural writing ^{lú}⸢SAG.MEŠ⸣-*ia*, and the possessive suffix -*šunu* in *elišunu*, both in line 12, could be taken as indicating that Sargon appointed governors in other Western polities as well (thus Andreas Fuchs, "Die Assyrer und das Westland," *Or* 83 (2014): 243–57, esp. 250); but the sign sequence ⸢SAG.MEŠ⸣, apart from not being absolutely certain, is perhaps rather a late echo of the dual-based Middle Assyrian term for eunuch, *ša–rēšēn*, while *elišunu*, apparently referring to the people, is also found in texts that clearly deal only with Hamath (see below, Texts 13–15).
33 Copy: Hugo Winckler, *Die Keilschrifttexte Sargons nach den Papierabklatschen und Originalen neu herausgegeben* (Leipzig: Hinrich'sche Buchhandlung, 1889), vol. 2, pl. 48. For a discussion of the text and a partial new edition, see Nadav Na'aman, "The Historical Portion of Sargon's Nimrud Inscription," *SAAB* 8 (1994): 17–20.

BCE, which is long before Sargon's next recorded major campaign to the Levant in 711 BCE,[34] it is generally assumed that the reference to Sargon being "the subduer of Judah" refers to the campaign of 720 BCE as well. In the Khorsabad Annals, to be discussed later (Text 7/10), Sargon claims that the fight against the enemy coalition led by Yau-bi'di was immediately followed by an Assyrian attack on Gaza in southern Palestine, and it is possible that the altercation with Judah happened as the Assyrian troops moved southwards in this direction, or back from there.[35] Despite the strong language used by Sargon in the Juniper Palace Inscription, it is evident that Judah did not lose its independence in the course of these events; but the Assyrian actions clearly left an impression on the Judeans. When in 711 BCE Yamani of Ashdod sought to implicate Judah in another rebellion, the Judean king did not oblige him, adopting instead a pro-Assyrian stance.[36]

Based on the reference to Judah in the Juniper Palace Inscription, both Andreas Fuchs and I tentatively suggested, years ago, that the fragmentary "Azekah inscription,"[37] which describes an Assyrian attack on the Judean city of Azekah – and fighting elsewhere in the region – at some point during the reign of King He-

---

[34] Note, however, that column ii of the Assur fragment VA 8424 (see Fuchs, *Die Annalen des Jahres 711 v. Chr.*, 28–29, 57) refers to the deportation of members of an unknown people to southern Palestine in Sargon's "fifth *palû*" – a chronological marker probably referring, in this text, to 716 BCE.

[35] Bas reliefs in Room V of Sargon's palace in Khorsabad show the Philistine cities of Amqarruna (Biblical Ekron) and Gabbutunu (Biblical Gibbethon), plus several additional cities, among them Ba'il-gazara and Sinu (see Fuchs, *Die Inschriften Sargons II. aus Khorsabad*, 277, 364), the latter of which is to be identified with Tell Siyānu, 50 km north of Arwad. Amqarruna and Gabbutunu might likewise have been attacked in the course of the Assyrian army's move to southern Palestine in 720 BCE (thus, among others, John Malcolm Russell, *The Writing on the Wall: Studies in the Architectural Context of Late Assyrian Palace Inscriptions* (Winona Lake IN: Eisenbrauns, 1999), 114–23), but it cannot be excluded that they were targeted some other time, perhaps as late as in 711 BCE. It has been suggested that one of the cities depicted in Room V for which no epigraph is extant is Samaria (thus Norma Franklin, "The Room V Reliefs at Dur-Sharrukin and Sargon II's Western Campaigns," *TA* 21 (1994): 255–75), but Younger, "The Fall of Samaria," 476, correctly points to the uncertainty of this proposal. For additional discussion, see the references listed above in note 2.

[36] See Fuchs, *Die Annalen des Jahres 711 v. Chr.*, 44–46, 73–74; id., "Die Assyrer und das Westland," 248–49.

[37] The most recent edition, with ample bibliography, is by A. Kirk Grayson and Jamie Novotny, *The Royal Inscriptions of Sennacherib, King of Assyria (704–681 BC), Part 2* (Winona Lake IN: Eisenbrauns, 2014), 350–52, no. 1015. For the *editio princeps* of the rejoined fragments, see Nadav Na'aman, "Sennacherib's 'Letter to God' on His Campaign to Judah," *BASOR* 214 (1974): 25–39.

zekiah, might describe events that happened in 720 BCE.³⁸ This idea did, however, not find widespread support. A few years ago, Nadav Na'aman provided strong, albeit perhaps not entirely conclusive arguments against it, reaffirming his earlier contention that the Azekah inscription deals with the famous attack on Judah conducted by Sennacherib in 701 BCE.³⁹

If Na'aman is right, there would be no other references to the subjugation of Judah in Sargon's inscriptions, which would make the one in the Juniper Palace Inscription even more puzzling. One way to deal with the problem would be to assume that the scribe who composed the text somehow confused the Kingdom of Israel with the Kingdom of Judah; but there is no parallel for such an error, and the characterization of Judah as "a far-away land" seems at odds with the idea.

It is worth noting, on the other hand, that the next Sargon inscription available to us, the king's Cylinder Inscription from Khorsabad, which covers events up to 713 BCE in a non-chronological sequence, briefly refers to a defeat over Israel, while completely ignoring Judah, as if the former had replaced the latter. After alluding, with a phrase identical to the one used in the Juniper Palace Inscription, to the battle of Der, and to skirmishes against Aramaean tribes in the Assyro-Babylonian border region (which we know also took place in 720 BCE), the text characterizes the Assyrian king as follows:

Text 6: Khorsabad Cylinder (covers events up to 713 BCE)⁴⁰

19) *mu-ri-ib* KUR **É-ḫu-um-ri-a** *rap-ši ša i-na* ᵘʳᵘ*ra-pi-ḫi* BAD₅.BAD₅-*ú* KUR *mu-uṣ-ri* GAR-*nu-ma* ¹*ḫa-a-nu-nu* LUGAL ᵘʳᵘ*ḫa-zi-te ka-mu-us-su ú-še-ri-ba* ᵘʳᵘ*aš-šur*

---

38 Fuchs, *Die Inschriften Sargons II. aus Khorsabad*, 314–15; Eckart Frahm, *Einleitung in die Sanherib-Inschriften* (Vienna: Institut für Orientalistik, 1997), 229–32. One of my main arguments for ascribing the text to the reign of Sargon was that its language and style are highly reminiscent of Sargon's "Letter to the god Assur."
39 Nadav Na'aman, "Sargon II's Second *Palû* according to the Khorsabad Annals," *TA* 34 (2007): 165–70. Na'aman argues quite convincingly that in Sargon's Khorsabad Annals, only 13 lines, and not 26, are missing from the account of the western campaign conducted in the king's second *palû*. This seems not enough to accommodate the lengthy report about an attack against Judah that Fuchs and Frahm had suggested might once have been included at this point – even though a short reference to such an attack would still fit into the gap. Na'aman also provides some other important arguments for dating the Azekah episode to 701 BCE. Attempts to date it to 712/711 BCE or the years after 689 BCE seem, altogether, unconvincing.
40 Edition: Fuchs, *Die Inschriften Sargons II. aus Khorsabad*, 29–44, 289–96. For a similar text, see Cyril J. Gadd, "Inscribed Prisms of Sargon II from Nimrud," *Iraq* 16 (1954): 173–201, esp. 198–201, ll. 17, 22.

20) *ka-šid* ⁱᵘ*ta-mu-di* ⁱᵘ*i-ba-di-di* ⁱᵘ*mar-si-i-ma-ni* ⁱᵘ*ḫa-ia-pa-a šá si-it-ta-šú-nu in-né-et-qa-am-ma ú-šar-mu-ú qé-reb* KUR **É-ḫu-um-ri-a**

"(Sargon), the one who made the vast land of **Bīt-Ḫumria** ("House of Omri," i.e., Israel) tremble, who inflicted a defeat on Egypt in the city of Rapiḫu, who had Ḫanunu, the king of Gaza, enter Assur in fetters, who conquered the Tamudi, Ibadidi, Marsimani, and Ḫayapâ, and had the rest of them, (once) they had been resettled, dwell in the land of **Bīt-Ḫumria**."

This is the first time in an extant Sargon inscription that some kind of punishment of Israel is mentioned, even though it remains unclear what Sargon exactly means when he claims to have made Israel "tremble." It is noteworthy that the remarks on Bīt-Ḫumria are separated in the Cylinder Inscription by several lines from those on the violent suppression of the revolt of Yau-bi'di (now for the first time called Ilu-bi'di), which is found later in the text:

25) ... *na-si-iḫ šur-uš* KUR *a-ma-at-te ša ma-šak* ᵐᵈ*i-lu-bi-i'-di ḫa-am-ma-'i-i iṣ-ru-pu na-ba-si-iš*

"(Sargon) ..., the one who tore out the root of the land of Hamath, who dyed the skin of Ilu-bi'di the rebel ruler (*ḫammā'u*, possibly wordplay with *ḫamatāyu* "Hamathean") red like *nabāsu*-wool."[41]

The sudden emphasis on the defeat of Bīt-Ḫumria ("House of Omri") in the Cylinder Inscription is surprising if one takes into account that the earlier Sargon texts have nothing to say about it. One wonders which specific event is actually alluded to here. An episode in 720 BCE not recorded in Sargon's earliest inscriptions? Such a scenario is to some extent suggested by the fact that the Cylinder Inscription juxtaposes the Bīt-Ḫumria episode with the Assyrian victory over Ḫanunu of Gaza, dated in Sargon's Khorsabad Annals (Text 7/10) to the king's second regnal year. Since the campaign against Gaza is not mentioned in Sargon's

---

[41] The exact meaning of this phrase is somewhat unclear. At first glance, the point seems to be that Ilu-bi'di's skin became "bloody red" in the process of the flaying to which his body was subjected. But Erica Reiner has pointed to a statement by Lactantius according to which the skin of the Roman emperor Valerian, after he had been flayed, "was dyed with vermilion (*infecta rubro colore*) and placed in the temple of the god of the Barbarians" as a reminder of the triumphal victory the Sasanians had achieved over him and his Roman troops. Something similar, she suggests, might have been done with Ilu-bi'di's skin; Erica Reiner, "The Reddling of Valerian," *ClQ* 56 (2006): 325–29; see also Shiyanthi Thavapalan, *The Meaning of Color in Ancient Mesopotamia* (PhD Dissertation, Yale University, 2017), 69. Drawing on Reiner, David Woods, "Lactantius, Valerian, and Halophilic Bacteria," *Mnemosyne* 61 (2008): 479–81, suggested that Valerian's skin became red because the Sasanians treated it with salt containing halophilic bacteria when they tried to preserve it.

earliest inscriptions, one wonders, however, whether it might not in fact have occurred some time after 720 BCE, and the same could apply to the assault on Bīt-Ḫumria. The deportation to Israel of the various Arab tribes mentioned in line 20 of the Cylinder Inscription clearly happened long after 720 BCE – in Sargon's Khorsabad Annals (Text 7/10, ll. 120–123), it is dated to the king's seventh *palû*, that is, 715 BCE.[42]

There is yet another possibility, however: the remark about Bīt-Ḫumria could refer to an incident that happened before 720 BCE. This last scenario is chiefly suggested by Sargon's aforementioned Annals from Khorsabad, a long, chronologically organized inscription from late in the king's reign, which covers events up to 707 BCE (an earlier annalistic text, Sargon's Annals from 711 BCE, is unfortunately poorly preserved, with the accounts of his first regnal years missing).[43] The Khorsabad Annals describe an attack on Samaria that is dated, quite unexpectedly, to the king's accession year. Regrettably, the passage is poorly preserved:

Text 7: Khorsabad Annals (covers events up to 707 BCE)[44]: Samaria

10) ...... *i-na* S[AG *šarrūtiya ša ina kussê šarrūti ušibuma* (?)]
11) [*agê bēlūti annapruma* (?) (...) ᵘ⁽⁻ᵘʳᵘ⁾*sa-me-r*]*i-na-a-a* [*ša itti šarri nakiriya* (or: *ālik pāniya*) *ana lā epēš ardūti* (?)]
12) [*u lā našê bilti idbubū igmelūma* (or: *ikmelūma*) *ēpušū tāḫāzu* (?) *ina emūq* DN(N) ......]
13) [......]
14) [...... *mu-š*]*ak-ši-i*[*d*] *er-net-ti-ia i*[*t-ti-šu-nu amdaḫiṣma* (?) ......]
15) [27 *lim* 2 ME 80/90 *nīšē āšib libbišu* (*adi narkabātišunu u ilāni tiklīšun*) *á*]*š-lu-la* 50 ᵍⁱˢGIGIR.MEŠ *ki-ṣir šar-ru-ti-ia i-na* [*libbišunu akṣurma sittātišunu* (?)]
16) [*ina qereb māt aššur ušaṣbit* (?) **samerina** *ú-t*]*er-ma* UGU *šá pa-na ú-še-šib*(or: *me*?) UN.MEŠ KUR.KUR.MEŠ *ki-šit-*[*ti qātēya ina libbi ušērib šūt-rēšiya*]

---

42 On the date(s) of Sargon's (and possible later) deportations to Samaria, see Nadav Na'aman and Ran Zadok, "Assyrian Deportations to the Province of Samerina in the Light of Two Cuneiform Tablets from Tell Hadid," *TA* 27 (2000): 159–88. For references in Sargon's inscriptions to deportations of various other people to "Ḫatti," Amurru, Hamath, and Damascus, see Grant Frame, "A 'New' Cylinder Inscription of Sargon II of Assyria from Melid," in *God(s), Trees, Kings, and Scholars: Neo-Assyrian and Related Studies in Honour of Simo Parpola*, ed. Mikko Luukko, Raija Mattila, and Saana Svärd (Helsinki: The Finnish Oriental Society, 2009), 65–82, esp. 77.
43 Fuchs, *Die Annalen des Jahres 711 v. Chr.*, 85, contends that the 711 BCE edition (whose preserved section dates all of Sargon's military accomplishments back by one year, assigning events of the fifth *palû* to the fourth, for example) did probably not yet include the episode of the conquest of Samaria. His arguments seem persuasive, even though some uncertainty remains.
44 Edition: Fuchs, *Die Inschriften Sargons II. aus Khorsabad*, 82–188.

17) [bēl–pāḫati elišunu aškunma biltu] ma-da-at-tu ki-i ša áš-šu-ri e-mid-su-nu-ti k[a-ri māt muṣuri kangu aptema]

Notes to the text: Line 10–11 tentatively restored after Text 1 (Ashur Charter), l. 16; the other equally uncertain restorations follow Text 8 (Nimrud Prism), iv 25–41 and Text 9 (Khorsabad Display Inscription), ll. 23–25 (see Tadmor, *JCS* 12:34). Becking, *The Fall of Samaria*, 39–44, questioned the restoration of ^{lú(-uru)}sa-me-r]i-na-a-a in line 11, but the parallels especially with the Nimrud Prism leave little doubt that it is correct. As kindly pointed out to me by Grant Frame shortly before the present volume went to press, there is some evidence that the alleged lines 12 and 13 actually do not exist. This would eliminate the long gap indicated for line 13. The restorations suggested for lines 11 and 12 could be distributed onto lines 11 and 14, but should be considered as highly conjectural. With regard to line 14, note that one of Sargon's new gates in Khorsabad bore the name *Šamaš-mušakšid-ernettiya*. The phrase UGU šá pa-na ú-še-ME in line 16 is odd, and it remains somewhat unclear whether one should read the last sign as -*šib* or as -*me*.

"... In [my] accession year, [when I had settled on my royal throne and had been crowned with the lordly crown (……)], the people of **Samaria**, [who had spoken and come to an agreement with a king who was my enemy to no longer do service and no longer bring tribute (or: who had … with a king who preceded me to no longer do service and no longer bring tribute, had become angry) and had done battle – with the strength provided by the god(s) ………],* who grant(s) my wishes, [I fought] with [them. 27,280/27,290 of the people living in its (Samaria's) midst *(together with their chariots and the gods in whom they trusted)*] I led away. From [their midst, I gathered together] fifty chariot (crew)s for my royal contingent. [*The rest of them I settled within Assyria*]. I resettled [**Samaria**], making it more *(populous)* than before. [I had] people from (various) lands I had conquered [enter it. One of my eunuchs I installed over them as a provincial governor]. I imposed [tribute] and taxes upon them as (if they were) Assyrians. [I opened the sealed] quay [of the land of Egypt] …"[45]

My restorations of the passage just quoted are largely based on another late Sargon text, which is known from two clay prisms from Nimrud. Here, the report about Samaria, of which crucial lines are again damaged, occurs in a non-chronological sequence of accounts of Sargon's military endeavors, after a description of the campaign against Carchemish (which happened in 717 BCE):

Text 8: Nimrud Prism (covers events up to 706 BCE),[46] col. iv

25) [^{lú(-uru)}sa]-*me-ri-na-a-a* ša it-ti LUGAL
26) [*nakiri*(or: *ālik pāni*)]-*ia a-na la e-peš ar-du-ti*

---

45 As already pointed out, later in the Annals, in a report about the seventh *palû* (= 715 BCE), Sargon claims that he settled various Arab tribes, including the Tamudi, in Samaria (*ina* ^{uru}*sa-me-ri-na ú-še-šib*) (Fuchs, *Die Inschriften Sargons II. aus Khorsabad*, 110, ll. 120–23).
46 Edition: Gadd, "Inscribed Prisms of Sargon II," 173–98. I have not been able to collate the text.

27) [u lā na]-še-e bil-ti
28) [id?-bu?-b]u?([x x (x)]▷—) ig(or: ik)-me-lu-ma e-pu-šú ta-ḫa-zu
29) [i-n]a e-muq DINGIR.MEŠ GAL.MEŠ E[N].MEŠ-ia
30) [i]t-ti-šú-nu am-da-ḫi-[iṣ-ma]
31) [2]0?+7 lim 2 me 80 UN.MEŠ a-di ᵍⁱˢGIG[IR.MEŠ-šú-nu]
32) ù DINGIR.MEŠ ti-ik-li-šú-un šal-la-t[i-iš]
33) am-nu 2 me ᵍⁱˢGIGIR.MEŠ ki-ṣir LUGA[L-ti-ia]
34) ina lìb-bi-šú-nu ak-ṣur-ʳmaʼ
35) si-it-ta-ti-šú-nu
36) i-na qé-reb KUR aš-šurᵏⁱ ú-šá-aṣ-bit
37) ᵘʳᵘsa-me-ri-na ú-ter-ma UGU šá pa-ni
38) ú-še-šib(or: me) UN.MEŠ KUR.KUR ki-šit-ti ŠUⁱⁱ-ia
39) i-na lìb-bi ú-še-rib ˡᵘ́šu-ut–SAG-ia
40) ˡᵘ́EN–NAM UGU-šú-nu áš-kun-ma
41) it-ti UN.MEŠ KUR aš-šurᵏⁱ am-nu-šú-nu-ti

Notes to the text: Line 28: The reading [id-bu-b]u ig-me-lu (which would make perfect sense if the passage is indeed about a Samarian conspiracy with an "enemy king") is new and, even though uncertain, in my view the only feasible one that has so far been suggested. Tadmor restored [a-ḫa-me]š ig-me-lu-ma,⁴⁷ but this seems at odds with Akkadian semantics. Dalley proposed to read [ibbalkitū/ikpudū] ikmilūma,⁴⁸ but if the copy is accurate, this restoration cannot be correct either.⁴⁹ Line 33: In her contribution to this volume, Karen Radner argues that the number 200 refers to chariot crews, whereas the number 50 in the Khorsabad Annals (Text 7, line 15) is used to count the chariots taken from Samaria.

"The people of **Samaria**, who had *spoken and come to an agreement* with a king [who was] my [*enemy*] to no longer do service and no longer bring tribute (or: who had … with a king [*who preceded*] me to no longer do service and no longer bring tribute, *had become angry*) and had done battle – with the strength provided by the great gods, my lords, I fought with them. 2?7,280 people together with [their] chariots and the gods in whom they trusted I counted [as] spoil. I gathered from their midst 200 chariot (crew)s for my royal contingent. The rest of them I settled within Assyria. I *resettled* **Samaria**, making it more (*populous*) than before. I had people from (various) lands I had conquered enter into it. One of my eunuchs I installed over them as a provincial governor, and I counted them among the people of Assyria (followed by a report about the opening of the "sealed quay" of Egypt)."

The Samaria accounts of the Khorsabad Annals and the Nimrud Prism are similar but not identical, which means that the restorations offered above for the former on the basis of the latter remain somewhat uncertain. Among the noteworthy features of the texts is the much discussed and theologically intriguing

---

47 Tadmor, "The Campaigns of Sargon II," 34.
48 Stephanie Dalley, "Foreign Chariotry and Cavalry in the Armies of Tiglath-Pileser III and Sargon II," *Iraq* 47 (1985): 31–48, esp. 36.
49 Younger, "The Fall of Samaria," 469–70, followed Dalley and tentatively translated "who agreed [and plotted] with a king [hostile to] me."

statement (preserved only in the Nimrud Prism) that Sargon took away "the gods of Samaria." Whether it is simply a *topos*, added to the account as a rhetorical-ideological flourish, or a reference to an actual event cannot be determined with certainty; it is worth mentioning, though, that the statement occurs only here.[50] Also remarkable is that the two texts mention the incorporation of substantial numbers of Samarian chariot (crew)s into the Assyrian army. The significance of this segment of the Samarian troops is confirmed by references to equestrian officers from Samaria in archival texts from Nimrud from the late eighth century,[51] and by Shalmaneser III's Kurkh inscription, which claims that the Israelites had provided 2,000(?) chariots for the army assembled for the battle of Qarqar in 853 BCE.[52]

One key problem with the passage in the Nimrud Prism is to establish whether Sargon claims, in line 26, that the people of Samaria rebelled during the reign "of a king who preceded me," that is, Shalmaneser V, or conspired with "a king who was my enemy," that is, Yau-bi'di. From a grammatical and semantic point of view, both restorations, *itti šarri ālik pāniya* and *itti šarri nakiriya*, are possible. Since the Khorsabad Annals date the episode to 722 BCE, it may at first glance seem more likely that the reference is to Sargon's unloved predecessor, and not to Yau-bi'di, whose revolt apparently happened later.[53] But things are not

---

[50] Note, however, that 2Kgs 18:34 (which is part of a message delivered by the Assyrian Chief Cupbearer to the people of Jerusalem in the name of King Sennacherib) seems to imply that the Assyrians had, in fact, once taken away "the gods of Samaria." For discussion, see the articles by Uehlinger and Na'aman mentioned above in n. 2.

[51] See Dalley, "Foreign Chariotry," 31–48.

[52] See A. Kirk Grayson, *Assyrian Rulers of the Early First Millennium BC II (858–745 BC)* (Toronto: University of Toronto Press, 1996), A.0.102 ii 91. Nadav Na'aman, "Two Notes on the Monolith Inscription of Shalmaneser III from Kurkh," *TA* 3 (1976): 89–106, esp. 97–102, has argued that the "2 *lim*" ("2,000") of the text may be a mistake for "2 *me*" ("200"). Since the signs LIM and ME are quite similar, this cannot be excluded, but some uncertainty remains; Grayson, in his edition, accepted the higher number. Even if this should turn out to be mistaken, the numbers given for the Israelite chariot (crew)s in the aforementioned inscriptions still seem to suggest that Israel may have been a more eminent political player in the ninth and eighth centuries BCE than many modern scholars, inspired by "minimalist" trends in recent biblical scholarship, have come to believe.

[53] There is also the issue that Sargon's inscriptions otherwise rarely use the title *šarru* for Yau-bi'di. It is not quite correct, however, as claimed by Dalley, "Foreign Chariotry," 36, that the title is not attested for him anywhere – some late Sargon texts (see below, Texts 13–15, l. 53) do call Yau-bi'di *šarru*. The Juniper Palace Inscription (Text 5) identifies him, moreover, as a *malku*, a title that is also found, as pointed out by Younger, "The Fall of Samaria," 471, in a passage that mentions Yau-bi'di together with other rulers (Fuchs, *Die Inschriften Sargons II. aus Khorsa-*

quite that clear – there is a way to interpret the evidence in line with the new restoration suggested by me for iv 28 of the Nimrud Prism, which presupposes that the text does allude to the Yau-bi'di revolt. The compilers of the Khorsabad Annals might have assigned a victory over Samaria achieved by the Assyrians in the immediate aftermath of their defeat of Yau-bi'di to Sargon's accession year, perhaps conflating it with a successful earlier Assyrian attack late in the reign of Shalmaneser,[54] while also adding remarks on actions taken against Samaria in the aftermath of the events of 720 BCE.

All this may seem unduly complicated, but one needs to keep in mind, as already realized by Tadmor,[55] that the ostensibly accurate chronological scaffolding of the Annals text is somewhat deceptive. The resettling of Samaria and its reorganization as a province, for example, occurred sometime after the quelling of the Yau-bi'di revolt in 720 BCE; the deportation of the Samarian people, also described in the Bible (2Kgs 17:6)[56] and undoubtedly a historical reality,[57] must have taken place over a longer period of time if one considers the logistical challenges;[58] and the commercial contacts with Egypt, likewise assigned by the Annals to 722 BCE, might, in fact, not have been initiated before 716 BCE.[59]

That the compilers of Sargon's Annals combined military actions the Assyrians had undertaken against Samaria at different points in time in an account of only one year, 722 BCE, to fill out the gap left by the king's inability to campaign

---

bad, 261, l. 22). Clearly, then, Sargon and his scribes were not entirely unwilling to grant Yau-bi'di royal status.

54 If Samaria was indeed conquered in 722 BCE (which we suggest below, in section 3), then Sargon, who assumed his office quite late in that year, in the tenth month, can hardly have experienced this event as king. If he participated at all in the assault on the city, then it was as a general of Shalmaneser V.

55 Tadmor, "The Campaigns of Sargon II," 22–40, 77–100.

56 The Biblical text claims that the Assyrian king placed the Israelites "in Halah (Ḫalaḫḫu in the Assyrian core area), Gozan (Guzana on the Khabur River), and Media." See Radner's chapter in this volume.

57 For evidence for the enlistment of equestrian officers from Samaria by the Assyrians, see Dalley, "Foreign Chariotry," 31–48, and the previous remarks. While the Assyrian reports about the deportation of the Israelites are in essence trustworthy, the accuracy of the numbers Sargon's inscriptions provide for the deported people can of course be questioned, even though they do not seem completely over the top; see Marco De Odorico, *The Use of Numbers and Quantifications in the Assyrian Royal Inscriptions* (Helsinki: The Neo-Assyrian Text Corpus Project, 1995), 52, 114–15.

58 Radner, in her contribution to this volume, stresses that the Israelites cannot have arrived in Media before 716 BCE. It is, of course, possible that they stayed in a third location before they were sent on their final journey.

59 See Tadmor, "The Campaigns of Sargon II," 35–36.

in the months following his accession[60] is therefore a possibility that deserves serious consideration. It may well be that they initially produced an account of this type for a text without chronological markers, such as the Nimrud Prism, and then simply copied it, perhaps with some adaptations, into the Annals. If this is what happened, one should not make too much of the fact that the Annals ascribe the Samarian rebellion to "the people of Samaria" and not to their king. Given the deceptive chronology of the account, one cannot exclude that the last king of Israel, Hoshea, remained in office until the end of the Assyrian siege, presumably in 722 BCE, and that the period in which the Samarians were kingless only began thereafter.[61]

In Sargon's so-called Display Inscription from Khorsabad, like the Nimrud Prism a late text that does not organize the king's military accomplishments chronologically, the victory over Samaria is described as well, in an abbreviated and slightly modified form:

Text 9: Khorsabad Display Inscription (covers events up to 707 BCE)[62]: Samaria

23) ...... ^{uru}*sa-me-ri-na al-me ak-šud*
24) 27 (var. 24) *lim 2 me 80* (var.: 90) UN.MEŠ *a-šib* ŠÀ-*šú áš-lu-la* 50 ^{giš}GIGIR.MEŠ *ina* ŠÀ-*šú-nu ak-ṣur-ma ù si-it-tu-ti i-nu-šú-nu ú-šá-ḫi-iz* ^{lú}*šu-ut*–SAG-*ia* UGU-*šú-nu áš-kun-ma* GÚ.UN LUGAL *maḫ-re-e*
25) *e-mid-su-nu-ti* ......

"... I besieged and conquered **Samaria**. 27,280/27,290/24,280 of the people living in its (Samaria's) midst I led away. From their midst, I gathered together fifty chariot (crew)s. I let the rest take up their *crafts* again. I installed over them one of my eunuchs and imposed on them tribute (as under) a previous king. ..."

The account follows a short report about the battle of Der and precedes one about Ḫanunu of Gaza, similar to the Annals. It differs from all the other descriptions of Sargon's confrontation with Samaria in two important respects. One is that it claims that Sargon "besieged and conquered" Samaria at some point.

---

60 That the scribes of Sargon's Khorsabad Annals reassigned the battles the Assyrians fought in Babylonia in 720 BCE to Sargon's "first year," i.e., 721 BCE, seems obvious; see Fuchs, *Die Inschriften Sargons II. aus Khorsabad*, 88–89, ll. 18–23.
61 The matter has a bearing on attempts to explain the confusing chronological data 2Kgs 17 and 2Kgs 18 provide for Hoshea. Much of this confusion would, of course, disappear if the statements made in 2Kgs 17:3–5 were to be understood for the most part as "a theological comment in narrative form" originating from the time when the books of Chronicles were composed, which is the argument made by Levin in his chapter in this volume.
62 Edition: Fuchs, *Die Inschriften Sargons II. aus Khorsabad*, 189–248.

This statement is in marked contrast to the Nimrud Prism, which only talks about "fighting" (*maḫāṣu*) with the Samarians. Particularly conspicuous is the use of the verb *lamû* "to besiege," a term that brings to mind the claim in 2Kgs 17:5 (and 18:9) that "the king of Assyria" (according to the context Shalmaneser) "besieged" (וַיָּצַר) Samaria. Whether we should consider the Display Inscription's reference to a siege of Samaria as a literary *topos*,[63] a lie,[64] or a statement that has a historical *fundamentum in re* – either in events from the end of the reign of Shalmaneser V or in incidents that happened in 720 BCE – remains somewhat unclear.

The second item setting the passage quoted above apart is the statement that a previous Assyrian king had once imposed tribute on Samaria. This can only be a reference to either Tiglath-pileser III or Shalmaneser V.

The texts from the last years of Sargon's reign also include detailed accounts of the Yau-bi'di episode. In the Khorsabad Annals, the episode is attributed to Sargon's second regnal year, as in the Ashur Charter (and the Najafehabad Stele), and follows an expanded report about the battle of Der and subsequent skirmishes with Aramaean tribesmen, now – falsely – reassigned to the king's first regnal year:

Text 10: Khorsabad Annals (covers events up to 707 BCE)[65]: Hamath

> 23) ...... *i-na 2-i BALA-ia* ᵐ*i-lu-b*[*i-i'-di* ᵏᵘʳ*amatāyu* ......]
> 24) [......] DAGAL-*tim i-na* ᵘʳᵘ*qar-qa-ri ú-p*[*a*]-*ḫir-ma ma-mit* [*ilāni rabûti* ......]
> 25) [...... *arpadda ṣimirra* ᵘʳᵘ]*di-maš-q*[*a* ᵘʳᵘ*s*]*a-me-ri-*[*na ittiya*] *u*[*š-bal*]-*k*[*it-ma* ......]

"... In my second regnal year, Ilu-bi'di [of Hamath ...] gathered [...] the vast [...] in the city of Qarqar and [... *transgressed*] the oath [(sworn) by the great gods ...]. He prompted [the cities of Arpad, Ṣimirra], Damascus, and **Samaria** to rebel [against me and ...]."

Another version of an annalistic Sargon text, only recently published and of uncertain date, provides a slightly better preserved, similar version of this episode:

---

[63] The expression *alme akšud* is extremely common in Neo-Assyrian royal inscriptions.
[64] It should be noted that the Khorsabad Display Inscription includes at least one evident historical falsehood: the claim in ll. 133–34 that Sargon had managed to lead Marduk-apla-iddina II and his family into captivity; see Fuchs, *Die Inschriften Sargons II. aus Khorsabad*, 351, n. 479.
[65] Edition: Fuchs, *Die Inschriften Sargons II. aus Khorsabad*, 82–188.

Text 11: Mosul Annals (covers events up to [...])[66]

4) [...... ina šanê] BALA-ia ᵐᵈia-ú–bi-i'-di
5) [amattāya lā bēl kussê lā šininti ekalli ša i/ana rē'ût] UN.MEŠ ši-mat-su la ši-mat
6) [...... ú?]-ri-d[a]m?-ma it-ti ˡᵘERIM.MEŠ ḫup-ši
7) [......nāš ka-b]a-bu ᵍᶦˢaz-ˈma¹-[ru]-ú ú-maš-šir-ma
8) [...... i-n]a ᵘʳᵘqar-qa-ri š[a] i-na GÚ
9) [arante ... ṣāb(ē)(?) ... rapašti(?) ú-paḫ-ḫi]r-ma ma-mit DINGIR.MEŠ GAL.MEŠ
10) [... māt amurru (rapaštu) (?) ultu S]AG.MEŠ-šá a-di še-p[i]-te-šá it-ti-ia
11) [ušbalkitma pâ ēdâ ušaškinma ikṣura (?) tāḫāzu (?) (...) a]-na KUR aš-šurᵏⁱ UN.[MEŠ]-šá ḪUL-tu
12) [lā ṭābtu uba"ima (......) i]l-qa-a še-ṭu-ú-tú ᵘ[ʳᵘ]ˈar?¹-[pad?-da?]
13) [(ᵘʳᵘ?...) ᵘʳᵘṣimirra (?) (ᵘʳᵘ?...) ᵘʳᵘ?...]-tu ᵘʳᵘdi-maš-qu ᵘʳᵘsa-mir-i-n[a]
14) [(upaḫḫirma) ana idišu uterra (?) (...) DU]MU.MEŠ KUR aš-šurᵏⁱ ša i-na qé-reb
15) [māt amatti (?) ......] ba-šu-ú ki-i DIŠ-en id-duk-ma
16) [napištu ul ēzib ......] ˈa?¹-na ᵈEN.ZU LUGAL DINGIR.MEŠ be-el KUR.KUR
17) [...... n]a-ki-ri mu-ḫal-liq za-ma-ni EN-ia
18) [(......) qātāya aššima(?) aššu(?) kašād(?)] KUR a-ma-at-ti sa-kap
19) [Yau-bi'di ......] MAR.TUᵏⁱ DAGAL-tim am-ḫur-ma
20) [......]-ú áš-šu UN.MEŠ-šú

Notes to the text: Lines 15 and 19 restored after Text 3 (Tell Tayinat Stele), ll. 5', 7'.

"[... In] my [second] regnal year, Yau-bi'di [of Hamath, (who was) not the rightful throne-holder, (who was) unfit for (living in) a palace, and as whose] fate it had not been decreed [that he would (ever) shepherd] the people, [...] came down [...] and together with a troop of commoners [... bearers of] shields and lances he left [...]. In the city of Qarqar, which is on the bank [of the Orontes, ...] he gathered [the troops of the vast land of Amurru (or: vast troops)] and [transgressed] the oath (sworn) by the great gods [...]. [He prompted the (vast) land of Amurru, from] its upper end to its lower end, [to rebel] against me, achieved unity (among its citizens), and prepared for battle (...)].

Against the land of Assyria and her people [he (Yau-bi'di) intended (to do)] evil, [things that were not good (...)], and he treated (them) with insolence. [He gathered] the cities of Arpad, [(...), Ṣimirra, (...) ...]tu, Damascus, and **Samaria** [and brought them to his side (...)]. He killed the citizens of Assyria who were present in [the land of Hamath ...] all together [and left no one alive (...)].

[I lifted my hands] to Sîn, the king of the gods and lord of the lands [..., who vanquishes] the foes and destroys the enemies, my lord, and implored him (to help me) [conquer] the land of Hamath, overthrow [Yau-bi'di and ...] the wide land of Amurru. (20) [...] they [...]. Because (of) his people [...] (remainder of text lost)."

---

[66] Edition: Eckart Frahm, "A Sculpted Slab with an Inscription of Sargon II Mentioning the Rebellion of Yau-bi'di of Hamath," *AoF* 40 (2013): 42–54.

This text, from an unknown place in the Assyrian heartland,[67] offers interesting additional details about Yau-bi'di's revolt, especially with regard to the killing spree on which his supporters went, but apart from apparently listing several additional cities involved in the insurrection, it provides few new data on Samaria, so there is no need to discuss it here at length. The same applies to the report about the revolt in Sargon's Display Inscription from Khorsabad, which is separated from the Samaria episode by a number of other campaign accounts and seems to be more stereotypical than the annalistic texts:

Text 12: Khorsabad Display Inscription (covers events up to 707 BCE)[68]: Hamath

> 33) ^{md}*ia-ú-bi-i'-di* ^{kur}*a-ma-ta-a-a ṣa-ab ḫup-ši la* EN ^{giš}GU.ZA ^{lú}*ḫat-tu-ú lem-nu a-na* LUGAL-*ut* KUR *a-ma-at-ti* ŠÀ-*šú ik-pu-ud-ma* ^{uru}*ar-pad-da* ^{uru}*ṣi-mir-ra* ^{uru}*di-maš-qa* ^{uru}***sa-me-ri-na***
> 34) *it-ti-ia uš-bal-kit-ma pa-a e-da-a ú-šá-áš-kin-ma ik-ṣu-ra* MÈ *um-ma-na-at gap-šá-a-ti* ^{d}*aš-šur ad-ke-ma ina* ^{uru}*qar-qa-ri* URU *na-ram-i-šú šá-a-šú a-di mun-daḫ-ṣe-šú*
> 35) *al-me ak-šud-su* ^{uru}*qar-qa-ru ina* ^{d}*gíra aq-mu šá-a-šú ma-šak-šú a-ku-uṣ ina qé-reb* URU.MEŠ *šú-nu-ti* EN *ḫi-iṭ-ṭi a-duk-ma su-lum-mu-ú ú-šá-áš-kin* 2 *me* ^{giš}GIGIR.MEŠ 6 *me* ^{anše}*pét-ḫal-lim*
> 36) *i-na* ŠÀ UN.MEŠ KUR *a-ma-at-ti ak-ṣur-ma* UGU *ki-ṣir* LUGAL-*ti-ia ú-rad-di* ......

"Yau-bi'di of Hamath, a commoner (who was) not the rightful throne-holder, an evil Hittite, set his heart on becoming the king of the land of Hamath. He prompted Arpad, Ṣimirra, Damascus, and **Samaria** to rebel against me, achieved unity (among them), and prepared for battle.

I mobilized the vast troops of Assur and besieged and captured him together with his fighters in Qarqar, the city he loved. I burnt Qarqar with fire. As for him, I flayed his skin. I killed those who had committed crimes and established peace in those cities. I gathered from among the people of Hamath 200 chariot (crew)s and 600 cavalry troops and added them to my royal contingent.

Noteworthy here is the remark that those who had committed crimes, that is, had opposed the Assyrians, had been killed by Sargon in the cities involved in the insurrection, including Samaria.

A few additional texts from late in Sargon's reign provide yet another account of Yau-bi'di's revolt. They include Sargon's stele from Cyprus, a cylinder

---

[67] For possible find spots, see the discussion in Frahm, "A Sculpted Slab," 52–53. In 2001, the slab was definitely in the Mosul Museum, but it may have been sent to Baghdad in 2003 and thus have escaped the destruction wrought upon the Assyrian artifacts in the Mosul Museum by supporters of ISIS in 2015.

[68] Edition: Fuchs, *Die Inschriften Sargons II. aus Khorsabad*, 189–248. Orthographical variants are not noted in the following.

inscription from Nineveh, and the so-called Borowski Stele, which was probably erected, like some earlier Sargon stelae, in the territory of Hamath:

Texts 13–15: Cyprus Stele,[69] Nineveh Cylinder,[70] Borowski Stele[71] (all apparently covering events up to 707 BCE)

Line count after the Cyprus Stele, orthographic variants not noted:

51) KUR *a-ma-at-tu a-na paṭ g*[*im-ri-šá*]
52) *a-bu-bi-iš as-p*[*u-un*]
53) ^{md}*ia-ú-bi-i'-di* LUGAL-*šú-nu*[72]
54) *a-di kim-ti-šú mun-daḫ-ṣ*[*e-e-šú*]
55) *šal-lat* KUR-*šú ka-mu-us-su*
56) *a-na* KUR *aš-šur*^{ki} *ub-la*
57) 2 *me* (var.: 3 *me*) ^{giš}GIGIR.MEŠ 6 *me* ^{anše}*pét-ḫal-lum*
58) (*na-áš*) ^{giš}*ka-ba-bu* ^{giš}*az-ma-re-e*
59) *i-na lìb-bi-šú-nu ak-ṣur-ma*
60) UGU *ki-ṣir* MAN-*ti-ia ú-rad-di*
61) 6 *lim* 3 *me* ^{lú}*aš-šur-a-a* EN *hi-iṭ-ṭi*
62) *ina qé-reb* KUR *ha-am-ma-ti ú-še-šib-ma*
63) ^{lú}*šu-ut*-SAG-*ia* ^{lú}EN-NAM
64) UGU-*šú-nu áš-kun-ma bíl-tu ma-da-at-tu*
65) *ú-kin* UGU-*šú-un*

"I swept away the land of Hamath, with all its territory, like a flood. I brought Yau-bi'di, their king, in fetters, together with his family and [his] fighters and (other) captives from his land to Assyria. 200/300 chariot (crew)s[73] and 600 cavalry, bearers of shields and lances I gathered together from among them and added to my royal contingent. I settled in the midst of the land of Hamath 6,300 Assyrians who had committed crimes. I appointed a eunuch of mine over them to serve as provincial governor and imposed upon them tribute and taxes."

---

69 Edition: Françoise Malbran-Labat, "Section 4: Inscription assyrienne (No. 4001)," in *Kition dans les textes*, ed. Marguerite Yon (Paris: Éditions Recherche sur les Civilisations, 2006), 345–54.
70 Edition: Reginald C. Thompson, "A Selection from the Cuneiform Historical Texts from Nineveh (1927–32)," *Iraq* 7 (1940): 85–131, esp. 86–89.
71 So called after its former owner, Elie Borowski. Edition: J. David Hawkins, "The New Sargon Stele from Hama," in *From the Upper Sea to the Lower Sea: Studies on the History of Assyria and Babylonia in Honour of A. K. Grayson*, ed. Grant Frame (Leiden / Istanbul: Nederlands Instituut voor het Nabije Oosten, 2004), 151–64.
72 The royal title of Yau-bi'di is preserved in the texts of the Nineveh Cylinder and (albeit the sign LUGAL is damaged) the Cyprus Stele; on the Borowski Stele, ll. 51–56 are lost.
73 Note that exactly the same number, 200, is given in the Nimrud Prism (Text 8) for chariot (crew)s from Samaria.

The Borowski Stele (Side B) has instead of ll. 61–65:

> 5) 6 lim 3 me ˡúaš-šur-a-a EN ḫi-iṭ-ṭi
> 6) gíl-la-su-nu a-miš-ma
> 7) re-e-ma ar-ši-šú-nu-ti-ma
> 8) ina qé-reb KUR.ḫa-am-ma-ti ú-še-šib-šú-nu-ti
> 9) GÚ.UN ma-da-tu za-bal ku-du-u-ri
> 10) a-lak KASKAL ki-i šá MAN.MEŠ AD.MEŠ-iá
> 11) a-na ᵐir-ḫu-le-na ᵏᵘʳa-ma-ta-a-a
> 12) e-mid-du e-mid-su-nu-ti

"I disregarded the guilt of 6,300 Assyrians who had committed crimes, had mercy on them, and settled them in the midst of the land of Hamath. I imposed upon them tribute, taxes, the bearing of the basket (i.e., corvée work), and (the duty) to go on campaigns, just as my royal forefathers had imposed (these things) on Irḫulena of Hamath (a contemporary of Shalmaneser III)."

What is particularly important here is Sargon's claim that he had sent to Hamath some 6,300 Assyrian "criminals," in all likelihood people who had opposed him in the wake of his accession to the throne. Given that Assyrian citizens in Hamath had been the explicit targets of Yau-bi'di's earlier rampage (see Texts 1 and 11), this forced move was probably not a reason for much joy for the individuals in question; one wonders, though, why Sargon was not concerned that the unfaithful Assyrians might make common cause with the people of Hamath.

There are a few minor references to Samaria and Hamath in other Sargon inscriptions, mostly from Khorsabad, on cylinder fragments, bull colossi, thresholds, and wall slabs. The texts in question, which list the king's military accomplishments in a non-chronological order, do not provide anything that would change in a major way the overall picture, but it seems worthwhile to quote at least those passages that mention Samaria and Bīt-Ḫumria, i.e., Israel, by name.

Texts 16–18 (all covering events up to 707 BCE)

Display Inscription XIV[74]

> 15) [á]š-lul ᵘʳᵘši-nu-uḫ-tú ᵘʳᵘ**sa-mer-i-na** ù gi-mir KUR É–**ḫu-um-ri-a**

"I plundered (or: I carried away people from) Šinuḫtu, **Samaria**, and all of **Bīt-Ḫumria**."

---

[74] Edition: Fuchs, *Die Inschriften Sargons II. aus Khorsabad*, 75–81.

Bull Inscription[75]

21) sa-pi-in ᵘʳᵘsa-me-ri-na ka-la KUR É–ḫu-um-ri-a KUR kas-ku

"(Sargon is) the one who crushed **Samaria**, all of **Bīt-Ḫumria** and the land of Kasku."

Threshold Inscription no. 4[76]

31–32) ka-ši-id ᵘʳᵘsa-mer-i-na ù gi-mir KUR É–ḫu-um-ri-a

"(Sargon is) the one who conquered **Samaria** and all of **Bīt-Ḫumria**."

Noteworthy in these summary accounts is the aggressive language used by Sargon, who talks about having "plundered," "crushed," and "conquered" Samaria. In light of the archaeological evidence, which does not suggest that the Assyrians inflicted any major destruction on Samaria, one is, however, probably well advised not to take all the aforementioned statements as accurate descriptions of what actually happened to the city.[77]

Sargon's main wife (MUNUS.É.GAL), at least later in his reign, was a woman by the name of Atalyā. As observed by Dalley, this name is reminiscent of that of the ninth century Israelite princess ᶜtlyh[w], who later married into the royal family of Judah (see 2Kgs 8:16–11:16).[78] Drawing on Dalley's idea that Atalyā might have been a Judean princess, it might seem tempting to assume that she was, in fact, of Israelite background, which, if true, would shed some interesting psychohistorical light on Sargon's approach towards Samaria; but the uncertainties in identifying Atalyā's true background are so substantial[79] that it seems preferable to abstain from further speculation.

---

75 Edition: Fuchs, *Die Inschriften Sargons II. aus Khorsabad*, 60–74.
76 Edition: Fuchs, *Die Inschriften Sargons II. aus Khorsabad*, 259–71.
77 Thus also Tappy, "The Final Years of Israelite Samaria."
78 Stephanie Dalley, "Yabâ, Atalyā and the Foreign Policy of Late Assyrian Kings," *SAAB* 12 (1998): 83–98.
79 For a linguistic discussion of the name, see Ran Zadok, "Neo-Assyrian Notes," in *Treasures on Camels' Humps ...: Historical and Literary Studies from the Ancient Near East Presented to Israel Eph'al*, ed. Mordechai Cogan and Dan'el Kahn (Jerusalem: Magnes Press, 2008), 312–30, esp. 327–29; for the problem in general, Eckart Frahm, "Family Matters: Psychohistorical Reflections on Sennacherib and His Times," in *Sennacherib at the Gates of Jerusalem: Story, History and Historiography*, ed. Isaac Kalimi and Seth Richardson (Leiden: Brill, 2014), 163–222, esp. 182–89, with earlier literature.

3 Conclusions and Final Thoughts

The main goal of the previous section was to provide readers with an opportunity to review in an unprejudiced way what Sargon's royal inscriptions have to say about the rebellion of Yau-bi'di of Hamath and the fall of Samaria. No systematic attempt was made to establish the actual chronology of the events and provide a historical synthesis. It would be somewhat cowardly, however, if the present author failed to conclude this article without a few remarks on these issues, however provisional they may be.

The point of departure for any discussion of the last years of the kingdom of Israel has to be the short note in the Babylonian Chronicle (i 27–28) that claims that Shalmaneser V, at an undetermined point after his accession to the Assyrian throne, "ravaged Samaria" (ᵘʳᵘšá-ma-ra-'i-in iḫ-te-pe').[80] The note confirms what 2Kgs 17:3–5 and 18:9–10 have to say about King Shalmaneser's crucial role in the downfall of Samaria. It also indicates something else, not sufficiently stressed in the secondary literature: the defeat of Samaria must have been a major turning point – otherwise, it would hardly have been the only deed ascribed to Shalmaneser in the Babylonian Chronicle.

It stands to reason that an event so important would also have been mentioned in the Assyrian Eponym Chronicle, which is, unfortunately, badly damaged for the period in question. Based on Millard's copy and edition of the only surviving fragment, K. 3202,[81] the historical events listed for the years 727 to 722 BCE are the following:

---

[80] Grayson, *Assyrian and Babylonian Chronicles*, 73. Some scholars have questioned whether the text is really about Samaria, suggesting the alternative reading ᵘʳᵘšá-ba-ra-'i-in, but Dubovský, after carefully studying the forms of the signs MA and BA on the Chronicle tablet, has convincingly demonstrated that the reading ᵘʳᵘšá-ma-ra-'i-in is to be preferred, which would confirm the Biblical passages talking about Shalmaneser as the conqueror of Samaria (Peter Dubovský, "Did Shalmaneser V Conquer the City of Samaria? An Investigation into the *ma/ba*-sign in Chronicle 1," *Or* 80 (2011): 423–35). The date of the devastation inflicted on Samaria is not specified in the Babylonian Chronicle – there is no need to assume, as Na'aman, "The Historical Background," 206–25, did, that the passage refers to an assault on the city in Shalmaneser's accession year, and the horizontal ruling in the text between the reference to the ravaging of Samaria and the following note about Shalmaneser's death in the tenth month of his fifth year (i.e., 722 BCE) does not, in my view, necessarily mean that Samaria was conquered before 722. For further discussion of these matters, and the meaning of *ḫepû* in the Babylonian Chronicle, see Becking, *The Fall of Samaria*, 22–25.

[81] Alan R. Millard, *The Eponyms of the Assyrian Empire 910–612 BC* (Helsinki: The Neo-Assyrian Text Corpus Project, 1994), 45–46, pl. 15: B 3. See also Jean-Jacques Glassner, *Mesopotamian*

727: *a-na* ᵘʳ[ᵘ ...] / [(...) SILIM-*ma-n*]*u*–MAŠ *ina* ᵍⁱ[ˢGU.ZA *ittūšib*]
726: *i-*[*na māti*]
725: *a-n*[*a* ...]
724: *a-n*[*a* ...]
723: *a-*[*na* ...]

722: [(...) *Šarru-ukīn ina kussê ittūšib* (...)]

727: (The army fought) against the city [...]; [(...)]⁸² Shalmaneser [sat] on the throne.
726: (The army / the king stayed) in [the land (of Assyria)].
725: (The army fought) against [...]
724: (The army fought) against [...]
723: (The army fought) against [...]

722: [(...)⁸³ Sargon [sat] on the throne. (...)]

Another fragment (Rm. 2, 97)⁸⁴ begins with two poorly preserved lines that either deal with the years 721 and 720 BCE, respectively, or with 720 BCE alone.⁸⁵ Tadmor, assuming the latter,⁸⁶ restored [*ana māt ḫat-t*]*i*⁸⁷ / [... *uššū ša bīt* DN *ša* GN *kar*]-*ru* "[(The army fought) against the land of] Ḫatti (i. e., northern Syria); [... the

---

Chronicles (Atlanta GA: Society of Biblical Literature, 2004), 174–75. Unfortunately, no photo of K. 3202 is available on the CDLI website, and I was unable to collate the fragment in London.
82 It is possible that the beginning of the line included a reference to the date of the king's accession to the throne, which occurred, according to the Babylonian Chronicle, on the 25ᵗʰ of Ṭebētu. For a parallel, see the Eponym Chronicle's reference to the accession of Tiglath-pileser in 745 BCE (Millard, *The Eponyms of the Assyrian Empire*, 43).
83 As in the entry for 727 BCE, there might have been a reference to the king's accession date, which in the case of Sargon was the 12ᵗʰ day of the month Ṭebētu, if we are to believe the Babylonian Chronicle. The beginning of the entry might have mentioned another military campaign, undertaken by Shalmaneser shortly before his death; for parallels, see the entries in the Eponym Chronicle for the years 727 and 705 (Millard, *The Eponyms of the Assyrian Empire*, 45, 48). Less likely is that there was a reference to the turmoil that seems to have accompanied Sargon's accession. Considering how late in the year this last event occurred, the entry did probably not include a reference to yet another episode.
84 Edition and copy: Millard, *The Eponyms of the Assyrian Empire*, 46, pl. 16: B 4.
85 The uncertainty is due to the fact that several entries in this Eponym Chronicle fragment run over more than one line.
86 Tadmor, "The Campaigns of Sargon II," 85.
87 The photo on the CDLI website confirms Millard's copy of the modest traces at the end of the line. The earlier copy by Carl Bezold, "Some Unpublished Assyrian 'Lists of Officials,'" *Proceedings of the Society of Biblical Archaeology* 11 (1889): 286–87, esp. pl. 3 after p. 286, does not indicate any traces for the line in question.

foundations of the temple of DN of the city of GN] were laid,"[88] which is, altogether, not implausible, albeit some uncertainty remains. In case the first two lines cover two years, an alternative restoration might be for the first one (721 BCE) [*ina* KU]R "[(The army / the king stayed) in the] land (of Assyria)," which would be in line with what is otherwise known about this year, and for the second (720 BCE) [*ana* ^{uru}*qar-qa*]-*ru* "[(The army fought) against] Qarqar" – even though it must be admitted that in light of the writing conventions of the Assyrian Eponym Chronicles, one would rather have expected *ana* ^{uru}*qar-qa-ri*.[89]

Both 2Kgs 17:3–6 and 2Kgs 18:9–10 claim that Shalmaneser conquered Samaria after a three year siege, a statement so specific that it should not be dismissed out of hand.[90] Judging from the entries the Eponym Chronicle provides for the years 727 and 726 BCE, this siege, if it really took place, cannot have begun before 725 BCE. It either lasted, therefore, from 725 to 723 BCE or from 724 to 722 BCE, ending with Samaria's downfall. While the nine regnal years attributed to Hoshea in the Bible could be taken as pointing towards the earlier dates,[91] Sargon's claim in his Annals (Text 7) that the conquest of Samaria occurred in his accession year is more easily explained if one assumes that the siege lasted from 724 to 722 BCE. Clearly, the siege was brought to a successful conclusion prior to Sargon's actual accession in the tenth month of 722 BCE. This is indicated by the aforementioned note in the Babylonian Chronicle, by the accounts in 2Kgs 17 and 18, which ascribe the final breakthrough to Shalmaneser, and by the fact that no military achievements are mentioned in Sargon's early Ashur Charter (Text 1) for the king's accession year and his first regnal year.

---

88 Tadmor's restoration of the second line follows Arthur Ungnad, "Eponymen," in *RlA* 2, ed. Erich Ebeling and Bruno Meissner (Berlin, de Gruyter: 1938), 412–57, esp. 433, and is inspired by the Eponym Chronicle's entries for the years 788 and 717 BCE. See also CAD K, 209a. Millard, *The Eponyms of the Assyrian Empire*, 46, and Glassner, *Mesopotamian Chronicles*, 174, refrained from offering any restorations.
89 It is also possible that the entry for 720 BCE, rather than mentioning the campaign to the Levant (in which the king did not participate, after all), dealt with the battles fought by the Assyrians in Babylonia in that year.
90 Note that the Assyrian Eponym Chronicle does occasionally refer to prolonged sieges. That of the city of Arpad is mentioned in the entries for the years 743 to 740 BCE (Millard, *The Eponyms of the Assyrian Empire*, 43–44).
91 See Becking, *The Fall of Samaria*, 52–53. Like others, Becking argues that Hoshea's first regnal year was 731 BCE. Note, however, that the chronological data the Bible provides for Hoshea produce so many problems that attempts to come up with a scenario that fits them all (and, moreover, takes into account the Biblical report about Hoshea's imprisonment prior to the Assyrian siege) appear somewhat quixotic, especially if Levin (this volume) is right and 2Kgs 17:3–5 is a late addition (see above, n. 61).

Sargon's later claim that it was actually he and not Shalmaneser who had conquered Samaria in 722 BCE[92] can be seen as an attempt to demonstrate, in a text that recorded the king's military successes on a year by year basis, that he had achieved great things from the very beginning, including in his accession year and his first regnal year – when he was, in fact, preoccupied by the internal unrest his power grab had caused.

This inner-Assyrian strife – whose existence can be inferred from several of Sargon's inscriptions[93] – did not remain unobserved in the empire's Western periphery. It prompted almost immediately an anti-Assyrian rebellion, which was headed by Yau-bi'di, a political leader apparently not of royal stock operating in the territory of Hamath. Several fairly new Assyrian provinces, among them Arpad, Ṣimirra, and Damascus, joined the insurrection.[94] The people of Samaria, who seem to have been kingless at this point but whose capital city had probably not yet been turned into the center of an Assyrian province, did so as well, despite the strenuous siege they had apparently suffered in the previous years.

In 720 BCE, after a bloody battle fought in and around Qarqar on the Orontes, an Assyrian army sent by Sargon managed to quell the rebellion, capture Yau-bi'di, and pacify the other participants in the insurgency. It stands to reason that the Israelites essentially surrendered to the Assyrian troops at this point, and that it was not necessary to subject Samaria to another siege.

Sargon's earliest inscriptions, most importantly the Ashur Charter, do not talk about how the Assyrians treated Samaria in the aftermath of their victory, but in an inscription from 713 BCE (Text 6), Sargon claims for himself to have "made Bīt-Ḫumria tremble." More detailed information on Samaria's fate is available from inscriptions from the last years of Sargon's reign (Texts 7–9, 16–18). These texts mention, among other things, the deportation of significant portions of the Samarian people, the enlistment of the Samarian chariot troops into the Assyrian army, the transformation of Samaria into an Assyrian province, and the resettlement of Samaria with Arabs. All these things probably happened in stages and over a longer period of time; the population transfer of the Arabs, for example, is dated in the Annals to 715 BCE. The texts now also claim that Sargon had "besieged, "conquered," and "crushed" Samaria (Texts 9 and 17), possibly alluding to the events of 722 BCE.

---

[92] That Sargon participated in some military capacity in the conquest of the city is possible but cannot be proven.
[93] See above Texts 1 and 13–15, and the discussion sections following them.
[94] Arpad had become a province in 740 BCE, Ṣimirra in 738 BCE, and Damascus in 732 BCE; see Bagg, *Die Assyrer und das Westland*, 235.

Most of the late Sargon inscriptions leave the timeline of the events concerning Samaria unspecified. Sargon's Annals, however, as pointed out earlier, fit them into a Procrustean bed of pseudo-chronology. They claim that it was in his accession year that Sargon defeated the Samarians, deported and replaced them with other people, and turned their land into a province. Judging by a parallel passage in the Nimrud Prism (Text 8), the account probably also claimed that the Samarians had made common cause with "an enemy king," an allusion, in all likelihood, to their alliance with Yau-bi'di. In other words: in the Annals, Sargon's scribes seem to have assigned events that happened at very different stages – from Shalmaneser's conquest of Samaria in 722 BCE, to the quelling of the insurrection in the West in 720 BCE, to the reorganization of Samaria and its hinterland in subsequent years – to Sargon's accession year, in which the king actually ruled for no more than two and a half months.[95]

Obviously, much of this reconstruction, although it follows in many ways earlier scholars such as Tadmor or Fuchs,[96] remains hypothetical. The problem is that the various written sources available for the last days of the kingdom of Israel contradict one another in crucial respects and cannot be fully reconciled. As already pointed out in the introduction, substantial progress will only be possible through future discoveries – for example of a manuscript of the Assyrian Eponym Chronicle with an undamaged account of the years 727 to 715 BCE. Until then, a full scholarly consensus regarding the events that led to the fall of Samaria will probably remain elusive.

---

95 For similar chronological manipulations in the inscriptions of Sargon's successor, see Liverani, "Critique of Variants and the Titulary of Sennacherib."
96 Tadmor, "The Campaigns of Sargon II," 22–40, 77–100; Fuchs, *Die Inschriften Sargons II. aus Khorsabad*, 457–58.

Frederick Mario Fales
Why Israel?

Reflections on Shalmaneser V's and Sargon II's Grand Strategy for the Levant

1 Introduction

This paper attempts to look at the theme of "the last days of Israel" from a historical perspective based mainly on Assyriological data and on a few gleanings from archaeological reports – although I am fully aware that a rich and well-attended conference, such as is gathered here on this theme, would never have been conceived and organized, if these two important bodies of data, together with the similarly crucial Biblical evidence and other sets of documentary materials, were devoid of ongoing controversy in their precise contextualization and mutual interfacing, in their chronological pinpointing, and in their overall implications. My specific approach to the theme is meant to tackle the subject from the point of view of a possible Assyrian "grand strategy" in the Levant after the demise of the last of the great Aramaean state, Damascus, in the third quarter of the 8th century BC. We may thus start by asking ourselves two basic questions: can a "grand strategy" of the Assyrian empire be said to have existed, at least at some point in time? And what could its mechanisms have been in the Levantine context? [1]

---

[1] A word on the state of art is due here. Research on the texts of the Neo-Assyrian imperial period – both of official-ideological and "everyday"/archival nature and scope – has flourished through well-funded national research programs and internationally coordinated scholarly efforts in the last 40 years. Felicitously, in these two first decades of the 21st century, a sufficient level of interpretation and publication in disseminated form has been reached as to allow not only the (few and dwindling) "inner circle" specialists, but also a vast (and growing) host of students of allied or connected disciplines, to participate in the construction of coherent overall perspectives regarding the history of Neo-Assyrian imperial period. All such perspectives – which often also include expertise on the complexity of the contemporaneous archaeological contexts – are to be considered equally welcome, insofar as they have enriched and are enriching the problematical terrain on which to cast the comprehensive historical description and evaluation of the Assyrian Empire – as the earliest of a set of military and political experiments in achieving "total supraregional rule" that characterized the Near East in the 1st millennium BCE and continued in the West into the subsequent millennium. As is often the case in developing intellectual horizons, a number of different interpretive models prove at this time to be mutually

2 The Grand Strategy of the Assyrians in the Levant: Setting the Stage

The first question ("can a grand strategy of the Assyrian state be said to have existed"?) shows, at least in my experience, the interesting feature of being acknowledged in general – i.e., even without need for an in-depth justification – by a number of Ancient Near Eastern scholars, both on the philological and the archaeological side of things, while it is considered debatable by others, most often operating in the realm of world history.[2] Apart from this, however, or rather prior to it, we may point out the problem of reaching an agreement on *what is* a "grand strategy". Now, as the modern political scientist C.S. Gray has it, "strategy is the bridge that relates military power to political purpose; (but) it is neither military power *per se* nor political purpose."[3] This dry but

---

competing for recognition on the stage – whether models involving benchmarks of comparative historical trial/validity (e. g., *pax assyriaca*, "militarism", or the so-called "Augustan threshold") or adaptations of pan-historical constructs to the scenario at hand (e. g., "World-Systems Theory"). At the same time, some prejudiced views, with forerunners going back to the very infancy of Assyriology in the late 19th century (e. g., concerning the Assyrians' alleged "greed", "outright cruelty", "disregard for other cultures") do not seem to have been fully eradicated through adequate "stress tests" as yet, but to have rather been (perhaps unconsciously) embedded within these new theoretical formulations. In a nutshell, therefore, this is an exciting time for Neo-Assyrian history – but it is also necessary that experimenting with new frameworks and concepts should be held under the tight control of common sense, *Wahrscheinlichkeit*, and the unyielding burden of "hard" evidence. For a broad overview of present-day historiographical approaches to the chronological and geographical scenario treated in the present contribution, cf. Joshua T. Walton, *The Regional Economy of the Southern Levant in the 8th-7th Centuries BCE*. (PhD thesis, Harvard University, 2015; https://dash.harvard.edu/handle/1/17467381). The quest for an Assyrian "Grand Strategy", as presented in this chapter, in which the conquest and annexation of the kingdom of Israel could be contextualized, implies no new interpretive model *per se*, but merely a heuristic attempt to project the event of the Fall of Samaria onto a wider geographical and chronological canvas, in order to evaluate the ensuing results.

2 See on the one hand, e. g., Bradley J. Parker, *The Mechanics of Empire: The Northern Frontier of Assyria as a Case Study in Imperial Dynamics* (Helsinki: The Neo-Assyrian Text Corpus Project, 2001); Frederick Mario Fales, *L'Impero Assiro: Storia e Amministrazione, IX–VII sec. a. C.* (Roma / Bari: Laterza, 2001); Simo Parpola, "Assyria's Expansion in the 8th and 7th Centuries and Its Long-Term Repercussions in the West," in *Symbiosis, Symbolism, and the Power of the Past*, ed. William G. Dever and Seymour Gitin (Winona Lake IN: Eisenbrauns, 2003): 99 – 111. On the other hand, see e. g., Reinhard Bernbeck, "Imperialist Networks: Ancient Assyria and the United States," *Present Pasts* 2 (2010): 142–68; Ariel M. Bagg, "Palestine under Assyrian Rule: A New Look at the Assyrian Imperial Policy in the West," *JAOS* 133 (2013): 119 – 44.

3 Colin S. Gray, *Modern Strategy* (Oxford: Oxford University Press, 1999), 17.

clear definition claims precise adaptations from the pioneering study by Carl von Clausewitz, *On War*,[4] and – in more recent days – from Sir Basil Henry Liddell Hart, according to whom strategy is "the art of distributing and applying military means to fulfill the aims of policy."[5] With these forerunners in mind, there is no doubt that Gray's definition of "strategy" indicates a link between specific military actions and their mid-to-long-term consequences in the future policy to be enforced or adapted vis-à-vis the vanquished: in other words, at least logically, war comes first, policy follows. I dare say that this approach might at first sight strike some as particularly fitting for the Assyrian historical evidence, although I will attempt to show that this is decidedly not the case.

We may now move to the expression "grand strategy," which originally was merely conceived as a broader and more extended form of strategy, and as such interchanged with "higher strategy" in Liddell Hart's definition; its role, as he stated, was "to co-ordinate and direct all the resources of a nation, or band of nations, toward the attainment of the political object of the war." This definition, in which "grand" meant, all said and done, a strategy executed through interconnections at the highest levels of the state, with the marshaling of the full range of the state's resources, may summon with ease (and some nostalgic pleasure) memory flashes of Churchill's resounding speeches and of D-day,[6] but it has been in recent decades superseded by a wider and more nuanced concept, in which the stakes are more evenly distributed between wartime and peacetime.

This we owe in particular to political theoreticians such as Edward N. Luttwak and Michael Walzer,[7] who have analyzed decision-making in war and peace, finding them to be of a fully different order, and in fact often oppositional, so as to require entirely varying perspectives and methods of planning and thinking. Hence a renewed definition of "grand strategy" by Luttwak himself, who applied it – most usefully for us – in his wide-ranging historical-political overviews of the Roman and the Byzantine empires: "Grand strategy is simply the level at

---

4 Carl von Clausewitz, *On War*, trans. Michael Howard and Peter Peret (Princeton NJ: Princeton University Press, 1976), 178
5 Basil H. Liddell Hart, *Strategy: The Indirect Approach* (London: Faber & Faber, 1976), 335.
6 In point of fact, Churchill seems to have been preoccupied by the interplay between politics and military strategy already since Word War I, marked by the Gallipoli disaster, 17 February 1915 to 9 January 1916, when he wrote "The distinction between politics and strategy diminishes as the point of view is raised. At the summit true politics and strategy are one." Winston S. Churchill, *The World Crisis, 1911–1918, Part 2: 1915* (New York: Scribner, 1923), 404–405, from a dispatch dated 1 June 1915, i.e., right in the middle of the battle of attrition at Gallipoli.
7 Edward N. Luttwak, *Strategy: The Logic of War and Peace* (Cambridge MA: Cambridge University Press, 1987); Michael Walzer, *Arguing about War* (New Haven CT: Yale University Press, 2004).

which knowledge and persuasion, or in modern terms intelligence and diplomacy, interact with military strength to determine outcomes in a world of other states with their own grand strategies."[8]

We need not further pursue the ways and means by which Luttwak illustrated the applications of this definition in the very complex, and very different, realities of the Roman and Byzantine empires: suffice it to say that both reconstructions of this sharp political-theorist-turned-historian had to deal with the empires' multiple internal alliances and efforts at creating inner structures of self-protection from outside perils. But, simply going back to his definition of "grand strategy" quoted above, I believe there is a small but clear body of Assyrian textual evidence that fits it to a certain extent, dating to the age of Tiglath-pileser III and especially of Sargon II, although precious little of this evidence concerns the scenario of the Levant.

A few years ago, I analyzed Neo-Assyrian letters for the presence of the clause *dibbī ṭābūti issīšu(nu) dabābu*, "to speak kindly to him (or: to them)," through which we can see the opening, maintaining, or last-resort offering of diplomatic, or in any case non-bellicose, relations between Assyria and a number of polities beyond its "inner" borders.[9] The best example regarding the Levant is, actually, from the age of Tiglath-pileser III, in a well-known letter written by Qurdi-Aššur-lamur, possibly the governor of Ṣimirra in Phoenicia, to be dated around 734 BCE.[10]

As a confirmation of the king's prior instruction – quoted at the outset of the letter – to "speak kindly" to the king of Tyre, the governor proceeds to describe a well-oiled mechanism of peaceful economic exploitation of this vassal polity by the Assyrians, whereby the Tyrians are allowed to occupy their wharves on the Mediterranean, to go in and out from the warehouses, and to conduct their business, by ascending Mount Lebanon and bringing down timber, on which the governor has taxes levied by tax inspectors controlling the entire Lebanon range and the coastal quays. So far, so good; but even more interestingly, the sole exception described in the same letter – that of the recalcitrant Sidonians – entails the im-

---

8 Edward N. Luttwak, *The Grand Strategy of the Byzantine Empire* (Cambridge MA: Cambridge University Press, 2009), 409.
9 Frederick Mario Fales, "'To Speak Kindly to him/them' as Item of Assyrian Political Discourse," in *Of God(s), Trees, Kings, and Scholars: Neo-Assyrian and Related Studies in Honour of Simo Parpola*, ed. Mikko Luukko, Saana Svärd and Raija Mattila (Helsinki: Finnish Oriental Society, 2009): 27–40.
10 This letter (ND 2715) has most recently been published by Mikko Luukko, *The Correspondence of Tiglath-pileser III and Sargon II from Calah/Nimrud* (Helsinki: The Neo-Assyrian Text Corpus Project, 2012), no. 22. Online version: http://oracc.museum.upenn.edu/saao/P224471.

mediate deployment of a well-known corps of military police (the Itu'eans) to terrify the lumberjacks on the mountain, and to bring the situation back to the desired state of fiscal normalcy. As Teddy Roosevelt used to say, "Speak softly, but carry a big stick," indeed!

But an even clearer case of what a policy of "kind words" traded between the Assyrians and the chiefs/representatives of foreign powers could entail as an alternative to the use of armed force, may be viewed in a letter written by Sargon himself to a subordinate, Aššur-šarru-uṣur. The latter had related to the king the news that king Midas of Phrygia had captured fourteen Cilician envoys on their way to the enemy state of Urartu, and delivered them to the Assyrians. This act of spontaneous detente prompted a joyous outburst on the part of the Mesopotamian ruler: "My gods Aššur, Šamaš, Bel and Nabû have now taken action, and without a battle [or any]thing, the Phrygian has given us his word and has become our ally!"[11]

In sum, as I noticed at the time, the policy of *dibbī ṭābūti*, "kind words," refers to a backdrop of political relations meant to extend the range of action of Assyrian suzerainty beyond the strict confines of its provincial system to vassal polities or external allies, ruling out (or minimizing to the least degree) recourse to armed force, whether threatened or carried out. The Akkadian expression – and its ensuing policy of "soft power" in a specific Assyrian formulation – seems to apply both to initial stages of a diplomatic agreement, as well as to consolidated situations of peaceful relations, and – as other types of texts show – even to last-minute offers of dialogue without recourse to arms, as e.g. the famous letter of Ashurbanipal to the citizens of Babylon, inciting them feelingly to submission, may show.[12] In this sense, even the second message of Rabshakeh, whatever one may think about its authenticity, authorship and date, might qualify as the expression of an Assyrian grand strategy in which "intelligence and diplomacy interact with military strength," as Luttwak put it:

---

[11] Simo Parpola, *The Correspondence of Sargon II, Part I: Letters from Assyria and the West* (Helsinki: Helsinki University Press, 1987), no. 1: 7–10. Online version: http://oracc.museum.upenn.edu/saao/P224485.

[12] This is the well-known letter ABL 301, written 23/II/652 BCE. For an edition see Simo Parpola, "Desperately Trying to Talk Sense: A Letter of Assurbanipal Concerning his Brother Šamaš-šumu-ukīn," in *From the Upper Sea to the Lower Sea: Studies on the History of Assyria and Babylonia in Honour of A. K. Grayson*, ed. Grant Frame (Leiden: Nederlands Instituut voor het Nabije Oosten, 2004): 227–34 and the discussion by Sanae Ito, *Royal Image and Political Thinking in the Letters of Assurbanipal* (PhD thesis, University of Helsinki, 2015; http://urn.fi/URN:ISBN:978-951-51-0973-6).

"Thus said the king of Assyria: make your peace with me and come out to me, so that you may all eat from your vines and your fig trees and drink water from your cisterns, until I come and take you away to a land like your own, a land of grain [fields] and vineyards, of bread and wine, of olive oil and honey, so that you may live and not die." (2Kgs 18:31–32).

In a nutshell, I would say that sufficient evidence may be summoned from Assyrian archival documentation, to counteract or at least to curb the monolithic impression that the official inscriptions of the Assyrian kings provide at a general and superficial perusal: that the sole actual strategy to be ascribed to the Assyrian empire was a warmongering and relentlessly militaristic one of territorial annexation, aimed at conquering all surrounding nations, at despoiling their resources, and at uprooting their inhabitants through mass deportation. This policy was indisputably carried out far and wide, but – for a comprehensive historical-political reconstruction of the Neo-Assyrian empire – it must be cast against an alternative set of decisions, which could lead to a delay or to an outright refraining from carrying out a set of assaults and destructions, for eminently strategic reasons.

The fact that the Assyrian royal inscriptions, due to their very nature as *res gestae* of the rulers with a specific emphasis on armed conquest and sometimes on the harsh punishments meted out to rebellious enemies, dedicate hardly any space to alternative choices of this kind, cannot at present – in the light of the quoted evidence present in epistolary or other "everyday" texts – be used to deny the picture of a "grand strategy" which seems to have used all available means to expand the range of Assyrian influence throughout Western Asia. And, just to take a step further in this debate, it may be observed that an imperial polity which took time and effort, as the Assyrians did, to establish a vast network of treaties and pacts with other state or tribal formations – as may be made out from the sum total of pieces/fragments of direct evidence and indirect mentions – would seem to have decidedly been endowed with at least a general "grand strategic" vision of its capacities as well as of its limits.

3 Tackling the Basic Issues: Who Conquered Samaria, and When?

We may now come to the issue of the possible application of Assyrian "grand strategy" to the fall of the kingdom of Israel, where we can see an initial policy of non-belligerence between Shalmaneser V and Hoshea of Israel which deteriorated into a situation of conflict, from 2Kgs 17:3–6 in combination with very limited Assyrian sources. Now, I am aware that many papers in this monograph will be dedicated to the long-standing problem of how many Assyrian kings conquered Samaria: one or two? To cut to the chase, I will state from the outset that I follow, by and large, the stance of Nadav Na'aman in his well-known contribution in *Biblica* of 1990, with his one-king hypothesis, centered on Sargon II.[13] Na'aman maintained, refining his teacher Hayim Tadmor's conclusions,

- that Shalmaneser V led a first campaign against Israel, making Hoshea his vassal, and that later he deposed him on the basis of the suspicion or evidence of a *double entente* with a king of Egypt named Sô,[14] and the refusal to pay tribute to Assyria, possibly deporting him, to be heard of no more; and
- that Sargon was, in point of fact, the actual conqueror of Samaria, and the author of the mass deportations to "Halah, the Habor –the river of Gozan– and the cities of the Medes," which find a parallel in Sargon's inscriptions, with his flaunting in the Nimrud prism of having removed 27,280 people to Assyria from the district of Samaria during his campaign to the west in 720 BC.[15] Now, a small number of Neo-Assyrian texts discovered in sites of the former Northern Kingdom and along the *Via Maris* have been analyzed as evidence of an Assyrian counter-deportation to Palestine (possibly from Babylonia), again attributed to Sargon.[16]

As for the major stumbling-block of the three-year long siege of the city, mentioned in 2Kgs 17:5, I have, for some time now, followed Andreas Fuchs' useful critical position on the extreme difficulty which Assyrian armies would have

---

[13] Nadav Na'aman, "The Historical Background to the Conquest of Samaria (720 BC)," *Bib* 71 (1990): 206–25.

[14] On the identity of the Egyptian king called Sô (*sw'*), I recall the studies by Duane L. Christensen, "The Identity of 'King So' in Egypt (2 Kings XVII 4)," *VT* 39 (1989): 140–53 (Tefnakht I of Sais); Alberto R. W. Green, "The Identity of King So of Egypt: an Alternative Interpretation," *JNES* 52 (1993): 99–108 (Piankhy / Piye of Kush), while others think of Osorkon IV of Tanis. See Robert Morkot's chapter in this volume.

[15] Andreas Fuchs, *Die Inschriften Sargons II aus Khorsabad* (Göttingen; Cuvillier, 1994), 196–97, 344: Display Inscription, ll. 23–24: "I fought with them (the Samarians) and I counted as spoil 27,280 people who lived therein, with their chariots and the Gods of their trust. Fifty chariots for my royal bodyguard I mustered from among them, and the rest of them I settled in the midst of Assyria. The city of Samaria I resettled and made it greater than before. People of the lands conquered by my own hands I brought there. My courtier I placed over them as a governor and I counted them with Assyrians."

[16] Nadav Na'aman and Ran Zadok, "Assyrian Deportations to the Province of Samerina in the Light of Two Cuneiform Tablets from Tel Hadid," *TA* 27 (2000): 159–88. For the deportations under Sargon, see already Nadav Na'aman, "Population Changes in Palestine following Assyrian Deportations," *TA* 20 (1993): 104–24.

had in undertaking an extensive siege of major fortified cities located at great distances from their homeland, much preferring to plunder the myriad of smaller sites around and to ravage the mainstay of their enemies, the rural environment.[17]

In the past few years I applied this approach to the problem of Sennacherib's alleged siege of Jerusalem,[18] where – following an interesting intuition by Davide Nadali on the meaning of the Assyrian expression "to shut the enemy up, like a bird in a cage"[19] – one may rather posit a blockade of fortresses, which isolated the besieged city within a confined area, opportunely made barren of all resources by the Assyrians, awaiting – in total isolation from any possible help – for famine to take its toll, thus causing Hezekiah's surrender.

This overall perspective, with its obvious advantages for the assailants, in terms of extensive duration and reduced human losses, vis-à-vis a more uncertain operation of actual siege beneath the walls of a major city (as we now can more clearly gauge from Eph'al's precious monograph on the subject),[20] has long had support among Assyriologists and some archaeologists.[21] However, other scholars still seem reluctant to abandon the traditional image of a veritable siege of Jerusalem, thus disregarding the vastness of the site (at least 60 hectares) and the obviously incomparable complexity of a possible siege-operation like the one actually enacted by Sennacherib at the site of Lachish, which, despite its relatively manageable size (20 to 30 hectares), forced the Assyrians to build a tall and vast siege-ramp under the pressure of unceasing enemy artillery.

In the case under examination, we should also take account of the fact that the archaeologically recorded destruction levels at Samaria attributable to this

---

17 Andreas Fuchs, "Über den Wert von Befestigungsanlagen," ZA 98 (2008): 45–99.
18 Frederick Mario Fales, "The Road to Judah: 701 BCE in the Context of Sennacherib's Political-Military Strategy," in Sennacherib at the Gates of Jerusalem: Story, History and Historiography, ed. Isaac Kalimi and Seth Richardson (Leiden: Brill 2014): 223–48.
19 Davide Nadali, "Sieges and Similes of Sieges in the Royal Annals: the Conquest of Damascus by Tiglath-pileser III," KASKAL 6 (2009): 137–49, esp. 139. One may even wonder whether the expression in 2Kgs 17:4: וַיַּעַצְרֵהוּ מֶלֶךְ אַשּׁוּר וַיַּאַסְרֵהוּ בֵּית כֶּלֶא did not originally refer to a situation of the same sort, and whether it was later substituted by the contents of the next verse.
20 Israel Eph'al, The City Besieged: Siege and Its Manifestations in the Ancient Near East (Leiden: Brill, 2009).
21 Cf. e.g. most recently Nazek Khalid Matty, Sennacherib's Campaign Against Judah and Jerusalem in 701 BC: A Historical Reconstruction (Berlin: de Gruyter, 2016), esp. 95–114, where the previous suggestions by Walter Mayer, William R. Gallagher and David Ussishkin on the solution of a blockade for Jerusalem are presented, and Nadali's hypothesis regarding Damascus is accepted – yielding a sum total of 9 cases of Assyrian blockades in all geographical scenarios between the late 8th and the late 7th centuries BCE.

phase are of quite limited character, and that they do not seem to have affected the interior of the city, thus making a wholesale destruction of the site rather improbable;[22] this point may be considered together with the fact that Sargon nowhere states that he has destroyed Samaria, but in fact claims to have fully resettled the city and "made it greater than before."[23] Thus, the traditional view of a double-armed conquest of Samaria, by Shalmaneser V and then again by Sargon, such as Tadmor and many others after him formulated, is open to many doubts.

Of course, if one wishes to keep to the fore the laconic passage in the Babylonian Chronicle referring to the "ravage" of Samaria[24] and to further integrate "Samaria" as the locale of royal activity in the fragmentary Assyrian Eponym List for the years 725–723 BCE,[25] it remains possible that it was the army of Shalmaneser V which in fact engaged in a long-lasting military operation against Samaria for the last three years of this ruler's reign, and that a reprise of the blockade under Sargon clinched the operation itself. If so, the three-year siege recorded in 2Kgs 17:5, although not resulting *per se* in the conquest of Samaria, would – whatever its actual degree of exactitude or even of likelihood – be aptly placed within the Biblical narrative, as an operational element logically antecedent to the fall of the city.

---

22 As noted by many authors, e.g. Ron E. Tappy, *The Archaeology of Israelite Samaria, Volume II: the Eighth Century BCE* (Winona Lake IN: Eisenbrauns, 2001), 562–63; and see already Na'aman, "The Historical Background," 220: "It is not clear whether Samaria was severely damaged in the course of its conquest; the scanty archaeological evidence hardly supports the claim of overall destruction. We may rather assume a continuity of urban life and rapid reconstruction of the city under the Assyrians, when Samaria became the capital of the province of Samerina."
23 Andreas Fuchs, *Die Inschriften Sargons II*, 88, 314: Annals, l. 16.
24 Cf. Jean-Jacques Glassner, *Mesopotamian Chronicles*, trans. Benjamin R. Foster (Atlanta GA: Scholars Press, 2004), 194–95, l. 28: "On the twenty-fifth day of the month of Tebet Shalmaneser (V) ascended the throne in Assyria <and Akkad>. He ravaged Samaria (URU.*Sa-ma/ba-ra-'-in*)." On the toponym, cf. Brad E. Kelle, "What's in a Name? Neo-Assyrian Designations for the Northern Kingdom and Their Implications for Israelite History and Biblical Interpretation," *JBL* 121 (2002): 639–66, esp. 662 and Peter Dubovský, "Did Shalmaneser V Conquer the City of Samaria? An Investigation into the *ma/ba*-sign in Chronicle 1," *Or* 80 (2011): 423–38 (whose collation confirmed the reading *ma*).
25 Alan R. Millard, *The Eponyms of the Assyrian Empire, 910–612 BC* (Helsinki: The Neo-Assyrian Text Corpus Project, 1994), 59.

4 The Importance of the Conquest of Israel for the Assyrian Empire

This said, we may move to the actual problem of *why* it was important for Sargon to subjugate Samaria – with the mention of this subjugation being repeated with relish throughout his annalistic and recapitulative official inscriptions.[26] Proceeding from the position that there is no single, main strategic reason to be found in the texts, I would like to take a double view of the matter, by pointing out first what Assyria stood to gain immediately in the area around Samaria itself, by making the city the capital of a new province, and secondly what longer-term and wider-ranging perspectives were opened by the fall of the Northern Kingdom.

As recalled by various authors, the earlier evidence of the Samaria ostraca[27] points to a flourishing production of olive oil and wine in the smaller sites around the capital of the Northern Kingdom. As Finkelstein puts it, "The ostraca refer to types of oil and wine, names of places and regions around the capital, and names of officials. Regardless of whether they represent shipments of olive oil and wine to the capital or another kind of interaction between the capital and countryside estates/towns, they certainly attest to a large-scale oil and wine 'industry' at that time." This picture is supported by small-size excavations and surveys performed in the area around the city.[28]

But the Northern Kingdom was also a gateway to the growing phenomenon of Eastern Mediterranean trade, as e.g. shown by the coastal sites of Atlit and especially Dor, with their multiple elements of archaeological information on sophisticated trade networks which involved the entire Mediterranean area from Phoenicia to Egypt, touching various ports in Palestine. One of the hallmarks in material culture for these networks is represented by the so-called "torpedo" storage jar, of remarkably standard shape and volume, found "in dozens of excavated sites in Lebanon and Israel, mainly along the coast (e.g., Sarepta and

---

26 Fuchs, *Die Inschriften Sargons II*, 457–58.
27 Cf., e.g., Ivan T. Kaufman, "The Samaria Ostraca: An Early Witness to Hebrew Writing," *BA* 45 (1982): 229–39, who posited a date of at least thirty years before the fall of the city, while the more recent analysis by Hermann M. Niemann, "A New Look at the Samaria Ostraca: The King-Clan Relationship," *TA* 35 (2008) 249–66, esp. 264, based on the breakdown of political power relations within the Northern Kingdom between the royal residence and tribal/clan elites, yields an early 8th century BCE dating.
28 Israel Finkelstein, *The Forgotten Kingdom: The Archaeology and History of Northern Israel*, Atlanta, GA: Society of Biblical Literature, 2013, 132.

Tyre) but also in inland sites located along trade routes (such as Hazor and Megiddo)."[29] Moreover, the well-known archaeological evidence from shipwrecks of "rounded and beamy" freighters, laden with prize wines, retrieved off the coast of Ashkelon,[30] indicates the presence of various hundreds of such jars in intact condition, which petrographic analysis showed to come from the Phoenician coast, with wine as their content, presumably destined to Egyptian buyers. The potential interest of the Assyrians for profits deriving from this – presumably well-established and thriving – commercial activity may be gauged *ex post* from the meticulous and tight-reined provisions regarding naval commerce already present in the letter of Qurdi-Aššur-lamur quoted above, and enforced on a larger scale by Esarhaddon on the Tyrian king Ba'alu in 676 BCE.[31]

A third aspect regards the extreme interest which the Assyrians demonstrate to have had concerning horses, with one of their favorite breeds represented by the equids called *Kusāyu*, i.e. "Nubian."[32] Undoubtedly, by Sargon's time, when the demand for steeds to be employed both for the ever-growing war effort (e.g. in Babylonia and the Zagros), as well as for the massive building operations at Dur-Šarruken grew exponentially, horses came to be bred within the confines of Assyria itself.[33] But certainly a letter like the following one shows that the Levant was one of the two gateways (the other being the Zagros mountains) through which this crucial technological "product" found its way to Assyria:

"I have received 45 horses for the country.[34] The emissaries (LÚ*.MAḪ. MEŠ) from the lands of Egypt (KUR.*Mu-ṣur-a-a*), Gaza (KUR.*Ha-za-ta-a-a*), Judah (KUR.*Ia-ú-du-a-a*), Moab

---

[29] Israel Finkelstein, Elena Zapassky, Yuval Gadot, Daniel M. Master, Lawrence E. Stager and Itzhak Benenson, "Phoenician 'Torpedo' Amphoras and Egypt: Standardization of Volume Based on Linear Dimensions," *AeL* 21 (2011): 249.
[30] R. D. Ballard, Lawrence E. Stager, Daniel Master, Dana Yoerger, David Mindell, Louis L. Whitcomb, Hanumant Singh and Dennis Piechota, "Iron Age Shipwrecks in Deep Water off Ashkelon, Israel," *AJA* 106 (2002): 151–68.
[31] See now Frederick Mario Fales, "Phoenicia in the Neo-Assyrian Period: an Updated Overview", *SAAB* 23 (2017): 181–295. For the treaty, see in particular 241–243.
[32] Lisa Heidorn, "The Horses of Kush," *JNES* 56 (1997): 105–14. Horses of Egyptian origin are attested also in the Bible: cf. Nadav Na'aman, *Ancient Israel and Its Neighbors: Interaction and Counteraction: Collected Essays*, vol. 1 (Winona Lake IN: Eisenbrauns, 2005), 7 on 1Kgs 10:28.
[33] Cf. Frederick Mario Fales, "Ethnicity in the Assyrian Empire: a View from the *Nisbe*, (I): Foreigners and 'Special' Inner Communities," in *Literature as Politics, Politics as Literature: Essays on the Ancient Near East in Honor of Peter Machinist*, ed. David S. Vanderhooft and Abraham Winitzer (Winona Lake IN: Eisenbrauns, 2013): 37–74, esp. 63.
[34] The formula *ša* KUR is often opposed to *ša* KASKAL, "for the campaign," and indicates that these horses were destined for use other than combat; but it is unclear whether such a subdivision was established already at the time of the request / provision, or whether it arose from

(KUR.*Ma-'a-ba-a-a*), and of the "sons of Ammon" (KUR.*Ba-an–Am-ma-na-a-a*) entered Kalhu on the 12th, their tributes in hand. A (further) 24 horses of (the emissary) of Gaza (KUR.*Ha-za-ta-a-a*) were (also) available."[35]

Again quoting Finkelstein, "before Assyria established direct contacts with Egypt in the late 8th century BCE, Israel was the source of these horses, which were brought from Egypt, bred and raised at Megiddo, and then sold to Assyria and other kingdoms in the north." Finkelstein bases this judgment on the analysis of the layout of Megiddo in the 8th century BCE, which should vindicate the description by Chicago archaeologists of the pillared buildings with unified plan in the newly reestablished urban plan as devoted to the stabling of horses.[36] But of course, as shown by the above letter – to be dated after the fall of Samaria – there was a veritable "rush" on the part of many polities in the area for the appropriation of the Nubian horse breed, and its redistribution (as commerce, or, in this case, ceremonial gifts) to Assyria.

And finally, we have men. As shown by Stephanie Dalley,[37] the Nimrud Horse Lists from the reign of Sargon show the presence of a unit made of top equestrian officers from Samaria, and it is the only unit from outside Assyria proper that is known as a national unit under its own city name. Already in his royal inscriptions, Sargon stated – with an unusual point of detail – that he had singled out a specialized military corps from among the Samarian deportees to Assyria: "200 chariots for my royal bodyguard I mustered from among them." Dalley also noted that already in 853 BCE, at the battle of Qarqar, Ahab of Israel had brought solely his chariotry to face Shalmaneser III's invasion, and thus suggested that – at a distance of some 130 years – chariotry could have been a traditional military technique that was still practiced in Samaria with particular skill.

Now for the second and final point. What longer-term perspectives were opened for the Assyrians by the fall of the Northern Kingdom? My answer to this question is simple, although I hope not viewable as simplistic: the fall of Samaria removed a possible obstacle for the Assyrian king to make his way to the southern sector of the veritable "isthmus" of territory of Palestine which reached the border with Egypt. With Samaria out of the way as an independent political entity, Sargon's action was quick and relentless: after his victory over

---

a decision by the Assyrian receiving authority (e,g, on the basis of the horses' type or physical conditions).
35 Parpola, *The Correspondence of Sargon II, Part I:* no. 110.
36 Finkelstein, *The Forgotten Kingdom*, 133–35.
37 Stephanie Dalley, "Foreign Chariotry and Cavalry in the Armies of Tiglath-Pileser III and Sargon II," *Iraq* 47 (1985): 31–48. See also Karen Radner's chapter in this volume.

Hamath and its allies (720 BCE), the Assyrian ruler led his troops towards Philistia, and his successive actions were marked by a drive to solidly establish Assyrian rule in the southernmost Levant. Such actions comprised the repression of rebellious cities, and keeping neighboring nomadic Northern Arabian tribes at bay, but especially – agreeing with another assertion by Na'aman – "pushing the Egyptians back to their homeland, with the intervening expanses of Sinai preventing any immediate threat to the Assyrian holdings in Philistia."[38] However, in the very same breath that the "clear and present danger" of Egyptian armed thrusts to the Levant was to be countered, Sargon's grand strategy foresaw the advantage, and actually the necessity, of keeping the flow of commerce with Egypt open and fluid: for this reason, he could state with pride in the same Nimrud prism inscription that "I opened the sealed h[ar]bour *(k[a]-a-ri)* of Egypt, mingled Assyrians and Egyptians together and made them trade with each other."[39]

---

[38] Nadav Na'aman, "The Brook of Egypt and Assyrian Policy on the Border of Egypt," *TA* 6 (1979): 83.
[39] Fuchs, *Die Inschriften Sargons II*, 88, 314: Annals, ll. 17–18.

Karen Radner
The "Lost Tribes of Israel" in the Context of the Resettlement Programme of the Assyrian Empire

1 Introduction

This paper deals with the "Lost Tribes of Israel," the people removed by the Assyrian authorities from the territories of the conquered kingdom of Israel and especially its capital city Samaria (Assyrian Samerina), to be resettled elsewhere in the Empire's vast holdings.

For the Assyrian Empire, such a procedure was routine. During the imperial period from the 9th to the 7th century BCE, an extensive, centrally directed resettlement programme saw population groups from all corners of the enormous geographical area under Assyrian control being moved across great distances, to be settled within the provinces making up the "land of Aššur." Populations within the boundaries of the Empire were relocated, replacing and being replaced by people who were themselves moved, in complex circular movements that were carefully planned and executed over the course of several years. Populations taken from outside the provincial system, however, were not replaced.

Assuming that the 43 cases where numbers are given in the Assyrian royal inscriptions are a representative sample of the 157 cases of mass resettlement attested in the period from the 9th to the mid-7th century, it has been calculated that these instances resulted in the relocation of 4.400,000 ± 900,000 people[1] – a gigantic figure, especially in a world whose population was a small fraction of today's. Even if one has qualms about accepting the figures given in the Assyrian royal inscriptions as accurate,[2] it is clear that from the viewpoint of the crown, resettling people across the Empire was a mass effort, meant to affect all lands under Assyrian rule.

Today, the Assyrian strategy of mass resettlement is often described with the loaded term "deportation" and the people affected are called "deportees" – most prominently in the title of Bustenay Oded's important monograph *Mass Deporta-*

---

[1] Bustenay Oded, *Mass Deportations and Deportees in the Neo-Assyrian Empire* (Wiesbaden: Harrassowitz, 1979), 19–21 with fn. 5.
[2] Cf. Marco De Odorico, *The Use of Numbers and Quantifications in the Assyrian Royal Inscriptions* (Helsinki: The Neo-Assyrian Text Corpus Project, 1995).

tions and Deportees in the Neo-Assyrian Empire. To a certain extent, the use of these terms is misleading, given the strong associations with concepts such as marginalisation and extermination that are simply not applicable. The Assyrian kings used the phrases "to count among the people of the land of Aššur" and "to turn into a part of the land of Aššur" in their inscriptions when referring to the integration of people and territories.[3] The explicit goal was the creation of an integrated, economically highly developed culture and society of "Assyrians": no longer seen as an ethnic label, "Assyrian" was from the 9th century onwards a designation referring to all the king's subjects, regardless of their origins.[4]

People were chosen for resettlement in a considered selection process, often in the aftermath of warfare that had reduced their original home to ruins. How exactly the Assyrian authorities handled the selection is unclear, although palace decorations from the reign of Tiglath-pileser III (r. 744–727 BCE) onwards illustrate proceedings by showing, usually in the context of the capture of enemy cities, pairs of scribes[5] logging people as well as booty. Very few administrative records of the Assyrian Empire have survived, despite the fact that these were originally written in duplicate, in Assyrian cuneiform and Aramaic alphabet script.[6] Alas, the preferred writing material of the Assyrian administration was wax-covered wooden writing boards, which allowed much more text to be recorded than the more durable clay tablets; and like the leather scrolls used for Aramaic, these did not endure the ravages of time.[7] The fragmentary records that have survived are hard to interpret, also due to the innate terseness of this internal documentation. Frederick Mario Fales and John Nicholas Postgate have interpreted various texts from Nineveh as lists of "deportees and displaced persons"[8] but what stage in the lengthy process of relocation they precisely document is difficult to assess. As Fales and Postgate state, these are lists of in-

---

[3] As discussed by Oded, *Mass Deportations*, 81–91.
[4] Cf. Peter Machinist, "Assyrians on Assyria in the First Millennium BC," in *Anfänge politischen Denkens in der Antike: die nahöstlichen Kulturen und die Griechen*, ed. Kurt Raaflaub (Munich: Oldenbourg, 1993): 77–104.
[5] John M. Russell, *Sennacherib's Palace without Rival at Nineveh* (Chicago / London: Chicago University Press, 1991), 28–31, with list of attestations in fn. 36.
[6] E.g., Karen Radner, "Schreiberkonventionen im assyrischen Reich: Sprachen und Schriftsysteme," in *Assur: Gott, Stadt und Land*, ed. Johannes Renger (Wiesbaden: Harrassowitz, 2011): 388.
[7] Frederick Mario Fales and John Nicholas Postgate, *Imperial Administrative Records, Part I: Palace and Temple Administration* (Helsinki: Helsinki University Press, 1992), XIII.
[8] Frederick Mario Fales and John Nicholas Postgate, *Imperial Administrative Records, Part II: Provincial and Military Administration* (Helsinki: Helsinki University Press, 1995), nos. 144–99.

dividuals "reduced to a sea of names,"⁹ lacking the context that might help us to harness them for our present purposes. However, it emerges unequivocally that professions and family ties were of key interest to the compilers of this data.

Whenever the Assyrian sources specify who was to be relocated, they name the urban elites, craftsmen, scholars and military men. The very best example is the summary of the people taken away from the Egyptian city of Memphis after its capture in 671 BCE according to an inscription of Esarhaddon (r. 680–669 BCE):

> "The seed of his father's house, descendants of earlier kings, [...] of his house; 'Third Men' (of chariot crews), charioteers, [...], rein-holders, archers, shield bearers; [...], incantation priests, dream interpreters (ḫarṭibē), [...], veterinarians, Egyptian scribes, [...], snake-charmers, together with their helpers; kāṣiru-craftsmen; singers; bakers, [cooks], brewers, (together with) their suppliers; [..., clothes] menders, hunters, leather workers, [...], wheelwrights, shipwrights, [...], iron-smiths, [...]."¹⁰

Although fragmentarily perservered, the order of the list is clear enough: it begins with the members of the royal family, followed by professional soldiers and then a wide range of highly trained experts as well as their support personnel. Oded¹¹ calculated that 85% of the documented cases of resettlement concern people that were transplanted to Central Assyria, the area between the cities Assur in the south, Nineveh in the north and Arbela in the east. Indeed, some of the Egyptian specialists mentioned in the inscription appear shortly after at Esarhaddon's court in Nineveh: three dream interpreters (ḫarṭibē), three Egyptian scribes and a physician (certainly a profession originally mentioned in the enumeration of the royal inscription) with an Egyptian name appear in a roster that identifies the scholars in the royal entourage.¹² In addition, private legal texts featuring Egyptians and even entire archives of Egyptian families have been

---

9 Fales and Postgate, *Imperial Administrative Records, Part II*, XXX.
10 Erle Leichty, *The Royal Inscriptions of Esarhaddon, King of Assyria (680–669 BC)* (Winona Lake IN: Eisenbrauns, 2011), no. 9, i' 6'–17'.
11 Oded, *Mass Deportations*, 28.
12 Fales and Postgate, *Imperial Administrative Records, Part I*, no. 1: ii 15 (physician Ṣihuru), rev. i 12–ii 7 (dream interpreters [A]guršî, Ra'ši and Ṣihû; Egyptian scribes Huru, Nimmurau and [Hu]ruaṣu); photograph: http://cdli.ucla.edu/P335693 (accessed 10/2017). Discussed by Karen Radner, "The Assyrian King and His Scholars: The Syro-Anatolian and the Egyptian Schools," in *Of God(s), Trees, Kings, and Scholars: Neo-Assyrian and Related Studies in Honour of Simo Parpola*, ed. Mikko Luukko, Saana Svärd and Raija Mattila (Helsinki: Finnish Oriental Society, 2009): 222–26.

found in Nineveh and Assur, demonstrating the presence of populations from the Nile in the cities of Assyrian heartland (Fig. 1).[13]

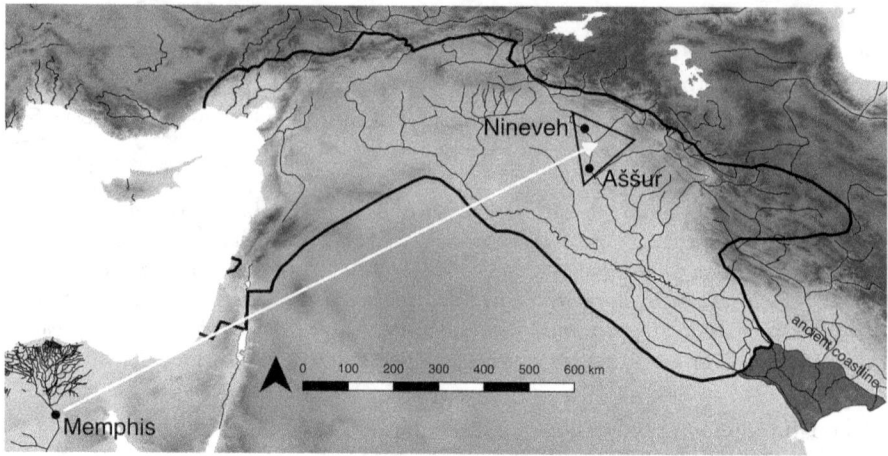

Fig. 1: The deportees taken from Memphis in 671 BCE were relocated in Central Assyria and can be traced in particular in Nineveh and Assur. The black line indicates the extent of the Assyrian provincial system whose areas were under direct Assyrian control in the year 670 BCE. As Memphis was beyond the provincial system, the authorities did not aim to replace the depleted population of the city. Map prepared by Andrea Squitieri after a draft of the author.

The specialists from conquered regions, such as the Egyptian experts, were to generate knowledge and wealth and to contribute to the economic and cultural development of the Empire. When the topic of resettlement is discussed in the royal inscriptions, they either employ a vocabulary of violence and pillage, fittingly for the context of war, or else the language of horticulture, which likens the deportees to precious trees that are uprooted and replanted in the best possible circumstances by that most conscientious of gardeners, the king of Assy-

---

13 Nineveh: Raija Mattila, *Legal Transactions of the Royal Court of Nineveh, Part II: Assurbanipal Through Sin-šarru-iškun* (Helsinki: Helsinki University Press, 2002), nos. 426–56, especially nos. 435 and 442 (private archive found near the Šamaš Gate); Assur: Betina Faist, *Alltagstexte aus neuassyrischen Archiven und Bibliotheken der Stadt Assur* (Wiesbaden: Harrassowitz, 2007), nos. 78–101, 114 ("Archive N31"); Karen Radner, "Die beiden neuassyrischen Privatarchive," in *Ausgrabungen in Assur: Wohnquartiere in der Weststadt, Teil 1*, ed. Peter A. Miglus, Karen Radner and Franciszek M. Stepniowski (Wiesbaden: Harrassowitz, 2016): 121–26 ("Archive N52b").

ria:¹⁴ just like the gardener transfers valuable plants to a nurturing new environment that they in turn will enhance, the wise ruler allocated his people where they best benefitted the Empire. In the case of carefully selected specialists, the Assyrian crown clearly regarded their resettlement as a privilege and an indication of high esteem. But the transplantation of people was certainly also used as a means of punishment, as we shall see below.

In general, the people selected for resettlement were moved together with their families and their possessions, and the authorities' key objective was clearly to keep them healthy and well supplied during their trek.¹⁵ But the resettlement programme of course brutally divided existing communities according to the needs of the Empire – into those who had to leave and those who were allowed to stay or, conversely, into those who were allowed to leave and those who had to stay. This was a highly effective way of minimising the risk of rebellion against the central authority.

In the following, we will discuss resettlement from and to Samaria, analysing one of several overlapping cycles for transportation in detail, before we turn to the Assyrian archival texts as a source for the fate of some of the people that were made to leave Samaria. Some of this material has long been connected to the "Lost Tribes" but other texts – in particular a letter concerning Samarians in Dur-Šarruken, the new capital city of Sargon II (r. 721–705 BCE), and a sale contract originally from Guzana – have not yet been considered in this context.

2 The Inhabitants of Samaria, Old and New: Where to and Whence from?

According to the testimony of 2Kgs 17 (Fig. 2), inhabitants of Samaria were moved to Halahhu, the region around Sargon's new capital city of Dur-Šarruken in Central Assyria;¹⁶ Guzana (Tell Halaf on the border between Turkey and Syria)¹⁷ on

---

14 Karen Radner, "How Did the Neo-Assyrian King Perceive His Land and Its Resources?" in *Rainfall and Agriculture in Northern Mesopotamia*, ed. Remko M. Jas (Leiden: Nederlands Instituut voor het Nabije Oosten, 2000): 233–46.
15 Karen Radner, "Economy, Society, and Daily Life in the Neo-Assyrian Period," in *A Companion to Assyria*, ed. Eckart Frahm (Wiley: Malden MA, 2017): 210–11.
16 Karen Radner, "Provinz. C. Assyrien," in *RlA* 11, ed. Michael P. Streck (2008): 54; Ariel Bagg, *Die Orts- und Gewässernamen der neuassyrischen Zeit, Teil 2: Zentralassyrien und benachbarte Gebiete, Ägypten und die arabische Halbinsel* (Wiesbaden: Reichert, 2017), 194–95.
17 Radner, "Provinz," 51; Bagg, *Die Orts- und Gewässernamen der neuassyrischen Zeit, Teil 2*, 187–89.

the Khabur River, a tributary of the Euphrates which joins that river near Deir ez-Zor; and the towns of the Medes. In turn, people from Northern Babylonia, namely Babylon, Kuthah / Cutha (Tell Ibrahim) and Sepharvaim, most probably the twin cities of Sippar,[18] from Hamath[19] in western Syria and from the unidentified city of Avva[20] were settled in Samaria and its towns:

> "In the 9th year of Hoshea, the king of Assyria captured Samaria and deported the Israelites to Assyria. He settled them in Halah, in Gozan on the Habor River and in the towns of the Medes." (2Kgs 17:6; translation: New International Version).
> "The king of Assyria brought people from Babylon, Kuthah, Avva, Hamath and Sepharvaim and settled them in the towns of Samaria to replace the Israelites. They took over Samaria and lived in its towns." (2Kgs 17:24; translation: New International Version).

As we shall see below, Assyrian archival sources firmly support the identification of Halah = Assyrian Halahhu and Gozan = Assyrian Guzana as a destination for people resettled from Samaria. At present, there is no explicit mention of Samarians in the provinces established in 716 BCE in Median territory, but there are

---

18 Namely Sippar-Yahrurum (Tell Abu Habbah) and Sippar-Amnanum (Tell ed-Der); see Hermann Gasche and Caroline Janssen, "Sippar," in *The Oxford Encyclopedia of Archaeology in the Ancient Near East* 5, ed. Eric M. Meyers (Oxford: Oxford University Press, 1997): 47–49. An alternative interpretation for SPRWYYM that, however, still places the site in Babylonia was suggested by Ran Zadok, "Geographical and Onomastic Notes," *Journal of the Ancient Near Eastern Society* 8 (1976): 115–16 who connected this place name with the city of Ša-barê (URU.Šá–bar-re-e), one of 39 fortified cities of the land of the Bit-Amukani that Sennacherib captured in 703 BCE: Albert Kirk Grayson and Jamie Novotny, *The Royal Inscriptions of Sennacherib, King of Assyria (704–681 BC), Part 1* (Winona Lake IN: Eisenbrauns, 2012), no. 1: 45; Kirk Grayson and Jamie Novotny, *The Royal Inscriptions of Sennacherib, King of Assyria (704–681 BC), Part 2* (Winona Lake IN: Eisenbrauns, 2014), no. 213: 44.
19 Ariel Bagg, *Die Orts- und Gewässernamen der neuassyrischen Zeit, Teil 1: Die Levante* (Wiesbaden: Reichert, 2008), 87–91.
20 As far as I can see, there are two toponyms in the Assyrian sources from the late 8th century BCE that could arguably match the name given in the Bible: (1) A city called Abâ in the Upper Tigris region, near modern Diyarbakır, is attested in a letter from an Assyrian official to Sargon II that mentions "these people from Abâ" (UN.MEŠ *an-nu-te* URU.*A-ba-a-a*) and the "pass of [Ab]â" (*né-ri-bi* [URU.*A-ba*]-*a*): Giovanni B. Lanfranchi and Simo Parpola, *The Correspondence of Sargon II, Part II: Letters from the Northern and Northeastern Provinces* (Helsinki: Helsinki University Press, 1990), no. 24: 7, 14–15; photograph: http://cdli.ucla.edu/P334350 (accessed 10/2017). We do not know about deportations from that particular region during the time of Sargon II. (2) A city called Amâ (URU.*A-ma-a*) on the Uqnu branch of the Tigris in Gambulu in eastern Babylonia that is mentioned in the very fitting context of Sargon's conquest of Babylonia in his Dur-Šarruken Annals, line 292: Andreas Fuchs, *Die Inschriften Sargons II. aus Khorsabad* (Göttingen: Cuvillier Verlag, 1994), 149, 330. On the latter see also Zadok, *Journal of the Ancient Near Eastern Society* 8 (1976): 120–21.

The "Lost Tribes of Israel" in the Context of the Resettlement Programme — 107

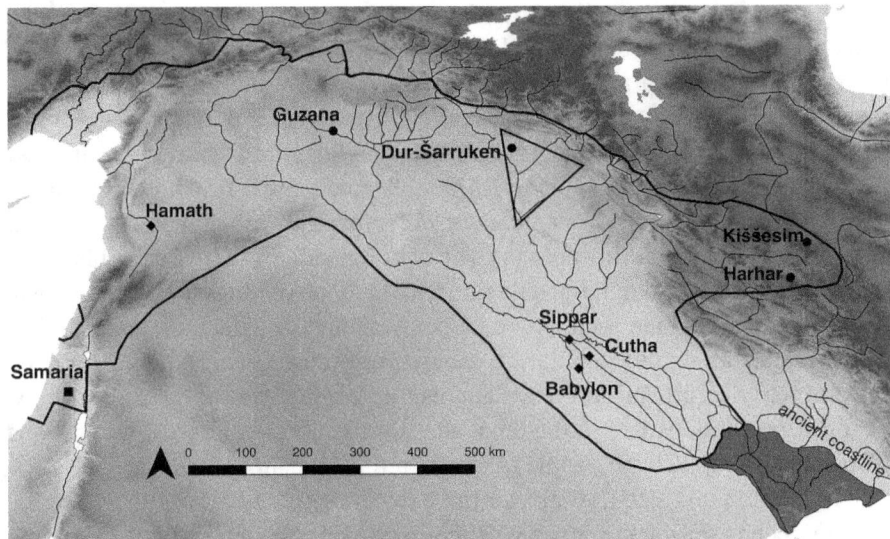

Fig. 2: According to the Book of Kings, the destinations of the people removed from Samaria are (marked with a circle symbol): Dur-Šarruken in the Halahhu region in the northern part of the roughly triangular Assyrian core region; Guzana on the Khabur river; and the "towns of the Medes," with the provincial centres Kišessim and Harhar. The places of origins of the people resettled in Samaria are (marked with a diamond symbol): the Northern Babylonian cities Babylon, Cutha and Sippar, and Hamath in western Syria; the location of Avva is presently uncertain. The black line indicates the extent of the Assyrian provincial system whose areas were under direct Assyrian control in the year 708 BCE. Map prepared by Andrea Squitieri after a draft of the author.

very limited archival sources available for this part of the Empire, and none discovered locally.[21]

---

[21] On the one hand, there is the correspondence of the Assyrian officials appointed by Sargon II to administrate the new province of Kar-Šarruken = Harhar, written in the period after it was established 716 BCE in Median territory: Andreas Fuchs and Simo Parpola, *The Correspondence of Sargon II, Part III: Letters from Babylonia and the Eastern Provinces* (Helsinki: Helsinki University Press, 2001), nos. 83–110; none of the letters refer explicitly to deportee populations. In addition, there is one private legal text from 715 BCE (Faist, *Alltagstexte*, no. 15) that documents the sale of a garden in Kar-Nabû, the new Assyrian designation for Kišešlu, an Assyrian-controlled settlement in the province of Harhar. This sale contract was unearthed in Assur but, as discussed by Karen Radner, "Assyria and the Medes," in *The Oxford Handbook of Ancient Iran*, ed. Daniel T. Potts (New York: Oxford University Press, 2013), 450, it was certainly written in Western Iran, as not only the location of the garden but also the involvement of the following witnesses suggests who must have been present at Kar-Nabû while the Assyrian army was active there:

The Assyrian sources allow us, to a certain extent, to recreate the geography and chronology of the complex and protracted arrangements required to relocate the people of Samaria and to replace them in their former home. The resettlement of Samaria took, at the very least, eight years, and possibly even longer. One region from where population groups were taken to Samaria was affected by Assyrian military action only in 715 BCE: Sargon's Dur-Šarruken Annals mention the transplantation of members of different Arab tribes (namely Tamudi, Ibadidi, Marsimani and Hayapâ) to the city of Samaria in that year.[22] This information highlights also that the data given in the Book of Kings is not exhaustive, as no mention is made there of Arabs being settled in Samaria. The territories from where these Arab population groups were taken were not incorporated into the Assyrian provincial system and as the Assyrian authorities only ever exchanged populations within the areas that they controlled directly, no one was dispatched to replace the people taken from the Arabian Peninsula.

Whether this is also the case for the Babylonian populations brought to Samaria depends on the chronology of their removal – before or after Babylonia seceded from the Empire. The region revolted during the murky circumstances that had brought Sargon to the throne, and in 721 BCE the Chaldean leader Marduk-apla-iddina of Bit-Yakin was appointed King of Babylon.[23] A first attempt to regain control in 720 BCE was unsuccessful, with Sargon's forces defeated at the Battle of Der, and Babylonia was lost to the Empire for twelve years. During that time, the Assyrian crown certainly would not have had the possibility, nor the inclination, to replenish its population. In 710 BCE, Sargon invaded again and eventually secured the Babylonian throne for himself. It is probable, although not certain, that the Northern Babylonian people settled in Samaria were taken as a consequence of Sargon's recapture of the region between 710 and 708 BCE. If this is accepted, then people were still being relocated to Samaria more than a decade after the city had been conquered. If one argues for an ear-

---

Samaš-belu-uṣur, identified in the text as an "Assyrian magnate" (and very probably the governor of Arzuhina); Emuq-Aššur, the commander of Kar-Nabû; the eunuch Tarditu-Aššur; and Ibû, a horse trader (that is, an agent in charge of procuring horses as part of Assyrian military activity). Vendor is Emuq-Aššur's Third Man, a member of the commander's chariot crew who is stated to have received the garden as a gift from the commander himself. No-one mentioned in the document, including the remaining witnesses, has any obvious Samarian connection.

22 Sargon's Dur-Šarruken Annals, lines 120–3; edition: Fuchs, *Die Inschriften Sargons II.*, 110, 320.

23 Karen Radner, "Revolts in the Assyrian Empire: Succession Wars, Rebellions Against a False King and Independence Movements," in *Revolt and Resistance in the Ancient Classical World and the Near East: In the Crucible of Empire*, ed. John J. Collins and Joseph G. Manning (Leiden: Brill, 2016): 51.

lier date of the uprooting of the Babylonian groups then the relocation of the Arabs in 715 BCE provides an end date.

3 An Example of Circular Interchange: Samaria – Kišessim – Assur – Hamath – Samaria

The resettlement of Samaria and its people necessitated several overlapping, circular movements, one of which can be reconstructed in full (Fig. 3). It is the route linking the towns of the Medes (in a region first conquered in 716 BCE) with Assur (where Medes are first attested in a text from 714 BCE) and Hamath (where Assyrians from the heartland were settled after their 720 BCE rebellion was subdued) and finally Samaria (where people from Hamath were relocated after the crushing of their own insurgency in 720 BCE).

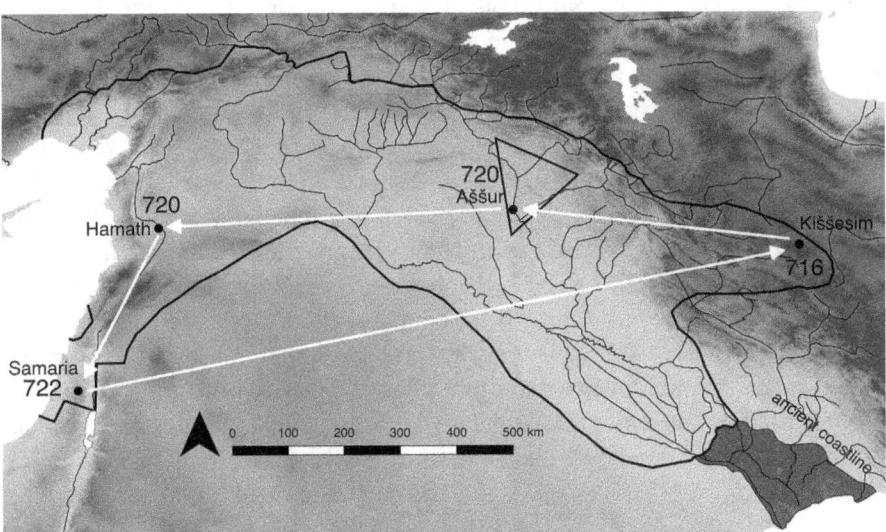

Fig. 3: One of many contemporaneous circular interchanges of people being moved across the Empire: People from Samaria, conquered in 722 BCE, are moved to Kišessim, one of the "towns of the Medes" first conquered in 716 BCE, whose residents are brought to Assur; in turn, after a revolt in 720 BCE, insurgents from Assur and other places in the roughly triangular Assyrian core region are relocated to Hamath after a rebellion there had been quelled in 720 BC; and people of Hamath are sent to Samaria. The black line indicates the extent of the Assyrian provincial system whose areas were under direct Assyrian control in the year 708 BCE. Map prepared by Andrea Squitieri after a draft of the author.

Let's start with the "towns of the Medes." In 716 BCE, Sargon created two new provinces in Median-controlled territory in the modern Iranian province of Hamadan; their centres were Kišessim, renamed Kar-Nergal ("Trading quay of the god Nergal"; corresponding to the settlement mound of modern Najafehabad) and Harhar, renamed Kar-Šarruken ("Sargon's trading quay"; corresponding to Tepe Giyan).[24] Serious complications plagued the establishment of these provinces, as Sargon's correspondence with his officials highlights. On the one hand, the local Assyrian administration suffered from the effects of the unforgiving weather conditions: snow and cold slowed down building up the necessary infrastructure[25] and frequently cut off the new provinces from all communication with Central Assyria.[26] On the other hand, local insurgence was a pressing problem: already in 715 BCE, the new provinces rose in rebellion on a scale that the local Assyrian officials were unable to contain, and the imperial army had to return in order to regain control. Once subdued, four of the most important Median strongholds were turned into Assyrian fortresses, with new names assigned to them that associated them with some of the most important Assyrian deities: Kišešlu became Kar-Nabû and Qindau was renamed Kar-Sîn while Anzaria was rebranded as Kar-Adad and Bit-Bagaia as Kar-Issar.[27] These and the two provincial centres are arguably the Book of Kings' "towns of the Medes," as the imperial resettlement programme now targeted these places: 4,820 persons were taken away according to Sargon's inscriptions, and in addition, 4,000 enemy warriors lost their heads as the consequence of the 715 BCE rebellion.[28] And yet, the conflict continued and the Assyrian army had to return twice more to assert the Empire's control. The troubles subsided only after 713 BCE, once a two-fold system of power saw the Assyrian provincial administration cooperate with the local city lords, who were left in power under the proviso that they formally accepted Assyrian sovereignty.[29] It is only at that time that the region can be reasonably assumed to become a viable destination for settlers brought in by the Assyrian crown. – The distance from Samaria to Kišessim is about 1,300 km, as the crow flies, with the Syrian Desert and the Zagros mountain range in between.

---

24 Radner, "Assyria and the Medes," 444–47.
25 Fuchs and Parpola, *The Correspondence of Sargon II, Part III*, nos. 85, 98, 100.
26 E.g., Fuchs and Parpola, *The Correspondence of Sargon II, Part III*, no. 83.
27 Radner, "Assyria and the Medes," 450.
28 Dur-Šarruken Annals, lines 109–15; 210–11; Dur-Šarruken Display Inscription, lines 64–65: edition: Fuchs, *Die Inschriften Sargons II.*, 108–109, 319.
29 Karen Radner, "An Assyrian View on the Medes," in *Continuity of Empire (?): Assyria, Media, Persia*, ed. Giovanni B. Lanfranchi, Michael Roaf and Robert Rollinger (Padova: s.a.r.g.o.n, 2003): 53–55.

Some of the people deported from the Median region were moved to the city of Assur where people from Hundur, the hinterland of Kišessim, are attested from the reign of Sargon II onward. The first attestation occurs in a detailed and meticulously dated log of a series of events that took place in the Ešarra temple at Assur in the year 714 BCE over a period of two days during the month of Ṭebet. An altar had been damaged when another heavy piece of temple furniture was being moved and the report served to record in detail the steps taken to repair the damage to the sacred objects and to restore equilibrium to the fragile temple atmosphere. The repairs included some apparently specialised polishing work undertaken by men from Hundur,[30] who must have been settled at some point before these events, most likely as part of the group of 4,820 people taken away from the new provinces in Iran in 715 BCE. Hundureans are very well attested in Assur in the 7th century BCE, when the private archives found in two adjoining buildings document the business affairs of an extended well-to-do family of Hundureans for the period from 681 BCE until the conquest of Assur in 614 BCE.[31] They can only be identified as the descendants of the erstwhile deportees because even a century after their ancestors had arrived in Assur, they still labelled themselves as "Hundurean" (presumably as this had now taken on a professional meaning); but none of the people attested in these texts bear Iranian names. – The distance from Kišessim to Assur is about 500 km, as the crow flies, with the massive Zagros mountain range in between.

Let's turn to the next stop on our circular route through the Empire, the city of Hamath. In the course of Sargon II's ascension to the throne, he met with opposition in the core region, including the city of Assur. By 720 BCE, he was able to crush this resistance against his rule. The inscription of a royal stele that once stood in the city of Hamath describes how he treated his detractors. Ever the merciful ruler, he refrained from killing them and instead had them moved to the war-torn city of Hamath; this relocation is clearly meant to punish and corresponds probably closest to our modern notions of a deportation:

---

30 Simo Parpola, *Assyrian Royal Rituals and Cultic Texts* (Helsinki: The Neo-Assyrian Text Corpus Project, 2017), no. 55: 17: KUR.*Hu-un-dir-a-a ú-ṣip-pu* "The Hundureans polished it."

31 Archives N9 and N10. Editions: Frederick Mario Fales and Liane Jakob-Rost, "Neo-Assyrian Texts from Assur: Private Archives in the Vorderasiatisches Museum of Berlin, Part 1," *SAAB* 5 (1991): 3–157; discussed by Kaisa Åkerman, "The 'Aussenhaken Area' in the City of Assur during the Second Half of the 7th Century BC," *SAAB* 13 (1999–2001): 217–72; Radner, "Assyria and the Medes," 447–49.

"I pardoned 6,300 guilty Assyrians and had mercy on them: I settled them in the city of Hamath. I imposed on them taxes and tribute, work obligations and conscription, just like my royal fathers had imposed on Irhulenu of Hamath." [32]

The western Syrian city of Hamath (modern Hama) is situated in the fertile Orontes valley. It had been the capital of the eponymous kingdom, whose most famous ruler was Irhulenu, a king of the 9th century BCE. From 738 BCE onwards, Tiglath-pileser III of Assyria invaded this kingdom and integrated it in two stages into the Assyrian Empire; in 732 BCE, Hamath became part of the newly established Assyrian province of Manṣuate.[33] During the troubled times when the Assyrian crown passed, under very unclear circumstances, from Shalmaneser V (r. 726–722 BCE) to Sargon II, Hamath was the centre of a large-scale insurrection. The western territories, including the cities Samaria and Damascus, managed to break free from Assyrian control and rallied behind one Ilu-bi'di ("God is behind me", alternatively written Yau-bi'di "Yahweh is behind me"). This "man of humble descent", as Sargon's Dur-Šarruken Display Inscription calls him,[34] aimed to resurrect the ancient kingdom of Hamath, with himself as its king. Sargon squashed these ambitions in 720 BCE, captured and executed Ilu-bi'di and wrecked the city of Hamath.[35] During this same tumultuous time, inhabitants of Central Assyria opposed Sargon's rise to power, and after the struggle for control was decided in his favour, they had to be removed from the Empire's power centre. Deporting them to Hamath achieved this, and by helping to rebuild the ruined city, they were meant to repay the mercy of their king, who had graciously refrained from executing them for their disloyalty. – The distance from Assur to Hamath is about 650 km, as the crow flies.

This brings us back to Samaria where, according to the Book of Kings, people from Hamath were settled to replace the deported Samarians. It is unclear whether this happened before or after Hamath supported the insurgence of Ilu-bi'di; both scenarios are possible although I find it more likely that the relocations were authorised by the Assyrian crown only in the aftermath of the defeat of the rebels in 720 BCE. The distance from Hamath to Samaria is about 350 km, as the crow flies.

---

32 J. David Hawkins, "The New Sargon Stele from Hama," in *From the Upper Sea to the Lower Sea: Studies in the History of Assyria and Babylonia in Honour of A. K. Grayson*, ed. Grant Frame (Leiden / Istanbul: Nederlands Instituut voor het Nabije Oosten, 2004), 156-57, 160 (Side B).
33 Radner, "Provinz," 62 no. 54, 66.
34 Dur-Šarruken Display Inscription, line 33: Fuchs, *Die Inschriften Sargons II.*, 200–201, 345.
35 Radner, "Revolts in the Assyrian Empire," 49–51.

We are fortunate in that the sources allow us to reconstruct this one complete cycle of many circular population exchanges that affected Samaria. This one cycle saw people being moved in various stages over a decade, between 722 BCE and (at least) 713 BCE. It highlights that within the regions of the provincial system, the Assyrian crown had no interest in creating empty spaces. Populations were replaced in complicated patterns that required a great deal of organisation and planning, but as we have already stated above, the meagre surviving administrative records do little to enlighten us about the specific personnel and processes involved.

4 Who Was Taken Away from Samaria?

Let's start again with the testimony of the Book of Kings.

> "It was reported to the king of Assyria: 'The people you deported and resettled in the towns of Samaria do not know what the god of that country requires. ...' Then the king of Assyria gave this order: "Have one of the priests (*kohanim*) you took captive from Samaria go back to live there and teach the people what the god of the land requires." (2Kgs 17:26, 27; translation: New International Version).

It identifies the *kohanim*, the "priests", as a group of people that had been removed from the towns of Samaria wholesale. The Assyrian sources do not specifically mention cultic experts from Samaria as deportees, but they certainly confirm that the Assyrian crown had selected highly trained specialists for relocation elsewhere in the Empire. Incidentally, the Assyrian references support resettlement of Samarians in two of the areas mentioned in the Book of Kings: Halahhu and Guzana in the Khabur valley.

4.1 Samarian Chariot Troops, Integrated into the Assyrian Royal Forces

When discussing the relocation of the people of Samaria, three inscriptions of Sargon II specifically mention the Samarian chariotry and its absorption into the Assyrian armed forces. The Display Inscription and the Annals from Sargon's palace in Dur-Šarruken (Khorsabad) feature 50 ^{giš}GIGIR.MEŠ while the inscription on a prism found at Kalhu list 2-*me* ^{giš}GIGIR.MEŠ. The apparent contradiction can be easily explained as the logogram ^{giš}GIGIR is used both for the chariot (*narkabtu*) and the men of the chariot crew (*bēl narkabti*). The Samarian chariot corps fought with heavily armed chariots whose crew consisted of four men each, so that 200 chariot troops correspond to the crews of 50 chariots.

(a) Sargon's Kalhu Prism, iv 31–41 (translation after Frahm in this volume, Text 8):[36]

> "27,280 people together with [their] chariots and the gods in whom they trusted I counted [as] spoil. I gathered from their midst 200 chariot (troop)s for my royal contingent. The rest of them I settled within Assyria. I resettled Samaria, making it more (populous) than before. I had people from (various) lands I had conquered enter into it. One of my eunuchs I installed over them as a provincial governor, and I counted them among the people of Assyria."

(b) Sargon's Dur-Šarruken Annals, lines 15–7 (translation after Frahm in this volume, Text 7):[37]

> "[27,280 of the people living in its (Samaria's) midst] I led away. From [their midst, I gathered together] fifty chariot (troop)s for my royal contingent. [The rest of them I settled within Assyria]. I resettled Samaria], making it more (populous) than before. [I had] people from (various) lands I had conquered [enter it. One of my eunuchs I installed over them as a provincial governor]. I imposed [tribute] and taxes upon them as (if they were) Assyrians."

(c) Sargon's Dur-Šarruken Display Inscription, lines 23–25 (translation after Frahm in this volume, Text 9):[38]

> "27,280 (Variants: 27,290; 24,280) of the people living in its (Samaria's) midst I led away. From their midst, I gathered together fifty chariots. I let the rest take up their crafts again. I installed over them one of my eunuchs and imposed on them tribute (as under) a previous king."

The armies of the 8th century BCE knew two chariot types.[39] The light version was drawn by two horses and manned by a three-man crew: the chariot driver, an archer as the fighter and the so-called "Third Man" who shielded the others.[40] The heavily armoured version was drawn by four horses and had a fourth crew member who provided additional protection (Fig. 4). These tank-like construc-

---

36 Edition: Cyril J. Gadd, "Inscribed Prisms of Sargon II from Nimrud," *Iraq* 16 (1954): 173–98.
37 Edition: Fuchs, *Die Inschriften Sargons II*, 87–88, 313–14.
38 Edition: Fuchs, *Die Inschriften Sargons II.*, 196–97, 344.
39 Robin Archer, "Chariotry to Cavalry: Developments in the Early First Millennium," in *New Perspectives on Ancient Warfare*, ed. Garrett G. Fagan and Matthew Trundle (Leiden: Brill, 2010): 76.
40 For the terminology see Karen Radner, *Die neuassyrischen Texte aus Tall Šēḫ Ḥamad* (Berlin: Reimer, 2002), 9–10.

tions were much taller than the lighter models, with wheel diameters of up to 2 meters. They were used to fire at enemy archers at close range, and while they lacked in speed they very effectively served the twin purposes of show-of-force and intimidation.⁴¹ The Samarian chariotry was of this second type.

Fig. 4: Tank-like chariot with a four-man crew consisting of driver, archer and two shield-bearers. Detail from the wall decoration of Assurbanipal's palace at Nineveh. Reproduced from T. Dezsö, *The Assyrian Army 1: The Structure of the Neo-Assyrian Army 2. Cavalry and Chariotry* (Budapest: Eötvös University Press, 2012): pl. 18 no. 31. Used with the author's kind permission.

The integration of fighters from defeated armies into the permanent Assyrian forces was routine and always focused on chariotry and cavalry, that is, those units with the most specialised training. The Samarian chariotry was not merely integrated into the Assyrian army, but specifically into the "royal contingent"

---

41 Andreas Fuchs, "Assyria at War: Strategy and Conduct," in *The Oxford Handbook of Cuneiform Culture*, ed. Karen Radner and Eleanor Robson (Oxford: Oxford University Press, 2011): 394.

(*kiṣir šarrūti*) of the armed forces that was under the direct command of the king.⁴²

Some of the members of the Samarian chariotry are attested about a decade later in an administrative text from Kalhu that matches groups of commanders of chariot teams (*rab urāte*) with their superior officers. The document may have been prepared in order to organise the armed forces that Sargon dispatched against Babylonia, as the text can be assigned to the period c. 710 – 708 BCE.⁴³ A group of thirteen commanders is associated with the city of Samaria:

> "Ibba-dalâ, Dalâ-ahi, Yāu-gâ, Atamru, Ahi-idri, Abdi-Milki, Bel-duri, Narmenâ, Gabbê, Sama', Ahi-idri, Bahî, Ahi-Yāu: in total, 13 (from) Samaria, command of Nabû-belu-ka'"in." ⁴⁴

The chariot team commanders mostly bear names with a clear West Semitic etymology and two have names formed with the divine element Yahweh: Yāu-gâ "Yahweh is exalted"⁴⁵ and Ahi-Yāu "My brother is Yahweh".⁴⁶

At about the same time, in 709 BCE, a private legal document found in Nineveh⁴⁷ mentions a chariot driver called Nadbi-Yāu ("Impelled by Yahweh"⁴⁸) as a witness to a slave sale, with Šumma-ilani, a chariot driver of the royal contingent, as the purchaser. As Šumma-ilani was a chariot driver of the royal corps, it is therefore likely that also his witness Nadbi-Yāu was a member of this part of the Assyrian armed forces. As we have seen, the Samarian chariotry was part of the royal contingent and several of its known members had Yahweh names. It therefore seems a reasonable hypothesis to identify also Nadbi-Yāu as one of the Samarian chariot corps.

---

42 For a discussion of *kiṣir šarrūti* see Tamás Dezső, *The Assyrian Army II. Recruitment and Logistics* (Budapest: Eötvös University Press, 2016), 16.
43 Stephanie Dalley and John Nicholas Postgate, *Texts from Fort Shalmaneser* (London: British School of Archaeology in Iraq, 1984), 176.
44 Dalley and Postgate, *Texts from Fort Shalmaneser*, no. 99 ii 16 – 23. Discussed by Stephanie Dalley, "Foreign Chariotry and Cavalry in the Armies of Tiglath-Pileser III and Sargon II," *Iraq* 47 (1985): 31– 48.
45 Daniel Schwemer, "Iāu-gâ," in *The Prosopography of the Neo-Assyrian Empire 2/I*, ed. Heather D. Baker (Helsinki: The Neo-Assyrian Text Corpus Project, 2000): 497.
46 Steven Cole, "Aḫi-Iāu," in *The Prosopography of the Neo-Assyrian Empire 1/I*, ed. Karen Radner (Helsinki: The Neo-Assyrian Text Corpus Project, 1998): 63 no. 1.
47 Theodore Kwasman and Simo Parpola, *Legal Transactions of the Royal Court of Nineveh, Part I: Tiglath-Pileser III through Esarhaddon* (Helsinki: Helsinki University Press, 1991), no. 34 rev. 9: ᵐ*Na-ad-bi–Ia-a-ú* LÚ.DIB–KUŠ.PA.MEŠ. Photograph: http://cdli.ucla.edu/P335181 (accessed 10/2017).
48 Kaisa Åkerman, "Nadbi-Iāu," in *The Prosopography of the Neo-Assyrian Empire 2/II*, ed. Heather D. Baker (Helsinki: The Neo-Assyrian Text Corpus Project, 2001): 915.

Finally, "Third Men from Samaria" (3-*šú*.MEŠ ᴷᵁᴿ*Sa-mir-na-a-a*, l. 6)⁴⁹ are mentioned alongside "Third Men from Hatti" (3-*šú*.MEŠ ᴷᵁᴿ*Ha-t*[*a*]-*a-a*, l. 10) and various other military personnel, including chariot fighters (EN–ᵍⁱˢGI[GIR.MEŠ], l. 5) as well as scouts (UŠ–*kib-si*.MEŠ, l. 1) and outriders (*kal-la-pu ši-pir-te*, l. 2), in a fragmentary administrative text from Kalhu recording food expenditure. We can certainly assign these "Third Men from Samaria" to the Samarian chariot corps of the royal contingent formed by Sargon II.

4.2 Samarian Artisans, Participating in the Construction of Dur-Šarruken

As we have already stated, Sargon's new capital Dur-Šarruken was constructed in the Halahhu region of the Assyrian heartland. A broken letter, whose author is unknown because of the fragmentary state of the tablet, is one of many items in Sargon's correspondence with his governors and high officials that deals with details concerning the construction of this new residence city, the king's pride and joy.⁵⁰ This letter is of interest to us because it mentions Samarians who were to contribute to these works. These included carpenters and potters (or perhaps better ceramic artists, as Dur-Šarruken's architectural decoration boasted elaborate ceramic features such as glazed brick panels⁵¹) who were to direct the work of the other deportee workers. The carpenters and potters are designated as *ummānu*, an Assyrian term used for "expert; specialist" that denotes a master of any discipline that requires extensive training and knowhow.

---

49 Stephanie Dalley and John Nicholas Postgate, *The Tablets from Fort Shalmaneser* (London: British School of Archaeology in Iraq, 1984), no. 121: 6. They read 3 ŠÚ.MEŠ KUR.*Sa-mir-na-a-a* and did not understand this and the parallel passage in l. 10, wondering in their commentary whether ŠÚ.MEŠ was a small measuring unit (Dalley and Postgate, *The Tablets from Fort Shalmaneser*, 238–39); they did not offer a translation of the fragmentary text. Later, Kyle Lawson Younger Jr., "The Deportations of the Israelites," *JBL* 117 (1998): 221 assumed that ŠÚ was used as a logogram for *kalû* and interpreted this as a reference to "three Samarian lamentation-priests." But given that the logogram ŠÚ is not at all used in the meaning *kalû* "lamenter" in Neo-Assyrian archival texts and in view of the otherwise exclusive presence of military personnel in our text, this interpretation cannot be maintained.
50 Simo Parpola, "The Construction of Dur-Sarrukin in Assyrian Royal Correspondence," in *Khorsabad, le palais de Sargon II, roi d'Assyrie*, ed. Annie Caubet (Paris: Louvre, 1995): 47–77.
51 E.g., on the façade of Room 18 of the royal palace: Gordon Loud and Charles B. Altman, *Khorsabad, Part 2: The Citadel and the Town* (Chicago: University of Chicago Press, 1938), 77; David Kertai, *The Architecture of Late Assyrian Royal Palaces* (Cambridge: Cambridge University Press, 2015), 120.

"What the king, my lord, wrote to me: 'Provide all the Samarians ([LÚ.Sa]-mir-i-na-a-a) in your charge with work in Dur-Šarruken.' – I subsequently sent word to the clan leaders (LÚ.na-si-ka-a-ni), saying: 'Collect all the carpenters and potters; let them come and direct the deportees (LÚ.hu-ub-te) who are in Dur-Šarruken.' But they did not agree to send them. Surely, if I had sent [threatening] letters to the clan leaders, saying: 'If indeed you do not send me experts (LÚ.um-ma-ni) to work for me, all the people who are here [will face dire consequences],' they would have promptly sent the experts to work for me. Now (however), following the king, my lord's instructions, I strictly [...] do not argue with any of the clan leaders. I have appointed the carpenters and potters [...]."[52]

Sargon's official had been commanded to negotiate with the clan leaders (nasīku, often translated as "sheikh"[53]) in order to organise the Samarian workforce and did so, although he clearly found the experience frustrating. Not only does this letter illustrate that the innate social structures of the resettled population group had been preserved, but also that the Assyrian authorities were expected to respect them, even if this caused friction and authority conflicts regarding the management of the deportee workers.

4.3 Samarians in Guzana

There are two Assyrian archival texts that demonstrate the presence of Samarians in Guzana (Tell Halaf). The first is a sale contract from the year 700 BCE featuring a Samarian selling real estate in that city whereas the second text is a letter from late in the reign of Esarhaddon that mentions a Samarian as the source of incriminating information about a prominent family in Guzana. Intriguingly, both texts have a Libyan connection.

---

52 Fuchs and Parpola, *The Correspondence of Sargon II, Part III*, no. 280; slightly adapted. Photograph: http://cdli.ucla.edu/P334710 (accessed 10/2017).
53 For a recent discussion of the term see Kyle Lawson Younger Jr., *A Political History of the Arameans: From Their Origins to the End of Their Polities* (Atlanta GA: SBL Press, 2016), 50 Table 2.2, 52, 56–57.

4.3.1 Guzana, 700 BCE: A Samarian Sells a Bathhouse

Although it is clear that the sale took place in Guzana the legal document recording this transaction was found in Assur, in an archive that has no obvious links to any of the parties involved ("Archive N18"[54]).

> "Instead of his seal he impressed his fingernail. Fingernail of Sama', Samarian, son of Šamaš-bel-ketti, from Guzana, owner of the bath being sold.
> A bath with its beams and doors, and the wall between Ribṣiṣi and Hallabeše, (property) of Sama' in the city of Guzana – Qišeraya, chief [...]ean, has contracted and bought it for fifty shekels of silver. The money is paid completely. The bathroom in question is acquired and purchased. Any revocation, lawsuit or litigation is void.
> Whoever in the future, at any time, whether Sama' or his sons, his grandsons, his brothers, his relatives or any litigant of his who seeks a lawsuit or litigation with Qišeraya and his sons, shall place ten minas of refined silver and one mina of pure gold in the lap of Adad who resides in Guzana; shall tie four white horses at the feet of Sîn who resides in Harran; and shall return the money tenfold to its owner. He shall contest in his lawsuit and not succeed.
> Witness Abba-...aya, scholar; witness Zanbalâ, Arab; witness Abarrâ, scholar of the temple of Adad; witness Uširihiuhurti, Egyptian; witness Adda-bi'di, merchant; witness Adad-ahu-uṣur, of the temple; witness Haia-ereš; witness Gabrî; witness Adda-sakâ son of Huiri; witness Palṭi-Yāu, visitor; witness Mizi-Yāu, visitor; witness Ah-abi, visitor; witness Mini-ahhe, leather worker of Il-nemeqi; witness Ṣiranû and Alara, his ...s; witness Buraya, chief beer brewer of the governor of Guzana; [witness ...]aya; witness Ni...ni; witness Nabû-ahu-[...], keeper of the tablet.
> Month Tishri (VII), first day, eponym year of Metunu (700 BCE).
> One shekel of silver for his fingernail."[55]

The seller is a Samarian[56] and resident of Guzana with the West Semitic name Sama' ("He has heard"); he shares that name with one of the Samarian team commanders in the royal cohort (see above, 4.1). Interestingly, his father has the Akkadian name Šamaš-bel-ketti ("The sun god is the lord of truth"). The

---

54 Olof Pedersén, *Archives and Libraries in the City of Assur: a Survey of the Material from the German Excavations, Part II* (Uppsala: Almqvist & Wiksell, 1986), 106–107.
55 First edition: Veysel Donbaz and Simo Parpola, *Neo-Assyrian Legal Texts in Istanbul* (Saarbrücken: SDV, 2001), no. 53; updated edition with important corrections: Charles Draper, "Two Libyan Names in a Seventh Century Sale Document From Assur," *Journal of Ancient Egyptian Interconnections* 7 (2015): 6.
56 The reading LÚ*.*Si-me-ri-na!-a-a* "Samarian" was first suggested by Simonetta Ponchia, Review of *Neo-Assyrian Legal Texts in Istanbul Studien zu den Assur-Texten* by Veysel Donbaz and Simo Parpola, *Or* 72 (2003): 275–76; accepted by Draper, "Two Libyan Names," 5, 12 fn. 14 (quoting also the approval of Ran Zadok, pers. comm.).

transaction is witnessed by some visitors to Guzana (Assyrian *ubāru*[57]) whose names include the divine element Yahweh: Palṭi-Yāu "My deliverance is Yahweh"[58] and ᵐ*Mi-zi–Ia*, perhaps for Mahsi-Yāu "Work of Yahweh"[59], as well as a man identified as an Egyptian with the Libyan name Uširihiuhurti; also the owner of an adjoining property bears a Libyan name: Hallabeše.[60]

As is customary in Neo-Assyrian contracts, the family members of the vendor are mentioned as potential litigants; this always reflects the actual family situation. In this case, not only are his (possibly future) sons and grandsons cited here but also his brothers and his relatives in general. This indicates that the Samarian Sama' is residing in Guzana with his extended family – evidence for the Assyrian policy to relocate entire family units. The deities who would benefit in case of litigation against the contract are the most prominent local gods: the storm god of Guzana and the moon god of nearby Harran.

4.3.2 Guzana, Late 670s BCE: A Samarian Informs on a Corrupt Scribe

Hallabeše the Samarian, a [...] of the king,[61] is mentioned in an anonymous letter to Esarhaddon (r. 680–669 BCE) that presents a detailed account of the crimes and misdemeanours of various prominent individuals in Guzana. The Samarian's testimony concerns the scribe Tarṣî, his wife Zazâ and their son who are accused of abusing their close relationship to a member of the royal family.[62]

The Samarian Hallabeše has a title or profession (unfortunately damaged) that links him to the king. His name is of Libyan origin, and he shares it with the neighbour of his fellow Samarian Sama' who sold a bathhouse in Guzana nearly three decades earlier. If this second link between Samarians in Guzana

---

57 For a discussion of the term see Draper, "Two Libyan Names," 12 fn. 19.
58 Daniel Schwemer, "Palṭī-Iāu," in *The Prosopography of the Neo-Assyrian Empire 3/I*, ed. Heather D. Baker (Helsinki: The Neo-Assyrian Text Corpus Project, 2002): 982.
59 Kaisa Åkerman, "Maḫsi-Iāu," in *The Prosopography of the Neo-Assyrian Empire 2/II*, ed. Heather D. Baker (Helsinki: The Neo-Assyrian Text Corpus Project, 2001): 675.
60 As discussed in detail by Draper, "Two Libyan Names," 1–15.
61 Mikko Luukko and Greta Van Buylaere, *The Political Correspondence of Esarhaddon* (Helsinki: Helsinki University Press, 2002), no. 63 rev. 9–10: " ᵐ*Hal-bi-šú* URU.*Sa-mir-i-na-a-a* [x x]x x LUGAL. Photograph: http://cdli.ucla.edu/P313461 (accessed 10/2017).
62 According to the letter, Aššur-zeru-ibni socialises with the sons of the king, goes regularly to Nineveh and does not only wear the golden bracelet and golden dagger that denote an Assyrian of the highest social standing but even a parasol – an item exclusively reserved for the royal family: Michael Roaf, "Schirm (parasol). B. Archäologisch," in *RlA* 12, ed. Michael P. Streck (2011): 192–94.

and this Libyan name is not merely a curious coincidence then we can take it as an indication that Charles Draper was correct when suggesting that the population deported from Samaria included people bearing Libyan names, presumably with roots in Egypt.[63]

4.3.3 Dur-Katlimmu, 656 and 602 BCE: More Samarians on the Khabur?

For completeness's sake, we will briefly mention the fact that there are a number of people with Yahweh names attested in the private legal records unearthed in the so-called Red House, an elite residence at Dur-Katlimmu (Tell Sheikh Hamad) on the Khabur river.

When an irrigated field was sold in 602 BCE, one of the adjoining fields is owned by Hazaqi-Yāu ("Yahweh is mighty"[64]), and the witnesses to the transaction include Dadi-larim son of Ahzi-Yāu ("Yahweh has taken"[65]) according to the sale contract documenting the transaction.[66] Michael Heltzer was the first to tentatively connect the mention of individuals with Yahweh names in this document with the resettlement of the people of Samaria in the Khabur valley a century earlier; but he also drew attention to other occasions that might have brought deportees from the southern Levant to the region.[67] He was not yet aware of a significantly earlier attestation for one Rapâ-Yāu ("Yahweh has healed"[68]) as a witness in another legal document from Dur-Katlimmu, a judicial settlement from 656 BCE.[69] There is also another attestation for a Yahweh name at Dur-Katlimmu in the fragment of an undated private letter.[70]

---

63 Draper, "Two Libyan Names," 4–5.
64 Daniel Schwemer, "Hazaqi-Iāu," in *The Prosopography of the Neo-Assyrian Empire 3/I*, ed. Heather D. Baker (Helsinki: The Neo-Assyrian Text Corpus Project, 2000): 469.
65 Gebhard J. Selz, "Ahzi-Iāu," in *The Prosopography of the Neo-Assyrian Empire 1/I*, ed. Karen Radner (Helsinki: The Neo-Assyrian Text Corpus Project, 1998): 88–9.
66 Radner, *Die neuassyrischen Texte aus Tall Šēḫ Ḥamad*, no. 37: 4: ᵐ*Ha-za-qi–Iá-a-u*; rev. 14: ᵐ*Aḫ-zi–Iá-a-u*. There is also Adad-milki-ereš son of ᵐ*Me-na-se-e* (rev. 13).
67 Michael Heltzer, "Some Remarks Concerning the Neo-Babylonian Tablets from Šēḫ Ḥamad," *SAAB* 8 (1994): 116.
68 Pierre Villard, "Rapâ-Iāu," in *The Prosopography of the Neo-Assyrian Empire 2/I*, ed. Heather D. Baker (Helsinki: The Neo-Assyrian Text Corpus Project, 2002): 1032–33.
69 Radner, *Die neuassyrischen Texte aus Tall Šēḫ Ḥamad*, no. 110b rev. 4: ᵐ[*Ra*]-*pa–Ia-u*.
70 Karen Radner, "Neue neuassyrische Texte aus Dur-Katlimmu: eine Schülertafel mit einer sumerisch-akkadischen Königshymne und andere Keilschriftfunde aus den Jahren 2003–2009," in *Dur-Katlimmu 2008 and Beyond*, ed. Hartmut Kühne (Wiesbaden: Harrassowitz, 2010): 185 no. 14: 5': [ᵐ]*Ia-a-ú–ra-qu-ut*.

It remains of course open whether the presence of persons with Yahweh names in Dur-Katlimmu during the 7th century BCE has anything to do with the resettlements of Samarians in Guzana, which lies about 160 km upstream from Dur-Katlimmu. But it is not entirely unlikely that there is a connection, given that we have encountered a significant number of Yahweh names among or in association with the resettled Samarians.

5 Conclusions

Some of the resettled Samarians attested in the Assyrian archival records did very well in their new surroundings: the military men were members of the royal contingent, arguably the most prestigious corps of the Assyrian armed forces; and in Guzana, we met a Samarian with an extended family who owned a real estate portfolio in the city and another very well-connected Samarian individual who mingled with the city's leading residents.

We cannot assess the economic standing of the Samarian potters and carpenters who we encountered at Dur-Šarruken, but their skill was clearly highly valued as King Sargon himself deemed them fit to contribute to the construction of his new capital in the Halahhu region of Central Assyria. In this case, we were able to observe that some of the innate social structures of the resettled population had not only been preserved but that the Assyrian authorities were expected to respect them.

Repeatedly, we found Samarians bearing Yahweh names, while in Guzana, we observed a curious connection with Libyan names that highlights how onomastics alone are not a reliable indicator of origin or ethnic or cultural identity. The kingdom of Israel was of course neither geographically nor politically isolated, and especially its capital Samaria is likely to have been a cosmopolitan city with sizeable groups of foreign residents when the Assyrian Empire annexed it.[71]

It is a matter of debate how many people of a particular local population were made to move. In the case of the kingdom of Israel, this question has received much attention as it underpins any assessment of the relationship between ancient Israelite and later Samaritan traditions.[72] It is moot, in my view, to try and quantify proportions. However, it is beyond any doubt that the Assyrian sources overwhelmingly associate resettlement with persons possessing spe-

---

[71] For the connection with Egypt and the Libyan-controlled kingdoms in the Nile Delta see Robert Morkot's chapter in this volume.
[72] Gary N. Knoppers, *Jews and Samaritans: The Origins and History of Their Early Relations* (New York: Oxford University Press, 2013), 18–44 for a critical assessment of debate.

cialised skills, with educated elites in the broadest sense: highly trained fighters, scribes and scholars, artisans and craftsmen of all kinds. Therefore, even if the resettlement programme affected only a relatively small percentage of the overall population, the absence of such specialists – which in the case of Samaria, as we have discussed, included chariot crews, potters and carpenters – would have massively eroded and changed local culture and local identity.

Robert G. Morkot
The End of the Kingdom of Israel: A View from the Nile Valley

1 Introduction

This paper is intended to present the current debates and disputes about the political geography of late-Libyan and early-Kushite Egypt (Fig. 1) that form one part of the context of the reign of Hoshea, and the end of the Kingdom of Israel. The Egyptological perspective on the end of the Kingdom of Israel is not fundamentally different now to how it was when Kenneth Kitchen published his ground-breaking study of the Libyan and Kushite periods in 1973.[1] Although there has been considerable research on the late Libyan period over the past two decades, this has largely concentrated on discussion of detail, in terms of chronologies, minutiae of dynastic affiliations and genealogies, and speculations on power bases. A radical proposal for re-ordering two Kushite rulers has repercussions for our understanding of the internal development of the dynasty, but does not fundamentally alter the view of the period around 730–725 BCE.

2 The Kushite 25th Dynasty

The starting point for establishing the Nile Valley context for the end of the Kingdom of Israel is the dating of the 25th Dynasty, originating in Kush (modern northern Sudan), and the phases of their domination of Egypt. The equation of the rulers named monumentally with those recorded by Manetho was established early in the development of Egyptology, and apparently supported by later discoveries.[2] These rulers were Shabaka (= Manetho's Sabacon), Shabataka (or Shebitqo = Sebichos) and Taharka (or Taharqo = Tar(a)cos). Taharka's successor

---

[1] Kenneth A. Kitchen, *The Third Intermediate Period in Egypt (1100–650 B.C.)* (Warminster: Aris & Phillips, 1973; second edition with supplement 1986, third edition with new preface 1996).
[2] Kitchen, *Third Intermediate Period*, 148–73; Robert Morkot and Stephen Quirke, "Inventing the 25th Dynasty: Turin Stela 1467 and the Construction of History," in *Begegnungen: Antike Kulturen im Niltal. Festgabe für Erika Endesfelder, Karl-Heinz Priese, Walter Friedrich Reineke und Steffen Wenig von Schülern und Mitarbeiten*, ed. Caris-Beatrice Arnst and Erika Endesfelder (Leipzig: Verlag Helmar Wodtke und Katharina Stegbauer, 2001): 349–63.

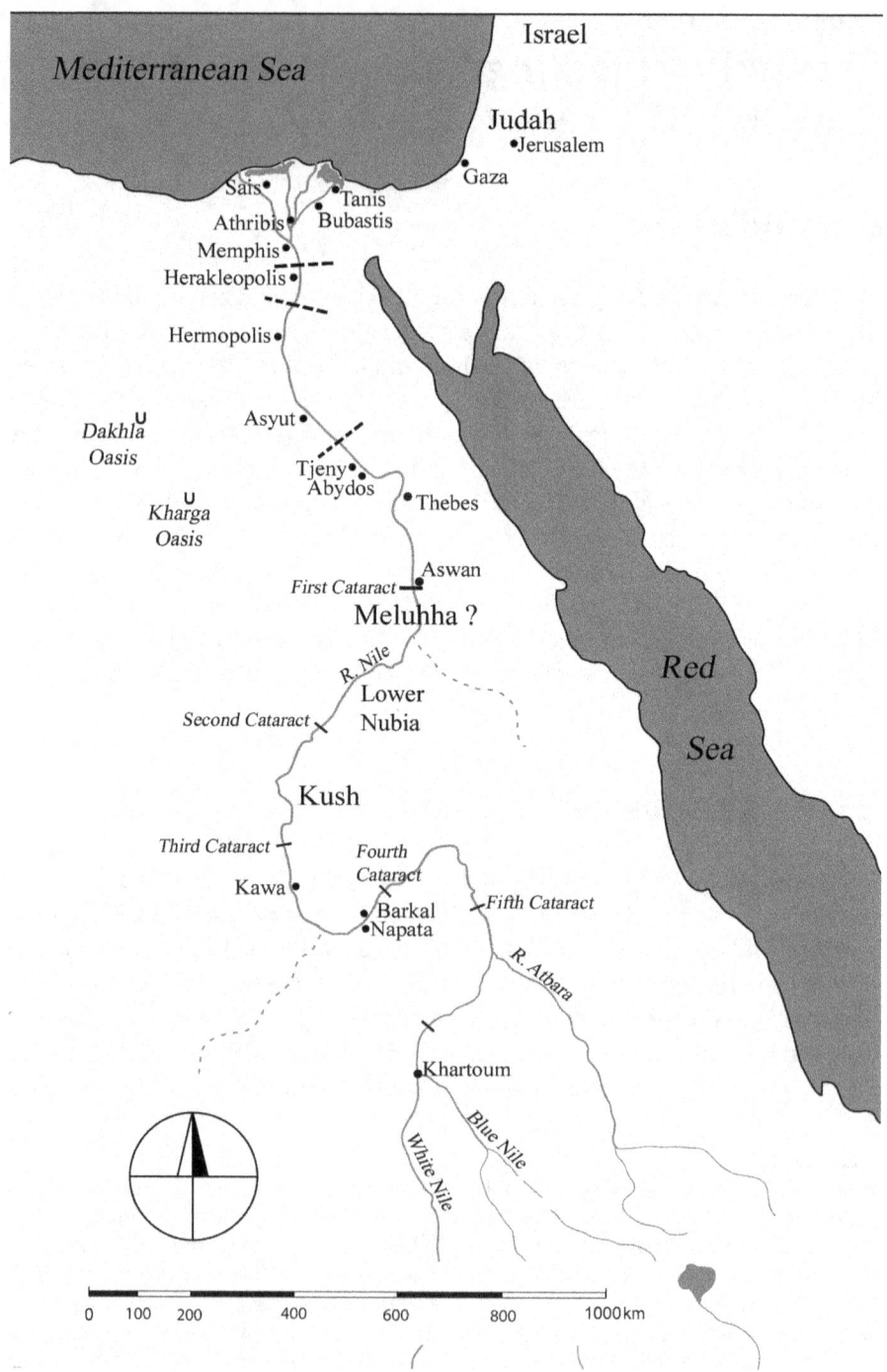

Fig. 1: Map of the Nile valley indicating the most important places discussed in this chapter (prepared by the author).

Tanutamun is recorded by Egyptian and Assyrian documents. The ordering of the predecessors of the dynasty, Alara, Kashta and Piye (Piankhy), was established through a range of inscriptional evidence.

The anchor date for the Kushites and, consequently, the late Libyan pharaohs, is the accession of Taharka in 690 BCE. The date is accepted as the earliest certain date in Egyptian history, all earlier dates being calculated from it, or based on the equation of the biblical Shishak with Shoshenq I,[3] or from Sothic dating. The reign of Taharka is linked to that of Psamtik I by the text of a stela recording the burial of a sacred Apis bull at Memphis, which states that its installation was in year 26 of the former ruler, its death in year 20 of the latter, and that the bull's age was 21 years.[4] Year 26 is the highest attested of Taharka, and as the exact dates for the 26th Dynasty are established (and can be linked to Assyrian, Babylonian, Persian dates and to Ptolemy's *Canon*), there is a consensus that the accession of Taharka fell in 690/689 BCE.[5]

The internal chronology of the Kushite dynasty thus becomes significant for the Egyptian context of the end of the Kingdom of Israel. The most important aspect from the perspective of Western Asiatic studies and Assyriology is the dating of the Kushite incursions into Egypt and the conflict of Piye and Tefnakht, and the implications for the years 730–720 BCE.

For the two immediate predecessors of Taharka there is inscriptional evidence from Egypt. Although Shabataka's highest regnal year so far documented is year 3, most scholars have assumed that the reign was longer.[6] The length of Shabaka's reign is more certain: the statue of Iti is dated to late in year 15.[7] With only one dated monument, the length of Shabataka's reign has always been calculated, using either the unreliable epitomes of Manetho, or the presumed accession date of Shabaka. Until further dated monuments can be confidently attrib-

---

3 Peter James and Peter G. van der Veen, eds., *Solomon and Shishak: Current perspectives from Archaeology, Epigraphy, History and Chronology* (Oxford: Archaeopress, 2015).
4 Stela 192: Kitchen, *Third Intermediate Period*, 161–63.
5 Cf. Anthony J. Spalinger, "The Foreign Policy of Egypt Preceding the Assyrian Conquest," *CdE* 53 (1978): 22–47; the arguments for Taharqo's accession in 689 BCE do not make much difference.
6 Kitchen, *Third Intermediate Period*, 154–61, esp. 154, §126 (i), although this is based on his calculation of the date for Shabaka's accession; Leo Depuydt, "The Date of Piye's Egyptian Campaign and the Chronology of the Twenty-fifth Dynasty," *JEA* 79 (1993): 274, uses the lack of monuments as one factor in arguing a minimal reign; Robert G. Morkot, "Kingship and Kinship in the Empire of Kush," in *Studien zum Antiken Sudan: Akten der 7. Internationalen Tagung für meroitistische Forschungen*, ed. Steffen Wenig (Wiesbaden: Harrassowitz, 1999): 205–207.
7 British Museum EA 24429: Kitchen, *Third Intermediate Period*, 153–54; Morkot, "Kingship and Kinship," 207.

uted to Shabataka, all that can be said is that his reign was not less than three years. With the accession of Taharqo in 690/689 BC, a strictly minimum chronology would set the beginning of Shabataka's reign at 693/2 BCE and that of Shabaka (with a full 15 years) at 708/7 BCE. The reign of Piye (Piankhy) is universally accepted as immediately preceding that of Shabaka, although its length is far less clear.[8]

Leo Depuydt adopted a minimal chronology as the only secure foundation, but later noted the criticisms of other writers, and felt obliged to clarify that the minimal date is not necessarily to be taken as an indication of the *actual* reign length.[9] The conventional interpretation of the ordering of Kushite rulers, their reign lengths and absolute dates are thus established with high (Kenneth Kitchen), low (Robert Morkot) and minimal (Morkot/Depuydt) alternatives.

	High	Low	Minimal
Piye	747–714	736–712	731–707
Shabaka	716–702	712–697	707–692
Shabataka	702–690	697–690	692–690
Taharka	690–664	690–664	690–664

On the assumption that the conflict between Piye and the Saite ruler Tefnakht occurred in years 19/20 of Piye's reign, the range is between 728/727 BC and 712 BC. The issue then becomes the reign length of Piye, which is certainly documented to year 24. Scenes relating to the *sed*-festival suggest he may have reigned for over 30 years, but a much disputed date on a bandage does not provide unequivocal evidence for a date higher than year 30.[10]

---

8 Kitchen, *Third Intermediate Period*, 151–53; Morkot, "Kinship and Kinship"; Robert G. Morkot, *The Black Pharaohs: Egypt's Nubian Rulers* (London: Rubicon Press, 2000), 167–74.
9 Depuydt, "The Date of Piye's Egyptian Campaign," 270–71 offers 708 BCE or (using a different accession dating system) an absolute minimum start-date of 706 BCE for Shabaqo. A minimal chronology had already previously been argued as 708/7 BCE for Shabaqo's year 1, see Peter J. James, I. J. Thorpe, Nikos Kokkinos, Robert G. Morkot and John A. Frankish, "Centuries of Darkness (Review Feature)," *Cambridge Archaeological Journal* 1 (1991): 230, 235, n. 2 (based on the analysis presented by Morkot at the 7. *Internationalen Tagung für meroitistische Forschungen* in 1992, eventually published as Morkot, "Kingship and Kinship").
10 BM EA 6640: Donald B. Redford, "Sais and the Kushite Invasions of the Eighth Century BC," *Journal of the American Research Center in Egypt* 22 (1985): 5–15, questioning year 40; Kitchen, *Third Intermediate Period*, 152 reading year 30+; Morkot, *Black Pharaohs*, 314 n. 9.

3 Recent Debates: the Inscription of Sargon II of Assyria at Tang-i Var in Iran

The most significant recent debates were generated by Grant Frame's publication of the inscription of Sargon II of Assyria (721–705 BCE) at Tang-i Var near Sanandaj in Kurdistan province of Iran.[11] Although a record of the campaign against Karalla, the annalistic preamble to the inscription contains another version of the well-known episode of Yamani of Ashdod's flight from the advancing Assyrian army.[12] The Tang-i Var inscription is the only version of the episode that records the name of the ruler of Meluhha (= Kush), which can only be understood as that of Shabataka (Shebitqo).

The Tang-i Var inscription has generated a voluminous Egyptological literature, the bulk of which has ignored the purpose of the Assyrian text. Frame observes that the Tang-i Var text almost certainly belongs to 706 BC, relating to the campaign to Karalla in that year, and must have been composed (and carved) before Sargon's death in 705 BCE. Frame also comments that the Display Inscription and the inscription from Room XIV of Sargon's palace in his new capital city Dur-Šarruken (Khorsabad) belong to the same year, as they refer to the completion of the construction of that city.[13]

The very brief annalistic preamble is not the purpose of the text, although it has drawn the lengthiest commentary from Egyptologists who put forward numerous new chronologies of the 25th Kushite Dynasty,[14] most claiming that Sar-

---

11 Grant Frame, "The Inscription of Sargon II at Tang-i Var," *Or* 68 (1999): 31–57.
12 Morkot, *Black Pharaohs*, 200–204 with references to the literature.
13 Frame "Inscription of Sargon II," 54.
14 Cf. David A. Aston, "Takeloth II, a King of the Herakleopolitan/Theban Twenty-third Dynasty Revisited: The Chronology of Dynasties 22 and 23," in *The Libyan Period in Egypt*, ed. Gerard P. F. Broekman, Robert J. Demarée and Olaf E. Kaper (Leuven: Peeters, 2009): 1–28; Gerard P. F. Broekman "The Egyptian Chronology from the Start of the Twenty-second until the End of the Twenty-fifth Dynasty: Facts, Suppositions and Arguments," *Journal of Egyptian History* 4 (2011): 40–80; Aidan Dodson, *Afterglow of Empire: Egypt from the Fall of the New Kingdom to the Saite Renaissance* (Cairo and New York: American University in Cairo Press, 2012), 195–201; Karl Jansen-Winkeln, "The Chronology of the Third Intermediate Period: Dyns. 22–24," in *Ancient Egyptian Chronology*, ed. Erik Hornung, Rolf Krauss and David A. Warburton (Leiden: Brill, 2006): 234–64; Dan'el Kahn, "The Inscription of Sargon II at Tang-i Var and the Chronology of Dynasty 25," *Or* 70 (2001): 1–18, id., "Divided Kingdom, Co-Regency, or Sole Rule in the Kingdom(s) of Egypt-and-Kush," *AeL* 16 (2006): 277–91; id., "Was There a Co-Regency in the 25th Dynasty?," *Mitteilungen der Sudanarchäologischen Gesellschaft* 17 (2006): 9–17; Rolf Krauss, "An Egyptian Chronology for Dynasties XIII to XXV," in *The Synchronisation of Civilisations in the Eastern Mediterranean in the Second Millennium B.C., vol. III: Proceedings of the*

gon's inscription can be interpreted as indicating that Shabataka was ruling Egypt by the date of the inscription, 706 BCE. This is a misinterpretation: Shabataka (if he was really intended to be named at all) is specified as ruler of Meluhha (= Kush), not of Egypt. When the original Egyptological responses made the incorrect assumption that the reference to Shabataka indicated he was ruling in Egypt by 706 BC, and perhaps at the time of Yamani's flight, this resulted in the following (very similar) chronologies:[15]

	Kahn 2001	Aston 2009	Jansen-Winkeln 2006	Krauss 2007	Broekman 2011	Dodson 2012
Shabaka	721– 707/6	721– 707/6	722/1– 707	722– 707	721– 707/6 (minimum)	722–707
Shabataka	707/6– 690	707/6– 690	707/6– 690	706– 691	706–691 (minimum)	707–690

Kitchen dismisses such dates as "quite simply ludicrous," giving two reasons: first, his belief that Shabaka removed all other kings from Egypt (making inexplicable the existence of Shilkanni, clearly a Delta ruler, in 716 BC); and second, that extending the reign of Shabataka "seems entirely unrealistic, given the almost non-existent state of date-lines so far attested from his reign."[16] The first point is not acceptable, as there must have been other kings (such as Gemenef-khonsu-bak) and *weru*-chiefs ruling in parts of the Delta throughout the Kushite hegemony (see further below).[17] There is, however, no evidence to justify

---

SCIEM 2000 2nd EuroConference, ed. Manfred Bietak and Ernst Czerny (Vienna: Austrian Academy of Sciences Press, 2007): 173–89.
15 The information in the following table derives from Kahn, "Inscription of Sargon II"; Aston, "Takeloth II," 5–6, 20; Jansen-Winkeln, "Chronology of the Third Intermediate Period," 258–61; Krauss, "An Egyptian Chronology," 187; Broekman, "The Egyptian Chronology," 57; and Dodson, *Afterglow of Empire*, 201.
16 Kenneth A. Kitchen, "The Third Intermediate Period in Egypt: An Overview of Fact & Fiction," in *The Libyan Period in Egypt*, ed. Gerard P. F. Broekman, Robert J. Demarée and Olaf E. Kaper (Leuven: Peeters, 2009): 161–202, esp. 163.
17 Note that not all the "kings" (*šarru*) listed by Esarhaddon were necessarily local "mayors" in Egyptian terms. Some cases are clear: e.g., Mantimeanhe, *šarru* of Ni, is the well-known Montjuemhat, Mayor of Thebes. Yet at least some of these were actual monarchs, as Kitchen, *Third Intermediate Period*, 395–97 accepts with respect to Niku I (672–664 BC) and Putubishti of Tanis, who he identifies as Sehetepib(en)re Pedubast II. From the finds at Tanis Kitchen acknowledges the possibility of a line of "kinglets," including Gemenef-khonsu-bak. Robert G. Morkot and Peter J. James, "Peftjauawybast, King of Nen-nesut: Genealogy, Art History, and

stretching the reign of Shabataka to some 16 years or more from the three attested, even if a reign longer than the documented three years seems more likely.

The most important point (somewhat obscured in Kitchen's argument) is that the new high dates derived from the Tang-i Var inscription run completely counter to the well-raked over evidence that the Kushites were not in direct control of Lower Egypt by 713/2 BCE, when Yamani of Ashdod made appeal to "Pirʻu of Muṣri" (that is, Pharaoh of Egypt) for help. This Pirʻu was certainly not a Kushite ruler, but is most probably identical with Šilkanni who sent a gift of horses from the Nile Delta region to Sargon II in 716 BCE according to the latter's inscriptions. The high dates advocated for Shabaka indicate the end of Piye's reign in 722/1 BCE – thereby pushing his accession backwards from Kitchen's 747 BCE to around 754 BCE.[18]

If Shabaka had already made Memphis his base in Egypt before 716 BCE, how could a local Delta dynast such as Šilkanni have dared to have independently sent a gift of horses to Sargon II? It seems a most unlikely scenario. If Shabaka were already established at Memphis, surely he himself would have sent the horses, especially as Šilkanni would have almost certainly obtained these from Kush in the first place.[19] The same problem recurs in 713/2 BCE when Yamani of Ashdod sent gifts not to the king of Kush, but to the pharaoh of Egypt ("Pirʻu of Muṣri"; arguably still Šilkanni), attempting to obtain help against the Assyrians. Sargon records that the Pirʻu was powerless to help and that after his expulsion from Ashdod, Yamani fled through Egypt to Meluhha, where he received sanctuary. Again, if Shabaka were based at Memphis, why would the decision not have been made there to give him asylum? Or, if Shabaka was the Pirʻu as some have claimed – was the flight to Meluhha some kind of subterfuge, in which Shabaqo was pretending to have no authority over the remote land of Meluhha? Again, a most unlikely scenario.

After the conflict with Tefnakht, Piye (who did not make his capital at Memphis, but retained control of Upper Egypt), Šilkanni/the Pirʻu would have remained at least the nominal vassal of the Kushite kings, but with enough independence to have diplomatic relations with the Assyrians, who were active on Egypt's very border. Kush and Meluhha seem very removed from all these pro-

---

the Chronology of Late-Libyan Egypt," *Antiguo Oriente* 7 (2009): 13–55 argue that the main 22nd Dynasty line (in the person of Shoshenq V) continued at Tanis until the reign of Shabaqo.
18 Kitchen, *Third Intermediate Period*, 589: Table 4.
19 For Kushite horses see Robert G. Morkot, "The Origin of the Kushite State: A Response to the Paper of László Török," in *Actes de la VIIIe Conférence Internationale des Études Nubiennes, vol. 1: Communications principales* (Villeneuve d'Ascq: Université Charles de Gaulle – Lille 3, 1995) 237–38; and Lisa Heidorn, "The Horses of Kush," *JNES* 56 (1997): 105–14.

ceedings; indeed, it is specifically described by Sargon as a remote country whose kings had not been in touch with Assyria before the extradition of Yamani. Unless we assume that this is mere hyperbole *and* that all Assyrian intelligence about Egypt at this period was virtually useless, we have to conclude that Shabaka's conquest of the north did not take place before c. 711 BCE. This renders the high dates derived from Tang-i Var, in which Shabaka's second year fell c. 720 BCE totally unworkable. Shabaka, after all, is first documented in Egypt in his second regnal year, and his defeat of the Saite ruler Bakanranef, by which he gained control of the whole of the Delta, is generally attributed to that same year.[20] Besides, as detailed above, any attempt to lengthen the reign of Shabataka on the evidence of the Tang-i Var inscription is misinterpreting the source. As Kitchen rightly notes, it has been 'glibly and superficially assumed' that Shabataka was reigning as pharaoh in Egypt in 706 BCE.[21] This misinterpretation of the evidence is having wider repercussions by being uncritically quoted: Jeffrey Blakely and James Hardin, citing Grant Frame, Donald Redford and Dan'el Kahn, state that Yamani was "eventually returned to Assyria … by Pharaoh Shebitku."[22]

4 Recent Debates: Re-Ordering the Kushite Kings

The debate has now gone even further in radically re-assessing the internal succession and chronology of the 25th Dynasty. Michael Bányai proposed the reversal of the generally accepted order of the Kushite kings Shabaka and Shabataka, arguing that the generally accepted readings of Manetho's Sabacon as Shabaka, and Manetho's Sebichos as Shabataka were wrong.[23] This has been followed by a number of writers: indeed, in the most recent defence of this interpretation, Claus Jurman notes that the order has now entered into one general history of

---

[20] Morkot, *Black Pharaohs*, 205–208.
[21] Kitchen, "Third Intermediate Period," 163: §§4, 6.
[22] Jeffrey A. Blakely and James W. Hardin, "Southwestern Judah in the Late Eighth Century B.C.E.," *BASOR* 326 (2002): 11–64.
[23] Michael Bányai, "Ein Vorschlag zur Chronologie der 25. Dynastie in Ägypten," *Journal of Egyptian History* 6 (2013): 46–129; Michael Bányai, with commentaries by Anke I. Blöbaum, Gerard Broekman, Karl Jansen-Winkeln, Claus Jurman, Dan'el Kahn, Angelika Lohwasser and Hans Neumann, "Die Reihenfolge der kuschitischen Könige," *Journal of Egyptian History* 8 (2015): 115–80.

Egypt as accepted truth.²⁴ Although this change in order post-dates the end of the kingdom of Israel, the repercussions impact on interpretation of the earlier phases of the dynasty.

Bányai's chronology adopts the minimalist chronology advocated by Depuydt but reverses the order of Shabaka and Shabataka and also builds in a large co-regency between Shabaka and Taharka that is not justified by the evidence, but necessitated to accommodate the known reign-length of Shabaka.

	Bányai 2013
Piye	735–708 BCE
Shabataka	708–696 BCE
Shabaka	698–684 BCE
Taharka	689–664 BCE

Jurman, supporting the reordering of the rulers, also follows a lower absolute chronology, thus maintaining the more conventional date for Piye's accession and, hence, the conflict with Tefnakht. On both Jurman's and Bányai's chronologies, the conflict between Piye and Tefnakht would have occurred around 715 BCE.

Frédéric Payraudeau accepts the reversal of rulers, and a thirty year long reign for Piye.²⁵ He therefore dates Piye's reign 744–714 BCE with the conflict with Tefnakht in 723 BCE, followed by an interruption to Kushite control of Upper Egypt by the obscure king Iny, around 720 BCE. In this scheme, Piye's successor Shabataka reigned 714–705 BCE, establishing himself in Egypt and defeating the Saite ruler Bakenranef in 712 BCE.

There are numerous issues of interpretation of the inscriptional evidence that have not yet been addressed by the proposers of this scheme. Our understanding of the royal genealogies and of the method of succession requires an almost complete revision.²⁶

---

24 Claus Jurman, "The Order of the Kushite Kings According to Sources from the Eastern Desert and Thebes, Or: Shabataka was here first!," *Journal of Egyptian History* 10 (2017): 124–51.
25 Frédéric Payraudeau, "Les obscures débuts de la domination soudanaise en Égypte (deuxième moitié du VIIIe s. av. J.-C.)," in *Comptes rendus des séances de l'Académie des Inscriptions et Belles-Lettres* 2014: 1597–611; also id., "Retour sur la Succession Shabaqo–Shabataqo," *NeHet: Revue numérique d'Égyptologie* 1 (2014): 115–27 (online: http://sfe-egyptologie.website/index.php/publications/la-revue-nehet; last accessed: 30 January 2018).
26 Morkot, " Kingship and Kinship."

5 Egyptian Involvement in Southwest Asia in the 8th and Early 7th Centuries BCE

The recorded interactions of Egypt with Israel, Judah and Assyria in the period preceding the reign of Sennacherib (704–681 BCE) are few, but have generated considerable literature. According to the Hebrew Bible, the first notable Egyptian activity was the sack of Jerusalem by "Shishak" in the reign of Rehoboam, generally dated to 925 BCE. Since François Champollion, Shishak's campaign has been connected with the relief of Shoshenq I on the "Bubastite Portal" of the temple of Karnak, despite the problems of linking the name lists there with the narrative of the Bible. This is not the place to discuss the campaign, or whether it represents an attempt by the new power in Egypt to re-assert some influence in southwestern Asia.[27]

The dynasty that descended from Shoshenq I (following Manetho, the 22nd Dynasty) was based in the eastern Delta at Per-Bast (Bubastis) and Tanis: they therefore controlled the route across north Sinai to Gaza. The dynasty ruled all of Egypt until the death of Osorkon II, when problems began, notably in the southern city of Thebes, and new, rival dynasties (or lines of the same family) competed for control. There is no consensus on the interpretation of the evidence for late-Libyan Egypt, into which the Kushites extended their power.

The next Egyptian involvement was relatively small-scale, when 1,000 soldiers were sent to join the coalition led by Hadad-idri of Damascus against the army of Shalmaneser III of Assyria (858–824 BCE) at the battle of Qarqar in 853 BCE. Kitchen attributes this involvement to Osorkon II, based on his reconstruction of the chronology, and is generally followed.[28]

Shalmaneser III continued to bring his armies to the Levant, and in 841 BCE achieved suzerainty over the rulers, recorded on the "Black Obelisk." Here, the usurper king of Israel, Jehu, is shown paying homage, and the tribute of the land of Muṣri is recorded. Kitchen[29] dates this event to the reign of Takeloth II, regarding the king as the direct successor of Osorkon II in Tanis: others consider Takeloth II a Theban or Herakleopolitan ruler.[30]

A major problem for defining the political and economic connections between Egypt and the kingdoms of Israel and Judah, and the Phoenician cities,

---

27 For discussion and references see Kitchen, *Third Intermediate Period*, 72–75, and James and van der Veen, *Solomon and Shishak*.
28 Kitchen, *Third Intermediate Period*, 325.
29 Kitchen, *Third Intermediate Period*, 327.
30 Aston, "Takeloth II."

is the lack of any significant amount of detailed economic evidence.[31] The records of the tribute presented by the Levantine cities and states to Assyria hints at trade with Egypt and (perhaps indirectly) Kush: ebony, ivory, elephant hides, and exotic animals are all mentioned. Some indication of the sorts of other commodities that were exported is given in the "Report of Wenamun" of the very late 20th Dynasty, whether or not the text is an actual report or a fictional account.[32] Whilst in Byblos to acquire timber, Wenamun received 500 rolls of papyrus from Nesubanebdjed and Tentamun, the rulers based in Tanis, along with vessels of gold and silver, and garments of "royal linen" (*byssos*) and "fine linen." High quality linen was an Egyptian product, and the best quality a royal monopoly, and there is evidence that it was dyed in cities such as Tyre before being made into garments which were then sent to Assyria. Papyrus production seems to have been entirely Egyptian, and the increase in the use of Aramaic probably saw an increase in its usage across Western Asia, and hence in its export. Papyrus too, varied in quality, and that made in the eastern Delta around Tanis was one of the best.

Egypt under Libyan rule continued to have a close relationship with Byblos, attested by the statue fragments of Shoshenq I, Osorkon I and Osorkon II found there. Trade presumably continued with other Phoenician cities such as Sidon, Tyre and Ashdod, although the direct evidence comes from the Kushite period: Taharka names Asiatic commodities such as timber and metal that were used in the building of the temple of Kawa during the first decade of his reign,[33] and a treaty with Esarhaddon specifically forbids Ba'alu of Tyre from engaging in trade with Egypt.[34] A letter of Sennacherib as Crown Prince to Sargon II lists contributions received by the royal palace, including elephant hides, rolls of papyrus, and garments made of *byssos*:[35] all Egyptian or Kushite products.

---

31 Moshe Elat, "The Economic Relations of the Neo-Assyrian Empire with Egypt," *JAOS* 98 (1978): 20–34; Robert G. Morkot, "North-East Africa and Trade at the Crossroads of the Nile Valley, the Mediterranean and the Red Sea," in *Dynamics of Production in the Ancient Near 1300–500 BC*, ed. Juan Carlos Moreno Garcia (Oxford and Philadelphia: Oxbow, 2016): 257–74.
32 Recent editions and discussions include Robert K. Ritner, *The Libyan Anarchy: Inscriptions from Egypt's Third Intermediate Period* (Atlanta: Society for Biblical Literature, 2009), 87–99 (no. 18) and Jean Winand, "The Report of Wenamun: A Journey in Ancient Egyptian Literature," in *Ramesside Studies in Honour of K. A. Kitchen*, ed. Mark Collier and Steven Snape (Bolton: Rutherford Press, 2009): 541–59.
33 Morkot, *Black Pharaohs*, 252–56.
34 Simo Parpola and Kazuko Watanabe, *Neo-Assyrian Treaties and Loyalty Oaths* (Helsinki: Helsinki University Press, 1988), no. 5.
35 Simo Parpola, *The Correspondence of Sargon II, Part I: Letters from Assyria and the West* (Helsinki: Helsinki University Press, 1987), no. 34.

Egyptian alabaster (calcite) vessels were another common export and have been excavated at Samaria,[36] and in the cemetery at Almuñecar in Spain.[37] Other vessels had hieroglyphic texts and cartouches added, presumably to increase their value.[38] The vessels presumably made their way from Tanis to one of the Levantine cities and thence to Spain. Scarabs carrying the names of the late-Libyan kings Pedubast, Pimay and Osorkon III, have been found at Carthage, Spain and in Italy.[39] The "Bocchoris vases" from Tarquinia (an original Egyptian product) and Lilybaeum (a non-Egyptian copy), along with other faience, give some indication of other types of manufactures exported.[40]

In the later years of the Libyan period there may have been a number of centres which were particularly involved in international trade. Tanis, both a royal residence city and situated on the sea, must have been one of these, with the names of successive 22nd Dynasty rulers, namely Shoshenq I, Osorkon I, Osorkon II, Takeloth II and Shoshenq III, occurring on items found abroad. Memphis too, remained important, as a major royal residence city and trading centre. In the western Delta, Sais may well have established early contacts with the Phoenicians. The Phoenician expansion along the North African coast would have required staging posts, and doubtless contacts would have been made with major towns nearby. Certainly the "Bocchoris vases" and scarabs suggest that Sais had contacts with the Phoenician traders.

Following Shalmaneser III (858–824 BCE), the next Assyrian ruler to be active in the west was Tiglath-pileser III (745–727 BCE). This is one of the few instances of specific contact between Egypt and Israel to be documented. The biblical episode of Hoshea's appeal to "So, king of Egypt" c. 725 BCE has been very extensively discussed and has a well-known and voluminous literature.[41] Earlier

---

36 George A. Reisner, Clarence S. Fisher and David G. Lyon, *Harvard Excavations at Samaria*, 1908–1910, vol. II (Cambridge, MA: Harvard University Press, 1924), pl. 56 (g), with name of Osorkon II.
37 Josep Padró i Parcerisa, *Egyptian-Type Documents from the Mediterranean Littoral of the Iberian Peninsula Before the Roman Conquest, vol. III: Study of the Material* (Leiden: E. J. Brill, 1985) pl. LXXVII (Takeloth II); pl. CXXVII.1 (Osorkon II).
38 Parcerisa, *Egyptian-Type Documents*, pl. CIX (Shoshenq III), pl. CXIV.1 (Osorkon II, copied from the original vessel).
39 Jean Vercoutter, *Les objets égyptiens et égyptisants du mobilier funéraire carthaginois* (Paris: Librairie orientaliste Paul Geuthner, 1945); Josep Padró i Parcerisa, *Egyptian-Type Documents from the Mediterranean Littoral of the Iberian Peninsula Before the Roman Conquest, vol. II: Study of the Material* (Leiden: Brill, 1983).
40 Glenn Markoe, *Phoenicians* (Berkeley: University of California Press, 2000), 158.
41 Kitchen, *Third Intermediate Period*, 372–75; Morkot, *Black Pharaohs*, 126–27, 310 n. 20; John Day, "The Problem of 'So, King of Egypt' in 2 Kings xvii 4," *VT* 42 (1992): 289–301.

Egyptologists, such as Flinders Petrie, identified "So" with Shabaka, arguing that he acted as a Viceroy or regent in Egypt for either Kashta or Piye of Kush. More recently, reading the name as a place, rather than person, was proposed by Donald Redford, who argued that "So" was a reference to Sau (Sais) and thus to Tefnakht.[42] Most writers prefer to understand "So" as an abbreviation for Osorkon, and usually number him 'IV,' arguing that the date of the events is far too late for an identification with Osorkon III. The ruler's identification with a specific, documented pharaoh is very largely dependent on the broader interpretations of the political geography and chronology of the period: hence there is a lack of consensus. Furthermore, in this volume, Christoph Levin raises doubts about the validity of this episode as recorded in the Book of Kings, regarding the name as an interpolation of the late Persian or Hellenistic period, and Timo Tekoniemi expands on the complexities of the traditions preserved in other sources. Clearly, without any corroborating Egyptian or Assyrian sources, the validity of the Book of Kings as a source, and hence the reality of the appeal to "So," is questionable.

Another considerable literature relates to the identification of Sargon II's opponent at the battle of Raphia in 720 BCE. "Sib'e," as the name in the Assyrian inscription was originally read, was once identified with the biblical "So, king of Egypt." Since the text clearly calls him "army leader," rather than "king," and the name has been re-read as Re'e, the Egyptian equivalent would be Raia. The question then becomes: which ruler of Egypt sent an army against the Assyrians? The logical answer would be: the leading ruler of Egypt at the time, which brings us back to the array of possible interpretations derived from chronological assumptions.

In 716 BCE, tribute was sent from Egypt to Sargon II by a king Šilkanni, acknowledged to be an "Osorkon."[43] It can only be assumed that despite Piye's suzerainty, Osorkon continued to be recognised as the most important of the Delta rulers, and hence in international terms the king of Egypt.

The other significant international event with repercussions in the Nile valley is the rebellion and flight of Yamani of Ashdod. In 712 BCE, Sargon II conquered Ashdod, expelling the "usurper" Yamani who fled as far as he could to escape the clutches of the Assyrians. A key passage in Sargon's records, as translated by A. Leo Oppenheim, states that Yamani "fled into the territory of Muṣri – which belongs (now) to Ethiopia (Meluhha) – and his (hiding) place could not

---

42 Redford, "Sais and the Kushite Invasions" and Donald B. Redford, *Egypt, Canaan, and Israel in Ancient Times* (Princeton, NJ: Princeton University Press, 1992).
43 Kitchen, *Third Intermediate Period*, 143, 376 n. 756; Morkot, *Black Pharaohs*, 128, 193 with references.

be detected."[44] Kenneth Kitchen understood this as meaning that Shabaka must have conquered Egypt "by 712 B.C. at the very latest,"[45] advocating 716 BCE for Shabaka's accession.[46]

First, it was pointed out long ago by Anthony Spalinger that the alleged *post quem* of 712 BCE for the invasion of Shabaka is based on a mistranslation by Oppenheim of the text.[47] Rather than saying that Yamani fled to Muṣri which "belongs" to Meluhha the correct reading is that he fled to Meluhha which borders on Egypt, or "to the border of Egypt which is at the territory of Meluhha."[48] The corrected translation is now generally accepted, including by Kitchen himself.[49] Hence, the Pirʻu of Muṣri to whom Yamani appealed for aid in 713/2 BCE was not a Kushite overlord of Egypt but the leading Delta dynast, possibly still Šilkanni. It follows that far from the Assyrian evidence supporting Kitchen's relatively high chronology, it would follow that 713/2 BCE *is* a firm *terminus post quem* for the conquest by Shabaka (or Shabataka, if following Bányai's revised order). The first year of Shabaka cannot have been as high as 716 BCE and hence cannot be used to calculate (by subtracting the known 14/15 years of his reign in Egypt) the accession of Shabataka to 702 BCE. There is no longer any concrete objection to a later date for the conquest of Egypt by Shabaka (or Shabataka), and hence a minimal dating for the 25th Dynasty (see above) with the latter's reign beginning even as late as 708/7 BCE.

The debates arising from the Tang-i Var inscription unnecessarily raised the dates for the Kushite invasion of Egypt by Shabaka and greatly extended the reign of Shabataka, in direct conflict with the Assyrian evidence. The proposed reversal of ordering of kings has carried some of the raised dating and extended reigns across into the new scheme. Only Claus Jurman has proposed a workable revision that adheres to the evidence. But whether it is "true" remains to be substantiated – numerous questions remain unanswered. So, despite the considerable discourse, the *actualité* of the Nile valley context to the end of the Kingdom of Israel remains essentially that argued broadly by Kitchen and other writers:

---

[44] A. Leo Oppenheim, "Babylonian and Assyrian Historical Texts," in *Ancient Near Eastern Texts Relating to the Old Testament*, ed. James B. Pritchard (Princeton NJ: Princeton University Press, 1969, 3rd edition), 285 (11–15), 286 (90–112).
[45] Kitchen, *Third Intermediate Period*, 144 (his emphasis).
[46] James *et al.*, "Centuries of Darkness (Review Feature)," 230, 235 n. 2.
[47] Spalinger, "The Year 712 BC," 97 n. 17.
[48] Alan R. Millard, as cited in Kitchen, *Third Intermediate Period*, 583.
[49] Kitchen, *Third Intermediate Period*, 583, xl: Redford, "Sais and the Kushite Invasions," 7 n. 11; Kahn, "Divided Kingdom," 279.

Kushite control of the Nile Valley into Upper Egypt; Libyan kingdoms in Middle and Lower Egypt, with numerous Libyan fiefdoms under lesser rulers.

6 The Political Geography of Late Libyan Egypt

Lengthily discussed, the principal source for the political geography of Egypt at the time of the Kushite incursion is the long narrative inscription of Piye (Piankhy) of Kush known variously as the "Victory Stela" or "Triumphal Stela."[50] Specifically concerned with the defeat of the Saite ruler Tefnakht, the text details the numerous rulers of Egypt, revealing that there were four "uraeus-wearers" – kings in the fullest pharaonic sense, along with the Libyan Great Chiefs and Chiefs of the Ma (Meshwesh) and the ruler of Sais.

The inscription is dated to New Year's Day of year 21 of the reign of Piye, and most of those who have discussed the events have assumed that they occurred in the two years immediately preceding, beginning in year 19.[51] The present writer's suggestion that the campaign should be attributed to year 4 or year 12 has not been accepted.[52] Giving an absolute date for the campaign is more difficult:[53] Kitchen, and Aston and Taylor, place the campaign in 728 BCE.[54] The recent discussions of the chronology of the 25th Dynasty have not specifically addressed the issue but generally imply a rather higher date if a long reign for Piye is accepted. Even adopting a minimal chronology for the 25th Dynasty, the evidence indicates that the Kushites controlled southern Egypt, and had vassal rulers in Middle Egypt, during the decade 730–720 BCE.

From the text of the Victory Stela we can state that the southernmost part of Egypt, centred on Thebes, was under Kushite control and that there was some sort of military presence that Piye – in Kush, at the time of Tefnakht's southward campaign – could send against the Saite army.[55] Another inscription of Piye, the "Sandstone Stela," is only partially preserved, but can be dated early in his reign, probably around year 3.[56] Altogether the evidence indicates that

---

50 Cairo JE 48862 and 47086–47089: Nicholas Grimal, *Études sur la propagande royale Égyptienne, vol. I: La stèle triomphale de Pi(ankh)y au Musée du Caire. JE 48862 et 47086–47089* (Cairo: Institut français d'Archéologie Orientale du Caire, 1981).
51 Morkot, *Black Pharaohs*, 167–68.
52 Morkot, *Black Pharaohs*, 172–74, 184, 200; Morkot and James, "Peftjauawybast," 15.
53 Morkot and James, "Peftjauawybast," 17–18.
54 Kitchen, *Third Intermediate Period*, 234; Aston and Taylor, "The Family of Takeloth III."
55 Morkot, *Black Pharaohs*, 182–85.
56 Morkot, "The Origin of the Kushite State;" id., *Black Pharaohs*, 169–74.

Piye was recognised as ruler in Thebes and Upper Egypt. His immediate predecessor is generally believed to have been Kashta and although the evidence for his reign and actions is slight, most writers have assumed that he began the process of Kushite expansion into Upper Egypt.[57] The most notable indicator of his ambition is the installation of his daughter, Amenirdis, as heiress to the priestly office of God's Wife of Amun, at Thebes. The incumbent was the Libyan princess, Shepenwepet daughter of Osorkon III. Although Kitchen argued that her brother Piye placed Amenirdis in this role, one must stress that all other God's Wives were installed by their fathers.

The northern limit of Kushite rule in Upper Egypt is not specified in any text, but somewhere between Abydos and Asyut seems likely. The early Libyan High Priest of Amun, Iuwelot, (son of Osorkon I) stated that his northern military boundary lay at the nome of Asyut.[58] Tjeny (Girga), slightly north of Abydos, was the base of Vizier in the later 25th Dynasty,[59] and the Ptolemaic administrative centre for the Thebaid, Ptolemais Hermiou, was in the same region.

The "Sandstone Stela" of Piye is important in carrying a speech of the god Amun of Thebes (*Waset*) who addresses the Kushite king as "Ruler of Egypt (*Kemet*)" and gives him the power to establish rulers, or not:[60]

> "He to whom I say 'You are a *wer*-Chief', he shall be a *wer*-Chief.
> He to whom I say 'You are not a Chief', he shall not be a *wer*-Chief.
> He to whom I say 'Make an appearance [i.e. as *nesut*-king]', he shall make an appearance.
> He to whom I say 'Do not make an appearance [as *nesut*-king],' he shall not make an appearance."

The distinction between the Chiefs (in Egyptian *wer/weru*) and those who "make appearance" as full kings is very clear, and reflected in the text of the "Victory Stela." We can see in these texts the Kushite confirmation of rulers in their positions, and perhaps deposition of opponents.[61] The later Assyrian list of Egyp-

---

57 Morkot, *Black Pharaohs*, 157–66.
58 "Stèle de l'apanage," Cairo JE 31882: Karl Jansen-Winkeln, *Inschriften der Spätzeit, Teil II: Die 22.–24. Dynastie* (Wiesbaden: Harrassowitz, 2007), 77–80 (no. 16.8); Ritner, *The Libyan Anarchy*, 271–78 (no. 69).
59 Morkot, *Black Pharaohs*, 275; Anthony Leahy "Nespamedu, 'King' of Thinis" *Göttinger Miszellen* 35 (1979), 31–39.
60 Morkot, *Black Pharaohs*, 179; Ritner *The Libyan Anarchy*, 461–64 (no. 143).
61 Morkot, "The Origin of the Kushite State," 231–32; id., *Black Pharaohs*, 179–80.

tian rulers, dating from 671 BCE[62] or, more conventionally, 667/6 BCE, indicates a similar process.

North of the Kushite-controlled Thebaid was the vassal-kingdom of Khmunu (Hermopolis) under the rule of Nimlot. This appears to be a new kingdom, and one possibly established by the Kushites. As Tefnakht and the Delta rulers advanced south, Nimlot defected, but was soon besieged by Piye's army.[63] Nimlot's identity and association with other dynasties has been the subject of discussion, but is not directly relevant to the issues here. It is possible that he was still ruler at the time of the Assyrian list which records a "Lamintu of Himunu," although most Egyptologists assume that this was a like-named grandson.[64]

North of Khmunu lay another vassal kingdom of Piye's centred on Nen-nesut (Herakleopolis), in a controlling position at the mouth of the Fayum, and in a very fertile part of Egypt. Its precise limits are not stated, but its southern border was presumably the northern border of Nimlot's kingdom. Nen-nesut controlled access to Memphis and the Delta from the south. It also included the fortresses at Teudjoi (el-Hiba) and Per-Sekhem-kheper-re that had been the seats of formidable royal representatives throughout the Libyan period. The kingdom appears to have been a new creation, although a number of Egyptologists, notably David Aston, have argued that it was the centre of the "23rd Dynasty." Piye's vassal ruler was Peftjauawybast who was related by marriage to the family of Takeloth III and Rudamun (both sons of Osorkon III). It has been generally assumed that he was a member of one of the Libyan royal families, although the suggestion of Morkot and James[65] that he could be identified with the like-named High Priest of Ptah and descendant of Osorkon II has not been widely accepted. The northern limit of Peftjauawybast's kingdom lay somewhere in the region of Medum, Lisht, and Tep-ihu.

Memphis, one of the largest and most significant cities, had been brought under his own rule by Tefnakht. The "Victory Stela" narrates Tefnakht's expanding power from his original power base in Sau (Sais) across the western Delta and southwards to Memphis.

The central and eastern Delta was controlled by Libyan chiefs of differing ranks.[66] There were also two full kings: Osorkon, who controlled Per-Bast (Bu-

---

[62] Herbert Verreth, "The Egyptian Eastern Border Region in Assyrian Sources," *JAOS* 119 (1999): 234–47.
[63] Morkot, *Black Pharaohs*, 182–83, 187–88.
[64] E.g., Anthony Leahy, "Royal Iconography and Dynastic Change, 750–725 BC: the Blue and Cap Crowns," *JEA* 78 (1992): 223–40.
[65] Morkot and James, "Peftjauawybast".
[66] Morkot, *Black Pharaohs*, 191–95.

bastis) and Iuput of Tent-remu. The identification of Iuput's centre of power is uncertain; Kitchen suggested Tell Muqdam.[67] The references to Osorkon seem to indicate that he had some considerable prestige amongst the rulers (or at least with Piye), and his seat of Per-Bast indicates he was in the line of rulers descended from Shoshenq I (conventionally termed "22nd Dynasty"). The "Victory Stela" names no separate ruler in Tanis: although the "22nd Dynasty" originated in Per-Bast, they were buried at Tanis and built extensively in the city. The rulers such as Gemenef-khonsu-bak and Pedubast, attested by monuments from Tanis, must thus be placed later than Osorkon and Piye.

Egyptological literature has been concerned with who these individual rulers were and how they relate (genealogically and geo-politically) to the scheme of dynasties derived from Manetho. There can hardly be said to be consensus: some preferring to see Osorkon III and his successors Takeloth III and Rudamun as the direct line from the 22nd Dynasty rulers Shoshenq I and Osorkon II, whilst others prefer to see them as an entirely separate "23rd Dynasty" that was based in Middle or Upper Egypt. Indeed, for some writers, the "23rd Dynasty" has become itinerant, wandering around Egypt in search of a power-base from Thebes, to Hermopolis and/or Herakleopolis (surely a reflection of the unsatisfactory nature of this particular reconstruction). Manetho's skeletal king-list has now been inflated with numerous rulers attested monumentally who have been ascribed to it for no good reason. In some chronologies there are contemporaneous "23rd" dynasties based in Tanis, Asyut, Hermopolis, Herakleopolis and Leontopolis.

The main issue is the identity of Osorkon of Per-Bast. Petrie and many Egyptologists of the late-19th and early-20th centuries identified him with Osorkon III, a well-documented pharaoh who installed his daughter, Shepenwepet I, in the significant religious office of God's Wife of Amun at Thebes. Shepenwepet I later adopted the Kushite princess, Amenirdis I, as her successor to the role, which establishes a direct link between the Libyan and Kushite dynasties. More recently, the equation with Osorkon III was abandoned, and Piye's opponent viewed as a far more obscure Osorkon 'IV.' The French team working at Tanis recovered a group of blocks carrying the name of an Osorkon with relief images in an "archaising" style.[68] Although the Prenomen, Usermaetre, is that of Osorkon III, the

---

[67] Kitchen, *Third Intermediate Period*, 129, 360–61.
[68] Robert G. Morkot, "All in the Detail: Some Further Observation on 'Archaism' and Style in Libyan-Kushite-Saite Egypt," in *Thebes in the First Millennium BC*, ed. Elena Pischikova, Julia Budka and Kenneth Griffin (Cambridge: Cambridge Scholars Publishing, 2014): 380–88; Robert G. Morkot and Peter J. James, "Dead-Reckoning the Start of the 22nd Dynasty: From Shoshenq V Back to Shoshenq I," in James and van der Veen, *Solomon and Shishak*, 20–41.

blocks have generally been attributed to Osorkon 'IV.' The identity of Osorkon does have bearing on the reference to Šilkanni.

The Kushite military action led by Piye captured Khmunu, relieved Nennesut, and stormed Memphis. Piye received the homage of all of the Libyan rulers with the exception of Tefnakht – in the Delta city of Hut-hery-ib (Athribis). The Kushite king then returned south, the *status quo ante* restored. Tefnakht took his oath of loyalty in Sais.

7 Summary and Conclusions

Irrespective of the alternative chronological and genealogical interpretations that have been proposed very recently, the broad view of Egypt at the time of Assyria's destruction of Samaria and the end of the Kingdom of Israel remains essentially the same. Summing up, these are the key points:

The Kushites controlled the Nile valley throughout Kush (modern northern Sudan) into southern Egypt. They had a power base in Thebes, with the northern limit of their control somewhere in the Abydos/Girga-Asyut region. There were vassal kingdoms north of Kushite territory in the Nile valley. Egypt was divided into five kingdoms and numerous smaller principalities.

The kingdom of Khmunu (Hermopolis) was ruled by Nimlot at the time of Piye's campaign. The kingdom of Nen-nesut (Herakleopolis) may have been a Kushite creation and no longer existed at the time of the Assyrian conquest in the 670s BCE. The Delta was divided between the principality of Sau (Sais) in the west, smaller principalities under Libyan Great Chiefs and Chiefs, and two kingdoms in the central and eastern Delta. Piye's opponent, Tefnakht, is only ever referred to by the title "Chief." A ruler with full pharaonic style called Tefnakht may be the same man, or a second Tefnakht; opinion is, unsurprisingly, divided. Bakenranef, who also had full pharaonic style, is the sole ruler attributed to Manetho's 24th Dynasty, and his defeat and death at the hands of Shabaka or Shabataka brought the whole of Egypt under Kushite rule. The location of the kingdom ruled by Iuput is less certain. In the eastern Delta, the royal line which was associated with Per-Bast in the reign of Piye appears to have come to an end. Bakenranef is attested from Tanis, and re-used monuments of other rulers have been excavated there, also documented by the Assyrian list of Egypt's rulers.

Finally, the evidence, albeit relatively limited, does indicate that there was significant trade between the Kushites, the Delta rulers of both Tanis and Sais, and the kingdoms and city states of Israel, Judah, and the Phoenician coast. It was in the interests of any Egyptian rulers to ensure that these states did not come under Assyrian domination and hence they would have become involved in the politics of the region. The capabilities and ambitions of the Kushite rulers were certainly greater than those of the Libyan pharaohs, and when they gained control of all of Egypt, their policy seems to have become more active, if not aggressive.

Part III: Views from Archaeology

Ron E. Tappy[1]
The Annals of Sargon II and the Archaeology of Samaria: Rhetorical Claims, Empirical Evidence

1 Introduction

The archaeology of Samaria and, by extension, the political history it reflects have emerged as vexing topics for those interested in the closing decade of Israelite sovereignty over this once grand capital city. Improved editions of key Assyrian texts in both hard copy and digital formats[2] and recent analyses of reliefs

---

[1] The bulk of this paper first appeared under the title "The Final Years of Israelite Samaria: Toward a Dialogue between Texts and Archaeology," in *Up to the Gates of Ekron: Essays on the Archaeology and History of the Eastern Mediterranean in Honor of Seymour Gitin*, ed. Sidnie White Crawford and Amnon Ben-Tor (Jerusalem: The W.F. Albright Institute of Archaeological Research and the Israel Exploration Society, 2007): 258–79. I am indebted to the editors and publishers of that Festschrift for granting me permission to reprint here a revised version of that article, which became the basis for my seminar presentation in Munich. Conferences such as the one organized by Shuichi Hasegawa, sponsored by the Japan Society for the Promotion of Science and held at the Schloss Nymphenburg on 15–17 March 2017, help open the way toward both solving some difficulties related to this historical period and generating new ideas and questions to consider. I am grateful to have been a participant in this stimulating event. – The following abbreviations are used in this chapter: *ANET* = James B. Pritchard, ed., *Ancient Near Eastern Texts Relating to the Old Testament* (Princeton NJ: Princeton University Press, 1955); *ARAB II* = Daniel David Luckenbill, *Ancient Records of Assyria and Babylonia*, vol. II (Chicago IL: The University of Chicago Press, 1926); *CAD* = *The Assyrian Dictionary of the Oriental Institute of the University of Chicago* (Chicago IL: University of Chicago Press, 1956–); *SS I* = John Winter Crowfoot, Kathleen Mary Kenyon and Eliezer L. Sukenik, *The Buildings at Samaria* (London: Palestine Exploration Fund, 1942); *SS III* = John Winter Crowfoot, Grace Mary Crowfoot, and Kathleen Mary Kenyon, *Samaria-Sebaste III: The Objects* (London: Palestine Exploration Fund, 1957).
[2] To printed volumes that have appeared since Albert Kirk Grayson, *Assyrian and Babylonian Chronicles* (Locust Valley NY: Augustin, 1975; repr. Winona Lake IN: Eisenbrauns, 2000), add Hayim Tadmor, *The Inscriptions of Tiglath-pileser III King of Assyria, Critical Editions, with Introductions, Translations and Commentary* (Jerusalem: Israel Academy of Sciences and Humanities, 1994); Alan R. Millard, *The Eponyms of the Assyrian Empire, 910–612 BC* (Helsinki: The Neo-Assyrian Text Corpus Project, 1994); Andreas Fuchs, *Die Inschriften Sargons II. aus Khorsabad* (Göttingen: Cuvillier Verlag: 1994); Hayim Tadmor and Shigeo Yamada, *The Royal Inscriptions of Tiglath-Pileser III (744–727 BC) and Shalmaneser V (726–722 BC), Kings of Assyria* (Winona Lake IN: Eisenbrauns, 2011). For relevant materials from the years following the fall of Samaria (Sennacherib), see Eckart Frahm, *Einleitung in die Sanherib-Inschriften* (Wien: Institut für Orientalis-

and epigraphs from the Assyrian palaces³ have supplemented a wave of renewed interest in the period spanning the years 732–720 BCE.⁴ Yet a perusal of the resultant publications reveals the absence of any consensus regarding the historical particulars that led to Samaria's decline. Moreover, uncertainties surrounding the archaeology of Samaria have compromised the success of these text-based studies in reaching firm conclusions founded on data drawn from different but mutually essential disciplines. A recent, detailed investigation into the archaeology of this site,⁵ however, now allows for a productive interdisciplinary effort to settle some of the historical and linguistic questions that remain.

One such question concerns the sequence and nature of Assyria's military activities against Samaria during the reigns of Shalmaneser V and Sargon II. What precisely does the Babylonian Chronicle (1.i.28) mean when it says of Shal-

---

tik der Universität, 1997), plus Albert Kirk Grayson and Jamie Novotny, *The Royal Inscriptions of Sennacherib, King of Assyria (704–681 BC), Part 1* (Winona Lake IN: Eisenbrauns, 2012); Albert Kirk Grayson and Jamie Novotny, *The Royal Inscriptions of Sennacherib, King of Assyria (704–681 BC), Part 2* (Winona Lake IN: Eisenbrauns, 2014). For excellent digital resources, see the tools now available in the Royal Inscriptions of the Neo-Assyrian Period (*RINAP*) Online (http://oracc.museum.upenn.edu/rinap/index.html) and other references cited in the "at-a-glance" glossaries for the corpora of Tiglath-pileser III, Esarhaddon and Assurbanipal presented in Jamie Novotny, "The Royal Inscriptions of Tiglath-Pileser III and Shalmaneser V: An At-a-Glance Glossary of the RINAP 1 Corpus," *SAAB* 19 (2011–12): 1–27; id., "The Royal Inscriptions of Esarhaddon: An At-a-Glance Glossary of the RINAP 4 Corpus," *SAAB* 19 (2011–12): 29–86; id., "The Royal Inscriptions of Sennacherib: An At-a-Glance Glossary of the RINAP 3 Corpus," *SAAB* 20 (2013–14): 79–129.

3 See, e.g., Pauline Albenda, *The Palace of Sargon, King of Assyria: Monumental Wall Reliefs at Dur-Sharrukin, from Original Drawings Made at the Time of their Discovery in 1843–1844 by Botta and Flandin* (Paris: Recherche sur les Civilisations, 1986); Christopher B. F. Walker, "The Epigraphs," in Pauline Albenda, *The Palace of Sargon, King of Assyria*, 107–14; Ruth Jacoby, "The Representation and Identification of Cities on Assyrian Reliefs," *IEJ* 41 (1991): 112–31; Norma Franklin, "The Room V Reliefs at Dur-Sharrukin and Sargon II's Western Campaigns," *TA* 21 (1994): 255–75.

4 After the groundbreaking article by Hayim Tadmor, "The Campaigns of Sargon II of Assur," *JCS* 12 (1958): 33–40, the principal studies include Nadav Na'aman, "The Historical Background to the Conquest of Samaria (720 BC)," *Bib* 71 (1990): 206–25; John H. Hayes and Jeffrey K. Kuan, "The Final Years of Samaria (730–720 BC)," *Bib* 72 (1991): 153–81; Bob Becking, *The Fall of Samaria: An Historical and Archaeological Summary* (Leiden: Brill, 1992); Gershon Galil, "The Last Years of the Kingdom of Israel and the Fall of Samaria," *CBQ* 57 (1995): 52–65; Gershon Galil, *The Chronology of the Kings of Israel and Judah* (Leiden: Brill: 1996); Kyle Lawson Younger Jr., "The Fall of Samaria in Light of Recent Research," *CBQ* 61 (1999): 461–82; M. Christine Tetley, "The Date of Samaria's Fall as a Reason for Rejecting the Hypothesis of Two Conquests," *CBQ* 64 (2002): 59–77 (see also n. 19 below).

5 Ron E. Tappy, *The Archaeology of Israelite Samaria, Vol. II: The Eighth Century BCE* (Winona Lake IN: Eisenbrauns, 2001).

maneser, ᵁᴿᵁŠa-ma-ra-ʾ-in iḫ-te-pi, "he broke (the city of) Samaria"? Or what did the scribes of Sargon intend when they chose the verbs lamû ("to surround, hem in, or besiege"),⁶ s/šapānu ("to devastate, flatten or level [as if by flood]"),⁷ kašādu ("to conquer"),⁸ râbu ("to shake, make tremble"),⁹ or šalālu ("to carry off, plunder [people or property]")¹⁰ to describe his activities against this city? Nimrud Prism iv 25–41,¹¹ which delineates more different types of actions against Samaria than any other single text, records that Sargon fought against the city (maḫāṣu); reckoned (or perhaps "delivered") its people, property, and gods as spoil (manû); formed or organized a chariot corp with Israelite charioteers and equipment (kaṣāru); resettled or reorganized Israelite deportees in the Assyrian homeland (ṣabātu); increased the population of the city (târu/atāru ... ù-še-me/ù-še-šib = šemû/[w]ašābu)¹² by bringing in (erēbu) peoples conquered elsewhere by his own hands (kišitti ŠU^II-ia); appointed his own governor over the reorganized city (šakānu); and counted all the affected individuals as citizens

---

6 The Great Summary Inscription (or *Die Große Prunkinschrift*) — Fuchs, *Die Inschriften Sargons II.*, 197, l. 23 (trans. ARAB II, § 55; Becking, *The Fall of Samaria*, 26).
7 The Bull Inscription (or *Die Inschrift auf den Stierkolossen*) — Fuchs, *Die Inschriften Sargons II.*, 63, l. 21 (trans. ARAB II, § 92; Becking, *The Fall of Samaria*, 33 = "to usurp").
8 The Great Summary Inscription — Fuchs, *Die Inschriften Sargons II.*, 197, l. 23 (trans. ARAB II, § 2; Becking, *The Fall of Samaria*, 26); the Palace Doors Inscription IV (or *Schwelleninschrift*, No. 4) — Fuchs, *Die Inschriften Sargons II.*, 261, ll. 31–32 (trans. ARAB II, § 99; Becking, *The Fall of Samaria*, 27); the Annals — Fuchs, *Die Inschriften Sargons II.*, 87–89, l. 14 (trans. ARAB II, § 4; ANET, 284; Becking, *The Fall of Samaria*, 37). Note also the use of kašādu in the Cylinder Inscription (or *Die Inschrift auf den Tonzylindern*, l. 20) as a generic reference to the conquest of various peoples (the Tamudi, Ibadidi, Marsimani, and Hayapâ) whom Sargon resettled in the region of Samaria.
9 The Cylinder Inscription — Fuchs, *Die Inschriften Sargons II.*, 34, l. 19 (trans. ARAB II, § 118; Becking, *The Fall of Samaria*, 32 = "to subjugate"); for similar content in the Annals, compare Fuchs, *Die Inschriften Sargons II.*, 110, ll. 120–23; trans. ARAB II, § 17).
10 The Small Summary Inscription (or *Die Kleine Prunkinschrift*) — Fuchs, *Die Inschriften Sargons II.*, 76, l. 15 (trans. ARAB II, § 80; ANET, 285; Becking, *The Fall of Samaria*, 27–28 = "to plunder"); the Annals — Fuchs, *Die Inschriften Sargons II.*, 87–9, l. 15 (trans. ARAB II, § 4; ANET, 284; Becking, *The Fall of Samaria*, 37 = "to plunder").
11 The Nimrud Prism, D (= ND 2601+3401+3417) and E (= ND 3400+3402+3408+3409) — Cyril John Gadd, "Inscribed Prisms of Sargon II from Nimrud," *Iraq* 16 (1954): 179–80, col. iv, ll. 37–39 (trans. Becking, *The Fall of Samaria*, 28–30; compare the Annals in Fuchs, *Die Inschriften Sargons II.*, 88, l. 16).
12 For a discussion of which pair of verbs best fits the context, see Stephanie Dalley, "Foreign Chariotry and Cavalry in the Armies of Tiglath-pileser III and Sargon II," *Iraq* 47 (1985): 36. Dalley chooses the latter readings.

of Assyria (*manû*).¹³ But do any of these terms imply a physical destruction of the capital's infrastructure, as most scholars have traditionally presumed? To reach a credible answer to these inquiries, one must assess the textual evidence against a backdrop provided by the actual archaeological record, and vice-versa. No study to date has pursued this symbiotic strategy as its principal method.

This investigation, then, evaluates the compatibility of the textual and archaeological evidence by proceeding on two distinct but related levels. First, it draws from the rich and varied language of conquest attested in eight major texts (especially the annalistic records) of Sargon II to describe his military tactics and feats against a host of cities and towns. A survey of semantic roots used by Assyrian scribes allows a fresh evaluation of the terminology relating specifically to Samaria, for which the catalogue of terms seems noticeably conservative in scope compared to the claims relating to other capital cities. Following an exploration of Sargon's battle rhetoric, the study examines several key but representative stratigraphic contexts in the archaeological record from Samaria. The result shows an appreciable degree of harmony between descriptions in the Assyrian texts and the depositional history of the site itself, a fact that enhances our understanding of the city's final days.

Such an enquiry uncovers perhaps a certain paradox between the two principal disciplines involved (broadly defined as textual studies and archaeology). At least when it comes to the late history of Israelite Samaria, it seems that textual scholars often approach the pertinent biblical passages, disassemble them into their smallest discernible parts, evaluate the sources behind and historical credibility of each part, and more often than not ultimately deem the received text with which they started a mere contrivance, a compilation so riddled with historiographic pitfalls that it can tell us little to nothing about what actually happened as the Israelite capital slowly collapsed. Archaeologists, on the other hand, suffer from the opposite hermeneutical hardship. They seldom begin with a body of evidence that even purports to represent a complete, logical, understandable, accurate entity. Consequently, they struggle with myriad bits of raw data that require detailed analysis and systemization as a first step toward deriving any credible interpretation. Rather than commencing with a whole though perhaps heavily redacted entity (such as a final text) that, over the course of close inspection, often breaks down into discordant parts, archaeologists who retrieve and

---

13 For other references to Samaria or the House (Dynasty) of Omri by Sargon II, see (a) the **Aššur Charter** — Henry W. F. Saggs, "Historical Texts and Fragments of Sargon II of Assyria: I. The 'Aššur Charter'," *Iraq* 37 (1975): 11–20, l. 20 (trans. *ARAB II*, § 133–35; Becking, *The Fall of Samaria*, 34–35) and (b) the **Annals** — Fuchs, *Die Inschriften Sargons II.*, 87–89, ll. 11, 25 (trans. *ARAB II*, § 4; *ANET*, 284; Becking, *The Fall of Samaria*, 37).

study material culture typically begin by facing a debris field of fragmentary data from which they must reconstruct, or at least extrapolate, coherent patterns that lend themselves to further, comparative analysis. In short, it has been my observation that higher critical biblical scholars tend to be splitters, while archaeologists — commonly and in one sense correctly charged with engaging in a "destructive science" — labor to be joiners; the methodologies range from intentional deconstruction on the one side to attempted reconstruction on the other. But certainly the interpretative challenges are legion on both sides. Neither texts (whether biblical or cuneiform) nor artifacts are above or beyond interpretation, a fact that will raise pertinent questions throughout each of the two-staged discussion that follows.

2 The Fall of Samaria and the Fallout from Scholarship

The official excavation reports on the work of the Joint Expedition in 1932–1934 and the British Expedition in 1935 typically exhibit a great deal of certainty regarding the chronology of nearly all phases of occupation at Samaria. Within this context of confidence, the two dates most highly touted as fixed beyond any reasonable doubt consist in the *terminus post quem* of Kenyon's "Period I" and the *terminus ante quem* of "Period V." According to the report, the destruction of the so-called Period V House and the contents of the associated Pit *i* stem directly from the assault against the city by the Assyrians around 720 BCE.[14] In both the official report and a subsequent popular account of Samaria's history, Kenyon referred to the "extensive destruction" of the site by Sargon II[15] and asserted that the archaeological record provided eloquent testimony to "the complete destruction of the capital city."[16]

Judging from the archaeological reporting by the excavators themselves, then, one might logically expect to find a single, substantial destruction level at Samaria, with the pottery-bearing loci situated in clearly datable and primary stratigraphic contexts.[17] Archaeologists working at sites in Syria-Palestine and

---

14 *SS I*, 107–108.
15 *SS III*, 199.
16 Kathleen Mary Kenyon, *Royal Cities of the Old Testament* (New York: Schocken, 1971), 133.
17 The excavation director, however, recognized the compromised nature of many of these deposits. For example, see Tappy, *The Archaeology of Israelite Samaria*, II, 175–76, for a discussion of the differing assessments by Crowfoot and Kenyon of the levels assigned to Period V. For an-

the Aegean world responded with uncritical approval both to Kenyon's historical evaluation of Period V and to her suggested terminal date for its depositional history.[18] It is essential, then, to determine whether a coherent destruction level exists somewhere in Periods V – VII at Samaria that might correlate to an Assyrian assault during the closing decade of Israelite sovereignty there.

Unlike the certainty of interpretations based on the archaeological reports, biblical and cuneiform studies have failed to produce clear or consistent results with regard to Assyria's actions at Samaria. Among other limitations, no consensus has emerged regarding even the number, let alone the character, of Assyrian military campaigns against the Israelite capital. Rather than seeing a single, major conflagration at Samaria, as did the excavators, literary analysts vary widely in the number of physical assaults against the city they purport to read in the Assyrian records.

A series of studies in the 1990s[19] took issue with Hayim Tadmor's article[20] in which he rejected earlier views holding that the section of the Babylonian Chronicle relating to Shalmaneser V referred not to Samaria but to some other city,[21] or that Shalmaneser alone conquered Samaria and exiled the Israelites,[22] or that Shalmaneser simply began the siege of Samaria in 724 while Sargon fin-

---

other example of interpretative tension in the written comments of the excavators, see Tappy, *The Archaeology of Israelite Samaria*, II, 491– 92 regarding the so-called Ivory House/Palace of King Ahab.

18 One analyst even declared that Period V represented one of three occupational phases at Samaria to which "*absolute dates* may be assigned" (John S. Holladay, *Ninth and Eighth Century Pottery from Northern Palestine* [unpublished Th.D. diss. Harvard University, Cambridge MA, 1966], 60, emphasis added). Holladay included Period III (1966, 60 – 65), Period V (1966, 65 – 77), and the deposit in Pit *i* (1966, 67 – 79) in his catalogue of precisely datable pottery periods at Samaria. Contrast, however, his subsequent comments on pp. 65 and 131.

19 Cited in n. 4 above. As a prelude to these articles, see Antti Laato, "New Viewpoints on the Chronology of the Kings of Judah and Israel," *ZAW* 98 (1986): 210 – 21, and Jeremy Hughes, *Secrets of the Times: Myths and History in Biblical Chronology* (Sheffield: Sheffield Academic Press, 1990).

20 Tadmor, "The Campaigns of Sargon II of Assur."

21 Hugo Winckler, "Nachtrag," *ZA* 2 (1887): 351– 52.

22 Albert T. Olmstead, "The Fall of Samaria," *AJSL* 21 (1904/05): 179 – 82; also, more recently, William W. Hallo, "From Qarqar to Carchemish: Assyria and Israel in the Light of New Discoveries," *BA* 23 (1960): 34 – 61; Alfred Jepsen, "Noch einmal zur israelitisch-jüdischen Chronologie," *VT* 18 (1968): 31 – 46; Julian Reade, "Mesopotamian Guidelines for Biblical Chronology," *SMS* 4 (1981): 1 – 9; Edwin R. Thiele, *The Mysterious Numbers of the Hebrew Kings* (Grand Rapids MI: Kregel, 1994; rev. edition); Hughes, *Secrets of the Times*.

ished it in the *first* year of his rule (722/21).²³ Instead, Tadmor formulated the "Two-Conquest Hypothesis," which held that Shalmaneser besieged the city in 723–722 but that Sargon ultimately "conquered" it in his first western campaign in 720 BCE (rather than in his accession year).

More recent investigations have offered various alternative proposals drawn solely from each reader's own understanding of the biblical and cuneiform texts. A thorough critique of the multifarious arguments of each study is unnecessary here, since concise summaries of recent scholarship are available.²⁴ In his survey, Gershon Galil presents the various studies in order of their appearance, while Kyle Lawson Younger Jr. groups the studies according to interpretive similarities. Here I need only note that Nadav Na'aman[25] argues for at least three Assyrian assaults against Samaria (with minimal physical damage to the city) during the penultimate decade of the eighth century BCE.[26] Hayes and Kuan, on the other hand, believe that Samaria submitted to Assyrian pressure (as a result of stated or implied military operations) on no fewer than four occasions during the 720s.[27] In two separate publications, Galil[28] suggested that Samaria remained loyal to Assyria until 723 BCE, when Shalmaneser V invaded the northern kingdom, conquered its outlying cities, and arrested Hoshea (Babylonian Chronicle; 2Kgs 17:5). The city's ministers and officers ran the government for the next two and a half years without appointing a new king. With a limited Assyrian force deployed at Samaria, the broad-scale siege became a blockade of the capital city that resembled the unfolding of events at Tyre. This uneasy situation continued until 720 BCE, when Sargon II finally conquered the city and initiated a resettlement of foreign populations there.[29]

---

23 Julius Lewy, *Die Chronologie der Könige von Israel und Juda* (Giessen: Töpelmann, 1927); Sigmund Mowinckel, "Die Chronologie der israelitischen und jüdischen Könige," *AcOr* 10 (1932): 161–277; William Foxwell Albright, "The Chronology of the Divided Monarchy of Israel," *BASOR* 100 (1945): 16–22; more recently, Knud Tage Andersen, "Noch einmal: Die Chronologie der Könige von Israel und Juda," *SJOT* 3 (1989): 1–45.
24 Galil, "The Last Years"; Younger, "The Fall of Samaria."
25 Na'aman, "The Historical Background to the Conquest of Samaria."
26 Believing that the evidence shows only a partial destruction of Samaria, Galil, "The Last Years of the Kingdom of Israel," 59, countered this position by noting, "it is difficult to imagine that Samaria escaped total destruction, despite the fact that three campaigns [would] have been directed against it in a period of less than eight years."
27 Hayes and Kuan, "The Final Years of Samaria."
28 Galil, "The Last Years;" Galil, *The Chronology of the Kings of Israel and Judah*.
29 In my judgment, it seems possible that Shalmaneser V had earlier employed the tactical strategy of a city-wide blockade at Samaria. Although 2Kgs 17:1–6 appears heavily redacted and therefore quite compromised in its ability to shed clear light onto history, the final recension of the text (*even if composite in nature*) might actually preserve some memory of a series of un-

Younger also sees two military campaigns against Samaria, with the first occurring in 722 BCE (during Hoshea's ninth year) under Shalmaneser V (2Kgs 17:6; 18:10) and the second coming after Sargon's defeat of the anti-Assyrian coalition at Qarqar in 720 BCE. Following this victory, Sargon moved very rapidly and briefly against Samaria before proceeding to sites farther south (e. g., Raphia). While Na'aman wondered how Samaria, if so weakened under its prolonged siege and capture by Shalmaneser V, could face Sargon's army already in 720 with any respectable fighting force or resistance, Younger argued the case from the opposite direction. For him, the physical and political spoliation of Samaria late in the reign of Shalmaneser V becomes not the historical problem but the historical reason why Sargon's raid could proceed with such swiftness and decisiveness and allow him to move southward so soon after his foray through the Ephraimite hill country.[30]

Focusing attention more on the regnal chronologies of Hoshea and Hezekiah than on the Assyrian texts, Tetley infers at least two major campaigns against Samaria by Tiglath-pileser III already in 733–32[31] and 727 (2Kgs 16:6). According to Tetley, the latter year marks the accession of Hoshea to the Israelite throne. While Shalmaneser V again "ravaged" Samaria around 723 BCE, the protracted three-

---

happy encounters between this Assyrian king and the king and people of Samaria. If so, the deteriorating relationship appears to have unfolded in at least three stages. First, Samaria was brought under vassal status and charged with tribute duties (וַיְהִי־לוֹ הוֹשֵׁעַ עֶבֶד וַיָּשֶׁב לוֹ מִנְחָה, v. 3). Later, after a breach in payments, the city was quarantined ("enclosed") and its king imprisoned. (Note the alliterative עצר... אסר, v. 4; cf. Akkadian *esēru*, which Sennacherib used in relation to Jerusalem.) As in the previous verse, these two terms do not constitute a simple redundancy; rather, they may once again allude to a two-tiered development. More than connoting just the arrest and incarceration of Hoshea, the two actions could signal the initial "restraining, hindering, or shutting up (as in 'hemming in')" of the scope of Hoshea's territorial rule followed by his own house arrest. These developments constitute the tipping point not only in the passage as it now stands but also in the sustainability of Samaria as capital. A blockade of the still unfallen *city* would allow the Assyrians a free hand throughout the *region* of Samaria (בְּכָל־הָאָרֶץ, v. 5). During this period, the capital itself lay under constant guard with its king imprisoned. At this point, Shalmaneser might easily have employed the metaphor used later by Sennacherib, for Hoshea was indeed penned up "like a bird in a cage." Finally, in the third strategic state and undoubtedly after significant damage to infrastructure across the kingdom, Shalmaneser V completed the conquest of Samaria (לכד ~ *ḫepû*) and initiated his deportation of its citizens (גלה, v. 6).

30 Samaria's weakened state may also argue for its relatively minor role in the Qarqar coalition, a fact reflected in its last-place listing in all the Assyrian sources and possibly also in the depictions on the palace reliefs (see Franklin, "The Room V Reliefs at Dur-Sharrukin," 255–75).
31 Cf. Assyrian Eponym Chronicles, edited by Millard, *The Eponyms of the Assyrian Empire*; 2Kgs 15:29.

year siege did not occur until 721 to 719/18 BCE, during Sargon's rule. This proposal, therefore, rejects Tadmor's double-conquest theory but devises a similar scenario for Tiglath-pileser III, with additional military efforts orchestrated by Shalmaneser V and Sargon II. Yet the thesis depends on two questionable actions: (1) retaining the old *Di-* reading at the beginning of the place name in the *AEC* entry for 728 BCE, and (2) restoring the missing place name in the *AEC* entry for 727 with "to Damascus." Neither premise is convincing.[32]

In sum, these and other studies generally agree that Samaria faced a series of attacks by more than one Assyrian leader and that the city's trouble culminated in a final major assault led by Sargon II in 720 BCE. All investigators seem to accept that both Shalmaneser V and Sargon II participated in the ultimate decline of the city; yet they rearrange and/or redate specific episodes within the conquest sequence and often see an increased number of military confrontations early in the 720s. All the studies tend to accept one crucial fact: however many times the Assyrians approached the capital at Samaria, the imperial army *physically destroyed* the city at some point (if not multiple times). From this burgeoning corpus of literary studies, then, one might expect to find one or more destruction levels in the archaeology of Samaria, while the official excavation report espoused a single, wholesale debris layer from this period. Most of these textual studies, however, fail to distinguish between literary references to Samaria the city and notices of Samaria the region. Similarly, none addresses directly and systematically the different Akkadian terms used to describe the military actions of the Assyrian kings.

---

32 Tetley must still accept Smith's old reading of *Di-* over Millard's new reading $^{al}Ḫi$- as the beginning of the place name in the entry for the year 728: George Smith, "On a New Fragment of the Assyrian Canon Belonging to the Reigns of Tiglath-pileser and Shalmaneser," *Transactions of the Society of Biblical Archaeology* 2 (1873): 321–22; Millard, *The Eponyms of the Assyrian Empire*, 59. Tetley's claim that the entry must "remain uncertain" since it is "partly illegible" (Tetley, "The Date of Samaria's Fall," 67) is misleading. Millard's transliteration is, in fact, derived not from a reconstructed text but from a witness in which the determinative and first letter of the place name are clear (Millard, *The Eponyms of the Assyrian Empire*, 45). Thus the reading seems more secure than Tetley allows, and it poses a serious obstacle to her confident rejection of the current understanding of Tiglath-pileser's activities in the west.

3 The Language of Conquest in the Annals of Sargon II

Drawing from the *Annals* of Sargon II, I have assembled a study sample of 327 literary references (mostly verbs) to represent the language of conquest chosen by this king to describe his military tactics and feats against a host of cities and towns.[33] Working with this broad dataset helps to place the description of events at Samaria in a much wider literary (if not historical) context. Whereas only one verb (*ḫepû*) occurs in Mesopotamian sources in conjunction with Shalmaneser V's actions against Samaria, Sargon II's scribes used thirteen different semantic roots spread over eight major texts to portray his relations with this city.[34] On at least two occasions in the *Annals* (ll. 209, 391a) Sargon himself employs the term *ḫepû*, but never in connection to his maneuvers at Samaria. The sample also shows that Sargon varied his terminology relating to the Israelite capital. Of the thirteen verbal roots, he used only three more than once, and only one of the three occurred multiple times. (*šalālu* appears twice, as does *manû*; *kašādu*, however, appears five times.) The principal concept that sets forth Sargon's activities at Samaria, then, centers on the term *kašādu*.

The nuanced meanings of this term illustrate an important hermeneutical principal that will apply to virtually all the Assyrian verbs cited in this study. As seen in the glossaries published by Novotny,[35] *kašādu* can mean "to conquer, to arrive" (in the texts of Tiglath-pileser III and Shalmaneser V), "to arrive, reach, capture, conquer, catch up with" (Sennacherib), or "to arrive, reach, conquer, achieve" (Esarhaddon). Modern translations of battlefield texts from the Neo-Assyrian kings consistently render *kašādu* as simply "to conquer," and that definition proves an adequate one for the present investigation. But nothing in the greater semantic range of *kašādu* inherently implies a physical destruction of a targeted city. Thus while I will often provide a basic definition (and, as needed, alternative translations) for Assyrian words as they appear in the following section, a full lexical study of those terms would not alter to any appreciable degree the argument of each section or the overall thesis as outlined above and devel-

---

33 The sample is based on the transliteration in Fuchs, *Die Inschriften Sargons II.*, 86–181, ll. 1–424 (cf. *ARAB II*, §§ 4–47), and all references follow his lineation. Fuchs collated his numbering system with those of both Hugo Winckler, *Die Keilschrifttexte Sargons nach den Papierabklatschen und Originalen neu herausgegeben*, *I–II* (Leipzig: Pfeiffer, 1889), and Arthur G. Lie, *The Inscriptions of Sargon II, King of Assyria. Part I: The Annals* (Paris: Geuthner, 1929).
34 See above, Introduction.
35 For references see above, n. 2.

oped throughout the paper. One could say that Sargon either "arrived at" or "conquered" Samaria without substantially altering my discussion. Rather than the variant meanings of individual verbs, then, the fact that virtually all the Neo-Assyrian kings used this same catalogue of terms and the idioms in which they were embedded raises a more vital hermeneutical concern: if the bulk of these expressions reflects merely propagandistic rhetoric that was in current standard usage throughout the duration of the Neo-Assyrian empire, what credible history can we draw from them? It is well known that historiographic issues plague the cuneiform sources as well as the biblical records.[36] The purpose of this paper, therefore, aims to examine the ways in which the Assyrian kings (Sargon in particular) chose *to present themselves* in the literary records they commissioned, and then to evaluate the historical veracity of those self-depictions against the physical remains from Samaria.

I have divided the Assyrian terms in my overall study sample into five broad categories. In categories 2 and 3, the discussion includes various sub-categories.

Category 1

The first set of terms describes Sargon's preparation for and procession to battle, the start of siege operations, and various symbolic actions (such as the offering of sacrifices) conducted at the successful completion of an operation. The actions extend from basic maneuvers to the more serious outset of a siege. As perhaps expected, the verbs *alāku* ("to go"; Gtn "to march") and *šapāru* ("to dispatch [an army]") appear most often in this list, but still not frequently (7× *alāku*; 4× *šapāru*). The term *lemû* ("to besiege") also denotes the beginning of a siege, and Sargon applied this concept to Samaria in the Great Summary Inscription. Interestingly, the kings whose reigns sandwiched that of Sargon — from Tiglath-pileser III to Esarhaddon — apparently did not use this term to signal the start of an assault. On two separate occasions relating to his preparations against Marduk-apla-iddina (Merodach-baladan) of Babylon (ll. 264, 329), Sargon says *akṣura ušmanni*, "I set (constructed) my camp in order."[37] In Nimrud

---

[36] See especially the works of Tadmor cited above; also Hayim Tadmor, "Observations on Assyrian Historiography," in *Essays on the Ancient Near East in Memory of Jacob Joel Finkelstein*, ed. Maria de Jong Ellis (Hamden CT: Archon Books, 1977): 209–13.

[37] Adam Zertal, "The Heart of the Monarchy: Patterns of Settlement and Historical Considerations of the Israelite Kingdom of Samaria," in *Studies in the Archaeology of the Iron Age in Israel and Jordan*, ed. Amihai Mazar (Sheffield: Sheffield Academic Press, 2001): 38–64, esp. 57–58, proposed the identification of an Assyrian military camp at the site of el-Qa'adeh, located

Prism IV: 34, the same verb (*kaṣāru*) describes Sargon's integration ("gathering" or "organizing") of 200 conscripted Israelite chariots, or perhaps charioteers, into his royal force. A number of other words occur in this category, but usually no more than one or two times each.

Category 2

The second class of terms includes generic references to various levels of the defeat and/or subjugation of a city, though the physical destruction of property is generally not mentioned in the same context. I have grouped these words under five sub-headings.

Sub-category 2.1

Some terms represent general references to the political collapse of cities or lands. The verb *kašādu* ("to conquer") or various expressions based on the derivative *kišittu* (e. g., *kišitti qātī[šu]-ia / Aššur / PN*, "the conquest of my own hands / of Aššur / of a specified place name") clearly constitute the most widely used concept within this group. Such instances occur at least 38 times in the study sample. A parallel phrase, *ina qātī uṣabbit*, "I captured/seized [the cavalry of Ursâ the Urartean] with my own hand") also appears (l. 134). The *Annals* employ two verbs, *šakānu* (ll. 326, 385) and *maḫāṣu* (l. 290), in idiomatic usage with *dabdû* to denote a general defeat or, more specifically, the bloody massacre of an army in pitched battle. The implication seems clear: the enemy was fought, hit, beaten, and the defeat (*dabdû*) was established/put in place. But again, neither term refers unequivocally to the demolition of urban architecture. Sargon also sometimes referred metaphorically to his victories through such images as "I enveloped or overwhelmed" (*saḫāpu*) like a storm (ll. 69, 296), with a net (ll. 86, 421), or with the splendor of Aššur (l. 165). On one occasion, the scribes used *kamû* with the phrase *kīma tibūt aribî* ("I captured/overwhelmed like a swarm of locusts" — with *aribî* ["locusts"] stemming from *erbu*), as a trenchant synonym for both *kašādu* and *saḫāpu*, a situation that extends Sargon's actions

---

only 10 km northeast of Samaria, and his suggestion that the camp served to support the siege of Samaria in 722 BCE remains somewhat tentative, since the majority of pottery from the site apparently dates to the late Iron Age and Persian periods.

to the defeat/killing (*dâku*) of citizens and the physical destruction of their capital by fire (*šarāpu*, "to burn"; ll. 86–87; see below, category no. 5).

Sub-category 2.2

At least two verbs relate directly to the deposition or subjugation of local leaders (*nakāru*, "to change," and *kanāšu*, "to make [someone] bow down"; ll. 244 and 391, respectively).

Sub-category 2.3

Various phrases describe psychological tactics employed by the Assyrians, some of which prompted self-destructive acts by enemy forces or towns. In such instances gloom[38] is cast (*nadû*, l. 190) and tortures are established (*šakānu*, ll. 163, 306) as great mourning grips the entire land (*bašû*, l. 162). Hapless subjects must seize the hand or feet of Sargon (*ṣabātu*, ll. 272d, 284, 286b, 294, 300) or even kiss his feet (*nasāqu*, l. 287). They may suffer having their own hands burned (*qamû*, l. 238) or pierced (*paṭāru*, l. 347; cf. "to incise"), exposure to public gaze (*kullumu*, "to show or reveal", l. 238), or parching thirst (*ṣabātu*, now with *laplaptu*, ll. 283–84). In extreme cases panic so "falls upon/overwhelms" the leaders or people that they can no longer coherently identify even the cause of their fear (*maqātu*, l. 307), and they may begin to lay waste to their own property (*ēdurūma ušaḫribu* < *ḫarābu*, l. 293), attempt to hide themselves by "crawling" to the farthest corners of distant mountains (*raqātu*, l. 303), or even end ("finish") their own life, as did Ursâ of Urarṭu (*napišta*[*zi*]-*šu iq-ti* < *qatû*, l. 165).

Sub-category 2.4

Certain terms connote the results of economic hardships imposed by Sargon on specific cities, such as his allowing the Assryian army to eat (*akālu*, l. 289) or cut down (*kašāṭu*, ll. 290, 358) local orchards, to cut the date palms (*nakāsu*, l. 358),[39]

---

38 *ARAB II*, § 23; the Akkadian term *akukūtu* is "a poetic synonym for fire," though it can also denote a rare and ominous red glow in the sky; see *CAD* A1 285a.
39 The *Annals* apply this same term to people in l. 349. In the Gtn Stem, *nakāsu* means "to breach repeatedly."

and to enclose (that is, blockade) the capital city (*esēru*, l. 357)[40] as the devastation occurs in the outlying kingdom[41] (see below).

Sub-category 2.5

The final subset of words in this group denotes the killing of people or enemy troops, though again these terms typically appear without further reference to the physical destruction of the towns inhabited by these individuals. The two most common verbs in this class include *dâku* ("to defeat, kill," ll. 87, 131, 134, 387a) and *maqātu* (Š = "to cut down", ll. 122,[42] 168, 376), both of which basically mean "to kill."[43] Less frequently the scribes used stronger terms, such as *napāṣu* ("to massacre, slaughter", l. 344), *šaqāru* ("to decimate", l. 346; D = "to pierce"[44]); *nakāsu* ("to cut down/off," in the sense of "to slaughter," l. 349), or *salāḫu* ("to sprinkle or bespatter with the venom of death," l. 350[45]), concepts which they set against the rare occurrence of *bulluṭu* (< *balāṭu*, "to spare [someone's life]," l. 387b).

Category 3

The third group of conquest terminology describes the reorganization of subjugated areas and, like the previous group, incorporates a number of sub-areas.

---

[40] The term *ṣabātu* may also appear in reference to the blockading or sealing of borders, as in the case of Muški and Urarṭu (Fuchs, *Die Inschriften Sargons II.*, 128, l. 219; ARAB II, § 27).
[41] In certain instances, such as Tiglath-pileser III at Damascus in 733 BCE and Sennacherib at the gates of Jerusalem in 701, Assyrian leaders may have appealed to their blockade of a city "as a face-saving device to cover for a failure to take the enemy's capital and punish the rebellious king" (Tadmor, *The Inscriptions of Tiglath-pileser III*, 79, n. 11').
[42] This passage claims that, after the slaughter, Sargon deported the surviving remnant and re-settled them in Samaria (see Fuchs, *Die Inschriften Sargons II.*, 320).
[43] Compare also *nêru* in l. 320. Both *nêru* and *dâku* sometimes appear in conjunction with *kašādu*.
[44] Sargon claims to have pierced the hand of an enemy with an arrow just as the enemy managed to slip away "like a mongoose through the gate of his city" (Fuchs, *Die Inschriften Sargons II.*, 334).
[45] See CAD I 139–40 for a discussion of *imat mūti*, "poisonous foam [or] slaver produced from the mouths of angry gods, demons, humans, and animals."

Sub-category 3.1

To recognize the installation of a new ruler (either a local citizen or an Assyrian official) on a recently subdued throne, Sargon most often employed the basic verb *šakānu*, "to put, place, set" or "to establish, deposit" (ll. 204, 340, 245, 254, 276, 386b, 409). He also *caused* someone to rise to a throne (Š-stem of [w]*ašābu*, "to make occupy"), assigned a specific person to rule over an area ([w]*âru*; D = "to commission," l. 386b), or commanded (lit. "spoke") a new ruler into power (*qabû*, ll. 183, 409).

Sub-category 3.2

In addition to sparing the deportation or even the life of a subordinate (see *balāṭu* above; also l. 272a), Sargon sometimes presented other incentives to local rulers by offering them cities (*šarāku* <in broken context> and *nadānu*, l. 198), increasing the area under their control (*rabû*; l. 198), and forgiving or disregarding their misdeeds (*mêšu*, l. 272e). Following Sargon, Sennacherib certainly employed the first two strategies by transferring cities and towns captured in the Shephelah of Judah to the control of Philistine kings at Ashdod, Ekron, and Gaza.[46]

Sub-category 3.3

When recording local cities that Sargon considered to be Assyrian property or the occupants of those cities, whom he reckoned as actual Assyrians, the *Annals* typically resort to the common notion of "counting" (*manû*; 14 occurrences in the study sample). To facilitate this status, Sargon regularly gathered people together under a ruler (*paḫāru*, l. 197), "led them away" to bring them within the Assyrian border (*abāku*, l. 281) — that is, within the boundary marked by a *kudurru*-stone — and made or "installed" them as vassals of Aššur (*emēdu tupšikki Aššur*, ll. 204, 423).

---

[46] Ron E. Tappy, "Historical and Geographical Notes on the 'Lowland Districts' of Judah in Joshua 15:33–47," *VT* 58 (2008): 381–403.

Sub-category 3.4

Sargon's treatment of the provincial capitals of Sippar, Nippur, Babylon, and Borsippa[47] provides a sequence of actions through which he generally reorganized local people or land holdings. The *Annals* set this treatment in stark contrast to the devastation laid on the city of Dūr-Yakīn. In the case of the capital cities, Sargon claims to have broken or "destroyed" their bonds (*abātu*), freed the people (lit. "allowed them to see the light of day"; note the idiom *nūra kullumu*, with *kullumu* D = "to show," Š = "to reveal"), returned their fields to them (*eṭēru*), returned the territories taken away from them by the Sutians ([w]*uttura* < *atāru*; again, lit. "increased" their domains), reestablished the independence of their affiliated cities (*šakānu*), returned the images of their captured gods, and restored ("increased"?) the revenues of these deities ([w]*uttura* < *atāru*). On the other hand, the area of Bīt-Yakīn (which included Dūr-Yakīn) he "totally divided" (*malmališ zâzu*, l. 383) as far as the Elamite border. After Sargon, the scribes of Sennacherib used the concept of dividing (*zâzu*) to refer to the distribution of enemy booty to the military, Assyrian governors, and leaders of Assyrian cultic centers. While Esarhaddon used the term when reassigning skilled soldiers, charioteers, shepherds, orchard keepers, and the like to Assyrian service, he also attached a greater territorial sense to the term in his claims that he occasionally divided a particular land "in its entirety" (*si-ḫir-ti-šá*, a reference to its entire circumference/perimeter) into two parts, over which he placed Assyrian officials as governors. The Chicago Assyrian Dictionary's rendering of Sargon's use of *malmališ*[48] suggests the latter tactic over a simple redistribution of spoils, and Fuchs also understands the term in that way.[49] This practice of splitting an existing political entity and placing the newly defined parts under different, more sympathetic leadership anticipates Sennacherib's wholesale transfer of Judahite polities to Philistine rulers in 701 BCE.

Sub-category 3.5

The two principal terms that record a resettling of captured peoples in a different city are the Š-stems of *erēbu* (ll. 161, 214, 305) and *[w]ašābu* (e. g., ll. 78, 203, 216, 253, 381, 409, 423), "to make enter" and "to make settle." The last reference

---

[47] Fuchs, *Die Inschriften Sargons II.*, 169, ll. 373–78; *ARAB II*, § 40.
[48] *CAD* M/1 170.
[49] Fuchs, *Die Inschriften Sargons II.*, 335.

under *erēbu* (l. 305) relates to the occupancy of Dūr-Ladīni by Sargon's warriors.⁵⁰ In one instance (*ú-še-šib*, l. 123), the *Annals* apply the term *ašābu* to the transfer of various Arab desert tribes to the former capital city of Samaria.

Sub-category 3.6

Local building projects in subdued cities are usually mentioned by way of the verb *nadû* (e. g., ll. 216, 219, 283) or the phrase *ana eššuti ēpuš* (*epēšu*, sometimes written *ú-še-piš*, ll. 114, 305). The terms can appear in connection with a statement that Sargon had "conquered" or "captured" a certain city (e. g., note the sequence *kašādu* ... *epēšu* in ll. 113–14), but without explicit reference to the physical destruction of those places. The *Annals* typically employ *nadû* to note the establishment of watch posts along the borders of districts (as in Kammānu in south-central Anatolia, just north of Sam'al and Carchemish; l. 216) or provinces (Gambūlu, in southern Mesopotamia north of Bīt-Yakīn, l. 283; compare the situation along the border of the Land of Muški, l. 219). An alternative verb for describing the strengthening of border fortresses is *danānu*, as with the cities along the boundary with Urarṭu (l. 218).

Sub-category 3.7

While this category relates in various ways to the last three sets of terms, the following words refer more specifically to the *administrative* takeover and reorganization of foreign cities. In fact, this section constitutes the aspect of conquest that the *Annals* most often address with regard to actions taken within a certain city. As demonstrated in the previous subset, building projects that receive mention typically relate to the strengthening and fortification of borders; the records actually say very little about specific inner-city construction projects or the particular uses of buildings the Assyrians themselves may have designed. Besides calling a city by a new name (indicated by the verbs *zakāru*, l. 275; *nakāru*, ll. 279, 298; or *qabû*, l. 280 — "to name, change, or simply state"), or linking ("binding") cities together in a larger administrative network (*rakāsu*, l. 220), the key term involved here is *ṣabātu*, normally translated "to seize" but in this

---

50 On the somewhat awkward wording of ll. 304–305 in the annalistic record, see Peter Dubovský, *Hezekiah and the Assyrian Spies: Reconstruction of the Neo-Assyrian Intelligence Services and Its Significance for 2 Kings 18–19* (Rome: Pontificio Istituto Biblico, 2006), 91, n. 199.

context meaning "to take over for administrative purposes" (or more generically "to reorganize administratively"; e. g., ll. 214, 215, 253, 275, 297, 408, 422). The phrase *ana eššūti aṣbat* occurs often in the inscriptions of Sargon, Sennacherib, Esarhaddon, and Ashurbanipal; it typically conveys a new administrative purpose behind the control and exploitation of captured towns.[51] Unfortunately, many older translations obscure this meaning by rendering the phrase simply as "I built/rebuilt anew."[52] For example, in what appears to represent an unusual turn of events, Sargon smashed (*ḫepû*) the provincial capital of Melīdi "like a pot" (l. 209), while taking over Til-Garimmu, a city of lesser status, for administrative purposes (l. 214). As noted above, the typical pattern would reverse the fates of these two locales.

Sub-category 3.8

Finally, a few terms occur in this broader category that pertain to the setting of annual tribute, taxes, or work assignments. Service, or more specifically work on lands held by a higher authority (*ilku*, "state service"; l. 215), as well as vassalage (*tupšikku*, "corvée labor," l. 215) were imposed (*emēdu*, ll. 216, 288) on the subjects of Sargon. Both tax (*biltu*) and tribute (*maddattu*) were imposed on the groups resettled in Samaria "as though they were Assyrians" (ll. 16–17) – a phrase that denotes particularly heavy requirements of tribute.[53] More figuratively, subjugated peoples must pull (*šâṭu*) the rope of Sargon's yoke (*abšānu*, ll. 254, 424).[54] The Assyrians firmly levied (*nadānu* or *kânu*, ll. 277–78) annual (*šattišam*) tribute on their subjects often in the form of interest (a *ṣibtu*-tax) on cattle, sheep, and goats (l. 288b).

---

[51] See *CAD* E 377b; *CAD* Ṣ 16b.
[52] Cf. the appropriate passages in *ARAB II*, §§ 26, 30, 33, 46, 47.
[53] Becking, *The Fall of Samaria*, 37, n. 75. Cf. Simo Parpola, *The Correspondence of Sargon II, Part I: Letters from Assyria and the West* (Helsinki: Helsinki University Press, 1987), no. 220: 4–5, for the corn tax and for evidence that Samaria sometimes proved delinquent in its payment of such taxes.
[54] *abšānu*, a loanword from Sumerian, appears only in relation to labor or corvée; it never denotes any part of a chariot or other equipment or even routine physical labor (*CAD* A1 66).

Category 4

The fourth type of literary reference in my study sample relates to the direct removal by Sargon himself, or the indirect receipt by the king, of the spoils of war, which may include people and property. The verb that most commonly describes this action — *šalālu*, "to carry off, plunder" — occurs at least twenty times in the study sample and appears in relation to "Samerina and the entire land of the Household/Dynasty of Omri" in the Small Summary Inscription from Room XIV of the palace at Khorsabad (see n. 10). The nominal cognate of this root — *šallatu* — also serves as a basic term for the spoils of war (as distinct from *maddattu*, "tribute payment"), and it combines with *būšu* ("goods, valuables, movable property," l. 223) to help clarify the intended meaning of *šalālu, kašādu, leqû*, etc., as acts of plunder, not necessarily of destructive violence. The *Annals* sometimes record the receipt (using the verb *maḫāru*) of spoils after stating simply that Sargon went to battle (*alāku*, ll. 128–3×, 168) or in connection with plundering operations (*šalālu*, l. 355–2×) or while making post-battle offerings (ll. 314, 316). Less often, the record states that Sargon received booty "at/after the defeat" of someone (l. 327), and *maḫāru* is connected with *kašādu*, "to conquer," only once in the sample (l. 113). On occasion, different series of verbs relate to the removal of specific types of goods, such as economic or natural resources (e.g., ores — *šakālu … balālu … amāru*, ll. 227–32) or military resources (*amāru … ṣabātu … [w]ašābu*, l. 279). The conscription of chariots (or charioteers) in the *Annals* and the binding together of draft animals employs the term *kaṣāru* (ll. 357, 411), as at Samaria in Nimrud Prism IV: 33–34. Sargon considered (lit. "counted," *manû*) these resources as spoils of war along with deportees and apparent cultic images (IV: 31–3).[55] At one point (l. 408) the official who led the royal army against the provincial capital of Melīdi opened (*petû*) the local treasury (*bīt niṣirti*) and "carried off" the booty to Sargon ([w]*abālu*; compare ll. 213, 422). After receiving such goods (lit. "taking them away," *ekēmu*; ll. 351, 387), Sargon stored or heaped them up for his own use (*qarānu ~ garānu*, l. 233).

---

[55] In view of the heavy taxation, plundering of military resources, and removal of cultic symbols imposed on Samaria, Hayes and Kuan, "The Final Years of Samaria," 178, seem incorrect in their assertion that during and after the fall of Samaria "no special penalties were imposed on the people and no reference is made to any special booty taken." Franklin, "The Room V Reliefs at Dur-Sharrukin," 264, has suggested that the upper registers of Slabs 4 and 5 in the Room V reliefs from Dur-Šarruken actually depict the removal of Samarian booty by Assyrian soldiers.

Category 5

Finally, and perhaps most significantly for discerning what actually transpired at Samaria, the last group of terms in my study sample clearly denotes the physical destruction of property in a conquered city. Sargon's treatment of ᵁᴿᵁ*Rapīḫu* (Raphia) following the battle at Qarqar in 720 BCE provides a prime example of such a fate. This local town was destroyed, devastated, and burned with fire (*ap-pul aq-qur i-na išāti áš-ru-up*; l. 57; < *napālu*, *naqāru*, and *šarāpu*) before Sargon claims to have carried off (*áš-lu-la* < *šalālu*) more than 9,000 people along with their possessions. The *Annals* make the physical nature of the affront against the city unmistakable.

These terms go far beyond the generic sense of "to capture," though they occasionally follow and expand that concept in the text. For example, when the cities of Šuandahul and Durdukka (between the Caspian Sea and Lake Urmia) planned rebellion by prying into affairs in the northern Zagros Mountains of northwestern Iran, during Sargon's third *palû* (ll. 58–67), the king marched forth (*alāku*) to conquer (*ana kašād*) those places. Ultimately, he smashed (*parāru*) and leveled to the ground (*manû*, lit. "reckoned them as ground") and carried off (*šalālu*) their people and possessions. Next comes the standard, second-level statement: "Those cities I destroyed (*napālu*), I devastated (*naqāru*), I burned with fire (*ina išāti ašrup* < *šarāpu*)."[56] Clearly, this triad of terms communicates more than mere control, subjugation, or conquest (*kašādu*) of a locale. Compare the battle at Dūr-Yakīn, in which Sargon besieged the city (*lemû*, l. 344), then massacred and decimated its warriors (ll. 344–46), pierced the hand of the local ruler (l. 347), slaughtered various groups of tribesmen (l. 349), bespattered the citizens with the venom of death (l. 350), removed the symbols of indigenous power (l. 351), caused the people to run wild and loose (l. 352), plundered and received the spoils (ll. 353–57), completely enclosed (blockaded?) the city (l. 357), ruined the local economy by cutting down orchards and date palms (l. 358), negated the effectiveness of the city's moat (l. 359), and then burned the town (this time using the term *qamû*) and demolished (*napālu*) and devastated (*naqāru*) its defenses by digging out (*nasāḫu*) their very foundations. The result gave the city the appearance of a denuded mound of ruins after a flood (*tīl abūbi*, l. 373). When the loyalty of Mitatti of Zikirtu collapsed during the med-

---

[56] *Annals*, ll. 58–65; see Fuchs, *Die Inschriften Sargons II.*, 91 (text), 315 (translation).

dling of Šuandahul and Durdukka (see above), Sargon even boasted that he burned Mitatti's royal city — Parda — with divine fire from the god Gibil (l. 132).[57]

Once in the study sample Sargon speaks of the destruction (ḫepû, l. 391a) of Muški, a concept that receives metaphoric clarification earlier in the *Annals* when of Melīdi he records *karpāniš aḫpi*, "I smashed it like a pot" (l. 209). Like the other verbs in this section, *ḫepû* also seems to imply the physical demolition of a conquered site. Though the Babylonian Chronicle (1.i.28) once attributes this same action to Shalmaneser V in his campaign against Samaria, Sargon II never employs this word with regard to the Israelite capital.

As expected, the devastation suggested by these terms leads to deportations and the removal of the spoils of war addressed earlier. But the emphatic statements that incorporate these more drastic actions generally do not proceed by speaking of an administrative reorganization of the town, a rebuilding of physical structures, resettlement programs, the imposition of taxes, etc. On the other hand, the passages that do include these types of restructuring measures rarely move beyond *kašādu* or *lemû* in describing the initial military side of the picture. In other words, the more extreme level of conquest language gives the impression that the city in question suffered complete devastation, with little regard to its future either as an independent municipality or as a functional part of the Assyrian Empire. This fate was not the case at Samaria.

Based on the archaeological reporting from Samaria, one might expect to find clear evidence for this type of conflagration both in the site's depositional history and in the historical texts associated with the city's final days. But, in fact, a coherent destruction level does not emerge from the empirical evidence recovered there, and nowhere in the records of Sargon does the graphic language of destruction occur in relation to the Israelite capital. Only in the Babylonian Chronicle, where *ḫepû* describes Shalmaneser V's assault against the city, can one identify a possible reference to its physical destruction. Judging from the two occurrences of this term in the later *Annals* of Sargon, it at least implies more than a mere plundering. Even so, "ravage" (a popular translation used by scholars) remains too vague a term in English to ascertain precisely what those who resort to this rendering really envision.

From this overview of Sargon II's language of conquest, it becomes clear that his scribes employed a fairly standard vocabulary to describe the various phases

---

57 "Among the troops of Mitatti of Zikirtu I directed a slaughter. I conquered three strong [fortified] cities, together with twenty-four towns in their neighborhood, and plundered them. I burned down his royal city Parda with the [fire-god] Gibil, and that same fellow [Mitatti] fled with the inhabitants of his land/country, and their abode was not to be found." See Fuchs, *Die Inschriften Sargons II.*, 111 (text), 320 (translation); *Annals*, ll. 130–33.

and facets of battle and conquest. In fact, the terminology outlined here proves quite typical of all Neo-Assyrian conquerors in the late-eighth and seventh centuries BCE.[58] Yet Sargon's overall use of this catalogue to relay his actions against Samaria seems noticeably conservative in scope. It also appears from this survey that the treatment routinely afforded the provincial capitals often differed (for the better) from that given the regular cities.[59] The physical evidence from Samaria corroborates this conclusion. While the Israelite capital was besieged, blockaded(?), heavily taxed and levied with tribute, plundered, and repopulated, it was not physically destroyed.

4 The Archaeology of Periods V–VII at Samaria: What it Does and Does Not Reveal

4.1 Building Period V (Figs. 1–2)[60]

The complexities of the depositional history encountered north of the main courtyard presented the Joint Expedition (Fig. 1) with various challenges in achieving a tenable reconstruction of the events attending the Assyrian takeover of the site. The excavation report indicates that floor levels associated with the rooms in this area remained intact only north of Wall 65. Leveling operations for a thick layer of "chocolate soil," dated to the sixth or fifth century BCE, had subsequently destroyed the Period V and most earlier floors south of Wall 65.[61] On the east, a large tract of Roman quarrying also encroached on these remains as far west as 645° E and destroyed at least half of Room *kq*.

Only a few architectural changes occurred between Kenyon's Periods IV–IVa and V.[62] Besides the subdivision of Pit *i*, the more prominent changes are represented by an entirely new series of well-built rooms to the south and west of the pit (Rooms *o*, *h*, *q*, *hq*, *kq*, and *s*; see Fig. 2). These chambers subsumed the southern half of former Rooms *a-d* (of Periods III–IV), overran the disturbed Area *e*, and continued eastward to take in the southern half of Room *hk*. Wall 65, which had constituted the southern border of an earlier set of chambers (Period IV

---

58 See *CAD* for appropriate parallels.
59 See, e.g., Sub-category 3.4 above, though the unusual turn of events at the provincial capital at Melīdi provides an exception.
60 In the following discussion, this phase plan relates to both Period V and Period VI (cf. *SS I*, 107, fig. 50).
61 *SS III*, 107.
62 Compare *SS I*, figs. 48–50.

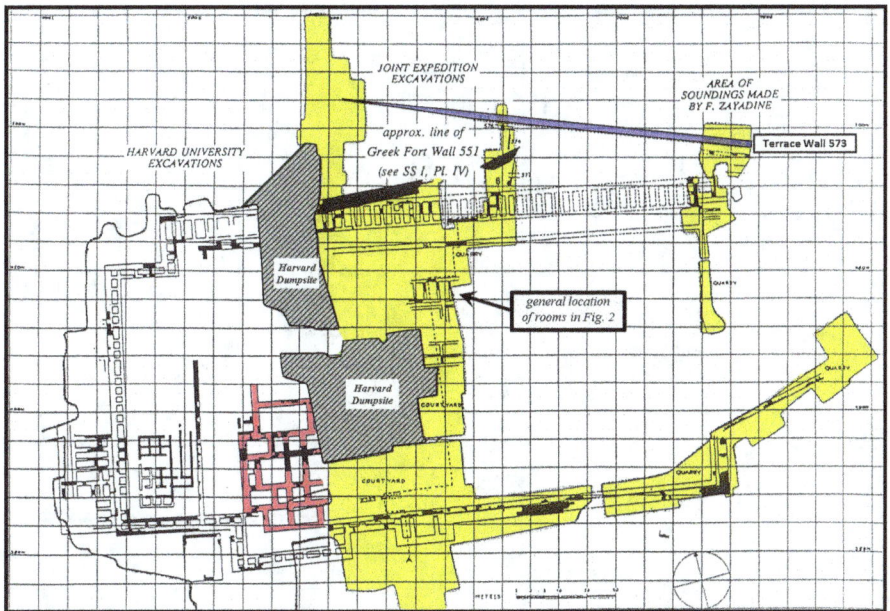

Fig. 1: General plan of the summit. Adapted from *SS I*, pl. II; courtesy of the Palestine Exploration Fund, London.

Rooms *o-h-q*), now separated *o-h-q-hq-kq* from other apparent spaces constructed to their south (e. g., Room *s*). The excavators maintained in various publications that a considerable deposit of destruction debris overlay even the few floors that survived in this area. Scrutiny of the available data, however, fails to validate this assertion.

The excavators reported that they recovered only a meager quantity of pottery from beneath the Period V house floors. In fact, the official report presents an astonishingly limited corpus to represent this important time-span (five jar fragments and three cooking pot rims). Furthermore, the report fails to demonstrate a clear correlation between the loci that yielded the published pottery and the area of the summit that revealed the most significant Period V construction activity. Five of the eight published fragments derive from two findspots located in Room *hk*, labeled in the field notes as Segment 125.144 and E Strip: Between Test Trench 2– Test Trench 3.[63] The excavators cut a lateral section through

---

[63] Cf. *SS III*, 118–19, fig. 8: 2–5, 8. In *SS III*, 118, Kenyon also assigned fig. 8: 1 to Room *hk*, but it appears that this jar came instead from Room *hq*.

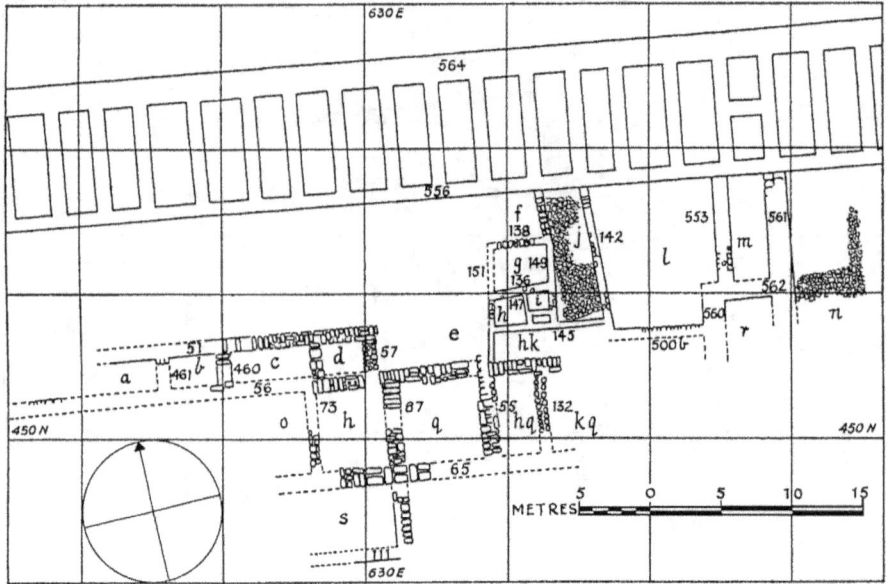

Fig. 2: Phase Plan of Building Periods V–VII. Reproduced from *SS I*, 107, fig. 50; courtesy of the Palestine Exploration Fund, London.

the northern half of Room *hk*, and Segment 125.144 lay on the western portion of this line, while E Strip: Btw TT2–TT3 ran along its eastern side. In Segment 125.144, a rather thick deposit of soil covered the purported Period IV floor, and the excavators identified it as Layer IIIe in 125.144 (old Room *h*) and Layer V in Btw TT2–TT3 (old Room *k*). They understood this layer as the only surviving Period V surface in the new Room *hk*.

Unpublished field notes, however, indicate that Layer III actually comprised "one of several levels making up III, above IIIb."[64] These records describe Layer III generally as a "hard yellow level" that contained examples of "hard, ringing wares," which prompted Kenyon to lower the estimated date of the deposit from her Period IV to Period V. Although the matrix of Layer III appears to have been more compact than some of the other fills along the northern courtyard and slopes, the overall thickness of the deposit (ca. 0.4 m) suggests that it in fact rep-

---

64 Kathleen Mary Kenyon, *Fieldbook Qk-l-m, Notes from the 1933 Season of Excavation*, 48a. Kenyon's hand-written, unpublished records from the Joint Expedition are now stored at the Palestine Exploration Fund in London. I am grateful to both Rupert L. Chapman III and Felicity Cobbing who, over the years, have granted me full access to these important materials.

resents a densely packed fill, not an Israelite surface, natural accumulation of soil, or pure occupational debris left on a surface from either Period IV or V.

Kenyon designated the portion of Layer III that actually ran up to the southern face of Wall 155 (on the northern side of Room *hk*) as Layer IIIo. Together, Layers III and IIIo yielded half of the published Period V assemblage.[65] The ceramic traditions reflected in two jar fragments[66] are at home in the mid-to-late eighth century, although they also extend into the seventh century BCE. Kenyon herself remarked on the general lateness of the hard, thin ware and full, light-colored slip exhibited by one of them.[67] Both fragments came from the thick fill of Layer III, but because of the secondary nature of this type of matrix, these items can help only to establish the *terminus post quem* for the deposition of that level. Two other fragments[68] belong to Layer IIIo and reflect ceramic traditions from the late Iron Age II period. One of these, the purported cooking pot rim[69] finds its best parallel among the late Iron II family of jars.[70] Holladay has noted that the holemouth forms represented by the other fragment,[71] with their wide mouths (32 cm) and thickened, slightly molded triangular ledges on the outer rim, "are ubiquitous in seventh century deposits."[72] In short, Level III appears to have been put in place sometime in the late eighth or early seventh century BCE.

A doubled-grooved, tripled-ridged fragment[73] emerges as the most typical seventh-century holemouth rim, although the tradition continues into the sixth century BCE. This piece came from Layer V in E Strip: Btw TT2–TT3, which Kenyon took to represent a 14-cm-thick floor belonging to Period V. But unpublished field sections show that this deposit deepens into a foundation trench for a later wall (125b) that replaced or repaired the broken or robbed Wall 56 along the southern border of Room *hk*.[74] Rather than depicting the principal Period V surface in this room, then, Layer V may actually represent the bot-

---

65 *SS III*, fig. 8: 2–3, 5, 8.
66 *SS III*, fig. 8: 2, 5.
67 *SS III*, fig. 8: 5.
68 *SS III*, fig. 8: 3, 8.
69 *SS III*, fig. 8: 8.
70 *SS III*, fig. 12: 10 (Period VIII). Kenyon, however, compared our fragment to *SS III*, figs. 11: 32 (Period VII) and 30: 26 (unstratified).
71 *SS III*, fig. 8: 3.
72 Holladay, *Ninth and Eighth Century Pottery*, 131, n. 119.
73 *SS III*, fig. 8: 4.
74 In the late Hellenistic period, yet another wall (which the excavators labeled Wall 125a) was built in this location. Kenyon herself acknowledged in her field notes that the phasing of this wall touched on at least three periods (Kenyon, *Fieldbook Qk-l-m*, 10).

tom striations of a subsequent fill and therefore might well postdate Period V altogether.

Although the excavation Segment *W of 124* also lay near the sequence of Walls 56–125b–125a, it extended southward from that point into Room *hq* and toward the summit, not northward into Room *hk*, as the excavation report sometimes seems to indicate.[75] The local stratigraphy in this area ran along both sides of Wall 132, which divided Rooms *hq* and *kq*. The earliest surviving deposits in this segment lay east of Wall 132W (Layers VIc–VIIc), and the construction of the wall cut these levels. An elongated, bag-shaped jar,[76] however, came from the deep deposit of fill poured against the western face of 132W (Layer VIII). This type of jar dates, in my judgment, at least as late as the seventh century BCE, although its floruit may fall slightly later still. The level in which it was found can hardly represent a surface of any kind, and the fact that the field notes indicate this matrix primarily yielded pottery forms from Periods I–IV attests to the mixed nature of its contents, as is characteristic of imported fill levels. One must therefore lower the *terminus post quem* (date of deposition) for this subfloor fill and whatever surface it might have supported to at least the seventh century BCE, that is, to well after the Assyrian conquest of Samaria.

Another field section, relating to Segment 509.126 in Room *j*, reveals three successive floor levels (Layers XI, X, and IX/paving stones) laid across massive deposits of construction debris and imported fills (Layers XII–XIV). While Layer XI reflects Ahab's extension of the courtyard north of Omri's original Enclosure Wall 161, comparative stratigraphic analysis shows that the intermediate Layer X corresponds directly to deposits that overran and sealed the remains of Period III Wall 160 (assigned by Kenyon to Jehu). These levels, then, probably date to sometime in the early eighth century BCE. The packing of Layer IX around the flat paving stones correlates well with surrounding deposits (e. g., Layer V, North of TT 2) dating to the second half of the eighth century BCE or possibly slightly later still. While no ivory fragments or burned, sooty materials appeared in these deposits, Layer IX yielded a short-flanged cooking pot rim.[77] A similar rim,[78] although of the elongated type with a flattened outer face and a deeper groove under the flange, came from Layer IX inside Room *n* farther to the east, again from soil packed around the stone paving. Deep fills and multiple robber trenches characterize the stratigraphy in Room *n* to the east of Wall

---

75 See Tappy, *The Archaeology of Israelite Samaria*, II, 190–97.
76 *SS III*, fig. 8: 1.
77 *SS III*, fig. 8: 7.
78 *SS III*, fig. 8: 6.

561. Certainly, then, these two fragments do not reflect the latest ceramic traditions associated with the so-called Period V House. Their respective styles appear with subtle variations throughout the tenth and early ninth centuries BCE, and Holladay correctly recognized these two specimens as early-ninth-century forms.[79] But the deposits that yielded these pieces represent secondary fills and packing used for laying flagstone floors during a later period. They in no way represent a massive conflagration from an assault against the city by any of the Neo-Assyrian rulers.

In sum, no stratigraphic or ceramic information gleaned thus far attests to a destruction event of any magnitude that might stem from the activities of Tiglath-pileser III (either during the years of the Syro-Ephraimite War or in a putative second campaign in 728/727 BCE[80]), Shalmaneser V (at any point during his reign), or even Sargon II (in 720 BCE). Within the amazingly scant ceramic assemblage, the mixture of ninth-century BCE cooking pot rims with jar forms from the seventh century BCE (or later) reveals the secondary nature of the pottery-bearing deposits assigned to Period V.

4.2 Building Period VI (Fig. 2)

Several basic facts must inform any summary of the layers and materials assigned to Period VI. First, only two principal deposits yielded the ceramic group assigned to this period. Kenyon described one of these as a "levelling contemporary with Wall 573" — a feature lying ca. 30 m north of the royal compound, on the middle terrace of the northern slope — and she identified its two pottery-bearing segments as North of 551 and 513.514. Pit *i* reportedly contained the second deposit, and she labeled the local stratigraphy Segments 122.125.19.121 and 122.126.19.121. Second, Kenyon remained unable to assign a reliable date to Wall 573 and held open two tentative alternatives: (1) this feature, which stood just inside the main road that curved around the northern slopes before approaching the eastern city gate, represented the final defensive structure constructed by the Israelites; or (2) the origins of the wall lay in one of the early construction projects commissioned by Sargon II after his takeover of the city. Third, Kenyon understood the limited Period V repertoire as indistinguishable from the collection assigned to Period VI. Ultimately, therefore, she placed Wall 573 in Period VI based solely on the claim of a strong ceramic affili-

---

[79] Holladay, *Ninth and Eighth Century Pottery*, 131.
[80] As suggested by Tetley, "The Date of Samaria's Fall."

ation with the latest vessels in Pit *i* on the summit. Fourth, Kenyon treated the pottery groups recovered from both contexts as examples of ceramic *horizons* (homogeneous materials reflecting a rather specific date and often deriving from destruction debris), not of ceramic *periods* (mixed materials that often come from imported fills and that show attributes which developed over a span of time).[81]

According to the official report, "the big raising of level contemporary with wall 573 … was only cleared in a trench 2 m wide between this wall and the northern casemate wall at c. 600 E."[82] A principal excavation segment lay north of Wall 551 (the massive Greek Fort Wall constructed in the late Hellenistic period, ca. mid-second century BCE) and all but one pottery fragment published from this area came from this particular locus. The field notes record only three main phases of activity here, each with various associated sub-levels: early Hellenistic (Layers I–IV); Israelite Period VI (Layer V); and Israelite Period I (Layers VI–VIII). Kenyon understood the Hellenistic deposits to predate the construction of Greek Fort Wall 551, and she assigned these levels to the late third or early second century BCE.

Kenyon's field notations describe the "decca" soil of Layer V[83] as "Period VI filling running up to 573."[84] Yet while published Section CD traces this deposit only as far as Robber Trench 578,[85] the field sections reveal that it continued northward to Robber Trench 573 as sub-Layer Va, and even beyond that point as sub-Layer Vb.[86] Significantly, these field records also reveal that Va lay "in R.T. 578, sealed by Vd, Period VI" and that Vb comprised "part of R.T. 573 (L.R. [= Late Roman])."[87] These data alone lead one to expect a very mixed as-

---

[81] See Holladay, *Ninth and Eighth Century Pottery*, 16, n. 36, for elaboration of these definitions.
[82] *SS III*, 119. Although no published section extended this far beyond the Casemate System, Section CD comes the closest to Wall 573 and reaches as far north (down-slope) as Wall 578, which ran almost contiguously to the southern face of 573 (see *SS I*, pl. II). Clearance operations conducted in 1965 by Fawzi Zayadine, "Samaria-Sebaste. Clearance and Excavations (October 1965–June 1967)," *ADAJ* 12 (1967–68): 77–80, revealed a wall fragment farther to the east (at 700°–715° E x 498° N), which he understood as the eastward extension of Kenyon's Wall 573. No stratigraphic connection exists between these two wall segments, and, in fact, Zayadine ultimately described his so-called Wall c as a "later addition" to 573. He dated the pottery taken from the foundation trench of this feature to the late eighth century BCE and noted that the group included a rim fragment apparently from an Assyrian-style bowl.
[83] This layer contributed all but one fragment illustrated in *SS III*, fig. 9.
[84] Kathleen Mary Kenyon, *Fieldbook Qn, Vols. I–II, Notes from the 1935 Season of Excavation* (unpublished ms. in the Palestine Exploration Fund, London), Vol. II, 118a.
[85] See n. 82 above.
[86] Tappy, *The Archaeology of Israelite Samaria*, II, 258, fig. 51.
[87] Kenyon, *Fieldbook Qn*, Vol. II, 118a.

semblage of ceramic traditions from this area. Moreover, that a number of robber trenches broke all stratigraphic connections between Wall 573 and Segment North of 551 further compromises the integrity of the overall deposit. Most of the pottery forms discovered here might easily derive from the earliest decades of Assyrian hegemony over the city (i.e., the late-eighth to early-seventh centuries BCE). This group includes two bowls,[88] a decanter,[89] a juglet,[90] and two braziers.[91] The fragment of "Samaria Ware,"[92] on the other hand, may come from the period leading up to 732 BCE. The mixed series of cooking pot rims[93] displays perhaps the longest chronological range, since these pieces reflect mainly variations on the flanged-style rims that existed during the ninth and eighth centuries BCE.

The latest pottery in this context, of course, suggests the turn of the eighth century as the earliest possible date of deposition for this deep fill. Ceramic parallels from Megiddo Stratum III support this conclusion.[94] But stratigraphically, at best this findspot represents a secondary context and a ceramic period, not a persuasive horizon. Moreover, none of the field notes relating to Segment North of 551 mentioned burned debris or even the scattered presence of charred ivory fragments. That is to say, the area produced no evidence of destruction by fire.

Unlike North of 551, located down the slope near the northern perimeter road, Segment 513.514 lay farther uphill and immediately outside the old Israelite Casemate System. It, too, yielded remains from three principal periods of activity: R.4 (Late Roman period, fourth century CE [Layers I – IV]); the Hellenistic period (mid-second century BCE [Layers V – VII]); and disparate deposits assigned to the Israelite period (Periods I and VI [Layers VIII – IX].[95] "Middenish-looking debris" appeared in Layer II, mixed with the natural overburden that covered this area. Beneath these levels, significant quantities of burnt matrix did not emerge until Layer V, the massive deposit of fill poured down the slope and against the Greek Fort Wall. Layer VI included steeply pitched, narrow bands of unconsolidated, "streaky, sooty" material separated by additional brownish fill. This stratigraphic situation does not reflect, then, an *in situ* destruction level, but instead successive rakings of debris from earlier periods down over

---

88 *SS III*, fig. 9: 1, 3.
89 *SS III*, fig. 9: 5.
90 *SS III*, fig. 9: 7.
91 *SS III*, fig. 9: 8 – 9.
92 *SS III*, fig. 9: 2.
93 *SS III*, fig. 9: 10 – 18.
94 For specific examples, see Tappy, *The Archaeology of Israelite Samaria, II*, 266 – 76, 285 – 94.
95 See Kenyon, *Fieldbook Qn, Vol. I*, 69a; *Vol. II*, 137a.

the northern slopes into a secondary context, where the debris served as basic leveling material.⁹⁶ A complete saucer, the only fragment from this area that did not come from North of 551, originated in Hellenistic Layer VI.⁹⁷

Back inside the Casemate System, in a service area lying below the central summit plateau, Pit *i* lay near the center of a poorly built cluster of rooms labeled *g*, *h*, *j*, and *hk*. Although Kenyon claimed to have removed the entire assemblage presented in *SS III*, Fig. 10:1–27 from two related layers (V–Va) located inside this pit, a detailed analysis of the unpublished excavation records reveals a different situation.⁹⁸ While Segment 122.125.19.121, which yielded the majority of fragments, took in the pit, it also extended southward to the higher rock of the central summit and Wall 56/125 at the southern boundary of Room *hk*. Similarly, the coordinates 122.126.19.121 included the pit but also the space to its north, perhaps as far as the northern perimeter of Room *g* (Wall 138), where the rock continued to decline and greater amounts of fill were required to achieve a suitable construction level.⁹⁹

Although Kenyon placed the origin of Pit *i* in her Period IV, she believed that it continued in use throughout Period V and that its contents reflected the Assyrian destruction of the city in 720 BCE. Elsewhere, however, she acknowledged that "the Period VII debris which overlay the floors of the rest of the house did not actually overlie the pit." Moreover, she interpreted the impressive quantity of pottery contained in the pit as "identical with that in the filling contemporary with wall 573."¹⁰⁰ Finally, she noted that this assemblage differed (at least in its significance) from the "few sherds of … harder ware, including some fragments of water decanters" that she excavated beneath the Period V House floors.¹⁰¹ That the upper courses of the pit stood at least as high in elevation as all the surrounding deposits and "considerably above the level of the adjoining rooms," together with Kenyon's acknowledgment that the putative "destruction" remains neither appeared *in situ* nor sealed nor even partly covered the open mouth of the pit, seem to indicate a functional life for this structure that

---

96 In an unpublished paper titled "Note of Levels. Samaria Excavations 1931–5. Q Area (Summit)" (available in the archives of the PEF in London), Kenyon herself described these deep fills as "material obtained by slicing off the highest deposits of the surrounding area."
97 *SS III*, fig. 9: 1. The daily excavation records show that Layer V and its related sub-deposits comprise a mixture of construction debris and leveling fills, and Layer VI is described as "H[ellenistic]. VI. Streaky, sooty, all part of G.F.W. [Greek Fort Wall] filling, but also R.T. [Robber Trench] 541" (Kenyon, *Fieldbook Qn, Vol. I*, 69a).
98 Tappy, *The Archaeology of Israelite Samaria*, II, 296–301, 341–46.
99 The main indicator, Wall 126, lay contiguous to the northern face of Wall 138.
100 *SS III*, 119–20.
101 *SS I*, 108.

either survived or postdated both the purported conflagration event and the post-destruction leveling operation.

The materials assigned to Pit *i*, therefore, do not appear to have come only from that specific installation. A slight majority of the published pottery (55.56%) reflects a series of rather late developments in Iron Age II ceramic traditions, that is, trends that arose or flourished after the Assyrian takeover of Samaria.[102] The largest collection of whole or nearly whole vessels (33.3%), however, appears to predate the so-called *Pax Assyriaca*, and many of the traditions might easily extend as far back as the ninth century BCE.[103] This dichotomy within the "pit assemblage" clearly militates against the position that "no serious question can be raised about the essential homogeneity of the group."[104] Differences also emerge between the stylish pottery of Pit *i* and that taken from the fills around Wall 573, which yielded a preponderance of thick, heavy bowls or braziers and utilitarian cooking pot forms. Thus, whereas Kenyon equated these two ceramic groups, I cannot. Actually, the Pit *i* corpus, with its examples of hard-fired ware, identifiable water decanters, etc., seems more akin to the few fragments recovered from beneath the Period V House floors. Yet Kenyon attempted to divorce these two groups. The better-preserved materials came from the area south of the pit (Segment 122.125.19.121), while the more fragmentary examples originated to its north and reflected the later phases of ceramic traditions attested by the overall group.

Thus a significant portion of the Period VI pottery appears to have derived from leveling debris surrounding Pit *i*, that is, from layers that Kenyon included in her Period VII. And since the latest materials in these unconsolidated fills span at least the first half of the seventh century BCE, the leveling activity itself must have occurred sometime during or after that point, not in 722–21 BCE or even during the period immediately following Sargon's subjugation of the city in 720 BCE. Multiple seal impressions recovered from the pit originated in Twenty-second Dynasty Egypt,[105] and Kenyon herself placed some of them in the late eighth or seventh century BCE, a conclusion that supports a post-Israelite date for these deposits. These seal impressions also suggest a period of peaceful Assyro-Egyptian contact at the site in the years following Israel's loss of political

---

[102] For whole or nearly whole forms, see *SS III*, fig. 10: 7–8, 15–17, 24–25; for the fragments, see *SS III*, fig. 10: 9–12, 13(?), 18–19, 27.
[103] For whole or nearly whole forms, see *SS III*, fig. 10: 1–6, 21–23; for the fragments, see *SS III*, fig. 10: 14, 20, 26. See also Tappy, *The Archaeology of Israelite Samaria*, II, 345, Table 43, for the specific segment — 122.125.19.121 or 122.126.19.121 — to which each entry in nn. 46–47 belongs.
[104] Holladay, *Ninth and Eighth Century Pottery*, 68.
[105] See Tappy, *The Archaeology of Israelite Samaria*, II, 245–46, 299.

autonomy.[106] In short, the entire interpretive framework that Kenyon and others have applied to the principal Period VI loci seems tendentious in nature.

4.3 Building Period VII (Fig. 2)[107]

Period VII does not represent a new phase of construction; rather, it consists in "a thick layer of debris, with much burnt matter, including a considerable quantity of burnt ivory"[108] that supposedly lay over the remains of the Period V rooms (although not Pit *i*) and stemmed from Assyria's sacking of the site around 720 BCE. The paltry nature of the Period V pottery repertoire, the lack of a stratigraphic connection between Periods V and VI, the apparent inaccuracy of field recordings relating to Pit *i*, and the fact that Pit *i* appears stratigraphically later than the Period VII debris pose serious questions for the excavators' archaeological and historical interpretations.

Four pottery-bearing loci from this period related to a single room or feature, while three additional segments ran through multiple rooms. The total space involved in this portion of fieldwork, however, remained quite limited (120 m², 449° – 464° N x 638° – 646° E) owing to substantial disturbances from the Persian through Roman periods that impinged on virtually all the surrounding areas.[109] Yet the excavators published a more diverse ceramic assemblage from the disparate contexts encountered here, and nearly 78 % of the entire published corpus of ivory fragments came from layers belonging to only two segments in this area (W of 124 and 19.51.14.20).[110]

---

106 See Graham I. Davies, *Megiddo* (Cambridge: Lutterworth, 1986), 102, 104.
107 Since the excavators did not include in the excavation report from the Joint Expedition a separate phase plan for their Period VII, the drawing for Periods V – VI must serve as our point of reference.
108 *SS III*, 97.
109 For example, a thick band of sticky chocolate soil deposited during the Persian period blanketed the entire area south of Wall 65 (see Fig. 2) and destroyed "all the latest Israelite deposits" beneath it. Similarly, substantial quarrying activities in the Roman period cut through at least half of Room *kq*. Kenyon noted further that the area covered by the old Room *k* (= Room *hk* and the northern half of Rooms *hq* and *kq*) was "completely disturbed by later walls and robber trenches" (*SS I*, 110).
110 See Tappy, *The Archaeology of Israelite Samaria*, II, 443 – 95 for a full locational analysis of the published ivories and Ron E. Tappy, "The Provenance of the Unpublished Ivories from Samaria," in *"I Will Speak the Riddles of Ancient Times" (Ps 78:2b): Archaeological and Historical Studies in Honor of Amihai Mazar on the Occasion of his Sixtieth Birthday*, ed. Aren M. Maeir and Pierre de Miroschedji (Winona Lake IN: Eisenbrauns, 2006): 637 – 56, for a similar study of a large group of unpublished fragments.

The single-feature segments include 19.51.14.20 (Room *e*), 122.125.19.121 and 125.144 (Room *hk*), and 504.503.509.508 (Room *l*). The heavily disturbed area inside Room *e* contributed five fragments from two layers, IVa and VIc. Layer IVa, which yielded several examples of thin, shallow, hard-ware bowls,[111] belonged to Segment 19.51.14.20, located immediately east of Wall 57 (The excavators labeled the matrix lying farther away from the wall Layer IVd.). While it remains difficult to determine whether or not this deposit actually abutted the wall, it clearly overlaid a rather wide cut that appears to represent a robber trench associated with the partial plundering of Wall 57. The deposition of Layer IVa, therefore, postdates the construction, use, and intentional dismantling of this wall. If Wall 57 belongs to the final days of Israelite control over Samaria, as the excavators believed, the matrix of Layer IVa most likely dates to a later period. Together, Layers IVa and IVd covered two separate pits or drains (both labeled Layer VIc) that yielded examples of a ceramic tradition which differed in many respects from the finer bowls of the stratigraphically later Layer IVa.[112] But again, since these pits intruded into levels that were apparently contemporary with the wall, their functional life may have either paralleled or postdated that of the wall.

Segment 122.125.19.121 lay near the previous area mentioned above, but on the eastern side of Wall 151, in the westernmost portion of Room *hk*. Unfortunately, the ancient robbing of walls in this area, including at least the partial plundering of Wall 151 itself, broke the stratigraphic connection between this segment and 19.51.14.20. A short, inwardly inclined, profiled storage jar rim with ridged neck[113] from Layer IIIz reflects a ceramic tradition that does not seem to have extended much beyond the eighth century BCE (notwithstanding a close parallel from a reportedly sixth-century context at Bethel).[114] Layer IIIz represents a trench cut by the excavators through the hard matrix of Layer III, which they tentatively assigned to their post-Israelite Period VIII.[115] An intact stand[116] came from a sooty deposit overlying Layer III in Segment 125.144, which also rested within the confines of Room *hk*. Although these forms are generally considered to hold little if any chronological value, their overall distribution at Megiddo begins in Stratum IV but concentrates in Strata III – II, and parallels appear in Ni-

---

111 *SS III*, fig. 11: 12, 15, 17.
112 *SS III*, fig. 11: 23, 28.
113 *SS III*, fig. 11: 25.
114 See William Foxwell Albright and James Leon Kelso, "The Excavation of Bethel (1934–1960)," *AASOR* 39 (1968), pl. 67: 11; compare also pl. 67: 1 and p. 75, § 299, n. 63.
115 Kenyon, *Fieldbook Qk-l-m*, 5a.
116 *SS III*, fig. 11: 35.

veau 1 (seventh century) at Tell el-Farah (N).[117] The stratigraphic context, however, does not help to refine the dating of the stand, since it came from a deposit of leveling fill that overran Walls 136 and 145 plus portions of Room *hk* and that supported a series of Hellenistic walls resting directly on (and in one instance set into) the mixed matrix of the fill.

Farther to the east, Segment 504.503.509.508 lay inside the western half of Room *l*, although it may not have actually abutted Wall 142. The excavators published a small group of five fragmentary vessels from this area, including two bowls made of hard-ringing ware[118] and three jar rim fragments.[119] One of the jars also exhibits a hard, thin ware while another represents a holemouth form[120] that came from Layer Va.z. Both field drawings and narratives indicate that this deposit comprised the backfill in a foundation trench for Wall 508a, from the "R.4 Period," or fourth century CE.[121] All the other pieces came from local Layer Va, a backfill poured against another wall (552) during Herodian building operations around 30 BCE.[122] The secondary nature of all these deposits, then, reduces the materials published from them to circumstantial evidence that does not directly reflect a conflagration at the site resulting from an Assyrian attack in the 720s BCE.

Three excavation tracts extended through more than one of the rooms on the northern side of the summit: Segments 120.121.19.126 (Rooms *e, f, g, kq*); 509.126 (Rooms *f, j, l*); and West of 124 (Rooms *hq, kq*). These areas yielded more than two-thirds of the entire ceramic assemblage published in support of Period VII. The first two segments focus on the irregularly built rooms (*e* through *l*) situated north of a rock scarp that defined the plateau of the central summit.

More than 43% of the entire Period VII pottery group came from Segment 120.121.19.126 alone, and three quarters of this corpus originated in Room *g*. The vertical distribution of these items concentrated in Layers VI (nine fragments) and VII (five fragments), with Layers V and VIII contributing one sherd each (Fig. 3). The midden-like matrix of Layer VIII lay over patches of a burnt plaster floor that rested on or very close to bedrock. This 20 cm-thick level contained the seventh-century jar rim fragment of hard, reddish ware.[123] A much

---

117 For parallels and a fuller discussion, see Tappy, *The Archaeology of Israelite Samaria, II*, 423–25.
118 *SS III*, fig. 11: 4, 6.
119 *SS III*, fig. 11: 30–31, 33.
120 *SS III*, fig. 11: 30.
121 See Tappy, *The Archaeology of Israelite Samaria, II*, 370, fig. 62.
122 See Tappy, *The Archaeology of Israelite Samaria, II*, 371–72, fig. 63.
123 *SS III*, fig. 11: 27.

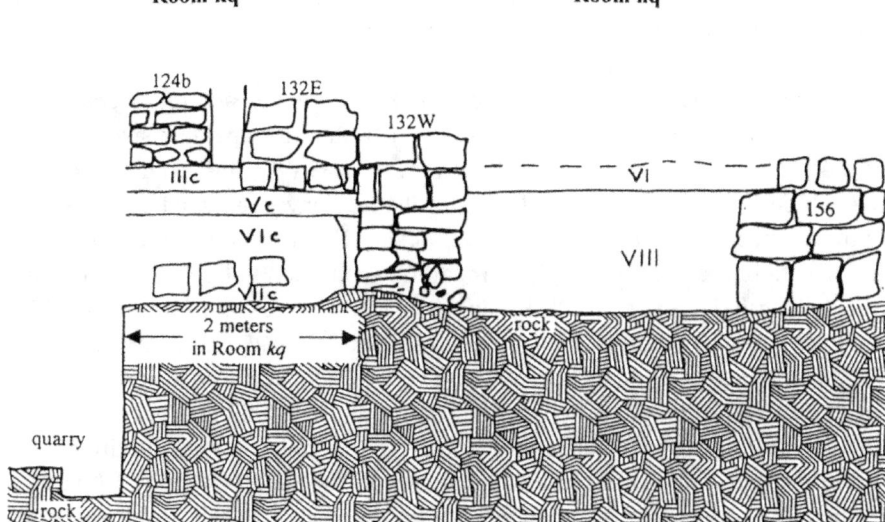

Fig. 3: Rooms hq and kq, view toward south. Reproduced from Kathleen Mary Kenyon, *Fieldbook Qk-l-m, Notes from the 1933 Season of Excavation*, 46a; courtesy of the Palestine Exploration Fund, London.

thicker deposit of rubble-filled earth (Layer VII) covered the surviving portion of VIII. The next layer actually consisted of two substantially thicker deposits of cleaner fill, both of which were labeled Layer VI. These levels do not reflect the remains of battle; rather, they appear to be routine fillings designed to raise or prepare a building level for the following phase of construction. For example, the double deposit of Layer VI became the subfloor makeup for the hard, yellow-colored clay of the Period VIII surface in Layer V, which did not remain intact across the entire area of Room g. The repertoire recovered from these combined levels dates almost exclusively to the seventh century BCE.[124] Moreover, the origins of all the published bowls from the earlier Layer VII lie in the seventh century,[125] and even the tall-necked jar fragment[126] from the debris of Layer VIII likely dates no earlier than the seventh century BCE. It may, in fact, represent a local imitation of a Neo-Assyrian form, but with the hard-fired red ware distinguishing it from the greenish-buff clay often used in the manufacture of true As-

---

124 From Layer VI, see *SS III*, fig. 11: 10, 18–20, 32, 34, 37; for Layer VIw, see fig. 11: 9. The profiled jar fragment in fig. 11: 24 represents the only piece belonging to the eighth century BCE.
125 *SS III*, fig. 11: 1, 5, 7, 14.
126 *SS III*, fig. 11: 27.

syrian vessels. If this piece does not represent an intrusive element in Layer VIII, then the *terminus post quem* of this and all successive layers belongs in the seventh century BCE or later.

Segment 509.126 reportedly spanned three laterally adjoining chambers: Rooms *f*, *j*, and *l* (with Room *l* actually constituting an open-air space). Three of the Period VII fragments published from this area[127] came from Layer IIa.f., the rubble lying beneath Floor IIa (a level that Kenyon equated with Layer V in the above-mentioned Segment 120.121.19.126). The field notes describe deposit IIa as a "floor sealing IIa.f. ... [that] apparently contains H[ellenistic] pottery, but this [is] poss[ibly] a mistake."[128] A single jar rim[129] came from Layer VIII, which the excavators correlated with Layer Va of Segment 504.503.509.508 and Layer IIa.f. mentioned above. In keeping with my earlier judgment regarding Layer Va, then, these deposits reflect a dumping of imported fill against the face of a much later feature.[130] That some of the ceramic forms contained in this matrix appear to stem from earlier traditions than many of the other Period VII vessels further supports its identification as imported secondary fill with an open *terminus post quem*.

Finally, Segment West of 124 ran primarily through the westernmost portion of Room *kq*, near the eastern face of Wall 132 (Fig. 2). It also, however, appears to have included levels lying on the opposite (western) side of 132, in Room *hq*. Both chambers belong to the better-constructed complex of rooms on the plateau of the central summit, just above the rock scarp that dropped down to Rooms *f* through *l*. As noted earlier, hardly any of *kq* survived the heavy Roman quarrying immediately to the east (Fig. 3).

The excavators published a series of five Period VII bowls that came from this segment. Once again, the results of both ceramic and stratigraphic analyses of this area concur with the conclusions reached for other segments. One bowl,[131] for instance, came from Room *kq* Layer IIIc, a mixed deposit of soot and hard yellow matrix situated just beneath the R.3 (late second century CE) Wall 124a. Kenyon herself described this and similar bowls as "all near the seventh century type with thickened rim, often nearly triangular in section."[132] While this form first appeared in significant numbers during the late eighth century, its floruit occurred in the seventh and even early-sixth centuries BCE. A thin-walled

---

127 *SS III*, fig. 11: 16, 21, 26.
128 Kenyon, *Fieldbook Qn*, Vol. II, 104a.
129 *SS III*, fig. 11: 29.
130 Wall 555; see Tappy, *The Archaeology of Israelite Samaria*, II, 373, fig. 64.
131 *SS III*, fig. 11: 3.
132 *SS III*, 127.

bowl,[133] with its flange pushed up and tapered out to a point, represents a related though possibly even later (sixth century?) form. It derived from Layer Vc, a possible floor level in Room *kq* that ran up to the eastern face of Wall 132W.[134] Although this surface may constitute a reliable late-Israelite locus, the ceramic assemblage it yielded again seems quite mixed.[135]

The bowls[136] reflect, in my judgment, a mixture of traits found in two Assyrian traditions. While the body forms of these vessels closely resemble the Assyrian Palace Ware (or "Table Service") motif, the rim designs (strongly everted and often curled out) and especially the ware of the Samaria exemplars find parallels in the Ring-Based Bowls from Assyria. Both items came from Layer VIw, that is, that portion of a possible floor (VI) disturbed during the construction of Late Hellenistic Wall 133.

The very hard, thin black ware, the shallow exterior ribbing on the upper carination, and the tall flaring upper sidewalls of one piece in particular[137] make it the best candidate for being an authentic Assyrian import. It very likely represents an imitation of a metal prototype. Moreover, its stratigraphic context (in Layer VII) — between tightly spaced, hard-packed surfaces that Kenyon dated to Periods V and VII — may provide the most reliable findspot of any item published in connection with this period. Yet the floors in question show no signs of a massive destruction event. Furthermore, the collective attributes of this bowl do not demand an indisputable date prior to the fall of Israelite Samaria. In fact, Kenyon herself cited "exact parallels" from Tell el-Farah (N) Niveau I and Tell Jemmeh,[138] and ultimately concluded that this innovative pottery entered Samaria only during the resettlement programs of Sargon II (programs which, according to more recent research, probably did not begin much before 716 BCE).

On the basis of a comparative ceramic analysis alone, the chronological distribution of the Period VII assemblage overall appears as follows: ca. 19% of the group could easily date to the eighth century BCE, perhaps even before the events of 722–720 BCE;[139] approximately 8% seem slightly later, nearer the turn of the century;[140] but more than 70% of the collection seem at home in

---

133 *SS III*, fig. 11: 8.
134 Tappy, *The Archaeology of Israelite Samaria*, II, 387, fig. 70.
135 Compare the bowl rim in *SS III*, fig. 11: 8 with Kenyon's statement in *Fieldbook Qk-l-m*, 21a that the overall character of the pottery seemed "fairly early."
136 *SS III*, fig. 11: 11, 13.
137 *SS III*, fig. 11: 22.
138 *SS III*, 97.
139 *SS III*, fig. 11: 16, 18, 21, 24–25, 29, 31.
140 *SS III*, fig. 11: 19–20, 35.

the heart of the seventh century or even later.[141] More than 68% of the published group came from Rooms *e*, *g*, and *l*, that is, from the smaller, more poorly constructed and often heavily disturbed chambers situated below the rock scarp that delineated the central summit plateau. Roughly one-third of these forms reflect clear or probable ties to Assyrian traditions, though undoubtedly most represent only local imitations of foreign prototypes.[142]

From a stratigraphic analysis, two crucial points clearly emerge. First, none of the deposits from which the excavators removed this pottery can date earlier than the seventh century BCE (with the possible exception of the thin accumulation of occupational debris in Layer VII of Segment West of 124). On the lower end, the depositional history germane to the published pottery extends even into the early Roman period. Second, none of the stratigraphy that contained the ceramic assemblage reflects a coherent, *in situ* destruction level,[143] that is, a wholesale conflagration that ultimately spread evenly across the entire site, as claimed by Kenyon. The leveling over of burnt debris and mixed pottery (which generally shows little to no trace of burning) occurred, according to Kenyon, "sufficiently long after Sargon's conquest for pottery brought by the newcomers ... to be lying about."[144] Furthermore, a larger problem remains in that the published corpus of pottery derives not from a single layer — burnt or not — but from a wide array of disparate deposits that include clean leveling fill, the tumble of rubble-filled matrix, hard-packed floor levels from different cultural phases, at least two post-Israelite pit fills, the backfill of a late foundation trench, other late (Hellenistic and Roman) disturbances of various kinds, and only a very few pockets of potentially primary occupational debris from any historical period.

5 Conclusions

Judging from the evidence reviewed above, neither the Assyrian texts nor the archaeology of Samaria points to a physical destruction of the city near the close of the third quarter of the eighth century BCE. Various factors may offer

---

141 From the seventh century, see *SS III*, fig. 11: 1–7, 9–15, 17, 22–23, 26–28, 30, 34, 37; for later periods, see *SS III*, fig. 11: 8, 32 and especially 33 from the Hellenistic period.
142 E.g., see *SS III*, fig. 11: 9–15, 17(?), 23, 26–27. On the other hand, the bowl in fig. 11: 22, the painted jug in fig. 11: 28, and the Assyrian bottle in fig. 11: 34 may represent actual imported pieces.
143 The excavators themselves acknowledged that none of the purported destruction debris appeared *in situ*: *SS I*, 110.
144 Kenyon, *Royal Cities of the Old Testament*, 133.

at least a partial explanation for this situation. For example, the early encounter between Hoshea and Shalmaneser V recalled by later writers may not have occurred inside Israel at all. The *AEC* records that, following Tiglath-pileser III's actions against Damascus and Israel in 733–732 BCE, he proceeded "to Shapiya" in 731.[145] While the assault against the city of Sarrabanu began during this expedition, it turned into a protracted siege that extended at least into 729 BCE,[146] and the Assyrians had apparently not yet subdued Shapiya even by the writing of Summary Inscription 7, that is, not before 729 BCE and perhaps later still.[147] So the arrival in the Shapiya-Sarrabanu region of Hoshea's diplomatic corps to offer Israel's tribute to Assyria may not have transpired until quite some time after the traditionally accepted year of 731 BCE, much closer to the accession of Shalmaneser V. If the king designate accompanied his father to receive the tribute, it seems reasonable to believe that the biblical writers accepted this occasion as the earliest real encounter between Shalmaneser V and Hoshea, although the contact did not occur during a military campaign against Samaria.

It also seems to have been common for Assyrian leaders during these years to blockade the capital city of a region and to ravage the countryside without capturing or destroying the political center itself. Tiglath-pileser III employed the term *esēru* for this sometimes unplanned strategy[148] in relation to the Urartian capital of Turushpa in 735 BCE,[149] Damascus in 733 BCE,[150] and Shapiya in 731 BCE.[151] Similarly, Sennacherib's later use of *esēru* in relation to Jerusalem may reflect his different approach to that city as compared with Lachish.[152] There is no reason to doubt that the intervening Assyrian rulers employed the same tactic — one that may help to explain further why we read of various sieges against Samaria (the region),[153] but remain unable to correlate coherent destruction levels from the capital city with the extant textual records.[154] As indicated

---

[145] Millard, *The Eponyms of the Assyrian Empire*, 59.
[146] Tadmor, *The Inscriptions of Tiglath-pileser III*, 161, n. 15.
[147] Tadmor, *The Inscriptions of Tiglath-pileser III*, 154, 163, n. 23.
[148] See above, Sub-category 2.4 and Category 3 with n. 40 on the language of conquest.
[149] Summary Inscription 1: 23–24 (Tadmor, *The Inscriptions of Tiglath-pileser III*, 125, nn. 23–24).
[150] Annal 23: 8'–9' (Tadmor, *The Inscriptions of Tiglath-pileser III*, 79, n. 11).
[151] Summary Inscription 7:23 (Tadmor, *The Inscriptions of Tiglath-pileser III*, 163, n. 23).
[152] See Tappy, "Historical and Geographical Notes."
[153] See the Palace Door Inscription IV: 32, the Small Display Inscription XIV: 15, the Cylinder Inscription l. 19, the Bull Inscription l. 21, and (for the sheer number of deportees mentioned) the Nimrud Prism iv 31.
[154] For destruction levels at Hill Country sites surrounding the city of Samaria, see Becking, *The Fall of Samaria*, 59–60, and, in greater detail with a balanced appraisal of the extent

earlier,[155] I believe that the final form of 2Kgs 17:4 may preserve an historical memory of Shalmaneser V's having implemented this strategy against the capital at Samaria. Interestingly, after Sennacherib's campaigns the term *esēru* does not appear in the records of Esarhaddon.

At any rate, the archaeological record of various northern sites around Samaria shows a consistent pattern of activity. Following the first substantial wave of military engagements throughout the northern valley areas during the decade of the 730s BCE, the Assyrians appear to have delayed regional administrative and building programs until after the final, political collapse of Israelite control over the capital in the late 720s.[156] After Stratum V at Hazor, even that site did not become a substantial citadel under the Assyrians until the time of Stratum III, with the intervening Stratum IV showing merely a small, unfortified settlement.

Yet once the Assyrians had firmly established control over a particular region and had selected (probably from economic interests) the most strategic sites they wished to rebuild and expand,[157] a much smoother transition between successive strata appears (e. g., Megiddo Strata III – II, Tell Keisan Levels 5 – 4a, 4b, etc.). Ultimately, the strategic importance of control over the more insular capital at Samaria was symbolic in nature — a signal that everything, from political center to outlying economic hubs, now belonged to Assyria. While a program to resettle foreign populations in Samaria and elsewhere began or at least accelerated during the rule of Sargon II (716 BCE on), the physical refurbishing of

---

and local impact of Israelite deportations, Gary N. Knoppers, "In Search of Post-Exilic Israel: Samaria after the Fall of the Northern Kingdom," in *In Search of Pre-Exilic Israel: Proceedings of the Oxford Old Testament Seminar*, ed. John Day (London: T&T Clark, 2004): 150 – 80. For a thorough and systematic archaeological assessment of sites in Galilee, Gilead, Samaria, and Philistia that are named in either the biblical or Neo-Assyrian texts and of sites that go unmentioned in these texts, see William G. Dever, "Archaeology and the Fall of the Northern Kingdom: What Really Happened?" in *Up to the Gates of Ekron: Essays on the Archaeology and History of the Eastern Mediterranean in Honor of Seymour Gitin*, ed. Sidnie White Crawford and Amnon Ben-Tor, (Jerusalem: The W. F. Albright Institute of Archaeological Research and the Israel Exploration Society, 2007): 78 – 92.

155 See above, n. 29.

156 Compare the transitions at Megiddo from Stratum IVA to III, at Ta'anach from Stratum IV to V, at Yoqne'am from Stratum 10 to 9, at Tell Abu Hawām from Stratum III to II, at Keisan from the occupational gap to Level 5, etc.

157 Compare Ekron and Gezer for parallels in the south: Amihai Mazar, "The Northern Shephelah in the Iron Age: Some Issues in Biblical History and Archaeology," in *Scripture and Other Artifacts: Essays on the Bible and Archaeology in Honor of Philip J. King*, ed. Michael D. Coogan, J. Cheryl Exum and Lawrence E. Stager (Louisville KY: Westminster John Knox, 1994): 247 – 67, esp. 260.

selected provincial centers (e.g., Megiddo more than Samaria) emerges from the archaeological record only during the late-eighth and seventh centuries BCE. Few traces of such a rebuilding effort have appeared in the depositional history of Samaria, apparently owing to the minimal destruction of the site by the Assyrians when they first "conquered" the city.

Norma Franklin
Megiddo and Jezreel Reflected in the Dying Embers of the Northern Kingdom of Israel

1 The Beginning of the End

In 746 BCE, Tiglath-pileser III came to the Assyrian throne as a usurper.[1] His foreign policy was markedly different to that of his predecessors: he enlarged the area of Assyrian control, annexed former client states and converted them into Assyrian provinces.[2] His rule marks the beginning of Assyria's imperial phase[3] and, significantly, also the beginning of the end of the Kingdom of Israel. The Northern Kingdom rebelled against Assyrian domination circa 734 BCE – an event heralded by the murder of Pekahiah, the son of Menahem, and the accession of Pekah to the Israelite throne in 736 BCE.[4] Tiglath-pileser responded to the general unrest in the region by conducting three campaigns[5] to the west, including at least one against Israel, between the years 734 and 732 BCE.[6] This resulted

---

[1] Stefan Zawadzki, "The Revolt of 746 BC and the Coming of Tiglath-pileser III to the Throne," *SAAB* 8 (1994): 53–54.
[2] Karen Radner, "Revolts in the Assyrian Empire: Succession Wars, Rebellions against a False King and Independence Movements," in *Revolts and Resistance in the Ancient Classical World and the Near East: In the Crucible of Empire*, ed. John J. Collins and Joseph G. Manning (Leiden: Brill, 2016): 47.
[3] Shigeo Yamada, "Inscriptions of Tiglath-pileser III: Chronographic-Literary Styles and the King's Portrait," *Orient* 49 (2014): 31.
[4] Nadav Na'aman, "Forced Participation in Alliances in the Course of the Assyrian Campaigns to the West," in *Ah, Assyria... Studies in Assyrian History and Ancient Near Eastern Historiography Presented to Hayim Tadmor*, ed. Mordechai Cogan and Israel Eph'al (Jerusalem: Magnes Press, 1991): 92–94.
[5] Tiglath-pileser conducted his 12th campaign (*palû*) in 734/733 BCE, along the Levantine Coast, travelling south via Šimirra-Tyre-Akzib-Akko-Dor-Ashkelon-Gaza. His 13th campaign was conducted from the area of Damascus and southeast of the River Jordan. It was only during the final, 14th campaign that Damascus was captured and the bulk of the Kingdom of Israel conquered, including Gezer. Samaria, the capital, and its immediate hinterland were spared and a new pro-Assyrian king, Hoshea, installed: Peter Dubovský, "Tiglath-pileser III's Campaigns in 734–732 B.C.: Historical Background of Isa 7; 2 Kgs 15–16 and 2 Chr 27–28," *Bib* 87 (1990): 158, 160–61.
[6] Hayim Tadmor, *The Inscriptions of Tiglath-pileser III King of Assyria. Critical Edition, with Introductions, Translations and Commentary* (Jerusalem: Israel Academy of Sciences and Humanities, 1994), 279–82; Nadav Na'aman, "Tiglath-pileser III's Campaign against Tyre and Israel (734–732 B.C.E.)," *TA* 22 (1995): 271.

in the incorporation of the Kingdom of Israel – except for the capital Samaria and its immediate hinterland – into the Assyrian Empire. The event is briefly recorded in 2Kgs 15:29 and contemporary Assyrian information is provided by Tiglath-pileser III's Summary Inscription, which states that Bit-Ḫumria, the Assyrian name for the Kingdom of Israel, had been captured[7] and gives its new borders,[8] while Tiglath-pileser's Annals describe the destruction and deportation from sixteen districts of Bit-Ḫumria.[9] The Kingdom of Israel was, in effect, no more; its only remnant was the rump state of Samaria, ruled by an Assyrian puppet-king, Hoshea.[10]

This paper focuses on Megiddo and Jezreel: the former was transformed into the provincial capital of Magiddû,[11] while the small settlement of Jezreel became a frontier site[12] on the border between Magiddû and Samaria.

2 Megiddo before Tiglath-pileser III

The Stratum IV[13] city of Megiddo on the eve of Tiglath-pileser's invasion was an incredible military and commercial enterprise that had been constructed some

---

[7] Tadmor, *The Inscriptions of Tiglath-pileser III*, Summ. 9 rev. 9' = Hayim Tadmor and Shigeo Yamada, *The Royal Inscriptions of Tiglath-pileser III (744–727 BC) and Shalmaneser V (726–722 BC), Kings of Assyria* (Winona Lake IN: Eisenbrauns, 2011), no. 49 rev. 9'.
[8] Tadmor, *The Inscriptions of Tiglath-pileser III*, Summ. 4: 6' = Tadmor and Yamada, *The Royal Inscriptions of Tiglath-pileser III*, no. 42: 6'.
[9] Tadmor, *The Inscriptions of Tiglath-pileser III*, Ann. 18: 3' = Tadmor and Yamada, *The Royal Inscriptions of Tiglath-pileser III*, no. 22: 3'; and Tadmor, *The Inscriptions of Tiglath-pileser III*, Ann. 24: 3' = Tadmor and Yamada, *The Royal Inscriptions of Tiglath-pileser III*, no. 21: 3'; cf. Kyle Lawson Younger Jr., "The Deportations of the Israelites," *JBL* 117 (1998): 206–207, 210.
[10] Hoshea was an Assyrian vassal, placed on the throne by Tiglath-pileser III, as recorded in Tadmor, *The Inscriptions of Tiglath-pileser III*, Summ. 4: 16'–9' = Tadmor and Yamada, *The Royal Inscriptions of Tiglath-pileser III*, no. 42: 16'–9'; cf. Kyle Lawson Younger Jr., "The Fall of Samaria in Light of Recent Research," *CBQ* 61 (1999): 478. This is the same policy that he employed some five years earlier (in 738 BCE), when he placed a puppet-king, Eni-ilu, over the reduced kingdom of Hamath: Na'aman, "Forced Participation in Alliances," 94.
[11] Ariel M. Bagg, "Palestine under Assyrian Rule: A New Look at Assyrian Imperial Policy in the West," *JAOS* 133 (2013): 123.
[12] For Assyrian frontier zone sites in the west, see Yifat Thareani, "The Empire and the 'Upper Sea': Assyrian Control Strategies along the Southern Levantine Coast," *BASOR* 375 (2016): 77–102.
[13] "Stratum IV" is the name for the stable city used by the team of the Oriental Institute of the University of Chicago (OIC). The name was changed to "Stratum IVA" following The Hebrew University of Jerusalem excavations conducted by Yigael Yadin in the late 1960s. "Stratum IV" will be used in this chapter.

fifty years earlier,[14] circa 782 BCE, during the early reign of Jeroboam II with the tacit agreement and logistical support of Adad-nerari III of Assyria (r. 810–783 BCE).[15] Its layout was reminiscent of a small-scale Assyrian arsenal, an *ekal māšarti*, used for muster in most major Assyrian cities. Although one cannot make a direct comparison between Megiddo and, for example, the *ekal māšarti* at Nineveh, which was the headquarters of the Assyrian army,[16] there are certain similarities. Both were built on a raised platform, had two courtyards and contained stone feeding troughs of similar size.

In addition to Megiddo's military role, its location on the Via Maris, the main highway linking Assyria with Egypt, also indicates that it was an important emporium. Megiddo's role as an Assyrian trading post (singular *bēt kāri*; plural *bēt karāni*) had been established when Israel was a client state under Adad-nerari III,[17] known to have established at least four new trading cities. While some of these trading posts were renamed with the prefix *Kār-* to designate their new role, there were also instances when the original city name continued to be used even by the Assyrians.[18] This appears to be the situation at Megiddo, which is mentioned by its original name in an Assyrian text[19] in the same line with cities known to be the seat of a *rab kāri* "Head of the trading post".[20]

Chariots were an essential part of both the Israelite and Assyrian armies. Consequently, horses were one of the main traded items in the ancient Near East, particularly large Kushite chariot horses from Egypt.[21] Megiddo was a city specifically constructed to deal with hundreds of horses, with two large stable complexes, one of which had two identical courtyards (Courtyards 977 and

---

14 It has been suggested that the life span of cities in the Iron Age is approximately 50 to 60 years: Amnon Ben-Tor, "Hazor and the Chronology of Northern Israel: a Reply to Israel Finkelstein," *BASOR* 317 (2000): 11. As noted by Israel Finkelstein, "Destructions: Megiddo as a Case Study," in *Exploring the Longue Durée: Essays in Honor of Lawrence E. Stager*, ed. David J. Schloen (Winona Lake IN: Eisenbrauns, 2009): 118–19, Megiddo Stratum IV (A) was not destroyed in 732 BCE.
15 See Norma Franklin, "Entering the Arena: The Megiddo Stables Reconsidered," in *Rethinking Israel: Studies in the History and Archaeology of Ancient Israel in Honor of Israel Finkelstein*, ed. Oded Lipschits, Yuval Gadot and Matthew Adams (Winona Lake IN: Eisenbrauns, 2017): 81–101.
16 Geoffrey Turner, "Tell Nebi Yūnus: The *Ekal Māšarti* of Nineveh," *Iraq* 32 (1970): 85.
17 Franklin, "Megiddo Stables Reconsidered."
18 Shigeo Yamada, "*Kārus* on the Frontiers of the Neo-Assyrian Empire," *Orient* 40 (2005): 58–62.
19 Fredrick Mario Fales and John Nicholas Postgate, *Imperial Administration Records, Part 2: Provincial and Military Administration* (Helsinki: University of Helsinki Press, 1995), no. 2.
20 A *rab kāri* would reside in the *kāru*: Yamada, "*Kārus* on the Frontiers," 77–81.
21 Deborah O. Cantrell, *The Horsemen of Israel: Horses and Chariotry in Monarchic Israel (Ninth–Eighth Centuries B.C.E.)* (Winona Lake IN: Eisenbrauns, 2011), 44–46.

1693) designed for chariot horses, which were stabled in the city and traded from it.²² A large facility such as the one at Megiddo could stable complete chariot squadrons of twenty and even fifty chariots, which is sixty to one hundred and fifty chariot horses at any one time.²³ Located on a major trade route, Megiddo would have been an important destination for Assyrian traders, in particular for the royal agents, the *tamkārū*, who traveled these trade routes, often accompanied by military personnel, in order to obtain whatever the Assyrian king needed, including horses.²⁴

This was the city that Tiglath-pileser took over. Clearly, there was no logic in destroying such a useful trading station and mustering facility; in fact, there were many reasons to preserve it intact and maintain its role.

3 Megiddo after Tiglath-pileser III

There is no sign of destruction at Megiddo from the time that Tiglath-pileser III launched his campaign(s) against Israel.²⁵ Megiddo presents a very different picture to that revealed by the surveys and excavations conducted in the area to the north of it, which shows that the region of the Upper Galilee was devastated in the 8th century BCE.²⁶ Its strategic location and economic potential²⁷ would have made Megiddo a natural candidate for the usual Assyrian practice of choosing a suitable pre-existing city and providing it with a residence for the governor.²⁸ Thus, Megiddo was made the administrative capital of a newly created Assyrian province named Magidû.

---

22 Specialized *bēt kāri* that dealt in the horse trade are known from the central Zagros region: Kyle Lawson Younger Jr., "The Assyrian Economic Impact on the Southern Levant in the Light of Recent Study," *IEJ* 65 (2015): 184–85 n. 14.
23 For the various sizes of a chariot squadrons and the number of squadron known to have been deployed, see Tamás Dezső, *The Assyrian Army I. The Structure of the Neo-Assyrian Army* (Budapest: Eötvös University Press, 2012), 136–47.
24 Karen Radner, "Traders in the Neo-Assyrian Period," in *Trade and Finance in Ancient Mesopotamia*, ed. Jan G. Dercksen (Istanbul: Nederlands Instituut voor het Nabije Oosten, 1999): 101–103, n. 10, n. 12.
25 Contra Nadav Na'aman, "Province System and Settlement Pattern in Southern Syria and Palestine in the Neo-Assyrian Period," in *Neo-Assyrian Geography*, ed. Mario Liverani (Rome: Università di Roma, 1995): 107; contra Younger, "Deportations of the Israelites," 213.
26 Zvi Gal, *Lower Galilee during the Iron Age* (Winona Lake IN: Eisenbrauns, 1992).
27 See Thareani, "Empire and the 'Upper Sea'," 79.
28 Karen Radner, "The Neo-Assyrian Empire," in *Imperien und Reiche in der Weltgeschichte*, ed. Michael Gehler and Robert Rollinger (Wiesbaden: Harrassowitz, 2014): 103.

Did this change of status mean that Megiddo was immediately rebuilt or redesigned to reflect its new position as an Assyrian provincial capital? While there is no doubt that Megiddo must have undergone some changes, the Assyrian city of Stratum III evolved very slowly.[29] According to the excavators, most walls of the buildings of this stratum were built directly on those of Stratum IV and there was no intervening accumulation of debris. During the life of Stratum III, buildings were frequently altered, sometimes even before completion.[30] An analysis of the gradual changes that the city underwent must reflect the changing role of Megiddo from an Israelite city to an Assyrian provincial capital: first as a capital of a frontier province, and later as a provincial capital functioning within the framework of the Assyrian Empire.

The earliest modification was the construction of a palace, a residence suitable for the Assyrian governor. Two large Assyrian residences, Buildings 1052 and 1369, were excavated by the Oriental Institute of Chicago (OIC). Building 1052[31] is the earlier of the two[32] and it is generally thought to be the original residence[33] for the governor, while Building 1369 represents a later addition.[34] The two buildings were connected by a suite of rooms consisting of Rooms 510 and 511 and a bathroom.[35] The enlargement of the Assyrian governor's palace and the addition of a bathroom must signify the growing importance of Megiddo and of

---

[29] Megiddo's slow transformation from Stratum IV to Stratum III is in complete contrast to the total makeover that the city underwent when Stratum IV was built (see Franklin, "Megiddo Stables Reconsidered"). Stratum III was calculated by the Oriental Institute of Chicago (OIC) to have lasted some 150 years from circa 780 to 650 BCE. If the inception of Stratum III is adjusted to the period of direct Assyrian rule, 734–732 BCE, Stratum III is still seen to be a long-lasting city, ca. a century, which evolved and changed slowly.
[30] Robert Lamon and Geoffrey M. Shipton, *Megiddo I: Seasons of 1925–34, Strata I–V* (Chicago IL: University of Chicago Press, 1939), 62.
[31] Building 1052 appears to be the only Assyrian building that has a regular, orthogonal plan. Gordon Loud, "An Architectural Formula for Assyrian Planning Based on the Results of Excavation of Khorsabad," *RA* 33 (1936): 160 noted that at Khorsabad courts in the majority of cases tend to approximate a square, although often due to having to fit into a city plan not a true square.
[32] Alexander Joffe, Eric Cline and Oded Lipschits, "Area H," in *Megiddo III: The 1992–1996 Seasons*, vol. 1, ed. Israel Finkelstein, David Ussishkin and Baruch Halpern (Tel Aviv: Emery and Claire Yass Publications in Archaeology, 2000): 160.
[33] Contra Ronny Reich, "The Stratigraphic Relationship between Palaces 1369 and 1052 (Stratum III) at Megiddo," *BASOR* 331 (2003): 39–44.
[34] Buildings 1052 and 1369 (Lamon and Shipton, *Megiddo I*, figs. 89 and 101, fig. 117) were rebuilt and adapted a number of times during the long period represented by Strata III and II (Lamon and Shipton, *Megiddo I*, 69).
[35] Lamon and Shipton, *Megiddo I*, 71.

its governor as the empire evolved. Interestingly, the area in the city that was chosen for the governor's palace was not suitable for sprawling monumental buildings. It was an area where the ground sloped steeply down[36] from elevation 167 m a.s.l. in the south (Grid Square O/8[37]) to elevation 153 m a.s.l. in the north (Grid Square L/8[38]): a drop of ca. 17 m over a distance of ca. 80 m. The large level area that formed the Southern Stable Complex would have been eminently suitable for the large-scale construction required for a palatial building, but it was not utilized. It has been noted previously that the public buildings (i.e., the stable complexes) were not destroyed when the Assyrians took over Megiddo, because they were still in use,[39] and that the transition was a gradual and peaceful one.[40] Therefore, I propose that the governor's residence was built on less suitable, sloping ground because the Southern Stable Complex continued to be used after the Assyrian takeover. Unfortunately, the available data regarding the Southern Stable Complex is not sufficient[41] to prove conclusively my theory regarding the longevity of the complex and the resultant location of the palace. However, the OIC did note that the stables had been used over a long period of time and that some of the pottery recovered from the floors of the Stratum IV complex might actually belong to Stratum III.[42]

Finally, the Southern Stable Complex was built over and elements from the stables were incorporated into the new domestic buildings. For example, pillars and troughs from Stable Unit 1612 were incorporated into the Stratum III Building 1423/1427[43] and two of the troughs in Stable Unit 1576 in Square R/6 continued to be used, *in situ*, in Stratum III. Four Assyrian underfloor bathtub burials were also found in the area of the former Southern Stable Complex and a fifth

---

36 Buildings 1052 and 1369, whose foundations resembled a small podium so that their interior surfaces could be at a uniform elevation, had external stone buttresses to strengthen and stabilize them (see Lamon and Shipton, *Megiddo* I, 70–71, figs. 81 and 89 Section A–B).
37 See Norma Franklin, "Revealing Stratum V at Megiddo," *BASOR* 342 (2006): 104, fig. 3.
38 See Lamon and Shipton, *Megiddo* I, fig. 89, Section A–B.
39 Israel Finkelstein and David Ussishkin, "Archaeological and Historical Conclusions," in *Megiddo* III, 598.
40 Baruch Halpern, "Centre and Sentry: Megiddo's Role in Transit, Administration and Trade," in *Megiddo* III, 563–64.
41 The Northern Stable Complex was discovered first and partially removed. The Southern Stable Complex was not removed. It was excavated near the end of Philip Langstaffe Orde Guy's tenure as director and, due to the pressure of work, the documentation is less detailed.
42 Lamon and Shipton, *Megiddo* I, 63.
43 Lamon and Shipton, *Megiddo* I, fig. 72.

was found slightly further north,⁴⁴ indicating a new Assyrian-influenced population. Fortunately, the longevity of the Northern Stable Complex is better documented.⁴⁵ It continued in use during Stratum III: Stable Unit 351 was adapted with the addition of mud-brick mangers or grain bins.⁴⁶ Eventually, when the stables were no longer needed, their mud-brick superstructure was deliberately pulled down—evident by a thick layer of mud-brick collapse in the aisles—in preparation for the construction of Stratum III.⁴⁷ One of the units, Stable Unit 404, was later incorporated into a Stratum III building.⁴⁸

The small domestic area exposed by the Tel Aviv University (TAU) excavations in their Area H also exhibits an extended period of use. TAU's Level H-3 was equated with the OIC's Stratum IV (IVA). The area was destroyed by fire, but the destruction was localized, with a 60 cm deep collapse containing many restorable vessels.⁴⁹ Of particular note was an Assyrian bottle (Vessel 1996/H/32/VS6) retrieved from Building Unit 8, a small domestic structure immediately below Building 1853 and an open courtyard north of Building 1369.⁵⁰ The locally manufactured bottle is significant for dating the end of Level H-3, and a recent study by Peter Van Der Veen⁵¹ has confirmed that this particular type of Assyrian bottle, known as a

---

44 Building 1060 in Sq. N/9 (Lamon and Shipton, *Megiddo* I, fig. 74) had five steps. At the lowest level there was an Assyrian bathtub. It is impossible to determine if this was an underfloor burial (robbed in antiquity) that was not recognized as such on excavation or if the Assyrian bathtub served as part of an installation in a subterranean room (Lamon and Shipton, *Megiddo* I, 63).
45 For example, the lime floor of Stable Unit 407 was reused by Stratum III rooms (452–458) signifying that they were built immediately after the unit ceased being used as a stable (Lamon and Shipton, *Megiddo* I, 74). Stable Unit 364 also continued in use during Stratum III and was reconstructed and enlarged during that period (Lamon and Shipton 1939, *Megiddo* I, 63–4). Stable Unit 351 also continued in use in Stratum III, and on excavation the troughs were found to be of mud-brick and rubble construction, causing the excavators to surmise that the original stone troughs had been discarded and the substitution made during the time of Stratum III (Lamon and Shipton, *Megiddo* I, 64 and fig. 76).
46 Lamon and Shipton, *Megiddo* I, 65, fig. 76.
47 Eric H. Cline, "Area L (the 1998–2000 Seasons)," in *Megiddo IV: The 1998–2002 Seasons*, vol. 1, ed. Israel Finkelstein, David Ussishkin and Baruch Halpern (Tel Aviv: Emery and Claire Yass Publications in Archaeology, 2006): 116.
48 See Lamon and Shipton, *Megiddo* I, figs. 49, 54, and 71.
49 Israel Finkelstein, Orna Zimhoni and Adi Kafri, "The Iron Age Pottery Assemblages from Areas F, K and H and Their Stratigraphic and Chronological Implications," in *Megiddo* III, 310.
50 That is, the Assyrian bottle was found below later additions to Stratum III (see Joffe, Cline and Lipschits, "Area H," 160) and may well denote the transition here from Stratum IV to Stratum III. See the following footnote.
51 The author is indebted to Peter Van Der Veen who noted that "based on my own observations on genuine Assyrian Palace Ware from the Assyrian heartland, there can be little doubt that the Neo-Assyrian dimpled beakers are a late Assyrian innovation which were only introduced from

Neo-Assyrian dimpled beaker, first appeared in Assyria during Sargon's reign and, consequently, locally made copies were an even later development.

So when did the gradual transition from Stratum IV to Stratum III take place and over how lengthy a time period? The transformation appears to have begun with the construction of Building 1052 for the newly appointed governor and ended when the stable complexes were finally built over and a new city gate was constructed.[52] It is presumed that whatever small population existed in Megiddo Stratum IV was deported at the same time that Tiglath-pileser III depopulated much of the Galilee.[53] However, possibly of greater importance is the question of when Megiddo was repopulated by the Assyrians. The Assyrians brought in deportees from the east between 716 and 708 BCE.[54] They would have required housing, and the proliferation of domestic buildings in Stratum III provides a clue. Jennifer Peersmann has argued that Megiddo was repopulated by Sargon some five years after the final fall of Samaria.[55] Baruch Halpern, on the other hand, noted that the Assyrian domestic area appears to be orientated with the east wing of Building 1369, suggesting that the domestic area was built only after the governor's palace had been extended to include that building.[56] He proposes, therefore, that the repopulation of Assyrian Megiddo may have taken place in the time of Sennacherib or even as late as Esarhaddon. Another clue is provided by the change, already apparent in 709 BCE, from chariotry to cavalry,[57] which would have made the chariot stable complexes and the deep-chambered gates obsolete. Eventually, the Southern Stable Complex became a well-organized domestic area, and four Assyrian bathtub burials[58] provide sound evidence for the ethnic origin of at least part of the population. Even if

---

the late 8th century BCE onwards (i.e. during the Sargonid period). Southern Levantine imitations therefore postdate the introduction in the central polity of Assyria" (pers. comm.).

52 Cantrell, *The Horsemen of Israel*, 76–86 has suggested that the deep chambers of the Stratum IV six-chambered city gate were designed to facilitate the harnessing of the chariot teams.

53 2Kgs 15:29 mentions the deportation of the residents of both Upper and Lower Galilee: Ijon, Abel-beth-maacah, Janoah, Kedesh, Hazor, Gilead and Galilee, including the land of Naphtali. No mention is made of Megiddo or Jezreel.

54 Nadav Na'aman, "Population Changes in Palestine Following the Assyrian Deportations," *TA* 20 (1993): 109–11; Nadav Na'aman and Ran Zadok, "Sargon II's Deportations to Israel and Philistia (716–708)," *JCS* 40 (1988): 42–46.

55 Jennifer Peersmann, "Assyrian Magiddu: The Town Planning of Stratum III," in *Megiddo* III, 532.

56 Halpern, "Centre and Sentry," 568.

57 Stephanie Dalley, "Foreign Chariotry and Cavalry in the Armies of Tiglath-pileser III and Sargon II," *Iraq* 47 (1985): 37–38.

58 A fifth bathtub burial was found slightly northwest of the Assyrian palace buildings.

a firm date is impossible to establish, it is evident that the Stratum III domestic quarters evolved slowly, starting with the construction of a small governor's palace circa 732 and possibly ending circa 701 BCE. The OIC attempted to divide Stratum III into IIIB (earlier) and III (later), observing that this simply reflects the rebuilding and renovation that took place throughout the period, while Stratum II is simply a continuation of the preceding phase.[59]

4 Jezreel before Tiglath-pileser III

Jezreel[60] on the eve of Tiglath-pileser's invasion was a military enclosure that had been constructed at more or less the same time as Megiddo, during the reign of Jeroboam II.[61] It too could be classified as an *ekal māšarti*,[62] albeit much smaller than the one at Megiddo; however, an 8th-century-BCE date for Jezreel and a correlation with the Stratum IV stable city of Megiddo is not universally accepted, so a brief account of the argument will be presented here.

The upper tell was excavated in the 1990s, but only three preliminary reports dealing almost exclusively with the Iron Age phases, pertinent to this paper, were published[63] and no final publication is expected.[64] The excavators uncovered a

---

59 Lamon and Shipton, *Megiddo* I, 62.
60 Jezreel consists of two sites: An upper tell, Tel Jezreel, is located on the summit of a rocky hill that was continuously inhabited until the middle of the last century. A lower tell, Tel 'Ein Jezreel, is located by the perennial spring of 'Ein Jezreel, which was inhabited until the late Roman period. Both sites had been plundered throughout the ages for building material and preservation is poor, complicating our understanding of the history and archaeology of Jezreel (greater Jezreel). The area of greater Jezreel was surveyed in 2012 and since 2013 the lower tell has been excavated by a team from the University of Haifa and the University of Evansville, led by Norma Franklin and Jennie Ebeling, respectively.
61 See Norma Franklin, "Jezreel before and after Jezebel," in *Israel in Transition: From Late Bronze II to Iron IIa (c. 1250 – 850 BCE)*, ed. Lester L. Grabbe (London: T&T Clark, 2008), 45 – 53.
62 Aster has pointed out that the enclosure at Jezreel also functioned as an *ekal māšarti* and to the fact that Jezreel is referred to in 1Kgs 21:1 as having a *heikal* (translated there as palace); the term is most likely derived from the Akkadian *ēkallu*, which is another reason to recognize Jezreel as an *ekal māšarti*, a military enclosure. See Shawn Zelig Aster, "The Function of the City of Jezreel and the Symbolism of Jezreel in Hosea 1–2," *JNES* 71 (2012): 39.
63 Excavations from 1990 to 1996 were conducted by a joint expedition of Tel Aviv University (TAU) and the British School of Archaeology in Jerusalem (BSAJ) and directed by David Ussishkin and John Woodhead, respectively.
64 A final report was in preparation by the Council for British Research in the Levant, but it has apparently been abandoned.

poorly preserved[65] Iron Age enclosure on the summit of the hill of Tel Jezreel, the date of which has been a controversial subject for the last two decades. Despite the "badly preserved strata",[66] the enclosure was attributed to the 9th century BCE, the period of the Omride dynasty "on the basis of the limited stratigraphic evidence and in accord with the biblical source",[67] and reaffirmed by David Ussishkin.[68] This is unfortunate, as archaeology in the latter half of 20th century should not have relied on the biblical narrative to determine the chronology of a site or to establish the date of a particular architectural feature.[69]

Only a selection of the Iron Age pottery was published and in the words of the late Orna Zimhoni: "Unfortunately, such an arbitrary collection may omit precisely the vessels which would enable us to determine the exact date of the assemblage." [70] Ceramic parallels for the published material were found in Megiddo Stratum V (i.e., VA–IVB) and Stratum IV (IVA),[71] which, at that time, was dated to the 10th–9th centuries BCE by Zimhoni, Ussishkin and other scholars. This meant that the published pottery associated with the Jezreel enclosure was "dated generally within the 10th to 9th centuries BCE".[72] Notably, following

---

[65] Preservation was poor due to stone robbing, various episodes of destruction and later building from the Iron Age through the Roman-Byzantine period and up to modern times. See David Ussishkin and John Woodhead, "Excavations at Tel Jezreel 1992–1993: Second Preliminary Report," *Levant* 26 (1994): 16.
[66] Ussishkin and Woodhead, "Excavations at Tel Jezreel 1992–1993," 3.
[67] David Ussishkin and John Woodhead, "Excavations at Tel Jezreel 1990–1991: Preliminary Report," *TA* 19 (1992): 53.
[68] David Ussishkin, "The Credibility of the Tel Jezreel Excavations: a Rejoinder to Amnon Ben-Tor," *TA* 27 (2000): 248; id., "Samaria, Jezreel, and Megiddo: Royal Centers of Omri and Ahab," in *Ahab Agonistes: the Rise and Fall of the Omri Dynasty*, ed. Lester L. Grabbe (London: T&T Clark, 2007): 301.
[69] The original dating of the Megiddo Stratum IV stables serves as an excellent example of how one should not use the biblical narrative as a chronological tool. Philip Langstaffe Orde Guy, *New Light from Armageddon: Second Provisional Report (1927–29) on the Excavations at Megiddo in Palestine* (Chicago IL: University of Chicago Press, 1931), 45–48 used the verses in 1Kgs 9:15–19 to link Stratum IV to Solomon and to place it the 10th century BCE.
[70] See Orna Zimhoni "The Iron Age Pottery from Tel Jezreel – an Interim Report," *TA* 19 (1992): 57–58. Zimhoni's study focused on the three most common vessel types: bowls, cooking pots, and storage jars, similar to her research strategy at Lachish (1990). Sadly, she passed away before she could study all the Jezreel pottery.
[71] Zimhoni, "Iron Age Pottery from Jezreel," 69. Stratum IVA and certain loci of Stratum IVB correspond to Stratum IV, the stable city; see Franklin, "Revealing Stratum V at Megiddo" and ead., "Megiddo Stables Reconsidered."
[72] Zimhoni, "Iron Age Pottery from Jezreel," 69.

Israel Finkelstein's low chronology correction[73] and TAU's excavation of the remaining Stratum IV stable units at Megiddo, pottery that was once attributed to the 10th and 9th centuries was down-dated to the 8th century BCE. Nonetheless, in an attempt to preserve a 9th-century-BCE date for the Jezreel enclosure, the Jezreel pottery was compared by Zimhoni with pottery that she mistakenly presumed belonged to Megiddo Stratum V (VA–IVB).[74] Unfortunately, the Megiddo pottery loci chosen for comparison were contained in the Stratum IV deep constructional fill below Courtyard 1693.[75] This courtyard is part of the stable city[76] and its constructional fill was laid down when this city was constructed in ca. 782 BCE. This misunderstanding preserved the illusion that the Jezreel enclosure was built in the 9th century, at the same time as Stratum V (Strata VA–IVB).

Following criticism on the comparison of the Jezreel enclosure with Megiddo Stratum V (i.e., VA–IVB[77]) and on the security of the loci that yielded the Jezreel pottery,[78] I analyzed the construction techniques used to build the Jezreel enclosure.[79] In brief, the enclosure phase at Jezreel and the Stratum IV stable city at Megiddo share similar construction methods that do not appear in the 9th century BCE, namely, an artificial podium to create a level plastered surface, built-up foundations, mixed ashlar and fieldstone construction, the use of strengthening

---

[73] Israel Finkelstein, "The Archaeology of the United Monarchy: An Alternative View," *Levant* 27 (1996): 177–87.
[74] Orna Zimhoni, "Clues from the Enclosure Fills: Pre-Omride Settlement at Tel Jezreel," *TA* 24 (1997): 91. Stratum VA and some loci of IVB belong to the multiphased Stratum V (see Franklin, "Revealing Stratum V at Megiddo"). Gordon Loud, the third director of the OIC excavations, had noted that Stratum V had no less than three phases (Lamon and Shipton, *Megiddo* I, 7, n. 4).
[75] Zimhoni thought that the pottery was from the floors of the pillared buildings, e.g., Building 1706 in Square Q/10, sealed below Courtyard 1693. However, although the pillared buildings belonged to a late phase of Stratum V (Franklin, "Revealing Stratum V at Megiddo," 107; Franklin, "Megiddo Stables Reconsidered," 94–5; Lamon and Shipton, *Megiddo* I, 3–5, figs. 5 and 8), the pottery reanalyzed by Zimhoni was contained within the Stratum IV constructional fill that buried the Stratum V pillared buildings. The fill would have been brought in from elsewhere on the site and, therefore, the pottery contained in it cannot be used to achieve a secure date. Unfortunately, further confusion was provided by the fact that the Stratum IV fill below Courtyard 1693 was registered as Locus -1693 (minus 1693) of Stratum V, while the constructional fill below the identical, adjacent courtyard, Courtyard 977, was registered as Locus 1674 of Stratum IV (Franklin, "Revealing Stratum V at Megiddo," 99).
[76] Lamon and Shipton, *Megiddo* I, 17, figs. 34, 43; Anabel Zarzecki-Peleg, *Yadin's Expedition to Megiddo: Final Report of the Archaeological Excavations (1960, 1966, 1967 and 1971/2 Seasons)* (Jerusalem: Publications of the Institute of Archaeology, 2016): 104, 209–10; Franklin, "Megiddo Stables Reconsidered," 94–95.
[77] Zarzecki-Peleg, *Yadin's Expedition to Megiddo*, 286.
[78] Ben-Tor, "Hazor and Chronology."
[79] Franklin, "Before and after Jezebel."

ashlar piers and marginal drafting. Collectively these are all 8th century BCE building techniques,[80] which means that the enclosure phase at Jezreel dates to the 8th century and, as correctly noted by Ussishkin and John Woodhead, functioned as a military base.[81]

Jezreel's role was to protect the principal route to the capital Samaria. Located at the junction of the Via Maris and the Ridge Route, the local highway running south to the capital, Samaria, Jezreel was also situated at the narrowest point of the Jezreel Valley, opposite the village of Shunem.[82] Together these two sites formed a bottleneck that controlled the route west to the Levantine Coast. Thus, during the apogee of the Northern Kingdom, when the enemy— whether Aramean or Assyrian—was located to the northeast, Jezreel had an important military function helping to protect the trade route to the coast and serving as an *ekal māšarti*, an arsenal and mustering station, for the Israelite capital.

5 Jezreel after Tiglath-pileser III

After 732 Jezreel's important role as the gatekeeper of Samaria was no longer relevant, but it still had a function, albeit a much diminished one, and the site was not destroyed.[83] The only destruction observed was a localized layer of burnt debris contained within the foundations of the enclosure's southeastern tower.[84] The pottery-rich debris from the tower, Locus 214, contained material that had collapsed into the basement from the tower's upper story.[85] Among it was a large group of restorable storage jars,[86] one of which is of particular interest:[87] this vessel has close parallels in the southern Coastal Plain and Judah[88] and is

---

80 Franklin, "Revealing Stratum V at Megiddo," 108.
81 Ussishkin and Woodhead, "Tel Jezreel 1992–1993," 47; David Ussishkin and John Woodhead, "Excavations at Tel Jezreel 1994–1996: Third Preliminary Report," *TA* 24 (1997): 70.
82 Shunem of 2Kgs 4, known today as Sulam.
83 Jezreel is mentioned in Hos 1:4–5, 2:2, 24 in reference to a historical event. Although there is no agreement as to which specific event is referenced, it is clearly a military and political one (or possibly more than one). See Aster, "Function of Jezreel," 33–34.
84 This localized destruction has often been interpreted incorrectly as the destruction of the entire enclosure; however, the enclosure was not destroyed and the excavators never claimed that it was; see Ussishkin and Woodhead, "Tel Jezreel 1992–1993," 46.
85 Ussishkin and Woodhead, "Tel Jezreel 1992–1993," 25–28.
86 Zimhoni, "Clues from Enclosure Fills," figs. 10–11.
87 Zimhoni, "Clues from Enclosure Fills," fig. 11: 5.
88 Orna Zimhoni, "Two Ceramic Assemblages from Lachish Levels III and II," *TA* 17 (1990): 27–29; fig. 17: 3, Group IIIE.

best known from contexts dating to the late 8th and 7th centuries BCE.[89] Evidence for 8th-century and later settlement was found across the site but, unfortunately, there were no secure loci. One example is the thick-rimmed cooking pots that were found in all excavated areas.[90] The base of a wedge-shaped decorated bowl found unstratified in Area D (Fig. 9: 3) suggests a 7th – 6th-centuries-BCE settlement.[91] Lastly, a late Iron Age, red-slipped, ring-based carinated bowl, wheel-burnished on the inside (Reg. No. 15538) was found intact in Sq. T/50; it imitates an Assyrian bronze bowl.[92] Further evidence for an 8th – 6th-century-BCE settlement at Jezreel was provided by the small finds. They include two ceramic horse heads that date to the 8th – 7th centuries BCE[93] and three weights (one hematite and two limestone) that compare with similar weights found in Megiddo Stratum III or II.[94] A fragment of a stone-carved incense bowl was also compared with examples from Megiddo Stratum III or II.[95] The Megiddo examples were published by Herbert May[96] and dated to the 7th and 8th centuries BCE. A nearly complete stone cosmetic palette was dated to between the 8th and 6th centuries BCE, and has parallels from Megiddo Strata I to III.[97] Four late Iron Age burials were excavated, three of which were very close together: Cists G.1239 and G.1260 and Assyrian bathtub Burial G.2000.[98] Grave 1260 contained burial goods: an alabaster palette dated to the 7th century BCE, a bronze mirror dating, possibly, to the Persian period and a bronze bowl.[99] Lastly, two LMLK stamped jar handles[100] provide evidence for activity ca. 701 BCE.[101] In short, the excavators documented 8th – 7th centuries BCE Iron Age material remains in all the excavated

---

89 Zimhoni, "Clues from Enclosure Fills," 100.
90 Zimhoni, "Iron Age Pottery from Jezreel," 68, fig. 9: 1–2.
91 Zimhoni, "Iron Age Pottery from Jezreel," 68.
92 Zimhoni, "Clues from Enclosure Fills," 108, fig. 15: 2.
93 Raz Kletter, "Clay Figurines and Scale Weights from Tel Jezreel," *TA* 24 (1997): 110.
94 Kletter, "Clay Figurines," 117.
95 Ussishkin and Woodhead, "Tel Jezreel 1992–1993," 40–1, fig. 56.
96 Herbert May, *Material Remains of the Megiddo Cult* (Chicago IL: University of Chicago Press, 1935), 19, pl. 18.
97 Ussishkin and Woodhead, "Tel Jezreel 1994–1996," 66–67, fig. 56; Lamon and Shipton, *Megiddo* I, pls. 108–11.
98 Ussishkin and Woodhead, "Tel Jezreel 1994–1996," 32–40, figs. 20, 22–23, 26, 31–34.
99 Ussishkin and Woodhead, "Tel Jezreel 1994–1996," 33–36, figs. 27–30.
100 The first was a surface find and was held by a local collector in Kibbutz Beit Alfa (information curtesy of Gabriel Barkay). The second, a *mmšt* stamp, was found in a salvage excavation; see Ora Yogev, "Tel Yizreel, 1987/1988," *Hadashot Arkheologiyot – Excavations and Surveys in Israel* 92–93 (1988/1989): 192, fig. 160.
101 Ussishkin and Woodhead, "Tel Jezreel 1990–1991," 10; and Gabriel Barkay, pers. comm.

squares that they presumed postdated the enclosure,[102] yet there were no small finds that they could attribute to a 9th century BCE enclosure.

Finally, eight iron arrowheads were retrieved from Areas A and F and, in the words of the excavators, "four or five of the iron arrowheads were found in a context *likely associated* with the Iron Age enclosure." They went on to state that "the discovery of iron arrowheads in the context of the enclosure is an important datum indicating the use of arrowheads in Palestine in the middle of the 9th century BCE."[103] However, more recent research conducted by Yulia Gottlieb has conclusively shown that iron arrowheads did not become common before the end of the 9th century BCE.[104] In addition, according to Gottlieb, only two of the Jezreel arrowheads can be dated with any certainty, specifically the two retrieved from debris in an installation (L154) near the enclosure's gatehouse, and they cannot be earlier than the 8th century BCE.[105]

An Excursus: the Communication Network

Once the Assyrians had annexed a region, it was linked to the imperial information network by a system of roads[106] known as the *hūl šarri*:[107] the King's Road or the Royal Road. This was a high-speed communications network essential to ensure efficient Assyrian administration. Sections of the *hūl šarri* were maintained

---

102 Ussishkin and Woodhead, "Tel Jezreel 1994–1996," 32.
103 Ibid. 64–66 fig. 55. This is an unfortunate example of circular reasoning, i.e., the date of the enclosure was dated, based on biblical evidence, to the 9th century, and the first appearance of iron arrowheads was therefore pushed back to the 9th century, though no examples appeared elsewhere earlier than the 8th century.
104 Yulia Gottlieb, "Beer-Sheba under Attack: A Study of Arrowheads and the Story of Destruction of the Iron Age Settlement," in *Beer-Sheba* III: *the Early Iron IIA Enclosed Settlement and the Late Iron IIA–Iron IIB Cities*, ed. Ze'ev Herzog and Lily Singer-Avitz (Tel Aviv: Emery and Claire Yass Publications in Archaeology, 2016): 1193.
105 Yulia Gottlieb, pers. comm.
106 Radner, "The Neo-Assyrian Empire," 103. While there are no Assyrian documents that mention the actual road system, much can be gleaned from Assyrian state letters; see Karen Radner, "An Imperial Communication Network: The State Correspondence of the Neo-Assyrian Empire," in *State Correspondence in the Ancient World: From New Kingdom Egypt to the Roman Empire*, ed. Karen Radner (Oxford: Oxford University Press, 2014): 64.
107 Karen Radner, "Royal Pen Pals: the Kings of Assyria in Correspondence with Officials, Clients and Total Strangers (8th and 7th Centuries BC)," in *Official Epistolography and the Language (s) of Power. Proceedings of the First International Conference of the Research Network Imperium and Officium*, ed. Stephan Procházka, Lucian Reinfandt and Sven Tost (Vienna: Austrian Academy of Sciences Press, 2015): 63.

by the relevant Assyrian provincial governor,[108] as they were vital for both administrative and military matters.[109]

Also in these newly conquered regions,[110] forts that served as outposts for an Assyrian garrison were established. They functioned as military centers and information hubs.[111] In this way Assyria was connected, via a network of fortresses, to the outlying areas facilitating the passage of messengers, armies and military supplies needed to control the provinces and convey revenue back to the heartland.[112] The *hūl šarri* was divided into stages (Ass. *mardētu*), and staging-posts (Ass. *bēt mardēti*, plural *bēt mardiāte*), which were set up at strategic locations, especially at intersections.[113] These *bēt mardiāte* were reserved solely for Assyrian use,[114] and were maintained by the local Assyrian governor. The term *mardētu* may refer to a strategic location along the route, such as an important intersection, rather than indicate the existence of an actual *bēt mardēti*.[115] In any case, it is unlikely that all *bēt mardiāte* were of a uniform layout or size. Rather, the appellation and function of the different stations must have been determined by their location within the empire and by the jurisdiction they were under — of a provincial governor or the Assyrian capital.[116]

---

108 Radner, "Imperial Communication Network," 68, 71.
109 Karlheinz Kessler, "'Royal Roads' and Other Questions of the Neo-Assyrian Communication System," in *Assyria 1995: Proceedings of the 10th Anniversary Symposium of the Neo-Assyrian Text Corpus Project*, ed. Simo Parpola and Robert M. Whiting (Helsinki: Neo-Assyrian Text Corpus Project, 1997): 129.
110 Although the Assyrian administrative letters that are available to us today deal almost exclusively with the Assyrian frontier region in the east, e.g., Urartu, similar correspondence must have once existed in the west.
111 Bradley J. Parker "Garrisoning the Empire: Aspects of the Construction and Maintenance of Forts on the Assyrian Frontier," *Iraq* 59 (1997): 77.
112 Fredrick Mario Fales, "Palatial Economy in Neo-Assyrian Documentation: An Overview," in *Palatial Economy in the Ancient Near East and in the Aegean: First Steps towards a Comprehensive Study and Analysis*, ed. Pierre Carlier, Francis Joannès, Françoise Rougemont and Julien Zurbach (Pisa: Serra, 2017): 273. A communication system was probably set up as early as the days of Shalmaneser III (858–824 BCE); see Radner, "Imperial Communication Network," 71; but the earliest reference dates to Adad-nerari III's time: Fales and Postgate, *Imperial Administration Records, Part 2*, no. 1: 9, 16; no. 2 rev 5; see Kessler, "Royal Roads," 130.
113 Radner, "Imperial Communication Network," 73.
114 Radner, "Imperial Communication Network," 73; Radner, "Royal Pen Pals," 63.
115 See Kessler, "Royal Roads," 134; it has also been suggested that the term *mardētu* denotes the distance between stages that could be ridden in one day: Natalie Naomi May, "Administrative and Other Reforms of Sargon II and Tiglath-pileser III," *SAAB* 21 (2015): 95.
116 Kessler, "Royal Roads," 135.

Radner has previously noted that no *bēt mardēti* has been recognized in the archaeological record;[117] however, Aster has recently identified one near Tel Hadid,[118] a site located on the direct route to Gezer.[119] Although Aster mentions forts designed for muster and for specifically provisioning the army *en route* to a campaign, he describes some of these staging posts as Assyrian administrative centers with specific characteristics, including agricultural installations.[120] Karen Radner notes that the *bēt mardiāte*, often located in pre-existing settlements, needed to have the necessary agricultural infrastructure required to support the Assyrian envoys and transport animals.[121] Therefore, an important prerequisite of a *bēt mardēti* would be a small but permanent civilian population to cultivate the land in order to provide provisions.[122]

6 The Role of Megiddo under Assyrian Rule

It is very probable that prior to the invasion of Tiglath-pileser III the Israelite chariot units were based at strategically located Megiddo rather than at Samaria,[123] which was buried deep in the mountainous heartland of ancient Israel. Furthermore, following Tiglath-pileser's invasion, it is questionable if Hoshea was allowed to keep more than a token chariot force at Samaria. Israelite chariots do not appear on the Khorsabad reliefs depicting Sargon's defeat of Samaria; only the Assyrian chariots are shown.[124] That is, by the time that Samaria fell, the major part of the Israelite chariot force may have been under Assyrian rule at Megiddo for more than a decade. It is recorded that following Sargon's final defeat of Samaria he incorporated an Israelite team of fifty chariots,[125] including

---

117 Radner, "Imperial Communication Network," 73.
118 Shawn Zelig Aster, "An Assyrian *bīt mardite* Near Tel Hadid?" *JNES* 74 (2017): 281.
119 Aster, "An Assyrian *bīt mardite*," 288.
120 Aster, "An Assyrian *bīt mardite*," 282–84.
121 Radner, "Imperial Communication Network," 73.
122 This is deduced from Aster's reading of two cuneiform tablets found at Tel Hadid, which testify to the presence of deportees (and whose task may have been to maintain the *bēt mardēti*): Aster, "An Assyrian *bīt mardite*," 287.
123 There is no evidence for the availability of stables or chariot facilities at Samaria, although only the acropolis has been excavated and any stable complexes must have been in the lower city.
124 Norman Franklin, "The Room V Reliefs at Dur-Sharrukin and Sargon II's Western Campaigns," *TA* 21 (1994): 270, fig. 8.
125 Cf. Radner's chapter in this volume. Note that a team of fifty chariots is unlikely to represent the full strength of the Israelite chariotry in 732 BCE.

thirteen equestrians whose title was *rab urâte* (team commander), into the Assyrian army, as a distinct Samarian unit. Stephanie Dalley pointed to the ambiguity regarding whether the chariot teams were deported or deployed locally, but rejected the idea of local deployment.[126] She did suggest, however, that the Israelite chariot teams were so professional that they could change allegiance as long as they would continue to employ their professional skills.[127] The Samarian team of fifty chariots based in the capital would have been an elite unit, and so, the mention of their redeployment by Sargon would have warranted a mention in the Assyrian annals. On the other hand, that Tiglath-pileser III must have commandeered the bulk of the Israelite chariot force when he captured Megiddo was apparently either considered not noteworthy or a relevant inscription did not survive.

Megiddo was not just the provincial capital of a newly created Assyrian province. It was also a military stronghold, an inferior version of an *ekal māšarti*, located on the *hūl šarri*. In an analysis of the Assyrian presence in the Upper Tigris region, Parker shows that the Assyrians used similar strongholds, located on the periphery, to launch military strikes and as supply depots enabling these strikes.[128] These peripheral strongholds were important communication centers for military matters and for the procurement of supplies, including horses.[129] From the time of Tiglath-pileser III the Assyrian military's requirement for horses could not be met solely by tribute; a royal horse agent (Ass. *tamkār sisē*) was employed to purchase horses for the Assyrian army.[130] The horse training and trading center at Megiddo was designed to deal with hundreds of horses at a time, training and selling them — not just as a chariot team of two or three horses, but as complete chariot squadrons of twenty or fifty chariots.[131] Megiddo's role thus continued as an established *bēt kāri* that specialized in the training and trading of horses. Similar specialized Assyrian trading posts are known from the central Zagros region.[132] A *bēt kāri* was originally established in Gaza by Tiglath-pileser III when he conquered the city in 734 BCE,[133] and Megiddo's location on the *hūl*

---

126 Dalley, "Foreign Chariotry and Cavalry," 34–36.
127 Dalley, "Foreign Chariotry and Cavalry," 39.
128 Bradley J. Parker, *The Mechanics of Empire: The Northern Frontier of Assyria as a Case Study in Imperial Dynamics* (Helsinki: The Neo-Assyrian Text Corpus Project, 2001), 265.
129 Parker, "Garrisoning the Empire," 79.
130 Dalley, "Foreign Chariotry and Cavalry," 31, 44–47.
131 See Franklin, "Megiddo Stables Reconsidered."
132 Younger, "Assyrian Economic Impact," 184–85, n. 14.
133 Yamada, "*Kārus* on the Frontiers," 64, 69.

šarri, which was also an important Assyrian trade route,¹³⁴ would have continued. Megiddo would have also been an invaluable asset to the Assyrians even after Tiglath-pileser III, particularly during the campaigns to the west of Shalmaneser V and Sargon II. In fact, even after Sargon's final annihilation of Samaria, his re-establishment of dominion over the Philistine coast and the opening up of the Gaza trading post, the *kāru* of Egypt, Megiddo's dual function as a specialized *bēt kāri* and as a military stronghold was still relevant. Possibly, Megiddo was still used as a mustering station by Sennacherib as late as 701 BCE, but with relative quiet in the west and the Assyrian policy of population transfer, new domestic quarters eventually replaced the stables. Cavalry forces took over from the chariot units, and at Megiddo the stable complexes and the chambered gates became obsolete and the full blown, orthogonal, planned city of Stratum III arose.

7 The Role of Jezreel under Assyrian Rule

Jezreel, located on the border with the rump state of Samaria, would have played a crucial role under Tiglath-pileser III by controlling access to and from Samaria. That is, Jezreel, once the gatekeeper that protected Samaria, had changed sides!

The Assyrian army travelled vast distances and there are various scenes on the Neo-Assyrian reliefs that depict the army camped and victualled en route to, or at, a battle site.¹³⁵ On average, the Assyrian army could cover twenty-two kilometers per day if it was marching with no battles, plundering or foraging on the way.¹³⁶ Camps were set up in strategic locations, often at a crossroad, but always where there was pasturage for the horses.¹³⁷ In unstable areas, usually on the fringes of the empire, a permanent camp (Ass. *birtu*, plural *birāti*) would be erected.¹³⁸ These military outposts were sometimes left abandoned, but with their walls intact, ready to be reused if necessary. This way, a temporary camp could be set up within a fortified area.¹³⁹ The camp could be oval, rectangular

---

134 These routes were vital for trade with Egypt: Younger, "Assyrian Economic Impact," 182–84, n. 9.
135 Fredrick Mario Fales and Monica Rigo, "Everyday Life and Food Practices in Assyrian Military Encampments," in *Paleonutrition and Food Practices in the Ancient Near East: Towards a Multidisciplinary Approach*, ed. Lucio Milano (Padova: s.a.r.g.o.n., 2014): 414.
136 Younger, "Fall of Samaria," 472.
137 Fales and Rigo, "Everyday Life and Food Practices," 415.
138 Fales and Rigo, "Everyday Life and Food Practices," 414.
139 Fales and Rigo, "Everyday Life and Food Practices," 417.

or even square in plan with a defensive wall.¹⁴⁰ Jezreel, a border site on the fringe of the empire, located at the intersection of the Via Maris, a major *hūl šarri*, with the road to Samaria, made it a perfect location for an Assyrian border outpost, a *birtu*.

Following the fall of Samaria, Jezreel's role as an Assyrian border outpost was no longer relevant; however, just as the *bēt mardēti* at Tel Hadid was on the direct route to Gezer,¹⁴¹ so Jezreel was on the direct route to Megiddo and on to the *kāru* of Gaza. Jezreel would have been an obvious choice to be transformed¹⁴² into a *bēt mardēti*. Located on the international highway in an area of agricultural fecundity, Jezreel could support a small but necessary civilian population to produce and process the grain and wine required to provision the Assyrian army. A large winery complex¹⁴³ and the ca. one hundred rock-cut underground storage pits ¹⁴⁴ dotted over the summit of Jezreel attest to its agricultural nature and suitability as a *bēt mardēti*.¹⁴⁵ This change of function is reflected in Hos 2:24:¹⁴⁶ "And the earth will produce grain and wine and oil, and they will cause Jezreel to produce" (וְהָאָרֶץ תַּעֲנֶה אֶת־הַדָּגָן וְאֶת־הַתִּירוֹשׁ וְאֶת־הַיִּצְהָר וְהֵם יַעֲנוּ אֶת־יִזְרְעֶאל).¹⁴⁷ A *bēt mardēti* had no need for large stable complexes,¹⁴⁸ although it was responsible for the fast envoy system (Ass. *kalliu*), which necessitated that a fresh pair of mules be available at each station.¹⁴⁹ They did not need a fancy stable.

---

140 Fales and Rigo, "Everyday Life and Food Practices," 415–16.
141 "Assyrian *bīt mardite*," 288.
142 Aster, "Function of Jezreel," 41 argues that Hos 1:2b–25 contains a vision regarding Jezreel changing its role, that is, Jezreel is transformed from a military compound to an agricultural center. Although this is interpreted as a vision of Hosea (Aster, "Function of Jezreel," 45) it was, in fact, a reality. Hosea, the only Northern Kingdom prophet, portrays the Northern Kingdom at the time of king Hoshea, cf. Nadav Na'aman, "The Book of Hosea as a Source for the Last Days of the Kingdom of Israel," *BZ* 59 (2015): 233–34, 236.
143 Norma Franklin, Jennie Ebeling and Philippe Guillaume, "An Ancient Winery in Jezreel," *Beit Mikra* 60 (2015): 9–18 (in Hebrew); Jennie Ebeling, Norma Franklin, and Philippe Guillaume, "The Jezreel Winery" (forthcoming).
144 Norma Franklin "Exploring the Function of Bell Shaped Pits: With a View to Iron Age Jezreel," in *Lawrence Stager Volume* (*Eretz-Israel*; in press): 76*–82*.
145 See Aster, "Assyrian *bīt mardite*," 287.
146 Hos 2:24 in the Hebrew or 2:22 in KJV and other versions.
147 See Aster, "Function of Jezreel," 36.
148 Radner, "Imperial Communication Network," 73.
149 Radner, "Royal Pen Pals," 64.

8 Summary and Conclusions

Neither Megiddo nor Jezreel were destroyed by Tiglath-pileser III in 732 BCE. In fact, the opposite is true: both sites were of use to the Assyrians as they expanded and controlled their empire in the west.

Megiddo's dual role as a regional *ekal māšarti* and as a *bēt kāri* specializing in the trade of trained chariot horses would have been an invaluable asset. Tiglath-pileser III chose Megiddo as the capital of the newly founded frontier province of Magiddû. Only following the final defeat of Samaria by Sargon II did Megiddo become a fully-fledged provincial capital; however, this did not happen overnight. It was only with the change from chariotry to cavalry that the stables were dismantled and Megiddo rebuilt to house a new population of Assyrian deportees.

Jezreel's role as a strategic fortified site, a minor *ekal māšarti*, and mustering station that protected the Israelite capital changed under Tiglath-pileser III to controlling the passage to Samaria. Located on the very fringe of the empire, in an unstable area, it could have served as a permanent camp, a *birtu*, for the Assyrians. Following the fall of Samaria, Jezreel's location on a major trade route, a *hūl šarri*, together with its agricultural potential, made it eminently suited to be turned into a *bēt mardēti* and continue to serve its Assyrian masters in a new way.

Part IV: **Working with the Book of Kings: the Text**

Timo Tekoniemi[1]
Between Two Differing Editions: Some Notable Text-Critical Variants in 2 Kings 17

1 Introduction

The chapter 2Kgs 17 is a well-known playfield (or minefield) for all sorts of literary and redaction critical theories. The first six verses of the chapter even contain some of the most challenging historical puzzles in the Book of Kings, as seen in the many contributions of this volume. While the historical and literary critical reconstructions have dominated the scholarly discussion, surprisingly little interest has been given to the text-critical challenges of the chapter. On the basis of some recently published commentaries on 2Kings one could even come to the conclusion that there are no notable text-critical variants in the chapter.

Based on Alfred Rahlfs' widely used "semi-critical" edition of the Septuagint this would indeed seem to be the case: the majority text of Septuagint 2Kings ("4 Reigns") agrees with the Masoretic text (MT) almost completely. However, this happens for a good reason: the majority of Greek witnesses attest to the so-called *kaige* revision, which harmonized the Greek text towards that of (proto-)MT.[2] There is, however, one textual tradition that has on many occasions escaped this Hebraizing revision, namely the Antiochian (*L*) tradition. Often original Old Greek (OG) readings can also be found in the daughter versions of the Septuagint (LXX), especially in the Old Latin (OL) traditions. Rahlfs was not yet aware of this *kaige* phenomenon, and because of this he in fact considered the Antiochian text form as inferior to the majority text.

Because of the *kaige* revision, many differences between the original Septuagint translation and the Masoretic text have likely been lost forever. However, in 2Kgs 17 the Antiochian text has clearly preserved some vestiges of the old text. Furthermore, the first third of the chapter has also been preserved in an Old Latin manuscript *Palimpsestus Vindobonensis* (La[115]), which has been recently

---
[1] I want to thank Tuukka Kauhanen for his kind and helpful remarks on an earlier draft of this paper.
[2] See James K. Aitken, "The Origins of ΚΑΙ ΓΕ," in *Biblical Greek in Context: Essays in Honour of John A. L. Lee*, ed. James K. Aitken and Trevor Evans (Leuven: Peeters, 2015): 21–40, for further information on the *kaige* revision.

concluded to often preserve a very old and reliable text.³ The manuscript seems to have often – if not always – escaped the *kaige* revision even when other witnesses have not. Therefore, especially when the Antiochian text and La¹¹⁵ agree against the majority text, we can in most cases be fairly sure that the reading is an ancient one.⁴

It has become evident in the research that already the *Vorlage* (i.e. the Hebrew base text) of Septuagint 1–2Kings differed drastically from the Masoretic edition of the books. This is especially noteworthy in 1Kings, where the *kaige* revision has not faded out the differences between the two editions. Even in 2Kings there can be found some differences in the compositional layout of these two main versions. In fact, 2Kgs 17 is likely to be one such passage where these editions originally differed from each other considerably.⁵

---

3 For the edition of La¹¹⁵ see Bonifatius Fischer, "Palimpsestus Vindobonensis: A Revised Edition of L115 for Samuel-Kings," *BIOSCS* 16 (1983): 13–87. For the characteristics of La¹¹⁵'s text, see Tuukka Kauhanen, "Septuagint in the West: the Significance of the Post-Lucianic Latin Witnesses for the Textual History of Kings," in *Die Septuaginta – Orte und Intentionen*, ed. Siegfried Kreuzer, Martin Meiser and Marcus Sigismund (Tübingen: Mohr Siebeck, 2016): 309–25; Timo Tekoniemi, "Is There a (Proto-)Lucianic Stratum in the Text of 1 Kings of the Old Latin Manuscript La115?" in *The Antiochean Text and the Antiochean Manuscripts*, ed. Kristin De Troyer (Göttingen: Vandenhoeck & Ruprecht, forthcoming). Some of the text of 2Kgs 17 has also preserved in the Old Latin witness La^M (also known as La$_{91-95}$); see for an edition of La^M Antonio Moreno, *Las Glosas Marginales de Vetus Latina en Las Biblias Vulgatas Españolas: 1–2 Reyes* (Madrid: CSIC, 1992), 97–144; and a study of some of its most notable readings by Julio Trebolle, "Readings of the Old Latin (Beuron 91–95) Reflecting "Additions" of the Antiochene Text in 3–4 Kingdoms," in *The Legacy of Barthélemy: 50 Years after Les Devanciers d'Aquila*, ed. Anneli Aejmelaeus and Tuukka Kauhanen (Göttingen: Vandenhoeck & Ruprecht, 2017), 120–45.

4 Even though some Lucianic readings may have very sporadically seeped into La¹¹⁵, for the most part the agreements between the two are proto-Lucianic; see Tekoniemi, "Is There a (Proto-)Lucianic Stratum." La¹¹⁵ does have, however, some highly intriguing characteristics in 2Kgs that are found nowhere else in the Greek tradition: the death narrative of Elisha (13:14–21) is transposed after verse 10:30; the chapter 16 is missing between 15 and 17 (and was likely originally situated after chapter 17); and in chapter 17 verse 7 is in a completely differing form from MT/LXX, verse 8 is missing, and verses 9–14 and 15–19 have been transposed with each other. As can be seen, a study of La¹¹⁵'s text in 2Kgs 17 could yield some interesting text-historical results.

5 See Julio Trebolle, "Textual Pluralism and Composition of the Books of Kings: 2 Kings 17,2–23," in *After Qumran: Old and Modern Editions of the Biblical Texts: the Historical Books*, ed. Hans Ausloos, Benedicte Lemmelijn and Julio Trebolle (Leuven: Peeters, 2012): 213–26; and Timo Tekoniemi, "On the Verge of Textual, Literary, and Redaction Criticism: The Case of 2 Kings 17:7," in *The Antiochean Text and the Antiochean Manuscripts*, ed. Kristin De Troyer (Göttingen: Vandenhoeck & Ruprecht, forthcoming).

In this paper three substantial text-critical cases will be analyzed. Most of them are interesting not only from the textual, but also from a broader methodological viewpoint, since their analysis could also have repercussions for the historical and literary theories of the chapter, or even the Book of Kings as a whole. This is indeed how text-criticism and literary criticism converge with each other: when the most original text is found in other witnesses than MT, also a reassessment of the literary theories bearing on the said text is in order.

2 Hoshea: The Worst or Not-So-Worst King of Israel?

2Kgs 17:2 has for long been a matter of debate because of its strange and unexpected judgment of Hoshea. Unlike what could be expected, according to the MT Hoshea "did evil in the eyes of Yahweh, *only not as much as the kings of Israel who were before him.*" Hoshea is thus apparently said to have been better than some, or even any, of the other kings of Israel. There is nothing in the text that would evoke such a lenient indiction, however, unless one takes the lack of a customary remark of Jeroboam's sin in verses 1–6 as an indication of him no more "walking in the sin of Jeroboam." As the last king of Israel, during whose reign the northern kingdom was exiled, the complete opposite could be expected, that is, Hoshea even being the most evil king of Israel.

To alleviate these problems, some scholars have proposed that possibly the turbulent political climate of Hoshea's reign did not simply allow Hoshea to focus on the cultic misdeeds of Israel's previous kings.[6] This idea runs into problems, however, when it is noted that even Zechariah, who only reigned for 6 months, and whose reign most probably was even more turbulent than that of Hoshea, is said in 2Kgs 15:9 to have sinned "like his fathers had done." On the other hand, according to the rabbinic tradition, Hoshea let the northern Israelites take freely part in the cult at Jerusalem,[7] which would have, of course,

---

[6] John Gray, *I & II Kings: A commentary* (London: SCM Press, 1964), 583 ("His comparative virtue according to Deuteronomic principles was a virtue of necessity"); Gwilym H. Jones, *1 and 2 Kings* (Grand Rapids MI / Cambridge: Eerdmans, 1984), 546. Some have also noted that Hoshea's valiant resistance against Assyria could have earned him this honor; see Norman H. Snaith, *I and II Kings* (New York: Abingdon Press, 1954), 278; Volkmar Fritz, *Das zweite Buch der Könige* (Zürich: Theologischer Verlag, 1998), 95. However, nowhere else does standing up to a foreign power by a king of Israel seem to evoke such positive evaluation.

[7] Cf. Taʿan. 30b–31a; Giṭ. 88a; B. Bat. 121b. This would be partly in line with the 2Chr 30:1–12, where Hezekiah sends letters to the northern Israelites, inviting them to take part in his Pass-

mitigated his blame even in the eyes of the Deuteronomistic Historian.[8] However, there are no traces of this in the text itself.

It has also been noted by the medieval rabbi Rashi that after Dan was lost to the Assyrians in 2Kgs 15:29, there would indeed be a good reason to argue why Hoshea simply *could* not have been as evil as his predecessor(s): with the loss of Dan also the blame for one of the golden calves of Jeroboam would have been canceled.[9] Therefore Hoshea only had the sole calf at Bethel under his rule from the beginning of his reign. Since the "sin of Jeroboam," usually equated with him making the calves, is the most important transgression Israel's kings are blamed for, Hoshea could have then indeed been at most only half as bad as any of the kings before him!

However, most theories have not taken into account the text-critical evidence, which gives a completely different picture of Hoshea: according to the Antiochian text and the Old Latin witnesses La[115] and La[M], Hoshea was indeed the most evil king of Israel: "And he did evil before Lord *more than all who were before him.*" As the reading of *L* is backed up by both OL witnesses, and can quite easily be translated back into Hebrew,[10] it is very likely that the reading is at least proto-Lucianic (and therefore not a "perversion of Lucian"[11]), and most probably Old Greek.[12]

---

over. The results were not stellar, however, and nothing is said about the king of Israel letting his people go freely, but according to the Chronicler some Israelites indeed do take part in the festivities.

8 To DtrH the "sin of Jeroboam" most likely was simply the decentralization of the Yahwistic cult from Jerusalem, not the making of the idolatrous golden calves; see Juha Pakkala, "Jeroboam without Bulls," *ZAW* 120 (2008): 501–25.

9 Arie Van der Kooij, "Zur Exegese von II Reg 17₂," *ZAW* 96 (1984): 109–12. Cf. *Miqra'ot Gedolot* 2Kgs 17:2. Rashi concludes that because there were no more calves to worship, Hoshea must have let the Israelites take part in the cult of Jerusalem.

10 The *Vorlage* likely read וַיַּעַשׂ הָרַע בְּעֵינֵי יְהוָה מִכֹּל אֲשֶׁר (הָיוּ) לְפָנָיו.

11 As noted by James Montgomery, *A Critical and Exegetical Commentary on the Books of Kings* (Edinburgh: T&T Clark, 1986, ed. Henry Snyder Gehman), 464, and later echoed by many other commentators.

12 Similarly Andrés Piquer, "What Text to Edit? The Oxford Hebrew Bible Edition of 2 Kings 17,1–23," in *After Qumran: Old and Modern Editions of the Biblical Texts: The Historical Books*, ed. Hans Ausloos, Benedicte Lemmelijn and Julio Trebolle (BETL 246; Leuven: Peeters, 2012): 227–43, esp. 230–31; Julio Trebolle, *Centena in Libros Samuelis et Regum: Variantes Textuales y Composición Literaria en los Libros de Samuel y Reyes* (Madrid: CSIC, 1989), 189.

Table 1: Textual Witnesses of 2 Kings 17:2			
MT	Rahlfs	L	OL
וַיַּעַשׂ הָרַע	καὶ ἐποίησεν τὸ πονηρὸν	καὶ ἐποίησεν τὸ πονηρὸν	et fecit male
בְּעֵינֵי יְהוָה	ἐν ὀφθαλμοῖς κυρίου	ἐνώπιον κυρίου	in conspectu dmī
רַק לֹא	πλὴν οὐχ	παρὰ πάντας	super omnes
כְּמַלְכֵי יִשְׂרָאֵל	ὡς οἱ βασιλεῖς Ισραηλ		
אֲשֶׁר הָיוּ	οἳ ἦσαν	τοὺς γενομένους	qui fuerunt
לְפָנָיו׃	ἔμπροσθεν αὐτοῦ	ἔμπροσθεν αὐτου.	ante eum
And he did evil in the eyes of Yahweh, *only not as much* as the kings of Israel who were before him.		And he did evil before Lord *more than all* who were before him.	

How should this difference between the texts be assessed? Many commentators, beginning with Bernhard Stade, have held that the reading "more than" is a late change motivated by the context: it would indeed be easier to see the last monarch of Israel as the most evil one, while him being not as evil as others could be argued to be ideologically the *lectio difficilior*.[13] On the other hand the fact that Hoshea does not seem to do anything to earn himself his judgment may just as well have prompted the MT editor, as Andrés Piquer notes, to change the judgment: it does indeed seem strange for such a minor character to possibly have been worse than Jeroboam or especially the Omride kings, the absolute epitomes of evil in the Book of Kings.[14] Furthermore, the arguments given above for making sense of the reading of MT could also be, at least to certain extent, reversed: for instance, it would not seem impossible that a later reviser, similarly to Rashi in the medieval times, noticed the second calf missing in the times of Hoshea – and, more importantly, the fact that Hoshea is also not accused of the "sin of Jeroboam" – and deducted that as a result of this he indeed *could* not have been the worst king of Israel.[15] Therefore both sides of the argument fail to convince completely on their own, as they are *reversible* with each other.[16] There is a need for cumulative evidence.

---

[13] Bernhard Stade, *The Books of Kings* (Leipzig: Hinrichs, 1904), 260. Similarly also Albert Šanda, *Die Bücher der Könige: Das Zweite Buch der Könige* (Münster: Aschendorffsche Verlagsbuchhandlung, 1912), 212, and many others.
[14] Piquer, "What Text to Edit," 237.
[15] Christoph Levin, "Die Frömmigkeit der Könige von Israel und Juda," in *Houses Full of All Good Things: Essays in Memory of Timo Veijola*, ed. Juha Pakkala and Martti Nissinen (Helsinki: Finnish Exegetical Society, 2008): 129–68, indeed assumes that Hoshea stopped with Jeroboam's sin: "Der letzte König *Hoschea* schließlich unterläßt die Sünde Jeroboams ganz" (156).
[16] See for discussion of the reversibility of text-critical arguments Adrian Schenker, "Man bittet um das Gegenargument! Von der Eigenart textkritischer Argumentation," *ZAW* 122 (2010): 53–63; and Ville Mäkipelto, Timo Tekoniemi and Miika Tucker, "Large-Scale Transposition as

The solution may be found when the other similar judgment formulae are text-critically assessed. While most Israelite kings are simply condemned for "doing evil in the eyes of Yahweh" without any comparisons, the Omride kings Omri (1Kgs 16:25), Ahab (16:30, 33), Ahaziah (22:54), and Joram (2Kgs 1:18b OG/3:2 MT) are all said to have been either worse (Omri, Ahab) or as evil (Ahaziah, Joram) as their predecessors. However, this picture changes somewhat after the textual evidence is taken into account: in 1Kgs 22:54 Ahaziah is in *L* said not to have provoked Yahweh "like all that his father had done" (כְּכֹל אֲשֶׁר־עָשָׂה אָבִיו) as in MT, but in fact παρὰ πάντας τοὺς γενομένους ἔμπροσθεν αὐτου, *"more than all who were before him."*[17] The fact that there is in two different places a similar difference between the witnesses raises a question: are these differences simply coincidental?[18]

The most important thing to note is that both Ahaziah and Hoshea rule after Ahab. This is important, since Ahab is often thought to be the main antagonist and evildoer in the Book of Kings, which is indeed the case on the basis of MT's text: no-one else after him is said to have been worse (although Ahaziah is said to have been *as* evil as him) than his predecessors. In OG this is of course not the case: even though Ahab is clearly the "main villain" of Kings, he is nevertheless

---

an Editorial Technique in the Textual History of the Hebrew Bible," *TC: A Journal of Biblical Textual Criticism* 22 (2017): 1–16.

17 The rest of the LXX witnesses give the text as κατὰ πάντα τὰ γενόμενα ἔμπροσθεν αὐτοῦ, "according to all that (τὰ) was before him." It seems like this text has been partially corrected towards the MT by *kaige* reviser by simply changing the preposition παρά of *L* to κατά, but leaving the "all [who/that] were before him" intact (the difference between the neuter plural of *kaige* and masculine plural of OG is significant in Greek only, since both translate the Hebrew אֲשֶׁר). Interestingly the Hexaplaric witnesses have not been further harmonized towards MT either. An accidental change κατα ~ παρα is possible, although not one of the likeliest of mistakes. The reading of *L* is also supported by La^M: *Et serviit Baalim et adoravit illi superponens in malitia universis quae gesta erant ante eum*. Adrian Schenker, *Älteste Textgeschichte der Königsbücher: Die hebräische Vorlage der ursprünglichen Septuaginta als älteste Textform der Königsbücher* (Fribourg: Academic Press, 2004), 100, also notes that in 2Kgs 1:18d (not found in MT) *L* has a harsher condemnation of Ahaziah, as *L* adds "and Yahweh became angry (*L* +towards him and) towards the house of Ahab." While this is true, this plus of *L* is probably best seen as a recensional Lucianic addition.

18 It is theoretically possible that the changes in *L* are in both cases due to the Lucianic reviser, but this does not seem very likely: while the reviser indeed changes many readings (for instance the use of the preposition παρά instead of ὑπὲρ [cf. 1Kgs 16:25, 33] may be recensional), he usually did it so that the meaning of the text did not notably change – at least as much as in these cases.

not the worst of the bunch, but only gets the third place after two quite insignificant kings (Ahaziah only rules for 2 years and Hoshea for 9 years).[19]

This is, in fact, not the only case where LXX gives a more ambivalent picture of Ahab: for example, Philippe Hugo argues that in 1Kgs 17–19 the picture of Ahab differs between the unrepentant evildoer of MT and a more ambivalent king of LXX.[20] Because of this, some scholars have proposed that LXX wanted to improve or "whitewash" the quite dark picture of Ahab given by MT for "midrashic purposes."[21] While not impossible, this does not seem very likely: it is more conceivable for evil characters to become more evil in the textual process than the opposite – especially when we are dealing with Ahab, the evildoer *par excellence*. In this case it seems that the picture of Ahab was indeed blackwashed by MT by later changing the judgments of two quite insignificant kings from being the most evil to either being as evil as Ahab or even to possibly being the least evil of all the kings of Israel.[22] Furthermore, in chapter 17 the king(s) of Israel are not blamed for the destruction, but the people, which is ideologically unusual in the Book of Kings.[23] It could be argued that the MT edition puts even more blame on the people (thus "democratizing" the sin of Jeroboam) by further trivializing the role of Hoshea. The "harmonized" reading of OG in 2Kgs 17:2 is thus likely the most original judgment of Hoshea.

This textual problem of verse 2 has further *redactional* significance. According to MT Hoshea, who "did what was wrong in the eyes of Yahweh, though not like the kings of Israel before him" seems to do nothing particularly wrong – apparently he did not even walk in the sin(s) of Jeroboam. This is of course baffling. If we are to understand, like the early rabbis, that Hoshea being the not-worst

---

[19] The late addition 1Kgs 21:25 further supports the idea of Ahab being seen as the most evil king. Even Manasseh, the reason for Judah's demise, is compared to Ahab and is told to have "made an Asherah, like Ahab had done" (2Kgs 21:3). Therefore Piquer, "What Text to Edit," 237, notes on Hoshea: "... MT tried to smoothen incongruities in the narrative, as it would certainly seem odd that this late minor monarch whose reign fills barely a couple lines in the narrative of Kings could be more evil than Jeroboam, who split Israel, or than Omri and Ahab, targets of choice of biblical invective against the Northern Kingdom."
[20] See Philippe Hugo, *Les deux Visages d'Élie* (Fribourg: Academic Press, 2006), 326–27; similarly Andrzej Turkanik, *Of Kings and Reigns: a Study of Translation Technique in the Gamma/Gamma Section of 3 Reigns (1 Kings)* (Tübingen: Mohr Siebeck, 2008), 207.
[21] David Gooding, "Ahab According to the Septuagint," *ZAW* 76 (1964): 269–80, esp. 277–79; idem, "Problems of Text and Midrash in the Third Book of Reigns," *Textus* 7 (1969): 1–29, esp. 26–27.
[22] Similarly Schenker, *Älteste Textgeschichte*, 116–22.
[23] Hartmut Rösel, "Why 2 Kings 17 Does Not Constitute a Chapter of Reflection in the 'Deuteronomic History'," *JBL* 128 (2009): 85–90, esp. 88–89.

king means that the worship of the calves in Bethel and/or Dan had already ceased,[24] the condemnation must come from late redactors, since it is unlikely that the calves were yet present in the Historian's text.[25] Of course, the fact that the OG gives in 17:2 a completely differing reading already shows us that even the passages we may have thought to be the most ancient ones could have been completely changed during later transmissional processes. Thus it is exceedingly important to conduct the text-critical work first, with no redactional preconceptions concerning the passages in question.

3 The Historical Problems of Verse 4: Adrammelek the Ethiopian and the Tribute of Hoshea

Verse 17:4 has incited quite a lot of discussion from the historical viewpoint, mainly because of the strange name of the Egyptian Pharaoh, "Sô, the king of Egypt," to whom Hoshea sent messengers.[26] Despite the several dynasties and Pharaohs reigning simultaneously at the time of Israel's last years,[27] no Pharaoh easily recognized as "Sô" seems to have ruled during Israel's demise. Therefore Sô has been identified with numerous Pharaohs, such as Tefnakht, Osorkon IV, or Piye, and sometimes not even as a personal name, but as a name of a city, Sais – while some have proposed that the "name" is in fact a job description for "commander" ($t3$), or, more likely, "king" (nsw).[28] No scholarly consensus has been formed on the identification of Sô.

---

24 As argued by Van der Kooij, "Zur Exegese," 111–12.
25 The calves in 1Kgs 12:28–30 are likely a late invention. See Pakkala, "Jeroboam's Sin and Bethel in 1Kgs 12:25–33," *BN* 112 (2002): 86–94.
26 The text of MT is clear and lucid, and most probably should not be emended in any way. Most of the emendations have indeed been born of the need to make the name "Sô" work in the historical context of the text, not because of problems of the text itself.
27 See Kenneth Kitchen, *The Third Intermediate Period in Egypt (1100–650 B. C.)* (Warminster: Aris & Phillips, 1973), 362–72.
28 For an overall picture of the problems pertaining to "Sô," see John Day, "The Problem of 'Sô, King of Egypt' in 2 Kings XVII 4," *VT* 42 (1992): 289–301.

Table 2: Textual Witnesses of 2 Kings 17:4

MT	Rahlfs	L	OL*
וַיִּמְצָא	καὶ εὗρεν	καὶ εὗρεν	et invenit
מֶלֶךְ־אַשּׁוּר	βασιλεὺς Ἀσσυρίων	βασιλεὺς Ἀσσυρίων	rex assyriorum
בְּהוֹשֵׁעַ קֶשֶׁר	ἐν τῷ Ωσηε ἀδικίαν,	ἐν τῷ Ωσηε ἐπιβουλήν,	in osee insidia
אֲשֶׁר שָׁלַח	ὅτι ἀπέστειλεν	διότι ἀπέστειλεν	et misit
מַלְאָכִים	ἀγγέλους πρὸς	ἀγγέλους πρὸς	nuntios *at*
אֶל־סוֹא	Σηγωρ	Αδραμέλεχ τὸν	adramalec
		Αἰθίοπα τὸν κατοικοῦντα	ethiopem habitātem
מֶלֶךְ־מִצְרַיִם	βασιλέα Αἰγύπτου	ἐν Αἰγύπτῳ.	in aegypto
וְלֹא־	καὶ οὐκ		
הֶעֱלָה	ἤνεγκεν	καὶ ἦν Ωσῆε φέρων	et offerebat osee
מִנְחָה לַמֶּלֶךְ	μαναα τῷ βασιλεῖ	δῶρα τῷ βασιλεῖ	munera regi
אַשּׁוּר	Ἀσσυρίων	Ἀσσυρίων	assyriorum
כְּשָׁנָה בְשָׁנָה		ἐνιαυτὸν κατ᾽ ἐνιαυτόν,	ab anno in annum
	ἐν τῷ ἐνιαυτῷ ἐκείνῳ,	ἐν δὲ τῷ ἐνιαυτῷ ἐκείνῳ	
		οὐκ ἤνεγκεν αὐτῷ μαναα.	
		καὶ ὕβρισε τὸν Ὡσῆε	et *iniuriam fecit ei*
		ὁ βασιλεὺς Ἀσσυρίων	rex assyriorum
			in chalee
וַיַּעַצְרֵהוּ	καὶ ἐπολιόρκησεν	καὶ ἐπολιόρκησεν αὐτὸν	
מֶלֶךְ	αὐτὸν ὁ βασιλεὺς		
אַשּׁוּר	Ἀσσυρίων		
וַיַּאַסְרֵהוּ	καὶ ἔδησεν αὐτὸν	καὶ ἔδησεν αὐτὸν	et tradidit eum
בֵּית כֶּלֶא:	ἐν οἴκῳ φυλακῆς.	ἐν οἴκῳ φυλακῆς.	in carcerem
And the king of Ashur found conspiracy (B: *offence*) in Hoshea, for he had sent messengers to Sô (B: *Sêgôr*), king of Egypt, and did not bear tribute to the king of Ashur as year by year (B: *that year*). And the king of Ashur shut him up and bound him in prison.		And the king of Assyrians found a plot in Hoshea, for he had sent messengers to Adrammelek the Ethiopian who was living in Egypt. And Hoshea bore tribute to the king of Assyrians year by year [L+ but in that year he did not bear him *manaa*]. And the king of Ashur maltreated (115+ *in Gilead*) Hoshea [L+: and besieged him] and bound him in prison.	

* La¹¹⁵ is in this verse partly supported by two other OL sources La^M and Sulpicius Severus, *I Chr* 47:1.

The Greek witnesses have rarely been considered when assessing this problem. Mostly they have been brushed aside as either irrelevant or as early attempts to make sense of the strange name "Sô."[29] As expected, most manuscripts indeed give simply the MT name or a variation of it, Σωα/Σωβα, or a corrupted form,

---

[29] See, e.g., Duane Christensen, "The Identity of King Sô in Egypt (2 Kings XVII 4)," *VT* 39 (1989): 140–53, esp. 141 ("... the most significant of the earliest attempts to eliminate "King So"..."); Donald Redford, "A Note on II Kings 17,4," *JSSEA* 11 (1981): 75–76, esp. 75 ("Lucian substituted"). Day, "The Problem of 'Sô, king of Egypt'," 298, also gives a lengthy mention of the Lucianic reading, but discusses it no further.

Σηγωρ.³⁰ However, the proto-Lucianic (= OG) text of L and the OL witnesses differs from the majority tradition, calling him, possibly even more strangely, "Adrammelek the Ethiopian, who dwelt in Egypt." Such a reading hardly came to be because of an accident, and OG clearly reflects an independent literary tradition from MT.³¹

Adrammelek is obviously neither an Ethiopian nor an Egyptian name, and on basis of its distribution it seems rather like a "stock-name" that could be used for different purposes: in 2Kgs 17:31 it reappears as a name of a foreign god and in 19:37 (= Isa 37:38) as a name of a son of Sennacherib – albeit there it could also be a genuine, corrupted historical name.³² There seems to be thus no historically relevant information in the name here – quite the contrary, the name seems like a literary construct. There is, however, one interesting and historically quite legitimate remark in the OG text that is lacking from MT: at the time of Hoshea's reign both upper and even lower Egypt seem to have been, at least nominally, under the rule of the Ethiopian 25th dynasty.³³ How should one then assess these two completely differing names, "Sô" and "Adrammelek"?

---

30 Σηγωρ B CI a f 64ᵗˣᵗ 381 55 158 244 318 342 372] Σωα A V 247 121 64ᵐᵍ-488 71 245; Σωβα rel. The reading Σηγωρ of B-tradition is not likely to stem from the majority text, and seems to be a transcription of צער; see Dominique Barthélemy, *Critique Textuelle de l'Ancien Testament*, vol. 1. (Göttingen: Vandenhoeck & Ruprecht, 1982), 408, according to whom this is "une assimilation malheureuse." This happenstance may be somehow connected to the textual confusion in the latter part of the verse, where even MT gives a double reading וַיַּאַסְרֵהוּ ... וַיַּעַצְרֵהוּ, and where the OG witnesses have the mysterious plus ὕβρισε (τὸν Ὡσῆ), ὑβρίζω possibly deriving from the same root as the mystical Σηγωρ, צער ("to be insignificant"; Targums: "hif./pi. to subordinate/shame").
31 Piquer, "What Text to Edit," 234–35, 238.
32 One has to wonder, whether this recurrence of the name in 17:31 has something to do with the mystical appearance or disappearance of Sô or Adrammelek in verse 17:4. Simo Parpola, "The Murderer of Sennacherib," *Death in Mesopotamia*, ed. Bendt Alster (Copenhagen: Akademisk Forlag, 1980): 171–82, esp. 174, has convincingly argued that the wrongly spelt name Adrammelek of 2Kgs 19:37 can indeed be found in the Assyrian sources as a son and murderer of Sennacherib in the form Arda-ᵈNIN.LÍL, to be read in Neo-Assyrian times as Arda-Mullissi. According to Parpola, the form Adrammelek can be explained as a scribal error (from the form "Ardamelos," for instance). While this is indeed likely, the reason for this "scribal mistake" may also be harmonization towards the two other mentions of the name "Adrammelek" before the one in 19:37. Piquer, "What Text to Edit," 235, hypothesizes that Hoshea may have been historically somehow linked to this murder and conspiracy, as shown by OG, but that the mention of his involvement in the text has become distorted in the long history of the text. Perhaps the name was even understood at some point as a sort of "stock-name for a conspirator" because of its appearance in 19:37, and was taken over from there.
33 Kitchen, *Third Intermediate Period*, 362–8; Donald Redford, *Egypt, Canaan, and Israel in Ancient Times* (Princeton NJ: Princeton University Press, 1992), 345–47.

Because of these unexpected traits of OG, Adrian Schenker argues that the MT tradition could, in fact, be reflecting a textual situation posterior to that of the OG.[34] First, Adrammelek's "job description" is completely lacking, and has to be deducted from the context: he could be anything from a mercenary to a king (which could, in a way, quite well reflect the confusing state of the Egyptian politics of the time). In MT there is no room for any confusion. On the other hand the name "Sô" is indeed much more Egyptian a name (possibly even a transcription of *nsw*, "king," or an abbreviation of (O)so(rkon)) than "Adrammelek," and it would be easy to see why the strange remark of an Ethiopian called Adrammelek who lives in Egypt would have later been changed into much more understandable and possibly even Egyptian-sounding "Sô, [that is:] king of Egypt": since the literary motive of Israelites depending on the help of Egypt and its king is somewhat common in the Hebrew Bible, also here it would make sense that Hoshea asked for help from "the king of Egypt."[35] Thirdly, the fact that the name "Adrammelek" confusingly appears in two completely differing contexts elsewhere makes it likely that MT has here smoothened a text that seems quite contradictory with itself: how could Hoshea send messengers to an Ethiopian, who concurrently seems to be a son of Sennacherib and, even more confusingly, is revered as a god by the later Mesopotamian inhabitants of the province of Samaria?[36] It is thus quite easy to see why the text would have been changed to the MT version, while the opposite, a change from the lucid MT to the somewhat strange and contradictory OG text, would be quite unexpected.

Stepping from the realm of textual criticism to that of literary theories, Julio Trebolle has argued that the narrative of the Assyrian king finding out about Hoshea's conspiracy in verse 4aα is itself a later interpolation to the verse, and that MT has in the verse overall a later version of the text.[37] Indeed, in OG version there seems to be a resumptive repetition (*Wiederaufnahme*) in verses 3b and 4aβ, both recounting the fact that "Hoshea bore tribute to the king of Assyria," indicating that 4aα might be a later interpolation.[38] Unlike in MT, in OG Hoshea never ceases paying tribute, which is surprising, since in MT version this

---

34 Schenker, *Älteste Textgeschichte*, 117–19.
35 Cf. 2Kgs 18:21, 24; Hos 7:11, 12:2; Jer 37:7–8; Isa 30:2–5, 31:1–2; Ezek 29:2–7.
36 See Matthieu Richelle, "Intentional Omissions in the Textual History of the Books of Kings: In Search of Methodological Criteria," *Sem* 58 (2016): 135–57, esp. 141–46, for a similar omission of contradicting information in 1Kgs 14:26.
37 Julio Trebolle, "La Caida de Samaria: Critica Textual, Literaria e Historica de 2 Re 17, 3–6," *Salmanticensis* 28 (1981): 137–52.
38 Trebolle, "La caida," 142, 146–47.

cessation seems to now be one of the main reasons why the Assyrian king invades Israel.³⁹ It is possible that MT has here slightly smoothed the logic of the text (*lectio facilior*) by having Hoshea also withhold his annual tribute on top of his conspiracy.⁴⁰

Even more surprising is the OG plus following the second remark of Hoshea's tribute: despite the yearly tribute, the king of Assyria ὕβρισε τὸν Ὡσῆ, "insulted/maltreated/injured Hoshea,"⁴¹ as if Hoshea was simply a *victim* of the whims of the king of Assyria. This reading becomes even more baffling if 4aα is deleted as a late addition: there would be in the text no apparent reason why Hoshea and Israel would have been invaded by Assyria, and Hoshea "maltreated" by their king. The situation could be compared to the similar enigmatic mention of king Josiah dying at the hands of Pharaoh Necho in 2Kgs 23:29. Such a text form would suit the minimalistic annalistic style of Kings,⁴² but would understandably seem strange to a later reviser. It seems thus likely that OG has preserved a more original version of verse 4, MT reflecting the final edition of the text.

The whole account of Hoshea asking for the help of Egypt against Assyria could thus be simply a late literary construct, borne from the common (theological) motive of futile dependence on Egypt, and a base text that seemed strange

---

39 One could also read this as a demonstration of Hoshea's cunning: even though he sent messengers to Egypt, he did not stop with the tribute so that his conspiracy would not become known.

40 Similarly Pablo Torijano, "Textual Criticism and the Text-Critical Edition of IV Regnorum: The Case of 17,2–6," in *After Qumran: Old and Modern Editions of the Biblical Texts: the Historical Books*, ed. Hans Ausloos, Bénédicte Lemmelijn and Julio Trebolle (Leuven: Peeters, 2012): 195–211, esp. 205–207. Similar, although apparently independent (a *Vorlage* different from [proto-]MT?), smoothing tendencies can be seen also in the *kaige* B-text. It is also good to note that the construct מִנְחָה + עלה of MT is above all cultic ("to offer burnt offerings"), not political (usually translated in 2Kgs 17:4 as "to pay tribute"), in its usage in the Hebrew Bible, and therefore somewhat unexpected here; cf. Ex 30:9, 40:29; Lev 14:20; Judg 13:19; Josh 22:23; 1Kgs 18:29, 36 (>LXX); 2Kgs 3:20; Isa 57:6, 66:3; Jer 14:12; Amos 5:22.

41 It is hard to confirm the *Vorlage* of this reading, since ὑβρίζω is a very rare verb in LXX; cf. 2Sam 19:44 (<קלל); Isa 13:3, 23:12; Jer 31:29 (<גאה). Apart from קלל, another plausible underlying verb could be צער, as noted above. If this was the case, it would be possible that either the *Vorlage* of ὕβρισε (<וי(י)צערהו?) or the MT reading (וַיַּעַצְרֵהוּ) has been borne out of a misreading of a similar looking verbal form – maybe the MT form was thus borne out of an accidental harmonization towards the phonologically quite similar וַיַּאַסְרֵהוּ.

42 The text of OG without 4aα would read thusly: "³Against him rose Shalmaneser, the king of Assyrians, and Hoshea became to him a servant, and he bore him tribute ⁴ᵃᵝ[*Wiederaufnahme*: and he was bearing him tribute] from year to year. And the king of Assyrians *insulted/maltreated/injured* Hoshea and put him in prison."

to a later reviser.⁴³ It is therefore unlikely that there is much historical data to be found in the remark, other than that there was, according to OG, an Ethiopian dynasty reigning in Egypt at the time, and that this dynasty was, at least at some point, thought to have been mighty enough to have had diplomatic relations with Israel.⁴⁴ The mention of "Sô, the king of Egypt" seems then like an even later, literarily-motivated harmonization.

4 A Vestment of a Yahwistic High Priest in Samaria?

In verse 17:17 there is a curious plus in *L* and La¹¹⁵: in addition to Israelites practicing divinations, they also "made an *ephod* and *teraphim*."

It is quite clear that this plus is not a result of some textual mishap, at least a typographical one. We are most probably dealing with a literary variant between MT and, very likely, OG.⁴⁵ When noted by commentators, the most common explanation for this plus is that this mention was a gloss-like addition made in LXX, either at the level of OG or some later copying stage.⁴⁶ The addition would have been made for the purpose of adding even more sins to the already lengthy listing of Israel's misdeeds.⁴⁷ The addition would have not been made

---

43 See similarly Christoph Levin in his chapter in this volume, who argues, quite convincingly, that verse 4 was likely not part of the most original version of the text. Here the text-critical considerations thus can indeed help further corroborate even purely literary critical theories.
44 Maybe even this could have been later deduced by a glossator, possibly from 2Kgs 19:9, where "Tirhakah, the *king of Ethiopia*," is mentioned.
45 Already Alfred Rahlfs, *Lucians Rezension der Königsbücher*. Septuaginta-Studien 2 (Göttingen: Vandenhoeck & Ruprecht, 1965), 290, classified this plus as "Vorlucianisches Gut in *L*." The plus is easily translatable back into Hebrew: ויעשׂו אפד ותרפים.
46 According to Mordechai Cogan and Hayim Tadmor, *II Kings: A New Translation with Introduction and Commentary* (New York: Doubleday, 1988), 205–206, this plus is indeed due to "the tendency of translators and copyists to add elements in catalogue-like listings" (although it is exceedingly unlikely that this plus is due to the Septuagint translator). See also Stade, *Kings*, 264, who notes: "… originally a marginal gloss. It seemed to a later reader as though this could not be dispensed with in the catalogue of Israel's heresies."
47 It could even be that this addition was made as a partial harmonization to the phrase found in 2Kgs 21:6 ("καὶ οἰωνίζετο καὶ ἐποίησεν θελητὴν"), but in that case the harmonizer would have done an extremely bad job at his attempt.

Table 2: Textual Witnesses of 2 Kings 17:17

MT	Rahlfs	L	OL
וַיַּעֲבִ֗ירוּ	καὶ διῆγον	καὶ διήγαγον	et perducebant
אֶת־בְּנֵיהֶ֤ם	τοὺς υἱοὺς αὐτῶν	τοὺς υἱοὺς αὐτῶν	filios suos
וְאֶת־בְּנֽוֹתֵיהֶם֙	καὶ τὰς θυγατέρας	καὶ τὰς θυγατέρας	et filias suas
בָּאֵ֔שׁ	αὐτῶν ἐν πυρὶ	αὐτῶν ἐν πύρι,	in igni
וַיִּקְסְמ֥וּ	καὶ ἐμαντεύοντο	καὶ ἐμαντεύοντο	et divinabant divinationes
קְסָמִ֖ים	μαντείας	μαντείαις	
וַיְנַחֵ֑שׁוּ	καὶ οἰωνίζοντο	καὶ οἰωνίζοντο οἰωνισμοῖς	
		καὶ ἐποίησαν ἐφοὺδ	et fecerunt ephud
		καὶ θεραφείμ	et teraphin
			et augurabantur
			et auspicabantur *
וַיִּֽתְמַכְּר֗וּ	καὶ ἐπράθησαν	καὶ ἐπράθησαν	
לַעֲשׂ֥וֹת	τοῦ ποιῆσαι	τοῦ ποιῆσαι	ut facerent
הָרַ֛ע	τὸ πονηρὸν	τὸ πονηρὸν	quod malum est
בְּעֵינֵ֥י	ἐν ὀφθαλμοῖς	ἐνώπιον	in conspectu
יְהוָ֖ה	κυρίου	Κυρίου	dm̅i̅ ut in indignatione̅
לְהַכְעִיסֽוֹ׃	παροργίσαι αὐτόν.	τοῦ παροργίσαι αὐτόν.	eum mitterent
And they made their sons and daughters pass through fire, divined divinations, and took omens. And they sold themselves to do evil in the eyes of Yahweh in order to provoke him.		And they made their sons and daughters pass through fire, divined divinations, augured by augurs, and made ephod and teraphim, and sold themselves to do evil before Lord in order to provoke him.	And they made their sons and daughters pass through fire, divined divinations, and made ephod and teraphim, and augured and took auspices in order to do what is evil before Lord in order to provoke him.

* Since *auspicabantur* is a very faulty rendering of ἐπράθησαν, it seems likely that the translator of La[115] either had a differing (corrupted?) *Vorlage* before him, or simply misunderstood the meaning of the verb form ἐπράθησαν as denoting here some sort of mantic practice (as the meaning of "selling (oneself) in order to do evil" is somewhat counter-intuitive to the matter at hand), which he then rendered as "taking auspices."

haphazardly, since both the *ephod* and *teraphim* are indeed at times used in divinatory practices.[48]

---

[48] *Ephod* is used for "asking Yahweh" in 1Sam 23:9–12 (LXX lacks verse 12), 30:7–8, and is in Exodus often mentioned in connection with the breast-plate where Urim and Thummim were positioned (Ex 25:7, 28:4, 15, 28 (>LXX), 29:5, 35:9, 27, 39:8, 21). *Teraphim* are used for divination in Ezek 21:21; and possibly Zech 10:2. *Teraphim* are also mentioned together with *ephod* in Judg 17:5, 18:14, 17, 18, 20; Hos 3:4 (different in LXX).

However, some scholars have also seen this plus as a part of the original Hebrew text.⁴⁹ As Schenker notes, it is actually not that clear whether "making *ephod* and *teraphim*" is even a sin in itself:⁵⁰ at least *ephod*, which is even twice consulted by David himself, was quite clearly considered a part of the legitimate cult and is nowhere denounced as such.⁵¹ The *teraphim*, on the other hand, are more often seen as a form of idolatry.⁵² Therefore we are in a tough spot: on one hand it would be quite understandable to have the sinful Israelites also "make *teraphim*," as they clearly at least at some point came to be seen as idolatrous devices. On the other hand making an *ephod* does not seem like a good sin (or sin at all) to add to the list. On the other hand, why would *teraphim* have been taken off the text if they worked so well in the context? Were they indeed simply added in OG or its Hebrew *Vorlage* as a gloss of sorts, possibly to increase the sinfulness of the Israelites?

The key to the problem may indeed lie in the *ephod*. While still somewhat enigmatic, it is quite clear that this usually quite lavishly adorned vestment was worn by priests, and therefore it was indeed part of the legitimate Yahwistic cult. Most importantly, even though an *ephod* of some kind (אֵפוֹד בָּד, "linen

---

49 August Klostermann, *Die Bücher Samuelis und der Könige* (Nördlingen: Beck, 1887), 454; Adrian Schenker, *Une Bible Archétype? Les parallèlles de Samuel-Rois et des Chroniques*, ed. Michaël Langlois (Paris: Les Éditions du Cerf, 2013), 162–64.
50 Schenker, *Une Bible*, 162–63: "On aurait donc deux fois, en 2 Rois 17,17 et 2 Rois 23,4, éliminé la mention de l'ephod d'un contexte païen créé par la décadence religieuse du roi Manassé" (163). Schenker's argument seems to be more about the text of Lucifer of Cagliari in 2Kgs 23:4 than it is about 17:17, and his argumentation does not really carry over from 23:4 to 17:17, as the contexts of these passages are so different (destruction of Samaria – reform of Josiah). That *ephod* was possibly omitted from the text in 23:4 does not in any way mean that it would be omitted here as well, especially when the "religious decadence" of Manasseh, to which Schenker seems to give the blame in 17:17 as well, could not even have affected the Israelites yet. See also Tuukka Kauhanen, *The Text of Kings and Lucifer of Cagliari* (Atlanta GA: SBL Press, 2017), 293, who contends that the addition of *ephod* in 2Kgs 23:4 may be simply due to Lucifer's own modification of the text.
51 There are nevertheless some texts that seem to criticize *ephod* in the Hebrew Bible. In Judg 8:27 Gideon makes an *ephod* in Ophrah, "and all Israel played the harlot with it there, so that it became a snare to Gideon and his household." Another story where *ephod* is criticized is the satirical story about Micah and his own temple(!) in Judg 17–18. However, the biggest problem about an *ephod* in these stories seems not to be its inherent unholiness (on the contrary, the *ephod* seems quite holy in both stories), but the fact that a *wrong person* has made an *ephod*, and even more so, *to the wrong place* (the Danites even take Micah's *ephod* with them to Dan). This way the case of 2Kgs 17:17 may be in a way parallel to the idea expressed in these stories as well: wrong people have made an *ephod* to a wrong place (in north).
52 See 1Sam 15:23; 2Kgs 23:24; Zeph 10:2.

ephod") is said to have been worn also by young Samuel and David,⁵³ it seems that *ephod* was understood to have been especially a garment of the high priest.⁵⁴ This understanding of the word would in turn create an implicational theological tension in the OG text: was there an *ephod* of a Yahwistic *high priest* in Israel/Samaria?⁵⁵ This, in turn, would imply that there was also a legitimate sanctuary of Yahweh in Samaria. This would have been something the later revisers of the Second Temple period saw as highly inappropriate.⁵⁶ Indeed, in 2Kgs 17:24–41 the chapter becomes increasingly "anti-Samaritan" in its polemic. Therefore it would not seem too strange if the mention of an *ephod* in context of Samaria would be omitted, even if it meant taking off the mention about the *teraphim* in connection to it.

Since verse 17 is situated in the "homiletical" portion of the chapter (17:7–41), which very likely comes from later redactors than the "annalistic" verses 1–6, this implicit notion of a Yahwistic high priesthood in Samaria can hardly be directly taken as describing a historical situation. However, a later omission of such a remark would seem much more suspicious, and possibly even more telling of a historically extremely likely Yahwistic sanctuary in Samaria. As noted by Juha Pakkala and Adrian Schenker, it seems likely that the Masoretic edition of Samuel-Kings is especially interested in omitting improper references to the illegitimate temple(s) of Yahweh, and even Baal, in Israel and Judah.⁵⁷ It would thus be expected that these Masoretic revisers were just as sensitive to possible illegitimate priestly garments in the Northern Kingdom as well.

5 Conclusions

The notion that there was excessive rewriting in chapter 2Kgs 17, as is assumed by most literary critics, is corroborated by the textual evidence: there seem to be two extant *editions* of chapter 17 preserved to us in textual witnesses, i.e. MT and

---

53 In 1Sam 2:18; 2Sam 6:14.
54 This was the understanding of the rabbinic writers as well; see Yehoshua M. Grintz, "Ephod," in *EncJud* 6 (Jerusalem: Keter Publishing House, 1972): 804–806; Carol Meyers, "Ephod," in *Anchor Bible Dictionary* 2 (New York: Doubleday, 1992): 550.
55 Both Judg 8:27 (Ophrah) and 17–18 (Dan) also have the "wrong ephod" in the area of the later Northern kingdom. These may both well be allusions to an illegitimate (high) priesthood in Samaria/Northern kingdom, similar to the case at hand.
56 Juha Pakkala, *God's Word Omitted: Omissions in the Transmission of the Hebrew Bible* (Göttingen: Vandenhoeck & Ruprecht, 2013), 233–34.
57 Pakkala, *God's Word Omitted*, 213–22, 231–37, 243–45; Schenker, *Älteste Textgeschichte*, 34–51, 149–66, 177–78.

LXX. It is clear that even complete rewriting of some verses has happened in either the MT or the OG editions of the chapter. Some details of the text change between the editions, whether it be the evil of Hoshea in 2Kgs 17:2 or the name of the Egyptian ruler in verse 17:4. There likely even were several omissions in the textual transmission of MT, most notably in verse 2Kgs 17:17, where the *ephod* of a Yahwistic high priest is mentioned in OG edition.

All of these textual remarks also have further repercussions to the use of this chapter as a witness to further scholarly assessments: if the text was indeed rewritten as extensively as seems to be the case, how much of the text – and of which edition – can be used for historical reconstructions, for example? If there is indeed a considerable possibility that the Old Greek has at times preserved a text form earlier than that of MT, it is methodologically questionable to discard such readings from the get-go without first conducting a meticulous study of their origins.

The extremely complicated literary-critical and redactional situation of chapter 17, and the Book of Kings as a whole, may also be further complicated by the text-critical evidence, since the different editions may occasionally have even completely differing texts in redactionally important passages. In the case of verse 17:2 it is indeed interesting to note that even a passage often thought to come from the *earliest* redactional stages may have been completely rewritten in the transmission process, and has now been transformed into a complete opposite of the original version in the latest form of the text attainable to us (either MT or OG).

A critical study of textual variants in 2Kgs 17 is thus not merely a matter of theoretical discussion of unimportant details, but likely of two widely variant *editions*, whose differences likely go back to a coherent revision on the part of one or the other – or even both. Because of this, the text-critical importance of the Septuagint should be taken most seriously both in this chapter, and in Samuel-Kings as a whole.

Dan'el Kahn
The Fall of Samaria: an Analysis of the Biblical Sources

1 Introduction: the Fall of Samaria in 2Kgs

The end of the Kingdom of Israel is described in Assyrian sources as well as biblical sources (2Kgs 17:3–6 and a similar description of the event in 2Kgs 18:9–11, synchronising the event with the reign of Hezekiah, king of Judah). The historical circumstances leading to the fall of the kingdom are described in a highly condensed paragraph. Several Assyrian campaigns against Israel are alluded to, as well as its subjugation, rebellion, siege, final capitulation and imprisonment of its last king, Hoshea. However, the Biblical account raises many questions about the order of events. Furthermore, there is an apparent discrepancy between the identity of the Assyrian conqueror in the Assyrian sources that claim that Sargon II of Assyria subdued Samaria and the Biblical accounts that claim that it was Shalmaneser V of Assyria.

In reconstructing the events, several scholars (e.g. Bob Becking, Mordechai Cogan and Hayim Tadmor, Nadav Na'aman, Gershon Galil etc.) suggested that the apparent chronological conundrums in 2Kgs 17:3–6 were caused by either the merging of two or more sources – an Israelite chronicle and a Judean one, an early chronicle and a late source, or a redactional addition of a late editor.

In this chapter, I propose a literary reading of the Biblical text, which may solve these problems. It is my contention that 2Kgs 17:3–6 is a coherent source. When paying attention to the pronouns of each verse it becomes clear that the paragraph about the fall of Samaria (2Kgs 17:3–6) is organised according to the following topics and not necessarily in chronological order: the deeds and the fate of the king of Israel; the fate of the kingdom and city; the fate of the inhabitants of Samaria. In contrast, 2Kgs 18:9–11 is a composite literary text. The synchronisms between Hezekiah, king of Judah, and Hoshea son of Elah, king of Israel, are the work of a redactor who inserted them into the narrative of Hezekiah in order to contrast between the fate of the most pious king of Judah and the fate of his kingdom, and the fate of Hoshea and the end of the kingdom of Israel.

I dedicate this chapter to the memory of my beloved son, Gilead Kahn *z"l*, who passed away on 1 March 2018.

2 Previous Analyses of 2Kgs 17:3–6 and Proposed Solutions

2Kgs 17:3–6 narrates the fall of Samaria from a historical perspective. It is followed by a theological explanation for the downfall of the Northern Kingdom. An additional historical version appears in 2Kgs 18:9–11. These two texts, as has been noted long ago, closely resemble each other, but are not entirely parallel. Vv. 3–4 in 2Kgs 17 are missing in 2Kgs 18, while 2Kgs 17:5–6 resemble 2Kgs 18:9–11.

I will first summarise the views of previous scholars. Two main attitudes can be detected in analysing 2Kgs 17: 3–6. The first attitude is to consider 2Kgs 17:3–4 and 5–6 (with its parallel in 18:9–11) as two parallel accounts of the same event from two different archival sources, whether Israelite, Judean or Assyrian. The second attitude is to see these verses as consecutive events from a single coherent source, with possible additions of the Deuteronomistic Historian, who wrote during the exile at the earliest.

After reviewing these suggestions and their merits and flaws, I will forward my understanding of the composition of 2Kgs 17:3–6 and 2Kgs 18:9–11. I will claim that 2Kgs 17:3–6 is a single literary source, and that the synchronisms between Hezekiah and the last days of Samaria as maintained in 2Kgs 18:9–11, are the work of a redactor and are not original. Therefore, they cannot be used in reconstructing the historical events that led to the fall of Samaria.

2.1 Two Parallel Accounts of the Same Event from Two Different Archives

In 1892 Hugo Winckler[1] noted discrepancies in the narrative of 2Kgs 17:3–6 between the imprisonment of Hoshea in v. 4b and the beginning of the siege in v. 5. He could not imagine that Samaria would endure a three-year siege without having a king and without nominating a new one. Furthermore, the redactor understood that the reign of Hoshea ended with the fall of Samaria in his ninth regnal year, and not at the beginning of the siege. Winckler was probably the first to

---

1 Hugo Winckler, *Alttestamentliche Untersuchungen* (Leipzig: Pfeiffer, 1892), 16–25 ("Beiträge zur quellenscheidung der Königsbücher").

suggest that 2Kgs 17:3–6 was composed of two units from different sources.² According to him, 2Kgs 17:3–4 originated from one source and described the subjugation and later imprisonment of Hoshea, whereas vv. 5–6 and its parallel, 2Kgs 18:9–11, stem from a different source and describe the fall of Samaria and the exile of its population. Winckler raised the question that if 2Kgs 17:3–6 were constituted from one source, how could 2Kgs 18:9–11, its parallel, fail to mention the imprisonment of Hoshea? He could not imagine that this detail was omitted because the parallel pericope dealt with the history of Judah. Thus, he concluded that this was proof that 2Kgs 17:3–6 was composed from two different sources. He did not explicitly state their origin, but it is clear from his discussion that in his view vv. 3–4 stemmed from an Israelite source that followed upon 2Kgs 15:30, describing the conspiracy of Hoshea who slew Pekah and rose to the throne.³

Immanuel Benzinger suggested that vv. 3–4 stem from the *Israelite annals*, accepting Winckler's division into two sources. Vv. 5–6 were regarded as deriving from *Judean annals*, attached by a later redactor, who used 2Kgs 18:9–12 as his source.⁴ Albert Šanda speculated that vv. 3–4 may derive from Hoshea's annals, whereas vv. 5–6 may derive from a *later compiler*.⁵ The "two sources hypothesis" was also adopted by many scholars, i.e. Rudolf Kittel,⁶ Charles F. Burney,⁷ Bernhard Stade and Friedrich Schwally,⁸ Martin Noth,⁹ John Gray,¹⁰ Richard D. Nelson,¹¹ Julio Trebolle,¹² Mordechai Cogan and Hayim Tadmor,¹³ and Bob

---

2 E.g., Otto Thenius, *Die Bücher der Könige* (Leipzig: Hirzel, 1873), 379–82, does not offer this explanation, and Frederic William Farrar, *The Second Book of Kings* (New York: Armstrong, 1894), 235–43 does not mention the possible existence of two sources either.
3 Winckler, *Alttestamentliche Untersuchungen*, 16–25.
4 Immanuel Benzinger, *Die Bücher der Könige* (Freiburg: Universitätsverlag, 1899), 172–73.
5 Albert Šanda, *Die Bücher der Könige* (Münster: Aschendorf, 1911), 217.
6 Rudolf Kittel, *Die Bücher der Könige* (Göttingen: Vandenhoeck & Ruprecht, 1900), 274.
7 Charles F. Burney, *Notes on the Hebrew Text of the Books of Kings* (Oxford: Clarendon, 1903), 328–30.
8 Bernhard Stade and Friedrich Schwally, *The Books of Kings* (Leipzig: Hinrichs, 1904), 48.
9 Martin Noth, *Überlieferungsgeschichtliche Studie: die sammelnden und bearbeitenden Geschichtswerke im Alten Testament* (Darmstadt: Wissenschaftliche Buchgesellschaft, 1963), 78.
10 John Gray, *I & II Kings: a Commentary* (Philadelphia: Westminster Press, 1975), 645–50.
11 Richard D. Nelson, *Double Redaction of the Deuteronomistic History* (Sheffield: JSOT Press, 1981), 61–62.
12 Julio Trebolle Barrera, "La caída de Samaría: crítica textual, literaria e histórica de 2 Re 17, 3–6," *Salmanticensis* 28 (1981): 137–52.
13 Mordechai Cogan and Hayim Tadmor, *II Kings* (New York: Doubleday, 1988), 196.

Becking.¹⁴ It thus became a wide consensus to regard these verses as stemming from two different sources, an Israelite, and a Judean source.

The detailed information about Hoshea's conspiracy, his alliance with Egypt, and his rebellion against Assyria is found in vv. 3–4, which shows knowledge of Israelite politics between the superpowers. Assigning these verses to an Israelite archival source is therefore certainly possible. On the other hand, vv. 5–6, which the majority of scholars regard as Judean, is understood by Shemaryahu Talmon as a factual Israelite annalistic notation, devoid of any derogatory connotations against the fate of the Kingdom of Israel.¹⁵ It would seem that there is no clear criteria to distinguish between the origins of the alleged sources. Furthermore, Nadav Na'aman has rightly stressed, ¹⁶ that there is no stylistic or linguistic difference between the two assumed sources. The passage is written in the same verbal patterns as many other passages in the Book of Kings including other episodes that refer to campaigns by Assyrian kings against Israel or Judah. It opens in the past *qatal* form followed by verbs with the *waw* consecutive *wayyiqtol* form. Hence, there are no established criteria to identify either of these verses as originating from an Israelite or Judean source, and the linguistic division seems artificial.

2.2 Brettler's View: the Use of an Assyrian Source, and Possible Later Editorial Work

The division of vv. 3–6 into two sources has been slightly revised by Marc Z. Brettler.¹⁷ Vv. 5–6 are regarded as based on an early source. Brettler speculates that they derive from an Assyrian text, based on the progression of the verbs, which follows that of the Assyrian annals (the king going up against a country, besieging and capturing it [*alme, akšud, ašlula*], exiling the inhabitants and settling them in foreign cities), and because of the list of cities in v. 6 to which the conquered people were exiled. Furthermore, Brettler claims that v. 6 originally opened with "he captured" (וילבוד), with a waw consecutive followed by the con-

---

14 Bob Becking, *The Fall of Samaria: an Historical and Archaeological Study* (Leiden: Brill, 1992), 47–53.
15 Shemaryahu Talmon, "Polemics and Apology in Biblical Historiography: 2 Kings 17:24–41," in Shemaryahu Talmon, *Literary Studies in the Hebrew Bible: Form and Content: Collected Studies* (Leiden: Brill, 1993): 141.
16 Nadav Na'aman, "The Historical Background to the Conquest of Samaria," *Bib* 71 (1990): 213.
17 Marc Z. Brettler, "Text in a Tell: 2 Kings 17 as History," in Marc Z. Brettler, *The Creation of History in Ancient Israel* (London/New York: Routledge, 1995): 112–18.

verted imperfect *wayyiqtol*, and not with the date "*In the ninth year of Hoshea the king of Assyria captured Samaria* (בִּשְׁנַת הַתְּשִׁעִית לְהוֹשֵׁעַ לָכַד מֶלֶךְ־אַשּׁוּר אֶת־שֹׁמְרוֹן)" for the following reasons:

1. The grammatical past form "he captured" (לכד) breaks the narrative sequence.
2. "In the ninth year" (בִּשְׁנַת הַתְּשִׁעִית) is a late addition, since the syntax of that verse is only found in texts which date to exile and later. Furthermore, if the source was Assyrian, the text would not date according to the regnal years of Hoshea. Therefore, the text must have been added later.

Therefore v. 6aα is regarded as an addition based on the regnal years of Hoshea mentioned in v. 1. Brettler mentions the double introduction of the king of Assyria, "he went up against" (עלה).[18] In addition, the text in vv. 4–5 suggests that the Northern Kingdom withstood a three-year siege after its king was exiled; this is also regarded by Brettler as unlikely. The similarities between the phrases that open v. 3 and v. 5 suggest to Brettler that this is a case of *Wiederaufnahme*. The reconstruction of v. 4 and v. 5 coming from different sources, resolves, in Brettler's opinion, the problem of Samaria enduring a three-year siege without a king. The repeated notices in v. 3a and v. 5a are the result of redactional activity. Therefore, a *later editor* found or created an additional fragment which offered background information concerning the political history of events that led up to the conquest of Samaria. This information *chronologically preceded the capture and exile of Samaria and was inserted as an introduction* to vv. 5–6. He marked the insertion with a *Wiederaufnahme*. The insertion names Shalmaneser, *incorrectly*, accepting Na'aman's suggestion that Samaria was conquered only once by Sargon [italics mine].

In order to prove that vv. 3–4 were an addition of a later editor, Brettler notes that the opening of the verse 3 עָלָיו עָלָה שַׁלְמַנְאֶסֶר מֶלֶךְ אַשּׁוּר does not occur in the Deuteronomistic History and is only found in 2Chr 36:6: עָלָיו עָלָה נְבוּכַדְנֶאצַּר מֶלֶךְ בָּבֶל וַיַּאַסְרֵהוּ בַּנְחֻשְׁתַּיִם לְהֹלִיכוֹ בָּבֶלָה ("*Against him* King Nebuchadnezzar of Babylon came up, and bound him with fetters to take him to Babylon.")

Brettler, therefore, regards this form as an exilic or post-exilic form, added to the original text. Furthermore, he deems the claim that Samaria was besieged for three years unhistorical, since the treatment of the city after its conquest following a three-year rebellion seems too mild. He regards it as an accidental mistake by a *Judean scribe or copyist* [italics mine], who turned the fact that Samaria was conquered in Sargon's third year into a three-year siege (however, it actually occurred in his second regnal year). According to Brettler, the origins of vv. 3–4 are

---

18 The king of Assyria is actually mentioned five times in these verses.

less clear. The elements of paying tribute, conspiring, ceasing to pay tribute, and being fettered are found in Assyrian royal inscriptions, and it is possible that they were based on Assyrian inscriptions as well. In most inscriptions the rebellious king is exiled to Assyria, rather than imprisoned. Furthermore, there is no specific material that requires access to Assyrian sources. The only concrete information in vv. 3–4, namely the names of Shalmaneser and So', king of Egypt, are regarded by Brettler as highly suspect and understood as two historical errors by the late editor. Brettler, therefore, concludes that vv. 3–4 were created to offer background information concerning the exile, and may not be from an old source at all, but created by an editor, structured to conform to the biblical pattern of being reliant on Egypt, and being sent in fetters to Mesopotamia (cf., however, the fate of Manasseh [2Chr. 33:11], Jehoiachin [2Kgs 24:12 no fetters mentioned] / Jehoiakim [2Chr. 36:6] and Zedekiah [2Kgs 25:7]).

Bustenay Oded, accepting Brettler's suggestion of an Assyrian source, adds that the imprisonment of Hoshea before the fall of Samaria was probably based on an Assyrian source, in which Shalmaneser might have boasted that he imprisoned Hoshea in his own town (*ina ālīšu esiršu*). According to Oded, Hoshea's fate was not elaborated upon, as in the case of other kings who were exiled, and Hoshea's imprisonment may have been superimposed upon Jehoiachin's fate. A second reason why Hoshea's fate was allegedly paralleled with Jehoiachin's is, according to Oded, the fact that Hoshea was not considered in v. 2 as bad as his predecessors, and therefore he was saved from death and imprisoned prior to the siege.[19]

2.3 Doubts Concerning Brettler's and Oded's Views

However, Brettler's and Oded's arguments can be refuted on grammatical, syntactical, methodological and historical grounds.

Whereas Brettler claimed that the description of the king going up against a country, besieging and capturing it,[20] exiling the inhabitants and settling them in foreign cities derive from Assyrian royal inscriptions, based on the progression of the verbs, it should be remembered that the Assyrian actions were standard tactics, and because of their standard occurrence in warfare, became stock phrases. In the biblical verses these verbs appear, but not only in 2Kgs

---

19 Bustanay Oded, "Issues in the Bible in Light of the Assyrian Inscriptions," *Beit Mikra: Journal for the Study of the Bible and Its World* 42 (1996): 4–6 (in Hebrew).
20 *alme* "I besieged," *akšud* "I conquered," *ašlula* "I carried off their spoils (including people)".

17. According to this logic, 2Kgs 18:13 describing the arrival of the Assyrian army in 701 BCE, besieging and conquering all the cities of Judah, should be considered to derive from an Assyrian royal inscription as well. But is this evidence of copying an Assyrian text, or a reflection of reality? Note that the harsher terms *appul* ("I destroyed"), *aqqur* ("I devastated") and *aqmû* ("I set on fire") are not used. This seems to correspond with the archaeological findings at Samaria.[21]

The elements of paying tribute, conspiring, ceasing to pay tribute, and being fettered are found in Assyrian royal inscriptions. However, since these elements were widely practiced in the ancient Near East and Egypt,[22] they do not have to be regarded as originating from Assyrian texts.

As Brettler noted, the list of destinations of the deportees resembles the habit of Assyrian royal inscriptions to specify deportations of exiles and their resettling in remote parts of the empire. However, the Assyrian kings, who deported the Israelites, did not specify the destination of the deportations. According to most royal inscriptions, exiles were deported to Assyria, or in broad terms to the east or to the west.[23] Only in very rare cases is the destination of the exiles specified and the names of towns mentioned.[24] In none of these cases do the Assyrian royal inscription specify the breaking down of the settlement of deportees into specific towns inside a region or their dispersal into several regions, as is the case of 2Kgs 17:6. Furthermore, the list resembles the list in 2Kgs 18:34. Does this mean that both should be regarded as based on an (unknown) Assyrian

---

21 Ron E. Tappy, "The Final Years of Israelite Samaria: Toward a Dialogue between Texts and Archaeology," in *Up to the Gates of Ekron: Essays on the Archaeology and History of the Eastern Mediterranean in Honor of Seymour Gitin,* ed. Sidnie White Crawford and Amnon Ben-Tor (Jerusalem: W. F. Albright Institute of Archaeological Research / Israel Exploration Society, 2007): 265, 275–76. Cf. the terminology in Nazek Khalid Matty, *Sennacherib's Campaign against Judah and Jerusalem in 701 BC: a Historical Reconstruction* (Berlin: de Gruyter, 2016), 41–46.
22 Cf. the terms used in Egyptian texts: Anthony John Spalinger, *Aspects of the Military Documents of the Ancient Egyptians* (New Haven: Yale University Press, 1982).
23 Cf. Bustenay Oded, *Mass Deportations and Deportees in the Neo-Assyrian Empire* (Wiesbaden: Harrassowitz, 1979) and Radner's chapter in this volume.
24 Tiglath-pileser III: Hayim Tadmor and Shigeo Yamada, *The Royal Inscriptions of Tiglath-pileser III (744–727 BC) and Shalmaneser V (726–722 BC), Kings of Assyria* (Winona Lake, IN: Eisenbrauns, 2011), no. 14: 8. Sargon II: Andreas Fuchs, *Die Inschriften Sargons II. aus Khorsabad* (Göttingen: Cuvillier Verlag, 1994), 290: Zyl. 19–20; 313–14 Ann 16–17; 315 Ann. 66–67; 320 Ann. 120–23; 324 Ann. 211–13; 324 Ann. 213–15; 335 Ann. 380–81; 346 Prunk. 49, 55–56, 57; 349 Prunk. 115–16; 351–52 Prunk. 138–39. Sennacherib: A. Kirk Grayson and Jamie Novotny, *The Royal Inscriptions of Sennacherib, King of Assyria (704–681 BC), Part 1* (Winona Lake IN: Eisenbrauns, 2012), no. 2: 24; no. 3: 24; no. 4: 22; no. 16 ii 24; no. 17 ii 42; no. 18 ii 19'.

royal inscription²⁵ of either Shalmaneser V or Sargon II that was somehow accessible to the Hebrew scribe?

As to Oded's claim that the imprisonment of Hoshea (ויאסרהו) before the fall of Samaria was based on an Assyrian source, in which Shalmaneser might have boasted that he imprisoned Hoshea in his own town (*ina āliišu esiršu*)²⁶: this contradicts the biblical text. Hoshea is arrested and set in prison (בית כלא), not kept in confinement in his town "like a bird in a cage". This description is used to denote the attempts to subdue leaders who were not caught by the Assyrian king. In the cases of confining the rulers of Damascus to their city in the days of Adad-nerari III, Shalmaneser III and Tiglath-pileser III, and of Sennacherib's campaign against Judah, there is no evidence of a prolonged siege. When the besieged cities finally surrendered in the cases of Adad-nerari III, Tiglath-pileser III and Sennacherib, the inscriptions do not describe the blockades and deportations of the respective kings in connection with their city's capture.²⁷ Oded's reconstruction of events is based on the assumption that Hoshea's imprisonment preceded the fall of the city. Oded then compares Hoshea's fate to that of Jehoiachin, who was kept alive.²⁸ However, we simply do not know anything of Hoshea's fate after his imprisonment, and it would be wrong to speculate about his fate based on an enigmatic evaluation of his reign in v. 2, which does not belong to the narrative of the fall of Samaria, but to the Deuteronomistic framework.

The issue of transferring motifs from Assyrian royal inscriptions to the Biblical sphere has been *en vogue* since Peter Machinist's seminal work on the subject in the Book of Isaiah and has found many adherents.²⁹ However, the methods by which these motifs would have been transferred have been questioned, and the issue should be approached with caution, as the studies of William Morrow show.³⁰ There is the possibility that the information about the fall of Samaria

---

25 Cf. Ehud Ben Zvi, "Who Wrote the Speech of Rabshakeh and When?," *JBL* 109 (1990): 88–91.
26 Etymologically and semantically, Hebrew אסר and Akkadian *esēru* are similar.
27 Davide Nadali, "Sieges and Similes of Sieges in the Royal Annals: the Conquest of Damascus by Tiglath-pileser III," *Kaskal* 6 (2009): 137–49.
28 Oded, "Issues in the Bible," 4–6.
29 Peter Machinist, "Assyria and Its Image in the First Isaiah," *JAOS* 103 (1983): 719–37. Adherents include e.g. Nili Wazana and Shawn Zelig Aster, to name just a few. Cf. Shawn Zelig Aster, "Transmission of Neo-Assyrian Claims of Empire to Judah in the Late Eighth Century BCE," *HUCA* 78 (2007): 1–44.
30 Cf. William S. Morrow, "Cuneiform Literacy and Deuteronomic Composition," *BO* 62 (2005): 204–13; William S. Morrow, "Tribute from Judah and the Transmission of Assyrian Propaganda," in *"My Spirit at Rest in the North Country" (Zechariah 6.8): Collected Communications to the XX*ᵗʰ

originates from an Assyrian inscription, but this hypothesis was neither successfully demonstrated by Brettler nor by Oded. Concrete evidence is still lacking.

As to Brettler's attempt to prove the existence of *a later redactor,* the claim that the syntax in v. 6 בִּשְׁנַת הַתְּשִׁעִית "in the ninth year" is late Biblical Hebrew[31] is incorrect. In contrast to Brettler's assertion, the clause "in the nth year of ..." occurs already in the Samaria ostraca (without the *n*, which is assimilated into the *t*).[32] These clauses should, therefore, not be regarded as later additions. Brettler's motivation in discarding the originality of this opening to v. 6 is that if the source had been Assyrian, as Brettler suggested, the text would not be dated according to the regnal years of Hoshea.[33] Indeed, this circular reasoning is problematic. Furthermore, Brettler's claim that the grammatical past form לכד ("captured") in v. 6 breaks the narrative sequence and is not in the converted imperfect, and that this is therefore another piece of evidence that the date is a late addition and the verb was changed,[34] is not precise. The verbal form opens the sequence of verbs following a time adverb, just as v. 3 opens with an indirect object followed by a verb in the *qatal* form and is followed by *wayyiqtol* forms.

Brettler assumes that vv. 3–4 are *late editorial additions.* Brettler's claim that the opening of the verse 3 עָלָיו עָלָה שַׁלְמַנְאֶסֶר מֶלֶךְ אַשּׁוּר does not occur in the Deuteronomistic History is correct. However, he uses the occurrence of this word order in 2Chr 36:6, clearly a post-exilic text, to claim that the same syntactic structure in v. 3 is a late form as well, that is to say, a late addition by a post-exilic redactor.[35] Unfortunately, the occurrence of the same syntax in the post-exilic Book of Chronicles misled Brettler, who took it as a sign of the lateness of the text. In both cases the sentence emphasises its adverbial complement. The information focuses on the fate of the attacked king. It is against him (Hoshea and Jehoiakim) that the foreign king campaigned. The emphasis is on the identity of the attacked king against some other option (Jehoiachin), and not on the fate of the capital city or kingdom.

Congress of the International Organization for the Study of the Old Testament, ed. Hermann Michael Niemann and Matthias Augustin (Frankfurt am Main: Peter Lang, 2011): 183–92.
31 Brettler, "Text in a Tell," 117.
32 Shmuel Ahituv and Anson F. Rainey, *Echoes from the Past: Hebrew and Cognate Inscriptions from the Biblical Period* (Jerusalem: Carta, 2008), 263.
33 Brettler, "Text in a Tell," 117.
34 Brettler, "Text in a Tell," 117 and n. 38.
35 Brettler, "Text in a Tell," 115.

Brettler suggests that in v. 5 there is a *Wiederaufnahme* of v. 3 where Shalmaneser, king of Assyria, "went up against".[36] However, the object of the sentence is different and the narrative does not resume where it digressed from its course. Thus, the similarity of verbs should not be seen as resumptive.

Brettler dismisses the data mentioning Shalmaneser as the conqueror of Samaria, and regards the length of the siege as unhistorical.[37] Whereas the Babylonian Chronicle explicitly mentions that Shalmaneser destroyed Samaria,[38] a three-year long siege is not incomprehensible, and was rejected only because of Brettler's preconceptions.

Finally, Brettler claims that v. 3 is added to conform to the biblical pattern of being reliant on Egypt.[39] However, where can this pattern be detected, except for Isaiah and Jeremiah, which are historical? Why should the information about conspiring with the king of Egypt be regarded as fictitious? At the end of the 8th century BCE there is evidence of Egyptian intervention in the Levant, as can be learned from Assyrian, biblical and classical texts,[40] and as a seal of Hoshea with Egyptian motifs testifies.[41]

2.4 The Composition of 2Kgs 18:9–11

In a century of scholarship, scholars from Hugo Winckler in 1892[42] to Bob Becking in 1992[43] have based their arguments for the existence of a second source describing the Fall of Samaria on the existence of 2Kgs 18:9–11, which partially parallels 2Kgs 17:5–6 and does not include 2Kgs 17:3–4. However, in 1990 Christof Hardmeier[44] proposed that two sources were assembled together in 2Kgs 18:9–11, on the following grounds:

---

36 Brettler, "Text in a Tell," 116.
37 Brettler, "Text in a Tell," 118.
38 Jean-Jacques Glassner, *Mesopotamian Chronicles* (Atlanta GA: Society of Biblical Literature, 2004), 195.
39 Brettler, "Text in a Tell," 118.
40 Dan'el Kahn. "The Inscription of Sargon II at Tang-i Var and the Chronology of Dynasty 25," *Or* 70 (2001): 1–18.
41 André Lemaire, "Royal Signature: Name of Israel's Last King Surfaces in a Private Collection," *BAR* 21 (1995): 48–52.
42 Winckler, *Alttestamentliche Untersuchungen*, 16–25.
43 Becking, *The Fall of Samaria*, 47–53.
44 Christof Hardmeier, *Prophetie im Streit vor dem Untergang Judas: Erzahlkommunikative Studien zur Entstehungssituation der Jesaja- und Jeremiaerzahlungen in II Reg 18–20 und Jer 37–40* (Berlin: de Gruyter, 1990), 101–108.

a. Two forms of the name of Hezekiah, king of Judah, occur in these three verses. In v. 9 king Hezekiahu is spelled הַמֶּלֶךְ חִזְקִיָּהוּ, whereas in v. 10 his name is spelled חִזְקִיָּה. This spelling occurs as well in v. 1 (the Deuteronomistic opening of the framework of the chapter) and in the so-called source A in 2Kgs 18:14–16, differing from the rest of the Sennacherib-Hezekiah narrative in 2Kgs 18:13–19:37.
b. The conquest of Samaria using the verb לכד occurs twice. In v. 10a the verb occurs in the direct object suffix conjugation and again in v. 10b in the passive voice.
c. Hoshea appears twice as king of Israel. One use of the title is redundant.
d. There is a double synchronism between the years of Hezekiah and Hoshea
e. There are two different systems of counting years in v. 9 and v. 10. In v. 9 the year is in absolute state, followed by the number in the ordinal with a definite article preceding it וַיְהִי בַּשָּׁנָה הָרְבִיעִית ("It happened in the fourth year of king Hezekiah"). In v. 10, the year is in the construct state, and the number in the cardinal without the article בִּשְׁנַת־שֵׁשׁ ("in year six").

Hardmeier suggests that the first source can be found in vv. 9–10a, and the second starts at v. 10b. According to him, vv. 9–10a open a narrative that continues with Sennacherib's campaign against Judah in 18:13. He assigns this source to the DtrN (Nomist) who worked in the exilic or post-exilic period, since he identifies this narrative structure in the description of the fall of Judah, and in the books of Jeremiah and Ezekiel.[45]

There are some weaknesses in Hardmeier's hypothesis. These can be divided into two aspects: the reconstruction of two alleged sources, and chronological aspects. I will start with the question of two sources in 18:9–10.

1. The reconstruction of two alleged sources
    a. If one eliminates the information of v. 9, the Assyrian king in v. 11 becomes anonymous.[46]
    b. According to Hardmeier's reconstruction, the information of alleged source 18:9–10a derives from 2Kgs 17:3–5a, whereas alleged source 18:10b–11 derives from 2Kgs 17:5b–6. The alleged redactor of both sources in 2Kgs 18:9–11 had either the two alleged sources of 17:3–4 and 5–6 in front of him, in which case he mixed the two sources and created two new sources, divided differently, or he had in front of him the entire

---

[45] Hardmeier, *Prophetie im Streit*, 108.
[46] Benjamin D. Thomas, *Hezekiah and the Compositional History of the Book of Kings* (Tübingen: Mohr Siebeck, 2014), 350.

paragraph 2Kgs 17:3–6. In that case, it is difficult to understand why he discarded a unified narrative in order to create two sources, with numerous problems.
2. Chronological aspects:
   a. The information of 18:9–10a is not fabricated at a late exilic date, and can be found in 17:5–6, and corroborated by the Babylonian Chronicle, where it is explicitly claimed that Samaria was destroyed by Shalmaneser V.[47]
   b. Hardmeier associates 18:9–10a, in which Hezekiahu is written with the longer and older spelling, to the post-exilic period, whereas he regarded the shorter writing as earlier. The biblical data leads to the opposite conclusion.[48]
   c. Hardmeier's identification of a narrative opening in v. 9 is correct, however dating it to the exilic/post-exilic period because of the occurrence of similar syntactic structures in the books of Jeremiah and Ezekiel is unnecessary. 2Kgs 18:13/Isa 36:1, which has a similar opening (the Sennacherib account), does not have to be regarded as post-exilic. On the contrary, it seems to be based on early material.

Consequently, even though Hardmeier's observations are valid, and cannot be ignored, his division into two hypothetical sources, of which at least one is exilic or even post-exilic, stitched together in v. 10b should be discarded. The solution is more complicated.

There are several additional factors, which have to be taken into account:
a. The chronology is Judean, but the events described, surprisingly, deal with Israelite history.
b. The pericope is detached from what precedes and from what follows.[49]
c. 18:9–11 appear in chapter 17 with minor changes and are, therefore, redundant.
d. Hezekiah is named without title, whereas Hoshea, appears with full name and title.
e. The subject changes from the king of Assyria in the singular in v. 9 to an unmentioned plural in v. 10a, and then to Samaria in passive singular in v. 10b.

---

47 Glassner, *Mesopotamian Chronicles*, 195.
48 Sara Japhet. "The Supposed Common Authorship of Chronicles and Ezra-Nehemia Investigated Anew," *VT* 18 (1968): 338–41; David Talshir, "A Reinvestigation of the Linguistic Relationship between Chronicles and Ezra-Nehemiah," *VT* 38 (1988): 175–76.
49 Galo W. Vera Chamaza, "Literarkritische Beobachtung zu 2 Kön. 18, 1–12," *BZ* 33 (1989): 228.

f. It seems that v. 9 originally ended in the middle of v. 10 with "and at the end of three years, they took it".

The synchronisms in 18:9–10 are regarded as authentic, original and historical by many scholars.[50] However, when scrutinizing these verses, I have come to the conclusion that these synchronisms cannot be relied upon to be historical for the following reasons:

g. All the synchronisms in the Book of Kings between the kings of Israel and Judah and vice versa have a similar syntactic form. The ones who differ from this form are suspected not to be authentic for various reasons.
h. All synchronisms in the Book of Kings are between the accession of a king and the regnal years of the other king.[51]
i. From the 35 synchronisms in the Book of Kings, the only synchronisms to open with the words וַיְהִי בַּשָּׁנָה הָרְבִיעִית ;וַיְהִי בִּשְׁנַת שָׁלֹשׁ ("and it happened in the nth year") are found in 2Kgs 18:1 and 9, respectively.
j. וַיְהִי בִּשְׁנַת usually opens royal narratives about wars or divine revelations to the prophets Jeremiah, Ezekiel and Zechariah,[52] whereas synchronisms open with the time clause בשנת without a narrative opening (except for 2Kgs 18:1).
k. There is no synchronism of events in the middle or end of a reign except in this case.
l. The double synchronism of years four and six in a space of one verse is unnecessary and unique.
m. In v. 9, the nominal clause opening with the feminine copula, הִיא הַשָּׁנָה הַשְּׁבִיעִית לְהוֹשֵׁעַ בֶּן־אֵלָה מֶלֶךְ יִשְׂרָאֵל ("which was the seventh year of king Hoshea son of Elah of Israel"), can be regarded as a gloss, similar to the gloss in Jer 25:1 which is omitted in the Septuagint.[53] This gloss is inserted into v. 9 and creates the first synchronism.

---

50 Becking, *The Fall of Samaria*, 47–53.
51 For a list of the synchronisms, see conveniently M. Christine Tetley, *The Reconstructed Chronology of the Divided Kingdom* (Winona Lake IN: Eisenbrauns, 2005), 35–39 and Hayim Tadmor, "Chronology," *Encyclopedia Miqra'it* 4 (1963), 251–54 (in Hebrew).
52 1Kgs 14:25; 2Kgs 12:7; 2Kgs 25:1; Jer 25:1; 28:1; 32:1; 36:1, 9; 52:4; Ezek 8:1; 20:1; 24:1; 26:1; 29:1, 17; 30:20; 31:1; 32:1, 17; 33:21; Zech 7:1.
53 See the dating in Jer 32:1. 2Kgs 25:8, and its parallel in Jer 52:12 have a similar structure. The clause occurs in LXX 4 Kgdms 25:8, but is omitted in the Septuagint of ch. 52. Note that these paragraphs have a parallel in Jer 39, where this verse is entirely omitted. The origin of these paragraphs is debated, and exceeds the scope of this paper.

n. The clause "In the sixth year of Hezekiah, which was the ninth year of king Hoshea of Israel, Samaria was taken" creates a strain in the sentence.

From the analysis of the synchronisms in 2Kgs 18:9–10, it becomes clear that they differ from the synchronisms in the Book of Kings in terms of syntax (v. 9 corresponds to the opening of narratives), and the use of synchronisms with events of the middle of the reign and not with the accession. At least one synchronism (year 6 of Hezekiah is year 9 of Hoshea) belongs orthographically to the dating used in the *Deuteronomistic strata*.[54]

Year 9 is the year found in the original description of the fall of Samaria (2Kgs 17:6), and is then coupled to Hezekiah's reign. There is a duplication of data, which does not add any new and significant information.

As Hardmeier noticed, v. 9 opens with a *narrative opening* ויהי followed by the date of an event, dating "in the fourth year of King Hezekiahu" (וַיְהִי בַּשָּׁנָה הָרְבִיעִית לַמֶּלֶךְ חִזְקִיָּהוּ).[55] The narrative opening remains, but the original continuation of that narrative is dislocated. The redactor was not interested in the events of Hezekiah's fourth regnal year, but wanted to *contrast the fall of Samaria with the reign of Hezekiah*. He mentioned Shalmaneser as the king of Assyria who came against Samaria in 18:9. This information is taken from 2Kgs 17:3. Since the name of Shalmaneser has been taken from 17:3 where he is said to have come up against Hoshea, the omission of the latter's fate from 2Kgs 18 should be understood as deliberate. The redactor was simply not interested in the fate of the king of Israel. As a consequence, the grammar of the sentence was changed and the emphasizing structure עליו was discarded. However, the *qatal* verbal form עלה of 2Kgs 17:3 remained unchanged. Thus, it can be concluded that 2Kgs 18:9 is dependent on information from 2Kgs 17:3, which is regarded by scholars as a separate independent source, allegedly not available to the author of 2Kgs 18:9–11.

The next information in the redactor's source was the date found in 2Kgs 17:5b–6 for Samaria's fall in Hoshea's ninth regnal year after a three-year siege. In order to connect the passages about the fall of Samaria with the date of the fourth regnal year of Hezekiah (which was available to him), the redactor calculated backwards three years from Hoshea's ninth regnal year. He arrived at year 7 of Hoshea, and added it in a gloss in the corresponding grammatical construction of a narrative, synchronising it with the date he had for Hezekiah: הִיא הַשָּׁנָה הַשְּׁבִיעִית לְהוֹשֵׁעַ בֶּן־אֵלָה מֶלֶךְ יִשְׂרָאֵל. He then added the information about

---

54 See the writing of the name Hezekiah חזקיה in 2Kgs 18:1.
55 Hardmeier, *Prophetie im Streit*, 107.

the Fall of Samaria in year 9 of Hoshea, as found in his source (2Kgs 17). By correlating the dates concerning the Fall of Samaria with the source about Hezekiah, he added to Hezekiah's fourth regnal year the three years of siege and arrived at Hezekiah's regnal year 6. He then synchronised it in the corresponding grammatical construction of an official date.

I concur with Hardmeier, that the paragraph originally opened a narrative. However, I do not accept his reconstruction of two sources in 18:9–11, and that the source of Hezekiah originally dealt with the fall of Samaria. I suggest that the opening of the narrative belonged to an alternative story, namely Hezekiah's illness and miraculous recovery (2Kgs 20:1; Isa 38:1), which was moved from its original location to follow the narrative of Jerusalem's divine salvation at a later editorial stage, although chronologically it clearly preceded the events of 701 BCE. In its current position it received the vague date בימים ההם "in those days".

Consequently, the synchronism cannot be used to correlate between the fall of Samaria and the reign of Hezekiah, and thus Hezekiah's accession should be determined to be in 715 BCE according to the data in 2Kgs 18:13.

Summing up this section, it can be seen that 2Kgs 18:9–11 cannot be regarded as an original primary source. It exhibits breaks in the text, duplications, redundancy, abrupt change in subject, glosses, different styles, and inconsistencies in the titles of kings and their orthography. All these elements are crude signs suggesting different sources stitched together. Furthermore, the synchronisms do not conform to the numerous synchronisms in the Book of Kings; it should, therefore, be regarded as a secondary composition. It seems that it was edited and inserted into its current position by the Deuteronomistic historian during the final years of the monarchy. The *raison d'etre* of these synchronisms is to relate the fall of Samaria and of the sinful king of Israel with the reign of Hezekiah, the most pious Davidic king, and to contrast their religious behaviour and eventually, between the fall of Samaria and the divine deliverance of Jerusalem. This contrast is intended to convey an ideological message for the inhabitants of Judah, namely that destruction and deportation are not unavoidable.

The narrative cannot be regarded as historical or chronologically accurate since Ahaz – a sinner in his own right – ruled as king of Judah during the fall of Samaria. Maintaining the original chronology as it appears in 2Kgs 18:13 would miss the point of the didactic pericope.

Let us return to the claim that the episode describing the fall of Samaria in 2Kgs 17:3–6 was composed by merging two sources (either an Israelite and a Judean source, or an Israelite or Assyrian source with later additions by a redactor), based on the existence of a parallel in 2Kgs 18:9–11. I hope I have shown that it has scant foundation. In the following, I will survey the suggestions of scholars who regarded 2Kgs 17:3–6 as a single source.

3 2Kgs 17:3–6: a Coherent Text?

John H. Hayes and Jeffrey K. Kuan[56] regard 2Kgs 17:3–6 as a coherent text, and the events described in it as consecutive. They argue that there were four Assyrian campaigns against Samaria; that Hoshea was imprisoned before the final three-year siege; that Shalmaneser V ravaged Samaria in 725–724 BCE; that the Samarians enthroned an anonymous king during the siege; that Samaria was conquered by Shalmaneser just before his death; and that Sargon needed to reconquer Samaria in 720 BCE.

However, without delving into the details of the research of Hayes and Kuan, since it exceeds the scope of this paper, there are chronological and historical problems.[57] There is no evidence of an unnamed king in Samaria following Hoshea, and the reliance of Hayes and Kuan on interpretations of the prophetic Book of Hoshea seems exaggerated.[58]

4 One Main Source with Later Redactional Additions / Corrections?

Shemaryahu Talmon[59] noted that the factual account [in vv. 5–6] did not contain any formulaic references to the misdeeds of Samaria's rulers which abound in the Book of Kings and are presented there as the causes of setbacks and disasters which befell their realm. Talmon continues "... Furthermore, such criticism is also absent from the parallel version of that notation in 18:9–11". He concludes that "the doubling of the account of the conquest of Samaria, together with the evident *deviation* of 17:5–6 *from the conceptual framework of the book of Kings*, suggests that this latter chronistic notion was *quoted from a northern source*. It may well be a fragment of Ephraimite annals" (italics mine). The presumed Eph-

---

[56] John H. Hayes, and Jeffrey K. Kuan, "The Final Years of Samaria," *Bib* 72 (1991): 153–81.
[57] K. Lawson Younger Jr., "The Fall Samaria in Light of Recent Research," *CBQ* 61 (1999): 481.
[58] See the chapter by M. Nissinen in this volume.
[59] Shemaryahu Talmon, "Polemics and Apology in Biblical Historiography: 2 Kings 17:24–41," in Shemaryahu Talmon, *Literary Studies in the Hebrew Bible: Form and Content: Collected Studies* (Leiden: Brill, 1993): 137–46.

raimite origin of 17:5–6 is supported by the absence of any synchronising formula of Hoshea's last years with the regnal years of the contemporaneous Judean king Hezekiah. Noting the *Wiederaufnahme* of v. 5 ויעל מלך אשור בכל הארץ from v. 3 עליו עלה שלמנאסר מלך אשור Talmon claims that the reference to Hoshea's conspiracy with Egypt, his refusal to pay tribute, and his ensuing arrest by the king of Assyria (v. 4) is a secondary insert into the originally shorter text. V. 4 is thus regarded as an insert into an original Israelite source which included 17:3–6 and vv. 24, 29–31.

However, Talmon says nothing about the origin of the information of v. 4. Furthermore, if only v. 4 was a late insertion, the text of v. 3 ends with Hoshea's submission, and paying yearly tribute, omitting his rebellion, and resumes with the Assyrian campaign against the entire land with no reason. If v. 3b should be considered a later addition as well, it is not clear why the additional information of v. 4 was needed at all. Nevertheless, as noted before, the mentioning of coming up against the king and the land should not be regarded as a *Wiederaufnahme*, and therefore v. 4 should not be seen as an insertion.

Vv. 5–6 may come from an original Israelite source as Talmon asserts, but his reasoning that the absence of criticism for the Israelite king and his subjects proves this can be challenged. It seems highly probable that, as in 2Kgs 18:12, there once existed an original theological reason in 2Kgs 17:9 for the punishment of Israel, as Ronnie Goldstein has suggested.[60]

Na'aman[61] regards 2Kgs 17:3–6, describing the fall of Samaria, as a single source, written by the Deuteronomistic Historian several hundred years after the events, using earlier sources, which Na'aman does not identify. According to Na'aman, the Deuteronomistic Historian found only one Assyrian king – Shalmaneser – in the biblical text and mistakenly assigned the fall of Samaria to him. In fact, it was Sargon who conquered Samaria, as his numerous inscriptions claim. According to the biblical data, Samaria was conquered in Hoshea's ninth regnal year after a three year prolonged siege. Na'aman claims that these data were the result of historical deductions on the part of the Deuteronomistic Historian, who mistakenly interpreted his source material (which included the defeat of Samaria three years after its rebellion and the incarceration of its king) as a prolonged siege which ended with the arrest of Hoshea in his ninth year. Na'aman assigned the fall of Samaria solely to the reign of Sargon. Thus, according to Na'aman, the Deuteronomistic Historian got all his facts wrong.

---

60 Ronnie Goldstein, "A Suggestion Regarding the Meaning of 2 Kings 17: 9 and the Composition of 2 Kings 17: 7–23," *VT* 63 (2013): 393–407.
61 Na'aman, "The Historical Background," 220–25.

Gershon Galil[62] notes that the knowledge of the author of the Book of Kings, who wrote approximately 150 years after the events, was only partial. He did not know that Judah remained a vassal following Sennacherib's campaign in 701 BCE, and similarly, he did not know that Hoshea was a vassal of Assyria already during the reign of Tiglath-pileser III. He thus inserted v. 3 describing Hoshea's subjugation to Shalmaneser. For this he invented an alleged campaign by Shalmaneser, which is not supported by extra-biblical evidence. The rest of Samaria's demise, according to Galil, was based on reliable sources originating from the book of the chronicles of the kings of Judah. Galil finds no evidence of an Israelite chronicle. According to his reconstruction of the original Judean chronicle, vv. 4–6 existed and described the fall of Samaria, according to the Judean regnal dates of Hezekiah, and that the regnal years of Hoshea were edited into the text, whereas the dating according to Hezekiah was omitted, along with the events of Hezekiah's fifth year. According to Galil, two campaigns were conducted against Samaria, one in Shalmaneser's reign after Hoshea rebelled in 723 BCE. At the advance of the Assyrian army, Hoshea went out of Samaria to submit to the Assyrians, in order to spare the kingdom, but was arrested. Assyria continued with the campaign to subdue Samaria, and besieged it from Shalmaneser's last year, Hezekiah's fourth regnal year 722 BCE. Upon the death of Shalmaneser the siege probably was eased due to lack of manpower and turned into a loose enclosure, but the Assyrian forces did not retreat.

Galil's reconstruction contradicts the synchronisms between the reign of Hoshea who ascended the throne in 732/1 BCE and that of Hezekiah, according to Galil. Hoshea's seventh year is 725 BCE, and his ninth year is 723 BCE. These dates should correspond respectively to Hezekiah's fourth regnal year, which Galil sets in 722 BCE, and the sixth regnal year, of Hezekiah who fell, according to Galil, in 720 BCE.

In summary, scholars who claim that the pericope describing the fall of Samaria originates from a single source, suggest numerous mistakes and late interpolations in the biblical text, in order to uphold their theories and fit them to the extra-biblical sources.

---

[62] Gershon Galil, "The Last Years of the Kingdom of Israel and the Fall of Samaria," *CBQ* 57 (1995): 52–65.

5 The Literary Solution

5.1 2Kgs 17:3–6 as a Literary Composition

I concur with Ernst Würthwein[63] and Trevor R. Hobbs[64] that in vv. 3–4 the author of the pericope concentrated on the deeds of Hoshea, his relations with the kings of Assyria and Egypt, and eventually his fate, whereas vv. 5–6, rather than recounting a different series of events which followed those in vv. 3–4, go over the same events, but this time with the emphasis on the effect of the invasion by the Assyrians on the city, land and population of Samaria. This can be demonstrated by following the verbs and pronouns in the different verses: in vv. 3–4 verbs and pronouns describe Hoshea in the third person singular וַיַּעַל, וַיְהִי, עָלָיו, וַיֹּאסְרֵהוּ, וַיַּעַצְרֵהוּ, וְלֹא הֶעֱלָה, שָׁלַח. After describing the fate of the king during the fall of the city in Hoshea's ninth regnal year (724/3 BCE), the author turns in v. 5 to describe the fate of the city of Samaria in the third person feminine וַיָּצַר עָלֶיהָ. Finally, the author describes in v. 6 the fate of the inhabitants of Samaria who are exiled to the Assyrian realm in the third person plural: וַיֶּגֶל אֶת־יִשְׂרָאֵל אַשּׁוּרָה וַיֹּשֶׁב אֹתָם בַּחְלַח וּבְחָבוֹר נְהַר גּוֹזָן וְעָרֵי מָדָי. This analysis solves all problems raised by scholars, and enables a historical reconstruction of events in the days of Shalmaneser V.

5.2 A Stylistic Parallel in Sennacherib's Royal Inscriptions

A fascinating parallel to this literary division of focus on the king, the town and the inhabitants can be found in the royal inscriptions of Sennacherib of Assyria and his third campaign to the West. As Tadmor has shown in his discussion about the historiographic writing of Sennacherib's scribes, the third campaign of Sennacherib can be divided into six episodes. These episodes were not necessarily organised in a chronological or geographical order, but in a literary one. Tadmor showed that four elements recur in these episodes:
a. The fate of the rebellious king and kingship (the king either escapes, is punished, receives pardon, remains in office, or is reinstalled);
b. The fate of his kingdom and its towns;
c. Taxes are levied on the re-subjugated towns; and

---

63 Ernst Würthwein, *Die Bücher der Könige: 1. Kön. 17–2. Kön. 25* (Göttingen: Vanderhoeck & Ruprecht, 1984), 393–94.
64 Trevor R. Hobbs, *2 Kings* (Waco TX: Word Books, 1985), 225–26.

d. The fate of the inhabitants is recounted.[65]

The literary composition and order of 2Kgs 17:3–6 is very similar. Firstly, the deeds of the king are described, from his subjugation, through his rebellious plotting, open rebellion and final imprisonment. No mention is made of a subsequent king of Israel, since Samaria was turned into a province without a local king. Consequently, in Sargon's inscriptions the Samaritans are rebelling and there is no mention of a king. Secondly, the fate of the kingdom and its capital is described. The land is destroyed and the capital city besieged, until it is conquered. Thirdly, no mention of yearly taxes is made after the conquest. And fourthly, the inhabitants of Samaria are exiled and resettled in the Assyrian Empire.

6 The Origin of the Text?

In the following section, I will summarise what can and cannot be said about the origin of the text. Admittedly, I cannot identify the origin, and this discussion will be purely hypothetical.

The information is dated to the reign of Hoshea. It describes the political events leading to the demise of the Kingdom of Israel. These events are not described in a derogative fashion.

As discussed above, it seems that 2Kgs 17:3–6 is not composed from two different chronicles, either from Israel or from Judah. Furthermore, chronicles (at least the Assyrian prototypes which are known to us) are normally shorter and do not elaborate upon details. There is no chronological listing of events according to the king's years (2Kgs 18:9–10 is shown to be a fictitious chronology). Furthermore, there is no clear annual development of the events. The events of the beginning of the reign, the submission, the conspiracy with Egypt, and the open rebellion are not dated, and the events of year 8 during the siege are entirely missing. Finally, the events are not chronologically ordered, as, e.g., the imprisonment of Hoshea is mentioned before the capture of the city.

Annals (at least the Assyrian annals) typically herald the deeds of the king victoriously in the first person singular, boasting about the king's accomplishments. This is not the case in 2Kgs 17:3–6. It seems, therefore, that the source

---

65 Hayim Tadmor, "Sennacherib's Campaign to Judah: Historical and Historiographical Considerations," in *"With My Many Chariots I Have Gone Up the Heights of the Mountains": Historical and Literary Studies on Ancient Mesopotamia and Israel*, ed. Mordechai Cogan (Jerusalem: Israel Exploration Society, 2011), 662–72.

is not extracted from Israelite royal annals, at least if they would have followed the known Mesopotamian template.

The composition exhibits literary traits, and it is clearly not ordered chronologically. It may derive from a sort of summary inscription of the reign, organised in a literary form.

Should the narrative be regarded as having an Assyrian, Israelite or Judean source? As for the claim that the information derives from an alleged Assyrian royal inscription of Shalmaneser V,[66] describing the Fall of Samaria – there is no concrete evidence for the existence of such a text on which 2Kgs 17:1–6 could have been based. However, if Ronnie Goldstein[67] is correct in identifying an early strata in 2Kgs 17:7–23, using Neo-Assyrian calques in 2Kgs 17:9, it can cautiously be accepted, that the original narrative imitated Neo-Assyrian treaty terminology, reflecting Israelite theology, which blamed the Kingdom of Israel for political covenantal trespass. The Israelites did not obey the Lord and broke his covenant, and for this were severely punished. Similar attempts to explain Israel's demise can be found in 2Kgs 18:12. Comparable accusations were forwarded in Ezek 17:11–21 by a Judean author against Zedekiah, the last Judean king, suggesting that he broke the covenant with god by rebelling against Babylonia.

I would therefore like to suggest, cautiously, that 2Kgs 17:3–6 may have been composed by Israelite court scribes in the short period following the destruction, when Israel became an Assyrian province and before it was reconquered by Sargon, who radically changed its demography and administration. Such a composition can be compared to the description of the end of the Kingdom of Judah by its own scribes. The narrative was eventually reworked and incorporated into the Book of Kings by Judean scribes, who stressed the cultic abominations and transgressions, which according to them, brought about the downfall of the kingdom of Israel.

---

66 See the suggestions by Brettler and Oded, discussed above in sections 2.2 and 2.3. Cf. also Novotny's chapter in this volume.
67 Goldstein, "A Suggestion Regarding the Meaning of 2 Kings 17: 9."

Christoph Levin
In Search of the Original Biblical Record of the Assyrian Conquest of Samaria

1 Introduction: Two Parallel Records

The conquest of Samaria by the Assyrian great king is recorded two times in the Book of Kings. The first account is to be found in 2Kgs 17:3–6 in the framework of the section that deals with king Hoshea of Israel. This is the place where one would expect it. The second account in 2Kgs 18:9–11 is part of the section that relates the history of king Hezekiah of Judah (Fig. 1).

9 וַיְהִי בַּשָּׁנָה הָרְבִיעִית לַמֶּלֶךְ חִזְקִיָּהוּ הִיא הַשָּׁנָה הַשְּׁבִיעִית לְהוֹשֵׁעַ בֶּן־אֵלָה מֶלֶךְ יִשְׂרָאֵל עָלָה שַׁלְמַנְאֶסֶר מֶלֶךְ־אַשּׁוּר	3 עָלָיו עָלָה שַׁלְמַנְאֶסֶר מֶלֶךְ אַשּׁוּר וַיְהִי־לוֹ הוֹשֵׁעַ עֶבֶד וַיָּשֶׁב לוֹ מִנְחָה: 4 וַיִּמְצָא מֶלֶךְ־אַשּׁוּר בְּהוֹשֵׁעַ קֶשֶׁר אֲשֶׁר שָׁלַח מַלְאָכִים אֶל־סוֹא מֶלֶךְ־מִצְרַיִם וְלֹא־הֶעֱלָה מִנְחָה לְמֶלֶךְ אַשּׁוּר כְּשָׁנָה בְשָׁנָה וַיַּעַצְרֵהוּ מֶלֶךְ אַשּׁוּר וַיַּאַסְרֵהוּ בֵּית כֶּלֶא: 5 וַיַּעַל מֶלֶךְ־אַשּׁוּר בְּכָל־הָאָרֶץ
עַל־שֹׁמְרוֹן וַיָּצַר עָלֶיהָ: 10 ‹וַיִּלְכְּדָהּ› מִקְצֵה שָׁלֹשׁ שָׁנִים בִּשְׁנַת־שֵׁשׁ לְחִזְקִיָּה הִיא שְׁנַת־תֵּשַׁע לְהוֹשֵׁעַ מֶלֶךְ יִשְׂרָאֵל נִלְכְּדָה שֹׁמְרוֹן: 11 וַיֶּגֶל מֶלֶךְ־אַשּׁוּר אֶת־יִשְׂרָאֵל אַשּׁוּרָה ‹וַיַּנִּחֵם› בַּחְלַח וּבְחָבוֹר נְהַר גּוֹזָן וְעָרֵי מָדָי: 12 עַל אֲשֶׁר לֹא־שָׁמְעוּ בְּקוֹל יְהוָה אֱלֹהֵיהֶם וַיַּעַבְרוּ אֶת־בְּרִיתוֹ אֵת כָּל־אֲשֶׁר צִוָּה מֹשֶׁה עֶבֶד יְהוָה וְלֹא שָׁמְעוּ וְלֹא עָשׂוּ:	וַיַּעַל שֹׁמְרוֹן וַיָּצַר עָלֶיהָ שָׁלֹשׁ שָׁנִים: 6 בִּשְׁנַת הַתְּשִׁיעִית לְהוֹשֵׁעַ לָכַד מֶלֶךְ־אַשּׁוּר אֶת־שֹׁמְרוֹן וַיֶּגֶל אֶת־יִשְׂרָאֵל אַשּׁוּרָה וַיֹּשֶׁב אֹתָם בַּחְלַח וּבְחָבוֹר נְהַר גּוֹזָן וְעָרֵי מָדָי:

Fig. 1: Synoptic table presenting the text of 2Kgs 17:3–6 (first column) and 2Kgs 18:9–12 (second column). Prepared by the author.

The second record is usually seen as secondary, and rightly so. The section disrupts the connection that originally existed between the note about Hezekiah's rebellion against the Assyrian king in 18:7b and the account of Sennacherib's campaign which is given from 18:13 onward: "He rebelled against the king of Assyria, and would not serve him. [...] In the fourteenth year of King Hezekiah Sennacherib king of Assyria came up against all the fortified cities of Judah and took them." These two phrases once followed one another immediately.[1]

In most parts, 18:9–11 corresponds almost verbatim with 17:3, 5–6. This is best explained by direct copying. It raises the question of why a record was repeated which every reader had already come across in the preceding section of the book. The answer might be found in those phrases that go beyond the *Vorlage* and have no equivalent in it: the synchronistic dates in 18:9, 10, and the theological comment in v. 12.

2 The Origin of 2Kgs 18:9–12

The first excess is the date of Shalmaneser's campaign in v. 9. It was put in front of the original beginning of the record:

וַיְהִי בַּשָּׁנָה הָרְבִיעִית לַמֶּלֶךְ חִזְקִיָּהוּ הִיא הַשָּׁנָה הַשְּׁבִיעִית לְהוֹשֵׁעַ בֶּן־אֵלָה מֶלֶךְ יִשְׂרָאֵל עָלָה שַׁלְמַנְאֶסֶר מֶלֶךְ־אַשּׁוּר

In the *fourth year of king Hezekiah, which was the seventh year of Hoshea son of Elah, king of Israel,* Shalmaneser king of Assyria came up.

A similar synchronism is added to the date of the conquest in v. 10:

‹וַיִּלְכְּדָהּ› מִקְצֵה שָׁלֹשׁ שָׁנִים בִּשְׁנַת־שֵׁשׁ לְחִזְקִיָּה הִיא שְׁנַת־תֵּשַׁע לְהוֹשֵׁעַ מֶלֶךְ יִשְׂרָאֵל נִלְכְּדָה שֹׁמְרוֹן

‹And he captured it›[2] *at the end of* three years. In the *sixth year of Hezekiah, which was the ninth year of Hoshea king of Israel,* Samaria *was captured.*

---

1 The note in 18:8 about a great victory over the Philistines "cannot be attributed to an authentic source" either, as Martin Noth, *The Deuteronomistic History* (Sheffield: Sheffield Academic Press, 1981; trans. J. Doull et al.), 132 n. 17, stated. The verse begins similarly to v. 4, compare הוּא הִכָּה אֶת־פְּלִשְׁתִּים "he was the one who smote the Philistines" with הוּא הֵסִיר אֶת־הַבָּמוֹת "he was the one who removed the high places." This is meaningful: Most probably the victory over the Philistines was invented because Hezekiah's piety should not go unrewarded. The combination עַזָּה וְאֶת־גְּבוּלֶיהָ "Gaza and its territory" is "objectionable, and we should expect גְּבוּלָהּ", so Bernhard Stade and Friedrich Schwally, *The Books of Kings* (Leipzig: Hinrich, 1904), 269. It may be borrowed from Judg 1:18: עַזָּה וְאֶת־גְּבוּלָהּ. The expression מִמִּגְדַּל נוֹצְרִים עַד־עִיר מִבְצָר "from watchtower to fortified city" (which is repeated in 2Kgs 17:9) is reminiscent of Josh 19:29: וְעַד־עִיר מִבְצַר־צֹר "to the fortified city of Tyre."
2 The Q^erê וַיִּלְכְּדֻהָ "and they captured it" is better vocalized as וַיִּלְכְּדָהּ "and he captured it" in accordance with the Septuagint, the Peshitta and the Vulgate. However, the Antiochian text reads

In the second case, there can again be little doubt that the synchronism is an expansion, compared to 17:5b–6:

וַיַּעַל שֹׁמְרוֹן וַיָּצַר עָלֶיהָ שָׁלֹשׁ שָׁנִים בִּשְׁנַת הַתְּשִׁיעִית לְהוֹשֵׁעַ לָכַד מֶלֶךְ־אַשּׁוּר אֶת־שֹׁמְרוֹן

He came up to Samaria, and he besieged it for three years. In the ninth year of Hoshea the king of Assyria captured Samaria.

In 17:5b the duration of the siege is given with "three years." In 18:10 the duration has become the date of the conquest: "And he captured it at the end (מִקְצֵה) of three years." In order to incorporate the synchronism, the verb וַיִּלְכְּדָהּ "and he captured it" had to be repeated towards the end of the verse: נִלְכְּדָה "it was captured." The doublet shows the secondary expansion. In the same process the subject מֶלֶךְ־אַשּׁוּר was moved to v. 11; compare וַיֶּגֶל מֶלֶךְ־אַשּׁוּר אֶת־יִשְׂרָאֵל אַשּׁוּרָה in 18:11 with וַיֶּגֶל אֶת־יִשְׂרָאֵל אַשּׁוּרָה in 17:6: "And he /the king of Assyria/ carried Israel away to Assyria."

There is one difficulty remaining. It relates to the form of the dating in 17:6. Instead of בִּשְׁנַת הַתְּשִׁיעִית לְהוֹשֵׁעַ "in the ninth year of Hoshea" one should expect either וַיְהִי בַּשָּׁנָה הַתְּשִׁיעִית לְהוֹשֵׁעַ "and it happened in the ninth year of Hoshea" (compare 18:9), or בִּשְׁנַת־תֵּשַׁע לְהוֹשֵׁעַ "in year nine of Hoshea," as in 18:10.[3] I would prefer the latter for the original reading. Possibly this was the reading at the time when the text was copied to 18:10, and it was later changed into the present form.

Why was the record of the conquest of Samaria expanded in such a way? The synchronisms relate the reign of the king of Judah to that of the king of Israel. It is emphasized that the conquest of Samaria took place exactly at the time when Hezekiah was king in Judah. Compared to 2Kgs 17, the version of 2Kgs 18 depicts a sharp contrast between the two kings: the wicked Hoshea who was punished and the pious Hezekiah who was saved.

This is quite in line with v. 12 where a reason is added to explain why Israel has been carried away to Assyria:

עַל אֲשֶׁר לֹא־שָׁמְעוּ בְּקוֹל יְהוָה אֱלֹהֵיהֶם וַיַּעַבְרוּ אֶת־בְּרִיתוֹ אֵת כָּל־אֲשֶׁר צִוָּה מֹשֶׁה עֶבֶד יְהוָה וְלֹא שָׁמְעוּ וְלֹא עָשׂוּ

Because they did not obey the voice of Yahweh their God but transgressed his covenant, all that Moses the servant of Yahweh commanded; they neither obeyed nor observed.

---

the plural καὶ κατελάβοντο; see Natalio Fernández Marcos and José Ramón Busto Saiz, *El Texto Antioqueno de la Biblia griega, 1–2 Reyes* (Madrid: Instituto de Filología del CSIC, 1992), 136.
3 There are more examples of the irregular style, however; see 2Kgs 25:1; Jer 28:1 $K^e tîb$; 32:1 $K^e tîb$; 46:2; 51:59; Ezra 7:8; and GKC §134p.

The addition of v. 12 was most clearly identified by Albert Šanda: "This verse certainly does not come from R [= the editor of the Book of Kings]. In this context one expects an objective report with no moralizing remarks."[4] The note adds to the historical details a theological rationale: Israel has sinned, and therefore had to suffer its awful fate.

The phrases used for this comment are familiar from the latest literary layers of the Book of Deuteronomy and from those books of the Old Testament which presuppose Deuteronomy. לֹא שָׁמַע בְּקוֹל יהוה "not to obey the voice of Yahweh" marks the disobedience to the Deuteronomic law, and later to the Torah in general.[5] The earliest instances relating to the divine law are to be found in Deut 28:1, 15.[6] עָבַר בְּרִית יהוה "to transgress the covenant of Yahweh"[7] (instead of the regular הֵפֵר בְּרִית "to break the covenant"[8]) presents the late concept in which Yahweh's covenant and the Torah are one and the same thing.

This is made clearer still by the apposition אֵת כָּל־אֲשֶׁר צִוָּה מֹשֶׁה עֶבֶד יהוה "all that Moses the servant of Yahweh commanded." The phrase is parallel to Josh 1:7, 13; 8:31, 33; 11:12; 22:2, 5; 1Chr 6:34. All of these instances belong to the literary sphere of the Priestly code or to the post-priestly Deuteronomism, roughly speaking. The title עֶבֶד יהוה as applied to Moses,[9] Joshua,[10] and David[11] is late throughout. This part of the verse may be a later clarification by another hand. It is added without a copula. The resumption of עַל אֲשֶׁר לֹא־שָׁמְעוּ "because they did not obey" by לֹא שָׁמְעוּ וְלֹא עָשׂוּ "they neither obeyed nor observed" at the end of the verse also supports this possibility.

The comment wants to assure the reader that the conquest of Samaria was due to Israel's sins. The defeat is interpreted as having been a divine punish-

---

[4] Albert Šanda, *Die Bücher der Könige*, vol. 2 (Münster: Aschendorff, 1912), 244 (my translation). Šanda continues: "R has added his judgment already in 17:21–23. The content [= of v. 12] is very reminiscent of 17:34–40."

[5] Num 14:22; Deut 8:20; 9:23; 28:15, 45, 62; Josh 5:6; Judg 2:2, 20; 6:10; 1Sam 12:15; 15:19; 28:18; 1Kgs 20:36; 2Kgs 18:12; Jer 3:25; 7:28; 9:12; 22:21; 32:23; 40:3; 42:21; 43:7; 44:23; cf. Zeph 3:2; Ps 106:25; Dan 9:10, 14.

[6] For the origin of the phrase see Christoph Levin, *Die Verheißung des neuen Bundes* (Göttingen: Vandenhoeck & Ruprecht, 1985), 108, n. 136.

[7] Deut 17:2; 29:11; Josh 7:11, 15; 23:16; 2Kgs 18:12; Jer 34:18; Hos 6:7; 8:1.

[8] פרר בְּרִית *hi.* "to break a covenant": profane/politically: 1Kgs 15:19/2Chr 16:3; Isa 33:8; Ezek 17:15, 16, 18, 19; related to the covenant with Yahweh, on the human side: Gen 17:14; Lev 26:15; Deut 31:16, 20; Isa 24:5; Jer 11:10; 31:32; Ezek 16:59; 44:7; on the divine side: Lev 26:44; Judg 2:1; Jer 14:21; Zech 11:10; cf. Jer 33:20f.

[9] Deut 34:5; Josh 1:1, 13, 15; 8:31, 33; 11:12; 12:6; 13:8; 14:7; 18:7; 22:2, 4, 5; 24:29; 2Kgs 18:12; 2Chr 1:3; 24:6.

[10] Josh 24:29; Judg 2:8.

[11] Ps 18:1; 36:1.

ment. With this statement we have a relative dating for the section 2Kgs 18:9 – 12 as a whole. "Therefore, the entire group of verses 9 – 12 is the work of a later postexilic redactor who, according to his way of thinking and his language, is in line with the author of 17:34 – 40."[12] It does not go back to the edition of the Deuteronomistic History in the 6th century BCE, but was added much later, towards the era when the Book of Kings had become the *Vorlage* for Chronicles and had been submitted to the theological doctrine of divine retribution which dominates Chronicles throughout. This doctrine can occasionally be observed in the earlier historical books as well, however mostly in the form of literary additions.

3 The Later Additions in 2Kgs 17:3 – 6

There is also a large part of the *Vorlage* 17:3 – 6 that is missing in 18:9 – 12:[13]

3 עָלָיו עָלָה שַׁלְמַנְאֶסֶר מֶלֶךְ אַשּׁוּר וַיְהִי־לוֹ הוֹשֵׁעַ עֶבֶד וַיָּשֶׁב לוֹ מִנְחָה: 4 וַיִּמְצָא מֶלֶךְ־אַשּׁוּר בְּהוֹשֵׁעַ קֶשֶׁר אֲשֶׁר שָׁלַח מַלְאָכִים אֶל־סוֹא מֶלֶךְ־מִצְרַיִם [וְלֹא־הֶעֱלָה מִנְחָה לְמֶלֶךְ אַשּׁוּר כְּשָׁנָה בְשָׁנָה] וַיַּעַצְרֵהוּ מֶלֶךְ אַשּׁוּר וַיַּאַסְרֵהוּ בֵּית כֶּלֶא: 5 וַיַּעַל מֶלֶךְ־אַשּׁוּר בְּכָל־הָאָרֶץ וַיַּעַל שֹׁמְרוֹן וַיָּצַר עָלֶיהָ שָׁלֹשׁ שָׁנִים:

> 3 *Against him* came up Shalmaneser king of Assyria, *and Hoshea became his vassal, and paid him tribute. 4 And the king of Assyria found conspiracy in Hoshea; for he had sent messengers to So, king of Egypt, [and offered no tribute to the king of Assyria, as he had done year by year]*[14] *and the king of Assyria restrained him, and bound him in prison. 5 And the king of Assyria came up in all the land and came up* to Samaria and besieged it for three years.

In the additional text, it is related that Shalmaneser's campaign was in the first instance directed against king Hoshea himself. As a consequence, Hoshea was pressed into vassalage and had to pay tribute every year. After some years Hoshea rebelled against his Assyrian overlord. He tried to establish diplomatic ties with some Egyptian king. Shalmaneser put him into prison and came up against the whole country.

This outline of the events confronts us with a number of difficulties:

(1) In his inscriptions, king Tiglath-pileser III claims that Hoshea came to rule as his vassal.[15] The assertion of 2Kgs 17:3 that Hoshea's vassalage had started only with Shalmaneser contradicts what is known from the Assyrian records.

---

12 Šanda, *Die Bücher der Könige*, vol. 2, 244 – 45 (my translation).
13 In the following translation, the minuses of 18:9 – 12 and the pluses of 17:3 – 6 are marked by italics.
14 Verse 4aβ is a later expansion. For the source-critical arguments see below.
15 Summary Inscription 4: 17 – 9, and Summary Inscription 9: rev. 9 – 10; text: Hayim Tadmor, *The Inscriptions of Tiglath-pileser III, King of Assyria* (Jerusalem: Israel Academy of Sciences

(2) Though the verb עלה is repeated no less than three times (עָלָה in v. 3 and וַיַּעַל twice in v. 5), there are no signs that the text wants to tell us of more than one campaign of Shalmaneser. This is in line with the date given by the parallel record in 2Kgs 18:9.

(3) However, it contradicts what is said in 17:4, namely that Hoshea paid his tribute "year by year" (בְּשָׁנָה בְשָׁנָה). This seems to indicate that several years passed between the beginning of Hoshea's vassalage and Shalmaneser's campaign against Samaria.

(4) From the sequence as the text tells it, one gets the impression that king Hoshea was put into prison prior to the siege of Samaria. This raises the question of who would have reigned in the city for the three years of the siege and could have led the resistance against the Assyrian campaign. "It is […] highly improbable that Israel remained for three years without a king, after the deposition of Hoshea, and, as a matter of fact, v. 6 states that the fall of the capital took place 'in the ninth year of Hoshea,' i.e. in his ninth reigning year."[16]

(5) There is an awkward doublet at the beginning of v. 5: וַיַּעַל מֶלֶךְ־אַשּׁוּר בְּכָל־הָאָרֶץ וַיַּעַל שֹׁמְרוֹן וַיָּצַר עָלֶיהָ "And the king of Assyria came up in all the land, and he came up to Samaria, and he besieged it." This is all the more striking since Shalmaneser must already have been in the land in order to bind Hoshea in prison, as is said immediately before in v. 4.

(6) The style of the passage is clumsy to some degree. In v. 5a the subject מֶלֶךְ־אַשּׁוּר is unnecessarily repeated though it does not change. Hebrew narratives usually try to avoid such redundancy.

(7) These observations are not due to modern criticism only, but are mirrored already in the textual tradition that in the case of the Old Greek or its *Vorlage* deviates from the Masoretic text quite remarkably, different to the surrounding verses.[17]

In order to solve these problems, Hugo Winckler proposed what could be called a documentary hypothesis. His idea was that two different sources had

---

and Humanities, 1994), 140 and 188 = Hayim Tadmor and Shigeo Yamada, *The Royal Inscriptions of Tiglath-pileser III (744–727 BC) and Shalmaneser V (726–722 BC), Kings of Assyria* (Winona Lake IN: Eisenbrauns, 2011), no. 42 and no. 49; translation: James B. Pritchard (ed.), *Ancient Near Eastern Texts Relating to the Old Testament* (Princeton NJ: Princeton University Press, 1955; 2nd edition), 284; William W. Hallo (ed.), *The Context of Scripture, vol. 2: Monumental Inscriptions from the Biblical World* (Leiden: Brill, 2000), nos. 117C and 117F; Mordechai Cogan, *The Raging Torrent: Historical Inscriptions from Assyria and Babylonia Relating to Israel* (Jerusalem: Carta, 2015; 2nd edition), 73 and 68.

16 Charles F. Burney, *Notes on the Hebrew Text of the Books of Kings* (Oxford: Clarendon, 1903), 328.

17 See the chapter of Timo Tekoniemi in this volume.

been interwoven in 2Kgs 17:3–6, both of them conveying the same historical event, but from different perspectives.[18] "It seems easiest to suppose that the first of the two biblical sections [i.e. in 2Kgs 17:3–6] presents a combination of two records of the same event, taken from *two different sources*, in such a way that ch. 17:3–4 is a second narrative of the events recorded in 17:5b–6, the latter taken from the same source as 18:9–11 with which it agrees almost word for word. At the least, this assumption would solve all of the contradictions and difficulties."[19] The one of these accounts, which according to Winckler is to be found in vv. 5–6, relates the rebellion of king Hoshea as well as his capture by Shalmaneser. The other account tells the conquest of Samaria roughly in the same form as it is also preserved in the parallel 18:9–10. Winckler maintains that both records are reliable in terms of history, Hoshea's rebellion having been the reason for Shalmaneser's campaign. From this follows that the capture of king Hoshea and the conquest of Samaria actually fell at the same time. So, for Winckler the two accounts are to be read as parallel versions, other than the present text wherein the editor of the Book of Kings set them in a sequence when he merged the two sources into a single record.

In accordance with the Assyrian sources – and contrary to 2Kgs 17:3 – Winckler holds that Hoshea came to the throne as a vassal of Tiglath-pileser. In order to solve the contradiction, Winckler states: "The whole difficulty would disappear if we assume that the editor read והיה לו עבד instead of ויהי לו עבד in 17:3. The meaning of his source would have been: 'Hoshea became king. Against him came up Shalmaneser *because* he was his vassal and had to pay him tribute. But the king of Assyria found treachery in him etc. and bound him in prison.'"[20] Unfortunately this reading has no basis in the textual transmission, as Winckler himself admits;[21] moreover, as Charles F. Burney stated, "such a construction is impossible,"[22] followed by Bernhard Stade and Friedrich Schwally: "Winckler's [...]

---

18 Hugo Winckler, "Beiträge zur quellenscheidung der Königsbücher," in id., *Alttestamentliche Untersuchungen* (Leipzig: Pfeiffer, 1892): 1–54, esp. 16–25. Winckler's hypothesis was accepted by Immanuel Benzinger, *Die Bücher der Könige* (Freiburg i.B.: Mohr Siebeck, 1899): 172–73; by Burney, *Notes*, 328–29; and by John Gray, *I & II Kings: A Commentary* (London: SCM Press, 1970; 2nd edition), 642: "Verses 3f. probably from the Annals of Israel, vv. 5f. from the Annals of Judah (cf. 18.9–11), both summarized, with vv. 3b–4a in loose parenthesis."
19 Winckler, "Beiträge zur quellenscheidung," 20 (my translation).
20 Winckler, "Beiträge zur quellenscheidung," 22 (my translation).
21 Winckler, "Beiträge zur quellenscheidung," 22, n. 3: "It is improbable that there is a mistake in *our* textual tradition, because all recensions, MT as well as LXX, witness ויהי."
22 Burney, *Notes*, 329, who nevertheless keeps Winckler's source critical hypothesis.

conjecture [...] maltreats the Hebrew language; *for Hosea was his vassal* is not in Hebrew: ויהיה הושע לו עבד."²³

However, Winckler's hypothesis is not completely obsolete. He rightly assumes that vv. 3–4 give another view of the events around the conquest of Samaria. But his solution is wrong: The other version does not go back to a different source. It constitutes a later comment on what was transmitted in one single source. It is an annotation that tells what should have happened for theological reasons but, as we know from the Assyrian sources, never happened in history. Those elements of the text that are missing in 18:9–10 did not exist at the time when the text had been copied there. They are scribal additions.

Above we have seen that the version of 2Kgs 18 is of very late origin because v. 12 shows features that are near to Chronicles. This is true also of 17:3b–5a. Whereas in 2Kgs 18 the emphasis is on the contrast between the two kings, the pious Hezekiah on the one hand, and the wicked Hoshea on the other, and the different fate of these two, it is no surprise that the editor who added 17:3b–5a also focused on Hoshea's personal guilt and his fate.

The addition follows the theological doctrine of retribution. Someone's fate had to be in line with someone's behavior. Because Hoshea was punished by the Assyrian king, he must have sinned against the Assyrian king. The scribe suggested that Hoshea rebelled against Shalmaneser. In order to demonstrate this, it is at first said that he became Shalmaneser's vassal: וַיְהִי־לוֹ הוֹשֵׁעַ עֶבֶד. Hoshea submitted to his overlord by paying tribute: וַיָּשֶׁב לוֹ מִנְחָה. The one who added these details did not care whether the sequence of events would be possible in terms of history. He simply wanted to sketch the initial situation that was later changed by Hoshea's rebellion.

The phrase מָצָא קֶשֶׁר בְּ- "to find conspiracy in someone" occurs only once more, in Jer 11:9: "Conspiracy is found (נִמְצָא קֶשֶׁר) among the people of Judah and the inhabitants of Jerusalem." In the historical books, except for 2Kgs 17:4 the noun קֶשֶׁר is used exclusively for a conspiracy against the king of Israel or Judah.²⁴ To indicate a rebellion against the Assyrian or Babylonian overlord the verb מרד is used (2Kgs 18:7; 24:1, 20). The scribe deviates from the terminology of the Book of Kings in favor of the language of prophecy. He indicates that Hoshea's rebellion against the Assyrian king was also directed against Yahweh.²⁵

---

23 Stade and Schwally, *The Books of Kings*, 260.
24 2Sam 15:12; 1Kgs 16:20; 2Kgs 11:14; 12:21; 14:19; 15:1, 30.
25 The Septuagint (*kaige*-recension) translates ἀδικία = שֶׁקֶר "deception," thus emphasizing the theological statement that may be implied. See Alfred Rahlfs and Robert Hanhart (eds.), *Septuaginta: Id est Vetus Testamentum graece iuxta LXX interpretes* (Stuttgart: Deutsche Bibelgesellschaft, 2006; 2ⁿᵈ edition), *sub loco*.

In order to illustrate Hoshea's disloyalty, it is said that he sent messengers to the Egyptian king of that time: אֲשֶׁר שָׁלַח מַלְאָכִים אֶל־סוֹא מֶלֶךְ־מִצְרַיִם "for he has sent messengers to Sō', king of Egypt." The purpose of the delegation is not indicated, but can easily be supplemented by the reader: Ahaz asked the king of Egypt for an alliance against the Assyrian king and offered him his submission. This action was seen as a severe fault by the theologians of the late Second Temple Period. We know from the Book of Chronicles that it meant sinning against the God Yahweh in a very strong way if the kings of Israel and Judah made alliances with foreign kings. As a consequence, each attempt is punished by military defeat or disaster.[26]

This doctrine may be labeled *Koalitionsverbot* ("prohibition of coalition with foreign powers"). It also found its way into the Book of Kings. In 2Kgs 16:7 it is said that king Ahaz of Judah called Tiglath-pileser for help when he was attacked by king Rezin of Aram and king Pekah of Israel. Here we read nearly the same expression as in 17:3:

וַיִּשְׁלַח אָחָז מַלְאָכִים אֶל־תִּגְלַת פְּלֶסֶר מֶלֶךְ־אַשּׁוּר לֵאמֹר עַבְדְּךָ וּבִנְךָ אָנִי עֲלֵה וְהוֹשִׁעֵנִי מִכַּף מֶלֶךְ־אֲרָם וּמִכַּף מֶלֶךְ יִשְׂרָאֵל הַקּוֹמִים עָלָי

And Ahaz sent messengers to Tiglath-pileser king of Assyria, saying: I am your servant and your son. Come up, and rescue me from the hand of the king of Aram and from the hand of the king of Israel who are attacking me.

This verse is a late addition to the record about Ahaz's submission to Tiglath-pileser when he was attacked by Rezin of Aram and Pekah of Israel. The original text is to be found in 2Kgs 16:5a, bα, 8, 9αβγ, b: "Then Rezin king of Aram and Pekah the son of Remaliah, king of Israel, came up to wage war on Jerusalem, and they besieged Ahaz. [...] So, Ahaz took the silver and gold that was found in the house of Yahweh and in the treasures of the king's house, and sent a present to the king of Assyria. [...] And the king of Assyria marched up against Damascus, and took it, carrying its people captive [...], and he killed Rezin." The addition stresses that with Ahaz's submission to the Assyrian king he refused the promise that Yahweh had given to David: "I will be his father, and he shall be my son" (2Sam 7:14). This behavior was counted as a severe fault.

The same doctrine is also to be found in the Book of Isaiah as well as in the Book of Hoshea. "Ephraim is like a dove, silly and without sense, calling to

---

[26] Older research was already aware of this doctrine. In more recent times it was especially investigated by Tetsuo Yamaga, "König Joschafat und seine Außenpolitik in den Chronikbüchern," *AJBI* 27 (2001): 59–154.

Egypt, going to Assyria" (Hos 7:11; cf. 12:2).²⁷ "Woe to the rebellious children, says Yahweh, who carry out a plan, but not mine; and who make a league, but not of my spirit, that they may add sin to sin; who set out to go down to Egypt, without asking for my counsel, to take refuge in the protection of Pharaoh, and to seek shelter in the shadow of Egypt!" (Isa 30:1–2; cf. 31:1). There are strong reasons to assume that statements like these do not go back to the prophets of the 8th century, but originate in the time of the Chronicler, i.e., in the Hellenistic era.

No one knows who סוֹא מֶלֶךְ־מִצְרַיִם "Sōʾ king of Egypt" could have been. "No known king of Egypt at this time (*ca.* 725 B.C.) bore this name, a circumstance all the more remarkable in view of the transparent nature of all the other Old Testament allusions to the names of Egyptian rulers."²⁸ The guessing game began already in the Antiochian text of the Septuagint (or its Hebrew *Vorlage*), which reads διότι ἀπέστειλεν ἀγγέλους πρὸς Ἀδραμέλεχ τὸν Αἰθίοπα τὸν κατοικοῦντα ἐν Αἰγύπτῳ "for he sent messengers to Adrammelech the Ethiopian who dwelt in Egypt."²⁹ With high probability this reading rests on Midrashic assumptions.³⁰ Possibly it is based on 2Kgs 19:37 where it is said that Adrammelech killed king Sennacherib of Assyria, in combination with 2Kgs 19:9 where it is said that the king of Assyria heard that king Tirhaka of Ethiopia went out to fight against him. The details may still reflect the original text which tells of an Egyptian king. Therefore, the title "king" is left out and Adrammelech, though being an Ethiopian, should have dwelled in Egypt.

---

27 James A. Montgomery and Henry Snyder Gehman, *The Books of Kings* (Edinburgh: T&T Clark, 1951), 465: "These shifting alliances of the day, now with Assyria, now with Egypt, are illustrated in the prophet Hoshea's scornful references (5:13; 7:8, 11, 16; 8:9; 11:5; 12:2; 14:4)." It is highly questionable whether these statements go back to the prophet himself.

28 John Day, "The Problem of 'So, King of Egypt' in 2 Kings xvii 4," *VT* 42 (1992): 289–301, esp. 289. Day presents a survey of the proposals produced so far. He finally argues in favor of the place name of Sais, the capital city of Tefnakht. This possibility was, however, rejected with strong arguments by, among others, Bernd Schipper, "Wer war 'So', König von Ägypten' (2 Kön 17,4)?" *BN* 92 (1998): 71–84, esp. 74–75.

29 Fernández Marcos and Busto Saiz, *El Texto Antioqueno*, 131–2. The reading is shared by the Codex Vindobonensis; see Bonifatius Fischer, "Palimpsestus Vindobonensis: A Revised Edition of L115 for Samuel-Kings," *BIOSCS* 16 (1983): 13–87, esp. 86.

30 Andrés Piquer Otero, "What Text to Edit? The *Oxford Hebrew Bible* Edition of 2 Kings 17,1–23," in *After Qumran: Old and Modern Editions of the Biblical Texts – the Historical Books*, ed. Hans Ausloos, Bénédicte Lemmelijn and Julio Trebolle Barrera (Leuven: Peeters, 2012): 227–43, esp. 233–35, still looks for some historical basis – to my mind this would be misconceiving the assumptive nature of the text.

It is mostly suggested that the name Sō' refers to Pharaoh Osorkon IV.³¹ But there is no clear indication for this suggestion, nor any linguistic support for it. Most probably the glossator did not refer to an individual king. The figure of this Pharaoh may be pure fantasy. Some scholars read his name Sō' as an abbreviated form of the Egyptian word for "king": *nj-św.t* → *nśw.t* → *nśw* → *Sō'*.³² This, however, cannot be proven either.³³ In any case we do not have to search in the 8th century BCE, because the note in 2Kgs 17:4 originates in the late Persian or early Hellenistic era.

In v. 4aβ there are some divergences in the textual transmission. Whereas the Hebrew text reads וְלֹא־הֶעֱלָה מִנְחָה לְמֶלֶךְ אַשּׁוּר כְּשָׁנָה בְשָׁנָה "and he offered no tribute to the king of Assyria, as he had done year by year,"³⁴ the Antiochian text³⁵ presents some explication: καὶ ἦν Ὡσῆε φέρων δῶρα τῷ βασιλεῖ ἀσσυρίων ἐνιαυτὸν κατ' ἐνιαυτὸν, ἐν δὲ τῷ ἐνιαυτῷ ἐκείνῳ οὐκ ἤνεγκεν αὐτῷ μαναά "And Hoshea brought gifts to the king of Assyria year by year, but that year he offered no tribute to him." This version seems to be much more natural since in v. 3 it is said only that Hoshea paid tribute to the king of Assyria (וַיָּשֶׁב לוֹ מִנְחָה) which does not unequivocally imply that he was to do so every year. However, the *lectio longior atque facilior* hardly presents the original reading. It is rather an indication that this detail of the rebellion was added only later. Again, the terminology is significant: The expression לֹא־הֶעֱלָה מִנְחָה "he did not offer tribute" is strange in this context because עלה מִנְחָה *hi.* is otherwise used exclusively for the grain-offering to Yahweh.³⁶ So we may conclude that this part of v. 4 is a still later addition.

Hoshea is said to have been punished for his disloyalty by Shalmaneser: וַיַּעַצְרֵהוּ מֶלֶךְ אַשּׁוּר וַיַּאַסְרֵהוּ בֵּית כֶּלֶא "the king of Assyria restrained him and bound

---

31 See (among many others) Manfred Görg, "So," *Neues Bibellexikon*, vol. 3, ed. Manfred Görg (Zürich: Benziger, 2001): 622; Schipper, "Wer war So'," 77–79.
32 This was first suggested by Herbert Donner, "The Separate States of Israel and Judah," in *Israelite and Judean History*, ed. John H. Hayes and J. Maxwell Miller (London: SCM Press, 1977): 381–434, esp. 433, followed by Rolf Krauss, "Sō, König von Ägypten – ein Deutungsvorschlag," *MDOG* 110 (1978): 49–54, who added some linguistic support, based on late evidence involving the history of language ("Rückschluß, der auf sprachgeschichtlich jungen Belegen beruht," 54). In any case the presupposition that "Sō'" is attested for the time around 725 BCE" (50, my translation) is to be doubted because 2Kgs 17:4 is historically unreliable.
33 See the strong objections referred to by Schipper, "Wer war So'," 80–81.
34 The Hebrew text is supported by the *kaige* recension of the Septuagint, see Rahlfs and Hanhart, *Septuaginta, sub loco*. For כְּשָׁנָה בְשָׁנָה the Greek text reads ἐν τῷ ἐνιαυτῷ ἐκείνῳ. It is doubtful whether this reading goes back to a different *Vorlage* (בַּשָּׁנָה הַהִיא).
35 According to the edition by Fernández Marcos and Busto Saiz, *El Texto Antioqueno*, 132.
36 Exod 30:9; 40:29; Lev 14:20; Josh 22:23; Isa 57:6; 66:3; Jer 14:12. See Otto Thenius, *Die Bücher der Könige* (Leipzig: Weidmann'sche Buchhandlung, 1849), 369: "העלה] it is to be noted that this word is otherwise used exclusively for *offering*" (my translation).

him in prison." Hoshea was bound, that means he had to share the fate that king Jehoahaz suffered from Pharaoh Necho (2Kgs 23:33), king Zedekiah from Nebuchadnezzar (2Kgs 25:7) and king Manasseh from the commanders of the Assyrian army (2Chr 33:11). Notably enough, in each of these four cases exactly the same verbal form is used: וַיַּאַסְרֵהוּ. The editor does not say what happened to Hoshea further on, but the reader of the Bible could appreciate that the other three kings were deported. This was also the case with king Jehoiachin, who is said in 2Kgs 25:27 to have finally been released from prison (בֵּית כֶּלֶא).

All in all, these are clear indications that the longer record of 2Kgs 17:3–5 as we now read it is to be understood as a theological comment in narrative form, originating around the time when the Book of Chronicles was about to be written. The details given are not intended to be read as historical information.

4 The Original Record

Finally, in order to restore the original biblical record of the Assyrian conquest of Samaria, we have to look at those parts of the text that are shared by both of the parallel sections in 2Kgs 17 and 2Kgs 18 accordingly. The text that is common to both records is what the scribe of 2Kgs 18:9–12 found in 2Kgs 17:3–6 when he copied it and added his comments to it, and into which the glossator of 2Kgs 17:3–6 inserted the additional details in vv. 3b–5a.

In 17:3 par. 18:9, עָלָה שַׁלְמַנְאֶסֶר מֶלֶךְ־אַשּׁוּר is common to both versions: "Shalmaneser the king of Assyria came up". However, it is hard to imagine that the perfect עָלָה was the original beginning – though there is also one example of it in 15:19: בָּא פוּל מֶלֶךְ־אַשּׁוּר עַל־הָאָרֶץ "Pul (i. e., Tiglath-pileser) the king of Assyria came against the land." Preferably, we have to look for some other reading.

One possibility is that the section began with the narrative וַיַּעַל, as is the case in 1Kgs 15:17: וַיַּעַל בַּעְשָׁא מֶלֶךְ־יִשְׂרָאֵל עַל־יְהוּדָה "Baasha king of Israel went up against Judah" and in 2Kgs 15:14: וַיַּעַל מְנַחֵם בֶּן־גָּדִי מִתִּרְצָה וַיָּבֹא שֹׁמְרוֹן "Menahem the son of Gadi came up from Tirzah and came to Samaria". Also, a temporal adverb can precede the verb, as in 2Kgs 12:18: אָז יַעֲלֶה חֲזָאֵל מֶלֶךְ אֲרָם וַיִּלָּחֶם עַל־גַּת וַיִּלְכְּדָהּ "At that time Hazael king of Aram went up and fought against Gath, and took it," and in 2Kgs 23:29: בְּיָמָיו עָלָה פַרְעֹה נְכֹה מֶלֶךְ־מִצְרַיִם עַל־מֶלֶךְ אַשּׁוּר עַל־נְהַר־פְּרָת "In his days Pharaoh Necho king of Egypt went up to the king of Assyria to the river Euphrates." Finally, an exact date could have been given, as in 1Kgs 14:25: וַיְהִי בַּשָּׁנָה הַחֲמִישִׁית לַמֶּלֶךְ רְחַבְעָם עָלָה שׁוּשַׁק מֶלֶךְ־מִצְרַיִם עַל־יְרוּשָׁלָ͏ִם "In the fifth year of king Rehoboam, Shishak king of Egypt came up against Jerusalem." Following the last example and taking in account the synchronism in 2Kgs 18:9 (which of course has to be shortened, as shown above) the original beginning could have been like this: וַיְהִי בַּשָּׁנָה הַשְּׁבִיעִית לַמֶּלֶךְ הוֹשֵׁעַ עָלָה שַׁלְמַנְאֶסֶר מֶלֶךְ־אַשּׁוּר עַל־שֹׁמְרוֹן "In the seventh year of king Hoshea Shalmaneser king of Assyria came up against Samaria." There are no means that help us decide among these alternatives. However, to my mind the last possibility is the most probable because it could also have provided the basis for the synchronism in 18:9, which otherwise must have been calculated from the ninth year of Hoshea in 17:6 and the three years of the siege in 17:5.

In any case, the pronoun עָלָיו which opens 17:3 cannot be original for it refers to the data given for king Hoshea in vv. 1–2. These data go back to another source: the synchronistic excerpt of the annals of the kings of Israel and Judah.[37] The present form of 17:3 is focused on the person of king Hoshea: עָלָיו עָלָה שַׁלְמַנְאֶסֶר "against him came up Shalmaneser." Because this is in line with the addition in vv. 3b–5a, the change of the original reading may go back to the same glossator. The new point he made is balanced by v. 5a: וַיַּעַל מֶלֶךְ־אַשּׁוּר בְּכָל־הָאָרֶץ "And the king of Assyria came up in all the land." That means: after punishing king Hoshea, the Assyrian king turned towards the whole land, taking up and continuing his campaign against Samaria. This is again an addition as can be seen from the double וַיַּעַל in v. 5b. Possibly the prefix עַל־ that is still preserved in 18:9 was lost in favor of וַיַּעַל, which resumes the original עָלָה of v. 3.

Because 17:6 par. 18:10–11 presents no major differences, as a result of our inquiry, we have the supposed original record so far:

⟨וַיְהִי בַּשָּׁנָה הַשְּׁבִיעִית לַמֶּלֶךְ הוֹשֵׁעַ⟩ עָלָה שַׁלְמַנְאֶסֶר מֶלֶךְ אַשּׁוּר ... ⟨עַל־⟩שֹׁמְרוֹן וַיָּצַר עָלֶיהָ שָׁלֹשׁ שָׁנִים בִּשְׁנַת ⟨תֵּשַׁע לְהוֹשֵׁעַ לָכַד מֶלֶךְ־אַשּׁוּר אֶת־שֹׁמְרוֹן⟩ וַיֶּגֶל אֶת־יִשְׂרָאֵל אַשּׁוּרָה וַיֹּשֶׁב אֹתָם בַּחְלַח וּבְחָבוֹר נְהַר גּוֹזָן וְעָרֵי מָדָי

In the seventh year of King Hoshea came up Shalmaneser king of Assyria, against Samaria and besieged it for three years. In the ninth year of Hoshea the king of Assyria captured Samaria, and he carried Israel away to Assyria, and placed them in Halah, and on the Habor, the river of Gozan, and in the cities of the Medes.

Like the similar records about military attacks of foreign kings that are recorded in the Book of Kings, this source is probably taken from an official document, used by the editor of the Book of Kings (i.e., the Deuteronomistic historian) when he composed his major work. It can be continued with the note in 2Kgs 17:24 about the re-settlement of Samaria:

---

[37] See Christoph Levin, "The Synchronistic Excerpt from the Annals of the Kings of Israel and Judah," in id., *Re-Reading the Scriptures: Essays on the Literary History of the Old Testament* (Tübingen: Mohr Siebeck, 2013): 183–93.

וַיָּבֵא מֶלֶךְ־אַשּׁוּר מִבָּבֶל וּמִכּוּתָה וּמֵעַוָּא וּמֵחֲמָת וּסְפַרְוַיִם [וַיֹּשֶׁב בְּעָרֵי שֹׁמְרוֹן תַּחַת בְּנֵי יִשְׂרָאֵל] וַיִּרְשׁוּ אֶת־שֹׁמְרוֹן וַיֵּשְׁבוּ בְּעָרֶיהָ

> And the king of Assyria brought people from Babylon, Cuthah, Avva, Hamath, and Sepharvaim [and made them dwell in the cities of Samaria instead of the Israelites];[38] and they took possession of Samaria, and dwelt in its cities.

The expression "Samaria and its cities" witnesses that "Samaria" is not the name of the city anymore, but of the Assyrian province. So, the document tells about the events in hindsight.

I may underline that in the Bible no more than this short account was originally recorded about the Assyrian conquest: one single campaign under the Assyrian king Shalmaneser. The siege lasted for three years, from Hoshea's seventh through his ninth year (in line with the biblical way of counting years). According to the dating, Hoshea's rule ended when Samaria was conquered, and together with it the kingdom of Israel came to its end. The conquest was followed by the deportation of the Israelites and by the resettlement of the newly installed Assyrian province.

Nothing is said about the reason why the Assyrian king came up against Samaria. This is what we also observe with the earlier Assyrian campaigns recorded in the Book of Kings: For Tiglath-pileser's campaign against king Menahem (2Kgs 15:19) and his campaign against king Pekah (2Kgs 15:29) no reason is given either. Whereas king Hezekiah of Judah is said to have rebelled against the Assyrian king (2Kgs 18:7), nothing similar is said of Hoshea. The personal fate of the king remains unclear as well. The end of the kingdom of Israel coincides with the conquest of Samaria. There is no period without a king. And, more important and unfortunately enough, there is nothing in the Bible that may help us decide between the two Assyrian kings, Shalmaneser and Sargon, who both claimed to have conquered Samaria, and about the question of whether the city was conquered one or two times.

---

38 Verse 24aβγ is a later addition. This can be recognized from the doubling וַיֹּשֶׁב בְּעָרֵי שֹׁמְרוֹן "he made (them) dwell in the cities of Samaria" along with וַיִּרְשׁוּ אֶת־שֹׁמְרוֹן וַיֵּשְׁבוּ בְּעָרֶיהָ "they took possession of Samaria, and dwelt in its cities." The addition emphasizes that the people from Babylon replaced the Israelite inhabitants completely: תַּחַת בְּנֵי יִשְׂרָאֵל "instead of the Israelites." This assertion may be due to anti-Samaritan polemics.

Part V: **Working with the Book of Kings:
the Chronological Framework**

Kristin Weingart
2 Kings 15–18: a Chronological Conundrum?

1 Introduction

One of the outstanding features of the Book of Kings is that it not only contains a plethora of chronological data but also applies a distinctive chronological framework as a basic structuring device for its presentation.[1] So it is hardly surprising that, compared with the preceding periods, historians of Israel consider themselves on firmer ground once they reach the monarchic period, and that precise chronological tables are usually provided from here onwards.[2] At the same time, the obvious differences between the various chronological tables[3] demonstrate, that the interpretation of the chronological material in Kings remains an ongoing

---

[1] The ordering principle has long been recognized, cf. e.g. Samuel Rolles Driver, *An Introduction to the Literature of the Old Testament*, International Theological Library (Edinburgh: Clark, 1891), 179: "In the arrangement of the reigns of the two series of kings a definite principle is followed by the compiler. When the narrative of a reign (in either series) has once been begun, it is continued to its close …; when it is ended, the reign or reigns of the other series, which have synchronized with it, are dealt with; the reign overlapping it at the end having been completed, the compiler resumes his narrative of the first series with the reign next following, and so on."

[2] See e.g. Herbert Donner, *Geschichte des Volkes Israel und seiner Nachbarn in Grundzügen*, Teil 2: *Von der Königszeit bis zu Alexander dem Großen, mit einem Ausblick auf die Geschichte des Judentums bis Bar Kochba* (Göttingen: Vandenhoeck & Ruprecht, 2001), 508. Accordingly, Christian Frevel, *Geschichte Israels* (Stuttgart: Kohlhammer, 2016), 31, distinguishes between a "Vorgeschichte Israels" and a "Geschichte Israels" which commences with the monarchic period (10th or rather 9th century BCE); only then does Israel become visible as a state entity and biblical as well as extra-biblical sources tend to provide more information.

[3] The examples of Pekah and Hezekiah in three more recent chronological studies by Antti Laato, *Guide to Biblical Chronology* (Sheffield: Phoenix, 2015), 113; M. Christine Tetley, *The Reconstructed Chronology of the Divided Kingdom* (Winona Lake IN: Eisenbrauns, 2005), 182–83; and Gershon Galil, *The Chronology of the Kings of Israel and Judah* (Leiden: Brill, 1996), Appendix A, may suffice:

Pekah 735/34–732/31 (Laato); 757–727 (Tetley); (750?)–732/21 (Galil)
Hezekiah 715/14–697/96 (Laato); 724–719/18 (Tetley*); 726–697/96 (Galil)

* Note that Tetley only lists Hezekiah's dates up to the fall of Samaria, which according to her reconstruction took place in 719/718 BCE.

task in biblical scholarship.[4] The reasons are manifold; they lie in the inconsistencies of the biblical data, their lack of compatibility with external data, but first and foremost in the fact that reconstructing a chronology remains an equation with several unknowns.[5] Ever since a ground breaking study by Julius Wellhausen[6] in 1875, the respective weighting and handling of the numerous factors of uncertainty have resulted in differing reconstructions.[7]

---

[4] The question itself is much older than the onset of historical-critical exegesis; attempts to elucidate the biblical chronology have accompanied the history of exegesis from its beginnings. Early examples include Josephus's systematizing treatment of the chronology of Kings in his *Antiquitates Judaicae* IXf, the rabbinic *Seder Olam Rabah* (SOR; critical edition: Chaim Joseph Milikowsky, *Seder Olam: A Rabbinic Chronography* [Diss. Yale University, 1981]), which already tries to minimize the surplus in Judean regnal years in comparison to those of the Israelite kings (see SOR 17; 19), or Eusebius' *Chronicon*, which includes diverging data of the ancient versions into its calculations.

[5] Joachim Begrich, *Die Chronologie der Könige von Israel und Juda und die Quellen des Rahmens der Königsbücher* (Tübingen: Mohr Siebeck, 1929), 55–101, systematically outlined the principal problems: (1) inconsistencies within the chronological data, e.g. conflicting synchronisms or sums of regnal years for Israel and Judah; (2) variant numerical data in the ancient versions; (3) uncertainties regarding the calendar in ancient Israel, e.g. the date of the New Year; (4) uncertainties regarding the counting methods for regnal years, i.e. postdating or antedating; and (5) frequent incompatibility with external data, i.e., Assyrian or Babylonian sources which enable one to date specific events with a greater degree of certainty. A sixth point not explicitly listed by Begrich concerns the occurrence of coregencies and their handling in chronological compilations.

[6] Julius Wellhausen, "Die Zeitrechnung des Buches der Könige seit der Theilung des Reiches," *JDT* 20 (1875): 607–40.

[7] While biblical scholars in the late 19th or early 20th centuries, like Wellhausen, tended to freely emend the biblical numbers or to combine data from the Masoretic Text (MT), the Greek textual tradition and early historiographers like Josephus in order to reach a consistent reconstruction (so e.g. Begrich, *Chronologie*), later studies put more trust in the Masoretic Text. Prominent examples are Edwin R. Thiele, *The Mysterious Numbers of the Hebrew Kings: a Reconstruction of the Chronology of the Kingdoms of Israel und Judah* (Exeter: Paternoster, 1965), who assumes multiple changes in the method of reckoning as well as frequent co-regencies in order to reconstruct a coherent system. On the other hand, John Haralson Hayes and Paul K. Hooker, *A New Chronology for the Kings of Israel and Judah and Its Implications for Biblical History and Literature* (Atlanta GA: Knox, 1988), work with different calendars in Israel and Judah to compensate for inconsistencies. At the same time it became increasingly clear that at least parts of the Greek textual tradition present separate chronological systems whose relation to the chronology of the MT has to be determined. E.g., James Donald Shenkel, *Chronology and Recensional Development in the Greek Text of Kings* (Cambridge MA: Harvard University Press, 1968), and Tetley, *Chronology*, see the MT chronology as a secondary adaptation of an older chronological system attested in the OG (for a critical appraisal of this position see e.g. Galil, *Chronology*, 127–44).

What applies to the reconstruction of the chronology of Kings as a whole is also true for 2Kgs 15–18. Despite the large amount of chronological material provided in these chapters, the reconstruction of a chronological framework remains difficult. Here again, the biblical data is characterized by a lack of inner consistency and outward compatibility.[8] The present paper, however, does not intend to add a further entry to the extensive list of proposals and counter proposals on the historic timeline for Israel and Judah. It differs from the overwhelming majority of past and present studies on the chronology of Kings

---

8 Besides the notorious issues of the sequence of events and the date of the fall of Samaria, which are discussed elsewhere in this volume, another problem is the excess of years in the biblical chronology compared to external data. Menahem is listed in two Assyrian sources as offering tribute to Tiglath-pileser III: firstly, in a royal stele from Iran (Hayim Tadmor, *The Inscriptions of Tiglath-pileser III, King of Assyria: Critical Edition, with Introductions, Translations and Commentary* [Jerusalem: Israel Academy of Sciences and Humanities, 1994], 106–107: IIIA 5 = Hayim Tadmor and Shigeo Yamada, *The Royal Inscriptions of Tiglath-pileser III (744–727 BC) and Shalmaneser V (726–722 BC), Kings of Assyria* (Winona Lake IN: Eisenbrauns, 2011), no. 35: iii 5) and secondly, the Calah Annals (Tadmor, *The Inscriptions of Tiglath-pileser III*, 68–69: Ann. 13*: 10 = Tadmor and Yamada, *The Royal Inscriptions of Tiglath-pileser III*, no. 14: 10 // Tadmor, *The Inscriptions of Tiglath-pileser III*, 89 Ann. 27: 2 = Tadmor and Yamada, *The Royal Inscriptions of Tiglath-pileser III*, no. 32: 2). The tribute mentioned in the Calah Annals was connected by Tadmor, *The Inscriptions of Tiglath-pileser III*, 276, with Tiglath-pileser's 8th *palû*, i.e. 738 BC. The list of the Iran stele seems to refer to an earlier tribute, probably paid in 740. Tiglath-pileser III also claims to have disposed of Pekah and installed Hoshea as king in Israel (Tadmor, *The Inscriptions of Tiglath-pileser III*, Summ. 4: 15′–19′ = Tadmor and Yamada, *The Royal Inscriptions of Tiglath-pileser III*, no. 42: 15′–19′, cf. Tadmor, *The Inscriptions of Tiglath-pileser III*, Summ. 13: 17′–18′ = Tadmor and Yamada, *The Royal Inscriptions of Tiglath-pileser III*, no. 44: 17′–18′). Hoshea is reported to have brought tribute to Tiglath-pileser III (Tadmor, *The Inscriptions of Tiglath-pileser III*, Summ. 9: rev. 9–11 = Tadmor and Yamada, *The Royal Inscriptions of Tiglath-pileser III*, no. 49: rev. 9–11). The latter probably refers to Tiglath-pileser's 15th *palû* in 731 BC: Tadmor, *The Inscriptions of Tiglath-pileser III*, 277–78; cf. Galil, *Chronology*, 65. Therefore, the regnal years listed for the Israelite kings after Menahem (Pekahiah 2 years, Pekah 20 years) clearly exceed the 7-year period indicated by the Assyrian material. The issue is usually resolved by (a) attributing a shorter reign to Pekah: 2 years: Begrich, *Chronologie*, 155; 4 years: Jeremy Hughes, *Secrets of the Times: Myth and History in Biblical Chronology* (Sheffield: JSOT Press, 1990), 204–205; Laato, *Guide*, 43–48; 5 years: Galil, *Chronology*, 65; (b) by identifying Pekahiah and Pekah: Wellhausen, "Zeitrechnung," 630–31; Julian Reade, "Mesopotamian Guidelines for Biblical Chronology," *SMS* 4 (1981): 5; or (c) by assuming a simultaneous (counter-)kingdom of Pekah beginning in the reign of Jerobeam II, Zechariah or Menahem: Julius Lewy, *Die Chronologie der Könige von Israel und Juda* (Gießen: Alfred Töpelmann, 1927), 18–19; Thiele, *Mysterious Numbers*, 114; H. J. Cook, "Pekah," *VT* 14 (1974): 121–35; Nadav Na'aman, "Historical and Chronological Notes on the Kingdoms of Israel and Judah in the Eight Century B.C.," *VT* 36 (1986): 74–82. Tetley, *Chronology*, 148–51, bases her reconstruction here on a variant in G-manuscript 127 and attributes 12 regnal years to Pekahiah.

whose aim was programmatically stated by Alfred Jepsen: to "develop a system which respects the tradition and fits in well with the established Assyrian and Babylonian synchronisms."⁹ The combination of both aspects has led to meticulous work on the extant sources and brought forth detailed reconstructions, but none of them proved able to prevail among the scholarly community. With regards to methodology, this approach has exerted a high pressure to correct or change the biblical data in order to reach an acceptable fit. The inner system of the biblical chronology, its underlying historical ideas as well as the relation of the chronological data to the narrative material in Kings tended to be overlooked in the process.¹⁰ For this reason, the present study focuses on the chronological data within 2Kgs 15–18 on their own right and intends to elucidate the chronological concept conveyed and the ways and means of its compilation. This will be done initially irrespective of the extra-biblical data for the historical period in question. Whether the biblical chronology and the extra biblical data can be reconciled or whether the expectation that they could is even justified, is a different matter – and outside the scope of this paper. A thorough understanding of the biblical chronology and its development, however, is a necessary prerequisite for its use in any historical reconstruction. It may help to differentiate between reliable data and numbers obtained by the redactor(s) through some calculation method (which is the main focus of the present paper) and can provide insights into the nature of the sources behind the synchronistic compilation as well as its underlying pragmatics.¹¹

2 Chronological Consistency and Inconsistency in 2Kgs 15–18

2Kgs 15–18 describe the last era of the Northern kingdom of Israel and the contemporaneous history of Judah. After the long reign of Jeroboam II, there are six

---

9 Alfred Jepsen, "Zur Chronologie der Könige von Israel und Juda. Eine Überprüfung," in *Untersuchungen zur israelitisch-jüdischen Chronologie*, ed. Alfred Jepsen and Robert Hanhart (Berlin: Toepelmann, 1964), 6.
10 A notable exception is Laato, *Guide*, who divides his study into three steps: (1) an explanation of the biblical traditions, (2) a presentation of the extrabiblical material, and (3) a demonstration of "how the biblical and ancient Jewish chronological traditions can be harmonized with extra-biblical material" (Laato, *Guide*, 2–3).
11 For a discussion of these broader questions see Kristin Weingart, *Gezählte Geschichte: Die synchronistischen Datierungen in den Königebüchern in literargeschichtlicher und historischer Perspektive* (forthcoming).

more Israelite kings, four of whom rule in parallel to the exceedingly long term of Azariah (Zechariah, Shallum, Menahem, and Pekahiah). They are followed by Pekah and Hoshea. At the same time, four Judean kings are listed; following Azariah, these are Jotham, Ahaz, and Hezekiah. The table in Fig. 1 shows the chronological data provided in 2Kgs 15–18.

2Ki		no. of regnal years	synchronism	age
15:1	Azariah	52	17th year of Jerobeam	16
15:8	Zechariah	6 months	38th year of Azariah	
15:13	Shallum	1 month	39th year of Azariah	
15:17	Menahem	10	39th year of Azariah	
15:23	Pekahiah	2	50th year of Azariah	
15:27	Pekah	20	52nd year of Azariah	
15:30	Hoshea		20th year of Jotham	
15:32	Jotham	16	2nd year of Pekah	25
16:1	Ahaz	16	17th year of Pekah	20
17:1	Hoshea	9	12th year of Ahaz	
17:6	fall of Samaria		9th year of Hoshea	
18:1	Hezekiah	29	3rd year of Hoshea	25
18:9f.	siege/fall of Samaria		4th/6th year of Hezekiah = 7th/9th year of Hoshea	

Fig. 1: Table illustrating the chronological data provided in 2Kgs 15–18. Prepared by the author.

Some of these data show a high degree of consistency. This is the case in the regnal year totals and synchronistic accession dates for the kings of Israel from Zechariah to Pekah (2Kgs 15:1, 8, 13, 23, 27). With the sole exception of Menahem, the reign lengths given fit the intervals indicated by the synchronisms. At the same time, it is evident that an accession year system (postdating) is applied in order to establish the total number of regnal years of each king.

The case of Pekahiah can serve as an example. His reign parallels the 50th, 51st, and 52nd year of Azariah. Therefore, he ascended to the throne some time in the 50th year of Azariah, which is treated as his accession year and not yet counted as a regnal year. The 51st and 52nd year of Azariah are attributed to him as regnal years, the sum of which adds up to two. As usual in cases of postdating a subtraction of the synchronisms equals the regnal years given.

For a case of the alternative counting method, i.e. antedating, see Nadab in 1Kgs 15:25, 33: His reign starts in the 2nd year of Asa, while his successor Baasha ascended to the throne in the 3rd year of Asa. However, he is also attributed a two-year-long reign. This implies, that the year of his accession, though shared with Jeroboam I is counted as a full regnal year as well. In the case of antedating, the subtraction of the synchronisms is always one year short in comparison with the number of regnal years listed.

The synchronistic date for Hezekiah's accession and the subsequent parallelization of dates for the conquest of Samaria between Hezekiah and Hoshea (2Kgs 17:6; 18:1, 9f.) are consistent as well. As in the case of the Israelite kings, postdating is also applied for the determination of Hezekiah's reign length.[12]

Despite these cases of chronological coherence, the overall compilation displays an apparent lack of consistency; conflicts and conspicuities are discernible in no less than seven instances:

(1) The sum of regnal years attributed to the Israelite kings after Jeroboam II is 41 years and 7 months. The reign lengths of the Judean kings in the same period add up to 53 years.[13]

(2) Menahem is listed with 10 regnal years (2Kgs 15:17), but the synchronistic dates of his accession (39th year of Azariah) and that of his successor Pekahiah (2Kgs 15:23: 50th year of Azariah) imply an 11-year reign.

(3) For the accession of Hoshea, two synchronistic dates are extant, neither of which easily agrees with the data for the Judean kings:
– 2Kgs 15:30 synchronizes the beginning of his reign with the 20th year of Jotham. However, according to 2Kgs 15:32, Jotham only reigned for 16 years, so there should not be a 20th year of Jotham.
– 2Kgs 17:1 dates his accession to the 12th year of Ahaz. However, if Ahaz reigned for 16 years and his successor Hezekiah came to the throne in the 3rd year of Hoshea, then Hoshea's accession should fall into the 13th year of Ahaz' reign.

(4) Jotham's regnal year total and accession date (2Kgs 15:32) in combination with the synchronistic date for his successor Ahaz (2Kgs 16:1) seem to indicate antedating, since the synchronistic dates imply a 15-year reign for Jotham and a regnal year total of 16 years is attributed to him. This differs from Hezekiah,

---

12 Hezekiah's 4th year can only parallel Hoshea's 7th year, if the initial period of Hezekiah's reign, which falls into Hoshea's 3rd year, is treated as an accession year. His 1st regnal year corresponds to Hoshea's 4th year and, accordingly, Hezekiah's 4th year coincides with Hoshea's 7th year.

13 For the Israelite kings, the numbers are: Zechariah 6 months, Shallum 1 month, Menahem 10 years, Pekahiah 2 years, Pekah 20 years, and Hoshea 9 years. For the Judean kings the same period is marked by the synchronistic dates for Zechariah's accession (38th year of Azariah) and Hoshea's 9th year (= 7th year of Hezekiah). Therefore the sum includes 14 years for Azariah, 16 years each for Jotham and Ahaz, and 7 years for Hezekiah. Assuming antedating for the reigns of the Judean kings and postdating for the Israelite ones would only reduce the difference in the totals.

whose data clearly indicate that postdating was used to determine the number of his regnal years.[14]

(5) The synchronistic date for Jotham's accession, i.e. the 2nd year of Pekah (2Kgs 15:32), is conspicuous. According to 2Kgs 15:27, Pekah's reign began in the 52nd year of Azariah, which is also the latter's last year. If Jotham had succeeded Azariah directly, his rule should have commenced in the 2nd year of Pekahiah (which would coincide with the accession year of Pekah). This, however, would render the subsequent synchronistic dates impossible, esp. the one for Ahaz (2Kgs 16:1: 17th year of Pekah). The present data seem to indicate an interregnum of 1–2 years between the end of Azariah's reign and the beginning of Jotham's.[15]

(6) The synchronistic dates for the accession of Ahaz (2Kgs 16:1) and Hezekiah (2Kgs 18:1) are incompatible with the number of regnal years attributed to Ahaz. Between the 17th year of Pekah and the 3rd year of Hoshea there is only room for 6 years, not 16.

(7) The issue of Ahaz's age has been a long noted *crux:* If Ahaz ascended to the throne at the age of 20 and ruled for 16 years (2Kgs 16:1), he would have been 36 when Hezekiah took over. Hezekiah, however, is said to have been 25 years old at the beginning of his reign (2Kgs 18:1). So Ahaz can only have been an 11-year old boy when Hezekiah was born. While this might be possible from a biological point of view, it is improbable and would remain a notable exception among the Judean kings who are usually around 20 years old when the heir to the throne is born.[16]

The remarkable density of chronological problems within 2Kgs 15–18 has yielded an even greater abundance of attempts to explain them.[17] These are inevitably connected with more comprehensive propositions regarding the compilation history of the chronological data in the Book of Kings and the system behind it, as well as the literary history and pragmatics of the regnal frame as its

---

14 See above, note 12.
15 Cf. Thiele, *Mysterious Numbers*, 110–11.
16 See the lists provided by Begrich, *Chronologie*, 164, although some of his corrections are unnecessary. Azariah is another notable exception: according to the data provided in 2Kgs 15:2, 33 he was at the age of 43 when Jotham was born.
17 Only a small selection of proposals can be mentioned or even reviewed in the present context, the more so as most of them necessarily go hand in hand with more general presuppositions on the development and organization principles of the synchronistic chronology in Kings. For collections of recent proposals see Robb Andrew Young, *Hezekiah in History and Tradition* (Leiden: Brill, 2012), 9–34, or Raik Heckl, "Hiskia," *wibilex* 2012 (https://www.bibelwissenschaft.de/stichwort/21346/; accessed 10/2017).

text base[18] on the one hand and the overall aim to achieve a compatibility of the biblical data with the external sources on the other.

Though not dealing with the latter issue, the propositions outlined in this paper depend on a more general understanding of the synchronistic chronology as a whole (see below). They will address two questions: which individual components of the overall conundrum within 2Kgs 15–18 are interconnected and how the current contradictory picture might have come about.

In contrast to the data for other periods, the textual witnesses for 2Kgs 15–18 offer only a very limited number of variants. Most of them originate from differing chronological concepts or from attempts to harmonize or minimize inconsistencies within the given material.[19]

An example of the former is the Greek manuscript 127[20] belonging to a family of manuscripts which attest the Antiochene text, which has a unique and systematic reworking of the whole synchronistic chronology in Kings.[21] For the latter, two examples may suffice: (1) According to the 12th cent. minuscule 245, Menahem reigned for 20 years. The synchronistic dates are adjusted accordingly: Shallum's reign and the beginning of Menahem's reign fall into the 30th year of Azariah in order to accommodate the date of Pekahiah's accession (50th year of

---

18 For the latter see the recent study by Benjamin D. Thomas, *Hezekiah and the Compositional History of the Book of Kings* (Tübingen: Mohr Siebeck, 2014), which also provides an overview of the older discussion.

19 Text critical examinations of the chronological data inevitably face a methodological problem: in order to determine whether a given variant resembles a correction, deviation or otherwise motivated change, the underlying chronological system must be understood. On the other hand, proposals on the design of the underlying system depend on the data that the assumed system is supposed to include. Thus the danger of arguing within a hermeneutic circle is ever present.

20 The nomenclature follows Alfred Rahlfs, *Verzeichnis der griechischen Handschriften des Alten Testaments* (Berlin: Weidmann, 1914).

21 See Shenkel, *Chronology*, 27–31. Tetley, *Chronology*, nevertheless bases parts of her chronological reconstruction on 127, because she believes it still contains a number of old, i.e. prae-MT, regnal year totals and synchronisms (63). 127 has the following variant regnal year totals in 2Kgs 15–18: Menahem 20 years, Pekahiah 12 years, and Pekah 30 years. The synchronistic dates are:

Zechariah	28th year of Azariah	Jotham	2nd year of Pekah
Shallum	28th year of Azariah	Ahaz	18th year of Pekah
Menahem	28th year of Azariah	Hezekiah	4th year of Hoshea
Pekahiah	40th year of Azariah		
Pekah	52th year of Azariah		
Hoshea	14th year of Ahaz		

Azariah).²² The beginning of Hezekiah's reign is dated to the 5ᵗʰ year of Hoshea, thus avoiding a contradiction with Hoshea's accession date (12ᵗʰ year of Ahaz) and the length of Ahaz' reign (16 years). (2) Codex Alexandrinus, the Antiochene manuscripts 19, 82, 93, and 108 as well as the minuscules 158 and 700 indicate a regnal year total of 10 years for Pekahiah. This reading is arguably a correction resulting from another attempt to harmonize the accession year of Pekahiah (50ᵗʰ year of Azariah), the regnal year total of Ahaz (16 years) and the accession date of Hoshea (12ᵗʰ year of Ahaz).²³

3 The Chronological Concept of the Synchronistic Framework in 2Kgs 15–18

The following observations are based on the proposition (to be defended below), that the synchronistic chronology in 2Kgs 15–18 was compiled on the basis of two sets of numbers: (1) a compilation of regnal year totals and synchronistic accession dates for the kings of Israel, and (2) a collection of regnal year totals for the kings of Judah. The synchronistic dates for the accession of the Judean kings were calculated by combining Judean regnal year totals and Israelite accession dates. In this respect 2Kgs 15–18 is consistent with other parts of the synchronistic chronology in Kings. The chronological compilation is best explained as a series of consecutive combinations interlacing the two sets of numbers, each combination being internally coherent but limited in range.²⁴

As noted in the beginning the chronological data for the Israelite kings, i.e. the combination of regnal year totals and accession dates are perfectly consistent – with the sole exception of Menahem (Fig. 2).

Menahem's case is peculiar, because the synchronistic dates indicate a reign of 11 years, but 2Kgs 15:17 attributes only 10 regnal years to him. This combination is not compatible with antedating, because Menahem's regnal years would

---

22 Minuscule 245 shows an analogous tendency to avoid contradictions in other parts of the synchronistic chronology as well, such as the chronological data on Omri (1Kgs 16:23), Joram (2Kgs 1:18ᵃ), or Azariah (2Kgs 15:1).
23 The other attested variants are: (1) Regnal year totals: 2Kgs 15:13 Shallum: 8 days (A); 2Kgs 15:23 Pekahiah: 10 years (A, 19, 82, 93, 108, 158, 700), 12 years (V, 52, 107, 489, et al.); 2Kgs 15:27 Pekah: 28 years (55, 56, 119, 372, 554); 2Kgs 18:1 Hezekiah: 25 years (130); (2) Synchronistic dates: 2Kgs 15:8 Zechariah: 28ᵗʰ year of Azariah (V, 92, 106, 120, 130, 134, 314, 489, 554); 2Kgs 15:27 Pekah: 62ⁿᵈ year of Azariah (489); 2Kgs 15:32 Jotham: 13ᵗʰ year of Pekah (71); 2Kgs 17:1 Hoshea: 10ᵗʰ year of Ahaz (82). For the variants in manuscripts 127 and 245, see above.
24 For a detailed discussion and justification see Weingart, *Gezählte Geschichte*.

Fig. 2: Diagram showing the chronological data for the kings of Israel provided in 2Kgs 15–18. Prepared by the author.

then amount to 12. Assuming postdating was used, a total of 11 regnal years would be expected, so the figure is still off by one year. The textual witnesses unanimously support the MT in this case, so to assume a mistake would be sheer conjecture. The synchronistic dates, on the other hand, are completely in line with the neighboring synchronisms for Zechariah and Shallum as well as Pekah; changing them would cause a series of new problems and is equally unfounded.

This curious number of regnal years for Menahem coincides, however, with the fact that the combination of reign lengths and accession dates for earlier Israelite kings point to antedating when counting their regnal years[25] while the data for the later kings (like Pekahiah) indicate postdating. It has been suggested by Gershon Galil that Menahem's data reflect a change from ante- to postdating prompted by the adoption of the Assyrian custom of differentiating between the accession year of a king and the first regnal year starting with the first New Year

---

[25] Ahaziah is the last Israelite king before Menahem with a complete and well attested set of dates. Here, the interplay of synchronistic accession date and regnal year total for Ahaziah (1Kgs 22:52) and synchronistic accession date for Joram (2Kgs 3:1) imply antedating. There is no regular introductory formula and accession date for Jehu, therefore the method of reckoning for Joram and Jehu remains unclear. The number of regnal years for Joash also presupposes antedating if one reads with greater parts of the G-tradition the synchronism "39th year of Jehoash" in 2Kgs 13:10. The MT has in 2Kgs 13:10 the synchronism "37th year of Jehoash" which conflicts with the neighboring synchronistic dates in 2Kgs 13:1 and 14:1. The MT-reading seems to result from an attempt to reconcile the date with the accession date of Jehoash (2Kgs 12:2 "7th year of Jehu"). There is no trace of a corresponding change in 2Kgs 13:1, which should read "21st year of Jehoash" if the MT were correct.

in the king's reign.[26] The narrative material on Menahem corroborates the suggestion; 2Kgs 15:9f. not only mentions the exceedingly high tribute of 1,000 talents of silver which Menahem paid but also reports the introduction of a taxation system in order to collect the necessary means. Following the Assyrian system with regard to the reckoning of regnal years could well have coincided with another change discernible in various texts whose exact date is hard to determine – the change of the New Year in Israel from autumn to spring.

Since the issue has been extensively discussed,[27] a short outline of its main features may suffice. The Gezer calendar as well as the traditions reflected in the various festival calendars in the Pentateuch (Ex 23:14–19; 34:18–26; Lev 23:1–14; Deut 16:1–7), although the texts themselves are mostly younger, indicate that in earlier pre-exilic times, the year began in the autumn.[28] Whenever the months are numbered, however, the first month seems to lie in the spring (see e.g. Ex 12:2; Jer 36:2). Together with the use of Babylonian month names this attests an adaptation of Assyrian and/or Babylonian calendars. While it is clear (cf. mRHSh 1:1) that in later postexilic times the New Year was transferred back to the autumn, the question remains when the interlude of a vernal New Year started. With regards to Judah the change is often associated with Josiah[29] or the Babylonian exile.[30] For Israel, the data is even sparser. Therefore, some

---

[26] Galil, *Chronology*, 62. For Galil, however, the change took place already during the reign of Joash. Galil is correct in pointing out that Menahem is not the first Israelite king mentioned in Assyrian sources as paying tribute. At least Jehu (cf. Albert Kirk Grayson, *Assyrian Rulers of the Early First Millennium BC II (858–754 BC)* [Toronto: Toronto University Press, 1996], A.0.102.88) and Joash (cf. Grayson, *Assyrian Rulers*, A.0.104.7, 8) were also Assyrian vassals. Unlike the case of Menahem, the OT does not indicate any influence on Israelite administrative matters, and the chronological data do not indicate an earlier change from ante- to postdating.
[27] For an overview and further references see e.g. Karl Jaroš, "Kalender," in *Neues Bibellexikon*, vol. 2, ed. Manfred Görg (1995): 429–32; James C. VanderKam, "Calendars: Ancient Israelite and Early Jewish," in *The Anchor Bible Dictionary*, vol. 1, ed. David Noel Freedman (1992): 813–20; as well as the discussions in Begrich, *Chronologie*, 66–90; Thiele, *Mysterious Numbers*, 29–33; Jack Finegan, *Handbook of Biblical Chronology: Principles of Time Reckoning in the Ancient World and Problems of Chronology in the Bible* (Peabody MA: Hendrickson, 1998), 29–35; 76–80; Laato, *Guide*, 14–16.
[28] According to Lev 25:8–9, sabbatical years and jubilees also begin in the autumn, although the text mentions the "seventh month," implying that the first month is in the spring. Thiele, *Mysterious Numbers*, 30–2, and Laato, *Guide*, 14–15, also point to 1Kgs 6:37–8 and 2Kgs 23 for additional support of an autumnal turn of the year; for the latter see already Begrich, *Chronologie*, 68–69.
[29] Begrich, *Chronologie*, 70–90; cf. Hayes and Hooker, *New Chronology*, 13.
[30] So e.g. Laato, *Guide*, 15, asserting a change coinciding with Jeconiah's exile and a transition period of parallel chronological systems up to Zedekiah. Thiele, *Mysterious Numbers*, 33, as-

scholars deny a shift in the chronological system altogether and assert either an autumnal year[31] or vernal year for Northern Israel's monarchic period as a whole. If a change of systems and New Year date is accepted, however, it is usually connected to Assyrian influence and dated into the 8th century BCE.[32] In this case, the chronological data for Menahem would offer a valuable clue.

A shift of the New Year from fall to spring in Israel, while the autumn date still remained unchanged in Judah, could well explain why Menahem was only attributed 10 regnal years although the synchronistic dates indicate an 11-year period in Judah.

If these assumptions are correct, they allow some conclusions regarding the nature of the material in which the chronological data for the Israelite kings was transmitted and which was used by the compiler of the synchronistic framework. A change of reckoning method and New Year date at a certain point with consequences for the interplay of regnal year totals and synchronisms does not point to a systematic (and potentially artificial) construction, but rather to continually kept records which reflect and incorporate such changes when they occur. This would add weight to the view that older official records like king lists and/or chronicles constitute the basis of (or at least parts of) the chronological data in the Book of Kings.[33] In contrast to the common view that these documents only contained regnal year totals, the correspondence between these totals and the synchronistic dates strongly suggests that such an older document, dealing with the kings of Israel, already included synchronistic accession dates.[34]

At least at the time the Israelite data was combined with the Judean material the synchronistic accession dates of the Israelite kings must have been present, for the combination with the Judean data obviously presupposes them. The regnal year totals for the Judean kings of this period amount to 52 years for Azariah

---

sumes a consistent adherence to an autumnal year in Judah for the whole monarchic period; Galil, *Chronology*, 9–10, on the other hand, reckons with a vernal year for the same period.
31 So e.g. Galil, *Chronology*, 9. Cf. Hayes and Hooker, *New Chronology*, 13, who additionally argue for differing autumnal New Year dates in Israel and Judah.
32 Jaroš, "Kalender," 431.
33 While many researchers would probably ascribe to this general proposition – see e.g. the influential study by Shoshana Bin-Nun, "Formulas from Royal Records of Israel and of Judah," *VT* 18 (1968): 414–32, or Nadav Na'aman, "The Temple Library of Jerusalem and the Composition of the Book of Kings," in *Congress Volume Leiden 2004*, ed. André Lemaire (Leiden: Brill, 2006): 129–52 – the form and content of these sources as well as the questions how and at what stage they reached the author(s) of the Book of Kings remain highly controversial; cf. the recent overview in Thomas, *Hezekiah*, 84–102.
34 Bin-Nun, "Formulas", 426, allowed for the possibility, that the synchronistic dates for the accession of Ahab, Ahaziah, Joram, and Jehoshaphat were already present in the older king lists.

(2Kgs 15:1), 16 years for Jotham (15:32), 16 years for Ahaz (2Kgs 16:1) and 29 years for Hezekiah (2Kgs 18:1). According to 2Kgs 18:9f, the first 6 regnal years of Hezekiah parallel the last 6 years of Hoshea. Using the synchronism of Hezekiah's accession and the subsequent chronological alignment of the fall of Samaria as an anchor, the combination shown in Fig. 3 emerges.

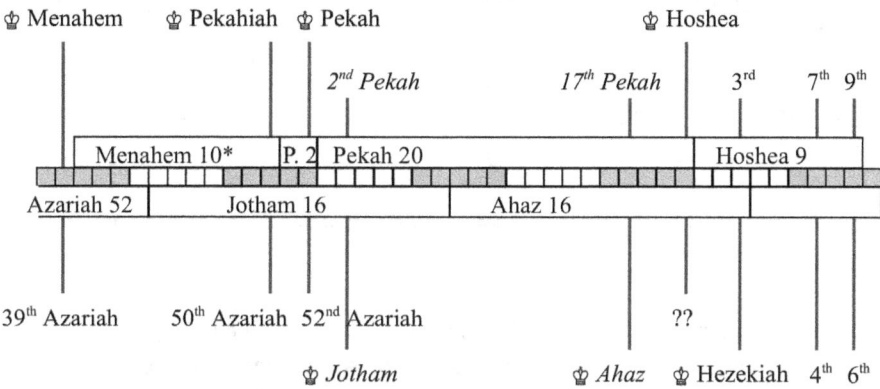

Fig. 3: Diagram showing the combined chronological data for Israel and Judah provided in 2Kgs 15–18. Prepared by the author.

It becomes immediately apparent that Ahaz's reign length is not compatible with the synchronistic dates for his and Hezekiah's accession. In addition, the total of 16 years for Ahaz also pushes the beginning of Jotham's reign well back into the time of Menahem and thus conflicts with the former's synchronization with Pekah (2Kgs 15:32). The synchronistic dates rather imply a reign length of only 6 years for Ahaz.[35] Assuming that an older number of 6 years was accidentally changed to 16 – possibly influenced by the regnal year total of Jotham (16 years) just a few verses earlier (15:33) – most of the neighboring synchronisms – Israelite as well as Judean – fall nicely into place (Fig. 4).

---

35 There is no textual witness for this date, but as Claus Schedl, "Textkritische Bemerkungen zu den Synchronismen der Könige von Israel und Juda," *VT* 12 (1962): 88–119, already pointed out, a change of 10 years is a rather frequent phenomenon within the chronological material. Such a change appears in Kings besides Chronicles (cf. 1Kgs 16:6,8/2Chr 16:1; 2Kgs 24:8/2Chr 36:9) or among the textual witnesses (cf. 1Kgs 15:2 Codex B "6 years he reigned in Jerusalem" / Codex A and minuscules 52 92 247 121 "16 years he reigned in Jerusalem"; 1Kgs 15:25 MT "2nd year of Asa" / Greek minuscule 501 "12th year of Asa"; 2Kgs 15:8 MT "38th year of Azariah" / Codex V and minuscules 92 106 120 127 130 134 314 489 554 "28th year of Azariah"; 2Kgs 15:27 MT "52nd year of Azariah" / minuscule 489 "62nd year of Azariah").

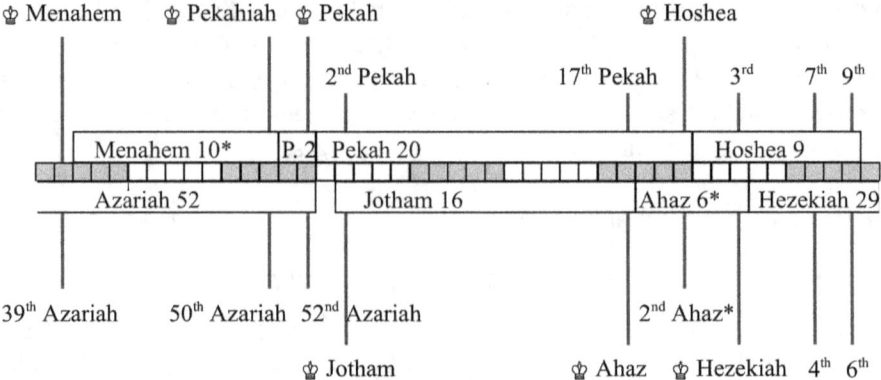

Fig. 4: Diagram showing the combined chronological data with a corrected regnal year total for Ahaz. Prepared by the author.

Only the synchronistic date for the accession of Hoshea (2Kgs 17:1), the 12th year of Ahaz, does not agree with this combination. One would expect the 2nd or 3rd year of Ahaz, depending on the exact date of his accession in the course of the year and its relation to the Judean New Year.

The synchronistic date for Jotham's accession, the 2nd year of Pekah, implies that an accession year is not taken into account in his case. Moreover, the current combination results in a gap between the 52nd year of Azariah and the beginning of Jotham's rule. As it seems, the regnal year totals with which the compiler had to work did not add up to the number of years required to cover the stretch of time indicated by the Israelite data.

The lack of an accession year points to a possible justification for this unusual combination in the eyes of the compiler:[36] in the chronological data for the Judean kings, there are only two instances of documented co-regencies or overlapping reigns – Jehoshaphat and Jehoram (2Kgs 8:16) and Amaziah and Azariah (2Kgs 14:22). In the former case, a short note in the regnal frame indicates that Jehoshaphat was still king when Jehoram began to reign (ובשנת חמש ליורם בן יהושפט מלך יהודה מלך יהורם בן יהושפט מלך ישראל אחאב).[37] In the latter,

---

[36] An alternative explanation would be an isolated instance of antedating. Considering the consistent use of postdating in the chronological data for the Judean kings, such a change would be hard to explain.

[37] Many commentators see ויהושפת מלך יהודה as a gloss secondarily inserted into the text and disturbing the usual sequence of the introductory formula (see e.g. Otto Thenius, *Die Bücher der Könige*, KEH [Leipzig: Hirzel, 1873], 312; Wellhausen, "Zeitrechnung," 616; Shenkel, *Chronology*, 73; Georg Hentschel, *2 Könige*, NEB [Würzburg: Echter Verlag, 1985], 37; Volkmar Fritz, *Das*

the narrative in 2Kgs 14:19–22 reports the circumstances of Amaziah's dismissal and Azariah's accession, while 14:22 seems to imply that there was a period in Azariah's reign which lay in the lifetime of his predecessor Amaziah. In both cases, the interplay of synchronistic dates and regnal year totals shows that no accession year is included, the beginning of the king's reign rather coincides with the first year counted as a regnal year.[38]

In the case at hand, the narrative description of the end of Azariah's reign provided the compiler with a suitable explanation for the chronological gap indicated: in his final years, Azariah suffered from a disease which impeded him from ruling, so Jotham functioned as an interim ruler (2Kgs 15:5: ויותם בן המלך על הבית שפט את עם הארץ). The result was a chronological concept which showed some peculiarities but remained within the reasonable and justifiable bounds provided by the narrative material on the kings of Judah.

In sum: the synchronistic chronology in 2Kgs 15–18 can be explained as a combination of data on the Israelite kings (regnal year totals and synchronistic accession dates) with regnal year totals for the Judean kings. It displays an application of certain compilation techniques (no accession year in case of co-regencies[39]) and methods of reckoning regnal years (postdating for Judah and a

---

zweite Buch der Könige, ZBK.AT [Zürich: TVZ, 1998], 43). The words are also missing in some textual witnesses (G[Nmin], Syh, S, V[Mss]), prompting the apparatus of the BHS to suggest their deletion. 8:16 obviously deviates from the usual regnal frame, but this marks the phrase rather as a *lectio difficilior probabilior:* a secondary adjustment to the regular formula is much more plausible than a later addition (Jürgen Werlitz, *Die Bücher der Könige* [Stuttgart: Katholisches Bibelwerk, 2002], 234; cf. Burke O. Long, *2 Kings* [Grand Rapids MI: Eerdmans, 1991], 108). Besides, it is hard to explain what information the assumed gloss ויהושפט מלך יהודה should have conveyed? That Jehoshaphat was king of Judah is implied by the filiation in v. 16b. However, if the phrase indicates a coregency, it has a recognizable function within the introductory formula and one does not have to assume a gloss or an interpolation.

38 Jehoram's accession is dated to the 5th year of Joram (2Kgs 8:16), the reign of his successor Ahaziah begins in the 12th year of Joram (2Kgs 8:25). Since Jehoram is said to have reigned for 8 years (8:17), no accession year is attributed to him. The case of Azariah is more complicated. The original date of his accession is probably the 17th year of Jeroboam (the number 27 seems to be another instance of a change of 10, see above note 35). The compiler probably understood the events related in 2Kgs 14:19–22 as a period in which the kingship was in dispute and assumed a temporary co-regency between Amaziah and Azariah (cf. Thiele, *Mysterious Numbers*; Galil, *Chronology*, 57–59). Accordingly Azariah's term does not begin in the 16th year of Jeroboam – as would be expected, if there had been an accession year –, but it is dated to the 17th year of Jeroboam.

39 Co-regencies or overlapping reigns are always indicated within the regnal frame itself or in the narrative material included for the respective kings (see below). In order to understand the chronological concept of the synchronistic framework of Kings on its own right, there is no need to postulate a greater number of co-regencies than indicated even though the assumption often

reasonable change from antedating to postdating with Menahem for Israel[40]) that is consistent with the compilation of data for other periods of the synchronistic chronology. The compilation itself further suggests a familiarity with narrative material fixed in between the introductory and closing formulae of the regnal frames.[41]

4 A Glimpse Behind the Synchronistic Framework

So far, it has been shown that the chronological data in 2Kgs 15–18 are no arbitrary collection of figures but bear witness to a thoughtfully designed synchronistic chronology which builds upon different materials and reflects a certain idea of the chronological sequence of the last five decades in the period of the divided kingdoms. Some of the discrepancies noted above have proven to be mere apparent ones once the compilation techniques were better understood. Other phenomena within the chronological data have not been addressed yet. They coincide with notable peculiarities in the narrative material within 2Kgs 15 f. as well

---

functions as an effective means to reconcile the biblical chronology with external data. Thiele, *Mysterious Numbers*, 61–65, e.g. presupposes seven cases of co-regency in his chronological reconstruction, six in Judah and one in Israel (see also Edwin R. Thiele, "Coregencies and Overlapping Reigns among the Hebrew Kings," *JBL* 93 [1974]: 174–200). Leslie McFall, "Some Missing Coregencies in Thiele's Chronology," *AUSS* 30 (1992): 35–58, wants to add another four. For a methodological critique, see Laato, *Guide*, 19–22.

40 There is no need to assume frequent and basically unmotivated changes in the praxis of regnal year reckoning in Israel and Judah as Thiele, *Mysterious Numbers* proposes. According to Thiele, Judah changed from postdating (Rehoboam – Jehoshaphat) to antedating (Jehoram – Jehoash) and back to postdating (Amaziah – Zedekiah). Israel changed from antedating to postdating at the time of Joash (see the table, p. 281–82).

41 This, of course, does not imply that all the material contained in the Book of Kings was already present, quite the contrary: many of the prophetic stories are in all likelihood later additions, cf. e.g. Hermann-Josef Stipp, *Elischa – Propheten – Gottesmänner: Die Kompositionsgeschichte des Elischazyklus und verwandter Texte, rekonstruiert auf der Basis von Text- und Literarkritik zu 1 Kön 20.22 und 2 Kön 2–7* (St. Ottilien: EOS Verlag, 1987), 253–67, 361–62; Steven L. McKenzie, *The Trouble with Kings: The Composition of the Book of Kings in the Deuteronomistic History* (Leiden: Brill, 1991), 88–93; Hermann-Josef Stipp, "Ahabs Buße und die Komposition des deuteronomistischen Geschichtswerks," *Bib* 76 (1995): 471–97; Erhard Blum, "Die Nabotüberlieferungen und die Kompositionsgeschichte der Vorderen Propheten," in *Schriftauslegung in der Schrift: Festschrift für Odil Hannes Steck*, ed. Reinhard G. Kratz, Thomas Krüger and Konrad Schmid (Berlin: de Gruyter, 2000): 111–28; or Susanne Otto, "The Composition of the Elijah-Elisha Stories and the Deuteronomistic History," *JSOT* 27 (2003): 487–508.

as components of the regnal frame and offer further insights into the development of the chronological concept found in the text.

One such notable feature is the double synchronism for the accession of Hoshea: 2Kgs 15:30 synchronizes the beginning of his reign with the 20th year of Jotham, 17:1 with the 12th year of Ahaz. As seen before, the first synchronism does not agree with Jotham's regnal year total of 16 years. If the proposed reign length of 6 years for Ahaz is correct, the second synchronism is impossible as well. It remains striking, however, that Hoshea's accession is synchronized with Jotham as well as with Ahaz.

Another peculiarity concerns the account of Jotham's reign in 2Kgs 15. Beyond the formulaic components usually given for any king, only two particulars of Jotham's reign, which is after all 16 years long, are mentioned: (a) construction measures undertaken on a temple gate (15:35b: הוא בנה את שער בית יהוה העליון), and (b) the beginning of Aramean and North Israelite hostilities against Judah (15:37: בימים ההם החל יהוה להשליח ביהודה רצין מלך ארם ואת פקח בן רמליהו). The same two issues recur in the account of Ahaz's reign, albeit in much more detail. 2Kgs 16:5–9 relate the joined effort of Rezin and Pekah to force Ahaz into an anti-Assyrian coalition and the latter's loyalty to the Assyrian king; vv. 10–18 describe various building measures at the Jerusalem temple, first and foremost the erection of an altar based on a model in Damascus (an undertaking presented in a highly critical angle within the Book of Kings). Compared to Ahaz, Jotham's depiction appears like an abridged and softened version of his highly problematic successor. Jotham's fields of activity are the same; he acts in a completely innocuous way, but the information given remains completely vague as well.

A third points concerns elements of the regnal frame, esp. the introductory formulae for Jotham and Ahaz. The evaluation of Jotham (2Kgs 15:34,35a) contains nothing extraordinary. It resembles the frequent type of assessment for Judean kings that is positive to a limited extend and links the cultic policies of a king to those of his father.[42] Ahaz, on the other hand, receives an unusually extensive and highly negative evaluation (2Kgs 16:2b–4), which connects him with the kings of Israel and, in the account of his sins, with the later Manasseh (2Kgs 16:3; cf. 2Kgs 21:6).[43] This evaluation is in line with the critical tendency of the account as a whole.

---

[42] The other examples are Asa 1Kgs 15:11ff; Jehoshaphat 1Kgs 22:43f; Joash 2Kgs 12:3f; Amaziah 2Kgs 14:3f; Azariah 2Kgs 15:3f.

[43] Cf. Hans-Detlef Hoffmann, *Reform und Reformen: Untersuchungen zu einem Grundthema der deuteronomistischen Geschichtsschreibung* (Zürich: TVZ, 1980), 39–40; Sang-Won Lee, "Den Ort, den JHWH erwählen wird ..., sollt ihr aufsuchen" (Dtn 12,5): Die Forderung der Kulteinheit im Deuteronomistischen Geschichtswerk (Diss. Universität Tübingen, 2015), 93.

On the other hand, the biographical information provided for Ahaz in the introductory formula is incomplete. While Jotham's formula contains the usual information (synchronistic date of accession, age at accession, regnal year total, residency, the king's mother), Ahaz' introduction lacks any information on his mother. This is striking, because all other introductory formulae for the kings of Judah (with the sole exception of Jehoram, 2Kgs 8:16–17, [44]) mention the king's mother, i.e. her name as well as her origin and/or patronym. Moreover, Ahaz's age at his accession, 20 years, is the only round number among all the Judean kings mentioned in the synchronistic account. This might just be a coincidence, but could also hint at an artificial construction like the round numbers in the regnal year totals of David (2Sam 5:4) and Solomon (1Kgs 11:42).

The following chart summarizes the textual phenomena described above:

	Jotham	Ahaz
biographical information	complete, specific	incomplete, generic
evaluation	generic	specific
narrative account	condensed, specific & duplicate	detailed, specific

The fact that among the two kings, there is only one complete and specific set of biographical information, and that the narrative account of Jotham comprises merely two notes, both of which double and soften up the information given for Ahaz, allow some insight into the content of the sources underlying the account in the Book of Kings and the methods and contributions of its compiler. It seems that the compiler worked with a certain set of information which he tried to adjust and to complete according to the requirements of the established framework. Assuming that contents of a specific nature point to data derived from source material the latter might have included:

- The two names Jotham and Ahaz,
- Two figures for regnal years: 16 years and 6 years[45],
- Possibly one figure for the age at accession,
- Data on one royal mother, and
- One account of the deeds of the king and the events during his reign.

---

[44] Here, however, information on another woman is provided: the king's wife, a daughter of Ahab (v. 18).
[45] Regarding the possibility that Ahaz might have reigned 6 years instead of 16, see above, p. 279.

Presenting Jotham and Ahaz as two successive kings, the compiler had to reconstruct what was missing:
– A second set of biographical information (age and the king's mother). Here, he used the material now provided for Jotham and constructed an introductory formula for Ahaz, leaving out the name of his mother because the required information was lacking and (possibly) creating a round number for the king's age at the beginning of his reign.
– A second account of the king's reign. Here, he used the extensive material now found for Ahaz and attributed similar activities and events to Jotham while depicting him as a less problematic king.

This led to a critical evaluation being provided for Ahaz while Jotham received the default evaluation of Judean kings who were not particularly bad but did not distinguish themselves as cult reformers either. The result was a rather colorless picture of Jotham and an artificially construed biographical frame for Ahaz. However, regardless of whether it was constructed to this aim or not, it helped to bridge Pekah's long reign of 20 years in the chronology – or at least a greater part of it, for two years remained unaccounted for.[46]

If this reconstruction of the source material is correct, it invites further speculation. Could it be that the information found there did not concern two consecutive kings but in fact only one king for whom two different names were included?[47] The fact that a king could bear multiple names is hardly surprising in ancient Near Eastern contexts as is well known from the numerous attestations of throne names in Egypt and Mesopotamia. There are at least some indications that attributing a new name to the king at the beginning of his reign was also practiced in Judah.[48] Remarkably, there are also two names for Jotham's prede-

---

46 See above, section 2, inconsistency (5).
47 This was already proposed by Knut Tage Andersen, "Noch einmal: die Chronologie der Könige von Israel und Juda," *SJOT* 2 (1989): 1–45, who argued that Jotham and Ahaz are to be identified and that there was only one Judean king between Azariah and Hezekiah: "Soviel ich sehe, kann aus diesem Zusammenfall nur die eine Schlußfolgerung gezogen werden, nämlich, daß *Jotham und Ahas historisch ein und dieselbe Person sind*, und zwar der Sohn von König Ussia und Königin Jerusa (2 Kön 15,32.33), der die Königswürde nach dem Vater übernahm" (18, emphasis in original).
48 Irrespective of whether one can follow Gerhard von Rad, "Das judäische Königsritual," *TLZ* 4 (1947): 211–16, in reconstructing a Judean coronation ceremony (cf. the critical appraisal by Markus Saur, "Königserhebungen im antiken Israel," in *Investitur- und Krönungsrituale: Herrschaftseinsetzungen im kulturellen Vergleich*, eds. Marian Steinicke and Stefan Weinfurter [Köln: Böhlau, 2005]: 29–42), he is probably right that carrying throne names was also common among the

cessor – Azariah and Uzziah[49], although the texts do not address the issue at all. If "Jotham" and "Ahaz" were indeed listed as two different names of one king in the sources underlying the synchronistic compilation, this might be the reason for the extent of data mentioned above. The data set only became "incomplete" when the compiler tried to construct a succession of two kings out of one. Combined with the fact that, according to 2Kgs 15, Azariah ruled for an unusually long time and that the transition to his successor is one of the few cases in which the text itself mentions particular circumstances which point to a coregency, it is conceivable that the two names refer to the period of coregency (Jotham) and – as a throne name – to the period of sole rule (Ahaz).[50] This could also be the rationale behind the two figures for the reign length: 16 years co-regency and 6 years of sole rule.

5 The Emergence of the Chronological Conundrum

Building upon the descriptive (section 1) and analytical (sections 3 and 4) steps undertaken so far, it is now possible to present a synthesis and trace the literary development of the chronological conundrum in 2Kgs 15–18.

The collection of data on the Israelite kings which formed the basis of the synchronistic chronology in the Book of Kings provided regnal year totals and synchronistic accession dates. With the exception of Pekah, it probably contained the regnal year totals still extant in the Masoretic text. With regards to Pekah, it may be assumed that the data set also included a date for the beginning of his reign as well as a regnal year total and, subsequently, an accession date for his successor Hoshea. There is no reason to doubt the 52nd year of Azariah as the beginning of Pekah's term. One can only speculate about the date for Hoshea's accession: it might have been the 2nd year of Ahaz, which would be reconcilable with the way the compiler of the synchronistic chronology conceptual-

---

Judean kings. Texts like Isa 9:6 or Jer 23:6 presuppose it; 2Kgs 23:34 and 24:17 report the renaming of Judean rulers by Egyptian or Babylonian kings.

49 Azariah: 2Kgs 14:21; 15:1, 6–8, 17, 23, 27; Uzziah: 2Kgs 15:13, 30, 32, 34; Isa 1:1; 6:1; 7:1; Hos 1:1; Amos 1:1; Zech 14:5; 2Chr 26; 27:2.

50 Notably, in the inscriptions of Tiglath-pileser III, Ahaz is mentioned as "Jehoahaz", i.e. with the theophoric element in the beginning of his name as in Jotham: Tadmor, *The Inscriptions of Tiglath-pileser III*, 170–1: Summ. 7: rev. 11' = Tadmor and Yamada, *The Royal Inscriptions of Tiglath-pileser III*, no. 47: rev. 11'): ^{m}*Ia-ú-ha-zi* ^{KUR}*Ia-ú-da-a-a*.

ized this period. Accordingly, Pekah's original reign length would have been 2 years (Fig. 5).

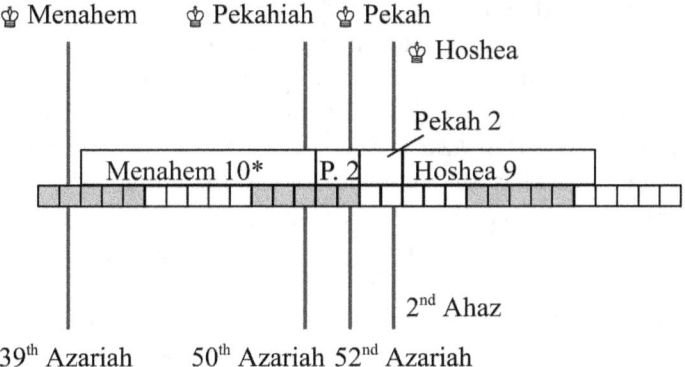

Fig. 5: Diagram showing the reconstructed chronological data for the kings of Israel. Prepared by the author.

At some point, the length of Pekah's reign was erroneously changed to 20 years. This change goes hand in hand with synchronizing Hoshea's accession with the 20th year of Jotham (2Kgs 15:30), because Pekah and Jotham began their respective terms in the same year. The consequence was a second synchronism for Hoshea's accession. Whether both changes took place together or one followed the other remains unknown.

This, however, was the state of affairs (see above, Fig. 2) when the Israelite data reached the compiler who tried to combine them with the regnal year totals of the Judean kings. He found the following synchronisms: 52nd year of Azariah for Pekah's accession and probably the 2nd year of Ahaz for Hoshea's, and combined these data with the regnal year totals he extracted from his Judean material, i.e. 16 years for Jotham, 6 years for Ahaz and 29 years for Hezekiah using the synchronistic alignment of Hoshea and Hezekiah as an anchor (see above, Fig. 4). In doing so, he had to fill the long stretch of time created by the prolongation of Pekah's reign to 20 years which could not be completely covered by the regnal years provided for the Judean kings.

In a final step, Ahaz' reign length was changed from 6 to 16 years (cf. above, Fig. 2), which contradicted a number of synchronisms but probably prompted the correction of the date for Hoshea's accession from the 2nd year of Ahaz to his 12th year.

This reconstruction including the identification of Jotham and Ahaz seems to aggravate the old crux in the chronological data of Hezekiah, namely his age when he came to the throne.⁵¹ There can be no doubt that Ahaz is Hezekiah's father; this is confirmed by a seal impression reading לחזקיהו אחז מלך יהודה.⁵² If – as proposed above – Jotham and Ahaz are one and the same king and the biographical information provided for Jotham (2Kgs 15:33) is likely to retain the original data, Jotham/Ahaz was 25 years old at the beginning of his reign. With a reign length of 6 years, this would make him 31 when his 25-year-old son Hezekiah succeeded him; and this is highly unlikely. Counting, however, from the beginning of a 16-year coregency with Azariah, he would be 47 at his death and 22 years old at the time Hezekiah was born. In this case, he fits in well with the other Judean kings. At the same time, another related riddle is solved: Azariah would have been 27 years old at the time his successor was born and not at the extraordinary age of 43.

Like many other issues of chronology, the synthesis of the chronological conundrum in 2Kgs 15–18 presented here requires a certain degree of conjecture and speculation. It should be understood, however, as an attempt to meet the first of Alfred Jepsen's two requirements for any chronological reconstruction; in elucidating the interaction of the numerical data and tracing their development, the tradition is respected – probably more so than by simply taking it as a point of departure, using only a suitable portion of the data and discarding the rest. This reconstruction now paves the way for tackling the second demand, i.e. the question of how this chronological concept might relate to the external data.

---

51 Recent treatments of the question were offered by Young, *Hezekiah*, 24–28, who argues that Ahaz was a brother of Jotham and by Heckl, "Hiskia," who has doubts about the chronological data provided in 2Kgs 16:2.
52 One such bulla was found in the Ophel Excavations, see Eilat Mazar, "A Seal Impression of King Hezekiah from the Ophel Excavations," in *The Ophel Excavations to the South of the Temple Mount 2009–2013: Final Reports, vol. I*, ed. Eilat Mazar (Jerusalem: Shoham, 2015): 629–40. Similar seal impressions had appeared earlier on the antiquities market and were published by: Nahman Avigad, *Hebrew Bullae from the Time of Jeremiah: Remnants of a Burnt Archive* (Jerusalem: Israel Exploration Society, 1986), no. 199; Robert Deutsch, "Lasting Impressions: New Bullae Reveal Egyptian Style Emblems on Judah's Royal Seals," *BAR* 28 (2002): 42–51, 60–62, and Frank Moore Cross, "King Hezekiah's Seal Bears Phoenician Imagery," *BAR* 25 (1999): 42–45, 60.

Steven L. McKenzie
The Last Days of Israel: Chronological Considerations

1 Introduction

This chapter surveys what I would consider the three main chronological problems in 2Kgs 15 and critiques solutions that have been offered for them. I have no solution of my own to offer except to suggest that the problems may be beyond complete resolution.[1]

The following table lists the kings of Israel from Jehu's revolt to the fall of the kingdom and their counterparts in Judah according to the Book of Kings. I begin with Jehu because his assassination of the kings of Israel and Judah marks a simultaneous starting point for the chronologies of the two kingdoms.[2] There are seven regnal accounts in 2Kgs 15: five kings of Israel (Zechariah, Shallum, Menahem, Pekahiah and Pekah) sandwiched by Uzziah and Jotham of Judah.

Israel	Judah
Jehu (2Kgs 10) – 28 yrs	Athaliah (2Kgs 11) – 7 yrs
Jehoahaz (2Kgs 13:1–9) – 17 yrs	Joash (2Kgs 12) – 40 yrs
Jehoash (2Kgs 13:10–13) – 16 yrs	Amaziah (2Kgs 14:1–20) – 29 yrs
Jeroboam II (2Kgs 14:22–29) – 41 yrs	Uzziah (Azariah) (2Kgs 14:21f; 15:1–7) – 52 yrs
Zechariah (2Kgs 15:8–12) – 6 mos	Jotham (2Kgs 15:32–38) – 16 yrs
Shallum (2Kgs 15:13–15) – 1 mo	Ahaz (2Kgs 16) – 16 yrs
Menahem (2Kgs 15:17–22) – 10 yrs	Hezekiah (2Kgs 18–20)

---

[1] I wish to thank to Shuichi Hasegawa for organizing this conference and for inviting me to take part in it. It was a pleasure for me to meet Kristin Weingart at this conference. Her intriguing paper, which is included in this volume, does offer a set of proposals, some of which are new. Since these are part of an ongoing project, "Gezählte Geschichte," that is not yet published and fully available for study and consideration, I offer no detailed critique here, though I do cite her paper, which she graciously provided to me, with some comments. My impression is that her work is a step forward with valuable insights about certain aspects of the chronological difficulties in 2Kgs 15–18, even though her overall solution is susceptible to some of the same criticisms as previous proposals.

[2] The joint starting point remains whether Jehu or the Aramaean author of the Tel Dan inscription was responsible for the assassinations. The *editio princeps* of the complete (reconstructed) inscription is Avraham Biran and Joseph Naveh, "The Tel Dan Inscription: A New Fragment," *IEJ* 45 (1995): 1–18. The controversies surrounding its interpretation are well beyond the scope of this paper.

Continued

Israel	Judah
Pekahiah (2Kgs 15:23–26) – 2 yrs	
Pekah (2Kgs 15:27–31) – 20 yrs	
Hoshea (2Kgs 17:1–4) – 9 yrs	

2 Chronological Discrepancies

The first problem is really a type or category of problems consisting of disagreements among the chronological data supplied in the chapter. These are significant disparities in numbers that go beyond minor discrepancies of a year or two that also exist but might be explained by differences in record keeping or the use of different calendars.[3] For instance, the reference in 15:1 to Azariah/Uzziah taking the throne of Judah in the twenty-seventh year of Jeroboam of Israel disagrees with the chronological references in 14:1–2, 17, 23, which indicate the fifteenth year of Jeroboam as that of Azariah's accession.

27th year of Jeroboam	15th year of Jeroboam
15:1: Azariah began to reign in 27th of Jeroboam	14:1–2: Amaziah (Azariah's father) accedes in 2nd (of 16) of Jehoash (Jeroboam's father) = Azariah's accession in 15th of Jeroboam 14:17: Amaziah lives 15 yrs after Jehoash's death = Azariah's accession in 15th of Jeroboam 14:23: Jeroboam accedes in 15th (of 29) of Amaziah = Azariah's accession in 15th of Jeroboam

---

3 The case of Menahem is particularly interesting in this regard. His accession is evidently dated to Azariah/ Uzziah's 39th year after Shallum's one-month reign (15:13–14). Azariah is credited with a 10-year reign in 15:17, but his succession by his son Pekahiah in Azariah's 50th year (15:23) indicates a reign of 11 years. Weingart, in her chapter in this volume, picks up on a suggestion by Gershon Galil, *The Chronology of the Kings of Israel & Judah* (Leiden: Brill, 1996), 62 that this reflects a change from ante- to postdating in Israel under the influence of Assyrian practice, which distinguished the accession year from the first regnal year following the New Year. She strengthens the suggestion with the observation that the formulae for kings before Menahem reflect antedating while those after him reflect postdating. But there are complications that make the suggestion inconclusive: (1) Galil actually argues that the change began already with Joash. (2) The records for quite a number of kings before Menahem are incomplete so that the regular practice of antedating for them is largely supposition. (3) Menahem was not the first Israelite king to be an Assyrian vassal, so it is not clear why a change in reckoning should have begun during his reign.

Similarly, 15:8, 13, 17 agree with each other in dating Zechariah's accession to Uzziah's thirty-eighth year, but they are at odds with 14:17, 23, which indicate that Zechariah acceded in Uzziah's twenty-sixth year (since Uzziah acceded in the fifteenth of Jeroboam's forty-one years).

38th year of Uzziah	26th year of Uzziah
15:8: In the 38th of Azariah, Zechariah became king (reigns 6 months)	14:17, 23: Uzziah's accession in Jeroboam's 15th (of 41) means Zechariah (Jeroboam's successor) accedes in Uzziah's 26th
15:13: Shallum accedes in Uzziah's 39th (reigns one month)	
15:17: Menahem accedes in Uzziah's 39th	

Such discrepancies are not peculiar to 2Kgs 15 but are relatively common in Kings, especially when the different textual witnesses are taken into consideration. A popular way of dealing with them has been to posit a combination of changing systems of record keeping along with coregencies. This approach is identified especially with Edwin R. Thiele and his book *The Mysterious Numbers of the Hebrew Kings*.[4] The approach is methodologically problematic because it cannot be proven false and because its application is often arbitrary. There is, moreover, a subtle agenda that drives its popularity: to show that the Bible's figures are all accurate; they are just based on different sources.

In the initial volume of the Harvard Semitic Monographs published in 1968, James Shenkel's *Chronology and Recensional Development in the Greek Text of Kings* offered a different solution — a text critical one. Shenkel argued against Thiele's approach that the MT's numbers were a systematic revision of the primitive and more consistent chronology preserved in the Old Greek (OG).[5] Shenkel's explanation has been adopted over the past five decades by such eminent text critics as Adrian Schenker and Julio Trebolle. Very recent research, however, has called this explanation into question on text-critical grounds. In an article published in the Trebolle Festschrift (2012) Ron Hendel argued that the OG re-

---

[4] Edwin R. Thiele, *The Mysterious Numbers of the Hebrew Kings* (Grand Rapids MI: Kregel, 1983; rev. edition).
[5] James Shenkel, *Chronology and Recensional Development in the Greek Text of Kings* (Cambridge MA: Harvard University Press, 1968).

vised the MT chronology rather than the other way around.[6] Hendel explains how in 1Kgs 16 the MT and OG construe the starting point of Omri's reign differently. The difference becomes clear in 16:29, where the MT dates Ahab's accession to the thirty-eighth year of Asa of Judah, while the OG dates it to the second year of Asa's son, Jehoshaphat, a difference of five years. The reason for this difference is that the MT construes the beginning of Omri's twelve-year reign from the point in 16:21 when half of the people followed Omri and half Tibni. This was, according to 16:15, the twenty-seventh year of Asa of Judah. The OG, on the other hand, dates Omri's reign from the point after Tibni had died, which was the thirty-first year of Asa. The OG's phrase *after Tibni* at the end of v. 22 makes its dating clear. Hendel contends that the MT's construal of v. 23 was idiosyncratic and therefore a kind of *lectio difficilior*. It is, therefore, more likely to have been altered by the OG's more "literal" construal than the other way around. That literal interpretation in turn led to (hyper)correction of the chronology in the OG in a manner typical of Second-Temple scribal hermeneutics.

I would add an argument in support of Hendel's case based on 2Kgs 8:16.[7] The chart in Fig. 1 illustrates the discussion that follows.

The OG is not extant here, but based on the foregoing figures in the OG chronology, it would have had Jehoram of Judah taking the throne in the second year of Ahaziah of Israel and reigning eleven years.[8] Since Ahaziah's reign spans the end of Jehoshaphat's and the beginning of Jehoram's in the OG, the proper place for the account of Jehoram's reign according to the OG chronology would have been immediately before the beginning of Israelite Joram's, i.e., between 2Kgs 1:17 and 1:18. Not coincidentally, this is where a single instance of OG chronology in MT is found, what Shenkel calls "a precious witness to the OG chronology in a Hebrew text."[9] The OG account of Jehoram was always in 2Kgs 8, where the MT has it, because of the occurrence of two historical presents—distinguishing features of the OG—in 8:22, 24, as Shenkel points out. This means that the OG placement and the OG numbers are at odds. The OG account of the reign of Jehoram is in the wrong place according to the "principles" of the composition of Kings. The

---

[6] Ron Hendel, "The Two Editions of the Royal Chronology in Kings," in *Textual Criticism and Dead Sea Scrolls Studies in Honour of Julio Trebolle Barrera*, ed. Andrés Piquer Otero and Pablo A. Torijano Morales (Leiden: Brill, 2012): 99–114.

[7] The argument is more fully developed in an article entitled "The Priority of the MT Chronology in Kings" that I have written for the forthcoming *Festschrift* for P. Kyle McCarter.

[8] So Shenkel, *Chronology*, 37–38, 68–82.

[9] Shenkel, *Chronology*, 74. The notice in the Lucianic witnesses at 1:17b in agreement with MT is hexaplaric and therefore the result of secondary adjustment.

MT		OG	
Israel	Judah	Israel	Judah
	Jehoshaphat (25 yrs) 1 Kgs 22:41-44		Jehoshaphat (25 yrs) 1 Kgs 16:28a-b
Ahaziah (17th of Jehoshaphat; reigned 2 yrs) 1 Kgs 22:52-54		Ahaziah (24th of Jehoshaphat; reigned 2 yrs) 1 Kgs 22:52-54	
			Jehoram (2nd of Ahaziah; reigned 11 yrs)
Joram (18th of Jehoshaphat; reigned 12 yrs) 2 Kgs 3:1-3		Joram (2nd of Jehoram; reigned 12 yrs) 2 Kgs 1:18a-d	
	Jehoram (5th of Joram; reigned 8 yrs) 2 Kgs 8:16-18		2 Kgs 8:16-18
	Ahaziah (12th of Joram; reigned 1 yr) 2 Kgs 8:25-27		Ahaziah (11th of Joram; 1 yr) 2 Kgs 8:25-27
Jehu (2 Kgs 9-10)	Jehu (2 Kgs 9-10)	Jehu (2 Kgs 9-10)	Jehu (2 Kgs 9-10)

Fig. 1: The differences between the OG and MT chronologies. Prepared by the author.

only way this could have happened is if the MT chronology was the older one. The OG introduced its revised figures into the MT's placement.

The systematic difference between the OG and MT chronologies is peculiar to the Omri dynasty and came to an end with Jehu's simultaneous slaughter of the kings of both Israel and Judah in 2Kgs 9. It therefore has no direct bearing on 2Kgs 15. Indirectly, however, this evidence shows that the MT chronology is primary. We must contend with the MT figures in 2Kgs 15 and cannot dismiss them as the result of scribal revision.

3 Regnal Totals

The totals for the kings of Israel and Judah are far apart for the period from the beginning of Azariah/Uzziah's reign to the fall of Samaria, as shown in the following table.

Judah	Israel
Azariah/Uzziah – 52	Jeroboam – 26[10]
Jotham – 16	Zechariah – 6 months
Ahaz – 16	Shallum – 1 month
Hezekiah – 6[11]	Menahem – 10
	Pekahiah – 2
	Pekah – 20
	Hoshea – 9
TOTAL: 90 years	TOTAL: 67 years, 7 months

Azariah's long reign and the administration of part of it by Jotham because of his father's skin disease (v 5) are unusual features of his account that have suggested a partial solution to this problem of the totals. Alfred Jepsen proposed that all of Jotham's reign and part of Ahaz's as well were included within Azariah's.[12] He pointed out the consistency in the ages of the kings of Judah at the births of their oldest sons as determined from the ages given for their successors when they ascended to the throne. The average age of Judahite kings at the time of the births of their oldest sons was twenty.[13] Jotham is reported to have been twenty-five years old when he became king (15:33). Assuming that his father Azariah was about twenty when Jotham was born, he would have been forty-five at Jotham's accession. Since Azariah himself became king at age 16 (2Kgs 15:2), Jotham's accession would have taken place in Azariah twenty-ninth regnal year. This was, following Jepsen, the year that Azariah became afflicted with skin disease and was removed to his quarantined residence (v 5).[14] The remaining twen-

---

[10] Numbered from the year of Uzziah's accession as calculated from 14:17, 23.

[11] The 84 years assigned to the reigns of Azariah, Jotham and Ahaz are too long for the allotted period, which covers 61–73 years. Figuring the start of Azariah's reign ca. 788 and the start of Hezekiah's reign in 727 = 61 years. If the beginning of Hezekiah's reign is dated to 715, the difference is 73 years. 2Kgs 18:10 dates the fall of Samaria to Hezekiah's sixth year (721 + 6 = 727). However, 18:13 dates the invasion of Sennacherib (701 BCE) to Hezekiah's 14th year, marking 715 as the start of his reign.

[12] Alfred Jepsen, "Zur Chronologie der Könige von Israel und Juda: Eine Überprüfung," in Untersuchungen zur israelitisch-jüdischen Chronologie, ed. A. Jepsen and R. Hanhart (Berlin: de Gruyter, 1964): 1–48.

[13] The exceptions are readily explained: Jepsen, "Zur Chronologie," 43.

[14] The exact sense of בבית החפשית is uncertain. The expression occurs in the HB only here and in variant form in the 2Chr 26:21 parallel. Because חפשי designates a person who is free from slavery (Exod 21:2, 5, 26, 27; Deut 15:12, 13, 18; Jer 34:9–11, 14, 16; Isa 58:6; Job 3:19) or exempt from taxes and conscription (1Sam 17:25), the present passage has been construed to mean that Azariah was exempted from kingly duties: Mordechai Cogan and Hayim Tadmor, *II Kings*

ty-three years attributed to his reign, then, included all of Jotham's sixteen years plus the first seven years of Ahaz's reign.

Jepsen's theory is attractive for its reduction of the total regnal years of the kings of Judah for the period from Azariah to the fall of Samaria from 90 to 67 years, which is very close to the total (68) for Israelite kings during the same period. However, there are some caveats. First, it is clear that this situation was atypical and should not be seen as a license for postulating coregencies throughout the history of the monarchy. Also, it may not be accurate to cast Jotham's *governing* (שפט) as "co-regency" since the text does not state that he was made king at this time and seems to avoid the root מלך. Thus, however the overlap between Uzziah and Jotham was understood by contemporaries, 2Kgs 15:7 construes their "reigns" as sequential, employing the regular succession formulae and indicating thereby that Jotham had an independent reign which began with the death of his father (v. 7).

Another serious problem is that despite the chronological assistance rendered by Jepsen's theory, sixty-seven years is still too large a total for the period, since the twenty years ascribed to Pekah must be reduced to six or seven, as we will see, yielding a total of fifty-four or fifty-five regnal years for Israel in this period. The total for Judah's kings must therefore be further reduced by a dozen years in order to correspond. This need for further reduction is the impetus behind appeals to additional coregencies, though the evidence for them is lacking. It seems more likely that one of the recorded numbers is erroneous. The suggestion to read *six* instead of *sixteen* in for the length of Jotham's reign (15:33) or of Ahaz's (16:2) may have merit.[15] While there is no textual evidence for the emendation, it is suspicious that both Jotham and Ahaz are credited with sixteen-year

---

(New York: Doubleday, 1988), 166 (citing Qimhi); James A. Montgomery, *A Critical and Exegetical Commentary on the Books of Kings* (Edinburgh: T&T Clark), 448. However, the occurrence of bṯḫptt in the Baal Cycle (Manfried Dietrich, Oswald Lorenz and José Sanmartín, *Die keilalphabetischen Texte aus Ugarit einschließlich der keilalphabetischen Texte außerhalb Ugarits, Teil 1: Transkription* [Kevelaer: Butzon & Bercker, 1976], no. 4 VIII 7–9) in the context of descent to the underworld (wrd. bṯḫptt.'arṣ // tspr.byrdm.'arṣ) suggests some other kind of meaning. My rendering tentatively follows Wilhelm Rudolph, "Ussias 'Haus der Freiheit,'" *ZAW* 89 (1977): 418–20, who suggests "house of freedom" as a euphemism actually meaning "house of no freedom" i.e., a place of isolation or quarantine. Unfortunately, he does not consider the Ugaritic evidence.

15 John Gray, *I & II Kings: A Commentary* (Philadelphia PA: Westminster, 1970; 2nd edition), 628–29 and Gwilym H. Jones, *1 and 2 Kings* (Grand Rapids MI: Eerdmans, 1984), 531 propose reading *6* for *16* in 15:33. Weingart in her chapter in this volume, following Claus Schedl "Textkritische Bemerkungen zu den Synchronismen der Könige von Israel und Juda," *VT* 12 (1962): 90–93, suggests it for Ahaz.

reigns. In that case, Uzziah's fifty-two years would have coincided with the reigns of Jotham and Ahaz and the first year of Hezekiah, yielding a total of fifty-seven years for the period. If we grant the possibility that Uzziah may have been eighteen when Jotham was born, this total is reduced to fifty-five, matching Israel's total.

It is obvious at this point, however, that the process has become quite speculative. Thus, while there seems to be something to Jepsen's theory, the further adjustments required to make it work remind us that it is still very much hypothetical.

4 Pekahiah (15:23 – 26) and Pekah (15:27 – 31)[16]

MT and G^B ascribe two years to Pekahiah's reign, while G^L reads *ten*. The numbers in 15:27, 32 accord with the two-year figure, but 17:1 (MT) assumes a ten-year reign for Pekahiah. Ten years is impossible according to the Assyrian evidence. The annals of Tiglath-pileser III (745 – 727 BCE) mention Menahem's payment of tribute in 738 BCE.[17] The annals and other inscriptions also note Tiglath-pileser's installation of Hoshea as king of Israel in 731/30 after the Assyrian campaigns against Pekah and Razon and the conquest of Damascus.[18] This leaves no

---

16 15:30b is secondary. It has Hoshea accede in the 20th year of Jotham and is in obvious contradiction of v. 33, where Jotham reigns 16 years. It reflects secondary calculation based on vv. 27, 32 where Pekah becomes king in the same year as Jotham though slightly before him. It is also absent from LXX[L], and is not a regular feature of conspiracy notices like the one in v 30a.
17 Hayim Tadmor and Shigeo Yamada, *The Royal Inscriptions of Tiglath-pileser III (744 – 727 BC), and Shalmaneser V (726 – 722 BC), Kings of Assyria* (Winona Lake IN: Eisenbrauns, 2011), nos. 14, 27, 32 and 35. The inscription from Iran (text 35) is undated. However, its list of tribute payers is apparently earlier, since it mentions Tubail (Itto-Baal) as king of Tyre instead of his successor, Hiram, who is mentioned in the annals (text 32 and reconstructed by Tadmor and Yamada in texts 14, 27). William H. Shea, "Menahem and Tiglath-pileser III," *JNES* 37 (1978): 43 – 49 and Nadav Na'aman, "Historical and Chronological Notes on the Kingdoms of Israel and Judah in the Eighth Century B.C.," *VT* 36 (1986): 81 date the Iran inscription to 740 BCE and correlate it with the notice of Menahem's payment in 2Kgs 15:19. Na'aman, "Historical and Chronological Notes," 82 argues further that Menahem made a second tribute payment in 738 and that this is the payment recorded in the annals. Shea, "Menahem," 49 denies that a second payment is necessary and thinks that Menahem's name was simply listed again as part of a general summary. But his argument does not adequately take into consideration the difference in genre between the annals and the non-annalistic text. The change in the name of the Tyrian king indicates the different settings of the two documents and nullifies the attempt of Thiele, *Mysterious Numbers*, 125 – 28 to date Menahem's payment early to 743 BCE.
18 See especially Na'aman, "Historical and Chronological Notes," 71 – 74.

more than nine years (738–730 inclusive) for the reigns of both Pekahiah and Pekah, where MT assigns twenty-two years, two for Pekahiah and twenty for Pekah. The main problem is the ascription of a twenty-year reign to Pekah.

Here several solutions have been proposed. Since the two names, Pekahiah and Pekah, are the same, the suggestion was made some time ago that they were historically identical.[19] If so, it would reduce the number of kings of Israel for this period and might help with the chronological problems by reducing the total number of regnal years required for the two kings. Nevertheless, there are cogent reasons for distinguishing them. First, the formula *lay with his ancestors* used for Menahem indicates royal succession.[20] That is, Pekahiah was Menahem's son, while Pekah has a distinct patronymic, Remaliah. Then there is the radical difference between the two kings embodied in the account of a *coup d'état* and assassination as well as the change of policy toward Assyria. Pekahiah might have altered his father's pro-Assyrian stance, but there would be no need to hide this by inventing another king with the same name and an overthrow. Finally, v. 25 raises the possibility that Pekah was from Gilead in Transjordan and hence had an entirely different origin from Pekahiah's. Apparently, therefore, the similarity of the names is coincidental or is to be explained in some other way.[21]

Among the other possibilities for explaining Pekah's inordinately long reign that have been put forward, the simplest is that the number *twenty* is a textual error.[22] This suggestion cannot be dismissed as easily as Na'aman would have it in view of the evidence for textual and chronological variation in Kings and especially in the present chapter.[23] Still, a clear understanding of how the error might have happened is necessary before this proposal can be fully convincing.[24]

---

19 Fritz Hommel, "Assyria," in *A Dictionary of the Bible*, vol. 1, ed. James Hastings (Edinburgh: T&T Clark, 1898): 186 argues that Pekahiah and Pekah were the same king who reigned only 2 years.
20 Matthew J. Suriano, *The Politics of Dead Kings* (Tübingen: Mohr Siebeck, 2010).
21 Dennis Olson, "Pekah," in *The Anchor Bible Dictionary*, vol. 5, ed. David Noel Freedman (New York: Doubleday, 1992): 214–15 suggests that it was a means for Pekah to claim legitimacy.
22 William Foxwell Albright, "The Chronology of the Divided Monarchy of Israel," *BASOR* 100 (1945): 21–22; William H. Barnes, *1–2 Kings* (Carol Stream IL: Tyndale House, 2012), 157. For additional scholars who adopt this position, see Na'aman, "Historical and Chronological Notes," 75, n. 9.
23 Na'aman, "Historical and Chronological Notes," 75.
24 The reading of *ten* (עשר) instead of *twenty* (עשרים) proposed by Gray, *Kings*, 64–65 and Martin Rehm, *Das zweite Buch der Könige* (Würzburg: Echter, 1982), 150 does not help because it is still more than the time allotted by the Assyrian evidence for Pekah's reign. The suggestion of Georg Hentschel, *2. Könige* (Würzburg: Echter, 1985), 71 that 16 years were added to Pekah's

Perhaps the most widely accepted explanation assumes the genuineness of the twenty-year reading and argues that it includes years spent by Pekah as the ruler of a rival kingdom in Transjordan beginning with the accession of Menahem, if not the end of Jeroboam II's reign.[25] Scholars who favor this view find allusions to the division in Kings and the Prophets.[26] But there is no clear reference in Kings to this division as there was for the factions of Zimri, Tibni, and Omri (1Kgs 16). A more serious problem is the reference in v. 25 to Pekah as Pekahiah's šālîš. It is hard to believe that Pekah would have served as the adjutant for two kings (Menahem and Pekahiah) while he was head of a rival kingdom. One pair of commentators even suggests that Pekahiah tried to solve the problem of Pekah's rivalry by giving him the rulership of Gilead.[27] Galil recognizes the problem and surmises that Pekah was an official appointed by Jeroboam II over Gilead and that the twenty years of his regnal tenure are calculated from that appointment.[28]

Two other proposals are similar to the rival kingdom theory.[29] One holds that Pekah considered himself the legitimate heir of the Jehu dynasty and therefore counted his regnal years from the end of Zechariah's or even Jeroboam II's reign, ignoring the reigns of Menahem and Pekahiah.[30] Alternatively, an early

---

4-year reign in an effort to accommodate the 16 years attributed to Jotham of Judah after it was forgotten that Jotham's years were incorporated within his father's (following Jepsen's theory) is ingenious but unprovable and unfalsifiable.

25 This view was conceived by Carl Lederer, *Die biblische Zeitrechnung vom Auszuge aus Ägypten bis zum Beginne der babylonischen Gefangenschaft* (Erlangen: Kleeberger, 1888), 135–38, developed by H. J. Cook, "Pekah," *VT* 14 (1964): 121–35, and advanced by Thiele, *Mysterious Numbers*, 129–32. Cf. James Maxwell Miller and John H. Hayes, *A History of Ancient Israel and Judah* (Louisville KY / London: Westminster John Knox, 2006; 2nd edition), 370–72.

26 Miller and Hayes, *History*, 371–2 appeal to the statement in 15:37 that Pekah with Razon had begun harassing Judah already in the reign of Jotham, when Pekah would not yet have been on the throne in Samaria. The observation is astute, but as they go on to point out, the organization of the material in Kings is often more theological than chronological. Pierre Buis, *Le Livre des Rois* (Paris: Librairie Lecoffre, 1997), 244–45 finds an allusion to the divided North in the reference to Manasseh devouring Ephraim and vice-versa in Isa 9:19–20. It is not clear, though, that the intertribal strife alluded to in this passage entails a separate Transjordan kingdom.

27 Richard D. Patterson and Hermann J. Austel, "1, 2 Kings," *The Expositor's Bible Commentary*, vol. 3 (Grand Rapids MI: Zondervan, 2005; revised edition): 887. They actually refer to Pekahiah "bringing Pekah into a position of prominence," but in context this must mean the rule over Gilead.

28 Galil, *Chronology*, 65–66.

29 Na'aman, "Historical and Chronological Notes," 76–80.

30 W. J. Chapman, "The Problem of Inconsequent Post-Dating in II Kings XV. 13, 17, and 23," *HUCA* 2 (1925): 59.

chronographer who considered Menahem and Pekahiah as usurpers counted back from the beginning of Pekah's reign to the end of the Jehu dynasty and attributed the intervening years to Pekah. Na'aman finds support for these theories in the supposition that both Jehu and Pekah, along with Elijah and Elisha, were from Gilead and that they all reflect a Gileadite strain of opposition to the Omrides and then to Menahem and Pekahiah as interlopers. The theory is ingenious and may be on to something in its perception of Gileadite roots behind these characters. But again there are questions. Elijah and Elisha are not always portrayed as opponents of the king. There is also no indication in Kings that Pekah was related to the Jehuids or had any grounds for being considered the legitimate heir of that dynasty. In short, the reason for the attribution of twenty years to Pekah's reign remains obscure. Fortunately, it does not seriously affect reconstruction of the overall chronology, but only because it is clear from non-biblical evidence that we are dealing with a period of at most nine years (738–731/30) rather than the twenty-two years that Kings ascribes to Pekahiah's and Pekah's reigns.

To conclude, there is no clear solution for these chronological problems in 2Kgs 15. While there were no doubt isolated scribal errors, these problems go beyond text-critical solutions. There may have been genuine sources containing historical data behind the regnal formulae in 2Kgs 15,[31] but they were either badly corrupted or badly misunderstood by author of Kings. Full restoration appears to be an impossibility. The explanations for Uzziah's extraordinarily long reign and for the reigns of Pekahiah and Pekah, for all the advantages they offer, are essentially scholarly conjectures. The main point of relevance for the topic of this conference is that chronological data preserved in 2Kgs 15, the densest collection of reports about the kings of the "last days of Israel," are essentially unusable for historical reconstruction.

---

31 See Weingart's chapter in this volume, which proposes that the chronological data in 2Kgs 15–18 are based on a list of regnal years and synchronistic accession years of Israelite kings and a set of regnal years for Judahite kings.

Part VI: **Working with the Book of Kings: the Narrative**

Christian Frevel
Wicked Usurpers and the Doom of Samaria
Further Views on the Angle of 2 Kings 15–17

1 Preliminary Remarks on the Credibility of Details in Historiography

In this paper I will argue that the chaotic portrayal of the last days of the kingdom of Israel follows the Judean bias more than it accurately reflects the course of historical events in the second half of the eighth century BCE. While some of the information is historically correct, the general impression is that the biblical description is intended to smear the northern state and its legitimacy. Accordingly, the general tendency in portraying the Northern Kingdom is to emphasize the coups in the last 25 years in Samaria. The usual assumption, that the greater part of information – particularly that given in 2Kgs 15 – is drawn from Samarian annals,[1] is misleading. This assumption is based on the principle that the biblical record is an accurate representation of history, rather than being largely invented. The biblical text is assumed to be correct unless strong arguments speak against it. This *a priori* assumption, that derives from credibility assessments of testimonies in legal proceedings, has to be questioned in many respects when it comes to historiography. Even detailed information can be invented. However, this does not necessarily mean that details indicate only the fictive inventiveness of authors. In this aspect, one has to agree with William G. Dever's statement that details have to be "left in the realm of possibility, unless they appear so fantastic that they lack any credibility."[2] But one has to bear in mind that not everything that is possible is probable, and not everything that is credible is factual.

This chapter was language-edited by Denise Bolton (Munich).

[1] See, e.g., Antoon Schoors, *The Kingdoms of Israel and Judah in the Eighth and Seventh Centuries B.C.E.* (Atlanta GA: Society of Biblical Literature, 2013), 12: "The accounts of these usurpations and other events must have been taken from some source, most likely the aforementioned annals (15:10, 14, 16, 19–20, 25, 29–30)."
[2] William G. Dever, *Beyond the Texts: An Archaeological Portrait of Ancient Israel and Judah* (Atlanta GA: Society of Biblical Literature, 2017), 366.

However, the opposite *a priori* assumption, that gives credibility to the extrabiblical accounts, is just as bad. Hence it is necessary to discuss aspects of historicity, literary composition, and tendencies of presentation ("Darstellungstendenzen") alike. The aim of this discussion is not to prove the biblical account right or wrong, but rather to evaluate its probability and accuracy. I use the portrayal of the last kings of Israel in 2Kgs 15 as a test case and I will demonstrate the account's bias.

While most of the studies have engaged in the trouble of dating and chronology, fewer studies have taken a closer look at the biblical representation of the eighth century BCE in 2Kgs 15, which is highly biased. The chapter mentions seven kings of Israel in total, including the last king of the Nimshide dynasty Zechariah, who is followed by the reigns of Shallum, Menahem, Pekahiah, Pekah, and finally the last king Hoshea. In focusing on the reported revolts, the present paper will not so much engage in chronological issues. This is not only due to the fact that the chronology is dealt with masterfully in this volume by Kristin Weingart and Stephen L. McKenzie; it is also on methodological account, because I have sincere doubts that we can fix the biblical chronology in the Book of Kings in exact figures. The following overview does not intend to settle the chronological issues under debate,[3] but is meant to provide a rough framework for the events discussed:

King's name	Length of reign according to the Bible	Assumed historical framework
Zechariah	6 months	747 BCE
Shallum	1 month	747–743 BCE
Menahem	10 years	747–738 BCE
Pekahiah	2 years	737–736 BCE
Pekah	20 years	735–733/2 BCE
Hoshea	9 years (following 2Kgs 18:10)	732–723 BCE

The lengthy presentation of the decline of the Northern Kingdom consists of 24 verses comprising almost 15 years up to the reign of the last king Hoshea. On the one hand, apart from the great reflection chapters and the narratives in the Book of Kings, no other period is characterized so extensively in historiographical respect. On the other hand, the historical information given in the annalistic script is scarce: no particular background of the four revolts is given, and the Assyrians are mentioned only twice, first in the reign of Menahem, and then in the reign of Pekah. The substantial loss of territory in 733/32 BCE in the 13th

---

3 Cf. Christian Frevel, *Geschichte Israels* (Stuttgart: Kohlhammer, 2016), 161–63.

and 14th *palû*, both named as *a-na* ᴷᵁᴿ*Di-maš-qa*,⁴ is related in almost only one sentence in 2Kgs 15:29.

The verse lists the Assyrian king Tiglath-pileser capturing cities in the north: Ijon, Abel-beth-maacah, Janoah, Kedesh, Hazor, Gilead, and Galilee. The biblical list concludes with "all the land of Naphtali" and a note on the mass deportation of people to Assyria (ויגלם אשורה). Although the report of the 12th *palû* is missing in the Kalḫu Annals, the Assyrian sources give some information on the 12th *palû* (*a-na* ᴷᵁᴿ*Pi-liš-ti* "against [the Land of] Philistia") and the 13th *palû* (*a-na* ᴷᵁᴿ*Di-maš-qa* "against [the land of] Damascus") and the subjugation of these lands. However, more detailed information on the annexation of the northern territory is completely missing.⁵ No further information is given on the political status of Samaria after the campaigns of Tiglath-Pileser III, let alone the status of the province after the conquest of Samaria.

Some peculiarities accompany the portrayal of the kings.⁶ While it holds true that the burial of the northern king is not generally part of the annalistic framework,⁷ the burial is mentioned with Baasha (1Kgs 16:6), Omri (1Kgs 16:28), Ahab (1Kgs 22:37), Jehu (2Kgs 10:35), Jehoahaz (2Kgs 13:9), Joash (2Kgs 13:13), and (if we accept the originality of the Antiochene text, which attests και εταφη εν Σαμαρεια)⁸ for Jeroboam II in 4Kgdms 14:29 – he is the last king bur-

---

4 For a proposed ordering of the campaigns see Peter Dubovský, "Tiglath-pileser III's Campaigns in 734–732 B.C.: Historical Background of Isa 7; 2 Kgs 15–16 and 2 Chr 27–28," *Bib* 87 (2006): 153–70, esp. 157–61; Hayim Tadmor, *The Inscriptions of Tiglath-pileser III, King of Assyria: Critical Edition with Introductions, Translations and Commentary* (Jerusalem: The Israel Academy of Sciences and Humanities, 1994), 232–82.
5 For the Assyrian point of view see the textual evidence assembled in Tadmor, *Inscriptions*, 27–215; and Manfred Weippert, *Historisches Textbuch zum Alten Testament* (Göttingen: Vandenhoeck & Ruprecht, 2010); further Kyle Lawson Younger Jr., "The Summary Inscription 9–10 (2.117F)," in *The Context of Scripture*, vol. 2: *Monumental Inscriptions from the Biblical World*, ed. William W. Hallo and Kyle Lawson Younger Jr. (Leiden: Brill, 2000): 291–92. For a quick overview see William W. Hallo's Introduction in Hallo and Younger, *The Context of Scripture*, vol. 2, xxi–xxvi; Heather D. Baker, "Tiglath-pileser III," in *RlA* 13, ed. Michael P. Streck (2014): 22; Hayim Tadmor and Shigeo Yamada, *The Royal Inscriptions of Tiglath-pileser III (744–727 BC) and Shalmaneser V (726–722 BC), Kings of Assyria* (Winona Lake IN: Eisenbrauns, 2011), 2–18, 232–37.
6 Note further the formula of the "sin of Jeroboam" (2Kgs 15:9, 24 לא סר מחטאות ירבעם, 2Kgs 15:18 לא סר מעל חטאות ירבעם, 2Kgs 15:28 לא סר מן־חטאות ירבעם; the evaluation formula can be found with Zechariah, Menahem, Pekaiah, Pekah. It is lacking with Shallum and Hoshea (in 2Kgs 17).
7 Notes on the burial are missing for Jeroboam, Nadab, Elah, Simri, Ahaziah, Joram, Jeroboam II (MT), and all following kings.
8 Natalio Fernandez Marcos and José Ramón Busto Saiz, *El Texto Antioqueno De la Biblia Griega II: 1–2 Reyes* (Madrid: C.S.I.C, 1992), 125.

ied in Samaria. Any further notice of burial is missing, particularly for the last kings of Israel. This already underlines that the composition of 2Kgs 15 is special. The murdered kings do not "pass away" and are not even buried. For Menahem, the only king who had a *legal* successor with his son Pekahiah, the pass-away-formula is used וישכב מנחם עם־אבתיו (2Kgs 15:22) but no burial is mentioned. Besides the evaluation formula, which is lacking for Shallum and emendated for the reign of Hoshea, it is the formulaic expression of the regicide, which is strikingly similar with all four revolts (Shallum, Menahem, Pekah, Hoshea), including the phrase קשר על (lacking with Menahem), נכה, and the following phrase וימיתהו וימלך תחתיו.[9]

Shallum v. 10	וַיִּקְשֹׁר עָלָיו שַׁלֻּם בֶּן־יָבֵשׁ וַיַּכֵּהוּ קָבָל־עָם וַיְמִיתֵהוּ וַיִּמְלֹךְ תַּחְתָּיו׃
Menahem v. 14b	וַיַּךְ אֶת־שַׁלּוּם בֶּן־יָבֵישׁ בְּשֹׁמְרוֹן וַיְמִיתֵהוּ וַיִּמְלֹךְ תַּחְתָּיו׃
Pekah v. 25	וַיִּקְשֹׁר עָלָיו פֶּקַח בֶּן־רְמַלְיָהוּ שָׁלִישׁוֹ וַיַּכֵּהוּ בְשֹׁמְרוֹן [...] וַיְמִיתֵהוּ וַיִּמְלֹךְ תַּחְתָּיו׃
Hoshea v. 30a	וַיִּקְשָׁר־קֶשֶׁר הוֹשֵׁעַ בֶּן־אֵלָה עַל־פֶּקַח בֶּן־רְמַלְיָהוּ וַיַּכֵּהוּ וַיְמִיתֵהוּ וַיִּמְלֹךְ תַּחְתָּיו

Table 1: The four revolts in 2Kgs 15

The verb קשר "to bind (together)" in the G-stem is the technical term used for conspiracies, particularly for military coups. Significantly, it is used in an intensifying compound with the noun קשר for Hoshea. The verb is also employed for Baasha (1Kgs 15:27); Zimri (1Kgs 16:9, 20); Jehu (2Kgs 9:14; 10:9); Shallum (2Kgs 15:10, 15); and the rebellions *against* Athaliah, Joash, Amaziah, and Amon (2Kgs 11:19; 12:20; 14:19; 21:23–24).

In the following I will try to evaluate the upheavals and regicides in the context of the portrayal of the northern monarchy 1Kgs 12–2Kgs 17.

2 The General Assessment of the North as Unstable Entity

The designation of the Northern Kingdom as unstable is deliberate. Of the 20 kings (including the unlucky Tibni, who – following 1Kgs 16:22 – was displaced allegedly without reigning as king) one half are irregular or illegitimate successors (Jeroboam I, Baasha, Zimri, Tibni, Omri, Jehu, Shallum, Menahem,

---

9 For the formula see also Peter Dubovský, "Why Did the Northern Kingdom Fall According to 2 Kings 15?," *Bib* 95:3 (2014): 321–46.

Pekah, Hoshea).¹⁰ This is in stark contrast to the supposed continuity of the Davidic dynasty in Jerusalem. The lengthy reign of Ahaz, who survived almost four Israelite kings, clearly underlines the contrast between stability and volatility. The historic background of this characteristic on both sides is difficult to evaluate in particular. While former studies in the history of kingdoms took the continuity of the Davidic kingdom for granted and the vicissitude of the Israelite monarchy as a historical characteristic of this political entity,¹¹ one has to be more cautious. I have argued elsewhere that the uninterrupted continuity of the Davidic dynasty is a Judean construct, at least before King Ahaz in Jerusalem.¹² As regards the northern monarchy, we have indications that the Omrides (Omri, Ahab, Ahaziah, and Jehoram) and the Nimshides (Jehu, Jehoahaz, Joash, Jeroboam II, and Zechariah) formed dynasties which reigned continuously over 50 or even 100 years.

All northern kings are portrayed as villains, and the Deuteronomists do not judge even a single ruler positively, making the assumption untenable that regicide was in fact the norm for the succession of power. Particularly if read against the background of the economic and political success of the Northern Kingdom, one cannot take the volatility as described in the biblical accounts as an evaluative starting point. On the other hand, the most successful periods under the reign of the Omrides and Nimshides are portrayed as dynastically more stable, so the biblical descriptions may have some foundation in historical fact. But strikingly, upheavals and regicides increase in the last 25 years of the kingdom of Samaria, a fact that was emphasized by Peter Dubovský as part of the Deuteronomistic reasoning regarding Samaria's demise: "the biblical text points to the first cause of the downfall of Samaria."¹³ Although the present paper has profited very much from Dubovský's sophisticated analysis, the suggestion that 2Kgs 15 not only "washes dirty laundry" but gives an implicit cause for the fall of Samaria in historical respect calls for some critique. His paper aims to understand the "dynamics latent in the society of the Northern

---

10 Based on various arguments, Peter Dubovský counts seven revolts during that time in the north. He sees the number as deliberate "in order to convey the idea of completeness": Dubovský, "Northern Kingdom," 325. Although this is a tempting argument, I doubt that the number of actual revolts was reduced in order to reach the number seven. I see, in particular, the exclusion of Omri as problematic, see below.
11 The impression is emphasized if the instability is compared against the long reigns of Azariah and Ahaz.
12 Frevel, *Geschichte Israels*, 178, 228.
13 Dubovský, "Northern Kingdom," 326.

Kingdom, which ... led to its fall,"[14] which is at the end itself a kind of a Deuteronomistic approach by taking the instability of the Northerners for granted. But isn't northern instability as a general feature and a 'birth defect' more rhetorically true than it is factually true? The "sin of Jeroboam" that drives the critique in the biblical portrayal of northern history is an invention of tradition rather than it is historically grounded. The term "invention of tradition" that Eric Hobsbawm introduced into the historian's vocabulary denotes supposed facts that evolve to mythic power in forming "history." These "facts" can be demonstrated as being projected backwards if not invented at all.[15] Recent evaluations of the "sin of Jeroboam" point exactly in that direction.[16] I have argued elsewhere that Jeroboam I's reign is, in fact, an invention to install a damaged eponym and to mark the birth of the Northern Kingdom as corrupted (see further below). Thus one should not build historiography on this highly colored portrayal to reconstruct deep historical structures. Moreover, had the *coups d'état* actually "ravaged the Northern Kingdom" as Dubovský is ready to assume? Assessed from the archaeological evidence this evaluation remains doubtful. While Dubovský can be praised for his detailed discussion, his blending of literary and historical analyses is open to some methodological critique. However, although being more skeptical, I agree with Dubovský in attempting to get somewhat behind the rhetoric of 2Kgs 15.

My approach to 2Kgs 15 is firstly to evaluate the literary design of the presentation and not to buy into its bias too quickly. And if historical information is lacking from the extra-biblical accounts, it should not be added from the Deuteronomistic narrative. 1Kgs 15–17 forms an unfavorable framework to the history of Samaria/Israel and does not aim to be a proper historical account. However, although most of the defamatory information is suspicious, there are actually no *strong* indications to question the biblical data for Israel in principle. Only some information can be proved more or less wrong by extra-biblical sources.

---

14 Dubovský, "Northern Kingdom," 321.
15 See Eric J. Hobsbawm, "Introduction: Inventing Traditions," in *The Invention of Tradition*, ed. Eric J. Hobsbawm and Terence O. Ranger (Cambridge: Cambridge University Press, 1983), 1–14.
16 See Frevel, *Geschichte Israels*, 148–51, 231; Angelika Berlejung, "Twisting Traditions: Programmatic Absence-Theology for the Northern Kingdom in I Kgs 12:26–33* (the 'Sin of Jeroboam')," *JNSL* 35 (2009): 1–42.

3 Destroyers, Subversive Forces, and Revolutions: The North as a Chaotic Entity

While it is not possible to go into every detail in this essay, I will now take a closer look at the portrayal of the northern state. I will briefly address each of the ten non-dynastic, irregular rulers of the Northern Kingdom with a short comment. This is to demonstrate the general tendency to devalue and denounce the North, on the one hand, and to highlight certain characteristics in the particular portrayals on the other hand. My thesis is that the portrayal of Israel as an unstable entity which is shaped by a chain of revolts is, more or less, invented; it is fabrication rather than fact.

3.1 Jeroboam I

From its very beginning in 1Kgs 11–14, the history of the North is already problematic. When does it become reliable? If we accept that, with regard to historicity, there was no United Monarchy (in the sense of a state that covered both the territory of Judah and Samaria, or an even larger territory that included the Negev, Shephelah, the Mediterranean coast, the hill country of Ephraim and Gilboa, and even Galilee, Bashan, and Gilead[17]) then there was no division of "kingdoms" at all. The struggle between Jeroboam I and Rehoboam over the succession to Solomon's throne, the opposition between the northern and southern tribes, and the historical reconstruction of a division of kingdoms are myth rather than history.[18] We cannot go into a detailed analysis here, but there are ample reasons to consider the biblical reconstruction in 1Kgs 11–14 as *invented tradition:* the double justification of the division in 1Kgs 11–12; the forced labor of Solomon; the election scene in Shechem; the establishment of Bethel and Dan as state sanctuaries; the resemblance between Jeroboam I (the dynastic founder) and Jeroboam II; and the Judean bias evident in the name-play of the "People's Contender" [Jeroboam: √ריב] and the "People's Expander" [Rehoboam: √רחב][19]

---

17 See Frevel, *Geschichte Israels*, 103–48.
18 See Frevel, *Geschichte Israels*, 148–65; id., "Disrupted or conjoined? A new proposal regarding the division of kingdoms in the history of Israel" (delivered at IOSOT Stellenbosch 2016, to be published 2018); id., "Ben Hadad I and his alleged campaign to the North in 1 Kings 15:17–20" (delivered at SBL Boston 2017, to be published 2018).
19 I am grateful to Jonathan Robker for this translation of my German pun "Volksweiter und Volksstreiter".

etc. Many arguments point in the direction that 1Kgs 11:26–14:30 is a literary account with only a few historic details, if there are any at all. With regard to a historical reconstruction of events, the first revolt by the people of Israel is neither directed against a Jerusalemite prerogative nor is the origin of Israel as an independent monarchy related to a *coup d'état*. In contrast to 1Kgs 11:26, Jeroboam I did not raise his hand against Solomon (וירם יד במלך) because of the corvée in Jerusalem, and he did not tear apart the northern tribes from the south. By *inventing* an upheaval that initiated the Northern Kingdom it became sinful from the moment of its foundation, even if Solomon is blamed (later?) for his misdoings (particularly for his mixed marriages and religious deviance). In sum: to build a history of the northern state based on the account in 1Kgs 11–14 is "skating on thin ice". From the historical side we cannot say anything safe about Jeroboam I, if he existed at all.

3.2 Baasha

Although presenting some details, the information about Baasha's reign is not very consistent. It is noted in formulaic manner that there was war between Asa and Baasha throughout his reign (1Kgs 15:16, and the repetition of the phrase in 1Kgs 15:32), and that he built Ramah to hinder Asa going north. Asa himself should have bribed the Arameans to push back Baasha. When Baasha was threatened by the Arameans, he withdrew from Ramah and built Tirzah (ויחדל מבנות את־הרמה וישב בתרצה, 1Kgs 15:21). Subsequently, Asa built Geba with the stones of Ramah (1Kgs 15:22). Although several places named Ramah are mentioned in the OT (Josh 13:26; 19:8, 29, 36 etc.), only the Ramah in Benjamin (Josh 18:25; Neh 11:33), *er-Rām* (today *al-Ram*, coord. OIG 1721.1402),[20] about five miles north of Jerusalem, can be taken into account for identification. Accordingly, the previously-mentioned Geba can be identified with *Ğeba* (coord. OIG 1749.1405), whereas Tirzah is *Tell el-Fārʿah* in the North (coord. OIG 1823.1882). The archaeological record cannot decide issues, but it is striking that neither Ramah, nor Geba, nor Tirzah show traces of building activities which can be attributed to Asa or Baasha. All these places show evidence of later building activities, mostly in the Iron IIB, if anything.

---

[20] Localizations are given following the map reference points of the so-called Palestine Grid 1923 (= OIG, "Old Israel Grid"). Add 500 to the latitude and 5000 to the longitude to receive the Israeli Transverse Mercator coordinates 1994 (= NIG, "New Israel Grid").

That the portrayal of Baasha's reign is drawn from literary sources rather than from historical records is further corroborated by the other information in 1Kgs 15. The text in 1Kgs 15 presents Baasha as an Aramean *protégé*, or at least as under Aramean influence (1Kgs 15:19), but neither his nor Asa's affiliation with Ben-Hadad (who is actually not found in the extra-biblical record at all) has left traces outside of the Bible. To make a long story short, many reasons suggest that this very Ben-Hadad and his influence on Israel is *invented*, as is the eponym of Aram by biblical scribes.[21]

Because the Aramean king Ben-Hadad defeated Israel following a bribe sent by Asa, the pressure on Judah should have stopped. 1Kgs 15:20 mentions the Aramean conquest of Ijon/*Tell ed-Dibbin* (coord. OIG 2052.3054), Dan/*Tell el-Qāḍī* (coord. OIG 2112.2948), Abel-bet-maacha/*Tell Ābil el-Qamḥ* (coord. OIG 2045.2962), the whole sea region of Kinneret, and the entire land of Naphtali. With many others, I have argued elsewhere that this does not reflect the situation in the early ninth century, but rather in the second half of the ninth century under the Aramean Hazael or even – since 1Kgs 15:20 is drawn from 2Kgs 15:29 – in the eighth century under Tiglath-pileser III.[22] This is supported by the archaeological record, which cannot be unfolded here.

Coming to Baasha's *coup d'etat*, we have to acknowledge the combination of standardized wording and supposed detailed information: Baasha started a revolution against Jeroboam's son Nadab (ויקשר עליו בעשא) and killed him at Gibbethon (ויכהו בעשא בגבתון, 1Kgs 15:27). After becoming king, he struck down all the offspring of the house of Jeroboam (הכה את־כל־בית ירבעם, 1Kgs 15:29). Further information is given on Baasha's ancestry. While his father's name בן־אחיה is inconspicuous (1Kgs 21:22; 2Kgs 9:9), the Hebrew לבית יששכר (1Kgs 15:27) is odd; it points to a place named Beth-Issachar, or a family named Issachar, rather than to the region of the tribe in the north. Strikingly, except for Ezra 2:36// Neh 7:39 the construction PN+לבית+PN is not used elsewhere. This may be the reason why the Vaticanus has ἐπὶ τὸν οἶκον Βελααν instead of לבית יששכר. The Antiochene text, in contrast, gives evidence for the variant ἐπὶ τὸν οἶκον Βεδδαμα τοῦ Ἰσσαχαρ. Whether this has to be taken as the oldest variant does not have to be decided here. Be that as it may, the additional information prevents the reader from identifying Baasha's father with the prophet Ahijah the Shilonite (1Kgs 11:29–30; 12:15; 14:2, 4). There has been much discussion on the specifica-

---

21 See the lengthy arguments in Frevel, "Ben Hadad I."
22 See Frevel, *Geschichte Israels*, 195; id., "Ben Hadad I"; Angelika Berlejung, "Nachbarn, Verwandte, Feinde und Gefährten: die 'Aramäer' im Alten Testament," in *The Arameans, Chaldeans, and Arabs in Babylonia and Palestine in the First Millennium B.C.*, ed. Angelika Berlejung and Michael P. Streck (Wiesbaden: Harrassowitz, 2013), 72–73.

tion that Baasha slayed Nadab in *Gibbethon* while the king of Israel besieged the city, which is said to be "Philistine" (אשר לפלשתים). This expression is attested only once more in 1Kgs 16:15, suggesting that the siege of Nadab was not successful at all. The narrative gives the impression that Baasha was part of Nadab's army and that he usurped the throne. After gaining power, as happens later with Jehu (2Kgs 10:11) and particularly Zimri (1Kgs 16:12), he killed all members of the house of Nadab (1Kgs 15:27). Gibbethon, the Assyrian Gabbutunu, is located in the vicinity of Gezer, either identified with *Tell el-Melat/Tell Mālāt* (coord. OIG 1374.1405) or less probably *Ras Abū Ḥamīd* (coord. OIG 1398.1456).[23] Strikingly, a siege of Gibbethon is mentioned on the eve of Omri's coup in 1Kgs 16:15. Omri and the people of Israel besieged Gibbethon while Zimri slayed Elah, the son of Baasha. When Omri heard about this he broke off the siege of Gibbethon and besieged Tirzah instead (1Kgs 16:17). The two notes on Gibbethon are part of a Deuteronomistic retribution-scheme, and are obviously related to each other. At least one, if not both of the notes was created for the purpose of correspondence. While it is not, in principle, impossible that in the face of changing Philistine power (including the decline of Ekron as the leading Philistine city) there were military struggles between "the Philistines" and Nadab in Gibbethon[24] (which was perhaps controlling the trade routes to the coast) it is not very likely. 1Kgs 15:27 mentions that Nadab laid siege to Gibbethon with the whole of Israel (וכל־ישראל צרים על־גבתון). The motif resembles the pointed participation of the people in Omri's revolt, where it makes perfect sense in legitimizing Omri. In 1Kgs 15:27 it is a borrowed motif.

The information on Baasha's illegitimate accession to the throne is now crisscrossed by the concluding comment about Baasha in 1Kgs 15:33, which is placed after the doublet of the war-note in v. 32. Whether Baasha conspired to overthrow Nadab (1Kgs 15:27–28) in Gibbethon or whether he accessed the throne more or less legitimately in 1Kgs 15:33 is open for discussion (and a fascinating topic), which cannot be unfolded here. But the composition as a whole

---

[23] The localization follows Stefan Timm, "Die territoriale Ausdehnung des Staates Israel zur Zeit der Omriden," *ZDPV* 96 (1980): 35; Ed Noort, *Die Seevölker in Palästina* (Kampen: Kok Pharos, 1994), 41; For Ras Abū Ḥamīd/Humeid see Steven M. Ortiz, "Gibbethon," in *Eerdmans Dictionary of the Bible*, ed. David Noel Freedman (Grand Rapids: Eerdmans, 2000): 500–501; Volkmar Fritz, "Das erste Buch der Könige," in *Zürcher Bibelkommentar: Altes Testament* 10:1 (Zürich: TVZ, 1996): 155; Manfred Görg, "Gibbeton," in *Neues Bibellexikon* 1, ed. Manfred Görg and Bernhard Lang (Düsseldorf: Patmos Verlag, 2001): 859; John L. Peterson, "Gibbethon (Place name)," in *Anchor Bible Dictionary*, ed. David Noel Freedman (New York: Doubleday, 1992): 1006–1007.
[24] Carl S. Ehrlich, *Philistines in Transition: a History from ca. 1000–730 BCE* (Leiden: Brill, 1996), 66–68.

casts doubt on Baasha's *coup d'état*. I support Šanda's astute view, that the whole chapter of 1Kgs 15 is more formulaic than it is historic: "Das ganze Kapitel ist eine Verquickung von Formeln des R, deuteronomistischen Phrasen und an wenigen Stellen auch von Worten der alten Quellen. Es ist ein Werk des R."[25] In sum, the revolt of Baasha – at least in its portrayal in 1Kgs 15 – is drawn from other biblical sources.

3.3 Zimri-Tibni-Omri

We will also not engage in speculation about the Omri-Tibni-Zimri entanglement here, although the alliteration of names is as suspicious as the rival kingdom of Tibni (1Kgs 16:21) is enigmatic. All names appear to be hypocoristic forms of Yahwistic names. While Zimri ("My praise is Yah") and Omri ("My life is Yah") are positive nominal-sentence-names, Tibni can be read, in parallel to Omri, as a mocking name denoting either "scarecrow" (from תבן "straw, chaff" with allusion to עמר "bind sheaves, clamp of ears") or "copy, piece" (from בנה or תבנית "to build"; "likeness, copy").[26] The legitimation of the military officer Omri by the people as an opponent to Zimri, who staged a revolt against the alcoholic Elah, makes Omri, on the one hand, a hero. On the other hand, Omri's takeover seems plausible,[27] if Zimri's act was judged a villainous regicide by the people. 1Kgs 16:9 classifies Zimri's act as a coup by using the phrase ויקשר עליו. Already this note introduces the opposition between Zimri and Omri, since both are army officers. While Zimri is a commander of half the king's chariots (1Kgs 16:9), Omri is a commander of the army (1Kgs 16:16). The subtle ironic difference makes sense because Omri overpowers Zimri. King Elah, the son of Baasha, is denounced as unable to lead Israel, because he drinks alcohol excessively in Tirzah (והוא בתרצה שתה שכור, 1Kgs 16:9) in the house of Arzah, the senior official of the palace. This ironic description proves him incompetent to govern, not only in the moment, but during the entire two years of his reign. Zimri then kills all the members of the royal family and of the reigning party in Tirzah (1Kgs 16:11).

---

25 Albert Šanda, *Die Bücher der Könige* (Münster: Aschendorf, 1911), 395.
26 See Martin Noth, *Die israelitischen Personennamen im Rahmen der gemeinsemitischen Namengebung* (Hildesheim: Olms, 1966), 232.
27 Dubovský, *Northern Kingdom*, 323 sees "several reasons to conclude that the ancient scribes did not classify it as a *coup d'état*", which makes the evaluation difficult from a historical standpoint. The parallel to the Jehu coup is obvious. Both have the same angle of evaluation, so that I tend to go with the first part of Dubovský's quote that "Omri's ascension to the throne bears several signs of a *coup d'état*" (323).

This is emphasized with the formulaic משתין בקיר "every male" (lit. "anyone, who is pissing at the wall") which is used in the context of regicide (1Sam 25:22, 34; 1Kgs 14:10; 21:21; 2Kgs 9:8). The extermination is emphasized with the phrase "any kinsmen and any friend" (וגאליו ורעהו) which is unique in this context. However, to attribute the end of the house of Baasha to Zimri, a monarch of only seven days, is to relieve Omri from regicide, and such a notion would most likely have originated in annals from the North. Omri battles in Gibbethon against the Philistines (see above) and is thus presented as "defender" of Israel. Even the Deuteronomistic fulfillment of the prophecy of the prophet Jehu (1Kgs 16:1–4, 12–13) makes the Zimri episode suspicious. His reign of seven days, as well as his suicide in Tirzah is construed.

The rival kingdom of Tibni has no reason to exist and sounds strange. It deliberately gets no regnal evaluation formula, and yet it might still have been historical. However, the reference to Tibni emphasizes the *basso continuo* of the chaos, disorientation, and ungovernability of the North.

3.4 Jehu

While there was no doubt about the account of Jehu's act of regicide, which launched the Nimshide dynasty (2Kgs 9–10), the discovery of an extra-biblical orthostat with an Aramaic inscription from Tel Dan in 1993 changed the situation completely.[28] In the most probable reconstruction, the author of the inscription (most likely the Aramean king Hazael) claims to have murdered both the Israelite king "Jehoram" and the King of the house of David "Ahaziahu." In contrast to Hazael's claim, the Bible ascribes the murder of these two kings (supposedly both Omrides[29] waging war together in Ramoth-Gilead against the Arameans) to Jehu, who usurped the throne of Joram and established his own dynasty (henceforth the Jehuite Dynasty) in the kingdom of Israel. Following 2Kgs 9:24–27, Jehu is the one who eliminated the last Omrides in Samaria and in Jer-

---

28 Shuichi Hasegawa, "The Historiographical Background for Jehu's Claim as the Murderer of Joram and Ahaziah," *AJBI* 37 (2011): 5–17; Frevel, *Geschichte Israels*, 110. The inscription was published by Avraham Biran and Joseph Naveh, "An Aramaic Stele Fragment from Tel Dan," *IEJ* 43 (1993): 81–98; id., "The Tel Dan Inscription: a New Fragment," *IEJ* 45 (2015): 1–18. The most recent discussion of the find context is Merja Alanne, *Tel Dan. An Archaeological and Biblical Study of the City of Dan from the Iron Age II to the Hellenistic Period* (PhD thesis, University of Helsinki, 2017).
29 For this assumption see Frevel, *Geschichte Israels*, 159.

usalem.³⁰ Many attempts have been made to reconcile the Aramaic inscription with the Bible. However, they mostly evince a harmonizing tendency or the effort to maintain the Bible's truth.³¹

Who was, then, the "real" murderer of Joram and Ahaziah? There is an ongoing discussion about whether the Aramean king Hazael is the mastermind behind the *coup d'état*, and whether he installed Jehu as Aramean vassal king in Samaria (and Joash in Jerusalem) after the victory over Israel and the killing of these kings.³² The issue becomes complicated if one compares the Assyrian sources that mention the tribute of Jehu, the man of *Bit-Ḫumri*, being paid to Shalmaneser III in his eighth regal year 841 BCE.³³ This would seem to exclude the possibility that he was an Aramean vassal. On the one hand, this may demonstrate that the Assyrians saw in Jehu a continuation of the Omride dynasty. On the other hand, the tribute shows clearly that Jehu was not an Aramean puppet at that time. We do not know much about the first years of Jehu's reign and how he behaved in foreign affairs after he gained power. It is still possible that Jehu was installed as an Aramean agent or vassal by Hazael (who killed Joram by himself or with his army) or that the Jehu coup was integrated immediately in the Aramean foreign policy strategy which failed under pressure from Shalmaneser III. However, this remains mere speculation. Following the general tendency of denouncing the North in the biblical record, and considering the character of the story in 2Kgs 9–10, stylizing this as an *intra*-Israelite development is perhaps too easy. Following Edward Lipiński, 2Kgs 8:28 may also give a clue for Hazael as the real wrong-doer.³⁴ Although the Tel Dan inscription cannot decide issues, it casts doubt on the portrayal of a Nimshide *coup d'état* as a military putsch which is parallel to the other revolts described in the Book of Kings.

---

30 For the killing of Athaliah as part of the Jehu coup see Frevel, *Geschichte Israels*, 159–62.
31 See Hasegawa, "Background," 9.
32 See positively e.g. William M. Schniedewind, "Tel Dan Stela: New Light on Aramaic and Jehu's Revolt," *BASOR* 302 (1996): 85; in contrast: Nadav Na'aman, "The Story of Jehu's Rebellion: Hazael's Inscription and the Biblical Narrative," *IEJ* 56 (2006): 162–63; id., "Three Notes of the Aramaic Inscription from Tel Dan," *IEJ* 50 (2000): 102–103. For discussion see Frevel, *Geschichte Israels*, 216; Jonathan Miles Robker, *The Jehu Revolution: A Royal Tradition of the Northern Kingdom and Its Ramifications* (Berlin: De Gruyter 2012), 219–24.
33 In addition to the Black Obelisk (2.113F) see also the Annals: Calah Bulls (2.113C), Marble Slab (2.113D), Kurba'il Statue (2.113E), cf. Hallo and Younger, *The Context of Scripture*, vol. 2, 267–70. For tribute in general see Jürgen Bär, *Der assyrische Tribut und seine Darstellung: Eine Untersuchung zur imperialen Ideologie im neuassyrischen Reich* (Neukirchen-Vluyn: Neukirchener Verlag, 1996).
34 Edward Lipiński, *The Aramaeans: Their Ancient History, Culture, Religion* (Leuven: Peeters, 2000), 379–80.

Jehu's accession definitely remains illegitimate, but it may not be evaluated as a sign of intrinsic instability in the Northern Kingdom.

3.5 Shallum

With Shallum's *coup d'etat* in 2Kgs 15:10 we enter the "last days of the kings of Israel." This revolt against Zechariah, the last member of the Jehuite dynasty and the son of Jeroboam II, who reigned for only six months (2Kgs 15:8), is also difficult to evaluate from a historiographic perspective. On the one hand, it is plausible that the royal succession after the successful reign of Jeroboam II may have been accompanied by turmoil and crisis. One would expect nothing else in turbulent times and under the shadow of growing pressure from the Assyrians like Tiglath-pileser III who ascended the throne in 745 BCE. Hence, the short reigns of Shallum and Menahem are reasonable in general. On the other hand, some issues of chronology and geography within these accounts cast doubt on the integrity of the Deuteronomistic report. In 2Kgs 15:10 we find the same phraseology as in the revolts before: ויקשר עליו שלם בן־יבש ויכהו קבל־עם וימיתהו וימלך תחתיו, "Shallum the son of Jabesh conspired against him, and struck him down at Ibleam, and killed him, and reigned in his stead." The peculiarities start with the name or origin of the king. Although the name is followed by a patronym (בן־), the name of his father can also be read as an indication of provenance. All other attestations of יבש/Ιαβις are related to the city in Transjordan albeit usually followed by גלעד. Miller and Hayes suggest a metathesis and take the Ephraimite town Jasib (*Yāsūf*, coord. OIG 1726.1865) as the hometown of Shallum[35] (although none of the ancient versions attest such a metathesis). The city of Jabesh in Transjordan can be identified with either *Tell Abū Charaz* (coord. OIG 2061.2007) or *Tell el-Maqlūb* (coord. OIG: 2144.2011).[36] Taking into account the biblical characterization (Judg 21:9–14; 1Sam 11:1–10; 31:11) it is a special place, from which separatist ambitions in critical situations are quite probable. Replacing the father's name with the city Jabesh would then parallel, in a way, the revolt of Shallum with the coup of Pekah, who is said to be accompanied by "fifty men of the Gileadites" (2Kgs 15:25). That there was turmoil in the important

---

[35] James Maxwell Miller and John H. Hayes, *A History of Ancient Israel and Judah* (Louisville: Westminster John Knox Press, 2006; 2nd edition), 376.

[36] For discussion see Erasmus Gass, "Jabesch," in *Das Wissenschaftliche Bibellexikon im Internet (www.wibilex.de)*, 2010 (https://www.bibelwissenschaft.de/stichwort/21995/, last access: 01/12/2017) and, on Tell el-Maqlūb, Volkmar Fritz, "Das zweite Buch der Könige," in *Zürcher Bibelkommentar. Altes Testament* 10:2 (Zürich: TVZ, 1998): 84–85.

transregional zone of Gilead, under Aramean control since the days of Jehu (2Kgs 10:32) and most probably under pressure as transition zone in the eighth century BCE (cf. 2Kgs 15:29), is quite imaginable. However, these textual and historical speculations cannot be based on further details.

Following the Masoretic Text, Shallum batters Zechariah קבל־עם, which is peculiar and transliterated in the Septuagint as καὶ Κεβλααμ. This text treats Keblaam as a companion. Keblaam is described in the Syrian text as 'his father' conspiring with Shallum.[37] The odd phrase קבל־עם is often translated "before the people" thus signifying the revolt and murder as a public affair. However, the phrase קבל־עם would have been used only here in this way and one has to stick to a late Aramaic adverb קבל "before" to make sense of it. Instead, the Antiochene text reads ἐν Ἰεβλαάμ ("in Ibleam")[38] and is probably older than the MT. Thus, the emendation of the text in Ibleam is one option that removes one oddity and uncovers another one. The site Ibleam is located in the direct neighborhood of Jenin/En Ganin (Ḫirbet Bel'ame, coord. OIG 1777.2058[39]) between Dothan and Jezreel. What makes this solution easy to dismiss is the fact that Ibleam at the ascent of Gur (במעלה־גור אשר את־יבלעם, 2Kgs 9:27) is the place where Jehu is said to have slain Ahaziah.[40] From a literary perspective, the Nimshide reign is framed by murder and "revenge" in Ibleam, which absolutely makes sense in the composition of Kings (see 2Kgs 15:12: "This was the promise of the LORD that he gave to Jehu, 'Your sons shall sit on the throne of Israel to the fourth generation.' And so it happened."). Again, the composition suggests that these regicides are not only understood as "historical" facts but also as a structural device.

3.6 Menahem

According to the biblical chronology Menahem usurped the throne after Shallum had reigned for only one month. In contrast to Shallum, who was from Transjordan, Menahem's origin is attributed to Tirzah, the former residence of the kings of Israel, which has to be located in *Tell el-Fār'ah* (North) (coord. OIG 1823.1882).

---

37 This is all the more evident when the order is reversed and the verbs are in plural, see the list of manuscripts in Dubovský, "Northern Kingdom," 327. This seems more or less due to the misreading of ιεβλααμ.
38 Marcos and Saiz, *Texto Antioqueno*, 126.
39 See Fritz, *Das zweite Buch der Könige*, 84.
40 For the itinerary see Shuichi Hasegawa, *Aram and Israel during the Jehuite Dynasty* (Berlin: De Gruyter, 2012), 32–33, 148–49.

Tirzah is the place where Omri started his revolution with a siege (1Kgs 16:17)[41] and Baasha, Elah, and Zimri resided (1Kgs 15:21, 33; 16:6, 8, 15, 23).[42] The only attestation we have to Menahems coup is the biblical text. The phrasing of this passage is slightly different compared to similar accounts: ויעל מנחם בן־גדי מתרצה ויבא שמרון ויך את־שלום בן־יביש בשמרון וימיתהו וימלך תחתיו, Menahem the son of Gadi came up from Tirzah and came to Samaria, and he struck down Shallum the son of Jabesh in Samaria and slew him, and reigned in his stead." (2Kgs 15:14) Besides the absence of the catch-phrase ויקשר עליו the order of notes is striking. Verse 15 presents the evaluation formula of Shallum referring back to his conspiracy in a formulaic expression which is almost identical to 1Kgs 16:20 and the conspiracy of Zimri. Verse 16 then inserts an אז sentence with regard to Menahem *before* the introductory synchronism of his reign. This important "information" introduces Menahem with incredible brutality without specifying, when "at that time" was. It may have been before, during, or after his revolution.

Whether Menahem was part of the royal family of the Nimshides or a member of the old Manassite elite in Tirzah (cf. Gaddi as representative of the Manassite tribe in Num 13:11) or perhaps even coming from Transjordan ("the Gadite"), is open for discussion.[43] If the latter is the case and בן־גדי has to be interpreted as a clan name (cf. 2Sam 23:36) or indicates the region (1Sam 13:7 ארץ גד; 24:5),[44] the origin of Menahem becomes parallel to the origin of Shallum from Jabesh (see above). This descent from Gilead is perhaps deliberately related. If so, it is also most relevant that his son was killed by 50 men from Gilead (2Kgs 15:25). Gilead in northern Transjordan is presented as a region in turmoil (perhaps following its eventful history as part of the northern state in the ninth and eighth century BCE). It may reflect a pro-Assyrian position arguing that

---

41 Note that this also fits the above-mentioned framing idea of Ibleam for the Nimshides and is supported further by the parallel of 1Kgs 16:20 with 2Kgs 15:15. One gets the impression that incidents and locations are put nicely together to emphasize divine providence.

42 For the "Tirzah polity" as a first cluster of power see Frevel, *Geschichte Israels*, 154; for a more biblically based portrait of Tirzah see Israel Finkelstein, *The Forgotten Kingdom: the Archaeology and History of Northern Israel* (Atlanta GA: Society of Biblical Literature, 2013), 66. For the archaeological record see also the overview of id., "Tell El-Far'ah (Tirzah) and the early days of the Northern Kingdom," *RB* 119 (2012): 331–46, focusing on Iron I and IIB while not discussing the Iron IIBC stratum VIIe.

43 Mordechai Cogan and Hayim Tadmor, *II Kings: a New Translation with Introduction and Commentary* (New Haven CT: Yale University Press, 1988), 171.

44 This is quite possible even if the conception of twelve tribes with Gad in Transjordan is mostly post-exilic.

only in subservience to Assur can a political connection between "the Gilead" and Israel be perpetuated.

If בן־גדי is not meant to link Shallum and Menahem, or does not reflect Transjordanian political background realities, Gad is the father's name,[45] and Menahem probably has a connection to Tirzah. One may speculate that Menahem is a partisan of the former Samarian elite who retired to the old regnal quarter in Tirzah when Shallum defeated the Nimshides and killed members of the royal house. It makes a lot of sense that the Samarian elite was superseded by the Shallum party, and may thus have fled to the old regnal quarter in Tirzah, about 8.5 miles east of Samaria, to organize a counter-revolution.

Dubovský points to the palace building 148 in Stratum VIId and to three patrician houses (no. 327, 328, 710) as possible evidence "that just before the collapse of Samaria the city of Tirzah reappeared as a new rival on the Israelite political scene."[46] He argues that Tirzah was destroyed by fire during the reign of Omri and that this forced him to move the capital to Samaria. Tirzah then "disappears ... from the biblical account, only to reappear again in the account of Menahem's usurpation."[47] In attributing Stratum VIId to the last days of the kingdom of Israel, Dubovský follows Alain Chambon. Since the significant prosperity of Stratum VIIb already postdates the move of the capital to Samaria by the Omrides in the ninth century, this prosperous phase may have been ended by Hazael.[48] After a short abandonment, Tirzah was rebuilt in Stratum VIIc which has to be taken together more or less with Stratum VIId. Stratum VIId then "consists of a large palatial complex in the north, medium-size domestic units in the center and smaller houses in the south. This architectural sequence seems to represent a three-tier hierarchy of citizens: a ruling class, wealthy families, and poorer families."[49] The pottery of Stratum VIIc and VIId "represents an

---

45 For the element Gad in personal names see Nahman Avigad and Banjamin Sass, *Corpus of West-Semitic Stamp Seals* (Jerusalem: Israel Academy of Sciences and Humanities, 1997), 491.
46 Dubovský, "Northern Kingdom," 332.
47 Peter Dubovský, "Menahem's Reign before the Assyrian Invasion (2 Kings 15:14–16)," in *Literature as Politics. Politics as Literature: Essays on the Ancient Near East in Honor of Peter Machinist*, ed. David S. Vanderhooft and Abraham Winitzer (Winona Lake IN: Eisenbrauns, 2013): 36.
48 See Finkelstein, "Tell El-Far'ah," 334. The attribution of the destruction level to Omri has produced various theories of rivalry between Samaria and Tirzah. See e.g. Bob Becking, "Menachem's Massacre of Tiphsat: At the Crossroads of Grammar and Memory (2 Kings 15,16)," in *History, Memory, Hebrew Scriptures: A Festschrift for Ehud Ben Zvi*, ed. Ian D. Wilson and Diana V. Edelman (Winona Lake IN: Eisenbrauns, 2015): 20.
49 Ze'ev Herzog and Lily Singer-Avitz, "Sub-Dividing the Iron Age IIA in Northern Israel: A Suggested Solution to the Chronological Debate," *TA* 33:2 (2006): 163–95, 175

8th-century assemblage"⁵⁰ parallel to Megiddo IVA which dates to the end of the eighth century.⁵¹ Israel Finkelstein has recently put *Tell el-Fārʿah* Stratum VIId in the very short period between 740/30–20.⁵² The eighth century heyday is parallel to other cities in the North. However, to attribute these structures to Menahem's agency and to imagine "tensions between Samaria and Tirzah since Tirzah became a military base for a new revolt"⁵³ is elaborate and remains mostly theoretical.

A further detail is noted in 2Kgs 15:16: "At that time Menahem sacked Tiphsah, all who were in it and its territory from Tirzah on; because they did not open it to him, he sacked it. He ripped open all the pregnant women in it." There are grammatical and exegetical problems with this verse, which have already been discussed at length by Bob Becking and Peter Dubovský. Let me briefly expound on four issues:

a) The preposition מן

One of the many problems of 2Kgs 15:16 is the understanding of the מן in מתרצה, which is usually translated to mean that Tirzah was the base from which Menahem sacked Tappuah or Tiphsah ("from Tirzah on"). If the מתרצה, which immediately follows the description of the first נכה-action and its three את-objects, is meant locally "from Tirzah" then one would expect a subsequent עד ("from Tirzah to …"). As an alternative to this understanding Dubovský suggested either to read the מתרצה as a declaration of Menahem's origin (thus doubling the מתרצה in v. 14) or as "from Tirzah" meaning that Menahem "attacked …, (the one who was) from Tirzah."⁵⁴ While admitting "insurmountable syntactical difficulties"⁵⁵ with the latter proposal, it can be ruled out. For the first interpretation, there is no need to mention the Menahem's origin again. Bob Becking added two further readings of מן, namely a causal "because of Tirzah" and a comparative "more than Tirzah."⁵⁶ Both remain problematic because they presume a context that

---

50 Herzog and Singer-Avitz, "Sub-Dividing", 176.
51 Lily Singer-Avitz, "The Pottery of Megiddo Strata III–II and a Proposed Subdivision of the Iron IIC Period in Northern Israel," *BASOR* 372 (2014): 123, 134.
52 Finkelstein, *Forgotten Kingdom*, 69.
53 Dubovský, "Menahem," 38. For the rivalry between Samaria and Tirzah see already fn. 49 and below.
54 Dubovský, "Menahem," 32.
55 Dubovský, "Menahem," 33.
56 Becking, "Menachem," 20.

is not mentioned in the text. They shall elliptically refer back to what had been done to Tirzah, that is Omri's siege on the city and the suicide of Zimri (1Kgs 16:18). For Becking, this is a counterstrike against the memory of a defeated group in the Northern Kingdom. However, the brutality of this event and its place in the collective memory as rivalry between Tirzah and Samaria remains only a guess (see below). 2Kgs 15:16 is not a "revenge for Omri's deeds and doings."[57] In sum, I agree with Dubovský that the only possible reading is the locational one: that Menahem is going out from Tirzah. Thus it becomes all the more important to understand the relation of Tirzah and Tiphsah (see c).

b) Menahem, the ripper

The atrocious act of ripping up pregnant women aims at razing out a population, since women in childbirth and offspring are killed alike. It is attested in biblical passages (2Kgs 8:12; Hos 14:1; Amos 1:13, cf. Isa 13:16, 18; Hos 10:14) and rarely in extra-biblical sources.[58] This is expressed by the use of the double verbs נכה and בקע (which are combined only in this verse). In biblical texts this cruel war crime occurs rarely. Amos 1:13 accuses Ammon of having ripped up pregnant women in Gilead to enlarge their territory (הרחיב את־גבולם). If Tiphsah could be attributed to Transjordan, Menahem (the Gadite?) could have been taking revenge for this Ammonite cruelty. But the location is almost excluded (see below c). The other two instances of ripping pregnant women in the Bible relate to the Arameans. In 2Kgs 8:12, Elisha weeps and prophesies that Hazael will dash little ones and rip the pregnant women of Israel. This corresponds to Hos 14:1. If we take Tiphsah at face value and locate it in Syria then it may be the north-eastern edge of the Aramean empire which is addressed here. Menahem then may take revenge for the Aramean cruelty committed by Hazael (2Kgs 8:12). But this implicit connection is also very elaborate.

In v. 15 the double נכה is striking. While the first clearly has Menahem as the subject, the second, in the כי-sentence, remains grammatically obscure. It has no object and no clear subject. The subject could be Menahem, but also the same

---

57 Becking, "Menachem," 20.
58 See Mordechai Cogan, "'Ripping Open Pregnant Women' in the Light of an Assyrian Analogue," *Journal of the Ancient Near Eastern Society* 103 (1983): 755–56; Peter Dubovský, "Ripping Open Pregnant Arab Women: Reliefs in Room L of Ashurbanipal's North Palace," *Or* 78 (2009): 394–419.

subject as in כי לא פתח.⁵⁹ Strikingly most translations change the subject with the narrative ויד. But if this is not the case, the subject of בקע "he ripped" opens up and does not necessarily have to be Menaham. If the subject of פתח is *not* the city as it is usually assumed to be, but should be read as "he did not open" (a masculine singular referring to a person), Hazael comes to mind, particularly on the literary level (2Kgs 8:12). Although it is the last and only other passage in the Book of Kings which uses also the verb בקע with הרה this might be too far-fetched. If the atrocious act by Menahem is not considered to be revenge, the solution may perhaps be found in the obscurity of "Tiphsah"?

c) Tiphsah

Tiphsah is mentioned only once more in 1Kgs 5:4 (Engl. 1Kgs 4:24) as the northern frontier of the Solomonic empire. It is usually identified with a city Tapsake/ Θαψακος or Θαψα, *latin:* Thapsa[cus], close to Carchemish at the river Euphrates, an important caravanserai identified either with *Qal'at el-Dibse* or *Qal'at Naǧm:*⁶⁰ "Tifsach war eine wichtige Karawanenstation am Eufrat, die in pers. Zeit wohl auch einen bedeutenden Grenzübergang von der transeufratischen in die zwischenstromländische Satrapie markierte."⁶¹ The siege of a city on the western shore of the Euphrates-knee seems very unlikely for Menahem. In acknowledging the "too far away location", the ancient versions read Θερσα Tirzah (LXX 2⁰ B A L⁺), θαιρα (A⁺), or ταφωε (L⁺) Tappuah.⁶² With the emendation of the text Menahem's crime comes closer to the core territory of the state of Israel. Tir-

---

59 Although the LXX has a plural ἤνοιξαν, the subject is *not necessarily* the city of Θερσα (or Tiphsah), as Bob Becking assumed. However, the city is the most probable subject even in the Hebrew text, because the suffixes of גבוליה (τὰ ἐν αὐτῇ καὶ τὰ ὅρια αὐτῆς) and ההרותיהrefer to Tiphsah.
60 See Wolfgang Röllig, "Thapsacus," in *Brill's New Pauly*, ed. Hubert Cancik and Helmuth Schneider (http://dx.doi.org/10.1163/1574-9347_bnp_e1206490, last access 21/12/2017).
61 Othmar Keel, Max Küchler and Christoph Uehlinger, *Orte und Landschaften der Bibel*, vol. 1: *Geographisch-geschichtliche Landeskunde* (Göttingen: Vandenhoeck and Ruprecht, 1984), 234. For an update to the archaeology of Carchemish see Nicolò Marchetti, "The 2014 joint Turco-Italian Excavations at Karkemish," *Kazi Sonuçlari Toplantisi* 37 (2016): 363–80 and id., "The Cultic District of Karkemish in the Lower Town," in *L'Archeologia del Sacro e L'Archeologie del Culto: Sabratha, Ebla, Ardea, Lanuvio*, ed. Paolo Matthiae (Rome: Bardi Edizioni, 2016), 373–414.
62 For the various traditions see Dubovský, *Menahem's Reign*, 31–32; for the Greek manuscripts see Alan England Brooke, Norman McLean and Henry St. John Thackeray, ed., *The Old Testament in Greek, According to the Text of Codex Vaticanus, Supplemented from Other Uncial Manuscripts, with a Critical Apparatus Containing the Variants of the Chief Ancient Authorities for the Text of the Septuagint* (Cambridge: Cambridge University Press, 2010).

zah does not make sense, because Menahem came originally from Tirzah and would have destroyed "his hometown" or the city where his action took its outcome (this may be the reason why Rahlfs reads Θαρσιλα). The Antiochene text Ταφώε is the Tappuah that is often favored in commentaries.[63] Tappuah has to be identified with Tell aš-Šēḫ/Abū Zarad, located about 20 km south of Tirzah[64] at the border between Ephraim and Manasse (Josh 17:8). At first glance this makes more sense if the given rationale כי לא פתח ("because he did not open") can be understood as a resistance against a reign of Menahem in the south. Whether there was a greater anti-Assyrian sentiment in the southern part of the land, or supporters of Shallum mounted an opposition against Menahem remains very speculative. Miller and Hayes suggested that Tappuah is very close to a village named Jashib (Yāsūf, coord. OIG 1726.1865) in Ephraim, which could be misread from Jabesh, the hometown of Shallum (see above). But why Tappuah if the revenge is actually directed against Jashib? Maybe there is another possibility to take Tiphsah metaphorically as will be elaborated in the next paragraph.

d) Why this brutality?

Does the reference mirror a struggle by the Israelite state for sovereignty in times of hardship? We come back to Bob Becking's idea that it may be "an act of revenge for Omri's deeds and doings" referring "back to the memory of a defeated group within the Northern Kingdom, which we rejected above"[65]. This may point in the right direction, but Zimri's suicide and Omri's cruelty are, in my understanding, already too far away in time to form the background to this reference. It is rather the revolt of Shallum and the end of the Nimshide dynasty that can be read as the background to Menahem's cruelty. If Menahem was not a member of the Nimshide dynastic family, he may nevertheless have been part of the elite.

---

63 Karl Elliger, "Studien aus dem Deutschen Evangelischen Institut für Altertumswissenschaften in Jerusalem, 42: Die Grenze zwischen Ephraim und Manasse," *Zeitschrift des Deutschen Palästina-Vereins* 53 (1930): 265–309, 292–93. See also Schoors, *Kingdoms of Israel and Judah*, 13; Jürgen Werlitz, *Die Bücher der Könige* (Stuttgart: Katholisches Bibelwerk, 2002), 265. For the Antiochene text see Marcos and Saiz, *Texto Antioqueno*, 126.
64 For the identification with Tell aš-Šēḫ/Abū Zarad (coord. OIG 1719.1679) see Siegfried Mittmann, ed., *Tübinger Bibelatlas* (Stuttgart: Deutsche Bibelgesellschaft, 2000). For the identification with Kirbet Beit Farr (A) (coord. OIG 1848.1831) see Adam Zertal, *The Eastern Valleys and the Fringes of the Desert*, vol. 2: *The Manasseh Hill Country Survey* (Leiden: Brill, 2007), 112, 443–44.
65 Becking, "Menachem," 20.

That he was *already* a king by the grace of the Assyrian ruler (see below) is not very likely, if we rely upon the established chronological framework. Tiglath-pileser III had not subdued Samaria in neither 743 nor 738 BCE.[66] According to the biblical chronology Menahem's revolt took place around 748 BCE when the Assyrian presence under Aššur-nerari V was non-existent in the Southern Levant. Menahem was certainly an Assyrian vassal and paid tribute to Pul only by 738 BCE.[67] Pul is the throne name of Tiglath-pileser (assyr. Tukulti-apil-Ešarra) after he ascended to the Babylonian throne in 729 BCE. Thus, naming Tiglath-pileser III Pul is most probably an anachronism, which attests to an editorial bias as the text was being produced.[68]

However, when and how Menahem became king is open for discussion. The "chronological conundrum" (Kristin Weingart; this volume) calls for caution as not only the dates of Pekah's reign are wrong. The common date of 738 BCE for the tribute as well as the ten-year duration of his reign are by no means clear.[69] Hayim Tadmor has argued that the tribute in 738 BCE was perhaps not the only tribute Menahem paid, and that the acknowledgment for the duration of his reign mentioned in 2Kgs 15:19 "was paid in 740 or even earlier"[70]. If so, the amount mentioned in the biblical text becomes also questionable in its relation to the "second" tribute in 738 BCE. The tribute mentioned in 2Kgs 15:19 is extraordinarily high but may not have been exaggerated, since 1000 talents of silver are also mentioned in the Summary Inscription 4: 18′ as the tribute of Hoshea, who was installed by the Assyrians.[71] Following Nadav Na'aman, the very high amount "fits the context of a heavy tribute paid by a newly installed

---

66 See Oswald Loretz and Walter Mayer, "Pūlu – Tiglatpileser III. und Menahem von Israel nach assyrischen Quellen und 2 Kön 15,19.20," *UF* 22 (1990): 226–27.
67 The tribute of Miniḫimme of Samerina (ᵐMi-ni-hi-im-⌈me⌉ ᴷᵁᴿSa-⌈me⌉-ri-i-na-a-⌈a⌉) is listed twice in the Calah Annals 13*: 10 and in the Iran-Stele IIIA: 5; see Tadmor, *Inscriptions*, 66, 106. For the tribute list of Tiglath-pileser III and the 1000 talents of silver see further Bob Becking, *The Fall of Samaria: An Historical and Archaeological Study* (Leiden: Brill 1992), 4, and the discussion below.
68 For other explanations see Hallo and Younger, *The Context of Scripture*, vol. 2, 285 and Loretz and Walter, "Pūlu – Tiglatpileser III," 221–31.
69 See the discussion in Tadmor, *Inscriptions*, 274–76. With the date 738 BCE I follow Weippert, *Historisches Textbuch zum Alten Testament*, 288, whereas Loretz and Mayer, "Pūlu – Tiglatpileser III," assume that Menahem paid tribute to Tiglath-pileser III already in 743 BCE, following the study of Edwin R. Thiele, whereas Fritz, *Das zweite Buch der Könige*, 86 dates the tribute to the year 740 BCE. See also Kristin Weingart's chapter in this volume.
70 Tadmor, *Inscriptions*, 276.
71 Cogan and Tadmor, *II Kings*, 172; Tadmor, *Inscriptions*, 141; for the parallel cases of Hulli of Tabal and Metenna of Tyre see Tadmor, *Inscriptions*, 276.

king in return for the recognition of the Assyrian king"[72]. This parallel may suggest that Menahem's ascension to the throne was illegitimate and perhaps related to Assyrian westward-expansion. At the very least he bought Assyrian support for his rule (see below).

If the figures given in the Bible are correct, but relate to an earlier tribute to the Assyrian king, Menahem either needed the help of the Assyrian power to enforce his power/campaign against the anti-Assyrian Shallum partisans, or he was indeed a king by the grace of the Assyrian king. The "text indicates that Tiglath-pileser intervened directly and personally to support the pro-Assyrian Menahem and to preserve his hold on the throne"[73].

Given that the relationship between the amount of the tribute paid and the political status of the vassal was commonly known, there is another possibility to explain 2Kgs 15:19: the figures for Menahem's tribute are not *historically* correct, but the Deuteronomistic editor, aware of this Assyrian practice, adds in this detail to paint Menahem as a wicked usurper.

The brutality shown to Tiphsah is given as paradigmatic example of his wickedness. But this elaborate possibility is only theoretical.

It is more probable that the figures are historically correct, and Menahem was seen as a usurper by Tiglath-pileser III. The biblical chronology is perhaps corrupted, and Menahem ascended the throne in Samaria, in fact, only in 738 BCE, or his tribute has to be dated earlier to 743–740 BCE,[74] as earlier studies were willing to assume. This opens the window to the suggestion that perhaps he directed a rival monarchy from Tirzah in the years before accessing the throne illegitimately in Samaria. This would fit the archaeological record of Tell el-Fārʿah (North) presented above.

The exceptional phrase להיות ידיו אתו להחזיק הממלכה בידו, "to that his hand might be with him to strengthen his kingdom in his hand" as the ratio of the tribute may give another hint for the subjection of Menahem to Tiglath-pileser III and the suggestion of a rival kingdom of Menahem. The phrase has two parts which can be read as a doublet or even seen as evidence for a pleonastic style. But since the LXX has only εἶναι τὴν χεῖρα αὐτοῦ μετ' αὐτοῦ, the second part להחזיק הממלכה בידו can be evaluated as a later gloss.[75] Interestingly enough the phrase is attested also with Amaziah, who erected a counter-kingdom in

---

[72] Nadav Na'aman, "Tiglath-pileser III's Campaigns against Tyre and Israel (734–732 BCE)," *TA* 22 (1995): 275 with reference to Tadmor, *Inscriptions*, 276.
[73] Miller and Hayes, *History*, 377.
[74] See the discussion Loretz and Mayer, "Pūlu – Tiglatpileser III," 226.
[75] See Marvin A. Sweeney, *I & II Kings: A Commentary* (Louisville KT: Westminster John Know Press, 2007), 373.

Lachish and who killed his servants (2Kgs 14:5), and with Jehoram in the context of the murder of his brothers (2Chr 21:4). By this, the suspicion is nurtured that Menahem's accession was 'special' in a way. It was irregular indeed, and supported by the Assyrians. Perhaps it was two-tiered process, and the second stage may also have been dearly bought with a bribe put into the hands of Tiglath-pileser III.

If we push this speculation even further, the enigmatic Tiphsah (given its original reading instead of Antiochene Ταφώε, Tappuah) gives a hidden clue to the revenge on Samaria, symbolizing the ideological transfer of Samaria in Assyrian realm ("because he had not opened" the city for the Assyrians). Tiphsah is a border city at the Euphrates and beyond there is clearly Assyrian territory.

The "payment and other tributes must have drained the wealth of Israel, broken the economic power of Israel, and financially ruined the Northern Kingdom"[76]. Menahem exacted the money from the people by imposing a tax on the wealthy. If the figures of the tribute are calculable and every rich man had to pay 50 silver shekels, as it is said in 2Kgs 15:20, Menahem was in need of 72,000 rich people. No matter how one looks at it, the given numbers cannot be sound. Dubovský has pointed to Lev 27:3. The idea of interpreting the figures theologically perhaps goes in the right direction.[77] Considering that this is a biased description of the North, these details may be intended to devalue Menahem's kingdom on an economic level. Be that as it may, the bribe did work and Tiglath-pileser III withdrew (ולא־עמד שם בארץ). This is only half of the truth, since the Assyrians were present shortly after this event at least in the 13th or 14th *palû* (see below). If the tribute of Menahem was meant to replace the anti-Assyrian policy of Shallum with the help of Tiglath-pileser III, the state of Israel was transferred into the second stage of vassalage.

To sum up, this in-depth historical discussion dealing with the scarcity of information about Menahem has come to some conclusions, which admittedly cannot be substantiated in terms of historical accuracy: in contrast to Shallum, Menahem seems to have taken a pro-Assyrian position. Shortly after the anti-Assyrian Shallum destroyed the Nimshides, and representatives of the ruling class had gained power in Samaria, he may have erected a rival kingdom in Tirzah. This may have formed the background for the biblical chronology which attributes a period of roughly ten years reign to him. Perhaps with an act of extraor-

---

76 Dubovský, "Northern Kingdom," 340.
77 Dubovský, "Northern Kingdom," 340. על כל־גבורי החיל can also denote the leading elite, which was allegedly in Samaria. Is this an additional hidden hint for the "revenge"-theory against the anti-Assyrian party? However, this is mere theory and cannot be substantiated. We do not know anything on the foreign policy of Shallum and a possible anti-Assyrian attitude.

dinary brutality he expanded his power from Tirzah to Samaria. For this very gambit he made use of the help of Tiglath-pileser III. The anti-Assyrian party grew mighty because of the heavy tribute he had to pay and they swept his achievements away at the end of his reign or shortly after his death. 2Kgs 15:22 says that he died naturally and was buried regularly, but the succession to this throne may be more tumultuous, as will be discussed below.

3.7 Pekah

The similarity between the names Pekah and Pekahiah, which differ only by their explicit theophoric elements and their patronyms, is suspicious. However, no other sources support the view, that they are the same person. As we have learned already, not all usurpers are named with explicit Yahwistic theophoric names, but we can find other indications that Pekahiah was conflated with Pekah by the biblical authors. Anyway, there are some quite interesting details in the description of this penultimate regicide. Pekah is said in 2Kgs 15:25 to be a captain שליש – a high officer of the reigning monarch or king's deputy. Therefore, the rebellion was kindled within the inner administration. This makes a lot of sense considering the controversies surrounding foreign policy. The שליש is a high military or administrative position (Ex 14:7; 15:4; 2Kgs 9:25; 10:25) and is in 1Kgs 9:22 separated from the עבדים, שרים, אנשי המלחמה, and the שרי רכבו ופרשיו. 2Kgs 7:2, 17, 19 suggests that שליש is the king's deputy. The next detail is the location of the regicide: like Shallum he is killed in Samaria, but notably in the palace. The ארמון בית־המלך is part of the king's palace, most probably the private rooms. It is mentioned only once more in the Zimri conspiracy in 1Kgs 16:18 as the place where the king committed suicide. Perhaps this also points to the close relation between Pekahiah and Pekah. On a textual level, the similarity between the names of the king and his captain emphasizes the close relationship between them. In addition, Dubovský argues that this location is used to inform the reader that "conspiracies, intrigues, and murders penetrated the whole kingdom; not even the most protected place of the kingdom — the keep of the royal palace — was safe enough to protect the king against conspirators."[78] Additionally, the special place links the Pekah revolt to the Zimri account. In my understanding, it is not meant to be especially climactic. The putsch is carried out by Pekah and fifty men of Gilead (2Kgs 15:25), and following the LXX, these are fifty of four hundred (ἀπὸ τῶν τετρακοσίων) in total.

---

78 Dubovský, "Northern Kingdom," 328.

Whether there is an official relationship between the usurper and these men is not said: they may be his combat-effective unit, but then Pekah would be only one of many captains (ὁ τριστάτης). It is striking that the region of Gilead receives special emphasis, as it does in the revolts of Shallum and Menahem. As argued above, Gilead was weak and had experienced frequent changes of sovereignty between Israel, the Arameans, and the Assyrians.[79] The region may have felt the growing pressure of Tiglath-pileser in 735 BCE first and foremost. Most enigmatic is the reference to את־ארגב ואת־האריה which is usually translated as "along with Argob and Arieh." It is possible that these are two individuals who took part in the revolution (so LXX μετὰ τοῦ Αργοβ καὶ μετὰ τοῦ Αρια καὶ μετ' αὐτοῦ πεντήκοντα ἄνδρες) or they are places, where the revolution first arose. Argob is the name of the region of Bashan, as noted in 1Kgs 4:13 and Deut 3:4, 13–14.[80] This is purely speculative, but it is striking that Transjordanian power is employed with the details of his revolution. Tiglath-pileser III raided Gilead to gain control over the Transjordanian trade route.[81] This may have preceded the conquest of Cis-Jordan described at the end of the reign of Pekah in 2Kgs 15:29. Another possibility is that the anti-Assyrian party toppled the reign in Samaria when Menahem died.[82] Be that as it may, the annexation of northern territory is connected to Pekah in the biblical text (2Kgs 15:29). The text mentions a military campaign of Tiglath-pileser, who is named here תגלת פלאסר for the first time (cf. 2Kgs 16:7, 10 for further references and 2Kgs 15:19 for Pul). This campaign is usually meant to be the 12th (*ana māt Pilišta*) 734 BCE or, more probably, the 13th and 14th *palû* of Tiglath-pileser III (733–732 BCE) (*ana māt Damašeq*).[83] It

---

[79] This is also the background of the Aramean conspiracy in the revolt of Pekah (cf. 2Kgs 15:37); cf. Miller and Hayes, *History*, 376. I will not discuss the so-called Syro-Ephraimite war in this chapter, but see Frevel, *Geschichte Israels*, 240.
[80] See Johannes Bremer, "Argob," in *Das Wissenschaftliche Bibellexikon im Internet* (www.wibilex.de), 2014 (https://www.bibelwissenschaft.de/stichwort/13757/, last access: 03/12/2017).
[81] See Meinders Dijkstra and Karel Vriezen, "The Assyrian Province of Gilead and the 'Myth of the Empty Land'," in *Exploring the Narrative: Jerusalem and Jordan in the Bronze and Iron Ages: Papers in Honour of Margreet Steiner*, ed. Eveline van der Steen, Jeanette Boertien and Noor Mulder-Hymans (London: Bloomsbury, 2015): 6–7.
[82] See Fritz, *Das zweite Buch der Könige*, 85.
[83] For the dating Weippert, *Historisches Textbuch zum Alten Testament*, 288, map in Cogan and Tadmor, *II Kings*, 180. Dubovský mentions that Transjordan was conquered in the 13th *palû* which he draws from Annals 23 and Summary Inscription 9 and 13, and the conquest of Ashtarot depicted in Nimrud. He proposes three phases coast, "Transjordan and epicentres (Damascus and Israel)" (Dubovský, "Tiglath-pileser III's Campaigns in 734–732 B.C.," 158.). The province of Magiddû was founded 733 BCE, the province of Dimašqa in 732 BCE; see the chart in Simo Parpola, "The National and Ethnic Identity in the Neo-Assyrian Empire and Assyrian Identity in Post-Empire Times," *Journal of Assyrian Academic Studies* 18 (2004): 5–22, appendix II.

is well known that the "he reigned twenty years" in 2Kgs 15:27 contradicts the chronology in several ways, most crucially the assumption that according to the vassal-list of Tiglath-pileser III the pre-predecessor Menahem payed tribute in ca. 738 BCE (see above). Taking this for granted, there is no time for Pekah (ass. *Paqaḫa*) to reign twenty years even without Pekahiah in between.[84] Be that as it may, the raid against Israel can best be placed in 734–732 BCE within the context of the annexation of Gaza and Damascus.[85] If we are forced to decide, it would fit our knowledge of the year 733 BCE best.[86]

The biblical text mentions the deportation of people and the conquest of eight areas in the north – moving from cities (Ijon, Abel-beth-maacah, Janoah, Kedesh, Hazor) to landscapes or regions (Gilead, Galilee) and from north to south. In adding the concluding element כל־ארץ נפתלי the list becomes different. Naphtali is not introduced by ואת and not determined by an article. The phrase is attested only once more in 1Kgs 15:20 to denote the territory taken by Ben-Hadad, but the latter appears to be dependent on 2Kgs 15:30 (see above). To bring up "all the land of Naphtali" after noting the cities in the Huleh valley is strange, because Ijon, Abel-beth-maacah, Kedesh, Janoah, and Hazor are all in the area which is commonly attributed to Naphtali. This very fact has nourished speculation that either Naphtali, or even the three regions of Gilead, Galilee, and Naphtali, are additions, not least because they are not listed in the alleged geographical order.[87] The list starts close to the Litani river in the North with Ijon, usually identified with Tell Dibbin (coord. OIG 2052.3054), then Abel-beth-maacah, the geographical "gate" to Palestine, *Tell Ābil el-Qamḥ* at the mouth of the Biqa valley (coord. OIG 2045.2962), going south to Janoah which is not Yenoʿam 5 km south from the outfall of the Sea of Galilee (coord. OIG 1982.2354), but rather *Tell en-Naʿameh/Tell an-Naʿimah* in the Huleh valley (coord. OIG 2058.2868). The next city Kedesh is usually identified with *Tel Qedesh* northwest of the Huleh swamp (coord. OIG 1997.2796), and the final city is Hazor identified with *Tell el-Qedaḥ* (coord. OIG 2035.2693) in the southwestern area of the Huleh basin. From this view, it is quite convincing to connect Galilee to the south, but the text mentions Gilead first and Galilee second. Scholars have

---

84 See Frevel, *Geschichte Israels*, 182–83.
85 See Na'aman, "Tiglath-pileser III's Campaigns," 268–78.
86 See Fritz, *Das zweite Buch der Könige*, 88–89.
87 See Ernst Würthwein, *Die Bücher der Könige*, vol. 2: *1 Kön 17:2–2 Kön 25* (Göttingen: Vandenhoeck & Ruprecht 1984), 384–85; Becking, *The Fall of Samaria*, 18; Fritz, *Das zweite Buch der Könige*, 88.

noted that the הגלילה is a more or less late form.⁸⁸ Considering the difference between the two object markers and the different phrase כל ארץ נפתלי, it has been argued that ואת־הגלעד ואת־הגלילה is a later addition. Both Gilead and Galilee are quite late additions which are intended to establish a larger territory of the North as conquered area. Perhaps it was influenced by Jdt 15:5, or the Maccabean revolt in 1Macc 5:17, 20, 55. If this is accepted, then כל ארץ נפתלי becomes the concluding summary of the cities in the north, which then only comprises the Huleh valley.⁸⁹ The important town of Dan, which was definitely destroyed by the Assyrians but later rebuilt as an administrative center, is (deliberately?) absent (but cf. 1Kgs 15:20). Despite this detailed discussion, most of the cities just mentioned show signs of significant destruction from Assyrian invaders in the archaeological record. Southern cities were also subject to the same destructive forces.⁹⁰ Tel Dan (Stratum II) was destroyed violently by Tiglath-pileser III. Domestic and public zones were affected alike. Bethsaida (et-Tell; Stratum Va) was destroyed by fire in intense warfare, Chinnereth (Tell el-ʿOreimeh; Stratum II) was almost completely destroyed. Although clear signs of destruction are undeniable, Yifat Thareani has recently argued against the view that the Assyrians totally emptied the land. "It seems that the archaeological evidence from Dan rules out the dominant theory that by the late eighth century BCE the Assyrians left the region as an 'empty cell'."⁹¹ After the Assyrian conquest, Dan prospered and this fact also argues against a total decline in the Huleh region. Thareani calls this a "middle-range" strategy which aimed at the economic exploitation of the region. We will not discuss the outcome of the campaign and the repercussions of the Assyrian strategy in the present paper. With Tiglath-pileser III's raid, Israel entered the final stage of vassalage that was accompanied by a significant loss of territory and the deportation of people.

---

88 The Galil is attested also in Josh 20:7; 21:32; 1Kgs 6:34; 9:11 ; 1Chr 6:61; Esth 1:6; Cant 5:14; and Isa 8:23. Only 2Kgs 15:29 reads גלילה.
89 See Naʾaman, "Tiglath-pileser III's Campaigns," 274; see James A. Montgomery, *A Critical and Exegetical Commentary on the Books of Kings* (New York: Scribner, 1951), 452; Würthwein, *Bücher der Könige*, 383; Cogan and Tadmor, *II Kings*, 174.
90 See Yifat Thareani, "Imperializing the Province: A Residence of a Neo-Assyrian City Governor at Tel Dan," *Levant* 48 (2016): 257–58; ead., "The Archaeological Character of an Imperial Frontier: Assyrian Control Policy in the Hula Valley," in *Archaeology and History of Empires: Models, Projects and Works in Progress in Northern Mesopotamia*, ed. Maria Grazia Masetti-Rouault and Olivier Rouault (2013 Paris conference, forthcoming). For the campaign see also Dubovský, "Tiglath-pileser III's Campaigns," 164–66, and Dijkstra and Vriezen, "The Assyrian Province of Gilead," 6–10.
91 Thareani, "Imperial Frontier," 14.

3.8 Hoshea

Whether Hoshea, the last king of Israel (who is not even mentioned by the conquerors of Samaria Shalmaneser V and Sargon II in 722/21 BCE),[92] was a usurper, or whether he was installed by Tiglath-pileser III, differs between the portrayal in 2Kgs 15:30 and the Assyrian Summary Inscription 4 (2.117C), line 11 (translation following K. Lawson Younger in CoS II:288): "Pekah,* their king, and I installed Hoshea [as king] over them." How Pekah was eliminated remains unclear, but the Assyrian sources are distinct about the fact that Hoshea was installed by the Assyrians.[93] In contrast, the biblical account is clear in its classification of Hoshea's accession as a revolt. It employs the classical formula in 2Kgs 15:30a, but in an intensified form that repeats the root על־פקח בן־רמליהו ויכהו וימיתהו וימלך תחתיו ויקשר־קשר הושע בן־אלה, "And Hoshea son of Elah conspired a conspiracy against Pekah son of Remaliah, attacked him, and killed him; he reigned in place of him."

Read against the sources, the historicity of Hoshea's *coup d'état* becomes doubtful. The situation is echoed in the Aramean inscription of the Tel Dan stele that claims the regicide of Joram (and Ahaziah), while 2Kgs 9:24–27 names Jehu as the killer of both (see above). While one has to admit that both reports are colored for propagandistic purposes, read against the Assyrian practice, the installation of Hoshea by the Assyrian king makes considerable sense. Perhaps it was also the Assyrian mastermind who drove the revolt against the disobedient Pekah, as Bob Becking suggested: "Beide Positionen sind von ihren jeweiligen Perspektiven geprägt und lassen sich in das Bild zusammenfügen, dass der assyrische König eine Revolte Hoscheas unterstützt haben könnte."[94] If this points us in the right direction, then also the last revolt in Samaria, which is pictured so vividly in many versions of the history of Israel, intentionally misinforms to promote a particular viewpoint.

---

[92] For the discussion on the conquest of Samaria see the chapters of Dan'el Kahn and Bob Becking in the present volume.

[93] For the installation of Hoshea as king see Tadmor, *The Inscriptions of Tiglath-pileser III*, 277–78; Weippert, *Historisches Textbuch zum Alten Testament*, 147–49; Kyle Lawson Younger, Jr., "The Summary Inscription 9–10 (2.117F)," and "The Summary Inscription 13 (2.117G)," in Hallo and Younger, *The Context of Scripture*, vol. 2, 291–92.

[94] Bob Becking, "Hoschea," in *Das Wissenschaftliche Bibellexikon im Internet (www.wibilex.de)*, 2012 (https://www.bibelwissenschaft.de/stichwort/21574/; last access: 04/12/2017).

4 The Built-in Weakness of the Northern State: Some Conclusions

This viewpoint is a very critical attitude towards the north, which does not attribute to it any continuity of governance beyond the Omride and Nimshide dynasties. This must be contrasted with the allegedly unbroken chain of Davidides in the south. However, this continuity becomes suspicious, when one considers how heavily biased this account is. When we consider the details of Solomon's succession and the accounts of Athaliah and Joash, Joram and Ahaziah, it is the continuity of the Davidic dynasty that becomes suspicious.[95] Anyway, the described instability of the Northern Kingdom is clearly the result of a Judean bias. Within this pattern, it is striking that all usurpers of the eighth century carry non-Yahwistic names. Is this by chance? I do not think so, but whether this is by chance, or partly deliberate, cannot be answered. Menahem (*Miniḫini*), Pekah (*Paqaḫa*), and Hoshea (*Auši'*) are attested in Assyrian sources as names of the northern monarchy, and Menahem or Shallum are names often attested extra-biblically. Hence, to be suspicious about the occurrence of non-Yahwistic names is probably being overly-cautious. However, it fits the pattern that the irregularities of the Northern Kingdom stand in direct contrast to God's will, as expressed in the unified Davidic kingdom in the south. One question has to be answered at the end of this argument: Why is there any continuity in the northern dynasties? It is striking that Omri, Ahab, Ahaziah, and Joram, and Jehu, Jehoahaz, Joash, Jeroboam, and Zechariah were conceived as dynasties, although they were sometimes judged more harshly than other kings of Samaria. I have no explanation, other than that these prosperous dynasties, which were all largely successful in economic, political, and religious governance, could not be easily disparaged by the Deuteronomists. Further historiographical studies are necessary to substantiate this.

Let me summarize these considerations with a few remarks. This paper focused on the portrayal of the last kings of Israel against the background of the string of revolts reported in the historical accounts in the Book of Kings. The revolts of Jeroboam, Baasha, Zimri, Tibni, Omri, Jehu, Shallum, Menahem, Pekah, and Hoshea have been considered in detail. The account of the 15 year period from 747–732 BCE in 2Kgs 15 was demonstrated to be a mix of historical and legendary construction. Only meager glimpses of 'historical' details are

---

[95] For the discontinuity of the Davidic dynasty see Frevel, *Geschichte Israels*, 192, 205–8, 216–21.

given in the biblical account. The single reports are linked very much with each other in terms of keywords, phrases, geography, and particular details. They form a continuous narrative of depravity, instability, and even immorality. This portrayal is not interested in historical correctness, but instead distorts the political history of Samaria deliberately. Particularly the detailed information on the Assyrian campaigns from the 12th to the 14th *palû* of Tiglath-pileser III (i.e., the years 743–743 BCE) is missing. Only the list of cities in the Huleh valley of the northern territory gives us a clue about the loss of Israelite sovereignty, although the portrayal does not reflect the creation of the province of Magiddû (in 732? BCE). The campaign to the Huleh basin is not related to the subjugation of Gilead and Galilee. This detail was added to the text by a later gloss for the purpose of historical accuracy. It has become clear, that the portrayal of the Northern Kingdom in 2Kgs 15 does not aim at a historically exact narration of the events. It is biased and interested in the instability of the Northern Kingdom in contrast with Davidic continuity. Whether Hoshea, Pekah, and even Menahem were indeed usurpers by revolution, or whether they were installed by the Assyrian power, remains thus open for discussion. But we have presented grounds to assume an Assyrian mastermind behind the revolts of Menahem and Hoshea rather than individual usurpers who acted on their own account.

This bias was particularly apparent in the fact that the text does not differentiate explicitly between pro- and contra-Assyrian foreign policy. In fact there are indications that Hoshea and Menahem pleaded (and if under constraint ...) for a more pro-Assyrian position, while Pekah established an anti-Assyrian policy. But almost nothing from the struggle in Israel between different positions can be drawn directly from the text. Most inviting to speculation was the often enigmatic information given about Menahem outside that in 2Kgs 15: the murder of Shallum; the role of Tirzah; the regional importance of Gilead; and the cruelty to Tiphsah, etc. We suggested that Menahem erected a rival kingdom in Tirzah and that he gained power in Samaria with the help of Tiglath-pileser III, paying a heavy tribute to gain power against the anti-Assyrian Shallum.

With regard to the earlier revolts, we argued that, in particular, the account of Jeroboam I, the putsch of Baasha, and the struggle of Zimri and Tibni were more or less inventions. The "sin of Jeroboam" was characterized as a very effective "invention of tradition" to blame the Northern Kingdom from its beginning. Methodologically speaking, the present paper took a very sceptical position on historicity for heuristic purposes. In discussing the textual evidence, we were unable to uncover sufficient reliable historical details in the biblical text. This paper has argued on the presumption that the history of the Northern Kingdom was compiled from administrative lists, which existed for the Omride and Nimshide kingdoms. However, almost all historiography *before* the Omrides is a retelling of later stories, details, and characterizations. This became particularly evident in the discussion of 1Kgs 15 and the presentation of the confrontation between Judah and Israel. The presentation of the Northern Kingdom is much more a fictive narrative than a factual history.

Michael Pietsch
Hoshea ben Elah, the Last King of Israel: Narrative and History in 2 Kings 17:1–6

1 Introduction

In the controversial discussion about the circumstances that led to the downfall of Samaria, there is still an important significance ascribed to the compact account of the events in 2Kgs 17:1–6.[1] The reason for this is not so much that the biblical narrative is considered to be of particularly historical value as a source, but rather the fact that the cuneiform sources provide contradictory reports as to which Assyrian ruler conquered Samaria. While the Babylonian Chronicle attributes the conquest to Shalmaneser V[2], his successor, Sargon II, claims for himself in contemporary inscriptions to have destroyed the city, deported its inhabitants, and incorporated the remaining Samarian state into the Assyrian provincial system.[3] This finding has been interpreted as either evidence for two separate military seizures of Samaria[4] or as an indication for a joint venture of both Assyrian kings.[5] In order to support their interpretation, both models

---

[1] The actual debate is briefly summarized in Christian Frevel, *Geschichte Israels* (Stuttgart: Kohlhammer, 2016), 234–45. The most thorough treatment of the problem is still offered by Bob Becking, *The Fall of Samaria: An Historical and Archaeological Study* (Leiden: Brill, 1992), cf. also Nadav Na'aman, "The Historical Background to the Conquest of Samaria (720 BC)," *Bib* 71 (1990): 206–25, and Stefan Timm, "Die Eroberung Samarias aus assyrisch-babylonischer Sicht," in id., *"Gott kommt von Teman ...": Kleine Schriften zur Geschichte Israels und Syrien-Palästinas*, ed. Claudia Bender and Michael Pietsch (Münster: Ugarit-Verlag, 2004): 103–20.
[2] The text of the Babylonian Chronicle dates from the 22nd year of the reign of the Persian king Darius II (i.e. 500 BC), but can be traced back to even older traditions. The Chronicle mentions that in the reign of Shalmaneser V, he "broke" (*ḫepû*) the city of Samaria: Albert Kirk Grayson, *Assyrian and Babylonian Chronicles* (Locus Valley NY: Augustin, 1975), 73.
[3] Cf. the prism inscription of Sargon II from Kalḫu/Nimrud, column IV, lines 25–41 (cf. Manfred Weippert, *Historisches Textbuch zum Alten Testament* [Göttingen: Vandenhoeck & Ruprecht, 2010], 301–302) and the somewhat contemporary annals of the king from Dūr-Šarrukēn/Ḫorsābād, lines 10–17, which text is, however, greatly damaged and often complemented by the parallel report from the Prism Inscription (cf. the critical discussion in Becking, *Fall*, 39–44).
[4] Cf. Hayim Tadmor, "The Campaigns of Sargon II," *JCS* 12 (1958): 22–40, 77–100, whose suggestion many have followed; cf. the literature listed in Becking, *Fall*, 38 note 78.
[5] Cf. Herbert Donner, *Israel unter den Völkern: Die Stellung der klassischen Propheten des 8. Jahrhunderts v. Chr. zur Außenpolitik der Könige von Israel und Juda* (Leiden: Brill, 1964), 65–66. Other supporters of this interpretation are mentioned in Becking, *Fall*, 33 note 56.

invoke particular passages from the biblical account in 2Kgs 17:1–6 that correspond to the respective cuneiform writings. But in doing so, the literary structure and narrative pragmatic of each text are not seriously taken into consideration. Such an analysis should, however, precede any historical interpretation. Therefore, this chapter will first discuss the narrative composition of the *res gestae* of the last king of Israel, Hoshea ben Elah, in 2Kgs 17:1–6. In the second part, based on the literary analysis of the episode what one can derive for a historical reconstruction of "the last days of the kings of Israel" will be considered.

2 2Kgs 17:1–6 as Narrative

The passage restarts the narrative plot in the Book of Kings by the syntactical construction *x-qāṭal* and the temporal modification "in the 12th year of Ahaz, the king of Judah," reaching back chronologically beyond the report of the death and burial of Ahaz in 2Kgs 16:19–20. The declaration of the nine-year reign of the last king of Israel in Samaria (cf. v. 1b) is taken up again by means of the stipulation "in the 9th year of Hoshea" (v. 6), which closes the literary sequence.[6] The syntactical structure of the section reveals a three-part composition, which is marked by the use of the element *x-qāṭal*: the actual narrative following the introductory regnal formula in vv. 1–2 starts with v. 3a as indicated by the syntactical construction *x-qāṭal* along with the introduction of the king of Assyria, Shalmaneser V. This is continued with a chain of narrative forms until v. 5 and ends with a note about the three-year siege of the city of Samaria by the Assyrians.[7] The use of a temporal adverb at the beginning of v. 6a (cf. *x-qāṭal*) marks yet another break and emphasizes the comment about the capture of the city and the deportation of its inhabitants as the final point of the sequence in contrast to what precedes it. This provides a clear structure of the text (Fig. 1), which goes from vv. 1–2, across vv. 3–5, ending in v. 6.

This observation dissuades the widespread assumption that vv. 3–4 and vv. 5–6 contain parallel accounts of the same event, which were taken from different archival collections.[8] This assumption is also contradicted by the fact that

---

[6] However, the title "the king of Assyria" occurs again in vv. 24–33, linking this passage back to the narrative in vv. 3–6 and supposing the identity of the Assyrian king mentioned in both texts.
[7] The chain of events is interrupted by a relative clause in v. 4a* giving some background information on the revolt of Hoshea, namely the request for help from the Egyptian pharao and the holding back of the regular tribute to the Assyrian overlord.
[8] This assumption goes back as far as Hugo Winckler, *Alttestamentliche Untersuchungen* (Leipzig: Eduard Pfeiffer, 1892), 15–25, who supposed that the twofold mention of a military cam-

vv. 1–2a   Dates of the reign of Hoshea ben Elah and negative royal judgment
          (*x-qāṭal* + *wayyiqṭol*)

v. 2b   Limitation of the royal judgment (textual background)

vv. 3–4a₁ Vassal status of Hoshea (v. 3) and the uncovering of the insurrection
          against the Assyrian sovereignty (*x-qāṭal* + *wayyiqṭol*)

v. 4a₂   Request for aid from Egypt and discontinuance of tribute
          (textual background)

vv. 4b–5 Capture of Hoshea and three-year siege of Samaria (*wayyiqṭol*)

v. 6   Conquest of Samaria "in the ninth year of Hoshea" and the
          deportation of Israel to Assyria (*x-qāṭal* + *wayyiqṭol*)

Fig. 1: The syntactic structure of 2Kgs 17:1–6. Prepared by the author.

in a synchronic reading the notice on the vassal status of Hoshea in v. 3 establishes the factual prerequisite for the Assyrian campaign described in vv. 4–6, and that without vv. 3–4, some of the syntactical references in vv. 5–6 were misleading.[9] Finally, the question remains: which type of archival material should

---

paign by Shalmaneser V against Samaria in v. 3a and v. 5a is due to the literary-critical technique of *Wiederaufnahme* indicating the use of two independent literary sources by the narrator. The first of which (represented in vv. 3b–4*) was originally connected to the historical account in 2Kgs 15:29, whereas the second (vv. 3a.4*.5–6) was related to 2Kgs 15:30. However, the starting point for Winckler's thesis was the observation that the biblical account neither fits with the report on the vassal status of Hoshea in the royal inscriptions of Tiglath-pileser III nor with the claim of Sargon II to have conquered the city of Samaria and deported its inhabitants. Regarding the narrative plot of the biblical account in 2Kgs 17:3–6 it is evident that the mentioning of the Assyrian king in v. 3a and in v. 5a is related to two different events as can easily be learned from their respective context. Therefore it is not necessary to regard them as a literary doublet or a case of redactional *Wiederaufnahme*. The narrative sequence from v. 4b to vv. 5–6 may seem a little awkward to modern interpreters, but it is not to be explained by means of source criticism.

9 Cf. Timm, "Eroberung," 103–104 with note 3. – Christoph Levin has clearly recognized the difficulties of a source-critical explanation of the literary structure of the passage and has argued in favor of a redaction-critical analysis based on a comparison with the parallel account in 2Kgs 18:9–11 (cf. his chapter in the present volume). He presupposes that 2Kgs 18:9–12 belong to a later editing in the account of the reign of Hezekiah, king of Judah. Its presentation of the

be considered as a source for the accounts? The Samarian royal court can hardly be considered.[10]

2.1 The Introductory Regnal Formula (vv. 1–2)

If we return to the beginning of the passage, it has already been said that the synchronistic dating of the beginning of Hoshea's regency in the 12th year of the Judean king Ahaz reaches back narratively to a point before the final verses of the previous chapter. In 2Kgs 15:29–30 the narrator has informed the reader more precisely that Hoshea came to power through a military coup (*qæšær*) against the ruling king Pekah after Tiglath-pileser III had annexed the (Upper) Galilee and the region of Gilead.[11] Hence, in the narrative plot of the Book of

---

events has been taken over from the report in 2Kgs 17:3–6 with only a little editorial reworking and the insertion of v. 12. Therefore only those textual elements from 2Kgs 17:3–6 which are also present in 2Kgs 18:9–11 can be assumed to be the original report of the events. This is to be confirmed by demonstrating that all the secondary elements in the narrative of 2Kgs 17:3–6 (cf. vv. 3b–5a*) share a common polemical bias discrediting the last king of Israel (cf. the textual variant in the Antiochene reading of v. 2b). Regarding the secondary origin of 2Kgs 18:9–12 Levin seems to be right. The passage interprets Samaria's demise as due to the peoples' (and their kings', respectively) breaking of the covenant with Yhwh by not obeying the Mosaic torah. By this means it contrasts Hezekiah's rebellion against Sennacherib, "the King of Assyria" (cf. 2Kgs 18:7b), with the revolt of Hoshea, for Hezekiah did follow the torah of Yhwh (cf. v. 6). It was his intention to explain why the rebellion of Hoshea led to the total loss of political sovereignty and the deportation of "all Israel" while Hezekiah, even after his revolt failed, had only to pay some heavy tribute to the Assyrians, but remained king in Jerusalem (cf. 2Kgs 18:13–16). The editor was neither interested in the reign of Hoshea itself nor in his personal fate. He used only the information from 2Kgs 17:3–6 which supports his own argument (e. g. the events mentioned in v. 3 would have weakened the antagonism between Hoshea and Hezekiah). If this proves to be correct, it is not possible to reconstruct any older textual layer in 2Kgs 17:3–6 by means of a comparison with the account in 2Kgs 18:9–11. The narrative plot in 2Kgs 17:3–6, however, shows no clear indication of a redactional reworking (cf. also the chapter by Dan'el Kahn in the present volume).
10 2Kgs 17:3–4* has often been assigned to a Northern tradition originating from the royal annals of the court in Samaria, but this assumption is not very probable (cf. Timm, "Eroberung," 104 note 3).
11 The events belong to the so-called Syro-Ephraimite War (cf. 2Kgs 16:5–9) dating to the years 733/32–732/31 BC according to the Eponym Chronicle for the reign of Tiglath-pileser III (cf. Weippert, *Textbuch*, 285–87). The narrator claims these territories for Israel, but at least Gilead seems to have been under Aramaean control at this time (cf. the chapter by Norma Franklin in the present volume). – Hoshea's rebellion is termed in the view of the reigning king Pekah as a military coup (*qæšær*, cf. 2Kgs 17:4a!), without any religious disqualification.

Kings, the note in v. 1 reminds the reader of Hoshea's violent seizing of power. The dating of this event in 2Kgs 15:30b, however, is in the 20th year of the reign of Jotham, the father of Ahaz, who reigned only 16 years according to 2Kgs 15:33. However, according to 2Kgs 16:1, Ahaz was crowned king in Jerusalem in the 17th year of Pekah, king of Israel. Since Pekah ruled 20 years, according to 2Kgs 15:27, Hoshea would have ascended the throne in the fourth year of Ahaz.[12]

The various chronological and text-critical problems apparent in the divergent statements do not need to be discussed here in detail.[13] Only a brief comment on the synchronism in 2Kgs 17:1 shall be given. The calculation that leads to the 12th year of Ahaz finds its point of origin, it seems, neither with the date of the beginning of the reign of Ahaz nor with the chronology of the reign of Pekah. Instead, it is to be found in the synchronism between Hezekiah, king of Judah, and Hoshea in 2Kgs 18:1. If this is right, it has to be assumed that the beginning of Hoshea's reign has been postdated and that his third regnal year overlapped with the 15th and 16th year of Ahaz.[14] The synchronistic dating of the capture of Samaria in 2Kgs 18:9–11, on the other hand, presupposes the synchronism in 18:1.[15] However, it is quite obvious that the system of synchron-

---

[12] The textual and historical difficulties regarding the synchronistic datings in the Book of Kings are discussed in further detail in the chapters by Christian Frevel and Kristin Weingart in the present volume.

[13] In the transmission of the Greek text different attempts have been made to harmonize the chronological problems present in the Masoretic text. However, no coherent chronological system has been reached in the history of textual transmission. Therefore it seems difficult to draw any firm conclusions from the textual variants with regard to different chronological systems within the sources used by the editor of the Book of Kings as did Joachim Begrich, *Die Chronologie der Könige von Israel und Juda und die Quellen des Rahmens der Königsbücher* (Tübingen: Mohr Siebeck, 1929), 102–15.

[14] This proposal would imply that the beginning of the calendrial year has been already transferred to spring-time in Samaria, while in Judah it still remained autumn – or at least the one responsible for the synchronism understood it in this way. Otherwise a short period of co-regency between both Judean kings not attested elsewhere has to be assumed; cf. the discussion in Erasmus Gaß, *Im Strudel der assyrischen Krise (2. Könige 18–19): Ein Beispiel biblischer Geschichtsdeutung* (Neukirchen-Vluyn: Neukirchener 2016), 7.

[15] Or is the synchronism in 2Kgs 18:1 made up by the editor responsible for the insertion of vv. 9–12 into the narrative contrasting the reigns of Hezekiah and Hoshea? In the narrative flow of the Book of Kings the reference to the nameless "King of Assyria" against whom Hezekiah rebelled (cf. 2Kgs 18:7b) points back to Shalmaneser V, who led Israel into exile (cf. 2Kgs 17:3–6, 24–28). This could explain the chronological contradiction between the regnal dates in v. 1 and the account of Sennacherib's campaign against Judah dated in the 14th year of Hezekiah according to 2Kgs 18:13–16.

istic dating in the Book of Kings is primarily a product of historiographic reasoning and cannot simply be taken as face value for historical queries.

Following the regnal dates of the king a historiographic evaluation of Hoshea's rule is given (v. 2): "He has committed evil in the eyes of Yhwh" (v. 2a). This is in accord with the same negative judgment all the kings of Israel receive (with the single exception of Jehu, cf. 2Kgs 10:30), albeit with one noteworthy qualification: "but not like the kings of Israel that came before him" (v. 2b). The reproach taken up against the last king of Israel differs from the usual theological pattern without offering a clearer reason in the text itself.[16] In this respect, the formulation differs from its closest parallel in 2Kgs 3:2–3. There, the negative judgment against Jehoram, king of Israel, the son of Ahab, is qualified because he supposedly acted against the cult of Baʻal, which his parents promoted.[17] He allowed, however, the "Sin of Jeroboam," the establishment of two golden calves as idols to be worshiped in Dan and Bethel (cf. 2Kgs 12:28–32), to continue, which led to a negative overall judgment of his reign. A similar argument was the basis of Jehu's evaluation in 2Kgs 10:28–31: Yhwh acknowledges that Jehu did "what is right in my eyes," in that he extinguished the cult of Baʻal and executed judgment against the Omride dynasty. But because

---

16 In the Antiochene text of the Septuagint there is no restriction to the negative evaluation of the king. On the contrary, it is explicitly said that he has done evil in the eyes of Yhwh *more than any other king of Israel before him* (παρὰ πάντας τοὺς γενομένους ἔμπροσθεν αὐτοῦ [= *mikkol ᵃšær hāyû lᵉpānâw*, cf. 1Kgs 14:9; 16:25, 30, 33]). The downfall of Samaria, it is reasoned, was due to the outstanding evil committed by its last king. This textual variant seems to correct the difficult Masoretic reading by referring to a more common phraseology to which textual priority cannot be ascribed. However, it has been argued that the phrase occurs in the Masoretic text one last time with regard to Ahab, who is stigmatized as the sinful king *par excellence* (cf. 1Kgs 16:30, 33). In the Antiochene text, on the other hand, it is also present in 1Kgs 22:54 (with regard to Ahaziah, Ahab's son und successor to the throne) and 2Kgs 17:2 indicating a use of the phrase not yet biased by the dogmatic stigmatization of king Ahab; cf. Julio C. Trebolle, "La caída de Samariá, critica textual, literaria e história de 2Re 17,3–6," *Salmanticensis* 28 (1981): 137–52, and the chapter by Timo Tekoniemi in the present volume. However, with regard to 1Kgs 22:54 the reading present in the rest of the Greek manuscripts (κατὰ πάντα τὰ γενόμενα ἔμπροσθεν αὐτοῦ) might have been reworked in the Antiochene textform to fit the more common expression. Therefore it does not seem reasonable to assume a dogmatic correction in the Masoretic text of 1Kgs 22:54 nor is the enigmatic reading in 2Kgs 17:2 due to a similar interest.

17 In 2Kgs 3:2b it is mentioned that Jehoram turned aside the pillar of Baʻal which his father had erected. This account contradicts 2Kgs 10:26–27, ascribing the destruction of the pillar of Baʻal in Samaria to Jehu. However, there is no other mention of Ahab erecting a pillar for Baʻal in the Book of Kings. The account may want to explain, why there is almost no polemic against the cult of Baʻal within the Elisha narratives (with exception of 2Kgs 3:13–14; 9:22 – both referring to the religious acts of Ahab and his wife Jezebel!) and why the prophet himself is partly acting on behalf of the Omride king (cf. 2Kgs 6–7).

he held fast to the "Sin of Jeroboam," the length of his dynasty is limited to four generations (vv. 29–30). This finding could point to the fact that the qualification of the negative judgment of the king in 2Kgs 17:2 purports that the worship of Yhwh in the form of the two golden calves at Dan and at Bethel were no longer continued in the time of Hoshea.[18] This is at least evident in the narrative plot of the Book of Kings for the Upper-Galilean city of Dan, which is located in the area that had been annexed by Tiglath-pileser III according to 2Kgs 15:29. Whether or not one can reckon with a loss of cultic image in Bethel due to the heavy tribute paid to the Assyrians is less certain regarding the many textual problems in Hos 10:5–6.

2.2 The Downfall of Samaria (vv. 3–6)

2.2.1 The Prologue (v. 3)

The course of events begins in v. 3 introduced by the syntactical construction *x-qāṭal*. By means of the precedence of the prepositional construction *'ālâw*, Hoshea's fate is emphasized and the focus on the king himself is continued beyond the introductory remarks: "*Against him* Shalmaneser, the king of Assyria, came up" (v. 3a). Mentioning Shalmaneser V by name marks, on the one hand, a chronological transition over and against the previous section in 2Kgs 15:17–16:20, where an Assyrian king, in the person of Tiglath-pileser III, enters the narrative stage of events for the first time in the Book of Kings.[19] On the other hand, it es-

---

18 Cf. Alexander Rofé, *The Prophetical Stories: The Narratives about the Prophets in the Hebrew Bible, their Literary Types and History* (Jerusalem: Magness Press, 1988), 98 with note 50: "According to the Rabbis, Hoshea son of Elah removed the *praesidia* (garrison troops) who had prevented the Israelites from making pilgrimages to Jerusalem (bGit 88a, bTa'an 28a, bBBat 121b)."
19 Tiglath-pileser III is introduced in 2Kgs 15:19–20 with the Assyrian name Pūl(u), by which he was known in Persian and Hellenistic times. The episode belongs to the reign of Menahem, king of Israel, who is mentioned among the tributaries of Tiglath-pileser III in a list dating to the year 738 BC (cf. Weippert, *Textbuch*, 288–90). The name Tiglath-pileser (III) first occurs in the biblical narrative in 2Kgs 15:29 during the reign of Pekah, king of Israel. He annexed Northern Galilee and the Transjordanian territories from Israel and led the people into exile. The second mentioning of the Assyrian king by name is related to the same event: the anti-Assyrian coalition defeated by the king in the years 733/32–732/31 BC (cf. 2Kgs 16:7–9). Hence, the narrative composition in 2Kgs 15–16 can be read as if Pul and Tiglath-pileser (III) were two different Assyrian kings (as is supposed in 1Chr 5:26!), who are opposed to different Israelite (and Judean) kings. In this case the reign of Tiglath-pileser III would have been narrowed down to the events related to the so-called Syro-Ephraimite War. Hoshea, the last king of Israel, is then linked to a new Assyrian king, Shalmaneser V.

tablishes to whom the title "the King of Assyria" refers, as a function of literary coherence, throughout the story (cf. vv. 4, 5, and 6). The narrator does not give a reason for the sudden appearance of the Assyrian king; there is also no exact temporal reference of the event within the reign of Hoshea. The idea of a vassal relationship between Hoshea and Tiglath-pileser III, the predecessor of Shalmaneser V on the Assyrian throne, is often referred to in order to understand the statement in v. 3a.[20] The Book of Kings, however, is not predisposed to report anything regarding such a relationship. Indeed, the mention of the Galilean and Transjordan territories of Israel annexed by Tiglath-pileser III in 2Kgs 15:29 could be interpreted as punishment for Pekah participating in an anti-Assyrian coalition in the view of 2Kgs 16:7–9, but it is only in 2Kgs 17:3b that Hoshea's status as an Assyrian vassal is reported for the first time.

This corresponds with the observation that v. 3 is not mentioning any attempt by Hoshea to throw off the Assyrian yoke, as is the case in v. 4a. In addition, the sudden appearance of Shalmaneser V and the resulting obligation of the king of Israel to pay tribute has a close parallel in connection with the first mention of an Assyrian ruler in the Book of Kings in the time of Menahem of Israel in 2Kgs 15:19–20. He, just like Hoshea, was able to affect an Assyrian withdrawal through the payment of a hefty tribute. The expansionistic politics of the Assyrian kings apparently did not need any further rationale. In the narrative framework of 2Kgs 17:3–6, the comment on Hoshea's vassal status sets the stage for the events evolving. It has an expository function for what follows.

2.2.2 Israel's Way into Exile (vv. 4–6)

The introductory function of v. 3 is also highlighted by the temporal phrase $k^e\check{s}\bar{a}n\bar{a}h\ b^e\check{s}\bar{a}n\bar{a}h$ ("from year to year, annually") in v. 4a separating the following events from what has preceded. A closer dating, however, is just as unclear as in the exposition. In other words, when exactly did Hoshea stop paying the annual tribute and began conspirative negotiations with Egypt is unknown to the narrator, or at least considered meaningless for his narrative presentation. The only fact important is the situation at hand that the last king of Israel – for unknown

---

20 Either the vassal status of Hoshea, mentioned in v. 3b, is paralleled to the notion of him paying tribute to Tiglath-pileser III in the royal inscriptions of the Assyrian king (cf. Weippert, *Textbuch*, 296), or – more commonly – it is assumed that the Israelite king participated in an anti-Assyrian revolt of some Syro-Palestinian vassal states subdued by Shalmaneser V shortly after his accession to the throne; cf. Mordechai Cogan and Hayim Tadmor, *II Kings: A New Translation with Introduction and Commentary* (New York: Doubleday, 1988), 198–99.

reasons – decided to revoke his loyalty to the king of Assyria, thereby setting the disastrous events in motion, which led to the decline of Samaria and the exile of Israel.

Whether there is something more to the difficult form of the name of the Egyptian king, *sô'*, in v. 4a, perhaps a shortened form of the name Osorkon (IV) or a misunderstood pharaonic title,[21] plays secondary role for the understanding of the narrative. For the South Palestinian petty states, Egypt is the closest ally, without whose military support an uprising against the supremacy of Assyria would be pointless.[22]

Although Hoshea's violation of loyalty precedes chronologically the second emergence of the Assyrian king, the narrator only mentions it in a circumstantial clause (textual background, cf. Fig. 1). The progress of the plot line (textual foreground) is dominated by the king of Assyria, who uncovered Hoshea's rebellion.[23] He is the main character (Fig. 2) in the narrative (cf. vv. 3a, 4a$_1$.b, 5–6).

v. 3a	Shalmaneser (V), *king of Assyria*
v. 3b	Hoshea (becoming a vassal of Assyria)
v. 4a$_1$	*King of Assyria*
v. 4a$_2$	Hoshea (violation of loyalty to the Assyrian king)
v. 4b	*King of Assyria*
v. 5	*King of Assyria*
v. 6	*King of Assyria*

Fig. 2: Acting characters in 2Kgs 17:3–6. Prepared by the author.

The exposure of the conspiracy resulted in Hoshea's arrest, the details of which remain vague. Neither battle nor siege are mentioned in v. 4b. Instead,

---

[21] Cf. the discussion of the various suggestions in Bernd U. Schipper, "Wer war 'Sō', König von Ägypten'?" *BN* 92 (1998): 71–84.
[22] Even Yamani of Ashdod sought Egyptian support for his anti-Assyrian activities (cf. Morkot in this volume, p. 131). Therefore the narrated world of the text can demand a certain degree of historical plausibility, but it is based on a more general pattern in Syro-Palestinian political affairs, whose only individual detail, the name of the pharao, remains obscure. Cf. the chapter of Robert Morkot in this volume.
[23] If Hoshea's rebellion is called a coup d'etat (*qæšær*), the negative qualification of the term is reasonable from the perspective of the Assyrian overlord. However, a religious disqualification of the last king of Israel is not necessarily implied (see above, note 11).

the personal consequences of the king are pointed out. He is captured by the Assyrians (*'ṣr*) and thrown into prison (*'sr* + *bêt kælæ'*).²⁴ The root *'sr* ("to bind, to tie") appears again later with the Judean kings Jehoahaz and Zedekiah, both of whom are led into captivity to Egypt and Babylon respectively (cf. 2Kgs 23:33; 25:7). If this was the case for Hoshea, as well, then his fate would symbolically point to that of Israel (cf. v. 6), but this is not explicitly said. The narrator is rather silent concerning the future wellbeing of the last king of Israel – he is captured and arrested, but still alive. In contrast to Necho II and Nebuchadnezzar II (cf. 2Kgs 23:34; 24:17), Shalmaneser V did not install a new king in Samaria. This implies that Hoshea is the last king of Israel known by the narrator, it does not imply, however, that his reign necessarily ended with his capture.²⁵

With the comment concerning the capture of Hoshea, the narrative comes to a relative end, as nothing else is said about the fate of the king, also the antagonism between Hoshea and the Assyrian king, which has dominated the narrative plot so far, comes to an end (cf. Fig. 2). But the question remains what the consequences might be for the people of Israel. Hence, the silence concerning a successor to the Samarian throne points forward to the portrayal of the siege and capture of the city in vv. 5–6.²⁶ The consecutive tempora in v. 5 drive the plot forward. After Hoshea's capture, the king of Assyria, still identifiable as Shalmaneser V according to the rhetorical outline of the text, claimed the remaining state of Samaria (v. 5a) and then moved against the capital city itself, which he besieged for three years (v. 5b). The verb *'ālāh* (Fig. 3), which functions as a keyword in vv. 3–5 (cf. vv. 3a, 4a, and 5a.b), evokes the threatening presence of the Assyrian king, which resulted in Hoshea's surrender earlier (cf. v. 3a), with-

---

24 Due to the course of events and according to the spatial references in the narrative plot the capture of Hoshea must have taken place outside the Samarian territory (cf. v. 5a). This has led to the assumption that the king had been summoned to Shalmaneser V and afterwards arrested (cf. Jehoahaz in 2Kgs 23:33). The meaning of the root *'ṣr* in the G-stem "to hold back" does not exclude this interpretation. The sequence of actions described by *'ṣr* and *'sr* (+ *bêt kælæ'*, cf. Judg 16:21, 25) is in accordance with the narrative plot: first Shalmaneser V arrested Hoshea before he sent him to jail.

25 This can be seen e.g. in the short account on Jehoiachin's release in 2Kgs 25:27–30 dating the event according to the regnal years of the imprisoned king (cf. v. 27). A similar chronological system is used in the Book of Ezekiel; cf. Ernst Kutsch, *Die chronologischen Daten des Ezechielbuches* (Freiburg: Universitätsverlag / Göttingen: Vandenhoeck & Ruprecht, 1985).

26 Hence, the literary analysis of the narrative plot in 2Kgs 17:3–6 confirms our earlier assumption that vv. 3–4 are neither taken from an independent textual source nor have they been added to the passage by a later editor (see above, notes 8–9).

out conflating both events into one.[27] At the same time, it points toward Hoshea's refusal to pay tribute in v. 4a: because he withheld his annual payment to the Assyrian king, the Great King marched to Samaria, which is named as the explicit target of the Assyrian advance here for the first time.[28]

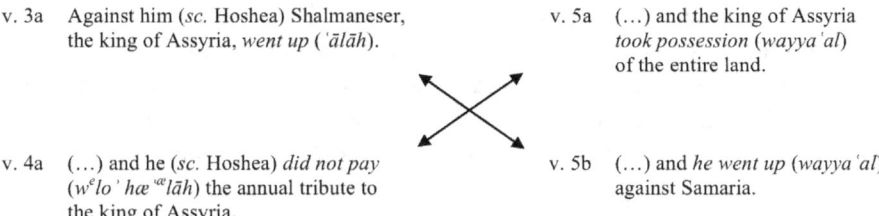

v. 3a   Against him (sc. Hoshea) Shalmaneser, the king of Assyria, *went up* (*'ālāh*).

v. 5a   (…) and the king of Assyria *took possession* (*wayya'al*) of the entire land.

v. 4a   (…) and he (sc. Hoshea) *did not pay* (*wᵉlo' hæ ᵃlāh*) the annual tribute to the king of Assyria.

v. 5b   (…) and *he went up* (*wayya'al*) against Samaria.

Fig. 3: The verb *'ālāh* as keyword in 2Kgs 17:3–5. Prepared by the author.

The consecutive chain of events in the middle section, which establishes a coherent structure through the repetition of the root *'lh*, arrives at its conclusion with the comment about the three-year siege of Samaria in v. 5b without reaching the end of the story. The actual beginning of the siege is not shared by the narrator, it is only possible to extrapolate it retrospectively by means of the temporal adverbial phrase "in the 9ᵗʰ year of Hoshea" at the beginning of v. 6 as it was done by a later editor in 2Kgs 18:9–12 synchronizing 2Kgs 17:5–6 with the reign of the Judean king Hezekiah. The much-discussed issue of whether it is plausible that Samaria was able to resist the siege of the Assyrian troops for three years does not seem to concern the narrator. He reckons that Hoshea, even while imprisoned, remains the legitimate king of Israel until its political

---

27 The mention of the Assyrian king campaigning against Samaria in v. 5a is not a literary doublet to the events mentioned in v. 3a, because in the first instance, Shalmaneser V subdued Hoshea and made him a vassal paying an annual tribute, while in the second, Samaria has been besieged and finally captured and the people sent to exile. There is also no reason to assume a later origin for the expression *bᵉkål hā'āræṣ* in v. 5a due to its absence in the parallel version of 2Kgs 18:9 as proposed by Immanuel Benzinger, *Die Bücher der Könige* (Freiburg im Breisgau: Mohr Siebeck, 1899), 173. The editor of 2Kgs 18:9–12 seems, instead, to have compiled both phrases from 2Kgs 17:3a and 5a into one. Due to his historiographic interest contrasting Hoshea with Hezekiah, he had to eliminate the first episode of his source text which mentions the last king of Israel paying tribute to the Assyrian overlord in order to rescue Samaria from becoming an Assyrian province as did Hezekiah in 2Kgs 18:13–16 (see above note 9).

28 The root *'ālāh* occurs twice, in v. 5 and in vv. 3–4. Is this a mere coincidence? However, the distribution of the root throughout the narrative shows a distinctive literary pattern (a–b–b'–a') according to which the conquest of the land (v. 5a) corresponds to the withholding of the annual tribute by Hoshea (v. 4a, cf. also the play on words with the roots *šwb* and *yšb* in vv. 3b and 6b).

sovereignty ended. The point at which this happened has already been mentioned in the regnal summary in v. 1b.

The reference to the 9th year of Hoshea at the beginning of v. 6 signals, on the one hand, the end of the siege of Samaria, and marks, on the other, a narrative break. It thus reveals the capture of the city and the deportation of its inhabitants as the pragmatic climax of the episode and connects the narrative arc back to the dates of Hoshea's reign in the introductory formula. The capture of the city, expressed with the verb *lākad* ("to catch, to capture"), does not necessarily imply its destruction but, instead, draws a parallel to the fate of its king.[29] The conquest of Samaria and the exile of its people are attributed to the same king that is identified at the beginning of the section as Shalmaneser V (cf. 2Kgs 18:9–11). He resettled the deportees in central Assyria and in the Northeastern border areas (v. 6b).[30] The expression *wayyošæb 'otām* in v. 6b phonetically assonates the notice of Hoshea paying tribute to the Assyrian king in v. 3b (*wayyāšæb lô minḥāh*). Instead of paying tribute, Israel itself is now brought to Assyria. The second confrontation with the Assyrians ended badly for Israel with the loss

---

[29] The root *lākad* with a personal object has the meaning "to catch," either humans (especially prisoners of war) or animals; with cities or territories as object it means "to take possession of, to conquer" (cf. Akkadian *kašādu*). It always implies violence and a loss of freedom, but not necessarily physical destruction; cf. Heinrich Groß, "לָכַד *lākad*," *ThWAT* 4 (1984): 573–76. Hence, on a literary level, the conquest of the city corresponds to the fate of its last king. In a historical perspective, however, the literary depiction of the events coincides with the archaeological record in *Sebaṣṭye* (Samaria), where no signs of a massive destruction of the city in the 8th century BC have been found; cf. Ron E. Tappy, *The Archaeology of Israelite Samaria*, vol. 2: *The Eighth Century BCE* (Winona Lake IN: Eisenbrauns, 2001), 558–75.

[30] The reference to the cities of the Medes may indicate that the deportations mentioned in v. 6b did not happen before the reign of Sargon II, who in 716 BC subdued the Eastern border region of the Assyrian empire and incorporated it into the Assyrian provincial system (cf. the chapter by Karen Radner in the present volume). However, the massive deportations carried out by the Assyrian kings over a long period led to an ongoing exchange of people from all parts of the Assyrian empire. Thus the deportation of the Samarians (as well as the resettlement of foreign people into the territory of Samaria, cf. 2Kgs 17:24) is not to be imagined as a single event, but has taken place over a period of time. It may well have started under the reign of Shalmaneser V and continued far into the time of Sargon II; cf. Bustenay Oded, *Mass Deportations and Deportees in the Neo Assyrian Empire* (Wiesbaden: Harrassowitz, 1979) and the chapter of Karen Radner in this volume. In 2Kgs 17:6 the continuing process of deportations has been reorganized in a single narrative plot and ascribed to "the King of Assyria". Whether the narrator had any particular knowledge about the settlement places of the deportees from Samaria (or their heirs) remains uncertain. There are references in the cuneiform sources to peoples possibly related to the deportees from Samaria in the regions mentioned in the biblical account until the end of the 7th century BC (cf. Becking, *Fall*, 61–93, and the chapter by Karen Radner in the present volume).

of political sovereignty and deportation of its people into a foreign country. The people finally share the same fate as their last king.

3 Who Conquered Samaria?

As mentioned at the beginning, the cuneiform sources contain contrasting information concerning the events leading up to the downfall of Samaria. Aside from the widely discussed alternatives of whether the capture of the city can be attributed to Shalmaneser V or Sargon II, there are further questions that arise when the biblical narrative in 2Kgs 17:3–6 is taken into consideration. If Shalmaneser V was responsible for the conquest of Samaria, at which point during his five-year reign did this take place? Was the capture of the city preceded by a three-year siege? Was the city handed over (by Hoshea) or was it taken by force? Was Samaria already made into an Assyrian province and the people deported under Shalmaneser V or did it all happen under Sargon II? Did Sargon II already overthrow Samaria in his accession year or not before his second *palû*? The list goes on, and the manifold problems cannot be discussed here in detail.[31] The following observations will merely give a brief sketch of what contribution the presentation of the events in 2Kgs 17:1–6, being aware of the narrative pragmatic of the passage, is able to bring to bear on the discussion concerning the historical circumstances of the conquest of Samaria as well as which (narrow) limits are hidden in such an endeavor. It is, however, not my primary interest to establish the historical validity of the biblical account, but to point to the various historical propositions, upon which its interpretations generally depend.

3.1 The Chronology

The first set of problems to address is about the chronology of events. Aside from the contradictory information contained in the synchronistic framework of the Book of Kings, which later have been reworked in the process of textual transmission,[32] we do not have any closer knowledge about the regnal dates of the

---

31 Cf. the discussion in the chapters by Eckart Frahm, Norma Franklin, Karen Radner and Ron Tappy in the present volume.
32 E. g., in the divergent textforms of the Septuagint the reigning years of the earlier kings Menahem, Pekahia, and Pekah have been (with variations) enlarged to fit the given synchronisms – a practice still in use in modern scholarship.

last king of Israel. Therefore it is nearly impossible to achieve a reliable set of data that can bear the weight of historical scrutiny. This is evident for the contradictory dates regarding the beginning of Hoshea's reign (cf. 2Kgs 15:30 with 17:1) and concerns just as much the synchronism between the downfall of Samaria and the reign of Hezekiah (cf. 2Kgs 18:1 with 18:9, 11), which stands in contradiction to the date of the third military campaign of Sennacherib, which took place in the year 701 BC, in the 14th year of Hezekiah (cf. 2Kgs 18:13).[33] However, the nine-year reign of Hoshea is often seen as historically reliable information, which has been used to firmly establish the date of the downfall of Samaria.[34] But when did it start? To more closely determine the date of Hoshea's accession to the throne, it is necessary to take a closer look at the royal inscriptions of Tiglath-pileser III.[35]

In his various summary inscriptions the Assyrian king mentions his submission of Israel, the installation of Hoshea as a vassal king, and the collection of tributary payments.[36] Because the summary inscriptions do not follow a chronological order, the date of these events can only be determined by a comparison with the Eponym Chronicle, which mentions for Tiglath-pileser III a military campaign against Damascus in the year 733/32 and 732/31 BC respectively, which most likely are related to the anti-Assyrian alliance also mentioned in 2Kgs 16:5–9.[37] It is often assumed that Samaria was already subdued during the first campaign of Tiglath-pileser III in the year 733/32 BC.[38] It is not clear, however, whether Hoshea's revolt, according to 2Kgs 15:30, occurred during

---

[33] Becking, *Fall*, 53–54, tried to harmonize both dates by ascribing the date in 2Kgs 18:13 to a military campaign of Sargon II to Palestine in the year 715 BC and assuming it was later erroneously connected with Sennacherib's siege of Jerusalem.

[34] Assuming the nine-year reign of Hoshea is certain, either the date of Hoshea's accession year or the date of the fall of Samaria vary in the scholarly debate; cf. Timm, "Eroberung," 115 note 49. On the other hand, some scholars have supposed a longer reign for the last king of Israel based on the cuneiform sources; cf. Rudolf Kittel, *Die Bücher der Könige* (Göttingen: Vandenhoeck & Ruprecht, 1900), 273–74 and Albrecht Šanda, *Die Bücher der Könige*, vol. 2: *Das zweite Buch der Könige* (Münster: Aschendorff, 1912), 211–12.

[35] Cf. the latest edition of the texts by Hayim Tadmor and Shigeo Yamada, *The Royal Inscriptions of Tiglath-pileser III. (744–727 BC) and Shalmaneser V. (726–722 BC), Kings of Assyria* (Winona Lake IN: Eisenbrauns, 2011).

[36] Cf. Weippert, *Textbuch*, 295, and Tadmor and Yamada, *Inscriptions*, 105–106, 112, 131–32.

[37] Cf. Weippert, *Textbuch*, 288. Tiglath-pileser III had already campaigned in Palestine in the year 734/33 BC in order to subdue a rebellion of the Philistine coastal cities and to secure the border to Egypt.

[38] Or did Israel lose parts of its territory already during Tiglath-pileser's campaign against Gaza in the year 734/33 BC? According to the archaeological record it seems that the coastal strip was no longer under Israelite control in the second half of the 8th century BC.

this conflict or followed shortly thereafter.[39] Tiglath-pileser III mentions that Hoshea paid his tribute in the South-Babylonian city of Sarrabānu.[40] Since the Assyrian king, according to the Eponym Chronicle, was engaged in a military campaign in this region in the year 731/30 BC, it would be obvious to connect the payment of tribute with these events.[41] If this tribute was Hoshea's first payment to the Assyrian suzerain, as is usually presumed, it would follow that the first year of Hoshea's reign was in the year 732/31 BC (or 731/30 BC respectively).[42]

This dating can be connected to the notice of the Babylonian Chronicle, which attributes the conquest of Samaria to Shalmaneser V (cf. 2Kgs 17:3–6), who reigned between 727 and 722 BC. An even more exact dating of the event, however, cannot be garnered from the text of the Babylonian Chronicle. The assumption that Shalmaneser V took possession of Samaria only at the end of his reign finds its basis on a misunderstanding of the compositional structure of the Chronicle.[43] Presupposing Hoshea's accession to the throne in Samaria in the

---

39 The wording of the Summary Inscription no. 13, lines 17–18, indicates that Pekah was murdered only after Tiglath-pileser III had annexed the Galilean and Transjordan territories of Israel (cf. Tadmor and Yamada, *Inscriptions*, 112) – perhaps to prevent any attempt to further support the former ally Rezin, king of Damascus, who withstood the Assyrian attack in 733/32 BC.
40 Summary Inscription no. 9, lines r. 10–11 (cf. Weippert, *Textbuch*, 295, and Tadmor and Yamada, *Inscriptions*, 132).
41 Cf. Rykle Borger and Hayim Tadmor, "Zwei Beiträge zur alttestamentlichen Wissenschaft aufgrund der Inschriften Tiglatpilesers III.," *ZAW* 94 (1982): 244–51, 244–49. The Babylonian Chronicle, however, mentions that Tiglath-pileser III did not defeat Nabû-mukin-zeri until the year 729/28 BC, when he became king of Babylon himself (cf. column I, lines 19–23). Therefore Hoshea could have paid his tribute to the Assyrian king in Sarrabānu at this later date as well; cf. Gaß, *Strudel*, 3–4. However, a date of Hoshea's coup years after Tiglath-pileser III had reorganized the political landscape of Syro-Palestine seems less probable.
42 The list of Western tributaries in the Summary Inscription of Tiglath-pileser III no. 7, r. 7–13 (cf. Weippert, *Textbuch*, 289–90), probably composed in the year 729/28 BC, fails to mention Samaria and Damascus, indicating that it may represent the political situation of the year 733/32 BC, when both rebelled against the Assyrian dominion; cf. Hayim Tadmor, *The Inscriptions of Tiglath-pileser III. King of Assyria: Critical Edition, with Introductions, Translations and Commentary* (Jerusalem: The Israel Academy of Sciences and Humanities, 1994), 268. The fragmentary character of the inscription, however, does allow different interpretations.
43 Cf. Becking, *Fall*, 24. – The Eponym Chronicle for Shalmaneser V is heavily damaged. In his 2nd to 4th year the king undertook military campaigns, but the names of his targets are not preserved. In his first regnal year (726/25 BC) he stayed in Assyria; cf. Alan R. Millard, *The Eponyms of the Assyrian Empire 910–612 BC* (Helsinki: The Neo-Assyrian Text Corpus Project, 1994), 59. The entry for his last year is too damaged to draw further conclusions. However, there are other hints to military activities carried out by Shalmaneser V in Southern Syria and Babylonia respectively, but their dating remains uncertain; cf. Timm, "Eroberung," 110–11. What can be

year 732/31 BC along with the information concerning his nine-year reign, a relative precise point in time for the conquest of Samaria by Shalmaneser V becomes apparent, which is compatible with the dates in the Babylonian Chronicle.[44] If instead, Sargon II has a right to his claim that he conquered Samaria in his accession year (i.e., 722/21 BC), then Hoshea could not have come into power before the year 730/29 BC, or else the reign of the last king of Israel must be calculated independent from the biblical chronology.

3.2 The Course of Events

What is the situation concerning the information the sources provide on the sequence of events? In the Babylonian Chronicle, it is only mentioned that Shalmaneser V "broke" Samaria (ḫepû). However, the Akkadian verb ḫepû is used in other passages of the Babylonian Chronicle as an expression indicating the conquest of cities and regions. For this reason, one can translate it "to conquer" or "to capture" without necessarily implying a violent destruction.[45] On the other hand, Sargon II presents the conquest of Samaria in a much more detailed manner: he fought against its people and conquered (kašādu) the city, deported its inhabitants, resettled deportees from other conquered areas, installed a provincial governor, and established tributes and taxes from the people. All of this sup-

---

said for sure is that Shalmaneser V did not capture Samaria earlier than his second regnal year (725/24 BC).

44 It is likely that Hoshea (together with other Western vassal states) took advantage of the political turmoil in the Assyrian homeland following Shalmaneser's V accession to the throne which forced the king to stay at home in his first regnal year (see above note 43). Did the king first subdue the revolt in Southern Babylonia, mentioned in an Aramaean letter from the 7th century BC (cf. KAI, no. 233, line 15), before he turned to the West?

45 Cf. Weippert, *Textbuch*, 296–97. However, Timm, "Eroberung," 107–108, concluded from a comparison of the account concerning the capture of the cities of Ḫarratum and Ḫirimma by Sennacherib in the Babylonian Chronicle (cf. column II, lines 24–25) with the parallel account in the Annals of the king (cf. column I, lines 54–63), that "ḫepû bedeutet im übertragenen Gebrauch der babylonischen Chronik grausamste Bestrafung der Gegner, Ablieferung schweren Tributs und administrative Neuordnung des eroberten Gebietes"; cf. also Becking, *Fall*, 24–25. But a closer analysis of the passage reveals that both cities have been treated by Sennacherib in quite different ways: regarding Ḫarratum, it is only said that the city had to pay heavy tribute. In the case of Ḫirimma, a violent destruction of the city, mutilation of the dead bodies of the enemies, and an administrative reorganization of its territory is mentioned. Both events have been summarized in the Babylonian Chronicle, with the term ḫepû used here in a more general sense of "to break (someone's resistance), to subdue"; cf. Na'aman, "Background," 211.

posedly occurred in the year of the king's accession to the throne according to the Annals of Sargon II from Dūr-Šarrukēn/Ḫorsābād.⁴⁶

The annals are dated, however, from later in the reign of the king.⁴⁷ The earlier inscriptions of Sargon II are not (yet) aware of these events and only mention Samaria in the context of the revolt of Ilu-bi'di of Hamath, which Sargon II surpressed in the second year of his reign (i. e., 720/19 BC).⁴⁸ The literary form of the portrayal in the annals follows already existing patterns and is linked to events that occurred over a period of time during the reign of Sargon II.⁴⁹ This could indicate that the author(s) of the royal annals freely constructed the campaign of Sargon II against Samaria in the accession year of the king, drawing on older material and imitating the typical style of Neo-Assyrian royal inscriptions. This may have been done to conceal the fact that Sargon II was not capable of any military undertakings due to the political turmoil in the wake of his claiming the throne.⁵⁰ Assuming this is correct, it would support the assertion of the Babylonian Chronicle that the conquest of Samaria occurred at the hand of Shalmaneser V.

The biblical tradition mentions a three-year siege, or more aptly stated, a blockade of Samaria, about which the Assyrian sources remain silent.⁵¹ It also

---

46 Cf. the Annals of Sargon II, lines 10–17. The fragmentary text of the annals is mostly restored according to the parallel account in the Prism Inscription of Sargon II from Kalḫu/Nimrud, column IV, lines 25–41; cf. Andreas Fuchs, *Die Inschriften Sargons II. aus Khorsabad* (Göttingen: Cuvullier, 1994, 87–88). The latter, however, does not allow a precise dating of the events. A shorter version of the story is preserved in the Summary Inscription of Sargon II from Dūr-Šarrukēn/Ḫorsābād, lines 23–25; cf. Weippert, *Textbuch*, 302.
47 The annals of Sargon II from Dūr-Šarrukēn/Ḫorsābād were not composed before his 15th *palû* (cf. Timm, "Eroberung," 115), the Prism-Inscription from Kalḫu/Nimrud dates from around the same time or shortly thereafter (see above note 3).
48 Cf. the Assur Charter of Sargon II, lines 16–28, probably written shortly after the events, and the recently discovered Tell Tayinat Stele of Sargon II; cf. Jacob Lauinger and Stephen Batiuk, "A Stele of Sargon II. at Tell Tayinat", *ZA* 105 (2015): 54–68, and the chapter by Eckart Frahm in the present volume.
49 Here a remarkable parallel to the biblical narrative in 2Kgs 17:3–6 can be noted, where a similar literary technique is to be observed; cf. already the remarks by John Gray, *I & II Kings: A Commentary* (London: SCM Press, 1977; third edition), 60–62.
50 Cf. the chapter by Eckart Frahm in the present volume. – The account in the annals that the military campaign against Samaria had already occurred in the accession year of Sargon II raises some logistical problems as well, because there are only a few weeks left between his accession to the throne on the 12th of Ṭebēt (cf. Babylonian Chronicle, column I, line 31) and the beginning of his first regnal year on the 1st of Nisān. Additionally the turmoil following the death of Shalmaneser V probably made it necessary for the king to stay at home.
51 The fragmentary text of the Eponym Chronicle for Shalmaneser V does not completely rule out a three-year siege of Samaria as mentioned in 2Kgs 17:5–6, but this would leave very little

appears unlikely that the city managed to muster the strength to resist the siege for a considerable time even after the capture of Hoshea.[52] Furthermore, one must reckon that the events as reported in 2Kgs 17:3–6 are ordered in a single continuous narrative plot even though historically they most likely occurred over a much longer period of time. This can be seen from the following observations: first the regions, in which the Israelites, according to 2Kgs 17:6b, are supposed to have been resettled, could only have been firmly incorporated in part into the Assyrian provincial system under Sargon II,[53] and second, considering the literary structure of the chapter, the resettlement of foreign deportees in the territory of Samaria (cf. 2Kgs 17:24) is ascribed to the same king of Assyria, who had conquered Israel and sent the people into exile and who the cuneiform sources identify as Sargon II.[54] Therefore the motif of the three-year siege of the city of Samaria is to be understood primarily as a narrative figure to develop the plot establishing a coherent literary thread. This, however, would be historically correct in that the procedure of transforming conquered regions into an Assyrian province, along with an expansive resettlement of the inhabitants, would require more time than would have been possible at the hand of Shalmaneser V alone, as the inscriptions of Sargon II confirm. A (short-lived) blockade of Samaria by

---

time for the other military campaigns the king had undertaken during his reign (see above note 44). However, the account from Menander mentioned by Josephus (cf. Ant. IX,13,2) in which Shalmaneser V besieged Tyros for five years is not to be connected to the fall of Samaria, but most probably belongs to another time; cf. Ariel M. Bagg, *Die Assyrer und das Westland: Studien zur historischen Geographie und Herrschaftspraxis in der Levante im 1. Jt. v.u.Z.* (Leuven: Peeters, 2011), 228–29. – In the Summary Inscription of Sargon II from Dūr-Šarrukēn/Ḫorsābād the king claims that he laid siege (*lemû*) against Samaria and conquered (*kašādu*) the city (cf. line 23), but this is the only passage in the royal inscriptions of Sargon II which mentions a siege of Samaria. Thus a three-year blockade would be in contrast to the reports of the event in the king's annals and in his Prism-Inscription from Kalḫu/Nimrud dating from around the same time. The contrary argument by M. Christine Tetley, "The Date of Samaria's Fall as a Reason for Rejecting the Hypothesis of Two Conquests," *CBQ* 64 (2002): 59–77, is not convincing.
52 Therefore J. Maxwell Miller and John H. Hayes, *A History of Ancient Israel and Judah* (Louisville KT: Westminster John Knox Press, 2006; second edition), 386–87, assumed that after Hoshea has been captured he was followed by another king on the throne in Samaria, whose name is not known to us anymore, but there is no evidence in the sources to foster their argument; cf. Gaß, *Strudel*, 14 note 52.
53 See above note 30.
54 Cf. the reference to some Arabic tribes Sargon II has resettled in Samaria in his Cylinder-Inscription from Dūr-Šarrukēn/Ḫorsābād. The episode is dated in the annals of the king to his 7th *palû* (715 BC), cf. Weippert, *Textbuch*, 305–306. Of course, this does not rule out the possibility that other deportees had been resettled in Samaria at an earlier time starting with the reign of Shalmaneser V.

Shalmaneser V might have happened, a three-year siege of the city, however, is historically less plausible.⁵⁵ Hence, the "king-less" resistence of Samaria seems to be a literary construct that does not need any historical explanation.

The same is true regarding the notice that Hoshea first became an Assyrian vassal under Shalmaneser V, at a time of his reign not precisely determined (cf. 2Kgs 17:3). According to the inscriptions of Tiglath-pileser III, Hoshea was from the beginning of his reign under Assyrian domination. For this reason, the events mentioned in v. 3 are often connected to a revolt of some vassal states in Southern Syria, which used the turmoil occurring in Assyria after the accession of Shalmaneser V as an occasion to throw off the Assyrian yoke.⁵⁶ The assumption that a group of Syro-Palestinian petty states took advantage of the political unrest in Assyria in order to build an anti-Assyrian coalition possesses a certain amount of plausibility.⁵⁷ This, however, serves more likely as the background for the rebellion, which led to the downfall of Samaria (cf. 2Kgs 17:4–6). The idea that Shalmaneser V mounted a second campaign against Samaria in such a short reign is less likely. Moreover, it remains unclear what reason there might have been for Hoshea (and his allies) to stage such a revolt later in the reign of the Assyrian king. If one takes into account that the narrator of the Book of Kings is silent about the vassal status of Hoshea under Tiglath-pileser III (cf. 2Kgs 15:30), and that 2Kgs 17:3 represents the narrative exposition for the report on the downfall of Samaria, then it seems to be futile to search for any historical cause for the first advance of Shalmaneser V against Hoshea.⁵⁸

Hoshea's insurgency against the Assyrian rule might be connected with a broader revolt of some Syro-Palestinian vassal states along with Egyptian support, about which little more is known, aside from the comment in 2Kgs

---

55 Cf. Hermann Michael Niemann, "Royal Samaria – Capital or Residence? or: The Foundation of the City of Samaria by Sargon II," in id., *History of Ancient Israel, Archaeology, and Bible: Collected Essays*, ed. Meik Gerhards (Münster: Ugarit-Verlag, 2015): 295–315, 305–307.
56 Cf. the discussion in Na'aman, "Background," 213–16, and Becking, *Fall*, 50–51.
57 However, this is not to be argued due to the reference from Menander in Josephus (see above note 51), but due to the fact that Shalmaneser V, according to the Eponym Chronicle, stayed at home in his first regnal year; cf. Jean-Jacques Glassner, *Mesopotamian Chronicles*, trans. Benjamin R. Foster (Atlanta GA: Society of Biblical Literature, 2004), 174. It can be reasoned that the struggle with his political adversaries in Assyria (and Babylonia) encouraged the Western vassal states to throw off the Assyrian yoke, but no further information has been preserved on the course of events in Assyria after Shalmaneser V acceded to the throne.
58 Cf. Gershon Galil, "The Last Years of the Kingdom of Israel and the Fall of Samaria," *CBQ* 57 (1995): 52–56, 62–63.

17:4a.⁵⁹ The identity of the Egyptian pharaoh, whose name (or title?) is *Sô'* in the biblical account, is unresolved.⁶⁰ In addition, it remains questionable whether the narrator had any closer knowledge about the political situation in that time, or whether his narrative is mandatory to a common historical pattern. The historical plausibility of an alliance with Egypt certainly cannot be denied. Such an endeavor, however, would have not likely been met with much success considering the unstable political conditions along with competing claims to power in Egypt at that time.⁶¹

4 In Conclusion

No matter how one wants to judge the details, each historical query of the events leading to the downfall of Samaria must take into consideration that the narrative in 2Kgs 17:3–6 pursues primarily an historiographic interest, which subsequently incorporates the individual narrative elements into the story. This makes an historical analysis palpably difficult, even when dispensing with the task of verifying its historical value. In this case, it leads to the result that the basic information concerning the dates in the narrative can be correlated with the cuneiform reports. The narrative does possess a general historical plausibility, but it does not allow a closer historical reconstruction of the course of events, which underlies many historicizing interpretations. Neither is the biblical account in 2Kgs 17:3–6 able to say what exactly happened in "the last days of the kings of Israel," nor should an historical reconstruction of the events be made the ultimate measure of the interpretation of the text. The 'biblical' answer to the question "Who conquered Samaria?" is just as unambigious as it is ambigious: "the King of Assyria".

---

59 Cf. Herbert Donner, *Geschichte Israels und seiner Nachbarn in Grundzügen,* vol. 2: *Von der Königszeit bis zu Alexander dem Großen: Mit einem Ausblick auf die Geschichte des Judentums bis Bar Kochba* (Göttingen: Vandenhoeck & Ruprecht, 1995; second edition), 345. Na'aman, "Background," 217–19, connects the account with an anti-Assyrian revolt following the accession of Sargon II to the throne subdued by the king in the year 720/19 BC. Thus he argues in favor of Sargon II as the Assyrian king, who conquered Samaria, but his proposal raises more questions than it can answer.
60 Cf. the discussion in Na'aman, "Background," 216–17, and Schipper, "Sō'."
61 Cf. Donner, *Königszeit,* 344–45.

Georg Hentschel
Did Hoshea of Israel Continue the Foreign Policy of His Predecessors?

1 Introduction

Why and how did the decline of the Northern Kingdom come about? Did Hoshea, its last king, have a chance to avert the fall of his kingdom? Peter Dubovský, when analysing 2Kgs 15, recently highlighted that some of the issues that may have contributed to the Fall of Samaria predate Hoshea's coming to power. Most importantly, perhaps, a series of *coups d'état* made the kingdom more and more unstable: "While the first three *coups d'état* are spread over almost 200 years, the last four took place within 20 years."[1] Dubovský also pointed to the rivalry between the tribes and the cities, to a gradual loss of executive power, to various atrocities, to the heavy burden of tribute due to the Assyrian Empire and to "Israel's wrong international policy."[2]

This assessment leads to our question for this chapter: Did Hoshea continue the disastrous policy of his predecessors on the throne of Israel, or did he try to find a way out? Can we even hope to achieve a satisfying answer? Are we in any position to assess the behaviour of a single person at the end of the eighth century BCE? Although it seems that we know the most important events only in rough outline, a great many articles and even monographs discuss the topic of the "Last Days of the Kingdom of Israel" in detail.

2 Hoshea's Predecessors

For a long time, the Northern Kingdom was strong enough to stand up against its enemies. According to the inscriptions of Shalmaneser III of Assyria, Ahab of Israel took part in the battle at Qarqar (853 BCE) with 2,000 chariots and 10,000 men[3] when he rose against the Assyrian Empire to defend the independence and sovereignty of the Levant, together with other regional kingdoms. But

---
[1] Peter Dubovský, "Why Did the Northern Kingdom Fall According to 2 Kings 15?" *Bib* 95 (2014): 321–46, esp. 326.
[2] Dubovský, "Why Did the Northern Kingdom Fall," 342–43.
[3] Albert Kirk Grayson, *Assyrian Rulers of the Early First Millennium BC II (858–754 BC)* (Toronto: Toronto University Press, 1996), A.0.102.2 ii 91–92.

only a decade later, in 841 BCE, the Assyrian evidence shows Jehu of Israel paying tribute to Shalmaneser III.[4] And he was not the only king of his dynasty who had to recognise the great power of Assyria, as Suichi Hasegawa presented in his survey about the biblical and Assyrian sources: Jehu's grandson Joash also paid tribute, to Adad-nerari III and perhaps in 796 BCE.[5] It was certainly not easy for a ruler of Israel to kneel down and to kiss the feet of the great king of Assyria. But did he have an alternative? The years after the Assyrian retreat from the Levant in 829 BCE and before the beginning of new campaigns in 805 BCE were difficult for the Northern Kingdom, because in these years Hazael and his son Ben-Hadad, the kings of Aram in Damascus, exercised their power over Israel. At that time, nobody would have imagined that one day Aram and Israel could be allies.

Jehu's dynasty ended with a conspiracy. Shallum killed Zechariah, the last king of the dynasty (2Kgs 15:10). Unfortunately we do not know anything about the reasons for this assassination. Marvin S. Sweeney assumes that Shallum "was likely motivated by an interest in changing Israel's alignment from Assyria to Aram."[6] But this is to be doubted, as during Jeroboam II's reign there was no Assyrian attack against Israel. On the contrary, Jeroboam was able to expand his territory (2Kgs 14:25). I prefer Dubovský's view that Zechariah's murder is a symptom of the instability of the Northern Kingdom and one of the reasons for its eventual downfall.[7]

Shallum's reign lasted only for one month (2Kgs 15:13), and then he was killed by Menahem. But this man did not form a conspiracy, as Shallum had (15:10.15).[8] According to Dubovský, the biblical author "wanted to underline the contrast between the *coups d'état* of Shallum, Pekah, and Hoshea, and of Menahem."[9] Perhaps this is an indication that Menahem's action was not unlawful. One may take the view that he wanted to rid the country of a murderer on the throne. Menahem came from Tirzah, which was in the time before Omri the res-

---

[4] Grayson, *Assyrian Rulers*, A.0.102.88.
[5] Grayson, *Assyrian Rulers*, A.0.104.7: 8; cf. Shuichi Hasegawa, *Aram and Israel during the Jehuite Dynasty* (Berlin/Boston MA: de Gruyter, 2012), 119.
[6] Marvin S. Sweeney, *I & II Kings: A Commentary* (Louisville KY: Westminster John Knox Press, 2007), 371. Cf. Peter Dubovský, "Suspicious Similiarities: a comparative Study of the Falls of Samaria and Jerusalem," in *The Fall of Jerusalem and the Rise of the Torah*, ed. Peter Dubovský, Dominik Markl and Jean-Pierre Sonnet (Tübingen: Mohr Siebeck, 2016): 47–71, esp. 58.
[7] Dubovský, "Why Did the Northern Kingdom Fall," 322–26.
[8] The author uses the narrative forms ויעל, ויבא and ויך, but not ויקשר.
[9] Peter Dubovský, "Menahem's Reign before the Assyrian Invasion (2 Kings 15:14–16)," in *Literature as Politics, Politics as Literature*, ed. David S. Vanderhooft and Abraham Winitzer (Winona Lake IN: Eisenbrauns, 2014): 29–45, esp. 34. Cf. 1Kgs 15:27–28; 16:9–10; 2Kgs 15:25, 30.

idence city of Israel's kings (1Kgs 14:17; 15:21, 33; 16:6, 8–9, 15, 17f.). The expression "from Tirzah" (2Kgs 15:16a) may indicate, according to Dubovský, "that he started his campaign in Tirzah and moved toward Tiphsah."[10] He succeeded in conquering the city of Tiphsah, if this name indeed belongs to the original text.[11] The majority of the Septuagint manuscripts explain that he ravaged Tiphsah, because "it had not opened its gates to him."[12] But the Hebrew text abstains from an explanation: "Indeed he did not (just) breach (it), but struck (it) down."[13] Do we have here an allusion to Solomon's realm, who is said to have reigned over the whole territory between Tiphsah and Gaza (1Kgs 5:4)? But how does this correspond with the next sentence, that Menahem committed cruelties? He is said to have "ripped open all pregnant women" (2Kgs 15:16d). Does he not perpetrate the same crime as Hazael, the king of Aram (8:12)? Menahem's image is contradictory.

A question of historical relevance remains. Did Menahem really reach Tiphsah on the banks of the Euphrates? Was he successful in a similar way to Jeroboam II (14:25)? A campaign towards the east would have been possible only in Menahem's first years, i.e. in 748 BCE.[14] After the accession of the mighty Tiglath-pileser III (r. 745–727 BCE) to the Assyrian throne there was no chance for such an adventure. The framework of the Book of Kings on Menahem reveals his weakness. He had to pay a heavy tribute to Tiglath-pileser III: "He gave him a thousand talents of silver to obtain his help in strengthening his hold on the kingdom" (15:19). Menahem's subjugation is confirmed by Tiglath-pileser's annals and also attested on his royal stele from Iran.[15] Probably this tribute was

---

10 Dubovský, "Menahem's Reign," 33.
11 Lucianic manuscripts read Ταφωε or Ταφοε "which corresponds to the city תפוח": so Dubovský, "Menahem's Reign," 30f. Tappuah may be identified with Tell Sheikh Abu Zarad, 15 km southeast of Nablus.
12 The Lucianic manuscripts read the singular of the verb, which corresponds to פתח.
13 Dubovský, "Menahem's Reign," 42.
14 Georg Hentschel, "Alter und Herkunft der Synchronismen in den Königsbüchern," *Nichts Neues unter der Sonne? Zeitvorstellungen im Alten Testament: Festschrift für Ernst-Joachim Waschke*, ed. Jens Kotjatko-Reeb, Benjamin Ziemer and Stefan Schorch (Berlin/Boston MA: de Gruyter, 2014): 171–85, esp. 182. Unfortunately, there are mistakes in the dates of his predecessors. Jeroboam reigned until 749 BCE. Zechariah had been killed six months later in 748 BCE. Shallum died yet in the same year and Menahem began to reign.
15 Annals: Hayim Tadmor, *The Inscriptions of Tiglath-pileser III, King of Assyria: Critical Edition, with Introductions, Translations and Commentary* (Jerusalem: Israel Academy of Sciences and Humanities, 1994), 68–9: Ann. 13*: 10 = Hayim Tadmor and Shigeo Yamada, *The Royal Inscriptions of Tiglath-pileser III (744–727 BC) and Shalmaneser V (726–722 BC), Kings of Assyria* (Winona Lake IN: Eisenbrauns, 2011), no. 14: 10; Tadmor, *Inscriptions*, 89 Ann. 27: 2 = Tadmor and Yamada, *Royal Inscriptions*, no. 32: 2; stele: Tadmor, *Inscriptions*, 106–107: IIIA 5 = Tadmor and

paid in the year 738 BCE. Because Menahem himself could not pay the tribute, he "laid a levy on all men of wealth in Israel and each had to give the king of Assyria fifty silver shekels" (15:20). By this levy, of course, the dissatisfaction of the population increased; as Dubovský puts it, "drawing on the wallets of 72,000 nobles must have severely undermined Menahem's popularity."[16] But the support of Tiglath-pileser was also very useful. When Menahem died – shortly after delivering the tribute – his son was able to ascend to the throne of the Northern Kingdom.

Menahem's son Pekahiah reigned for just two years. The circumstances of his assassination show how difficult the situation had become in the meantime. Pekahiah was killed "in the safest place of the kingdom", and "not even the most protected place of the kingdom – the keep of the royal palace in Samaria – was safe enough to protect the king against conspirators," as Dubovský stresses.[17] That was possible because Pekah, Pekahiah's assassin, belonged to the centre of power. He was "Pekahiah's third man, i.e. the officer of the king's entourage."[18] But Pekah was not alone: he headed a conspiracy, with fifty men from Gilead at his side, and was, according to Becking, possibly "an exponent of a Transjordan political party."[19] Tomoo Ishida already discerned "a power struggle between Gileadites and the men of Manasseh in the changes of dynasties."[20]

But the regicide was not only the result of tensions among the tribes. Pekahiah followed his father Menahem's foreign policy. Is it possible that his murderer Pekah opposed this and wanted to terminate Israel's subjugation to the Assyrians? If we want to find out about Pekah's political views, we cannot ignore the campaign against Jerusalem. Rezin of Damascus and Pekah went together southwards and besieged Ahaz of Judah (2Kgs 16:5; Isa 7:1, 2). They wanted to appoint a new king (Isa 7:5). Can we hypothesise that Ahaz was not willing to join their anti-Assyrian coalition? To quote John Bright, Ahaz "saw no course save to appeal to Tiglath-pileser for aid,"[21] which turned the tide: Pekah and Re-

---

Yamada, *Royal Inscriptions*, no. 35: iii 5. Cf. Manfred Weippert, "Menachem von Israel und seine Zeitzeugen in einer Steleninschrift des assyrischen Königs Tiglathpileser III aus dem Iran," *ZDPV* 89 (1973): 26–53.
16 Dubovský, "Why Did the Northern Kingdom Fall," 340.
17 Dubovský, "Why Did the Northern Kingdom Fall," 328.
18 Dubovský, "Why Did the Northern Kingdom Fall," 328.
19 Bob Becking, *The Fall of Samaria: An Historical and Archaeological Study* (Leiden: Brill, 1992), 6.
20 Tomoo Ishida, *The Royal Dynasties in Ancient Israel* (Berlin/New York: de Gruyter, 1977), 176.
21 John Bright, *A History of Israel* (London: SCM Press, 1977; 4th revised edition), 272.

zin's campaign against Ahaz – the so-called Syro-Ephraimitic war – failed (2Kgs 16:5; Isa 7:2).

But are the accounts in 2Kgs 16 and Isa 7 reliable? Some scholars doubt that there ever was a Syro-Ephraimitic war, because it is "known only from the Bible."[22] To quote Bustenay Oded, "We do not know of a single clear-cut, indisputable example of a war fought against a state in Syria or Palestine because it refused to join an anti-Assyrian alliance;"[23] "The causes of such wars were internal and regional, not external and international;"[24] and "The Syro-Ephraimite war, then, originated in an Arameo-Israelite alliance against Judah, and its aim was to dislodge Judah from Transjordania."[25] This hypothesis presupposes that "Azri-Yau of the land of Yaūdi" is identical with the Judean king Azariah or Uzziah and that one accepts the idea that he "became sole master of regions that had previously been under Israelite or joint Judeo-Israelite rule, and rapidly made himself into the strongest political and military force in Palestine and southern Syria."[26] However, the identification of Azri-Yau with Azariah or Uzziah is very dubious.[27]

Oded's final objection against the reality of a Syro-Ephraimitic war concerns the order of events: "If the primary aim of Damascus and Samaria was to form an alliance of states against Assyria, it is not clear why they should weaken themselves by a prolonged war against Jerusalem, thereby exposing their northern flank to the Assyrian forces."[28]

Was there ever even a chance for Rezin and Pekah to campaign against Judah and to besiege Jerusalem? The biblical text gives the impression that the events immediately followed each other very quickly: Rezin's and Pekah's common campaign against Jerusalem; Ahaz's call for help; and Tiglath-pileser's victory. In reality, however, Tiglath-pileser took three years to fight against his western enemies. The Assyrian inscriptions enable us to reconstruct Tiglath-pileser's campaigns in the years 734, 733 and 732 BC.[29] At the very latest, when Ti-

---

22 Roger Tomes, "The Reason for the Syro-Ephraimite War," *JSOT* 59 (1993): 55–71, esp. 61.
23 Bustenay Oded, "The Historical Background of the Syro-Ephraimitic War Reconsidered," *CBQ* 34 (1972): 153–65, esp. 154.
24 Oded, "Historical Background," 154; cf. Tomes, "The Reason for the Syro-Ephraimite War," 70.
25 Oded, "Historical Background," 161.
26 Oded, "Historical Background," 160.
27 Cf. Herbert Donner, *Geschichte des Volkes Israel und seiner Nachbarn in Grundzügen*, vol. 2 (Göttingen: Vandenhoeck & Ruprecht, 1995; 2nd edition), 335–36.
28 Oded, "Historical Background," 153.
29 Peter Dubovský, "Tiglath-pileser III's Campaigns in 734–732 B.C.: Historical Background of Isa 7; 2 Kgs 15–16 and 2 Chr 27–28," *Bib* 87 (2006): 153–70.

glath-pileser III started his campaigns in 734 BCE, Rezin and Pekah had to withdraw from Jerusalem, even if Tiglath-pileser went only against Philistia, i.e., against the Levantine coast and the centre of resistance of Gaza. The Assyrian king did not immediately attack Rezin, as the Book of Kings (16:9) would have it, but instead followed a strategy of encirclement. In the next year, in 733 BCE, he conquered Transjordan and fought against Rezin south of Damascus; he "won the battle in the field but was unable to capture … Damascus."[30] One year later, in 732 BCE, he occupied the Galilee (2Kgs 15:29) and "turned finally against Damascus, captured it, and executed Rezin" (2Kgs 16:9).[31]

The events of the Syro-Ephraimitic war reveal the international power structure.[32] As Dubovský puts it, "Pekah deliberately broke off the natural connections with Judah and formed a coalition with Israel's former enemy – Aram."[33] As Oded stresses, "In this alliance the dominant partner was the Aramean," noting that "Rezin is always mentioned before Pekah (2Kgs 15:37; 16:5; Isa 7:1, 4, 5, 8; 2Chr 28:5–6);" he therefore argues that Pekah "had gained the throne through Rezin's favour and active support."[34] Becking is also convinced that "The driving force behind the revolt of Pekah in 736 BCE must have been the Aramaean king Razyān of Damascus."[35]

Pekah's disastrous policy resulted in his downfall. Unfortunately, we do not know for sure who overthrew him. The inscriptions of Tiglath-pileser III leave it open whether the Assyrian forces or the people of Samaria brought him down. However, according to the Bible, it was Hoshea who killed him (2Kgs 15:30).

3 Hoshea's International Policy, and the Time after Him

Did Hoshea turn away from the anti-Assyrian policy of his predeceesor Pekah? According to the Assyrian inscriptions, Tiglath-pileser appointed Hoshea as

---

[30] Dubovský, "Tiglath-pileser III's Campaigns," 160.
[31] Dubovský, "Tiglath-pileser III's Campaigns," 161.
[32] Joachim Begrich, "Der Syrisch-Ephraimitische Krieg und seine weltpolitischen Zusammenhänge," *ZDMG* 83 (1929): 213–37, esp. 220, challenged the opinion that this war was an isolated event, expressing his own take on the matter already in the title of his article.
[33] Dubovský, "Why Did the Northern Kingdom Fall," 341.
[34] Oded, "Historical Background," 163.
[35] Becking, *Fall of Samaria*, 6.

king of Israel.[36] He trusted him to pursue a friendly policy towards Assyria. Therefore Israel remained a vassal state and did not become an Assyrian province, unlike Damascus. Hoshea paid his first tribute in 731 BCE, when Tiglath-pileser III was already far away, campaigning against the town Sarrabanu in southern Babylonia.[37] The Bible, however, does not present Hoshea as a ruler who was appointed by the Assyrian overlord Tiglath-pileser. According to 2Kgs 15:30, Hoshea himself formed a conspiracy against Pekah, attacked him, killed him and usurped the throne. As Gershon Galil stresses, "Consequently, the author of Kings believed that Hoshea was not an Assyrian vassal at the beginning of his reign."[38]

Did something change after Tiglath-pileser's death, when his son Shalmaneser V came to power during the month of Ṭebet in 727 BCE? That is at least the impression we get in the framework for Hoshea (2Kgs 17:3): "Shalmaneser king of Assyria marched against him, and Hoshea became his vassal and rendered him tribute." Did Shalmaneser really conduct a campaign against Hoshea? Nadav Na'aman is convinced "that v. 3 most probably refers to unrest and perhaps even rebellion that broke out in the West upon the death of the great emperor and the accession of his son, Shalmaneser V."[39] However, according to Kyle Lawson Younger Jr., the Assyrian Eponym Chronicles do not mention a campaign against the West during the years 728 and 727.[40] Moreover, there was not enough time for a military clash. Shalmaneser's accession year covered only few months (25 Ṭebet – Nisan 726), and Shalmaneser remained in his first year "in the land."[41] The biblical text in 2Kgs 17:3 corrects the impression that Hoshea had become an independent king by himself (15:30) and emphasises that Hoshea was Shalmaneser's vassal and paid his tribute to the new great emperor.[42]

---

[36] Tadmor, *Inscriptions*, Summ. 4: 15′–19′ = Tadmor and Yamada, *Royal Inscriptions*, no. 42: 15′–19′; fragmentary parallel: Tadmor, *Inscriptions*, Summ. 13: 17′–18′ = Tadmor and Yamada, *Royal Inscriptions*, no. 44: 17′–18′. Cf. Manfred Weippert, *Historisches Textbuch zum Alten Testament* (Göttingen: Vandenhoeck & Ruprecht, 2010), 295.
[37] Tadmor, *Inscriptions*, Summ. 9: rev. 9–11 = Tadmor and Yamada, *Royal Inscriptions*, no. 49: rev. 9–11.
[38] Gershon Galil, "The Last Years of the Kingdom of Israel and the Fall of Samaria," *CBQ* 57 (1995): 52–64, esp. 63.
[39] Nadav Na'aman, "The Historical Background of the Fall of Samaria (720 BC)," *Bib* 71 (1990): 206–25, esp. 214.
[40] Cf. Kyle Lawson Younger Jr., "The Fall of Samaria in Light of Recent Research," *CBQ* 61 (1999): 461–82, esp. 464.
[41] Cf. Lawson Younger, "Fall of Samaria," 464.
[42] Cf. John H. Hayes and Jeffrey K. Kuan, "The Final Years of Samaria (730–720 B.C.)," *Bib* 72 (1991): 153–81, esp. 163: 2Kgs 17:3 involves "a voluntary submission without military encounter."

The next biblical verse (17:4) makes it clear that this situation did not continue during Shalmaneser's reign. At some point, the Assyrian king discovered that Hoshea had sent messengers to So, the king of Egypt[43] and did no longer pay his tribute. Shalmaneser could not tolerate such behaviour. How did Hoshea get caught up in this? Egypt was at that time a divided country that could not help Israel to fight against Assyria.[44] There was no internal or external crisis in Assyria at that time. Hoshea's decision was a far-reaching political mistake.

The biblical author continues with a surprising turn of events (2Kgs 17:4c, d): "The king of Assyria arrested him and put him in prison." Why was it so easy to arrest Hoshea? Did he simply obey an order of the Assyrian king?[45] Why did he not remain behind the walls of his capital city of Samaria?[46] Did he go to the Assyrian king because he wanted to explain the difficult atmosphere inside Samaria to him? Galil supports this interpretation: "At that time Hoshea probably went forth from Samaria to meet the king of Assyria in a last-minute attempt to attain a compromise and prevent the conquest of the Israelite cities and the fall of Samaria."[47] But can we trust in the reliability of the biblical narrator? He probably wrote down this detail many years later. On the other side, we can compare the fate of Josiah of Judah (2Kgs 23:29) whom Pharaoh Necho put to death "as soon as he had seen him."[48] Moreover, we should bear in mind that Hoshea was perhaps not the driving force in the insurrection against Assyria. Hoshea's imprisonment did not break the resistance of the Samarians. They remained stubborn enemies of Assyria even when Sargon II began to rule, as we are yet to see. Perhaps the people of Samaria had put Hoshea under pressure to send messengers to So in Egypt. If we take all this into consideration, then

---

[43] There is a discussion about the name "So." Is it the name of a city or the name of a king in Egypt? From the use of the preposition אל we can see that So is not a toponym, cf. Bernd Ulrich Schipper, "Wer war So, König von Ägypten?" *BN* 92 (1998): 71–84, esp. 74–75. The most powerful rulers at that time were the Nubian leader Piye and Tefnakht, a prince on the western side of the Delta. But "from a geographic point of view, Osorkon's IV's kingdom was the nearest Delta principality to the land of Israel," so Pnina Galpaz-Feller, "Is That So? (2 Kings XVII 4)," *RB* 107 (2000): 338–47, esp. 344. The historical circumstances point to Osorkon IV, argues Schipper, "Wer war So," 82, pointing out that also from a linguistic point of view, it is at least possible that So is an abbreviation of the name *Wsrkn*.
[44] Cf. Donner, *Geschichte des Volkes Israel*, 345.
[45] Na'aman, "Historical Background," 218.
[46] Hayes and Kuan, "Final Years of Samaria," 162, think, however, that Hoshea had been taken "in the course of some military conflict."
[47] Galil, "Last Years of the Kingdom of Israel," 60. Similarly Jeremy Hughes, *Secrets of the Times: Myth and History in Biblical Chronology* (Sheffield: JSOT Press, 1990), 205–206: Hoshea "apparently decided to abandon his revolt, and went to offer his submission and pay tribute."
[48] Cf. Na'aman, "Historical Background," 218.

it is at least possible to assume that Hoshea had wanted to negotiate with the Assyrian king. That the latter did not kill Hoshea is perhaps an argument in favour of this interpretation.

The Samarians did not install a new king instead of Hoshea,[49] but continued their resistance. The Assyrian king invaded the country and besieged Samaria for three years (2Kgs 17:5). "In the ninth year of Hoshea he captured Samaria" (2Kgs 17:6a; cf. 18:9.10). But it is doubtful whether the Assyrians needed three years to besiege Samaria and to capture it. The archaeological evidence points against it. Herrmann Michael Niemann emphasised "that there are no traces of destruction that could be attributed to the Assyrians between 724 and 720 BCE."[50] Samaria was not a mighty stronghold: "Only the palace residence was fortified ... to resist, for example, an Aramean razzia or an attack from regional or local rival, but the lack of water would not permit a long siege."[51] As Galil states, "The Assyrian army encamped in Samaria was probably of limited scope, and the siege may possibly have turned into a blockade."[52]

Which Assyrian king punished Hoshea and captured Samaria for the first time, Shalmaneser V or Sargon II? The biblical text mentions Shalmaneser just one time (17:3a) and talks later about the "Assyrian king" (17:4a, c, 5a, 6a). I assume that it probably was Shalmaneser V, as this is in accordance with the Babylonian Chronicle which mentions only one event during Shalmaneser's reign: Samaria was taken.[53] While this much is clear, the exact meaning of the verb used here – *iḫtepi* (perfect of *ḫepû*) – is widely disputed: whereas e. g. Nadav Na'aman stresses "that other verbs were selected to designate the breaking of walls after a siege,"[54] Bob Becking is convinced that the Babylonian Chronicle refers to an actual capture of Samaria."[55] In any case, it seems clear that Shalmaneser was able to inflict a substantial defeat on the people of Samaria.

We come to the same conclusion if we take the chronological data into account. The Assyrian king captured Samaria "in the ninth year of Hoshea" (17:6a). That was Hoshea's last year on the throne, because he reigned no longer

---

49 Cf. Galil, "Last Years of the Kingdom of Israel," 60.
50 Herrmann Michael Niemann, "Royal Samaria – Capital or Residence? or: The Foundation of the City of Samaria by Sargon II.," in *Ahab Agonistes: The Rise and Fall of the Omri Dynasty*, ed. Lester L. Grabbe (London: T&T Clark, 2007): 184–207, esp. 189.
51 Niemann, "Royal Samaria," 201.
52 Galil, "Last Years of the Kingdom of Israel," 60.
53 Babylonian Chronicle 1 i 28; see Albert Kirk Grayson, *Assyrian and Babylonian Chronicles* (Locust Valley NY: Augustin, 1975), 69–87.
54 Na'aman, "Historical Background," 211.
55 Becking, *Fall of Samaria*, 25.

than nine years (17:1). When he paid his first tribute to Tiglath-pileser III, his first regnal year had already begun. That was probably in the year 731 BCE. He started therefore his ninth year in 723 BCE. Because Shalmaneser V reigned until the month of Tebet 722 BCE, the capture of Samaria must have still fallen into his reign. This result does not change, of course, if Hoshea had been imprisoned before his ninth year.

While no extant Assyrian inscription ascribes the Fall of Samaria to Shalmaneser, there are many texts that unanimously testify that Sargon II captured Samaria and deported its people.[56] However, these events belong to another context. When Sargon II seized power in 722 BCE, there was wide resistance, and Babylon and Elam rose against Assyria;[57] but he could stop their advances. In his second year (720 BCE), he fought against a rebellion in the western Assyrian provinces, including Damascus and Samerina (Ass. Samaria), centred on Hamath and headed by Ilu-bi'di. The people of Samaria did not want to face the loss of independence. They reacted in a similar way to what they had done after Hoshea's imprisonment. Sargon II defeated the rebellion, and also Samaria. I take it that the references refer to the conquest of Samaria. Sargon II knew the stubborn resistance of Samaria and deported therefore more than 27,000 people, as he claimed in his inscriptions. He became the "conqueror of Samaria and the whole land of Bit-Humria".[58] It is interesting, as Gershon Galil has pointed out, that Sargon's inscriptions do not mention Hoshea or any other king of Samaria.[59]

4 Conclusions

Did Hoshea's predecessors pursue a disastrous foreign policy? Dubovský showed that several causes contributed to the downfall of the Northern Kingdom. The main danger was surely the great power Assyria, especially after the enthronement of Tiglath-pileser III (r. 745–727 BCE). Did Israel's kings respect the great king? Menahem submitted to Assyria at the end of his reign, in 738 BCE, and paid a heavy tribute (15:19). Because he laid a levy on all men of wealth in Israel (15:20), he probably provoked or increased anti-Assyrian feelings among the peo-

---

56 All known texts are collected in Frahm's chapter in this volume. For a selection in translation cf. *TUAT* I/4, 379, 382–83, 385–87.
57 Bright, *A History of Israel*, 278.
58 Threshold Inscription IV 31–2 (= Frahm's Text 18). Cf. Niemann, "Royal Samaria," 194.
59 Galil, "Last Years of the Kingdom of Israel," 55, cites the Nimrud Prism (= Frahm's Text 8) passage regarding Sargon's enemies in Samaria and asks: "Why is there a general reference to the Samarians, without mentioning the name of their king (as was usual)?"

ple of Israel. Therefore, it was easier for Pekah to overthrow Pekahiah, Menahem's son. Pekah pursued an anti-Assyrian policy. That can be concluded from the common campaign against Jerusalem headed by Rezin, the Aramean king of Damascus (16:5; Isa 7,1.2). Rezin and Pekah wanted to appoint a new king in Jerusalem (Isa 7:5) and to enlarge their anti-Assyrian coalition. However, the operation failed. Pekah lost several towns in the North, Galilee and Gilead (15.29) and was left with only the small vassal-state Ephraim. Pekah's disastrous policy resulted in his downfall even though we do not know who overthrew him: Tiglath-pileser, the people of Samaria or his successor Hoshea (cf. 15:30).

Which foreign policy pursued Hoshea? Tiglath-pileser claimed that he appointed Hoshea. That suggests that Hoshea wanted to end Pekah's anti-Assyrian policy. Hoshea paid the tribute "year by year" (17:4). But in the end he sent messengers to an Egyptian ruler, perhaps Osorkon IV. Why did he risk such an adventure? Did the court or the people of Samaria put Hoshea under pressure? Why did he meet with Shalmaneser V who then imprisoned him? The people of Samaria continued their resistance anyway. Samaria was captured for the first time in Hoshea's ninth year, when he did not reign anymore (723 BCE). The anti-Assyrian attitude flared up again when resistance rose in the western provinces of the Assyrian Empire against Sargon II in his second year (720 BCE). Now Israel went down because the leadership of Samaria did not recognise the limitations of their might and failed to acknowledge the great power of the Assyrians.

Part VII: **Reflections in the Prophets**

Martti Nissinen
The Book of Hosea and the Last Days of the Northern Kingdom

The Methodological Problem

1 How Can We Reach the Eighth Century BCE?

The essays published in this volume demonstrate that the historical reconstruction of the last decades of the Kingdom of Israel is a meaningful enterprise. Some significant problems notwithstanding, it is possible to base such a reconstruction on a number of biblical and Assyrian texts. Whatever took place within the Northern Kingdom during the very last years of its existence is a tricky question, however, because there are hardly any sources where such knowledge could be drawn from. Nadav Na'aman has recently argued that "Hosea is the only available source for discussing the kingdom's internal affairs in the second half of the eighth century BCE; hence the great importance of elucidating the potential contribution of Hosea for the historical investigation."[1] This statement, of course, implies a great deal of confidence in the possibility that significant parts of the Book of Hosea actually date to the late eighth century BCE which, evidently, is no longer a matter of course.

The question of the dating of, not only the Book of Hosea, but also of the prophetic books in general has become a serious and manifold methodological problem.[2] How can the eighth century datings, or any datings predating the old-

---

[1] Nadav Na'aman, "The Book of Hosea as a Source for the Last Days of the Kingdom of Israel," *BZ* 59 (2015): 232–56, esp. 234.
[2] For recent discussion, see, e.g., Reinhard G. Kratz, *The Prophets of Israel* (Winona Lake IN: Eisenbrauns, 2015); id., "Probleme der Prophetenforschung," in id., *Prophetenstudien: Kleine Schriften II* (Tübingen: Mohr Siebeck, 2011), 3–17; Brad E. Kelle, "The Phenomenon of Israelite Prophecy in Contemporary Scholarship," *CurBR* 12 (2014): 275–320; Jörg Jeremias, "Das Rätsel der Schriftprophetie," *ZAW* 125 (2013): 93–117; David M. Carr, *The Formation of the Hebrew Bible: A New Reconstruction* (New York: Oxford University Press, 2011), 317–38; Erhard Blum, "Israels Prophetie im altorientalischen Kontext: Anmerkungen zu neueren religionsgeschichtlichen Thesen," in *"From Ebla to Stellenbosch": Syro-Palestinian Religions and the Hebrew Bible*, ed. Izak Cornelius and Louis C. Jonker (Wiesbaden: Harrassowitz, 2008): 81–115; Hans M. Barstad, "What Prophets Do: Reflections on Past Reality in the Book of Jeremiah," in *Prophecy in the Book of Jeremiah*, ed. Hans M. Barstad and Reinhard G. Kratz (Berlin: de Gruyter, 2009): 10–32;

est manuscript evidence, be methodologically justified? Can the eighth century be assumed as the date of any part of the Book of Hosea unless the opposite is proven? Can textual growth caused by centuries of transmission be identified in the text available to us so that more or less precise dates could be given to the textual layers thus recognized? Or should one, rather, date the book as a whole — and if so, to which period of time? How can the material in the Book of Hosea be compared to other sources, biblical as well as non-biblical, in a historically responsible way? The view of the Book of Hosea as a historical document depends essentially on the answers given to these methodological questions, which I attempt to address in this chapter.[3]

First of all, in my view, datings of the Book of Hosea or any prophetic book should not be based on default positions preferring the alleged lifetime of the prophet after whom the book is named. Every dating must be argued for, we cannot date texts for the sake of convenience. Any principle of the type "innocent until proven guilty" should not be applied to texts that are neither accused of anything nor in need of being defended. Therefore, the practice of dating Hoseanic passages routinely to the eighth century without an argument to justify it is unacceptable. This practice may emerge from the often unspoken preference of the prophet for the later editors, early datings for late datings, or textual unity for disunity.[4] Preferences like this are, however, difficult to reconcile with the documented evidence of textual transmission. Drawing historical conclusions from the Book of Hosea (or any other book) on the basis of such default positions is likely to introduce errors into the historical record.

Uwe Becker, "Die Wiederentdeckung des Prophetenbuches: Tendenzen und Aufgaben der gegenwärtigen Prophetenforschung," *BTZ* 21 (2004): 30–60.

3 Cf. my previous musings in, e.g., Martti Nissinen, *Ancient Prophecy: Near Eastern, Biblical, and Greek Perspectives* (Oxford: Oxford University Press, 2017), 144–67; id., "Comparing Prophetic Sources: Principles and a Test Case," in *Prophecy and the Prophets in Ancient Israel*, ed. John Day (London: T&T Clark, 2010): 3–24; id., "The Historical Dilemma of Biblical Prophetic Studies," in *Prophecy in the Book of Jeremiah*, ed. Hans M. Barstad and Reinhard G. Kratz (Berlin: de Gruyter, 2009): 103–20.

4 For a good representation of this view, see Francis I. Andersen and David Noel Freedman, *Hosea: A New Translation with Introduction and Commentary* (Garden City NY: Doubleday, 1980), 59: "In both cases [scil. the unity of the Book of Hosea and the integrity of the text] our premise and point of departure are conservative, that the book is essentially the work of a single person, and that the text is basically sound. These are hardly ringing affirmations; they are more like defensive desperation. If the opposite were true, if many hands and voices could be found from the book, then we would have the thankless and ultimately fruitless task of apportioning the work among a variety of people whose existence is hypothetical, and whose only distinguishing mark is some obscurity or inconsistency in the text."

How could such errors, then, be avoided? At the very least we must be aware of the nature of our source material. The oldest "hard" evidence of the existence of the Book of Hosea (like any other book of the Hebrew Bible) comes from the Dead Sea Scrolls. Parts of the Book of Hosea have been preserved in three scrolls, that is, 4QXII^c, 4QXII^d and 4QXII^g, all dating to the first half of the first century BCE.[5] This material alone, together with the Old Greek translation of the Book of Hosea which in some cases is arguably translated from a Hebrew text different from the Masoretic text,[6] demonstrates that textual transmission not only preserved ancient texts but also changed them.[7] We may assume that the texts transmitted in the Scrolls often date back several centuries, but the documented evidence of textual growth makes it impossible to believe that any of the available manuscripts provides us with a text that had remained unchanged for such a long time.[8] In the case of Hosea, the documented changes are usually less than dramatic, but they testify to actual scribal interventions to the text that cannot be dismissed either.[9] This is why any dating beyond the age of the extant manuscript material requires a diachronic theory concerning the transmission of the given text through a long period of time. Creating such a theory, however, immediately raises further methodological questions. While extant textual evidence shows that the idea of textual growth is not based on imagination, detecting the early phases of textual transmission on the basis of the text itself without empirical evidence is a matter of ongoing debate.

---

5 See Brian Webster, "Chronological Index of the Texts from the Judaean Desert," in *The Texts from the Judaean Desert: Indices and an Introduction to the Discoveries in the Judaean Desert Series*, ed. Emanuel Tov (Oxford: Clarendon Press, 2002): 393, 397. Taken together, these fragments include the following verses at least partially: 1:6–9; 2:1–5, 13–19, 22–25; 3:1–5; 4:1–19; 5:1; 6:3, 8–11; 7:1, 12–16; 8:1; 9:1–4, 9–17; 10:1–14; 11:2–5, 6–11; 12:1–15; 13:1, 3–13, 15; 14:1, 3–6, 9–10; see the convenient translation of the Dead Sea Scrolls material in Martin Abegg, Peter Flint and Eugene Ulrich, *The Dead Sea Scrolls Bible* (New York: Harper, 1999), 420–27.
6 For instance, the Greek text of Hos 13:4 must have been translated from a *Vorlage* much longer than the MT but similar to 4QXII^g.
7 For 4QXII^c, see Hanne von Weissenberg, "Changing Scripture? Scribal Corrections in MS 4QXII^c," in *Changes in Scripture: Rewriting and Interpreting Authoritative Traditions in the Second Temple Period*, ed. Hanne von Weissenberg, Juha Pakkala and Marko Marttila (Berlin: de Gruyter, 2011): 247–71.
8 For examples of documented evidence of textual growth, see Reinhard Müller, Juha Pakkala and Bas ter Haar Romeny, *Evidence of Editing: Growth and Change of Texts in the Hebrew Bible* (Atlanta GA: SBL Press, 2014).
9 Cf. von Weissenberg, "Changing Scripture," 269: "Even the smaller, individual scribal additions and corrections in manuscripts illustrate the minor forms of growth in the texts. They attest to the scribal contribution to the development of the texts that became the Hebrew Bible."

Diachronic analysis is, of course, the most traditional way of approaching the Book of Hosea in academic biblical studies, and has been practiced by many scholars over the last decades, myself included. Traditionally, the diachronic enterprise has been motivated by the search of the original message of the prophet by way of separating later additions from the original text and identifying the oldest material, which is often virtually equated with the words once uttered by the prophet Hosea. The ripest fruit carried by this branch of methodology can be found in the work of Jörg Jeremias, according to whom the essential contents of the Book of Hosea date back to the last years of the Northern Kingdom and the time immediately following the catastrophe: "Das Buch Hosea hat seine entscheidende Prägung im untergegangenen Nordreich erhalten."[10] According to Jeremias, the earliest form of the book is essentially the work of his disciples, who had collected and interpreted the prophet's words, whereas the book as we know it was edited and augmented in Judah after the collapse of the Northern Kingdom. A similar line of thought has been followed by many scholars.[11]

Another type of diachronic analysis of the Book of Hosea is not concerned with finding the prophet's message or even the original core of the book but reckon with a complicated process of redaction and/or *Fortschreibung* over a long period of time.[12] These studies have typically identified only scattered remains of material datable to the eighth century BCE, shifting the emphasis from the prophet and his disciples to the scribal circles of the monarchic and postmonarchic periods.

---

10 Jeremias, "Das Rätsel der Schriftprophetie," 113; cf. many well-known works of Jörg Jeremias, e.g., *Studien zur Theologie des Alten Testaments* (Tübingen: Mohr Siebeck, 2015, ed. Friedhelm Hartenstein and Jutta Krispenz,), 269–87 (= "Die Anfänge der Schriftprophetie," 1996) and 311–25 (= "Prophetenwort und Prophetenbuch: Zur Rekonstruktion mündlicher Verkündung der Propheten," 1990); *Hosea und Amos: Studien zu den Anfängen des Dodekapropheton* (Tübingen: Mohr Siebeck, 1996); *Der Prophet Hosea* (Göttingen: Vandenhoeck & Ruprecht, 1983).
11 E.g., Na'aman, "The Book of Hosea as a Source," 255–56 dates Hosea's prophecies to the time of Hoshea, the last king of Israel, and the earliest scroll to the time immediately after the Assyrian annexation of the kingdom (720 BCE).
12 E.g., Roman Vielhauer, *Das Werden des Buches Hosea: eine redaktionsgeschichtliche Untersuchung* (Berlin: de Gruyter, 2007); Susanne Rudnig-Zelt, *Hoseastudien: Redaktionskritische Untersuchungen zur Genese des Hoseabuches* (Göttingen: Vandenhoeck & Ruprecht, 2006); Henrik Pfeiffer, *Das Heiligtum von Bethel im Spiegel des Hoseabuches* (Göttingen: Vandenhoeck & Ruprecht, 1999); Martti Nissinen, *Prophetie, Redaktion und Fortschreibung im Hoseabuch: Studien zum Werdegang eines Prophetenbuches im Lichte von Hos 4 und 11* (Kevelaer: Butzon & Bercker and Neukirchen-Vluyn: Neukirchener Verlag, 1991); Gale A. Yee, *Composition and Redaction in the Book of Hosea: a Redaction Critical Investigation* (Atlanta GA: Scholars Press, 1987); cf. Reinhard G. Kratz, "Die Redaktion der Prophetenbücher," in id., *Prophetenstudien*, 32–48.

Diachronic studies reconstructing the emergence of the Book of Hosea have done their best to remove the illusionary innocence with regard to the textual transmission and its relation to historical events. Since, however, no two scholars arrive at the same conclusion but the results typically vary from study to study, many colleagues have found it difficult to decide on whose analysis is the more reliable one. Therefore, the possibility of unfolding the process of textual growth with a precision that could reveal even relative datings of each individual passage in the book has been seriously questioned. The ever-changing results of diachronic analyses have been found frustrating enough for many scholars to abandon them altogether and to read the texts synchronically, giving up the attempt to reconstruct the hypothetical phases of textual transmission.

Textual growth in prophetic books is not usually denied altogether, although acknowledging its existence often does not go beyond lip-service. Some scholars say they are reading the "final form" of the text; however, there is no such thing as the final form of any biblical book, unless modern editions of the Masoretic text are regarded as such.[13] Of course, any given form of the text can form the basis of an analysis that does not attempt to go historically beyond the textual witness itself. However, if we want to relate the Book of Hosea historically with the last days of the Northern Kingdom, the so-called "final form" readings clearly lead to an impasse.

A synchronic reading of the Book of Hosea does not as such require an eighth-century BCE setting, even though this very often seems to be assumed. A synchronic analysis can take the text as the product of postmonarchical readerships, relating the text of the Book of Hosea to a later historical period when one can suppose the text to have reached more or less the shape known to us from existing textual evidence. Thus, for instance, Ehud Ben Zvi consistently reads the book as the product of the literati of the late Persian period.[14] This way of reading the text neither denies the possibility that some parts of the book indeed have earlier origins, nor enables sorting these parts out. Historical links can be made to the time chosen as the setting of the alleged (re-)readership of the book, but historical connections with the events of the eighth century BCE fall entirely out of scope.

---

13 Cf., e.g., Eugene Ulrich, "Our Sharper Focus on the Bible and Theology Thanks to the Dead Sea Scrolls," *CBQ* 66 (2004): 1–24; Anneli Aejmelaeus, "Licence to Kill? Deut 13:10 and the Prerequisites of Textual Criticism," in *Verbum et calamus: Semitic and Related Studies in Honour of the Sixtieth Birthday of Professor Tapani Harviainen*, ed. Hannu Juusola, Juha Laulainen and Heikki Palva (Helsinki: Finnish Oriental Society, 2004): 1–22.
14 Ehud Ben Zvi, *Hosea* (FOTL 21 A/1; Grand Rapids MI: Eerdmans, 2005); cf. James M. Bos, *Reconsidering the Date and Provenance of the Book of Hosea: The Case of Persia-Period Yehud* (LHBOTS 580; London: Bloomsbury, 2013).

The methodological problem of relating the Book of Hosea to the last days of the Northern Kingdom, thus, consists of the following components:

(1) The oldest manuscript evidence from the Dead Sea Scrolls is enough to demonstrate that textual development and growth took place; however, coming from the first century BCE, it documents only the very latest phases of textual transmission and does not help to date individual passages of the book to older periods.

(2) There are good grounds to assume that the text of the Book of Hosea existed in some form several centuries earlier than the Dead Sea Scrolls. The book is one of the "Twelve Prophets" already in the oldest textual witnesses, but one can assume that the books included in this collection existed as individual scrolls before they were joined together in several phases, and that each phase of transmission is likely to have transformed the text.[15] However, the late date of the earliest textual witnesses makes it impossible simply to equate the extant textual evidence with any earlier form of the text. The Book of Hosea as we know it is already part of a larger composition and the product of a long chain of textual transmission, but no documented evidence is available to help with the reconstruction of this process. This is essentially due to the tendency of the texts themselves to hide rather than to reveal their editorial history.[16]

(3) If we want to establish a direct historical connection from the Book of Hosea to the last days of the Northern Kingdom, we should be able to date at least some parts of Hosea to this period of time. Diachronic studies detecting the oldest parts of the Book of Hosea have yielded exact results, but these have been varying enough to raise suspicions about the viability of even the diachronic methodology. The ever-changing results of ever-greater precision have been seen as pointing towards problems in the method itself. But the task cannot

---

15 For theories concerning the history of redaction of the "Book of the Twelve," see, e. g., Jakob Wöhrle, *Die frühen Sammlungen des Zwölfprophetenbuches: Entstehung und Komposition* (Berlin: de Gruyter, 2006); Aaron Schart, *Die Entstehung des Zwölfprophetenbuches: Neubearbeitungen von Amos im Rahmen schriftenübergreifender Redaktionsprozesse* (Berlin: de Gruyter, 1998); James D. Nogalski, *Literary Precursors to the Book of the Twelve* (Berlin: de Gruyter, 1993); cf. Ben Zvi who finds it impossible to reconstruct redactional processes from the existing text. For two different views of the "Twelve Hypothesis", see Ehud Ben Zvi and James D. Nogalski, *Two Sides of a Coin: Juxtaposing Views on Interpreting the Book of the Twelve/The Twelve Prophetic Books* (with an introduction by Thomas Römer; Piscataway NJ: Gorgias Press, 2009).

16 According to Ehud Ben Zvi, "the ongoing process of redaction was not bent on promoting, or archiving and analyzing itself; instead its function was to shape a series of texts in which the last, if successful, was meant to supersede and erase the memory of the previous one" ("Is the Twelve Hypothesis Likely from an Ancient Reader's Perspective?" in Ben Zvi and Nogalski, *Two Sides of a Coin*, 46–96, esp. 59).

be fulfilled by way of synchronic reading either unless the book as a whole is dated to the 730s–720s, which is not viable for reasons just mentioned.

So have we ended up in a cul-de-sac: if synchronic analysis is not the way to go and the results of diachronic studies are found to be disappointing, what else can we do other than give up entirely on the task of connecting the Book of Hosea with the last days of the Kingdom of Israel? Or is there a historically responsible way of doing this?

2 Historical Echoes from the Eighth Century?

Perhaps we could try circumventing the problems of diachronic methodology by way of looking for clues in the text that seem to point towards an eighth-century date, and, if possible, comparing such clues with the available historical data of the last days of the kingdom of Israel. If they seem to fit this documentary environment, they could be dated to the same period of time. The best candidates for an early date would be passages that do not show clear signs of intertextual influence, and are not to be taken as *Fortschreibung* of earlier texts but rather as belonging to the source materials of an early collection upon which the Book of Hosea has grown.

As many contributions to this volume demonstrate, the fall of Samaria and the subsequent de- and repopulations of the area can indeed be confirmed by Assyrian sources and even by archaeological evidence.[17] The problem is rather how to reconstruct the internal affairs of the kingdom of Israel, of which there is no documentation outside of, or even within, the Hebrew Bible. The following three examples may illustrate the case.

(1) A contemporary reflection of a disturbing political event could perhaps be found in Hos 7:3–7, a highly enigmatic passage that seems to reflect on the murder

---

17 For archaeological evidence of the devastation, see Zvi Gal, *Lower Galilee during the Iron Age* (Winona Lake IN: Eisenbrauns, 1992), 108–109. Cf. Avraham Faust, "Settlement, Economy, and Demography under Assyrian Rule in the West: The Territories of the Former Kingdom of Israel as a Test Case," *JAOS* 135 (2015): 765–89, who concludes that the Assyrians "did not really care about the fate of the areas they conquered. They carried off whatever they could and their investment was minimal" (782). However, the Assyrians did not just plunder but also, for example, looked after the water supply in Samaria as reported in a letter from the time of Sargon II: Simo Parpola, *The Correspondence of Sargon II, Part I: Letters from Assyria and the West* (Helsinki: Helsinki University Press, 1987), no. 255. According to Angelika Berlejung, "The Assyrians in the West: Assyrianization, Colonialism, Indifference, or Developmental Policy?" in *Congress Volume Helsinki 2010*, ed. Martti Nissinen (Leiden: Brill 2012): 21–60, esp. 48), "[s]uccess was maximal profit with minimal investment."

of a king, perhaps one of the successors of Jeroboam II. Of the last kings of Israel only Menahem is said to have died peacefully, whereas his predecessors Zechariah and Shallum as well as his followers Pekahiah and Pekah were killed. A rather laconic report of the four coups d'état that took place after Jeroboam II can be found in 2Kgs 15:8–31, a passage probably based on court chronicles that were used as sources of the Deuteronomistic History.[18] Hos 7:3–7 seems to give a metaphoric account of the day when one of the kings was murdered. The actors "make glad" (7:3) the unsuspecting king and his officials, who get drunk, presumably in the privacy of the royal palace. They become easy prey for the murderers who, compared with a heated oven, just wait "from the kneading of the dough until it is leavened," that is, for the opportunity to "devour their rulers" (7:7). Compared to the account of 2Kgs, such an event could best be identified with the murder of Pekahiah, committed by his captain (šālîš) Pekah, who conspired against him with fifty Gileadites and attacked him in the citadel of the palace (2Kgs 15:25).[19] This is what I argued in my master's thesis in 1984, and I would still like to agree with myself. The passage is probably neither interpreting a pre-existing text in the Book of Hosea nor is it dependent on another biblical text outside the book, hence it could belong to the material from which the early version of the book is composed.[20] However, I have to admit that the link between Hos 7:3–7 and Pekahiah's murder derives from what is visible through the keyhole provided by 2Kgs 15:25. The two sources seem to connect nicely, but the connection depends entirely on what we happen to see.

(2) Further echoes from the last days of the Northern Kingdom, either contemporary or slightly later, can be heard in passages of the Book of Hosea that reflect the Fall of Samaria. The demise of the Northern Kingdom, or Ephraim (the name may refer to the truncated kingdom in the time of the last king Hoshea[21]), is reflected in several passages that sound like fragments of laments (9:10–17; 11:1–5). Some passages in the Book of Hosea could be imagined to

---

[18] For court chronicles as the sources of the Deuteronomistic history, see Lester L. Grabbe, *1 & 2 Kings: An Introduction and Study Guide: History and Story in Ancient Israel* (London: Bloomsbury, 2017), 21–28; cf., e. g., Ernst Würthwein, *Die Bücher der Könige: 1. Kön. 17–2. Kön. 25* (Göttingen: Vandenhoeck & Ruprecht, 1984), 376–84.

[19] Pekahiah has not been among the prime suspects in this murder case; see, however, Andrew Alexander Macintosh, *A Critical and Exegetical Commentary on Hosea* (Edinburgh: T&T Clark, 1997), 256.

[20] Cf. Vielhauer, *Das Werden des Buches Hosea*, 86–92, according to whom verses 7:5–6 go back to oral words of northern origin and the remaining verses to the oldest written layer (*erste Verschriftung*). Rudnig-Zelt, *Hoseastudien*, 212–30, sees a pre-exilic core in the passage (verses 7:4b, 5b), however, without a reference to the murder of a king.

[21] Thus Na'aman, "The Book of Hosea as a Source," 238–39.

go back to contemporary laments; for instance, Hos 10:5–8 could be based on something like the following:[22]

l ['glwt byt 'wn]	For [the calf of Beth-Awen[23]]
ygwrw škn šmrwn	the inhabitants of Samaria tremble.
ky 'bl 'lyw 'mw	Its people mourn for it,
wkmryw 'lyw ygylw	its priests wail over it
['l kbwdw ky glh mmnw]	[over its glory that has departed from it[24]].
gm 'wtw l'šwr ywbl	The thing itself is carried to Assyria
mnḥh lmlky rb	as tribute to the Great King[25].
bšnh 'prym yqḥ	Ephraim has received shame,
wybwš yśr'l m'ṣtw	and Israel is ashamed for his own counsel.
ndmh šmrwn mlkh	Samaria and its king perish
kqṣp 'l pny mym	like a splinter on the face of the waters.
[wnšmdw bmwt 'wn ḥṭ't yśr'l	[The high places of Awen, the sin of Israel, shall be destroyed.
qwṣ wdrdr y'lh 'l mzbḥwtm]	Thorn and thistle shall grow up on their altars.][26]
w'mrw lhrym kswnw	They shall say to the mountains: "Cover us!"
wlgb'wt nplw 'lynw	and to the hills: "Fall on us!"

---

22 This reconstruction is based on my analysis in Nissinen, *Prophetie, Redaktion und Fortschreibung*, 309–12; cf. the different reconstructions of Pfeiffer, *Das Heiligtum von Bethel*, 103–17; Vielhauer, *Das Werden des Hoseabuches*, 165–72; Melanie Köhlmoos, *Bet-El – Erinnerungen an eine Stadt: Perspektiven der alttestamentlichen Bet-El-Überlieferung* (Tübingen: Mohr Siebeck, 2007), 126–31.
23 The peculiar and pejorative expression ʻeglôt Bêt-āwen (pl. fem.) is probably inspired by the Deuteronomistic polemics against the calf of Bethel, replacing the original name of the object to which the sg. masc. suffixes in the following bicolon refer.
24 This sentence probably serves as a secondary explanation of the masculine suffix in ʻālâw "for it/over it," which is not applicable to ʻeglôt.
25 Adopting the usual reading malkî rāb instead of melek yāreb (MT).
26 Verse 8a reads like a later, prosaic theological interpretation of the original lament.

This passage may originally refer to the transportation of a precious item, presumably, a divine statue, to Assyria.²⁷ It resonates well with the Nimrud Prism of Sargon II, which reads: "[The inhabitants of Sa]maria who agreed [and plotted] with a king [hostile to] me, not to endure servitude and not to bring tribute to Assur and who did battle, I fought against them with the power of great gods, my lords. I counted as spoil 27,280 people together with their chariots and gods in which they trusted" (lines iv 25–32).²⁸ One could easily imagine laments like the one possibly quoted in Hos 10:5–8* to have been uttered after the fall of Samaria, if not by prophets, then perhaps by professional lamenters similarly to the ones known from Assyrian records.²⁹

Prophecy and lament are related performances both in the Hebrew Bible and in the ancient Near Eastern sources,³⁰ and the literary reflection of the fate of the city of Samaria and the Kingdom of Israel may have been inspired by source texts representing both genres. The Mesopotamian *kalû*'s were not only singers but also scribes who wrote divinatory texts.³¹ If this was true also in Samaria (which can only be speculated), this could explain the early textualization of such laments. Laments like Hos 10:5–8* could have belonged to the material comprising the first beginnings of what we know as the Book of Hosea.³² The later redactors have subsequently used this material as a tool of criticism against

---

27 Cf. Köhlmoos, *Bet-El*, 135–38.
28 See C. J. Gadd, "Inscribed Prisms of Sargon II from Nimrud," *Iraq* 16 (1954): 173–201, esp. 179–80. For other texts of Sargon II related to the conquest of Samaria, see the chapter of Frahm in this volume
29 However, the assumed reference to Samarian lamenters in a text from Calah – read as 3 ŠÚ.MEŠ KUR.*Sa-mir-na-a-a* by Stephanie Dalley and J. N. Postgate, *The Tablets from Fort Shalmaneser* (London: British School of Archaeology in Iraq, 1984), no. 121: 6 and, assuming that ŠÚ was used as a logogram for *kalû*, interpreted as a reference to "three Samarian lamentation-priests" by Kyle Lawson Younger Jr., "The Deportations of the Israelites," *JBL* 117 (1998): 221 – cannot be used as evidence for the existence of Samarian lamenters, as the passage needs to be read 3-*šú*.MEŠ KUR.*Sa-mir-na-a-a*, meaning "Third Men (of a chariot crew) from Samaria" (pers. comm., Karen Radner); cf. also Radner's chapter in this volume.
30 Cf. Martti Nissinen, "Biblical Prophecy from a Near Eastern Perspective: The Cases of Divine Kingship and Divine Possession," in *Congress Volume Ljubljana 2007*, ed. André Lemaire (Leiden: Brill, 2010): 441–68, esp. 458–61.
31 See, e.g., Francesca Rochberg, *In the Path of the Moon: Babylonian Celestial Divination and Its Legacy* (Studies in Ancient Magic and Divination 6; Leiden: Brill, 2010), 247.
32 I am, thus, suggesting an earlier date to this passage than Vielhauer, *Das Werden des Buches Hosea*, 176–77, 227–78, according to whom already the basic layer of Hos 10:1–8 is Deuteronomistic. This is probably true for the *Kultpolemik* in chapter 10 in general, but not necessarily for the source material used by the editors.

past and/or contemporary religious practices referred to with the pejorative designation designation *'āwen* ("iniquity").

(3) My third example is the possible reference to the so-called Syro-Ephraimite war in 734–732 BCE. This war can be reconstructed from biblical texts only (2Kgs 16:5; 2Chr 28:5–8; Isa 7:1–9), but, if it actually took place, as scholars usually assume, it may be interpreted as an act of hostility towards Ahaz, the king of Judah, who refused to join the anti-Assyrian alliance.[33] A contemporary echo of it is usually heard in Hos 5:8–14*.[34] The alarm blown in three cities from south to north, Gibeah, Ramah, and Beth-Awen (scil. Bethel) (5:8), as well as the accusation of the princes of Judah acting "like those who remove the landmark" (5:10) give the impression of a Judahite attack to the area of the Kingdom of Israel and refer to Ephraim's resorting to the help of Assyria (5:13). Nothing of this is known from other sources which rather present the Northern Kingdom as attacking Judah, and this is exactly the reason why it could be interpreted as a reference to historical events rather than as interpretation or *Fortschreibung* of an already existing text. Hence, the text could be interpreted as referring to events of the Syro-Ephraimite war unknown from other sources, such as the attack of Judah on Israel and Israel's turning to Assyria for help. The passage is now embedded and reworked in the context of the Book of Hosea, but the old oracle could originate from either Israel or Judah.

Of course, the passage can be interpreted otherwise. Na'aman, for example, dates the counter-attack of Judah to the time of Hoshea, the last king of Israel, when Israel was at its weakest.[35] Ben Zvi, on the other hand, does not see a compelling reason to connect the passage with the historical circumstances of the last days of the kingdom of Israel: "The text as it stands does not lead to such

---

33 See, e.g., Nadav Na'aman, "Let Other Kingdoms Struggle with the Great Powers – You, Judah, Pay the Tribute and Hope for the Best: The Foreign Policy of the Kings of Judah in the Ninth–Eighth Centuries BCE," in *Isaiah's Vision of Peace in Biblical and Modern International Relations: Swords into Plowshares*, ed. Raymond Cohen and Raymond Westbrook (New York: Palgrave MacMillan, 2008): 55–73, esp. 62–64.
34 Thus the majority of scholars following Albrecht Alt, "Hosea 5,8–6,6: ein Krieg und seine Folgen in prophetischer Beleuchtung," *NKZ* 30 (1919): 537–68, repr. in id., *Kleine Schriften zur Geschichte des Volkes Israel*, vol. 2 (Munich: Beck, 1953): 163–87. Even Vielhauer, *Das Werden des Buches Hosea*, 225–26 finds remnants of oral proclamation from the last days of the Northern Kingdom in verses 5:8–11*, whereas the written text in verses 5:8–14 belongs to the late 8th century layer (*erste Ergänzungsschicht*) written from the perspective of Judah. Rudnig-Zelt, *Hoseastudien*, 157–77, reconstructs a complicated editorial process, dating the polemics against Samaria to its latest phases.
35 Na'aman, "The Book of Hosea as a Source," 239–40.

a reading" which is also unknown to ancient readerships who knew about the Syro-Ephraimite war on the basis of biblical texts.[36]

Ben Zvi is right in stressing that the reconstructions of the historical scenery behind passages in the Book of Hosea are based on the assumption that the texts directly reflect the historical prophet's oral speeches and should, therefore, be given a historical setting within his lifetime. "Given that there are only a limited number of political events during that period that are known and potentially relevant, the only question is which one would fit better a particular speech."[37] This easily leads to a chain of circular arguments causing erroneous historical conclusions. On the other hand, if one follows the principal that when writing history, all potential sources should be considered and nothing should be ruled out *a priori*, even secondary sources such as prophetic books deserve to be critically scrutinized.[38] Therefore, the possibility that a given passage in the Book of Hosea actually provides a keyhole view into the historical landscape, however narrow, should not be dismissed at the outset, even though the secondary nature of the evidence should never be forgotten. Individual passages of the Book of Hosea may contain reminiscences of real historical events, but they always appear recontextualized in literary settings created by scribes who may or may not have been aware of the actual historical reference.

Many other texts in the Book of Hosea, most recently collected by Na'aman,[39] could be highlighted to demonstrate the original connection of the text with the fall of Samaria and the last days of the Kingdom of Israel. The problem with using such clues as evidence of events that took place in the 730s–720s BCE is that, however nicely they seem to fit our picture of that period of time, there is always the risk of *potest, ergo* and circular reasoning. For example, the recurrent juxtaposing of Egypt and Assyria (Hos 7:11; 9:3; 11:5, 11; 12:1) undoubtedly makes sense with regard to the political maneuvers of Hoshea, the last king of Israel—provided that they actually took place and 2Kgs 17:3b–5a is not later historical speculation as suggested by Christoph Levin elsewhere in this volume. The problem is, evidently, that the parallelism of Egypt and Assyria could be used by any subsequent writer reflecting on the event. For later readers, the names can stand for Ptolemaic Egypt and Seleucid Syria.[40] Even Sa-

---

36 Ben Zvi, *Hosea*, 140.
37 Ben Zvi, *Hosea*, 141.
38 See Lester L. Grabbe, *Ancient Israel: What Do We Know and How Do We Know It?* (London: T&T Clark 2007), 35–36.
39 Na'aman, "The Book of Hosea as a Source," *passim*.
40 Cf. Christoph Levin, *The Old Testament: A Brief Introduction* (Princeton NJ: Princeton University Press, 2005), 133 with regard to Hos 7:8–11.

maria was still there, providing itself continually as a target for theological criticism for circles who considered that the wrong kind of Yahwism was practiced in the north.[41] Therefore—and this is generally the problem with the dating of individual passages in Hosea—even if an eighth-century setting makes sense, it cannot automatically be preferred.

3 Evidence or Reflection of Eighth-Century Events?

I am convinced that the beginnings of the Book of Hosea must be sought from the last days of the Northern Kingdom or shortly thereafter. It is virtually impossible to imagine the emergence of the Book of Hosea without the contemporary experiences of the end of the Northern Kingdom. The fall of Samaria must be considered the decisive event that triggered the emergence of the book, in whatever way this happened over the subsequent centuries. It is usually assumed that the redaction and transmission of the book took place in Judah, not only because of the multiple mentions of Judah, which are often ascribed to a specific redaction, but also because of the harsh criticism of Israel, Ephraim, and Samaria throughout the book.[42] However, this criticism does not need to derive from the eighth century only, since, as Christoph Levin has argued, there was enough reason for it even later when the Samari(t)an society and worship gradually became an issue to the (religious) elite of Jerusalem.[43] The echoes on the last days of the Northern Kingdom in what may have constituted the earliest form of the Book of Hosea were readily available for interpretations of the subsequent generations who likewise reflected their relationship with what took place in the Northern Kingdom.

It is, thus, problematic to quote verses of the Book of Hosea as quasi-eyewitness reports of events that took place in the 730s–720s BCE, even if we have good grounds to assume that some material in the book indeed dates back to this historical period. Some passages in Hosea, like the ones discussed above,

---

41 As Gary N. Knoppers, *Jews and Samaritans: The Origins and History of Their Early Relations* (Oxford: Oxford University Press, 2013) emphasizes, there was no absolute breakdown of relations between Yehud and Samaria in the first centuries BCE but, rather, a considerable cultural and religious overlap. The debate on the common heritage and religious identity is evidence of the overlap and continuity, not of the breakdown.
42 See, e.g., Jeremias, *Der Prophet Hosea*, 18–19 and *passim*.
43 Levin, *The Old Testament*, 129–33; cf. the late "Samariapolemik" reconstructed by Rudnig-Zelt, *Hoseastudien*, 271–73.

undeniably give the impression of contemporary experience, indeed making sense when compared to what we know about the last days of the Kingdom of Israel from other sources. However, even these passages rarely reveal historical data that could not even theoretically go back to later reflection. *Potest,* we can say quite often, but we should be careful with the *ergo.*

Without suggesting anything that has not been said and done before, I would like to argue that if any part of the Book of Hosea actually derives from a time not too distant from the last days of the kingdom of Israel (and I do believe this to be the case to some extent), such passages can only be identified by way of the diachronic method and comparative analysis. Individual parts of the Book of Hosea should not be dated randomly but the dating of each passage should be based on a well-argued theory concerning the emergence, growth, and transmission of the text of the Book of Hosea. The methodological problem is how to sort datable passages out from a text that is the product of a process of long textual transmission, and if there is a great deal of uncertainty about this, one should be cautious about making precise contemporary connections between the last days of the Kingdom of Israel and the literary work we call the Book of Hosea. This is why it is so difficult to detect independent historical information in the Book of Hosea that could be *reliably* used as *evidence of* the last days of the Northern Kingdom. Even texts that seem to connect well with historical circumstances known from other sources may go back to subsequent reflection and *Fortschreibung.*

However, the book can be used as a powerful document of the *reflection and interpretation* of this historical event. The event itself is real. The fall of the Northern Kingdom and its capital Samaria is something that can be historically reconstructed from the available sources. It would be nonsensical to deny the connection of the Book of Hosea with this event, but the nature of the connection is evidently more complicated than a simple contemporary eyewitness response. The book and the historical event are rather linked through social memory, which creates an indirect connection between the text and the shared past — not only through remembering but also by way of forgetting.[44]

---

44 Cf. Ehud Ben Zvi, "Remembering Hosea: The Prophet Hosea as a Site of Memory in the Persian Period Yehud," in *Poets, Prophets, and Texts in Play: Studies in Biblical Poetry and Prophecy in Honour of Francis Landy,* ed. Ehud Ben Zvi, Claudia V. Camp, David M. Gunn, and Aaron W. Hughes (London: T & T Clark, 2015): 37–57. For social memory and the collective past, see also Geoffrey Cubitt, *History and Memory* (Manchester: Manchester University Press, 2007), 199–249.

H. G. M. Williamson
Isaiah and the Fall of the Kingdom of Israel

Isaiah of Jerusalem lived during the closing decades of the existence of the neighbouring Kingdom of Israel and for some twenty years, at least, thereafter. Although he refers on a number of occasions to what Biblical scholars label "The Northern Kingdom," his references tend to be concentrated on events a decade or so before the final fall of Samaria. His allusions to the latter are generally oblique, using the fate of Samaria as a warning of the danger in which the southern Judah and Jerusalem stand if they continue with their present policies and lifestyle.

In terms of political history, with which this volume is chiefly concerned, it is therefore clear that our harvest from Isaiah will be meagre. In addition to that, however, I shall in this paper try also to outline some of the ideological implications that follow from the fall of Samaria. In terms of the history of religion and the language that gives expression to it, we may find that Isaiah, both as historical prophet and as book, has much to contribute.

It should come as no surprise if I stress finally by way of introduction that by almost universal consent only a modest amount of what is found in the book of Isaiah actually derives straight from the eighth century. From chapter 40 onwards, despite many references to Jacob and Israel, all the material was written in the sixth and later centuries, of course. Equally, all agree that a good deal in chapters 1–39 also comes from the time after Isaiah himself, but exactly what is more controversial. In a historical study, such as the present one, that is obviously a matter for concern, and I shall have space to make only a few remarks to justify the positions I adopt. What it is important to bear in mind, however, is that while I am undertaking a severely diachronic analysis that does not mean that we should simply discard the later material. Rather, we should value it highly as first-hand evidence of the later reception of material that may have applied originally to Israel and Samaria. That reception, from earliest days on, is important evidence of the great impact on the development of subsequent thought that Isaiah had.

I want to begin with terminology, and specifically with the ways in which Isaiah labelled the Northern Kingdom. The so-called refrain poem in 9:7–20 makes for a good starting point. In chapter 9 we have three stanzas, each closed by an almost identical refrain in verses 11, 16, and 20. The same form of wording recurs in 5:25, with the following verses, 5:26–29, apparently comprising the final stanza of the poem.¹ This final stanza tells of the advance of an unnamed but invincible enemy who we may presume is God's final agent of judgment for the various sins enumerated in the preceding stanzas. It is likely that the occurrence of the refrain in 5:25 marks the end, therefore, of the original fourth stanza, only two lines of which have been preserved in 5:25a. I refer to my discussions elsewhere to explain how and why this dislocation may have taken place.²

Once a few obvious minor later expansions (such as 9:14) have been parenthesised, the four complete stanzas which now remain are of remarkably similar length and poetic shape, though we should probably not use this to force them into exact conformity with each other, as Gray was tempted to do.³ This raises an interesting point with regard to the first stanza in verses 7–11. MT has six and a half lines, which certainly seems unlikely. There has probably been some severe damage to the text of verse 8, as I argue at length in the textual notes to my forthcoming commentary, so that the length of the present text of the stanza should not deflect us from construing verse 7 as an independent heading to the whole poem. That it is so is demanded by the observation that this is the only stanza which has a generalised introduction: "The Lord has sent a word against Jacob and it will fall upon Israel." In addition, the titles of those addressed are immediately changed in verse 8, where the specific indictment begins: "But all the people did evil, Ephraim and the residents of Samaria." Verse 8 therefore clearly refers to the inhabitants of the Northern Kingdom, and that will then account also for the use of the name Israel in v. 11 following.

In verse 7, however, which on this view introduces the whole of the poem, we find that those addressed are "Jacob and ... Israel." Although most of the rest of the poem is most easily construed with reference to the Northern Kingdom (the

---

1 The tenses used support this view, since they are generally indicative of the past in 9:7–20 but they shift to a future orientation in 5:26–29 (predominantly either imperfect or *waw* + perfect).
2 See Hugh G. M. Williamson, *A Critical and Exegetical Commentary on Isaiah 1–27*, vol. 1: *Isaiah 1–5* (London: T&T Clark, 2006), 400–403, together with the relevant passage in the forthcoming volume 2; see also id., "Commenting on the Unknown: Reflections on Isaiah 9:7–20," in *The Genre of Biblical Commentary: Essays in Honor of John E. Hartley on the Occasion of his 75th Birthday*, ed. Timothy D. Finlay and William Yarchin (Eugene OR: Pickwick, 2015): 184–95. Against the inclusion of 10:1–4 in this poem, despite the recurrence of the refrain at 10:4b, see Hugh G. M. Williamson, "'An Initial Problem': The Setting and Purpose of Isaiah 10:1–4," in *The Book of Isaiah: Enduring Questions Answered Anew: Essays Honoring Joseph Blenkinsopp and His Contribution to the Study of Isaiah*, ed. Richard J. Bautch and J. Todd Hibbard (Grand Rapids MI: Eerdmans, 2014): 11–20.
3 G. Buchanan Gray, *A Critical and Exegetical Commentary on the Book of Isaiah I-XXVII* (Edinburgh: T&T Clark, 1912), 177; see too more recently Herbert Donner, *Israel unter den Völkern* (Leiden: Brill, 1964), 66–69.

reference to Ephraim and Manasseh in verse 20 is only the most obvious indication of this), Judah is also included (again, see verse 20 for a direct mention[4]). It is therefore probable that the names in verse 7 are not synonymous with those in verse 8, as many commentators have assumed,[5] but rather that Israel and Jacob are used to cover a wider audience, including both kingdoms.

Because, as we shall see later, this is a matter of considerable historical importance, it will be worthwhile to see if this kind of distinction in terminology is a consistent feature of Isaiah's own sayings or whether our poem is an exception to some other rule.

A superficial survey indicates that elsewhere too Isaiah referred to the Northern Kingdom in comparable terms. In 8:1–4, which is part of Isaiah's own first-person commentary on the so-called Syro-Ephraimite crisis of 734–732 BCE, the coalition partners are referred to as Samaria and Damascus (v. 4), and the threat against them is again explicitly Assyria.

Similarly, there is a longer account of this same crisis in chapter 7. This is told in the third person and cannot derive directly from Isaiah but reaches us, as with the comparable narratives in chapters 20 and 36–39, from some separate, Deuteronomistically-inspired narrator. He had access to reasonable historical memory, however, as the other passages just mentioned clearly indicate, so that we need not doubt that he incorporated a fair substance of Isaiah's own words. Here, in the introduction in verse 1, which has a close parallel in 2Kgs 16:5, Pekah is identified as king of Israel. This is standard terminology in the his-

---

[4] Ronald E. Clements, *Isaiah 1–39* (Grand Rapids MI: Eerdmans and London: Marshall, Morgan & Scott, 1980), 69, proposes that this clause should be regarded as "a redactor's addition who has sought to bring out more forcefully that the final defeat of the Northern Kingdom arose because the people there refused to reunite with Judah and accept the Davidic monarchy." In his view, the original prophecy concerned only the Northern Kingdom in its final decade. In view of the familiarity with this kind of Judean gloss in Hosea, it is, perhaps, surprising that this suggestion has not been more widely adopted. The reason is presumably that it is not so certain as Clements maintains that the poem originally referred exclusively to the Northern Kingdom, and also that, as a Judean author, Isaiah would himself no doubt have had an interest in the effect of his observations on his own nation. In my opinion, the first colon of the verse would, on its own, have been a curiously weak poetic ending to the stanza. The poetic shape of the passage certainly favours retaining the phrase here.

[5] See, for instance, Karl Marti, *Das Buch Jesaja* (Tübingen: Mohr Siebeck, 1900), 96; John Skinner, *The Book of the Prophet Isaiah, Chapters i-xxxix* (Cambridge: Cambridge University Press, 1897), 78; Gray, *Isaiah 1–XXVII*, 183; Jesper Høgenhaven, *Gott und Volk bei Jesaja: eine Untersuchung zur biblischen Theologie* (Leiden: Brill, 1988), 8; J. J. M. Roberts, *First Isaiah: A Commentary* (Minneapolis MI: Fortress, 2015), 160; more cautiously Hans Wildberger, *Jesaja 1–12* (Neukirchen-Vluyn: Neukirchener Verlag, 1980; 2nd edition), 214 = id., *Isaiah 1–12: a Commentary*, trans. Thomas H. Trapp (Minneapolis MI: Fortress, 1991), 230.

torical books and we need not doubt that the wording derives from that same circle. It will not directly reflect Isaiah's own preferred terminology. When we get into the narrative proper immediately following, however, we find that the Northern Kingdom is referred to rather as Ephraim (vv. 2, 5, 9, 17) with Samaria as its "head" (v. 9). This therefore exactly parallels the use in 9:7.

The same terminology appears in 11:13: "Then the jealousy towards Ephraim will depart, and those who are hostile to Judah will be cut off; Ephraim will not envy Judah, and Judah will not show hostility towards Ephraim." This verse appears in a passage whose introduction and conclusion in verses 11–12 and 15–16 show conclusively that it cannot be earlier than the exilic period. Indeed, the links between these verses and parts of chapters 40–55 are striking. There are reasons to question the original internal unity of this passage, however.[6] First, verse 11 (with which 12 is joined by content) and verses 15–16 are more prosaic than the verses which they enclose. This kind of distinction is admittedly not as clear cut as we might wish in the modern world and there are undoubtedly gradations of style in classical Hebrew where the boundaries between poetry and prose are blurred. I do not, however, take the extreme view that claims that it is a mistake to use the term poetry at all. Whatever labels we use, however, the use of prose particles, lack of parallelism, the use of a long list of place names, and uneven line length combine to indicate that there is a difference of style between the two sections I have mentioned and the remainder of the passage.

Second, the first and last parts of the passage are closely associated thematically with each other. They concentrate on the regathering of those in the diaspora, and as already mentioned they come very close to some of the themes and forms of expression that we find in Isaiah 40–55. The middle section, by contrast, speaks of the reunion of the sharply opposed factions within the land and of their military triumphs over the traditional enemies of Israel and Judah (a theme, incidentally, in which Isaiah 40–55 shows no interest whatsoever). While it is possible imaginatively to join these two very different topics, the passage itself does not furnish any such join,[7] and the fact that it returns at the end to the theme with which it began tends to highlight the difference.

---

[6] The following discussion represents a revision of the position that I argued in Hugh G. M. Williamson, *The Book Called Isaiah: Deutero-Isaiah's Role in Composition and Redaction* (Oxford: Clarendon, 1994), 125–41, where I treated the passage as a unity, including verses 13–14. I now agree with those who have been critical of the way I handled those two verses. For fuller details on the points summarised here, see my forthcoming commentary on Isaiah 6–12.

[7] Cf. Bernhard Duhm, *Das Buch Jesaia* (Göttingen: Vandenhoeck & Ruprecht, 1892; 4th edition, 1922), 109: "13 und 14 schieben sich ungeschickt zwischen v. 11f. und v. 15f. ein."

The most plausible trigger for verses 13–14 is the refrain poem in chapter 9. There too we read of enmity between Ephraim and Judah (9:20), and there too the "Philistines in the west" and "Aram in the east" are depicted as the archetypical enemies of Israel (9:11). Our two verses seem to represent an idealised reversal of the bad situation which was depicted in that poem. It may therefore be suggested that these two verses were developed independently as some sort of responsive expansion of that longer poem and that this was later picked up by the author of our passage. Whether by Isaiah or a later close imitator, the use of the name Ephraim again fits the pattern we have been tracing.

With chapter 17 we get back on to slightly firmer ground. This is one of the long selections of "Oracles Against the Nations" in chapters 13–23, and again there are differences of opinion as to which may be from Isaiah himself, and equally which parts of even early oracles may have been added later. Chapter 17 is an oracle concerning Damascus, and it seems to predict her downfall. Given that this is known to have happened in 732 BCE, many commentators favour the view that the chapter at least contains some very early material. This whole debate has recently been well summarised by Paul M. Cook, and in my opinion he then advances a very convincing argument, based on the different ways in which the otherwise similar titles to each oracle are used, for isolating four of them as being among the material assembled at the earliest stage in the development of the book. These are the oracles about Philistia (14:28–32), Moab (chapters 15–16), Damascus (chapter 17), and Egypt (chapter 19).[8] While our chapter 17 has undoubtedly gone through some stages of later expansion, verses 1b and the first part of 3 at least seem to belong together as part of the primary layer, as agreed by even the most radical of modern analyses, and here too we find that the Northern Kingdom (with whom, of course, Damascus was in alliance at the point where her history impinged especially on Judah) is referred to initially as Ephraim (this was later expanded to "the children of Israel").[9]

---

8 Paul M. Cook, *A Sign and a Wonder: the Redactional Formation of Isaiah 18–20* (Leiden: Brill, 2011), 1–47.
9 For this minimal analysis, see, e.g., Scholastika Deck, *Die Gerichtsbotschaft Jesajas: Charakter und Begründung* (Würzburg: Echter Verlag, 1991), 53–55, 78–79; Uwe Becker, *Jesaja – von der Botschaft zum Buch* (Göttingen: Vandenhoeck & Ruprecht, 1997), 274–75. Matthijs de Jong, *Isaiah among the Ancient Near Eastern Prophets: A Comparative Study of the Earliest Stages of the Isaiah Tradition and the Neo-Assyrian Prophecies* (Leiden: Brill, 2007), 146–47, is similar, though he also retains part of verse 2; see too Heide-Marie Pfaff, *Die Entwicklung des Restgedankens in Jesaja 1–39* (Frankfurt am Main: Peter Lang, 1996), 85–88. For a more generous, though still critical, analysis of the whole chapter see Donner, *Israel unter den Völkern*, 38–42; Michael E. W. Thompson, *Situation and Theology: Old Testament Interpretations of the Syro-Ephraimite War* (Sheffield: Almond, 1982), 42–45; Høgenhaven, *Gott und Volk bei Jesaia*, 106–7.

The relationship of verses 4–6 with verses 1–3 is less clear. On the one hand, the introductory "And it shall come to pass on that day" is very often used elsewhere to indicate a subsequent addition or expansion. On the other hand there is little in the verses themselves to point to a substantially later date. It seems to announce the future downfall of "the glory of Jacob." We have not met this designation previously, though we shall need to look later at two or three other occurrences of it; we shall find that it can certainly be used (against what we might at first suppose) for the Southern Kingdom of Judah. In the context following verses 1–3, however, it is difficult not to suppose that it refers here to the Northern Kingdom, Ephraim, though why there should be a change of name here is not agreed. Is it possible that we have two originally separate poetic units in verses 1–3 and 4–6 which have here been combined (we may note the use of the catchword "glory" in verses 3 and 4)? If so, the possibility presents itself that verses 4–6 have in view not the fate of Israel in the aftermath of the Syro-Ephraimite crisis but rather the later eventual fall to the Assyrians in 720 (or whenever precisely it was).[10] If so, it would furnish one of only very few direct references to that particular event.

A final passage that demands our attention in this section of our study is 28:1–4, on which I still adhere to the view that I argued already more than twenty years ago.[11] Although it is generally agreed to start a significant new section in the book, it is striking that it has no heading, in contrast with 1:1, 2:1, and 13:1, as well as the different form of heading in 6:1 and 14:28. In addition, it is curious to find a woe-saying directed towards the Northern Kingdom opening a series of woe sayings in the following chapters which seem most naturally to be related to the situation in Judah just before 701 BCE, twenty years or so after the fall of Samaria. It is therefore perhaps helpful to recall that we only consider that it starts a new section in the book because it follows chapters 24–27, which stand out as a distinct section of their own. While the conclusion is thus entirely justified so far as the present shape of the book is concerned, the situation looks very different when we recall that 24–27 was certainly added quite late in the composition history of the book. Before that, 28:1–4 will have followed straight after the other oracles against the nations, and in fact there is no reason why we should not simply assume that it was originally one of those, introduced

---

[10] For the possibility that some of the material in the following verses also refers to the Northern Kingdom, see Willem A. M. Beuken, "From Damascus to Mount Zion: a Journey Through the Land of the Harvester (Isaiah 17–18)," in *'Enlarge the Site of Your Tent': the City as Unifying Theme in Isaiah*, ed. Archibald L. H. M. van Wieringen and Annemarieke van der Woude (Leiden: Brill, 2011): 63–80.

[11] See Williamson, *The Book Called Isaiah*, 184–88, where the case is set out in fuller detail.

by "woe" just like 18:1. Rather like Amos 1–2 in reverse, a series of oracles against various nations led originally to Judah's nearest neighbour and was then turned to Judah herself with a series of woe and *massa'* oracles in the remainder of 28–31. Without going into further detail here, it suffices to note that the Northern Kingdom is again called Ephraim (vv. 1 and 3).

Moving slightly further afield, we find comparably that in the early poem in 10:5–9, 13–15[12] Assyria is addressed directly but the reference is to her dealings with "a godless nation" (v. 6). While some have argued that this refers to Judah[13] or to both kingdoms together,[14] I strongly agree with the majority view that the reference is exclusively to the Northern Kingdom,[15] for the following reasons: (i) in verse 6 the "godless nation" echoes the language of 9:16, while the further description of them as people "who arouse my fury" uses a word for fury which does not derive from the previous verse (anger and rage) but rather from 9:18; as we have already seen, the people in view in 9:16 and 18 are Ephraim and Samaria. (ii) The reference to taking spoil and plunder (also in v. 6) recalls the name of the child Maher-shalal-hash-baz in 8:1–4 and in the explanation in v. 4 the "spoil" is linked directly with Samaria. (iii) The continuation of verse 6 by stating that they will be made into "something that is trampled down like mud in the streets" clearly recalls 28:3, where we are told that "the crown of the drunkards of Ephraim will be trampled under foot." Thus all four clauses in verse 6 have close parallels elsewhere in the early material in Isaiah that refers explicitly to Ephraim, Israel, or Samaria; (iv) finally, the sequence of cities conquered by

---

[12] In my opinion, which again is shared by many others, verses 10–11 and verse 12 represent later additions in which the lessons of the Northern Kingdom are reapplied to the Southern. I give reasons for this conclusion, together with fuller bibliography, in "Idols in Isaiah in the Light of Isaiah 10:10–11," in *New Perspectives on Old Testament Prophecy and History: Essays in Honour of Hans M. Barstad*, ed. Rannfrid I. Thelle, Terje Stordalen and Mervyn E. J. Richardson (Leiden: Brill, 2015): 17–28.

[13] E.g., Marti, *Das Buch Jesaja*, 105; Johann Fischer, *Das Buch Isaias übersetzt und erklärt: Kapitel 1–39* (Bonn: Hanstein, 1937), 94.

[14] E.g., August Dillmann, *Der Prophet Jesaia* (Leipzig: Hirzel, 1890; 5th edition), 105; Edward J. Young, *The Book of Isaiah: The English Text, with Introduction, Exposition, and Notes* (Grand Rapids MI: Eerdmans, 1965), 360; Clements, *Isaiah 1–39*, 110–11.

[15] E.g., Wilhelm Gesenius, *Philologisch-kritischer und historischer Commentar über den Jesaia* (Leipzig: Vogel, 1821), 391; Ferdinand Hitzig, *Der Prophet Jesaja* (Heidelberg: Winter, 1833), 126; Otto Procksch, *Jesaia I* (Leipzig: Deichert, 1930), 164; Josef Schreiner, *Sion-Jerusalem Jahwehs Königssitz: Theologie der Heiligen Stadt im Alten Testament* (Munich: Kösel, 1963), 264; de Jong, *Isaiah among the Ancient Near Eastern Prophets*, 128; Arie van der Kooij, "'Nimrod, a Mighty Hunter before the Lord!' Assyrian Royal Ideology as Perceived in the Hebrew Bible," *Journal for Semitics* 21 (2012): 15; Konrad Schmid, "Die Anfänge des Jesajabuchs," in *Congress Volume Munich 2013*, ed. Christl M. Maier (Leiden: Brill, 2014): 435.

the Assyrian as listed in verse 9 reaches its climax with Samaria. Now, it may well be that, rather as in the case of the sequence in 7:8–9a, the reader is meant tacitly to conclude from this that the same could apply by extension to Jerusalem, but that is not the same thing as saying that Jerusalem is directly mentioned here. The whole structure of the passage leads up to, and should therefore be referred to, Samaria. Since Damascus is referred to as a city which Assyria has already conquered (see v. 9), we must assume that this passage is later than 732 BCE, when the northern part of Israel was also annexed, and that it has in view the final fall of Samaria to the Assyrians a decade or so later.[16] The use of the name Samaria is thus entirely appropriate here, and again we should note that the name Israel is not used in this connection.

---

16 A more precise date is difficult to determine. In my view, the reference to the defeat of Carchemish in verse 9 means that it cannot be earlier than 717 BCE; see J. David Hawkins, "Karkamiš," in *RlA* 5, ed. Dietz Otto Edzard (1980): 441, 445; Karen Radner, "Provinz. C. Assyrien," in *RlA* 11, ed. Michael P. Streck (2008): 58. Some have thought that the failure to list Ashdod, which was subjugated by the Assyrians in 711 BCE, indicates a date earlier than that, hence quite narrowly between 717 and 711 BCE: e. g., Procksch, *Jesaia*, 166; Schreiner, *Sion-Jerusalem*, 265; Walter Dietrich, *Jesaja und die Politik* (Munich: Kaiser, 1976), 118; Hermann Barth, *Die Jesaja-Worte in der Josiazeit: Israel und Assur als Thema einer produktiven Neuinterpretation der Jesajaüberlieferung* (Neukirchen-Vluyn: Neukirchener Verlag, 1977), 26; Høgenhaven, *Gott und Volk bei Jesaja*, 118; Francolino J. Gonçalves, *L'Expédition de Sennachérib en Palestine dans la littérature hébraïque ancienne* (Paris: Gabalda, 1986), 260; but this particular argument is weak. There is no suggestion that every city conquered by Assyria should be included, and Ashdod would not have suited the north-south arrangement of the list so well, given that it is south of Samaria; see correctly Erich Bosshard-Nepustil, *Rezeptionen von Jesaia 1–39 im Zwölfprophetenbuch: Untersuchungen zur literarischen Verbindung von Prophetenbüchern in babylonischer und persischer Zeit* (Freiburg: Universitätsverlag and Göttingen: Vandenhoeck & Ruprecht, 1997), 240–41 n. 6. Others, therefore, have claimed that the passage should best be set immediately prior to the Assyrian invasion in 701 BCE in the course of Hezekiah's revolt: e. g., Duhm, *Jesaia*, 97; Skinner, *Isaiah*, 83–84; Marti, *Jesaja*, 105; Edward J. Kissane, *The Book of Isaiah, Translated from a Critically Revised Hebrew Text with Commentary*, 1: *i–xxxix* (Dublin: Browne and Nolan, 1941), 123; Paul Auvray, *Isaïe 1–39* (Paris: Gabalda, 1972), 135; William R. Gallagher, *Sennacherib's Campaign to Judah: New Studies* (Leiden: Brill, 1999), 85–86; Joseph Blenkinsopp, *Isaiah 1–39: a New Translation with Introduction and Commentary* (New York: Doubleday, 2000), 254. Clements, *Isaiah 1–39*, 110, not unreasonably rejects this latter opinion on the ground that "Isaiah condemned the alliance on which Hezekiah's revolt was based, and foretold its disastrous outcome." It may be noted in addition that this date is often supported by the reference to Jerusalem in verse 11, but if that verse is secondary, as most rightly believe, then that part of the argument loses its force. While there can be no final certainty, therefore (so Gray, *Isaiah I–XXVII*, 196; Wildberger, *Jesaja 1–12*, 393–94 [= *Isaiah 1–12*, 415]; Clements, *Isaiah 1–39*, 110; Deck, *Die Gerichtsbotschaft Jesajas*, 39), the earlier date, possibly in connection with the Ashdod rebellion, which began in 713, is to be preferred.

I mentioned that at 17:4 we find the expression "the glory of Jacob" in relation to the Northern Kingdom and that some scholars attribute this to Isaiah himself. It follows that we should also survey other uses of Jacob in chapters 1–39.[17] The name appears as part of the divine titles "the God of Jacob" in 2:3, and "the Holy One of Jacob" in 29:23; in the expression "house of Jacob" in 2:5, 6; 8:17; 10:20; 14:1 (second occurrence of the name in that verse); 29:22 (first occurrence); and in a more free-standing manner in 9:7; 10:21; 14:1 (first occurrence); 17:4; 27:6, 9; 29:22 (second occurrence). Of these, the majority should certainly be dated well after the time of Isaiah himself. In most cases this would not be in serious dispute, though a few are less certain. In my opinion a serious case for Isaianic authorship can be maintained in relation only to 2:6; 8:17; 9:7; and 17:6.[18]

Isaiah 2:6 introduces the famous poem against human hubris with the words "You have abandoned your people, the house of Jacob." Even among those who (like myself) are sympathetic to the largely Isaianic origin of this verse there are some who hold, on quite strong grounds, that our particular phrase was added only redactionally well after Isaiah's time.[19] In that case it would not be relevant for our present inquiry.

Taking it as original for the sake of argument, it has occasionally been thought that the reference here is exclusively to the Northern Kingdom.[20] This depends in part on construing the phrase "house of Jacob" as a vocative and in part on the suggestion that in authentically Isaianic sayings Jacob always refers to the Northern Kingdom. Neither supposition is beyond challenge, however. So far as the syntax of the verse is concerned, the versions are divided and so cannot settle the matter either way. More tellingly, the construal as vocative results in an awkward shift from second person address here to third person in the immedi-

---

17 See also Wolfgang Werner, *Eschatologische Texte in Jesaja 1–39: Messias, Heiliger Rest, Völker* (Würzburg: Echter, 1982), 112–14; Høgenhaven, *Gott und Volk bei Jesaja*, 16–17; for usage in the second half of the book, see Hugh G. M. Williamson, "Jacob in Isaiah 40–66," in *Continuity and Discontinuity: Chronological and Thematic Development in Isaiah 40–66*, ed. Lena-Sofia Tiemeyer and Hans M. Barstad (Göttingen: Vandenhoeck & Ruprecht, 2014): 219–29. Some of the passages in the first half, such as 14:1, come very close to what we find in the distinctive terminology of chapters 40–48 in particular.
18 For 2:1–4 as exilic, see Williamson, *Isaiah 1–5*, 173–78. 2:5 is a redactional join between 2–4 and 6–19, the name Jacob being one of the important connecting elements.
19 See, for instance, Marvin A. Sweeney, *Isaiah 1–39 with an Introduction to Prophetic Literature* (Grand Rapids MI: Eerdmans, 1996), 102.
20 See especially J. J. M. Roberts, "Isaiah 2 and the Prophet's Message to the North," *JQR* 75 (1984–85): 290–308, and Roberts, *First Isaiah*, 44.

ately following lines,[21] and in addition, as Gesenius observed long ago, outside of purely secular contexts the verb נטש is usually used with God as subject.[22] On the second argument, the evidence that in Isaiah Jacob only ever refers to the Northern Kingdom seems to me quite unjustified. 8:17, to which I shall turn next, seems categorically to rule out this proposal, and in the present chapter (which in this argument is taken as a whole), verse 3 seems equally clear. As we shall see later, the God of Jacob seems to be peculiarly associated with the Jerusalem temple, so that it is difficult to envisage that Judah would not at least be included in a reference such as the present one. The choice of title was probably determined by religio-historical rather than crudely political considerations. If authentic, its reference in 2:6 will therefore coincide with 8:17, to which I now turn.

This verse comes right at the end of the first-person material included in chapters 6 and 8. While I agree that verse 18 immediately following should be attributed to a later redactor, there is no good reason to include verse 17 with this, as has occasionally been suggested.[23] In particular, it is difficult to suppose that verses 16–17 do not predate 30:8. It would be very odd to have a much later writer indicating that Isaiah would still see God's deliverance within his own lifetime; such a "mistake" is more readily intelligible as a reflection of Isaiah's own thinking early on in his ministry.

This is the only place in this block of first-person material where (the house of) Jacob is mentioned at all. Just before, in verse 14 we find the unique expression "the two houses of Israel," which I will discuss more fully below. I suggest that in the present instance the referent is the same (i.e. a name that was inclusive of those in both kingdoms). It is suitable at this concluding point of the passage which began with the temple vision that we should revert to a peculiarly cult-based title to indicate the temporary withdrawal of God's protecting favour to his people (broadly conceived). In fact fuller study could show that all three main elements in the verse (the verbs to describe Isaiah's action, the clause to describe God's action, and the phrase which identifies the people affected) are

---

21 See Marvin A. Sweeney, *Isaiah 1–4 and the Post-Exilic Understanding of the Isaianic Tradition* (Berlin: de Gruyter, 1988), 139–40, including a helpfully full survey of the versional evidence.
22 Gesenius, *Philologisch-kritischer und historischer Commentar über den Jesaia*, 182.
23 For both points see my arguments in Hugh G. M. Williamson, "A Sign and a Portent in Isaiah 8.18," in *Studies in the Text and Versions of the Hebrew Bible in Honour of Robert Gordon*, ed. Geoffrey Khan and Diana Lipton (Leiden: Brill, 2012): 77–86, and id.,"Isaiah: Prophet of Weal or Woe?" in *"Thus Speaks Ishtar of Arbela": Prophecy in Israel, Assyria, and Egypt in the Neo-Assyrian Period*, ed. Robert P. Gordon and Hans M. Bartsad (Winona Lake IN: Eisenbrauns, 2013): 287–91.

all drawn from a similar cultic milieu. Judah must certainly at least be included, therefore, in Isaiah's understanding of the house of Jacob.

This conclusion fits perfectly with what I have already written with regard to 9:7, where Jacob is also used in an inclusive sense. In sum, 8:17 and 9:7 go together. If the occurrence in 2:6 is original (which is uncertain), it too could fit the same picture, though a reference there to Judah alone seems contextually more probable. This leaves only 17:4 as a possible reference to the Northern Kingdom alone, though it is equally disputed whether this verse should be ascribed to Isaiah.

I conclude this survey of nomenclature relating to the Northern Kingdom, therefore, by stating that Isaiah generally referred to it as Ephraim, occasionally Samaria, and perhaps once Jacob. He uses the name Israel in relation to it only when that is firmly subsumed from a literary perspective to the dominant Ephraim title, never, so far as we have seen, in isolation. These findings therefore raise in an acute form the question why Isaiah avoided almost completely the use of the name Israel in the way that we might have regarded as standard for the Northern Kingdom.[24]

An important clue comes in the first-person material in chapter 8. We have already noted the use of Samaria in verses 1–4, and this is followed in verses 5–8a with an indictment against "this people," whom I take to be Judah.[25] While it is clear that the sayings in 1–4 and 5–8 have been joined redactionally, that does not entail as a necessary consequence that this could only have happened very late. For a host of reasons relating to literary inter-connections and theological consistency which cannot all be itemised here, the literary integrity

---

24 To my embarrassment I was not aware until her participation in the conference that underlies this volume of the important and detailed monograph of Kristin Weingart, *Stämmevolk – Staatsvolk – Gottesvolk? Studien zur Verwendung des Israel-Namens im Alten Testament* (Tübingen: Mohr Siebeck, 2014). While inevitably there are points of difference between us (e. g., on the interpretation of Isa 5:7), we seem to be running along parallel lines in regard to some of the major issues which I now go on to address (see especially her pp. 190–227, 342–44, and 360–64, though other parts of the book are also relevant). Rather than completely rework my original draft in the light of her research, I have therefore decided to keep this part of the text more or less as first written in order that readers can distinguish more clearly how we have worked independently to reach our broadly compatible conclusions as well as to compare them and decide which they prefer on matters of detail.

25 I have discussed this in advance of my forthcoming commentary in Hugh G. M. Williamson, "The Waters of Shiloah (Isaiah 8:5–8)," in *The Fire Signals of Lachish: Studies in the Archaeology and History of Israel in the Late Bronze Age, Iron Age, and Persian Period in Honor of David Ussishkin*, ed. Israel Finkelstein and Nadav Na'aman (Winona Lake IN: Eisenbrauns, 2011): 331–43.

of 6:1–11+8:1–8a, 11–17 seems to me too strong to deny.[26] It is therefore no coincidence that after these sayings against Samaria and Judah, the two are drawn together in the following passage with a reference to the downfall of "the two houses of Israel." From Isaiah's own pen, therefore, we have here clear evidence that he considered Israel to be a name which embraced both Ephraim/Samaria and Judah/Jerusalem. In other words, in terms of political realities on the ground he favoured using ancient tribal designations together with reference to the capital cities whereas he preferred to reserve the name Israel for some sort of overarching unity between the two.[27]

Because of uncertainties about the dating of oracles within Isaiah's own lifetime it is difficult to be certain whether there are other passages which support this view from the years prior to the fall of Samaria.[28] The strongest candidate is in the Song of the Vineyard in 5:1–7. While the date of this passage cannot be certainly established, I have argued elsewhere that for several reasons it fits most naturally into the first part of Isaiah's ministry.[29] In the concluding verse, we read that "the vineyard of the Lord of Hosts is the House of Israel, and the people of Judah are the planting in which he took delight." There are three possible ways of understanding the relationship between these two names: they

---

[26] For full argumentation, see my forthcoming commentary. Some of the arguments are presented in a preliminary way in Williamson, "Isaiah: Prophet of Weal or Woe?"

[27] For a different approach to this expression, see the important study by Reinhard G. Kratz, "The Two Houses of Israel," in *Let Us Go up to Zion: Essays in Honour of H.G.M. Williamson on the Occasion of his Sixty-Fifth Birthday*, ed. Iain Provan and Mark J. Boda (Leiden: Brill, 2012): 167–79. He rightly makes the point that in this context "house" has to be understood politically rather than just culturally or religiously (in contrast, for instance, with "house of Jacob"). Encouraged by the reception of the passage in CD, he ties the present passage diachronically, however, with 7:17 and so finds the use of Israel to be much later than Isaiah, being part of the "all-Israel" perspective which he finds developing in the later Isaiah tradition. As I shall elaborate a little later in this essay, I find it possible to believe that Isaiah held together a sense of the two contemporary kingdoms with an inherited appreciation of their greater unity. So far as 7:17 is concerned, I agree that 7:1–17 can only have been written and later incorporated in the book well after Isaiah's lifetime. At the same time, it may well include a sound memory of some of Isaiah's own words (allowances, of course, have to be made for alteration over time). To the extent that 7:17 comes into this category, I agree that it may well reflect his understanding that this greater unity derived from a period which we now call the United Monarchy. Whether he was historically correct in this (as many still think) or not (as others hold) is not something which need affect the exegesis of his sayings.

[28] 1:3, for example, seems to refer to the people as a whole under the name Israel, but in my view and that of many others, this was not written as early as the time when the Northern Kingdom still existed; see Williamson, *Isaiah 1–5*, 28–30.

[29] See Williamson, *Isaiah 1–5*, 330–31.

could be synonymous, they could be completely distinct (referring to the northern and southern kingdoms respectively), or it could be a case where the first name is further specified by the second. Although the second possibility has been quite popular,[30] it seems the least likely here. The vineyard and the "planting in which he took delight" are clearly not two wholly separate elements but at the least overlap in some measure, and it would be very strange if Judah were not also included within the referent of the vineyard. Similarly, to make the two terms completely synonymous, as in the first possibility,[31] also seems unlikely. If this passage dates from early in the prophet's ministry, when the Northern Kingdom still existed, such usage would at the least be confusing. The third possibility, by contrast, has much to commend it.[32] It fits best the form of parallelism here (nearer definition), and it fits exactly with Isaiah's use of Israel already noted, namely the people of God as a whole.

More promising in this regard is, I believe, the divine title "the Holy One of Israel." While this title comes twelve times in Isaiah 1–39, not all occurrences by any means can be ascribed to Isaiah himself. Indeed, in a study of this title in the book as a whole, I have argued elsewhere that probably only 5:19; 30:11, 12, 25; 31:1 go back to Isaiah himself, and these probably all come from the period leading immediately up to 701 BCE.[33] There is no evidence that Isaiah himself coined this expression, and indeed, if he had, we should have expected to find it in the account of his vision in chapter 6, with its related cry in the Trisagion. Rather, it

---

[30] E.g. Clements, *Isaiah 1–39*, 59–60; Gale E. Yee, "A Form-Critical Study of Isaiah 5:1–7 as a Song and a Juridical Parable," *CBQ* 43 (1981): 37–38; Renatus Porath, *Die Sozialkritik im Jesajabuch: Redaktionsgeschichtliche Analyse* (Frankfurt: Peter Lang, 1994), 183–84; Klaus Seybold, "Das Weinberglied des Propheten Jesaja (5,1–7)," in id., *Die Sprache der Propheten: Studien zur Literaturgeschichte der Prophetie* (Zürich: Pano, 1999): 117.
[31] So Wildberger, *Jesaja 1–12*, 171–72 (= *Isaiah 1–12*, 184–85); Willy Schottroff, "Das Weinberglied Jesajas (Jes 5 $_{1-7}$): Ein Beitrag zur Geschichte der Parabel," *ZAW* 82 (1970): 89; Kirsten Nielsen, *There Is Hope for a Tree: The Tree as Metaphor in Isaiah* (Sheffield: Sheffield Academic Press, 1989), 108–14 (though she allows that it may have been reapplied to the Northern Kingdom in a later reinterpretation).
[32] Cf. Anders J. Bjørndalen, *Untersuchungen zur allegorischen Rede der Propheten Amos und Jesaja* (Berlin: de Gruyter, 1986), 316–18, who lists many earlier commentators who adopted this view; add now Lukas M. Muntingh, "The Name 'Israel' and Related Terms in the Book of Isaiah," in *Studies in Isaiah: OTWSA 22, 1979, and OTWSA 23, 1980*, ed. Wouter C. van Wyk (Pretoria: Society for the Study of the Old Testament, 1982): 159–82; Hubert Irsigler, "Speech Acts and Intention in the 'Song of the Vineyard' Isaiah 5:1–7," *OTE* 10 (1997): 64; Willem A. M. Beuken, *Jesaja 1–12* (Freiburg: Herder, 2003), 138.
[33] See Hugh G. M. Williamson, "Isaiah and the Holy One of Israel," in *Biblical Hebrew, Biblical Texts: Essays in Memory of Michael P. Weitzman*, ed. Ada Rapoport-Albert and Gillian Greenberg (Sheffield: Sheffield Academic Press, 2001): 22–38.

is my belief that its occurrence three times in the Psalter (Pss 71:22; 78:41; 89:19) indicates that it may have been an infrequently used title in the liturgy; whether or not these three Psalms pre-date Isaiah (and many would argue that they do not), it is more probable that they reflect ancient liturgical use (which, of course, is notoriously conservative) than that they have picked the title up from Isaiah or the later Isaiah tradition.[34]

I should make a similar case for "the God of Jacob," which astonishingly comes in the Zion Psalm 46:8, 12, as well as in a number of other psalms: 20:1; 24:6 (by a probable emendation); 75:10; 76:7; 81:2, 5; 84:9; 94:7; 146:5 (again without regard to the question whether these particular psalms are early, though a strong case can be made for that in some instances)[35] and likewise the even commoner title "the God of Israel" (some 200 occurrences in all, though in only three instances can any sort of case be made for use by Isaiah himself[36]) along with the rare "Strong One of Israel" (Isa 1:24, almost certainly Isaianic), which sits alongside the commoner "Strong One of Jacob" elsewhere (Gen 49:24; Isa 49:26; 60:16; Ps 132:2, 5).[37] All this needs to be contrasted with the fact that we never find even once any such title as "the God of Judah,"[38] which might have been expected if the Southern Kingdom was from its earliest origins a completely separate entity from the Northern Kingdom but one which happened to share in the worship of the same deity. For whatever reason,[39] so far

---

34 Contrast, in this regard, the only other occurrences of the title outside Isaiah, in 2Kgs 19:22; Jer 50:29; 51:5.
35 The title "God of Jacob" occurs at Isa 2:3, but in my opinion this is in a passage which dates to the exilic period. For "the house of Jacob" in verses 5 and 6, see above.
36 See Høgenhaven, *Gott und Volk bei Jesaja*, 14–16.
37 I am well aware of the discussion about the vocalization of the first element in these divine titles, but as it is the name Israel/Jacob which is my primary concern here that may be left aside for the moment. For some introductory considerations, see Williamson, *Isaiah 1–5*, 141–42. By contrast, "the Rock of Israel" (30:29) probably, and "the Light of Israel" (10:17) almost certainly, come in passages which are later than Isaiah; on the latter, see Hugh G. M. Williamson, "A New Divine Title in Isaiah 10.17," in *Open-Mindedness in the Bible and Beyond: A Volume of Studies in Honour of Bob Becking*, ed. Marjo C. A. Korpel and Lester L. Grabbe (London: T&T Clark, 2015): 315–20.
38 *Contra* Philip R. Davies, *The Origins of Biblical Israel* (New York and London: T&T Clark, 2007), 22.
39 Usually this has been explained as the natural consequence of the fact that a once united nation divided into two after the death of Solomon. For those who find themselves unable historically to accept that there ever was such a United Monarchy – in terms of contributors to the present volume, see especially Christian Frevel, *Geschichte Israels* (Stuttgart: Kohlhammer, 2015) – it would presumably be necessary to speculate about some form of common tribal symbiosis

as I am aware we find here the historically unprecedented situation of two nations in the ancient Near East sharing in the worship of the same deity. The language of the liturgy reflects this and in my opinion demands a much stronger historical explanation than the supposition that the name Israel only came to be used in Judah after the fall of Samaria;[40] it is difficult to see why that admittedly seismic event should have been the trigger for so fundamental a change of direction in the religion of a neighbouring country. Rather, it can only have given momentum for some underlying religious usage to be extended into the social and even political spheres. Isaiah, for his part, was not creating, but rather drawing on and developing traditions with which he was familiar from his participation in public worship.[41]

The extent to which this development in terminology took root can hardly be overestimated. The fact that we have found that so many of the passages that include the names Israel and Jacob with reference to the Southern Kingdom are probably to be dated after Isaiah's time is already an early indication. As we move into the unquestionably later sections of the book as a whole, this becomes even more pronounced.[42] And of course there are plenty of other books to which we might later turn our attention.[43] The view that all this was a completely novel appropriation of the name of one country by another fails to offer any explanation as to why anyone should have thought of doing so in the first place. Unless there was any prior sense in Judah that somehow they had some stake in the

---

which ante-dated the development of the political monarchy first in the north and then later in the south.

40 The most persuasive proponent of this alternative view is undoubtedly Reinhard G. Kratz, "Israel in the Book of Isaiah," *JSOT* 31 (2006): 103–28 = id., "Israel im Jesajabuch," in *Die unwiderstehliche Wahrheit: Studien zur alttestamentlichen Prophetie. Festschrift für Arndt Meinhold*, ed. Rüdiger Lux and Ernst-Joachim Waschke (Leipzig: Evangelische Verlagsanstalt, 2006): 85–103 (reprinted in Reinhard G. Kratz, *Prophetenstudien: Kleine Schriften II* [Tübingen: Mohr Siebeck, 2011], 160–76). This position has been developed even further by, e.g., Wolfgang Schütte, "Wie wurde Juda israelitisiert?" *ZAW* 124 (2012): 52–72, but unfortunately he gives no attention in his article to the material in Isaiah 1–39.

41 I note here the likelihood, in view of such divine titles as "God of Jacob" and "Lord of Hosts," that these names may have come to have their close association with the Jerusalem cult from their original attachment to the ark. I acknowledge, however, that this depends on ascribing greater historical credibility to some of the historical narratives in Samuel and Kings than some are able to share.

42 See, e.g., Kratz, "Israel in the Book of Isaiah," and for a distinctive nuance Gary N. Knoppers, "Who or What is Israel in Trito-Isaiah?" in Provan and Boda, ed., *Let us Go up to Zion*, 153–65.

43 Perhaps I may be allowed to refer for one much later example to Hugh G. M. Williamson, *Israel in the Books of Chronicles* (Cambridge: Cambridge University Press, 1977).

name and all that it signified, the fall of Samaria and the probable influx of refugees could hardly have been an adequate cause. Isaiah is one of the very few authors whose writings have survived who lived through those turbulent decades,[44] and our survey has revealed that he was acutely sensitive to the powerful associations that names can evoke. While the two kingdoms still existed he referred to them primarily under tribal designations, supplemented with the names of their capital cities, and he reserved the more evocative names of Israel and Jacob for their wider unity as expressed not by political labels but in the language of ancient cult and liturgy. It was precisely the loss of one of these political entities (the other followed later as well, of course) that freed him and his successors to turn more boldly to their application to the survivors, initially as the continuing kingdom of Judah together with those who survived of the Northern Kingdom either as refugees or as residents elsewhere, and eventually to an exclusively social, cultural, and religious community without strict geographical definition at all.

---

44 For a parallel (and partially overlapping) study to the present one which also includes evidence from Isaiah's contemporary Micah, see Hugh G. M. Williamson, "Judah as Israel in Eighth-Century Prophecy," in *A God of Faithfulness: Essays in Honour of J. Gordon McConville on his 60th Birthday*, ed. Jamie A. Grant, Alison Lo and Gordon J. Wenham (New York and London: T&T Clark, 2011): 81–95.

Indices

1 General index

Abel-beth-maacah (Tell Ābil el-Qamḥ) 196, 305, 311, 329
Abydos 140, 143
Adad-nerari III 191, 203, 236, 356
Adrammelech 218–221, 260
Aguršî 103
Ahab 98, 152, 172, 216, 217, 278, 284, 292, 305, 307, 332, 340, 355
Ahaz 9, 12, 243, 259, 271–275, 279, 280, 283–289, 294–296, 307, 336, 338, 339, 358, 359, 379
Ahaziah 216, 217, 278, 282, 292, 293, 305, 307, 315, 317, 331, 332, 340
Ahaziahu 314
Ahijah 311
Ahi-Yau 116
Ahzi-Yau 121
Akko 189
Akzib 189
Alara 119, 127
Amâ 106
Amaziah 280–283, 289, 306, 325
Amenirdis I 140, 142
Ammon 98, 321
Amon 306
Amqarruna (Ekron) 67
Amun 140
Amurru 60, 62, 70, 77
Anatolia 163
Anzaria 110
Apis 127
Apku (Tell Abu Marya) 38
Arabia, Arabs 42, 70, 71, 85, 99, 108, 109, 119, 163, 352
Aram 7, 9, 259, 262, 311, 356, 357, 360, 387
Aramaic 39, 57, 102, 135, 314, 315, 317
Aramaean(s) 68, 76, 87, 200, 283, 289, 310, 311, 314, 315, 317, 321, 328, 331, 338, 359, 360, 363, 365
Arbela 103
archaeology, archaeological evidence 1, 2, 8, 11, 12, 22, 24–27, 30, 31, 37, 41, 55, 56, 81, 87, 88, 94–98, 147–208, 235, 308, 310, 318, 330, 348, 375
– Atlit 96
– Bethsaida 330
– Carchemish 322
– Chinnereth 330
– Dor 96
– Jezreel 8, 12, 197–202
– Megiddo 8, 12, 190–197
– Samaria 8, 12, 30, 27, 28, 55, 56, 81, 94, 95, 147–187, 235, 346, 363, 375
– Tell Dan 330
– Tell el-Fārʻah 325
– Tell el-Ful 26
– Tell Hadid 204
– Tell Qudadi 26
Arda-Mullissi 220
Argob 328
Arieh 328
Arpad 60, 61, 64, 76–78, 84, 85
Arslan Tash 40
Arumâ 47
Arwad 67
Arzah 313
Arzuhina 108
Asa 271, 279, 283, 292, 310, 311
Ashdod 67, 129, 131, 135, 137, 161, 343, 390
Asherah 217
Ashkelon 97, 189
Ashtarot 328
Ashurbanipal 50, 52, 91, 115, 148, 164
Ashurnasirpal II 44, 51
Ashur / Assur / Aššur (city) 38, 40, 41, 43, 44, 52, 67, 69, 103, 104, 107, 109, 111, 112, 119, 219
Ashur / Assur / Aššur (god) 46, 52, 59, 60, 62–65, 78, 91, 101, 102, 158, 161, 319, 378
Assyria, Assyrian(s) passim
Asyut 140, 142, 143
Aššur-etel-ilāni 51
Aššur-nerari V 324

Aššur-šarru-uṣur 91
Aštammaku 65
Atalyā 43, 81
Athaliah 289, 306, 315, 332
Atlit 96
Auši' (see also Hoshea) 332
Avva 106, 107, 264
Awen 377
Azariah 271–276, 278–281, 283, 285–291, 294, 295, 307, 359
Azekah 67, 68
Azri-Yau 58, 359

Ba'al 226, 295, 340
Ba'alu 97, 135
Ba'il-gazara 67
Baasha 262, 271, 305, 307, 310–314, 318, 332–334
Babylon 5, 43, 50, 91, 106–108, 157, 162, 233, 264, 344, 349, 364
Babylonia 42, 50, 52, 75, 84, 93, 97, 106, 108, 116, 349, 350, 353, 361
Bakanranef 132, 133, 143
Bashan 309
Bel 91
Ben-Hadad 311, 329, 356
Beth-Awen (see also Bethel) 377, 379
Bethel 214, 218, 309, 340, 341, 377, 379
Beth-Issachar 311
Bethsaida (et-Tell) 330
Biqa Valley 329
Bit-Amukani 106
Bit-Bagaia 110
Bit-Ḫumria 37, 41, 42, 44–49, 52, 53, 69, 70, 80, 81, 85, 150, 165, 172, 190, 315, 364
Bit-Yakin 108, 162, 163
Book of Chronicles 75, 237, 246, 255, 258, 259, 262, 279
Book of Deuteronomy 254
Book of Ezekiel 239–241, 344
Book of Hosea 1, 7, 13, 369–382, 385
Book of Isaiah 1, 7, 13, 236, 259, 383–398
Book of Jeremiah 238–241
Book of Kings passim
Book of Samuel 227, 397

Books of the Prophets 5, 7, 8, 298
"Book of the Twelve" 374
Borsippa 162
Bubastis (Per-Bast) 134, 141–143
Byblos 135

Calah → see Kalḫu
Carchemish 71, 163, 322, 390
Carthage 136
cavalry 65, 72, 78, 79, 115, 196, 206, 208
Chaldean 108
chariots, chariotry 49, 63, 65, 71–75, 78, 79, 85, 93, 98, 103, 108, 113–117, 123, 149, 158, 162, 164, 165, 191, 192, 196, 204–206, 208, 313, 355, 378
Chinnereth (Tell el-'Oreimeh) 330
Cilician 91
Cis-Jordan 328
Cutha 107, 264
Cyprus 43, 78
Dadi-larim 121

Damascus 7, 9, 58, 60, 61, 64, 70, 76–78, 85, 87, 94, 112, 134, 155, 160, 185, 189, 236, 259, 283, 296, 305, 327–329, 348, 349, 356, 358–361, 364, 365, 385, 387, 390
Dan (Tell el-Qāḍī) 214, 218, 225, 309, 311, 340, 341
Darius II 335
David 225, 226, 254, 259, 284, 314
Davidic dynasty 243, 307, 332, 333, 385
Deir ez-Zor 106
Delta 12, 130–138, 141, 143
deportation, resettlement 10, 12, 21, 49, 53, 70, 74, 93, 101–124, 149, 154, 165–167, 185, 190, 204, 235, 236, 243, 264, 305, 329, 330, 336–338, 346, 350, 352, 364
Der 63, 66, 68, 75, 76, 108
Deuteronomistic History/Historian 9, 21, 214, 230, 233, 236, 237, 239, 242, 243, 245, 255, 263, 307, 308, 312, 314, 316, 325, 332, 376, 377, 378, 385
Dimašqa (province; see also Damascus) 328
Diyarbakır 106

Dor   96, 189
Dothan   317
Dur-Yakin   162, 166
Dur-Katlimmu (Tell Sheikh Hamad)   121, 122
Dur-Ladini   163
Dur-Šarruken (Khorsabad)   43, 45, 46, 55, 61, 63, 67, 68, 70, 71, 75, 78, 80, 97, 105, 107, 112–114, 117, 122, 129, 165, 193, 204, 351
Durdukka   166

Egypt, Egyptian(s)   97, 99, 103, 119, 127, 130, 131, 133–144, 191, 206, 218–223, 227, 232, 234, 238, 245, 247, 255, 259, 260, 262, 285, 336, 342–344, 348, 352, 362, 365, 380, 387
– 20th Dynasty   135
– 22nd Dynasty   131, 134, 136, 142, 177
– 23rd Dynasty   141, 142
– 24th Dynasty   143
– 25th Dynasty   125, 129, 132, 138–140, 220
Eḫursaggalkurkurra   52
'Ein Jezreel   197
Ekron   32, 63, 67, 161, 186, 312
Elah   229, 241, 252, 305, 312, 318, 331, 335–337, 341
Elam, Elamite(s)   50, 60, 63, 66, 162, 364
el-Hiba (Teudjoi)   141
Elijah   299
Elisha   212, 299, 321, 340
Emuq-Aššur   108
Eni-ilu   190
Ephraim, Ephraimite   13, 154, 244, 259, 298, 309, 316, 323, 365, 376, 377, 379, 381, 384–389, 393, 394
er-Rām (al-Ram)   310
Esarhaddon   39–41, 47, 48, 50–52, 97, 103, 118, 120, 135, 148, 156, 157, 162, 164, 186, 196
Ešarra   111
Ethiopia, Ethiopian   137, 218–221, 223, 260
Euphrates   106, 262, 322, 326, 357
Eusebius   268
Exodus   224

Ezekiel (prophet; see also Book of Ezekiel)   241
Ezida   49, 51, 52

Fayum   141

Gabbutunu (see also Gibbethon)   67, 312
Gad   318, 319
Gaddi   318
Gadi   262, 318
Gadite   318, 321
Galil   330
Galilee, Galilean   186, 192, 196, 305, 329, 330, 333, 338, 341, 342, 349, 360, 365
Gambulu   163
Gath   262
Gaza   67, 69, 75, 97, 98, 134, 161, 189, 205–207, 252, 329, 348, 357, 360
Gazru   42
Geba (Ǧeba)   310
Gemenef-khonsu-bak   130, 142
Gezer   42, 186, 189, 204, 207, 277, 312
Gibbethon   67, 311, 312, 314
Gibeah   379
Gibil   167
Gideon   225
Gilboa   309
Gilead, Gileadite(s)   13, 186, 196, 219, 297–299, 305, 309, 316–319, 321, 327–330, 333, 338, 358, 365, 376
Gozan / Guzana (Tell Halaf)   74, 93, 105–107, 113, 118–120, 122, 263
"grand strategy"   11, 87–99
Greece, Greek   6, 12, 174, 175, 211, 212, 214, 216, 219, 227, 256, 268, 274, 279, 291, 340
Gur   317

Habor → see Khabur
Hadad-idri   134
Halah / Ḫalaḫḫu   74, 93, 105–107, 113, 117, 122, 263
Hamadan   110
Hamath (Hama), Hamathean   44, 55, 58–62, 64–66, 69, 70, 76–80, 82, 85, 99, 106, 107, 109, 111, 112, 190, 264, 351, 364

Ḫanunu 69, 75
Ḫarḫar (Tepe Giyan) 107, 110
Ḫarran 119, 120
Ḫarratum 350
Ḫatarikka 62
Ḫatti 70, 83
Ḫayapâ 69, 108, 149
Hazael 262, 311, 314, 315, 319, 321, 322, 356, 257
Ḫazaqi-Yau 121
Hazor (Tell el-Qedaḥ) 186, 196, 305, 329
Herakleopolis, Herakleopolitan 134, 141–142, 262
Hermopolis 141–143
Hezekiah 68, 94, 154, 213, 229, 230, 239, 240, 242, 243, 245, 246, 251–253, 258, 264, 267, 271–275, 279, 280, 285, 287–289, 294, 295, 337–339, 345, 348
– accession 243, 272, 275, 279
Hezekiahu 239, 240, 242
Ḫinatuna 47
Hiram 296
Ḫirbet Bel'ame 317
Ḫirimma 350
horse(s) 11, 62, 65, 97, 98, 108, 114, 119, 131, 191, 192, 201, 205, 206, 208
Hosea (prophet; see also Book of Hosea) 207, 258, 372
Hoshea passim
– accession 154, 272, 275, 280, 283, 286, 287, 331, 348, 349
– capture 35, 52, 257, 337, 344, 352, 362
– "evil of Hoshea" 213–218, 227, 340
– imprisonment 84, 154, 229, 230, 231, 234, 236, 244, 248, 345, 362, 364, 365
– vassalage 93, 190, 246, 255–257, 337, 342, 345, 348, 350, 353, 361
Huleh 329, 330, 333
Hulli 324
Humbanigaš 60, 66
Ḫundur, Ḫundureans 111
Huru 103
Huruaşu 103

Ibadidi 69, 108, 149
Ibleam 316, 317, 318
Ibû 108
Ijon (Tell ed-Dibbin) 196, 305, 311, 329
Ilu-bi'di (see also Yau-bi'di) 58, 69, 76, 112, 351, 364
Iny 133
Iran 40, 41, 43, 129, 166, 269, 296, 357
Irḫulena 80, 112
Isaiah (prophet; see also Book of Isaiah) 238, 383–398
Israel, Israelite(s) passim
Israelite annals 231, 232
Issachar 311
Iti 127
Itto-Baal (Tubail) 296
Itu'eans 91
Iuput 142, 143
Iuwelot 140

Jabesh 316, 318, 323
Jacob 13, 383–385, 388, 391–393, 396–398
Janoah 196, 305, 329
Jashib (Yāsūf) 316, 323
Jeconiah 277
Jehoahaz 262, 286, 289, 305, 307, 332, 344
Jehoash 276, 282, 289, 290
Jehoiachin 234, 236, 237, 262, 344
Jehoiakim 234, 237
Jehoram 280–282, 284, 292, 293, 307, 314, 326, 340
Jehoshaphat 278, 280–283, 292, 293
Jehu (prophet) 314
Jehu (king) 134, 172, 276, 277, 289, 293, 298, 305–307, 312–317, 331, 332, 340, 356
Jehuids, Jehuite dynasty 299, 314, 316
Jenin/En Ganin (Ḫirbet Bel'ame) 317
Jeremiah (prophet; see also Book of Jeremiah) 238, 241
Jeroboam I 272, 306, 308–310, 333
Jeroboam II 191, 213–215, 217, 269, 270, 272, 281, 289–291, 294, 298, 305, 307–309, 311, 316, 332, 356, 357, 376
Jerusalem, Jerusalemite 26, 27, 53, 94, 134, 154, 160, 185, 213, 214, 243, 258, 259, 262, 279, 307, 310, 314, 315, 338,

339, 341, 348, 358–360, 365, 381, 383, 390, 392, 394, 397
Jerusalem temple   283, 392
Jezebel   340
Jezreel   8, 12, 189–202, 206–208, 317
Joash   276, 277, 282, 283, 289, 290, 305–307, 315, 332, 356
Joram   216, 275, 276, 278, 281, 292, 293, 305, 314, 315, 331, 332
Jordan (river)   189
Josephus   36, 38, 268, 352, 353
Joshua   254
Josiah   222, 225, 277, 362
Jotham   12, 271–275, 279–281, 283–289, 294–296, 298, 339
Judah, Judean   passim
Judean annals   231

Kalḫu/Calah (Nimrud)   37, 40, 41, 43, 49, 51, 52, 55, 66, 71, 73, 98, 113, 116, 117, 328, 335, 351, 352, 378
Kammānu   163
Kar-Adad   110
Karalla   129
Kar-Issar   110
Kar-Nabû   107, 108
Karnak   134
Kar-Nergal   110
Kar-Šarruken (Tepe Giyan)   107, 110
Kashta   127, 137, 140
Kasku   81
Keblaam   317
Kedesh   196, 305, 329
Khabur (Habor)   74, 93, 106, 107, 113, 121, 263
Khmunu (Hermopolis)   141, 143
Khorsabad → see Dur-Šarruken
Kišešlu   107, 110
Kirbet Beit Farr   323
Kišessim   107, 109–111
Kullania (Tell Tayinat)   63
Kurdistan (Irak)   41
Kurdistan (Iran)   129
kur'a   62
Kush, Kushite(s)   12, 93, 125, 127–135, 137–144, 191
Kuthah / Cutha (Tell Ibrahim)   106

Lachish   27, 42, 94, 185, 198, 326
Lachish reliefs   42
Lake Urmia   166
Lamintu   141
"language of conquest"   12, 150–168, 185
Latin   6, 211, 212
Lebanon   90, 96
Leontopolis   142
Levant, Levantine   passim
Libya, Libyan   12, 118–122, 125, 127, 131, 134–136, 139–144
Lilybaeum   136
Lisht   141
Litani   329
"Lost Tribes of Israel"   101–123
Lucian, Lucianic   212, 214, 216, 219, 220
Lucifer of Cagliari   225

Ma (Meshwesh)   139
Maccabean revolt   330
Magiddû (province; see also Megiddo)   190, 192, 208, 328, 333
Maher-shalal-hash-baz   389
Maḫsi-Yau   120
Manasseh   225, 234, 262, 283, 298, 323, 358, 385
Manassites, Manassite tribe   23, 318
Manetho   125, 127, 132, 134, 142, 143
Manṣuate   112
Marduk   50
Mantimeanhe (Montjuemhat)   130
Marduk-apla-iddina II (Merodach-baladan)   52, 76, 108, 157
Marsimani   69, 108, 149
Marum   47
Media(n), Medes   74, 106, 107, 109–111, 263, 346
Mediterranean   26, 90, 96, 309
Medum   141
Megiddo (see also Magiddû)   8, 12, 97, 98, 175, 179, 186, 187, 189–192, 194, 196–199, 201, 204–208, 320
Melidi   164–168
Meluḫḫa (Kush)   129–131, 137, 138
Memphis   103, 104, 127, 131, 136, 141, 142
Menahem (Minihini)   12, 189, 262, 264, 269–272, 274–280, 282, 287, 289–

291, 294, 296–299, 304–306, 316–326, 328, 329, 332, 333, 341, 342, 347, 356–358, 364, 365, 376
Menander 352, 353
Merodach-baladan → see Marduk-apla-iddina II
Meshwesh (Ma) 139
Mesopotamia, Mesopotamian 21, 91, 156, 163, 221, 234, 249, 285
Metanna 324
Micah 225, 398
Midas 91
Mila Mergi 41
Miniḫimme 324
Miniḫini (see also Menahem) 332
Mitatti 166, 167
Moab 97, 387
Montjuemhat 130
Mosaic torah 338
Moses 253, 254
Mount Lebanon 90
Muṣaṣir 43, 46
Muṣri 131, 134, 136–138
Muški 160, 163, 167

Nablus 357
Nabû 49, 51, 52, 91
Nabû-mukin-zeri 349
Nadab 271, 305, 311, 312
Nadbi-Yau 116
Nahal Oren 24
Naphtali 196, 305, 311, 329
Nebuchadnezzar II 27, 233, 262, 344
Necho 222, 262, 362
Necho II 344
Negev 309
Nen-nesut (Herakleopolis) 141–143
Nesubanebdjed 135
New Year (Judean) 268, 280, 290
– change of New Year 12, 276–278
Ni 130
Niku I 130
Nile 104, 125, 126, 131, 137–139, 143
Nimlot 141, 143
Nimmurau 103
Nimrud → see Kalḫu

Nimshide(s) 304, 314, 315, 317–319, 323, 326, 332, 333
Nineveh 42, 43, 79, 102–104, 115, 116, 120, 191
Nippur 162
North African coast 136
Northern Kingdom passim
Nubian 97, 98, 362

Omri 69, 216, 217, 275, 292, 293, 298, 299, 305–307, 312–314, 318, 319, 321, 323, 332, 356
Omride(s) 197, 215, 216, 307, 314, 315, 319, 332, 333, 340
Ophel Excavations 288
Ophrah 225
"Oracles Against the Nations" 387–389
Orontes 61, 63, 77, 85, 112
(O)so(rkon) 221
Osorkon I 135, 136, 140
Osorkon II 134–136, 141, 142
Osorkon III 136, 137, 140–142
Osorkon IV 93, 137, 142, 218, 261, 343, 362, 365
Osorkon of Per-Bast 142

Palestine 22, 31, 42, 67, 93, 96, 98, 202, 310, 329, 348, 359
Palṭi-Yau 119, 120
Paqaḫa (see also Pekah) 329, 332
Parda 167
Pedubast 136, 142
Peftjauawybast 141
Pekah (Paqaḫa) 42, 47–49, 189, 231, 259, 264, 267, 269–276, 279, 280, 283, 285–287, 289, 290, 294–299, 304–307, 316, 324, 327–329, 331–333, 338, 339, 341, 342, 347, 349, 356, 358–361, 365, 376, 385
Pekahiah 189, 269–276, 279, 280, 287, 289, 290, 294, 296–199, 304–306, 327, 329, 347, 358, 365, 376
Pentateuch 277
Per-Bast (Bubastis) 134, 141–143
Per-Sekhem-kheper-re 141
Peshitta 252

1 General index — 407

Philistia, Philistine(s)   67, 99, 161, 162, 186, 206, 252, 305, 312, 314, 348, 360, 387
Phoenicia, Phoenician(s)   11, 38, 90, 96, 134–136, 143
Phrygia   91
Piankhy (see also Piye)   93, 127, 128, 139
Pimay   136
Pir'u   131, 138
Piye (Piankhy)   93, 127, 128, 133, 137, 139–143, 218, 362
Psamtik I   127
Ptah   141
Ptolemais Hermiou   140
Ptolemy   127
Pul(u)   262, 324, 328, 341
Putubishti   130

Qal'at el-Dibse   322
Qal'at Naǧm   322
Qarqar   63–65, 73, 77, 78, 84, 85, 98, 134, 154, 166, 355
Qarqūr   63
Qindau (Kar-Sîn)   110
Qišeraya   119
Que   38
Qurdi-Aššur-lamur   90, 97

Rabshakeh   91
Ramah   310, 379
Ramoth-Gilead   314
Rapâ-Yau   121
Raphia   137, 154, 166
Rapiḫu (see also Raphia)   69, 166
Ras Abū Ḥamīd   312
Rashi   214, 215
Ra'ši   103
Razon   296, 298
Razyān   360
Re'e (Raia)   137
Rehoboam   134, 262, 282, 309
Remaliah   259, 297, 331
Rezin   259, 283, 349, 358–360, 365
Rudamun   141, 142

Sabacon (see also Shabaka)   125, 132
Ša-barê   106

Sais (Sau)   93, 136, 137, 139, 141–143, 218, 260
Saite ruler   128, 132, 133, 139
Sama'   116, 119, 120
Sam'al   38, 163
Samaria (Samerina), Samarians   passim
– archaeological evidence   8, 12, 30, 27f, 55f, 81, 94, 95, 147–187, 346, 363, 235, 346, 363, 375
– three-year siege   12, 93, 95, 230, 233, 238, 242, 244, 336, 345, 347, 351–353
– "two-conquests hypothesis"   10, 30, 31, 95, 153, 155
– Yahwistic high priest?   223–227
Samarian/Ephraimite annals   244, 303
Šamaš   91
Šamaš-bel-ketti   119
Šamaš-belu-uṣur   108
Šamaš-mušakšid-ernettiya (gate)   71
Samerina (see also Samaria)   30, 70, 101, 165, 324, 364
Samuel (prophet; see also Book of Samuel)   226
Sanandaj   129
Sarepta   96
Sargon II   passim
Sarrabanu   185, 349, 361
Satrapie   322
Scythians   25
Sea of Galilee   329
Sebaṣtye (see also Samaria)   346
Sebichos   125, 132
Sehetepib(en)re Pedubast II (Putubishti of Tanis)   130
Sennacherib   39, 42, 47, 50, 52, 53, 68, 73, 94, 106, 134, 135, 147, 154, 156, 160–162, 164, 185, 186, 196, 206, 220, 221, 235, 236, 239, 240, 246, 247, 252, 260, 294, 338, 339, 348, 350
Sepharvaim   106, 264
Septuagint   6, 211, 212, 223, 227, 241, 252, 258, 260, 261, 317
Shabaka (Sabacon)   125, 127, 128, 130–133, 137, 138, 143
Shabataka (Shebitqo)   125, 127–133, 138, 143

Shallum   271, 272, 274–276, 289, 290, 291, 294, 304–306, 316–319, 323, 325–328, 332, 333, 356, 357, 376
Shalmaneser III   65, 73, 80, 98, 134, 136, 203, 236, 315, 355, 356
Shalmaneser V   passim
Shapiya   185
Shechem   309
Shepenwepet I   140, 142
Shephelah   161
Shishak   127, 134, 262
Shoshenq I   127, 131, 134, 135, 136, 142
Shoshenq III   136
Shunem (Sulam)   200
"Sib'e" (now: Re'e)   137
Sidon, Sidonian   90, 135
Simri   305
Sîn   77, 119
"sin of Jeroboam"   213–215, 217, 305, 308, 333, 340, 341
Sîn-šarru-iškun   52
Sinai   99, 134
Sinu (Tell Siyānu)   67
Sippar   106, 107, 162
Solomon   198, 284, 309, 310, 332, 357, 396
Solomonic empire   322
Sō'   93, 136, 137, 218–221, 223, 234, 255, 259–261, 353, 362
Southern Kingdom   2, 7, 9, 13, 388, 395–397
Sudan   125, 143
Sulam (Shunem)   200
Sutians   162
synchronisms
– Assyrian and Babylonian   270
– Hezekiah – Hoshea   229, 230, 239, 241–243, 246, 252, 253, 262, 263, 272
– Israel and Judah   241, 268, 271, 274, 276, 278, 279, 283, 287, 318, 339, 347, 348
Syria, Syrian   42, 43, 61, 317, 321, 352, 359, 380
Syrian Desert   110
Syria-Palestine, Syro-Palestine   152, 342, 343, 349, 352

Syro-Ephraimite War   2, 7, 9, 173, 328, 338, 341, 359, 360, 379, 380, 385, 388
Ṣihû   103
Ṣihuru   103
Ṣimirra   60, 61, 64, 76–78, 85, 90, 189
Šilkanni   130, 131, 137, 138, 143
Šinuḫtu   80
Šuandahul   166, 167
Šumma-ilani   116

Ta'anach   186
Tabal   324
Taharka (Tar(a)cos)   125, 127, 128, 133, 135
Takeloth II   134, 136, 262
Takeloth III   141, 142
Tamudi   69, 71, 108, 149
Tang-i Var   129, 131, 132, 138
Tanis   93, 130, 131, 134–136, 142, 143
Tanutamun   127
Tappuah (Tell aš-Šēḫ/Abū Zarad)   320, 322, 323, 326, 357
Tapsake / Thapsa[cus]   322
Tar(a)cos (→ see also Taharka)   125
Tarditu-Aššur   108
Tarquinia   136
Tarṣî   120
Tefnakht   93, 127, 128, 131, 133, 137, 139, 141, 143, 218, 260, 362
Tel Dan   289, 314, 315, 330, 331
Tel 'Ein Jezreel   197
Tel Hadid   204, 207
Tel Jezreel   197, 198
Tell Ābil el-Qamḥ (Abel-beth-maacah)   329
Tell Abū Charaz   316
Tell Abu Hawām   186
Tell Abu Marya (Apku)   38
Tell Asharneh   61, 62, 63, 65
Tell aš-Šēḫ/Abū Zarad (Tappuah)   323, 357
Tell el-Fār'ah (Tirzah)   180, 183, 310, 317, 320, 325
Tell el-Ful   26
Tell el-Maqlūb   316
Tell el-Melat/Tell Mālāt   312
Tell el-'Oreimeh (Chinnereth)   330
Tell el-Qāḍī (Dan)   311
Tell el-Qedaḥ (Hazor)   329
Tell en-Na'ameh   329

Tell Halaf (see also Guzana)   105, 118
Tell Jemmeh   183
Tell Keisan   186
Tell Muqdam   142
Tell Qudadi (Tell esh-Shuna)   26
Tel Qedesh   329
temple of Karnak   134
temple of Kawa   135
temple(s) of Yahweh   226
Tentamun   135
Tepe Giyan (see also Kar-Šarruken, Ḫarḫar)   110
Tep-ihu   141
Teudjoi (el-Hiba)   141
Thebaid   140, 141
Thebes, Theban   130, 134, 139, 140, 142, 143
Tibni   292, 298, 306, 313, 314, 332, 333
Tiglath-pileser III   passim
Til-Garimmu   164
Tiphsah   320–323, 325, 326, 333, 357
Tirhaka   223, 260
Tirzah (Tell el-Fārʻah)   262, 310, 312–314, 317–323, 325–327, 333, 356, 357
Tjeny (Girga)   140, 143
trade(rs)   11, 26, 27, 31, 96, 97, 108, 135, 136, 143, 191, 192, 200, 205, 206, 208, 312, 328
Transeuphratene   57
Transjordan, Transjordanian   297, 298, 316–319, 321, 328, 341, 342, 349, 359, 360
Trisagion   395
Tubail (Itto-Baal)   296
Turkey   43, 105
Turushpa   185
Tyre/Tyros, Tyrian   38, 90, 96, 97, 135, 153, 185, 189, 252, 296, 324, 352

Ulūlāyu (see also Shalmaneser V)   36
Upper Tigris region   106, 205
Urarṭu, Urarṭian   42, 43, 46, 91, 158, 160, 163, 185, 203

Ursâ   158, 159
Uruk   52
Usermaetre   142
Uširihiuhurti   119, 120
Uzziah   286, 289–291, 293–296, 299, 359

Vale of Ayalon   42
Valerian   69
Via Maris   26, 31, 93, 191, 200, 207
Vulgate   252

Waset   140
Wenamun   135

Yabâ   39
Yahweh, YHWH   58, 116, 120–122, 213, 215, 217, 224, 226, 253, 254, 258–261, 338, 340, 341
Yahwistic cult   214, 225
Yahwistic high priest → see Samaria
Yahwistic names   28, 58, 313, 327, 332
Yahwism   381
Yamani   67, 129–132, 137, 138, 343
Yarkon   26
Yāsūf (Jashib)   316
Yaṭbite   47
Yau-biʼdi (see also Ilu-biʼdi)   58, 60–67, 73, 74, 76–80, 82, 85, 86, 112
Yaudi   359
Yau-gâ   116
Yehud   381
Yenoʻam   329
Yoqneʻam   186
Zagros   42, 64, 97, 110, 111, 166, 192, 205
Zazâ   120
Zechariah   213, 241, 269, 271, 272, 274–276, 289, 291, 294, 298, 304, 305, 307, 316, 317, 356, 357, 376
Zedekiah   234, 249, 262, 277, 282, 344
Zikirtu   166, 167
Zimri   298, 306, 312–314, 318, 321, 323, 327, 332, 333

2 Words

Akkadian

3-šú.meš   117, 378
esēru   154, 160, 185, 186, 236
ḫammā'u   69

ḫepû   82, 154, 156, 164, 167, 335, 350, 363
"kalû" → see 3-šú.meš
nasīku   118

Hebrew

אסר / 'sr   154, 236, 344
ephod   223–226
החפשית תבי   294
teraphim   223–226
בן־גדי   318, 319
לכד / lākad   154, 233, 237, 239, 346

מִנְחָה / minḫāh   222, 261, 346
נכה   306, 320, 321
עלה / 'ālāh   222, 233, 242, 256, 261, 263, 344, 345
קשר / qæšær   258, 306, 338
שליש / šālîš   298, 327, 376

3 Texts

Hebrew Bible / Old Testament

Gen 49:24	396	Judg 18:14, 17, 18, 20	224
		Judg 21:9–14	316
Exod 12:2	277		
Exod 14:7	327	1Sam 2:18	226
Exod 15:4	327	1Sam 11:1–10	316
Exod 21:2, 5, 26, 27	294	1Sam 13:7	318
Exod 23:14–19	277	1Sam 15:23	225
Exod 25:7	224	1Sam 17:25	294
Exod 28:4, 15, 28	224	1Sam 23:9–12	224
Exod 29:5	224	1Sam 24:5	318
Exod 30:9	222	1Sam 25:22, 34	314
Exod 34:18–26	277	1Sam 30:7–8	224
Exod 35:9, 27	224	1Sam 31:11	316
Exod 39:8, 21	224		
Exod 40:29	222	2Sam 5:4	284
		2Sam 6:14	226
Lev 14:20	222	2Sam 19:44	222
Lev 23:1–14	277	2Sam 23:36	318
Lev 25:8–9	277		
Lev 27:3	326	1Kgs 4:13	328
		1Kgs 5:4	322, 357
Num 13:11	318	1Kgs 6:34	330
		1Kgs 6:37–38	277
Deut 3:4, 13–14	328	1Kgs 9:11	330
Deut 15:12, 13, 18	294	1Kgs 9:22	327
Deut 16:1–7	277	1Kgs 10:28	97
Deut 28:1, 15	254	1Kgs 11–14	309, 310
		1Kgs 11:26–14:30	310
Josh 13:26	310	1Kgs 11:29–30	311
Josh 17:8	323	1Kgs 11:42	284
Josh 18:25	310	1Kgs 12–2Kgs 17	306
Josh 19:8, 29, 36	310	1Kgs 12:15	311
Josh 20:7	330	1Kgs 12:28–30	218
Josh 21:32	330	1Kgs 14:2, 4	311
Josh 22:23	222	1Kgs 14:9	340
		1Kgs 14:10	314
Judg 1:18	252	1Kgs 14:17	357
Judg 8:27	225, 226	1Kgs 14:25	241, 262
Judg 13:19	222	1Kgs 14:26	221
Judg 16:21, 25	344	1Kgs 15	311, 313, 333
Judg 17–18	225, 226	1Kgs 15–17	308
Judg 17:5	224	1Kgs 15:2	279

1Kgs 15:11	283	2Kgs 6–7	340
1Kgs 15:16	310	2Kgs 7:2, 17, 19	327
1Kgs 15:17	262	2Kgs 8	292
1Kgs 15:19	311	2Kgs 8:12	321, 322, 357
1Kgs 15:20	311, 329, 330	2Kgs 8:15	321
1Kgs 15:21	318, 357	2Kgs 8:16–18	280, 281, 284, 292, 293
1Kgs 15:25	271, 279		
1Kgs 15:27–28	306, 311, 312, 356	2Kgs 8:22, 24	292
1Kgs 15:29	311	2Kgs 8:25–27	281, 293
1Kgs 15:32	310, 312	2Kgs 8:28	315
1Kgs 15:33	271, 312, 318, 357	2Kgs 9–10	293, 314, 315
1Kgs 16	292, 298	2Kgs 9–14 and 15–19	212
1Kgs 16:1–4	314	2Kgs 9:8	314
1Kgs 16:6	279, 305, 318, 357	2Kgs 9:9	311
1Kgs 16:8–9	279, 318, 357	2Kgs 9:14	306
1Kgs 16:9–10	306, 313, 356	2Kgs 9:22	340
1Kgs 16:11	313	2Kgs 9:24–27	314, 317, 327, 331
1Kgs 16:12–13	312, 314	2Kgs 10	289
1Kgs 16:15	292, 312, 318, 357	2Kgs 10:9	306
1Kgs 16:16	313	2Kgs 10:11	312
1Kgs 16:17	312, 318, 357	2Kgs 10:25	327
1Kgs 16:18	321, 327	2Kgs 10:26–27	340
1Kgs 16:20	306, 318	2Kgs 10:28–31	212, 340
1Kgs 16:21	292, 313	2Kgs 10:32	317
1Kgs 16:22	292, 306	2Kgs 10:35	305
1Kgs 16:23	275, 292, 318	2Kgs 11	289
1Kgs 16:25	216, 340	2Kgs 11:19	306
1Kgs 16:28	293, 305	2Kgs 12	289
1Kgs 16:29	292	2Kgs 12:2	276
1Kgs 16:30	216, 340	2Kgs 12:3	283
1Kgs 16:33	216, 340	2Kgs 12:7	241
1Kgs 17–19	217	2Kgs 12:18	262
1Kgs 18:29, 36	222	2Kgs 12:20	306
1Kgs 21:1	197	2Kgs 12:28–32	340
1Kgs 21:21	314	2Kgs 13:1–9 and 10–13	276, 289, 305
1Kgs 21:22	311	2Kgs 13:14–21	212
1Kgs 21:25	217	2Kgs 14:1–2	276, 290
1Kgs 22:37	305	2Kgs 14:1–20	289
1Kgs 22:41–44	283, 293	2Kgs 14:3	283
1Kgs 22:52–54	216, 276, 293, 340	2Kgs 14:5	326
		2Kgs 14:17	290, 291, 294
2Kgs	10, 212, 229	2Kgs 14:19–22	280, 281, 286, 289, 306
2Kgs 1:17	292		
2Kgs 1:18	216, 275, 292, 293	2Kgs 14:22–29	289
2Kgs 3:1–3	276, 293, 340	2Kgs 14:23	290, 291, 294
2Kgs 3:13–14	340	2Kgs 14:25	356, 357
2Kgs 3:20	222		

2Kgs 15	13, 283, 286, 289, 291, 293, 299, 303, 304, 306–308, 332, 333, 355	2Kgs 15:27	271, 273, 275, 279, 286, 296, 329, 339
		2Kgs 15:27–31	290, 296
		2Kgs 15:28	305
2Kgs 15–16	3, 47, 341	2Kgs 15:29	154, 190, 214, 264, 305, 311, 317, 328, 330, 337, 341, 342, 360, 365
2Kgs 15–17	303		
2Kgs 15–18	5, 12, 53, 267, 269–271, 273–276, 279, 281, 282, 286, 288, 289, 299		
		2Kgs 15:29–30	303, 338
		2Kgs 15:30	231, 272, 283, 286, 287, 296, 329, 331, 337, 339, 348, 352, 356, 360, 361, 365
2Kgs 15:1	271, 275, 279, 286, 290		
2Kgs 15:1–7	289		
2Kgs 15:2	273, 294	2Kgs 15:32	272, 273, 275, 279, 286, 296
2Kgs 15:3	283		
2Kgs 15:5	281, 294	2Kgs 15:32–33	285
2Kgs 15:6–8	286	2Kgs 15:32–38	289
2Kgs 15:7	295	2Kgs 15:33	273, 288, 294–296, 339
2Kgs 15:8	271, 275, 279, 291, 316		
		2Kgs 15:34	283, 286
2Kgs 15:8–12	289	2Kgs 15:35	283
2Kgs 15:8–31	376	2Kgs 15:37	298, 328, 360
2Kgs 15:9	213, 277, 305	2Kgs 16	7, 9, 212, 359
2Kgs 15:10	303, 306, 316, 356	2Kgs 16:1	272, 273, 279, 339
2Kgs 15:12	317	2Kgs 16:2	288, 295
2Kgs 15:13–15	271, 275, 286, 289–291, 356	2Kgs 16:2b–4	283
		2Kgs 16:3	283
2Kgs 15:14	262, 303, 318	2Kgs 16:5	358–360, 365, 379, 385
2Kgs 15:15	306, 318, 356		
2Kgs 15:16	303, 318, 320, 321, 357	2Kgs 16:5–9	283, 338, 348
		2Kgs 16:6	154
2Kgs 15:17	272, 275, 286, 290, 291	2Kgs 16:7–9	341, 342
		2Kgs 16:7, 10	328
2Kgs 15:17–22	289	2Kgs 16:9	360
2Kgs 15:17–16:20	341	2Kgs 16:10–18	283
2Kgs 15:18	305	2Kgs 16:19–20	336
2Kgs 15:19	264, 296, 324, 325, 328, 357, 364	2Kgs 17	12, 13, 75, 105, 211, 212, 226, 227, 235, 240, 243, 305
2Kgs 15:19–20	303, 341, 342		
2Kgs 15:20	326, 358, 364	2Kgs 17 and 18	38, 52, 53
2Kgs 15:22	306, 327	2Kgs 17:1	272, 275, 280, 296, 339, 348, 364
2Kgs 15:23	271, 272, 275, 286, 290		
		2Kgs 17:1–2	263
2Kgs 15:23–26	290, 296	2Kgs 17:1–4	290
2Kgs 15:24	305	2Kgs 17:1–6	18, 20, 29, 153, 213, 226, 249, 335, 336, 347
2Kgs 15:25	42, 47, 48, 303, 316, 318, 327, 356, 376		

2Kgs 17:1–24	4	2Kgs 18:1–12	4
2Kgs 17:2	213–215, 217, 218, 227, 234, 236, 340, 341	2Kgs 18:4	252
		2Kgs 18:7	252, 264, 338, 339
		2Kgs 18:8	252
2Kgs 17:3	233, 237, 238, 242, 263, 342, 345, 352, 361, 363	2Kgs 18:9–10	10, 239–242, 248, 263, 272, 279, 345, 363
2Kgs 17:3–4	12, 230–232, 234, 237–239, 258, 338	2Kgs 18:9–11	12, 18, 20, 29, 229–231, 238, 240, 242–244, 251, 337–339, 346, 348
2Kgs 17:3–5	239, 262, 345, 380		
2Kgs 17:3–6	10, 12, 37, 92, 229–231, 240, 243–245, 247–249, 251, 255, 262, 337–339, 342–344, 347, 349, 351–353	2Kgs 18:9–12	37, 231, 262, 337, 338, 345
		2Kgs 18:10	154, 239–241, 294, 304
		2Kgs 18:10–11	263
2Kgs 17:4	94, 186, 218–220, 222, 227, 261, 338, 352, 362, 363, 365	2Kgs 18:11	239
		2Kgs 18:12	245, 249, 252
		2Kgs 18:13	235, 239, 240, 243, 252, 294, 348
2Kgs 17:4–5	233	2Kgs 18:13–16	338, 339, 345
2Kgs 17:4–6	352	2Kgs 18:13–19:37	239
2Kgs 17:5	93, 95, 153, 233, 238, 263, 345, 363	2Kgs 18:14–16	239
2Kgs 17:5–6	12, 232, 238, 239, 240, 242, 244, 245, 345, 351	2Kgs 18:21, 24	221
		2Kgs 18:31–32	92
		2Kgs 18:34	73, 235
2Kgs 17:6	154, 233, 235, 237, 242, 263, 272, 346, 352, 363	2Kgs 19:9	223
		2Kgs 19:22	396
		2Kgs 19:37	220
2Kgs 17:7	212	2Kgs 20:1	243
2Kgs 17:7–20	29	2Kgs 21:3	217
2Kgs 17:7–23	249	2Kgs 21:6	223, 283
2Kgs 17:7–41	226	2Kgs 21:23–24	306
2Kgs 17:9	245, 249, 252	2Kgs 23	277
2Kgs 17:17	223–225, 227	2Kgs 23:4	225
2Kgs 17:21–23	29	2Kgs 23:24	225
2Kgs 17:24	106, 245, 263, 346, 352,	2Kgs 23:29	222, 262, 362
		2Kgs 23:33	262, 344
2Kgs 17:24–28	339	2Kgs 23:34	286, 344
2Kgs 17:24–41	226	2Kgs 24:8	279
2Kgs 17:26, 27	113	2Kgs 24:12	234
2Kgs 17:29–31	245	2Kgs 24:17	286, 344
2Kgs 17:31	220	2Kgs 25:1	241
2Kgs 18	75, 242	2Kgs 25:7	234, 262, 344
2Kgs 18–20	289	2Kgs 25:8	241
2Kgs 18:1	241, 242, 272, 273, 275, 279, 339, 348	2Kgs 25:27	262
		2Kgs 25:27–30	344

1Chr 5:6	3	Isa 2:1	388
1Chr 5:26	3, 341	Isa 2:1–4	391
1Chr 6:61	330	Isa 2:3	391, 396
		Isa 2:5	391, 396
2Chr 16:1	279	Isa 2:6	391–393, 396
2Chr 21:4	326	Isa 5:1–7	394
2Chr 26	286	Isa 5:7	393
2Chr 26:21	294	Isa 5:19	395
2Chr 27:2	286	Isa 5:25	383, 384
2Chr 28:5–6	360	Isa 5:26–29	383, 384
2Chr 28:5–8	379	Isa 6	395
2Chr 28:16–21	3	Isa 6 and 8	392
2Chr 30:1–12	213	Isa 6–9	9
2Chr 33:11	234, 262	Isa 6–12	386
2Chr 36:6	233, 234, 237	Isa 6–19	391
2Chr 36:9	279	Isa 6:1	286, 388
		Isa 6:1–11	394
Ezra 2:36	311	Isa 7	3, 9, 359, 385
		Isa 7–8	7
Neh 7:39	311	Isa 7:1	286, 358, 360, 365
Neh 11:33	310	Isa 7:1–9	379
		Isa 7:1–17	394
Esth 1:6	330	Isa 7:2	358, 359, 365
		Isa 7:4	360
Job 3:19	294	Isa 7:5	358, 360, 365
		Isa 7:8	360
Pss 20:1	396	Isa 7:8–9a	390
Pss 24:6	396	Isa 7:17	394
Pss 46:8, 12	396	Isa 8	393
Pss 71:22	396	Isa 8:1–4	385, 389, 393
Pss 75:10	396	Isa 8:1–8	394
Pss 76:7	396	Isa 8:1–10	3
Pss 78:41	396	Isa 8:5–8a	393
Pss 81:2, 5	396	Isa 8:11–17	394
Pss 84:9	396	Isa 8:16–17	392
Pss 89:1	396	Isa 8:17	391–393
Pss 94:7	396	Isa 8:18	392
Pss 132:2, 5	396	Isa 8:23	3, 330
Pss 146:5	396	Isa 9	387
		Isa 9:6	286
Cant 5:14	330	Isa 9:7	385, 386, 391, 393
		Isa 9:7–20	383, 384
Isa 1–39	383, 391, 395	Isa 9:8	385
Isa 1:1	286, 388	Isa 9:11	387
Isa 1:3	394	Isa 9:14	384
Isa 1:24	396	Isa 9:16	389
Isa 2–4	391	Isa 9:18	389

Isa 9:19–20	298	Isa 30:11, 12, 25	395
Isa 9:20	385, 387	Isa 31:1	395
Isa 10:4	389	Isa 31:1–2	221
Isa 10:5–9	389	Isa 36–39	385
Isa 10:6	389	Isa 36:1	240
Isa 10:9	3, 390	Isa 37:38	220
Isa 10:10–12	389	Isa 38:1	243
Isa 10:11	390	Isa 40	383
Isa 10:13–15	389	Isa 40–48	391
Isa 10:20	391	Isa 40–55	386
Isa 10:21	391	Isa 49:26	396
Isa 10:27–32	4	Isa 57:6	222
Isa 11:11–12	386	Isa 58:6	294
Isa 11:13–14	386, 387	Isa 60:16	396
Isa 11:15–16	386	Isa 66:3	222
Isa 13–23	387		
Isa 13:1	388	Jer 14:12	222
Isa 13:3	222	Jer 23:6	286
Isa 13:16, 18	321	Jer 25:1	241
Isa 14:1	391	Jer 28:1	241
Isa 14:4b–21	4	Jer 31:29	222
Isa 14:28	388	Jer 32:1	241
Isa 14:28–32	387	Jer 34:9–11, 14, 16	294
Isa 15–16	387	Jer 36:1, 9	241
Isa 17	387	Jer 36:2	277
Isa 17:1	387	Jer 37:7–8	221
Isa 17:1–3	3, 388	Jer 39	241
Isa 17:2	387	Jer 50:29	396
Isa 17:3a	387	Jer 51:5	396
Isa 17:4	391, 393	Jer 52:4	241
Isa 17:4–6	388	Jer 52:12	241
Isa 17:6	391		
Isa 18:1	389	Ezek 8:1	241
Isa 19	387	Ezek 17:11–21	249
Isa 20	385	Ezek 20:1	241
Isa 20:1	4	Ezek 21:21	224
Isa 23:12	222	Ezek 24:1	241
Isa 24–27	388	Ezek 26:1	241
Isa 27:6, 9	391	Ezek 29:1, 17	241
Isa 28–31	389	Ezek 29:2–7	221
Isa 28:1	389	Ezek 30:20	241
Isa 28:1–4	388	Ezek 31:1	241
Isa 28:3	389	Ezek 32:1, 17	241
Isa 29:22	391	Ezek 33:21	241
Isa 29:23	391		
Isa 30:2–5	221	Hos 1:1	286
Isa 30:8	392	Hos 1:2b–25	207

Hos 1:4–5	200	Hos 10:5–6	341
Hos 1:6–9	371	Hos 10:5–8	377, 378
Hos 2:1–5	371	Hos 10:14	321
Hos 2:2	200	Hos 11:1–5	376
Hos 2:13–19	371	Hos 11:2–5	371
Hos 2:22–25	371	Hos 11:5, 11	380
Hos 2:24	200, 207	Hos 11:6–11	371
Hos 3:1–5	371	Hos 12:1	380
Hos 3:4	224	Hos 12:1–15	371
Hos 4:1–19	371	Hos 12:2	221
Hos 5:1	371	Hos 13:1, 3–13, 15	371
Hos 5:8–14	379	Hos 13:4	371
Hos 6:3	371	Hos 14:1	321, 371
Hos 6:8–11	371	Hos 14:3–6	371
Hos 7:1	371	Hos 14:9–10	371
Hos 7:3–7	375, 376	Hos 7:12–16	371
Hos 7:8–11	380		
Hos 7:11	221, 380	Amos 1–2	389
Hos 7:12–16	371	Amos 1:1	286
Hos 8:1	371	Amos 1:13	321
Hos 9:1–4	371	Amos 5:22	222
Hos 9:3	380	Amos 6:2	3
Hos 9:9–17	371		
Hos 9:10–17	376	Zech 7:1	241
Hos 10:1–8	378	Zech 10:2	224, 225
Hos 10:1–14	371	Zech 14:5	286

Apocrypha

1Macc 5:17, 20, 55   330   Jdt 15:5   330

Septuagint and related manuscripts

2^0 322
4Kgdms 14:29   305
4Kgdms 25:8   241
A   220, 322
$A^\dagger$ 322
Antiochene/Antiochian text   6, 211, 212, 214, 261, 274, 275, 305, 311, 317, 323, 326, 338, 340
Antiochene mss. 19, 82, 93, and 108   275
B   219, 220, 322
Codex A   279
Codex Alexandrinus   275
Codex B   279
Codex V   279
Codex Vaticanus   311

G^B 296
G^L 296
kaige revision   211, 212, 216, 222, 258, 261
L   219, 220, 223
$L^\dagger$ 322
La^{115} (*Palimpsestus Vindobonensis*)   211, 212, 214, 223, 260
La^M (also known as La$_{91-95}$)   212, 214, 216
Lucianic recension   6, 212, 216, 292, 357
LXX^L 296
minuscule 52   279
minuscule 92   279
minuscule 121   279
minuscule 106   279
minuscule 120   279

minuscule 127   274, 275, 279
minuscule 130   279
minuscule 134   279
minuscule 158   275
minuscule 245   274, 275
minuscule 247   279
minuscule 314   279
minuscule 489   279
minuscule 501   279
minuscule 554   279
minuscule 700   275
Palimpsestus Vindobonensis → see La^{115}
Septuagint (LXX)   6, 211, 212, 216, 217, 222–224, 227, 241, 296, 322, 325, 327, 328, 347, 357
V   220, 275
Vetus Latina   6

Classical and Ancient Christian writings
Eusebius, *Chronicon*   268
Lucifer of Cagliari   225
Sulpicius Severus, *I Chr* 47:1   219

Dead Sea Scrolls
4QXII^c 371
4QXII^d 371
4QXII^g 371

Josephus
A.J./Ant. IX 13,2   352
A.J./Ant. IX 15   38
A.J./Ant. IX 16   38
A.J./Ant. IXf   268

Mishnah, Talmud, and related literature
B. Bat. 121b   213
Giṭ. 88a   213
Ta'an. 30b–31a   213

Other Rabbinic works
Seder Olam Rabah   268

Aramaean inscriptions
KAI, no. 233, l. 15   350
"Tel Dan Stele"   289, 314, 315, 331

Ostraca
Lachish   27
Samaria   27, 96, 237

Seals and seal impressions
from Egypt   177
of Hezekiah   288
of Hoshea   238

Ancient Near Eastern texts

Historiographical texts

Assyrian Eponym List and Chronicle   3, 4, 37, 39, 50, 57, 82–84, 86, 95, 154, 338, 348, 349, 351, 352, 361
Babylonian Chronicles   3–5, 10, 30, 36–38, 60, 83, 95, 152, 153, 238, 240, 335, 349–351, 363
– i 19–23   349
– i 24–28   30, 37, 38, 57, 82, 95, 148, 167, 363
– i 29–31   38, 351
– ii 24–25   350
Babylonian King List A   36
Ptolemaic Canon   36

Assyrian royal inscriptions

Shalmaneser III:

"Black Obelisk"   134, 315
– epigraph (RIMA 3, A.0.102.88)   356
"Calah Bulls"   315
"Kurba'il Statue"   315
"Kurkh Inscription" (RIMA 3, A.0.102.2), ii 91–92   73, 355
"Marble Slab"   315

Adad-nerari III:

"Tell al-Rimah Stele" (RIMA 3, A.0.104.7), l. 8   356

Tiglath-pileser III:

"(Calah) Annals"   40, 41, 45, 47, 48, 190, 296, 305, 357
– Ann. 3 (RINAP 1, 27)   296
– l. 3   41, 357
– Ann. 13* (RINAP 1, 14)   296
– l. 8   235
– l. 10   41, 269, 324, 357
– Ann. 18 (RINAP 1, 22)
– ll. 1′–8′a   41, 47
– l. 3′   190
– Ann. 23 (RINAP 1, 20)   328
– ll. 8′–9′   185
– Ann. 24 (RINAP 1, 21)
– ll. 1′–11′   41, 47
– l. 3′   190
– Ann. 27 (RINAP 1, 32)   296
– l. 2   41, 269, 357

"Iran Stele" (RINAP 1, 35), iii 5   41, 269, 296, 324, 357

"Summary Inscriptions" (RINAP 1, 39–52)   41, 348
– Summ. 1 (RINAP 1, 39), ll. 23–24   185
– Summ. 4 (RINAP 1, 42)
– l. 6′   190
– l. 11′   331
– ll. 15′–19′   42, 48, 190, 269, 324, 361
– Summ. 7 (RINAP 1, 47)
– l. 23   185
– rev. 7–13   349
– rev. 11′   286
– Summ. 9 (RINAP 1, 49)   328, 331
– rev. 9–11   190, 269, 349, 361
– Summ. 13 (RINAP 1, 44)   328, 331
– ll. 17′–18′   42, 269, 349, 361

Shalmaneser V:

"Lion weights"   37

Sargon II:

"Annals" → see "Khorsabad Annals"

"Ashur Charter"   38, 43, 44, 51, 60, 61, 63, 76, 84
– ll. 16–28   59, 64, 71, 150, 351

"Borowski Stele"   79
– side B 5–12   80

"Bull Inscription"   45
– l. 21   81, 149, 185

"Cyprus Stele"   78
– ll. 51–65   79

"Hama Stele"   112

"Juniper Palace Inscription"   66–68, 73
– ll. 7–8   66

"(Khorsabad) Annals"   12, 44, 67, 69, 70,
    73–76, 84, 86, 108, 113, 147–187, 351
– ll. 10–18   70–72, 95, 99, 114, 149, 235,
    335, 351
– ll. 23–25   76, 114
– ll. 66–67   235
– ll. 109–115   110
– ll. 120–123   108, 235
– ll. 210–215   110, 235
– ll. 380–381   235

"Khorsabad Cylinder"   51, 68, 70, 352
– ll. 19–20   68f., 149, 185, 235
– l. 25   69

"Khorsabad Display Inscription"   45, 49,
    76, 77, 113, 129
– ll. 23–25   30, 71, 75, 93, 149, 157, 351,
    352
– ll. 33–36   60, 64, 65, 78, 112
– ll. 55–57   235
– ll. 64–65   110
– ll. 115–116   235
– ll. 138–139   235

"(Khorsabad) Display Inscription XIV", l. 15
    45, 80, 129, 149, 165, 166, 185

"Letter to the God Assur" ("Sargon's Eighth
    Campaign")   43, 44, 46, 68

"Mosul Annals"
– ll. 4–20   77
– ll. 5, 14–15, 18   60
– ll. 6–11   63

"Najafehabad Stele"   64–66, 76
– rev. 4–13   64f.

"Nimrud Prism"   72–76, 86, 93, 99, 364
– iv 25–32   378
– iv 25–41   71, 72, 149, 335, 351

– iv 31–33   49, 165, 166, 185
– iv 31–41   114
– iv 33–34   157, 158, 165, 166
– iv 37–39   185

"Nineveh Cylinder"   79

"Tang-i Var Inscription"   129, 131, 132, 138

"Tell Asharneh Stele"   44, 61, 63, 65, 66
– B 1′–12′ and C 1′–9′   62
– B 11′   60

"Tell Tayinat Stele"   44, 63, 66, 351
– ll. 1′–10′   63f.
– ll. 5′–7′   60, 77

"Threshold Inscription no. 4", ll. 31–32
    46, 81, 149, 185, 364

Sennacherib

RINAP 3, 4, ll. 52–58   53
RINAP 3, 22, iii 27b–49   53
RINAP 3, 1015   67, 68

Esarhaddon

RINAP 4, 9 i′ 6′–17′   103

Letters and administrative texts

Assur

StAT 2, 53   119

Dur-Katlimmu

BATSH 6, 37   121
BATSH 6, 110b   121
StCh 1, 185 no. 14   121

Kalḫu

CTN 3, 121   117, 378
Nimrud Horse Lists   98
SAA 19, 22   90
SAA 19, 8–11   37

Nineveh

ABL 301   91
SAA 1, 1   91
SAA 1, 110   98
SAA 1, 220   164

SAA 1, 255   375
SAA 6, 34   116
SAA 15, 280   118
SAA 16, 63   120
SAA 20, 55   111

Other Texts

Egyptian royal inscriptions
– Osorkon   142
– Piye   139–142

"Report of Wenamun"   135

Baal Cycle   295

www.ingramcontent.com/pod-product-compliance
Lightning Source LLC
Chambersburg PA
CBHW051554230426
43668CB00013B/1844